T0311780

ADVANCED TEXTS IN ECONOMETRICS

General Editors

Manuel Arellano   Guido Imbens   Grayham E. Mizon
Adrian Pagan   Mark Watson

Advisory Editor

C. W. J. Granger

Other Advanced Texts in Econometrics

ARCH: Selected Readings
Edited by Robert F. Engle

Asymptotic Theory for Integrated Processes
By H. Peter Boswijk

Bayesian Inference in Dynamic Econometric Models
By Luc Bauwens, Michel Lubrano, and Jean-François Richard

Co-integration, Error Correction, and the Econometric Analysis of Non-Stationary Data
By Anindya Banerjee, Juan J. Dolado, John W. Galbraith, and David Hendry

Dynamic Econometrics
By David F. Hendry

Finite Sample Econometrics
By Aman Ullah

Generalized Method of Moments
By Alastair Hall

Likelihood-Based Inference in Cointegrated Vector Autoregressive Models
By Søren Johansen

Long-Run Econometric Relationships: Readings in Cointegration
Edited by R. F. Engle and C. W. J. Granger

Micro-Econometrics for Policy, Program, and Treatment Effect
By Myoung-jae Lee

Modelling Econometric Series: Readings in Econometric Methodology
Edited by C. W. J. Granger

Modelling Non-Linear Economic Relationships
By Clive W. J. Granger and Timo Teräsvirta

Modelling Seasonality
Edited by S. Hylleberg

Non-Stationary Times Series Analysis and Cointegration
Edited by Colin P. Hargeaves

Outlier Robust Analysis of Economic Time Series
By André Lucas, Philip Hans Franses, and Dick van Dijk

Panel Data Econometrics
By Manuel Arellano

Periodicity and Stochastic Trends in Economic Time Series
By Philip Hans Franses

Progressive Modelling: Non-nested Testing and Encompassing
Edited by Massimiliano Marcellino and Grayham E. Mizon

Reading in Unobserved Components
Edited by Andrew Harvey and Tommaso Proietti

Stochastic Limit Theory: An Introduction for Econometricians
By James Davidson

Stochastic Volatility
Edited by Neil Shephard

Testing Exogeneity
Edited by Neil R. Ericsson and John S. Irons

The Econometrics of Macroeconomic Modelling
By Gunnar Bårdsen, Øyvind Eitrheim, Eilev S. Jansen, and Ragnar Nymoen

Time Series with Long Memory
Edited by Peter M. Robinson

Time-Series-Based Econometrics: Unit Roots and Co-integrations
By Michio Hatanaka

Workbook on Cointegration
By Peter Reinhard Hansen and Søren Johansen

STOCHASTIC VOLATILITY

Selected Readings

Edited by

NEIL SHEPHARD

OXFORD

UNIVERSITY PRESS

*This book has been printed digitally and produced in a standard specification
in order to ensure its continuing availability*

OXFORD
UNIVERSITY PRESS

Great Clarendon Street, Oxford OX2 6DP

Oxford University Press is a department of the University of Oxford.
It furthers the University's objective of excellence in research, scholarship,
and education by publishing worldwide in

Oxford New York

Auckland   Cape Town Dar es Salaam Hong Kong Karachi
Kuala Lumpur Madrid Melbourne Mexico City   Nairobi
New Delhi Shanghai Taipei Toronto
With offices in
Argentina Austria Brazil Chile Czech Republic France Greece
Guatemala Hungary Italy Japan South Korea Poland Portugal
Singapore Switzerland Thailand Turkey Ukraine Vietnam

Oxford is a registered trade mark of Oxford University Press
in the UK and in certain other countries

Published in the United States
by Oxford University Press Inc., New York

© Neil Shephard, 2005

The moral rights of the author have been asserted

Database right Oxford University Press (maker)

Reprinted 2007

ISBN 978-0-19-925720-1

Contents

List of Contributors

Andersen, Torben, Finance Department, Kellogg School of Management, Northwestern University, 2001 Sheridan Rd, Evanston, IL 60208, U.S.A.

Barndorff-Nielsen, Ole E., Department of Mathematical Sciences, University of Aarhus, Ny Munkegade, DK-8000 Aarhus C, Denmark.

Bollerslev, Tim, Department of Economics, Duke University, Box 90097, Durham, NC 27708-0097, U.S.A.

Chernov, Mikhail, Columbia Business School, Columbia University, 3022 Broadway, Uris Hall 413, New York, NY 10027, U.S.A.

Clark, Peter, Graduate School of Management, University of California, Davis, CA 95616-8609, U.S.A.

Comte, Fabienne, UFR Biomédicale, Université René Descartes-Paris 5, 45 rue des Saints-Pères, 75270 Paris cedex 06, France.

Diebold, Frank, Department of Economics, University of Pennsylvania, 3718 Locust Walk, Philadelphia, PA 19104-6297, U.S.A.

Gallant, A. Ronald, Fuqua School of Business, Duke University, DUMC Box 90120, W425, Durham, NC 27708-0120, U.S.A.

Ghysels, Eric, Department of Economics, University of North Carolina – Chapel Hill, Gardner Hall, CB 3305 Chapel Hill, NC 27599-3305, U.S.A.

Harvey, Andrew, Department of Economics, University of Cambridge, Sidgwick Avenue, Cambridge CB3 9DD, U.K.

Heston, Steven, Department of Finance, Robert H Smith School of Business, University of Maryland, Van Munching Hall, College Park, MD 20742, U.S.A.

Hsieh, David, Fuqua School of Business, Duke University, Box 90120, 134 Towerview Drive, Durham NC 27708-0120, U.S.A.

Hull, John, Finance Group, Joseph L. Rotman School of Management, University of Toronto, 105 St. George Street, Toronto, Ontario M5S 3E6, Canada.

Jacquier, Eric, 3000 Cote Sainte-Catherine, Finance Department, H.E.C. Montreal, Montreal PQ H3T 2A7, Canada.

Kim, Sangjoon, RBS Securities Japan Limited, Riverside Yomiuri Building, 36-2 Nihonbashi-Hakozakicho, Chuo-ku, Tokyo 103-0015, Japan.

Labys, Paul, Charles River Associates, Inc., Salt Lake City, U.S.A.

Melino, Angelo, Department of Economics, University of Toronto, 150 St. George Street, Toronto, Ontario M5S 3G7, Canada.

Nerlove, Marc, Department of Agricultural and Resource Economics, University of Maryland, College Park, MD 20742, U.S.A.

Polson, Nicholas, Chicago Business School, University of Chicago, 1101 East 58th Street, Chicago, IL 60637, U.S.A.

Renault, Eric, Department of Economics, University of North Carolina, Chapel Hill, Gardner Hall, CB 3305 Chapel Hill, NC 27599–3305, U.S.A.

Rosenberg, Barr

Rossi, Peter, Chicago Business School, University of Chicago, 1101 East 58th Street, Chicago, IL 60637, U.S.A.

Ruiz, Esther, Department of Statistics, Universidad Carlos III de Madrid, C/ Madrid, 126–28903, Getafe, Madrid, Spain.

Shephard, Neil, Nuffeld College, University of Oxford, Oxford OX1 1NF, U.K.

Siddhartha, Chib, John M. Olin School of Business, Washington University in St. Louis, Campus Box 1133, 1 Brookings Drive, St. Louis, MO 63130, U.S.A.

Taylor, Stephen, Department of Accounting and Finance, Management School, Lancaster University, Lancaster LA1 4YX, U.K.

Tauchen, George, Department of Economics, Duke University, Box 90097, Durham, NC 27708-0097, U.S.A.

Turnbull, Stuart, Department of Finance, Bauer College of Business, University of Houston, 334 Mel Hall, Houston, TX 77204-6021, U.S.A.

White, Alan, Finance Group, Joseph L. Rotman School of Management, University of Toronto, 105 St. George Street, Toronto, Ontario M5S 3E6, Canada.

General Introduction

NEIL SHEPHARD

Overview

Stochastic volatility (SV) is the main concept used in the fields of financial economics and mathematical finance to deal with time-varying volatility in financial markets. In this book I bring together some of the main papers which have influenced the field of the econometrics of stochastic volatility with the hope that this will allow students and scholars to place this literature in a wider context. We will see that the development of this subject has been highly multi-disciplinary, with results drawn from financial economics, probability theory and econometrics, blending to produce methods and models which have aided our understanding of the realistic pricing of options, efficient asset allocation and accurate risk assessment.

Time-varying volatility and codependence is endemic in financial markets. Only for very low frequency data, such as monthly or yearly asset returns, do these effects tend to take a back seat and the assumption of homogeneity seems not to be entirely unreasonable. This has been known for a long time, early comments include Mandelbrot (1963), Fama (1965) and Officer (1973). It was also clear to the founding fathers of modern continuous time finance that homogeneity was an unrealistic if convenient simplification, e.g. Black and Scholes (1972, p. 416) wrote "... there is evidence of non-stationarity in the variance. More work must be done to predict variances using the information available." Heterogeneity has deep implications for the theory and practice of financial economics and econometrics. In particular, asset pricing theory is dominated by the idea that higher rewards may be expected when we face higher risks, but these risks change through time in complicated ways. Some of the changes in the level of risk can be modelled stochastically, where the level of volatility and degree of codependence between assets is allowed to change over time. Such models allow us to explain, for example, empirically observed departures from Black–Scholes–Merton prices for options and understand why we should expect to see occasional dramatic moves in financial markets. More generally, as with all good modern econometrics, they bring the application of economics closer to the empirical reality of the world we live in, allowing us to make better decisions, inspire new theory and improve model building.

This volume appears around 10 years after the publication of the readings volume by Engle (1995) on autoregressive conditional heteroskedasticity (ARCH) models. These days ARCH processes are often described as SV, but I have not followed that nomenclature here as it allows me to delineate this volume from the one on ARCH. The essential feature of ARCH models is that they explicitly model the conditional variance of returns given past returns observed by the econometrician. This one-step-ahead prediction approach to volatility modelling is very powerful, particularly in the field of risk management. It is convenient from an econometric viewpoint as it immediately delivers the likelihood function as the product of one-step-ahead predictive densities.

In the SV approach the predictive distribution of returns is specified indirectly, via the structure of the model, rather than explicitly. For a small number of SV models this predictive distribution can be calculated explicitly (e.g. Shephard (1994) and Uhlig (1997)). Most of the time it has to be computed numerically. This move away from direct one-step-ahead predictions has some advantages. In particular in continuous time it is more convenient, and perhaps more natural, to model directly the volatility of asset prices as having its own stochastic process without immediately worrying about the implied one-step-ahead distribution of returns recorded over some arbitrary period used by the econometrician, such as a day or a month. This raises some difficulties as the likelihood function for SV models is not directly available, much to the frustration of econometricians in the late 1980s and 1990s.

Since the mid-1980s continuous time SV has dominated the option pricing literature in mathematical finance and financial economics. At the same time econometricians have struggled to come to terms with the difficulties of estimating and testing these models. In response, in the 1990s they developed novel simulation strategies to efficiently estimate SV models. These computationally intensive methods mean that, given enough coding and computing time, we can now more or less efficiently estimate fully parametric SV models. This has lead to refinements of the models, with many earlier tractable models being rejected from an empirical viewpoint. The resulting enriched SV literature has been brought far closer to the empirical realities we face in financial markets.

From the late 1990s SV models have taken centre stage in the econometric analysis of volatility forecasting using high frequency data based on realised volatility and related concepts. The reason for this is that the econometric analysis of realised volatility is generally based on continuous time processes and so SV is central. The close connections between SV and realised volatility have allowed financial econometricians to harness the enriched information set available through the use of high frequency data to improve, by an order of magnitude, the accuracy of their volatility forecasts over that traditionally offered by ARCH models based on daily observations. This has broadened the applications of SV into the important arena of risk assessment and asset allocation.

In this introduction I will briefly outline some of the literature on SV models, providing links to the papers reprinted in this book. I have organised the discussion into models, inference, options and realised volatility. The SV literature has grown rather organically, with a variety of papers playing important roles for particular branches of the literature. This reflects the multidisciplinary nature of the research on this topic and has made my task of selecting the papers particularly difficult. Inevitably my selection of articles to appear in this book has been highly subjective. I hope that the authors of the many interesting papers on this topic which I have not included will forgive my choice.

The outline of this Chapter is as follows. In section 2 I will trace the origins of SV and provide links with the basic models used today in the literature. In section 3 I will briefly discuss some of the innovations in the second generation of SV models. These include the use of long-memory volatility processes, the introduction of jumps into the price and volatility processes and the use of SV in interest rate models. The section will finish by discussing various multivariate SV models. In section 4 I will briefly discuss the literature on conducting inference for SV models. In section 5 I will talk about the use of SV to price options. This application was, for around 15 years, the major motivation for the study of SV models as they seemed to provide a natural way to extend the Black–Scholes–Merton framework to cover more empirically realistic situations. In section 6 I will consider the connection of SV with the literature on realised volatility.

The origin of SV models

The modern treatment of SV is almost all in continuous time, but quite a lot of the older papers were in discrete time. Typically early econometricians in this subject used discrete time models, while financial mathematicians and option pricing financial economists tended to work in continuous time. It was only in the mid-1990s that econometricians started getting to grips with the continuous time versions of the models. The origins of SV are messy. I will give five accounts, which attribute the subject to different sets of people.

Clark (1973) introduced Bochner's (1949) time-changed Brownian motion (BM) into financial economics (see also Blattberg and Gonedes (1974, Section 3)). He wrote down a model for the log-price M as

$$M_t = W_{\tau_t}, \ t \geq 0, \tag{1}$$

where W is Brownian motion (BM), t is continuous time and τ is a time-change. The definition of a time-change is a non-negative process with non-decreasing sample paths. In econometrics this is often also called a subordinator, which is unfortunate as probability theory reserves this name for the special case of a time-change with independent and stationary increments (i.e. equally spaced increments of τ are i.i.d.). I think econometricians should follow the probabilists in this aspect and so I will refer to τ solely as a time-change, reserving the word subordinator for its more specialised technical meaning. Clark studied various properties of log-prices in cases where W and τ are independent processes. Then $M_t|\tau_t \sim N(0, \tau_t)$. Thus, marginally, the increments of M are a normal mixture, which means they are symmetric but can be fat tailed (see also Press (1967), Praetz (1972)). Further, now extending Clark, so long (for each t) as $E\sqrt{\tau_t} < \infty$ then M is a martingale (written $M \in \mathcal{M}$) for this is necessary and sufficient to ensure that $E|M_t| < \infty$. More generally if (for each t) $\tau_t < \infty$ then M is a local martingale (written $M \in \mathcal{M}_{loc}$)—which is a convenient generalisation of a martingale in financial economics. Hence Clark was solely modelling the instantly risky component of the log of an asset price, written Y, which in modern semimartingale (written $Y \in \mathcal{SM}$) notation we would write as

$$Y = A + M.$$

In this notation the increments of A can be thought of as the instantly available reward component of the asset price, which compensates the investor for being exposed to the risky increments of M. The A process is assumed to be of finite variation (written $A \in \mathcal{FV}$), which informally means that the sum of the absolute values of the increments of this process measured over very small time intervals is finite. A simple model for A would be $A_t = \mu t + \beta \tau_t$, where β is thought of as a risk premium. This would mean that $Y_t|\tau_t \sim N(\mu t + \beta \tau_t, \tau_t)$.

In some of his paper Clark regarded τ as a deterministic function of observables, such as the volume of the asset traded. This work was followed by influential articles by Tauchen and Pitts (1983), Andersen (1994), Andersen (1996) and later by Ané and Geman (2000). In other parts of the paper he regarded τ as latent. It is perhaps the latter approach which has had more immediate impact. The main part of the Clark paper dealt with the case where τ was a subordinator and assumed $W \perp\!\!\!\perp \tau$ (that is W is independent of τ). He compared possible parametric models for τ using various datasets, rejecting the stable hypothesis earlier suggested by Mandelbrot (1963) and Mandelbrot and Taylor (1967). This broad framework of models, built by time-changing BM using a subordinator, is now called a type-G Lévy process for M. It has been influential in the recent mathematical finance literature. Leading references include Madan and Seneta (1990), Eberlein and Keller (1995), Barndorff-Nielsen (1998) and Carr, Geman, Madan, and Yor (2002).

Clark's paper is very important and, from the viewpoint of financial economics, very novel. It showed financial economists that they could move away from BM without resorting to empirically unattractive stable processes. Clark's arguments were in continuous time, which nicely matches much of the modern literature. However, a careful reading of the paper leads to the conclusion that it does not really deal with time-varying volatility in the modern sense. In the Clark paper no mechanism is proposed that would explicitly generate volatility clustering in M by modelling τ as having serially dependent increments.

To the best of my understanding the first published direct volatility clustering SV paper is that by Taylor (1982) (see also Taylor (1980)). This is a neglected paper, with the literature usually attributing his work on SV to his seminal book Taylor (1986), which was the first lengthy published treatment of the problem of volatility modelling in finance. I emphasise the 1982 paper as it appeared without knowledge of Engle (1982) on modelling the volatility of inflation.

Taylor's paper is in discrete time, although I will link this to the continuous time notation used above. He modelled daily returns, computed as the difference of log-prices

$$y_i = Y(i) - Y(i-1), \quad i = 1, 2, \ldots,$$

where I have assumed that $t = 1$ represents one day to simplify the exposition. In his equation (3) he modelled the risky part of returns,

$$m_i = M_i - M_{i-1}$$

as a product process

$$m_i = \sigma_i \varepsilon_i. \tag{2}$$

Taylor assumed ε has a mean of zero and unit variance, while σ is some non-negative process, finishing the model by assuming $\varepsilon \perp\!\!\!\perp \sigma$. The key feature of this model is that the signs of m are determined by ε, while the time-varying σ delivers volatility clustering and fat tails in the marginal distribution of m. Taylor modelled ε as an autoregression and

$$\sigma_i = \exp(h_i/2),$$

where h is a non-zero mean Gaussian linear process. The leading example of this is the first order autoregression

$$h_{i+1} = \mu + \phi(h_i - \mu) + \eta_i, \tag{3}$$

where η is a zero mean, Gaussian white noise process. In the modern SV literature the model for ε is typically simplified to an i.i.d. process, for we deal with the predictability of asset prices through the A process rather than via M. This is now often called the log-normal SV model in the case where ε is also assumed to be Gaussian. In general, M is always a local martingale, while it is a martingale so long as $E(\sigma_i) < \infty$, which holds for the parametric models considered by Taylor as long as h is stationary.

A key feature of SV, which is not discussed by Taylor, is that it can deal with leverage effects. Leverage effects are associated with the work of Black (1976) and Nelson (1991), and can be implemented in discrete time SV models by negatively correlating the Gaussian ε_i and η_i. This still implies that $M \in \mathcal{M}_{loc}$, but allows the direction of returns to influence future movements in the volatility process, with falls in prices associated with rises in subsequent volatility. This is important empirically for equity prices but less so for exchange rates where the previous independence assumption roughly holds in practice. Leverage effects also generate skewness, via the dynamics of the model, in the distribution of $(M_{i+s} - M_i)|\sigma_i$ for $s \geq 2$, although $(M_{i+1} - M_i)|\sigma_i$ continues to be symmetric. This is a major reason for the success of these types of models in option pricing where skewness seems endemic.

Taylor's discussion of the product process was predated by a decade in the unpublished Rosenberg (1972). I believe this noteworthy paper has been more or less lost to the modern SV literature, although one can find references to it in the work of, for example, Merton (1976a). It is clear from my discussions with other researchers in this field that it was indirectly influential on a number of very early SV option pricing scholars (who I will discuss in a moment), but that econometricians are largely unaware of it.

Rosenberg introduces product processes, empirically demonstrating that time-varying volatility is partially forecastable and so breaks with the earlier work by Clark, Press, etc. In section 2 he develops some of the properties of product processes. The comment below (2.12) suggests an understanding of aggregational Gaussianity of returns over increasing time intervals (see Diebold (1988)). In section 3 he predates a variety of econometric methods for analysing heteroskedasticity. In particular in (3.4) he regresses log squared returns on various predetermined explanatory variables. This method for dealing with heteroskedasticity echoes earlier work by Bartlett and Kendall (1946) and was advocated in the context of regression by Harvey (1976), while its use with unobserved volatility processes was popularised by Harvey, Ruiz, and Shephard (1994). In (3.6) he writes, ignoring regressor terms, the squared returns in terms of the volatility plus a white noise error term. In section 3.3 he uses moving averages of squared data, while (3.17) is remarkably close to the GARCH(p,q) model introduced by Engle (1982) and Bollerslev (1986). In particular in the case where u_i is exactly zero he produces the GARCH model. However, this vital degenerate case is not explicitly mentioned. Thus what is missing, compared to the ARCH approach, is that σ_i^2 could be explicitly written as the conditional variance of returns—which, in my view, is the main insight in Engle (1982). This degenerate case is key as it produces a one-step-ahead conditional model for returns given past data, which is important from an economic viewpoint and immediately yields a likelihood function. The latter greatly eases the estimation and testing of ARCH models. Rosenberg also did not derive any of the stochastic properties of these ARCH type model. However, having said that, this is by far the closest precursor of the ARCH class of models I have seen.

The product process (2) is a key modelling idea and will reappear quite often in this Introduction. In continuous time the standard SV model of the risky part of a price process is the stochastic integral

$$M_t = \int_0^t \sigma_s \mathrm{d} W_s, \qquad (4)$$

where the non-negative spot volatility σ is assumed to have càdlàg sample paths (which implies it can possess jumps). Such integrals are often written in the rather attractive, concise notation

$$M = \sigma \bullet W,$$

where $\bullet$ denotes stochastic integration (e.g. Protter (2004)). The squared volatility process is often called the spot variance or variation. I follow the latter nomenclature here. There is no necessity for σ and W to be independent, but when they are we obtain the important simplification that $M_t | \int_0^t \sigma_s^2 ds \sim N\left(0, \int_0^t \sigma_s^2 ds\right)$, which aids understanding, computation and immediately links the model structure to the time-change BM model (1) of Clark.

The first use of continuous time SV models in financial economics was, to my knowledge, in the unpublished Johnson (1979) who studied the pricing of options using time-changing volatility models in continuous time. This paper evolved into Johnson and Shanno (1987). Wiggins (1987) studied similar types of problems, recording his work first in his 1986 MIT Ph.D. thesis. The most well known paper in this area is Hull and White (1987) who allowed the spot volatility process to follow a diffusion. Each of these authors was motivated by a desire to generalise the Black and Scholes (1973) and Merton (1973) approach to option pricing models to deal with volatility clustering. In the Hull and White approach the spot variation process is written out as the solution to the univariate stochastic differential equation (SDE)

$$d\sigma^2 = \alpha(\sigma^2)dt + \omega(\sigma^2)dB,$$

where B is a second Brownian motion and $\omega(.)$ is a non-negative deterministic function. The process they spent most time on in their paper was originally parameterised as a linear process for $\log \sigma^2$. In particular they often focused on

$$d \log \sigma^2 = \alpha(\mu - \log \sigma^2)dt + \omega dB, \quad \alpha > 0,$$

which is a Gaussian OU process. The log-normal SV model in Taylor (1982) can be thought of as an Euler discretisation of this continuous time model over a unit time period

$$M_{t+1} - M_t = \sigma_t(W_{t+1} - W_t),$$
$$\log \sigma_{t+1}^2 - \log \sigma_t^2 = \alpha(\mu - \log \sigma_t^2) + \omega(B_{t+1} - B_t).$$

Ito's formula implies that the log-normal OU model can be written as

$$d\sigma^2 = \alpha\sigma^2\left\{\mu + e^{\omega^2/2} - \log \sigma^2\right\}dt + \omega\sigma^2 dB.$$

Other standard models of this type are the square root process used in this context by Heston (1993) and the so-called GARCH diffusion introduced by Nelson (1990). By potentially correlating the increments of W and B, Hull and White produced the first coherent and explicit leverage model in financial economics. It motivated the later econometric work of Nelson (1991) on EGARCH models.

In the general diffusion-based models the volatility was specified to be Markovian and to have a continuous sample path. Note this is a constraint on the general SV structure (4) which makes neither of these assumptions. Research in the late 1990s and early 2000s has shown that more complicated volatility dynamics are needed to model either options data or high frequency return data. Leading extensions to the model are to allow jumps into the volatility SDE (e.g. Barndorff-Nielsen and Shephard (2001) and Eraker, Johannes, and Polson (2003)) or to model the volatility process as a function of a number of separate stochastic processes or factors (e.g. Chernov, Gallant, Ghysels, and Tauchen (2003), Barndorff-Nielsen and Shephard (2001)). Chernov, Gallant, Ghysels, and Tauchen (2003) is particularly good at teasing out the empirical relevance of particular parts and extensions of SV models.

The SV models given by (4) have continuous sample paths even if σ does not. For $M \in \mathcal{M}_{loc}$ we need to assume (for every t) that $\int_0^t \sigma_s^2 \mathrm{d}s < \infty$, while a necessary and sufficient condition for $M \in \mathcal{M}$ is that $\mathrm{E}\sqrt{\int_0^t \sigma_s^2 \mathrm{d}s} < \infty$.

At first sight the construction of SV models looks rather ad hoc. However, the probability literature has demonstrated that they and their time-changed BM relatives are fundamental. This theoretical development will be the fifth strand of literature that I think of as representing the origins of modern stochastic volatility research. I will now discuss some of it. Suppose we simply assume that $M \in \mathcal{M}_{loc}^c$, a process with continuous local martingale sample paths. Then the celebrated Dambis–Dubins–Schwartz Theorem (cf., for example, Rogers and Williams (1996, p. 64)) shows that M can be written as a time-changed Brownian motion. Further the time-change is the quadratic variation (QV) process

$$[M]_t = \mathrm{p} - \lim_{n \to \infty} \sum_{j=1}^n (M_{t_j} - M_{t_j-1})^2, \tag{5}$$

for any sequence of partitions $t_0 = 0 < t_1 < \ldots < t_n = t$ with $\sup_j\{t_j - t_{j-1}\} \to 0$ for $n \to \infty$ (e.g. Jacod and Shiryaev (1987, p. 55)). What is more, as M has continuous sample paths, so must $[M]$. Under the stronger condition that $[M]$ is absolutely continuous, then M can be written as a stochastic volatility process. This latter result, which is called the martingale representation theorem, is due to Doob (1953)[1]. Taken together this implies that time-changed BMs are canonical

---

[1] An example of a continuous local martingale which has no SV representation is a time-change Brownian motion where the time-change takes the form of the so-called "devil's staircase," which is continuous and non-decreasing but not absolutely continuous (see, for example, Munroe (1953, Section 27)). This relates to the work of, for example, Calvet and Fisher (2002) on multifractals.

in continuous sample path price processes and SV models are special cases of this class. A consequence of the fact that for continuous sample path time-change BM, $[M] = \tau$ is that in the SV case

$$[M]_t = \int_0^t \sigma_s^2 ds,$$

the integrated variation of the SV model. This implies that the left derivative of the QV process is σ_{t-}^2, the spot variation just before time t. Of course if σ^2 has continuous sample paths then $\partial[M]_t/\partial t = \sigma_t^2$.

Although the time-changed BM is a slightly more general class than the SV framework, SV models are perhaps somewhat more convenient as they have an elegant multivariate generalisation. In particular, write a p-dimensional price process M as

$$M = \Theta \bullet W,$$

where Θ is a matrix process whose elements are all càdlàg, W is a multivariate BM process and the (ll)-element of Θ has the property that

$$\int_0^t \Theta_{(ll)s} ds < \infty, \quad l = 1, 2, \dots, p.$$

Again a key feature of this model class is that the QV process,

$$[M]_t = p - \lim_{n \to \infty} \sum_{j=1}^n (M_{t_j} - M_{t_j-1})(M_{t_j} - M_{t_j-1})',$$

has the property that

$$[M]_t = \int_0^t \Theta_s \Theta_s' ds,$$

the integrated covariation. Further, the SV class is closed under stochastic integration. In particular with M as a vector SV process, then

$$U = \Psi \bullet M = (\Psi\Theta) \bullet W = \Theta^* \bullet W$$

is again a SV process. This is attractive as we can think of U as the value of a set of portfolios constructed out of SV processes. In particular if M is a vector of SV processes, then each element of U is also a SV process. Hence this class is closed under marginalisation. This desirable feature is not true for ARCH models.

Second generation model building

Univariate models

Long memory

In the first generation of SV models the volatility process was given by a simple SDE driven by a BM. This means that the spot volatility was a Markov process. There is considerable empirical evidence that, whether the volatility is measured using high frequency data over a couple of years or using daily data recorded over decades, the dependence in the volatility structure initially decays quickly at short lags but the decay slows at longer lags (e.g. Engle and Lee (1999)). There are a number of possible causes for this. One argument is that long memory effects are generated by the aggregation of the behaviour of different agents who are trading using different time horizons (e.g. Granger (1980)). A recent volume of readings on the econometrics of long memory is given in Robinson (2003). Leading advocates of this line of argument in financial econometrics are Dacorogna, Gencay, Müller, Olsen, and Pictet (2001), Andersen and Bollerslev (1997a) and Andersen and Bollerslev (1998b) who have been motivated by their careful empirical findings using high frequency data. A second line of argument is that the long-memory effects are spurious, generated by a shifting level in the average level of volatility through time (e.g. Diebold and Inoue (2001)). In this discussion we will not judge the relative merits of these different approaches.

In the SV literature considerable progress has been made on working with both discrete and continuous time long memory SV. This is, in principle, straightforward. We just need to specify a long-memory model for σ in discrete or continuous time.

In independent and concurrent work Breidt, Crato, and de Lima (1998) and Harvey (1998) looked at discrete time models where the log of the volatility was modelled as a fractionally integrated process. They showed this could be handled econometrically by moment estimators which, although not efficient, were computationally simple.

In continuous time there is work on modelling the log of volatility as fractionally integrated Brownian motion by Comte and Renault (1998) and Gloter and Hoffmann (2004). More recent work, which is econometrically easier to deal with, is the square root model driven by fractionally integrated BM introduced in an influential paper by Comte, Coutin, and Renault (2003) and the infinite superposition of non-negative OU processes introduced by Barndorff-Nielsen (2001). These two models have the advantage that it may be possible to perform options pricing calculations using them without great computational cost. Ohanissian, Russell, and Tsay (2003) have used implied volatilities to compare the predictions from the Comte, Coutin, and Renault (2003) long memory model with a model with spurious long memory generated through shifts. Their empirical evidence favours the use of genuine long memory models. See also the work of Taylor (2000) on this topic.

Jumps

In detailed empirical work a number of researchers have supplemented standard SV models by adding jumps to the price process or to the volatility dynamics. This follows, of course, earlier work by Merton (1976*b*) on adding jumps to diffusions. Bates (1996) was particularly important as it showed the need to include jumps in addition to SV, at least when volatility is Markovian. Eraker, Johannes, and Polson (2003) deals with the efficient inference of these types of models. A radical departure in SV models was put forward by Barndorff-Nielsen and Shephard (2001) who suggested building volatility models out of pure jump processes. In particular they wrote, in their simplest model, that σ^2 follows the solution to the SDE

$$\mathrm{d}\sigma_t^2 = -\lambda\sigma_t^2\mathrm{d}t + \mathrm{d}z_{\lambda t}, \quad \lambda > 0,$$

and where z is a subordinator (recall this is a process with non-negative increments, which are independent and stationary). The rather odd-looking timing $z_{\lambda t}$ is present to ensure that the stationary distribution of σ^2 does not depend upon λ. Closed form option pricing based on this non-Gaussian OU model structure is studied briefly in Barndorff-Nielsen and Shephard (2001) and in detail by Nicolato and Venardos (2003). This work is related to the earliest paper I know of which puts jumps in the volatility process. Bookstaber and Pomerantz (1989) wrote down a non-Gaussian OU model for σ, not σ^2, in the special case where z is a finite activity gamma process. This type of process is often called "shot noise" in the probability literature. All these non-Gaussian OU processes are special cases of the affine class advocated by Duffie, Pan, and Singleton (2000) and Duffie, Filipovic, and Schachermayer (2003). Extensions from the OU structure to continuous time ARMA processes have been developed by Brockwell (2004) and Brockwell and Marquardt (2004), while Andersen (1994) discusses various autoregressive type volatility models.

I have found the approach of Carr, Geman, Madan, and Yor (2003), Geman, Madan, and Yor (2001) and Carr and Wu (2004) stimulating. They define the martingale component of prices as a time-change Lévy process, generalising Clark's time-change of Brownian motion. Empirical evidence given by Barndorff-Nielsen and Shephard (2003*b*) suggested these rather simple models are potentially well fitting in practice. Clearly if one built the time-change of the pure jump Lévy process out of an integrated non-Gaussian OU process then the resulting process would not have any Brownian components in the continuous time price process. This is a rather radical departure from the usual continuous time models used in financial economics.

Another set of papers which allow volatility to jump is the Markov switching literature. This is usually phrased in discrete time, with the volatility stochastically moving between a finite number of fixed regimes. Leading examples of this include Hamilton and Susmel (1994), Cai (1994), Lam, Li, and So (1998), Elliott, Hunter, and Jamieson (1998) and Calvet and Fisher (2002). See also some of statistical theory associated with these types of models is discussed in Genon-Catalot, Jeantheau, and Larédo (2000).

Interest rate models

Stochastic volatility has been used to model the innovations to the short-rate, the rate of interest paid over short periods of time. The standard approach in financial economics is to model the short-rate by a univariate diffusion, but it is well known that such Markov processes, however elaborate their drift or diffusion, cannot capture the dynamics observed in empirical work. Early papers on this topic are Chan, Karolyi, Longstaff, and Sanders (1992) and Longstaff and Schwartz (1992), while Nissen, Koedijk, Schotman, and Wolff (1997) is a detailed empirical study. Andersen and Lund (1997) studied processes with SV innovations

$$\mathrm{d}r_t = \kappa(\mu - r_t)\mathrm{d}t + \sigma_t r_t^\gamma \mathrm{d}W_t.$$

We may expect the short-rate to be stationary and the mean reversion is modelled using the linear drift. The volatility of the rate is expected to increase with the level of the rate, which accounts for the r^γ effects where $\gamma \geq 1/2$. When the volatility is constant the r^γ term would also enforce a reflecting boundary at zero for the short rate (so long as the volatility is sufficiently small compared to the drift), which is convenient as the short-rate is not expected to become negative. It is less clear to me if this is the case with stochastic volatility. Elaborations on this type of model have been advocated by for example Ahn, Dittmar, and Gallant (2002), Andersen, Benzoni, and Lund (2002), Bansal and Zhou (2002) and Dai and Singleton (2000).

Multivariate models

In an important paper Diebold and Nerlove (1989) introduced volatility clustering into traditional factor models, which are used in many areas of asset pricing. Their paper was in discrete time. They allowed each factor to have its own internal dynamic structure, which they parameterised as an ARCH process. The factors are not latent which means that this is a multivariate SV model. In continuous time their type of model would have the following interpretation

$$M = \sum_{j=1}^{J} (\beta_{(j)} \bullet F_{(j)}) + G,$$

where the factors $F_{(1)}, F_{(2)}, \ldots, F_{(J)}$ are independent univariate SV models and G is correlated multivariate BM. This structure has the advantage that if time-invariant portfolios are made of assets whose prices follow this type of process, then the risky part of prices will also have a factor structure of this type. Some of the related papers on the econometrics of this topic include King, Sentana, and Wadhwani (1994), Sentana (1998), Pitt and Shephard (1999b) and Fiorentini,

Sentana, and Shephard (2004), who all fit this kind of model. These papers assume that the factor loading vectors are constant through time.

A more limited multivariate discrete time model was put forward by Harvey, Ruiz, and Shephard (1994) who allowed $M = C(\Theta \bullet W)$, where Θ is a diagonal matrix process and C is a fixed matrix of constants with a unit leading diagonal. This means that the risky part of prices is simply a rotation of a p-dimensional vector of univariate SV processes. In principle the elements $\Theta_{(ll)}$ can be dependent over l, which means the univariate SV processes are uncorrelated but not independent. This model is close to the multivariate ARCH model of Bollerslev (1990) for although the M process can exhibit quite complicated volatility clustering, the correlation structure between the assets is constant through time.

Inference based on return data

Moment based inference

A major difficulty with the use of discrete but particularly continuous time SV models is that traditionally they have been hard to estimate in comparison with their ARCH cousins. In ARCH models, by construction, the likelihood (or quasi-likelihood) function is readily available. In SV models this is not the case, which leads to two streams of literature originating in the 1990s. First, there is a literature on computationally intensive methods which approximate the efficiency of likelihood based inference arbitrarily well, but at the cost of the use of specialised and time-consuming techniques. Second, a large number of papers have built relatively simple, inefficient estimators based on easily computable moments of the model. It is the second literature which we will briefly discuss before focusing on the former.

The task is to carry out inference based on a sequence of returns $y = (y_1, \ldots, y_T)'$ from which we will attempt to learn about $\theta = (\theta_1, \ldots, \theta_K)'$, the parameters of the SV model. The early SV paper by Taylor (1982) calibrated his discrete time model using the method of moments. A similar but more extensive approach was used by Melino and Turnbull (1990) in continuous time. Their paper used an Euler approximation of their model before computing the moments. Systematic studies, using a GMM approach, of which moments to heavily weight in discrete time SV models was given in Andersen and Sørensen (1996), Genon-Catalot, Jeantheau, and Larédo (1999), Genon-Catalot, Jeantheau, and Larédo (2000), Sørensen (2000), Gloter (2000) and Hoffmann (2002).

A difficulty with using moment based estimators for continuous time SV models is that it is not straightforward to compute the moments of the discrete returns y from the continuous time models. In the case of no leverage, general results for the second order properties of y and their squares were given in Barndorff-Nielsen and Shephard (2001). Some quite general results under leverage are also given in Meddahi (2001), who focuses on a special class of volatility models which are widely applicable and particularly tractable.

In the discrete time log-normal SV models described by (2) and (3), the approach advocated by Harvey, Ruiz, and Shephard (1994) has been influential.

This method, which also appears in the unpublished 1988 MIT Ph.D. thesis of Dan Nelson, in Scott (1987) and the early unpublished drafts of Melino and Turnbull (1990), was the first readily applicable method which both gave parameter estimates, and filtered and smoothed estimates of the underlying volatility process. Their approach was to remove the predictable part of the returns, so we think of $Y = M$ again, and work with $\log y_i^2 = h_i + \log \varepsilon_i^2$, which linearises the process into a signal (log-volatility) plus noise model. If the volatility has short memory then this form of the model can be handled using the Kalman filter, while long memory models are often dealt with in the frequency domain (Breidt, Crato, and de Lima (1998) and Harvey (1998)). Either way this delivers a Gaussian quasi-likelihood which can be used to estimate the parameters of the model. The linearised model is non-Gaussian due to the long left hand tail of $\log \varepsilon_i^2$ which generates outliers when ε_i is small. Comparisons of the performance of this estimator with the fully efficient Bayesian estimators I will discuss in a moment is given in Jacquier, Polson, and Rossi (1994), which shows in Monte Carlo experiments that it is reasonable but quite significantly inefficient.

Simulation based inference
In the early to mid-1990s a number of econometricians started to develop and use simulation based inference devices to tackle SV models. Their hope was that they could win significant efficiency gains by using these more computationally intensive methods. Concurrently two approaches were brought forward. The first was the application of Markov chain Monte Carlo (MCMC) techniques, which came into econometrics from the image processing and statistical physics literatures, to perform likelihood based inference. The second was the development of indirect inference or the so-called efficient method of moments. This second approach is, to my knowledge, a new and quite general statistical estimation procedure. To discuss these methods it will be convenient to focus on the simplest discrete time log-normal SV model given by (2) and (3).

MCMC allows us to simulate from high dimensional posterior densities, a simple example of which is the smoothing variables $h|y$, θ, where $h = (h_1, \ldots, h_T)'$ are the discrete time unobserved log-volatilities. The earliest published use of MCMC methods on SV models is Shephard (1993) who noted that SV models were a special case of a Markov random field and so MCMC could be used to carry out the simulation of $h|y$, θ in $O(T)$ flops. This means the simulation output inside an EM algorithm can be used to approximate the maximum likelihood estimator of θ. This parametric inference method, which was the first fully efficient inference methods for SV models published in the literature, is quite clunky as it has a lot of tuning constants and is slow to converge numerically. In an influential paper, whose initial drafts I believe were written concurrently and independently from the drafts of Shephard's paper, Jacquier, Polson, and Rossi (1994) demonstrated that a more elegant inference algorithm could be developed by becoming Bayesian and using the MCMC algorithm to simulate from h, $\theta|y$, again in $O(T)$ flops. The exact details of their sampler do not really matter as subsequent researchers have produced computationally simpler and numerically more efficient methods (of course they have the same statistical efficiency!). What is important is that once Jacquier, Polson, and Rossi (1994) had an ability to compute many simulations from this $T + K$ dimensional random variable (recall there are K parameters), they could discard the h variables and simply record the many draws from $\theta|y$. Summarising these draws then allows them to perform fully efficient parametric inference in a relatively sleek way. See Chib (2001) for a wider view of MCMC methods.

A subsequent paper by Kim, Shephard, and Chib (1998) gives quite an extensive discussion of various alternative methods for actually implementing the MCMC algorithm. This is a subtle issue and makes a very large difference to the computational efficiency of the methods. There have been quite a number of papers on developing MCMC algorithms for various extensions of the basic SV model (e.g. Wong (1999), Meyer and Yu (2000), Jacquier, Polson, and Rossi (2003), Yu (2003)).

Kim, Shephard, and Chib (1998) also introduced the first genuine filtering method for recursively sampling from

$$h_1, \ldots, h_i|y_1, \ldots, y_{i-1}, \theta, \ i = 1, 2, \ldots, T,$$

in a total of $O(T)$ flops[2]. These draws allow us to estimate by simulation $E(\sigma_i^2|y_1, \ldots, y_{t-1}, \theta)$, the corresponding density and the density of $y_i|y_1, \ldots, y_{t-1}, \theta$. This was carried out via a so-called particle filter (see, for example, Gordon, Salmond, and Smith (1993), Doucet, de Freitas, and Gordon (2001) and Pitt and Shephard (1999a) for more details. The latter paper focuses its examples explicitly on SV models). Johannes, Polson, and Stroud (2002) discusses using these methods on continuous time SV models, while an alternative strategy for performing a kind of filtering is the reprojection algorithm of Gallant and Tauchen (1998). As well as being of substantial scientific interest for decision making, the advantage of having a filtering method is that it allows us to compute marginal likelihoods for model comparison and one-step-ahead predictions for model testing. This allowed us to see if these SV models actually fit the data.

Although these MCMC based papers are mostly couched in discrete time, a key advantage of the general approach is that it can be adapted to deal with continuous time models by the idea of augmentation. This was mentioned in Kim, Shephard, and Chib (1998), but fully worked out in Elerian, Chib, and Shephard (2001), Eraker (2001) and Roberts and Stramer (2001). In passing we should also mention the literature on maximum simulated likelihood estimation, which maximises an estimate of the log-likelihood function computed by simulation. General contributions to this literature include Hendry and Richard (1991), Durbin and Koopman (1997), Shephard and Pitt (1997) and Durbin and

---

[2] Of course one could repeatedly reuse MCMC methods to perform filtering, but each simulation would cost $O(t)$ flops, so processing the entire sample would cost $O(T^2)$ flops which is usually regarded as being unacceptable.

Koopman (2001). The applications of these methods to the SV problem include Danielsson (1994), Sandmann and Koopman (1998), Durbin and Koopman (2001) and Durham and Gallant (2002). The corresponding results on inference for continuous time models is given in the seminal paper by Pedersen (1995), as well as additional contributions by Elerian, Chib, and Shephard (2001), Brandt and Santa-Clara (2002), Durham and Gallant (2002) and Durham (2003).

The work on particle filters is related to Foster and Nelson (1996) (note also the work of Genon-Catalot, Laredo, and Picard (1992) and Hansen (1995)). They provided an asymptotic distribution theory for an estimator of $\Theta_t \Theta_t'$, the spot (not integrated) covariance. Their idea was to compute a local covariance from the lagged data, e.g.

$$\widehat{\Theta_t \Theta_t'} = \hbar^{-1} \sum_{j=1}^{M} (Y_{t-hj/M} - Y_{t-h(j-1)/M})(Y_{t-hj/M} - Y_{t-h(j-1)/M})'.$$

They then studied its behaviour as $M \to \infty$ and $h \downarrow 0$ under some assumptions. This "double asymptotics" yields a Gaussian limit theory so long as $h \downarrow 0$ and $M \to \infty$ at the correct, connected rates. This work is related to the realised volatility literature discussed in section 6.

As I discussed above, the use of MCMC methods to perform inference on SV models is important, but it really amounted to the careful importation of existing technology from the statistics literatures. A more novel approach was introduced by Smith (1993) and later developed by Gourieroux, Monfort, and Renault (1993) and Gallant and Tauchen (1996) into what is now called indirect inference or the efficient method of moments. Throughout their development of this rather general fully parametric simulation method both Gourieroux, Monfort, and Renault (1993) and Gallant and Tauchen (1996) had very much in mind the task of performing reasonably efficient inference on SV models. Early applications include Engle and Lee (1996) and Monfardini (1998). Gallant, Hsieh, and Tauchen (1997) give an extensive discussion of the use of these methods in practice. Here I will briefly give a stylised version of this approach, using different notation.

Suppose there is an alternative plausible model for the returns whose density, $g(y; \psi)$, is easy to compute and, for simplicity of exposition, has $\dim(\psi) = \dim(\theta)$. The model g is often called the auxiliary model. I suppose it is a good description of the data. Think of it, for simplicity of exposition, as GARCH. Then compute its MLE, which we write as $\hat{\psi}$. We assume this is a regular problem so that

$$\left. \frac{\partial \log g(y; \psi)}{\partial \psi} \right|_{\psi = \hat{\psi}} = 0,$$

recalling that y is the observed return vector. Now suppose we simulate a very long process from the SV model using parameters θ, which we denote by y^+ and evaluate the score not using the data but this simulation. This produces

$$\left. \frac{\partial \log g(y^+;\psi)}{\partial \psi} \right|_{\psi=\hat{\psi}}, \quad y^+ \sim f(y;\theta).$$

Then we could move θ around until the score is again zero, but now under the simulation. Write the point where this happens as $\tilde{\theta}$. It is called the indirect inference estimator. It has been derived via the auxiliary model. Notice the data only enters the estimation procedure via the statistic $\hat{\psi}$. This procedure is not necessarily very efficient. Clearly it would be if g were the likelihood of the SV model and the simulation was very long. Gallant and Tauchen emphasise that the econometrician should try to use very well fitting g models for this procedure and have particular recipes for obtaining this. This work has been influential: leading applications of the method include Ahn, Dittmar, and Gallant (2002), Andersen, Benzoni, and Lund (2002), Bansal and Zhou (2002), Chernov and Ghysels (2000), Dai and Singleton (2000) and Andersen and Lund (1997).

Options

Models
A large number of papers have used SV models as the basis for realistic modelling of option prices. Almost all the literature on this topic is in continuous time, an exception being the early work carried out by Taylor (1986). The development of continuous time SV models was driven by the desire to produce more accurate option pricing formulae. These continuous time models were reviewed at the start of this paper. We just recall the central role played by Johnson (1979), Johnson and Shanno (1987) and Wiggins (1987). The most well-known paper in this area is by Hull and White (1987), who looked at a diffusion volatility model with leverage effects. They assumed that volatility risk was unrewarded and priced their options either by approximation or by simulation. Hull and White (1987) indicated that SV models could produce smiles and skews in option prices, which are frequency observed in market data. The skew is particularly important in practice and Renault and Touzi (1996) and Renault (1997) prove that can be achieved in SV models via leverage effects. Other related papers around this time include Scott (1987), Hull and White (1988), Chesney and Scott (1989) and Scott (1991). Melino and Turnbull (1990) was an early paper, first written in 1987, which estimated SV models using return data and then assessed how well these models predicted the prices of options. Their experimentation with simulation to allow the estimation of parameters inside an option pricing model leads naturally into the later work by Duffie and Singleton (1993) on simulated method of moments. A systematic study of this type of problem is given in Renault (1997). The book length discussion by Fouque, Papanicolaou, and Sircar (2000) allows one to access some of the mathematical finance literature

on this topic, particularly from their viewpoint of fast reverting volatility processes.

The first analytic option pricing formula was developed by Stein and Stein (1991) who modelled σ as a Gaussian OU process. A European option could then be computed using a single Fourier inverse. In this literature, such a level of computational complexity is called "closed form." A modelling difficulty with the Stein and Stein approach is that the volatility process could go negative. Heston (1993) overcame this by employing a square root volatility process. The only other closed form solution I know of is the one based on the Barndorff-Nielsen and Shephard (2001) class of non-Gaussian OU SV models. Nicolato and Venardos (2003) provide a detailed study of such option pricing solutions. See also the textbook exposition in Cont and Tankov (2004, ch. 15). Slightly harder computationally to deal with is the more general affine class of models highlighted by Duffie, Pan, and Singleton (2000) and Duffie, Filipovic, and Schachermayer (2003), which can be thought of as flowing from Stein and Stein (1991) and Heston (1993). They need the user to solve a differential equation inside a numerical Fourier inverse to price options. Carr and Wu (2004) is a stimulating paper for option pricing on time-change Lévy processes, while Hobson and Rogers (1998) and Jeantheau (2004) try to recapture completeness in stochastic volatility modelling.

Econometrics of SV option pricing

In theory, option prices themselves should provide rich information for estimating and testing volatility models. In the Black–Scholes–Merton world, a single option price would allow us to determine uniquely the volatility with no measurement error. Such "estimates" are called implied volatilities in the literature and play a key role in much applied work with option data. Of course, in practice implied volatilities are not constant through time, across maturities or strike prices. This is the result predicted by SV models.

In this subsection I will discuss the econometrics of options in the context of the stochastic discount factor (SDF) approach, which has a long history in financial economics and is emphasised in, for example, Cochrane (2001) and Garcia, Ghysels, and Renault (2004). The exposition I will give here is heavily influenced by the latter paper. For simplicity I will assume interest rates are constant. We start with the standard Black–Scholes (BS) problem, which will take a little time to recall, before being able to rapidly deal with the SV extension. We model

$$\mathrm{d}\log Y = (r + p - \sigma^2/2)\mathrm{d}t + \sigma \mathrm{d}W, \quad \mathrm{d}\log \widetilde{M} = h\mathrm{d}t + b\mathrm{d}W,$$

where $\widetilde{M}$ is the SDF process, r the riskless short rate, and σ, h, b and p, the risk premium, are assumed constant for the moment.

We will price all contingent payoffs $g(Y_T)$ as $C_t = \mathrm{E}\left(\frac{\widetilde{M}_T}{\widetilde{M}_t} g(Y_T)|\mathcal{F}_t\right)$, the expected discounted value of the claim where $T > t$. For this model to make financial sense we require that $\tilde{M}_t Y_t$ and $\tilde{M}_t \exp(tr)$ are local martingales, which is enough to mean that adding other independent BMs to the $\log \tilde{M}$ process makes no difference to C or Y, the observables. These two local martingale constraints imply, respectively, $p + b\sigma = 0$ and $h = -r - b^2/2$. Restating the processes, we have that

$$d \log Y = \left(r + p - \frac{\sigma^2}{2} \right) dt + \sigma dW, \quad d \log \tilde{M} = \left(-r - \frac{p^2}{2\sigma^2} \right) dt - \frac{p}{\sigma} dW.$$

In the BS case $g(Y_T) = \max(Y_T - K, 0)$, so writing $\varepsilon = (W_T - W_t)/\sqrt{T - t}$, $m_t = \log \tilde{M}_t, k = \log K$ and $y_t = \log Y_t$, then

$$C_t^{BS}(\sigma^2) = C_{1t} - C_{2t},$$

$$C_{1t} = \int_\gamma \exp(m_T - m_t + y_T) f_N(\varepsilon; 0, 1) d\varepsilon,$$

$$C_{2t} = K \int_\gamma \exp(m_T - m_t) f_N(\varepsilon; 0, 1) d\varepsilon,$$

where $\gamma = \{\varepsilon : Y_T > K\}$ and $f_N(x; \mu, \sigma^2)$ denotes a normal density with mean μ and variance σ^2. Then, writing Φ as the distribution function of a standard normal and $s = T - t$ then

$$C_{2t} = K \exp\left\{ \left(-r - \frac{p^2}{2\sigma^2} \right) s \right\} \int_\gamma \exp\left(-\frac{p}{\sigma} \sqrt{s}\varepsilon \right) f_N(\varepsilon; 0, 1) d\varepsilon$$

$$= K \exp\{-rs\} \int_\gamma f_N\left(\varepsilon; -\frac{p}{\sigma} \sqrt{s}, 1 \right) d\varepsilon$$

$$= K \exp\{-rs\} \Phi\left(\frac{y_t + \left(r + p - \frac{\sigma^2}{2} \right) s - k}{\sigma \sqrt{s}} - \frac{p}{\sigma} \sqrt{s} \right)$$

$$= K \exp\{-rs\} \Phi\left(\frac{\log Y_t + \left(r - \frac{\sigma^2}{2} \right) s - \log K}{\sigma \sqrt{s}} \right).$$

Similar arguments imply

$$C_{1t} = \int_\Theta \exp\left\{ y_t + \left(r + p - \frac{\sigma^2}{2} - r - \frac{p^2}{2\sigma^2} \right) s + \left(\sigma - \frac{p}{\sigma} \right) \sqrt{s}\varepsilon \right\} f_N(\varepsilon; 0, 1) d\varepsilon$$

$$= Y_t \int_\Theta f_N\left(\varepsilon; \left(\sigma - \frac{p}{\sigma} \right) \sqrt{s}, 1 \right) d\varepsilon$$

$$= Y_t \Phi\left(\frac{y_t + \left(r + p - \frac{\sigma^2}{2} \right) s - k}{\sigma \sqrt{s}} - \left(\sigma - \frac{p}{\sigma} \right) \sqrt{s} \right) = Y_t \Phi\left(\frac{\log Y_t + \left(r + \frac{\sigma^2}{2} \right) s - \log K}{\sigma \sqrt{s}} \right).$$

Taken together we have that in this framework, the bivariate continuous time process (C^{BS}, Y) is driven by a single source of randomness W.

When we move to the standard SV model we can remove this degeneracy. The functional form for the SV Y process is unchanged, but we now allow

$$\mathrm{d}\log \widetilde{M} = h\mathrm{d}t + a\mathrm{d}B + b\mathrm{d}W, \quad \mathrm{d}\sigma^2 = \alpha\mathrm{d}t + \omega\mathrm{d}B,$$

where we assume that $B \perp\!\!\!\perp W$ to simplify the exposition. The SV structure will mean that p will have to change through time in response to the moving σ^2. We continue to maintain that r is constant. In this case B is again redundant in the SDF (but not in the volatility) so the usual SDF conditions again imply $h = -r - \frac{1}{2}a^2$ and $p + b\sigma = 0$. This implies that the move to the SV case has little impact, except that the sample path of σ^2 is random, but independent of W. So the generalised BS (GBS) price is

$$C_t^{GBS}(\sigma_t^2) = E\left(\frac{\widetilde{M}_T}{\widetilde{M}_t} g(Y_T)|\mathcal{F}_t\right)$$

$$= E\left\{E\left(\frac{\widetilde{M}_T}{\widetilde{M}_t} g(Y_T)|\mathcal{F}_t, \frac{1}{T-t}\int_t^T \sigma_u^2 \mathrm{d}u\right)\right\}$$

$$= E\left\{C_t^{BS}\left(\frac{1}{T-t}\int_t^T \sigma_u^2 \mathrm{d}u\right)|\sigma_t^2, Y_t\right\},$$

the expected BS price, averaged over the random integrated variance starting at the initial spot variance σ_t^2. Now C^{GBS} is a function of both Y_t and σ_t^2, which means that (C^{GBS}, Y) is not degenerate. From an econometric viewpoint this is an important step, meaning inference on options is just the problem of making inference on a complicated bivariate diffusion process.

When we allow leverage back into the model, the analysis becomes slightly more complicated algebraically, but empirically much more interesting as this can produce skews in the options. A detailed discussion of this case from a SDF viewpoint is given in the excellent survey by Garcia, Ghysels, and Renault (2004). A simpler extension is to the case where σ^2 has multiple diffusive factors which I will write as $\sigma^{2(1)}, \ldots, \sigma^{2(K)}$, each of which is Markov of course. Then

$$C_t^{GBS} = E\left\{C_t^{BS}\left(\frac{1}{T-t}\int_t^T \sigma_u^2 \mathrm{d}u\right)|\sigma_t^{2(1)}, \ldots, \sigma_t^{2(K)}, Y_t\right\}.$$

Hence in this setup (C^{GBS}, Y) is not sufficient to exactly backout all of $\sigma_t^{2(1)}, \ldots, \sigma_t^{2(K)}$ when $K > 1$. Econometrically this is again a key insight, complicating inference considerably, for now we have to study partially observed diffusions.

In some recent work econometricians have been trying to use data from underlying assets and option markets to jointly model the dynamics of

(C^{GBS}, Y). The advantage of this joint estimation is that we can pool information across data types and estimate all relevant effects which influence Y, σ^2 and $\tilde{M}$. An early paper on this, which focused on the Heston (1993) model for volatility, was by Chernov and Ghysels (2000) who used EMM methods. I also found the paper by Pan (2002) to be highly informative on this issue, while Pastorello, Patilea, and Renault (2003) develop some interesting tools for dealing with these kind of unobserved processes. These papers also deal with leverage effects and often include jumps. Other papers on this topic include Bates (1996), Das and Sundaram (1999), and Bates (2000). The first of these papers has been particularly influential.

Realised volatility

Traditionally inference for SV models has been regarded as difficult. In the late 1990s and early 2000s these difficulties seem to have disappeared, allowing these models to be handled at least as easily as their ARCH cousins. This placed SV models at the centre of volatility research, not just for options but also for risk assessment and asset allocation. The reason for this is twofold.

The first innovation is the advent of commonly available, very informative high frequency data, such as either minute-by-minute return data or entire records of quote or transaction price data for particular financial instruments. The first exposure many econometricians had to this were the famous Olsen datasets, discussed in detail in the seminal work of Dacorogna, Gencay, Müller, Olsen, and Pictet (2001). Later econometricians started to use data from the main equity exchanges in the U.S. and Europe. This moved us away from thinking about a fixed time interval, such as a day, into the realm where, at least in theory, it is useful to think of the price process at different time horizons based on differing information sets. This means that continuous time models take centre stage, which in turn puts the spot light on SV. The highly informative nature of the data means that the emphasis on statistical efficiency becomes slightly less pressing, instead it is most important to have a modelling approach which is coherent across time scales.

The second innovation was a series of papers by econometricians which showed how to use this high frequency data to estimate the increments of the quadratic variation (QV) process and then to use this estimate to project QV into the future in order to predict future levels of volatility. This literature goes under the general heading of realised variation. In this section I will discuss some of the key papers, outlining the main ideas. The literature starts with three independent, concurrent papers by Andersen and Bollerslev (1998*a*), Barndorff-Nielsen and Shephard (2001) and Comte and Renault (1998) which introduced the main ideas. Some of this work echoes earlier important contributions from Merton (1976*a*) and Merton (1980), who started the trend of estimating quadratic variation from empirical observations. See also the influential empirical work based on this style of approach by Poterba and Summers (1986), Schwert (1989), Hsieh (1991), Taylor and Xu (1997) and Christensen and Prabhala (1998).

In realised variation we use high frequency data to estimate the QV process. Let δ denote a time period between high frequency observations. Then we compute the associated vector returns as

$$y_j = Y(\delta j) - Y(\delta(j-1)), \quad j = 1, 2, 3, \ldots,$$

and calculate the *realised QV process* as

$$[Y_\delta]_t = \sum_{j=1}^{\lfloor t/\delta \rfloor} y_j y_j'.$$

Then by the definition of the QV process, as $\delta \downarrow 0$ so $[Y_\delta]_t \xrightarrow{p} [Y]_t$, which the probability literature has shown is well behaved if $Y \in \mathcal{SM}$. If $A \in \mathcal{FV}^c$, then $[Y] = [M]$, while if we additionally assume that M is SV then $[Y_\delta]_t \xrightarrow{p} \int_0^t \Theta_s \Theta_s' ds$.

In practice it makes sense to look at the increments of the quadratic variation process. Suppose we are interested in analysing daily return data, but in addition have higher frequency data measured at the time interval δ. Write the j-th high frequency observation on the i-th day as

$$y_{i,j} = Y(i + \delta j) - Y(i + \delta(j-1)), \quad j = 1, 2, 3, \ldots, \lfloor 1/\delta \rfloor,$$

where $\lfloor x \rfloor$ is the largest integer less than or equal to x, then the i-th daily realised variation is defined as

$$V(Y_\delta)_i = \sum_{j=1}^{\lfloor 1/\delta \rfloor} y_{i,j} y_{i,j}' \xrightarrow{p} V(Y)_i = [Y]_i - [Y]_{i-1},$$

the i-th daily quadratic variation. The diagonal elements of $V(Y_\delta)_i$ are called realised variations or variances and their square roots are called realised volatilities. They obviously have important historical importance, allowing us to see how past volatilities have changed through time.

There is also a rather practical reason for looking at daily increments. Volatility clustering has strong intraday patterns caused by social norms and timetabled macroeconomic and financial announcements. This makes it hard to exploit high frequency data by building temporally stable intraday ARCH models (see, e.g. the careful work of Andersen and Bollerslev (1997b)). However, daily realised variations are somewhat robust to these types of intraday patterns, in the same way as yearly inflation is somewhat insensitive to seasonal fluctuations in the price level. Realised variations are the daily difference on a realised QV process. It was this mundane line of thought that influenced me to start work on realised volatility, after being struck by how complicated and unstable properly fitting high frequency models of returns were.

Andersen, Bollerslev, Diebold, and Labys (2001) and Andersen, Bollerslev, Diebold, and Labys (2003) have shown that to forecast the volatility of future asset returns, then a key input should be predictions of future daily quadratic variation. Recall, from Ito's formula, that if $Y \in \mathcal{SM}^c$, then

$$
\begin{aligned}
YY' &= [Y] + Y' \bullet Y + Y \bullet Y' \\
&= [Y] + Y \bullet A' + A \bullet Y' + Y \bullet M' + Y' \bullet M.
\end{aligned}
$$

So if $M \in \mathcal{M}$, then writing $\mathcal{F}_t$ as the filtration generated by the continuous history of Y_t up to time t then

$$
E(Y_t Y_t'|\mathcal{F}_0) = E([Y]_t|\mathcal{F}_0) + E\left(\int_0^t Y_s \mathrm{d}A_s'|\mathcal{F}_0\right) + E\left(\int_0^t Y_s' \mathrm{d}A_s|\mathcal{F}_0\right).
$$

In practice, over small intervals of time, the second and third of these terms will be small, which means that

$$
E(Y_t Y_t'|\mathcal{F}_0) \simeq E([Y]_t|\mathcal{F}_0).
$$

In terms of realised covariations this means that when we want to forecast the outer product of future returns given current data

$$
E(y_i y_i'|\mathcal{F}_{i-1}) \simeq E(V(Y)_i|\mathcal{F}_{i-1}).
$$

Of course we can also consistently estimate previous realised covariations, and indeed Andersen et al have been building models of future covariation by projecting the past realised covariations into the future. Andersen, Bollerslev, Diebold, and Labys (2003) and Andersen, Bollerslev, and Meddahi (2004) are fine examples of this line of work. An extensive review of some of this material, placed in a wider context, is given by Andersen, Bollerslev, and Diebold (2004).

A difficulty with this line of argument is that the QV theory only tells us that $V(Y_\delta)_i \xrightarrow{p} V(Y)_i$, it gives no impression of the size of $V(Y_\delta)_i - V(Y)_i$. Barndorff-Nielsen and Shephard (2002) have strengthened the consistency result to provide a central limit theory for the univariate version of this object. They showed that

$$
\frac{\delta^{-1/2}([Y_\delta]_t - [Y]_t)}{\sqrt{2 \int_0^t \sigma_s^4 \mathrm{d}s}} \xrightarrow{d} N(0, 1),
$$

while giving a method for consistently estimating the integrated quarticity $\int_0^t \sigma_s^4 \mathrm{d}s$ using high frequency data. This analysis was generalised to the multivariate case by Barndorff-Nielsen and Shephard (2004b). See also the earlier unpublished paper by Jacod (1994). Additional insights into the accuracy of the realised variation estimator for the QV process are given in Andreou and Ghysels

(2002) and Meddahi (2003). This type of analysis greatly simplifies parametric estimation of SV models for we can now have estimates of the volatility quantities SV models directly parameterise. Barndorff-Nielsen and Shephard (2002) and Bollerslev and Zhou (2002) study this topic from different perspectives.

In the very recent past there have been various elaborations to this literature. I will briefly mention two. First, there has been some interest in studying the impact of market microstructure effects on the estimates of realised covariation. This causes the estimator of the QV to become biased. Leading papers on this topic are Corsi, Zumbach, Müller, and Dacorogna (2001), Bandi and Russell (2003), Hansen and Lunde (2003) and Zhang, Mykland, and Aït-Sahalia (2003). Second, one can estimate the QV of the continuous component of prices in the presence of jumps using the so-called realised bipower variation process. This was introduced by Barndorff-Nielsen and Shephard (2004c) and Barndorff-Nielsen and Shephard (2003a). It has been used for forecasting future volatilities by Andersen, Bollerslev, and Diebold (2003), while a multivariate version of bipower variation has been introduced by Barndorff-Nielsen and Shephard (2004a).

Conclusion

Inevitably my discussion of the papers in this book, and the associated literature, is partial. I have mostly focused on the areas which have been of considerable interest to econometricians. However, much very stimulating additional work has been carried out in other areas of the SV literature. I would additionally point the interested reader to the paper by Ghysels, Harvey, and Renault (1996) which reviews some of the older papers on stochastic volatility, the review paper on volatility forecasting using high frequency data by Andersen, Bollerslev, and Diebold (2004) and the econometrics of option pricing paper by Garcia, Ghysels, and Renault (2004).

Acknowledgements

My research is supported by the UK's ESRC through the grant "High frequency financial econometrics based upon power variation." I thank Torben Andersen, Ole Barndorff-Nielsen, Clive Bowsher, Sir David Cox, Valentine Genon-Catalot, Eric Jacquier, Jeremy Large, Angelo Melino, Hsueh Ling Qu, Anders Rahbek and Eric Renault for comments on an earlier version of this Chapter and Tim Bollerslev and David Hendry for their advice when advice was needed. The detailed suggestions from Eric Ghysels and Michael Johannes were remarkably helpful—I am greatly in their debt. Finally, I would like to thank Barr Rosenberg for allowing me to publish his paper for the first time and Michael Johannes, Geert Bekaert and Bill Sharpe for putting me in contact with him.

References

Ahn, D.-H., Dittmar, R. F., and Gallant, A. R. (2002). Quadratic term structure models: Theory and evidence. *Review of Financial Studies* 15, 243–88.

Andersen, T. G. (1994). Stochastic autoregressive volatility: a framework for volatility modelling. *Mathematical Finance* 4, 75–102.

—— (1996). Return volatility and trading volume: an information flow interpretation of stochastic volatility. *Journal of Finance* 51, 169–204.

—— Benzoni, L., and Lund. J. (2002). An empirical investigation of continuous-time equity return models. *Journal of Finance* 57, 1239–84.

—— Bollerslev, T. (1997a). Heterogeneous information arrivals and return volatility dynamics: Uncovering the long-run in high frequency returns. *Journal of Finance* 52, 975–1005.

—— Bollerslev, T. (1997b). Intraday periodicity and volatility persistence in financial markets. *Journal of Empirical Finance* 4, 115–58.

—— —— (1998a). Answering the skeptics: yes, standard volatility models to provide accurate forecasts. *International Economic Review* 39, 885–905.

—— —— (1998b). Deutsche mark-dollar volatility: intraday activity patterns, macroeconomic announcements, and longer run dependencies. *Journal of Finance* 53, 219–65.

—— —— Diebold, F. X. (2003). Some like it smooth, and some like it rough: untangling continuous and jump components in measuring, modeling and forecasting asset return volatility. Unpublished paper: Economics Dept, Duke University.

—— —— —— (2004). Parametric and non-parametric measurement of volatility. In Ait-Sahalia L. and Hansen, L. P. (eds.), *Handbook of Financial Econometrics*, Amsterdam: North Holland. Forthcoming.

—— —— —— Labys, P. (2001). The distribution of exchange rate volatility. *Journal of the American Statistical Association* 96, 42–55. Correction published in 2003, volume 98, page 501.

—— —— —— —— (2003). Modeling and forecasting realized volatility. *Econometrica* 71, 579–625.

—— —— Meddahi, N. (2004). Analytic evaluation of volatility forecasts. *International Economic Review* 45, Forthcoming.

—— Lund, J. (1997). Estimating continuous-time stochastic volatility models of the short term interest rate. *Journal of Econometrics* 2, 343–77.

—— Sørensen, B. E. (1996). GMM estimation of a stochastic volatility model: a Monte Carlo study. *Journal of Business and Economic Statistics* 14, 328–52.

Andreou, E. and Ghysels, E. (2002). Rolling-sampling volatility estimators: some new theoretical, simulation and empirical results. *Journal of Business and Economic Statistics* 20, 363–76.

Ané, T. and Geman, H. (2000). Order flow, transaction clock and normality of asset returns. *Journal of Finance* 55, 2259–84.

Bandi, F. M. and Russell, J. R. (2003). Microstructure noise, realized volatility, and optimal sampling. Unpublished paper presented at the Realized volatility conference, Montreal, 8 November, 2003.

Bansal, R. and Zhou, H. (2002). Term structure of interest rates with regime shifts. *Journal of Finance* 57, 1997–2043.

Barndorff-Nielsen, O. E. (1998). Processes of normal inverse Gaussian type. *Finance and Stochastics* 2, 41–68.

—— (2001). Superposition of Ornstein–Uhlenbeck type processes. *Theory of Probability and its Applications* 45, 175–94.

—— Shephard, N. (2001). Non-Gaussian Ornstein–Uhlenbeck-based models and some of their uses in financial economics (with discussion). *Journal of the Royal Statistical Society, Series B* 63, 167–241.

—— —— (2002). Econometric analysis of realised volatility and its use in estimating stochastic volatility models. *Journal of the Royal Statistical Society, Series B* 64, 253–80.

—— —— (2003*a*). Econometrics of testing for jumps in financial economics using bipower variation. Unpublished discussion paper: Nuffield College, Oxford.

—— —— (2003*b*). Impact of jumps on returns and realised variances: econometric analysis of time-deformed Lévy processes. *Journal of Econometrics*, Forthcoming.

—— —— (2004*a*). Bipower covariation: measuring and testing jumps in multivariate price processes. Unpublished paper: Nuffield College, Oxford.

—— —— (2004*b*). Econometric analysis of realised covariation: high frequency covariance, regression and correlation in financial economics. *Econometrica* 72, 885–925.

—— —— (2004*c*). Power and bipower variation with stochastic volatility and jumps (with discussion). *Journal of Financial Econometrics* 2, 1–48.

Bartlett, M. S. and Kendall, D. G. (1946). The statistical analysis of variance-heterogeneity and the logarithmic transformation. *Supplement to the Journal of the Royal Statistical Society* 8, 128–38.

Bates, D. S. (1996). Jumps and stochastic volatility: Exchange rate processes implicit in deutsche mark options. *Review of Financial Studies* 9, 69–107.

—— (2000). Post-'97 crash fears in the S-&P 500 futures option market. *Journal of Econometrics* 94, 181–238.

Black, F. (1976). Studies of stock price volatility changes. *Proceedings of the Business and Economic Statistics Section, American Statistical Association* 177–81.

—— Scholes, M. (1972). The valuation of options contracts and a test of market efficiency. *Journal of Finance* 27, 399–418.

—— —— (1973). The pricing of options and corporate liabilities. *Journal of Political Economy* 81, 637–54.

Blattberg, R. C. and Gonedes, N. J. (1974). A comparison of the stable and student distributions as models for stock prices. *Journal of Business* 47, 244–80.

Bochner, S. (1949). Diffusion equation and stochastic processes. *Proceedings of the National Academy of Science of the United States of America* 85, 369–70.

Bollerslev, T. (1986). Generalised autoregressive conditional heteroskedasticity. *Journal of Econometrics* 51, 307–27.

—— (1990). Modelling the coherence in short-run nominal exchange rates: a multivariate generalized ARCH approach. *Review of Economics and Statistics* 72, 498–505.

—— Zhou, H. (2002). Estimating stochastic volatility diffusion using conditional moments of integrated volatility. *Journal of Econometrics* 109, 33–65.

Bookstaber, R. M. and Pomerantz, S. (1989). An information-based model for market volatility. *Financial Analysts Journal* 45, 37–46.

Brandt, M. W. and Santa-Clara, P. (2002). Simulated likelihood estimation of diffusions with an application to exchange rates dynamics in incomplete markets. *Journal of Financial Economics* 63, 161–210.

Breidt, F. J., Crato, N., and de Lima, P. (1998). On the detection and estimation of long memory in stochastic volatility. *Journal of Econometrics* 83, 325–48.

Brockwell, P. J. (2004). Representations of continuous-time ARMA processes. *Journal of Applied Probability* 41A, 375–82.

—— Marquardt, T. (2004). Levy-driven and fractionally integrated ARMA processes with continuous time parameter. *Statistica Sinica*. Forthcoming.

Cai, J. (1994). A Markov model of unconditional variance in ARCH. *Journal of Business and Economic Statistics* 12, 309–16.

Calvet, L. and Fisher, A. (2002). Multifractality in asset returns: theory and evidence. *Review of Economics and Statistics* 84, 381–406.

Carr, P., Geman, H., Madan, D. B., and Yor, M. (2002). The fine structure of asset returns: an empirical investigation. *Journal of Business* 75, 305–32.

—— Geman, —— —— (2003). Stochastic volatility for Lévy processes. *Mathematical Finance* 13, 345–82.

—— Wu, L. (2004). Time-changed Lévy processes and option pricing. *Journal of Financial Economics* 113–41.

Chan, K. C., Karolyi, G. A., Longstaff, F. A., and Sanders, A. B. (1992). An empirical comparison of alternative models of the short-term interest rate. *Journal of Finance* 47, 1209–27.

Chernov, M., Gallant, A. R., Ghysels, E., and Tauchen, G. (2003). Alternative models of stock price dynamics. *Journal of Econometrics* 116, 225–57.

Chernov, M. and Ghysels, E. (2000). A study towards a unified approach to the joint estimation of objective and risk neutral measures for the purpose of options valuation. *Journal of Financial Economics* 56, 407–58.

Chesney, M. and Scott, L. O. (1989). Pricing European options: a comparison of the modified Black–Scholes model and a random variance model. *Journal of Financial and Qualitative Analysis* 24, 267–84.

Chib, S. (2001). Markov chain Monte Carlo methods: computation and inference. In Heckman, J. J. and Leamer, E. (eds.), *Handbook of Econometrics*, Volume 5, pp. 3569–649. Amsterdam: North-Holland.

Christensen, B. J. and Prabhala, N. R. (1998). The relation between implied and realized volatility. *Journal of Financial Economics* 37, 125–50.

Clark, P. K. (1973). A subordinated stochastic process model with fixed variance for speculative prices. *Econometrica* 41, 135–56.

Cochrane, J. H. (2001). *Asset Pricing*. Princeton: Princeton University Press.

Comte, F., Coutin, L., and Renault, E. (2003). Affine fractional stochastic volatility models. Unpublished paper: University of Montreal.

—— Renault, E. (1998). Long memory in continuous-time stochastic volatility models. *Mathematical Finance* 8, 291–323.

Cont, R. and Tankov, P. (2004). *Financial Modelling with Jump Processes*. London: Chapman & Hall.

Corsi, F., Zumbach, G., Müller, U. A., and Dacorogna, M. M. (2001). Consistent high-precision volatility from high-frequency data. *Economic Notes* 30, 183–204.

Dacorogna, M. M., Gencay, R., U. A. Müller, Olsen, R. B., and Pictet, O. V. (2001). *An Introduction to High-Frequency Finance*. San Diego: Academic Press.

Dai, Q. and Singleton, K. J. (2000). Specification analysis of affine term structure models. *Journal of Finance* 55, 1943–78.

Danielsson, J. (1994). Stochastic volatility in asset prices: estimation with simulated maximum likelihood. *Journal of Econometrics* 61, 375–400.

Das, S. R. and Sundaram, R. (1999). Of smiles and smirks: A term structure perspective. *Journal of Financial and Quantitative Analysis* 34, 211–40.

Diebold, F. and Inoue, A. (2001). Long memory and regime switching. *Journal of Econometrics* 105, 131–59.

Diebold, F. X. (1988). *Empirical Modelling of Exchange Rate Dynamics*. New York: Springer-Verlag.

—— Nerlove, M. (1989). The dynamics of exchange rate volatility: a multivariate latent factor ARCH model. *Journal of Applied Econometrics* 4, 1–21.

Doob, J. L. (1953). *Stochastic Processes*. New York: John Wiley & Sons.

Doucet, A., N. de Freitas, and Gordon, N. J. (2001). *Sequential Monte Carlo Methods in Practice*. New York: Springer-Verlag.

Duffie, D., Filipovic, D., and Schachermayer, W. (2003). Affine processes and applications in finance. *Annals of Applied Probability* 13, 984–1053.

—— Pan, J., and Singleton, K. J. (2000). Transform analysis and asset pricing for affine jump-diffusions. *Econometrica* 68, 1343–76.

—— Singleton, K. J. (1993). Simulated moments estimation of Markov models of asset proces. *Econometrica* 61, 929–52.

Durbin, J. and Koopman, S. J. (1997). Monte Carlo maximum likelihood estimation of non-Gaussian state space model. *Biometrika* 84, 669–84.

—— —— (2001). *Time Series Analysis by State Space Methods*. Oxford: Oxford University Press.

Durham, G. (2003). Likelihood-based specification analysis of continuous-time models of the short-term interest rate. *Journal of Financial Economics* 70, 463–87.

—— Gallant, A. R. (2002). Numerical techniques for maximum likelihood estimation of continuous-time diffusion processes (with discussion). *Journal of Business and Economic Statistics* 20, 297–338.

Eberlein, E. and Keller, U. (1995). Hyperbolic distributions in finance. *Bernoulli* 1, 281–99.

Elerian, O., Chib, S., and Shephard, N. (2001). Likelihood inference for discretely observed non-linear diffusions. *Econometrica* 69, 959–93.

Elliott, R. J., Hunter, W. C., and Jamieson, B. M. (1998). Drift and volatility estimation in discrete time. *Journal of Economic Dynamics and Control* 22, 209–18.

Engle, R. F. (1982). Autoregressive conditional heteroskedasticity with estimates of the variance of the United Kingdom inflation. *Econometrica* 50, 987–1007.

—— (1995). *ARCH: Selected Readings*. Oxford: Oxford University Press.

—— and Lee, G. G. J. (1996). Estimating diffusion models of stochastic volatility. In Rossi, P. E. (ed.), *Modelling Stock Market Volatility—Bridging the GAP to Continuous Time*, pp. 333–84. Academic Press.

—— —— (1999). A permanent and transitory component model of stock return volatility. In Engle, R. F. and White, H. (eds.), *Cointegration, Causality, and Forecasting. A Festschrift in Honour of Clive W. J. Granger*, pp. 475–97. Oxford: Oxford University Press.

Eraker, B. (2001). Markov chain Monte Carlo analysis of diffusion models with application to finance. *Journal of Business and Economic Statistics* 19, 177–91.

—— Johannes, M., and Polson, N. G. (2003). The impact of jumps in returns and volatility. *Journal of Finance* 53, 1269–300.

Fama, E. F. (1965). The behaviour of stock market prices. *Journal of Business* 38, 34–105.

Fiorentini, G., Sentana, E., and Shephard, N. (2004). Likelihood-based estimation of latent generalised ARCH structures. *Econometrica* 72, 1481–1517.

Foster, D. P. and Nelson, D. B. (1996). Continuous record asymptotics for rolling sample variance estimators. *Econometrica* 64, 139–74.

Fouque, J.-P., Papanicolaou, G., and Sircar, K. R. (2000). *Derivatives in Financial Markets with Stochastic Volatility*. Cambridge: Cambridge University Press.

Gallant, A. R., Hsieh, D. A., and Tauchen, G. (1997). Estimation of stochastic volatility models with diagnostics. *Journal of Econometrics* 81, 159–92.

Gallant, A. R. and Tauchen, G. (1996). Which moments to match. *Econometric Theory* 12, 657–81.

——— (1998). Reprojection partially observed systems with applications to interest rate diffusions. *Journal of the American Statistical Association* 93, 10–24.

Garcia, R., Ghysels, E., and Renault, E. (2004). The econometrics of option pricing. In Y. Ait-Sahalia and Hansen, L. P. (eds.), *Handbook of Financial Econometrics*. Amsterdam: North Holland. Forthcoming.

Geman, H., Madan, D. B., and Yor, M. (2001). Time changes for Lévy processes. *Mathematical Finance* 11, 79–96.

Genon-Catalot, V., Jeantheau, T., and Larédo, C. (1999). Parameter estimation for discretely observed stochastic volatility models. *Bernoulli* 5, 855–72.

——— (2000). Stochastic volatility as hidden Markov models and statistical applications. *Bernoulli* 6, 1051–79.

——— Larédo, C., and Picard, D. (1992). Non-parametric estimation of the diffusion coefficient by wavelet methods. *Scandinavian Journal of Statistics* 19, 317–35.

Ghysels, E., Harvey, A. C., and Renault, E. (1996). Stochastic volatility. In Rao, C. R. and Maddala, G. S. (eds.), *Statistical Methods in Finance* 119–91. Amsterdam: North-Holland.

Gloter, A. (2000). Estimation of the volatility diffusion coefficient for a stochastic volatility model. *Comptes Rendus Mathematique, Academie des Sciences Paris Series* 1330, 243–8.

——— Hoffmann, M. (2004). Stochastic volatility and fractional Brownian motion. *Stochastic Processes and Their Applications* 113, 143–72.

Gordon, N. J., Salmond, D. J., and Smith, A. F. M. (1993). A novel approach to nonlinear and non-Gaussian Bayesian state estimation. *IEE-Proceedings F* 140, 107–13.

Gourieroux, C., Monfort, A., and Renault, E. (1993). Indirect inference. *Journal of Applied Econometrics* 8, S85–S118.

Granger, C. W. J. (1980). Long memory relationships and the aggregation of dynamic models. *Journal of Econometrics* 14, 227–38.

Hamilton, J. D. and Susmel, R. (1994). Autoregressive conditional heteroskedasticity and changes in regimes. *Journal of Econometrics* 64, 307–33.

Hansen, B. E. (1995). Regression with non-stationary volatility. *Econometrica* 63, 1113–32.

Hansen, P. R. and Lunde, A. (2003). An optimal and unbiased measure of realized variance based on intermittent high-frequency data. Unpublished paper, presented at the Realized volatility conference, Montreal, 7 November 2003.

Harvey, A. C. (1976). Estimating regression models with multiplicative heteroskedasticity. *Econometrica* 44, 461–5.

——— (1998). Long memory in stochastic volatility. In Knight, J. and Satchell, S. (eds.), *Forecasting Volatility in Financial Markets* 307–20. Oxford: Butterworth-Heinemann.

——— Ruiz, E., and Shephard, N. (1994). Multivariate stochastic variance models. *Review of Economic Studies* 61, 247–64.

Hendry, D. F. and Richard, J. F. (1991). Likelihood evaluation for dynamic latent variable models. In Amman, H. M., Delsley, D. A., and Pau, L. F. (eds.), *Computational Economics and Econometrics* 3–17. Dordrecht: Kluwer.

Heston, S. L. (1993). A closed-form solution for options with stochastic volatility, with applications to bond and currency options. *Review of Financial Studies* 6, 327–43.

Hobson, D. G. and Rogers, L. C. G. (1998). Complete models with stochastic volatility. *Mathematical Finance* 8, 27–48.

Hoffmann, M. (2002). Rate of convergence for parametric estimation in stochastic volatility models. *Stochastic Processes and their Application* 97, 147–70.

Hsieh, D. (1991). Chaos and nonlinear dynamics: Application to financial markets. *Journal of Finance* 46, 1839–77.

Hull, J. and White, A. (1987). The pricing of options on assets with stochastic volatilities. *Journal of Finance* 42, 281–300.

——— ——— (1988). An analysis of the bias in option prices caused by stochastic volatility. *Advances in Futures and Options Pricing Research* 3, 29–61.

Jacod, J. (1994). Limit of random measures associated with the increments of a Brownian semimartingale. Unpublished paper: Laboratorie de Probabilities, Universite P and M Curie, Paris.

——— Shiryaev, A. N. (1987). *Limit Theorems for Stochastic Processes*. Berlin: Springer-Verlag.

Jacquier, E., Polson, N. G., and Rossi, P. E. (1994). Bayesian analysis of stochastic volatility models (with discussion). *Journal of Business and Economic Statistics* 12, 371–417.

——— ——— ——— (2003). Stochastic volatility models: Univariate and multivariate extensions. *Journal of Econometrics*. Forthcoming.

Jeantheau, T. (2004). A link between complete models with stochastic volatility and ARCH models. *Finance and Stochastics* 8, 111–31.

Johannes, M., Polson, N. G., and Stroud, J. (2002). Nonlinear filtering of stochastic differential equations with jumps. Unpublished paper: Graduate School of Business, Columbia University.

Johnson, H. (1979). Option pricing when the variance rate is changing. Working paper, University of California, Los Angeles.

——— Shanno, D. (1987). Option pricing when the variance is changing. *Journal of Financial and Quantitative Analysis* 22, 143–51.

Kim, S., Shephard, N., and Chib, S. (1998). Stochastic volatility: likelihood inference and comparison with ARCH models. *Review of Economic Studies* 65, 361–93.

King, M., Sentana, E., and Wadhwani, S. (1994). Volatility and links between national stock markets. *Econometrica* 62, 901–33.

Lam, K., Li, W. K., and So, M. K. P. (1998). A stochastic volatility model with markov switching. *Journal of Business and Economic Statistics* 16, 244–53.

Longstaff, F. and Schwartz, E. (1992). Interest rate volatility and the term structure: A two-factor general equilibrium model. *Journal of Finance* 47, 1259–82.

Madan, D. B. and Seneta, E. (1990). The VG model for share market returns. *Journal of Business* 63, 511–24.

Mandelbrot, B. (1963). The variation of certain speculative prices. *Journal of Business* 36, 394–419.

——— Taylor, H. (1967). On the distribution of stock price differences. *Operations Research* 15, 1057–62.

Meddahi, N. (2001). An eigenfunction approach for volatility modeling. Unpublished paper: University of Montreal.

——— (2003). ARMA representation of integrated and realized variances. *The Econometrics Journal* 6, 334–55.

Melino, A. and Turnbull, S. M. (1990). Pricing foreign currency options with stochastic volatility. *Journal of Econometrics* 45, 239–65.

Merton, R. C. (1973). Rational theory of option pricing. *Bell Journal of Economics and Management Science* 4, 141–83.

—— (1976a). The impact on option pricing of specification error in the underlying stock price returns. *Journal of Finance* 31, 333–50.

—— (1976b). Option pricing when underlying stock returns are discontinuous. *Journal of Financial Economics* 3, 125–44.

—— (1980). On estimating the expected return on the market: An exploratory investigation. *Journal of Financial Economics* 8, 323–61.

Meyer, R. and Yu, J. (2000). BUGS for a Bayesian analysis of stochastic volatility models. *The Econometrics Journal* 3, 198–215.

Monfardini, C. (1998). Estimating stochastic volatility models through indirect inference. *The Econometrics Journal* 1, C113–C28.

Munroe, M. E. (1953). *Introduction to Measure and Integration*. Cambridge, MA: Addison-Wesley Publishing Company, Inc.

Nelson, D. B. (1990). ARCH models as diffusion approximations. *Journal of Econometrics* 45, 7–38.

—— (1991). Conditional heteroskedasticity in asset pricing: a new approach. *Econometrica* 59, 347–70.

Nicolato, E. and Venardos, E. (2003). Option pricing in stochastic volatility models of the Ornstein–Uhlenbeck type. *Mathematical Finance* 13, 445–66.

Nissen, F., Koedijk, C. G., Schotman, P., and Wolff, C. C. P. (1997). The dynamics of short term interest rate volatility reconsidered. *European Finance Review* 1, 105–30.

Officer, R. R. (1973). The variability of the market factor of the New York stock exchange. *Journal of Business* 46, 434–53.

Ohanissian, A., Russell, J. R., and Tsay, R. S. (2003). True or spurious long memory in volatility: does it matter for pricing options. Unpublished paper: Graduate School of Business, University of Chicago.

Pan, J. (2002). The jump-risk premia implicit in option prices: evidence from an integrated time-series study. *Journal of Financial Economics* 63, 3–50.

Pastorello, S., Patilea, V., and Renault, E. (2003). Iterative and recursive estimation in structural non-adaptive models. *Journal of Business and Economic Statistics* 21, 449–509.

Pédersen, A. R. (1995). A new approach to maximum likelihood estimation for stochastic differential equations on discrete observations. *Scandinavian Journal of Statistics* 27, 55–71.

Pitt, M. K. and Shephard, N. (1999a). Filtering via simulation: auxiliary particle filter. *Journal of the American Statistical Association* 94, 590–9.

—— —— (1999b). Time varying covariances: a factor stochastic volatility approach (with discussion). In Bernardo, J. M., Berger, J. O., Dawid, A. P., and Smith, A. F. M. (eds.), *Bayesian Statistics* 6, 547–70. Oxford: Oxford University Press.

Poterba, J. and Summers, L. (1986). The persistence of volatility and stock market fluctuations. *American Economic Review* 76, 1124–41.

Praetz, P. D. (1972). The distribution of share prices. *Journal of Business* 45, 45–55.

Press, S. J. (1967). A compound events model for security prices. *Journal of Business* 40, 317 35.

Protter, P. (2004). *Stochastic Integration and Differential Equations*. New York: Springer-Verlag.

Renault, E. (1997). Econometric models of option pricing errors. In Kreps, D. M. and Wallis, K. F. (eds.), *Advances in Economics and Econometrics: Theory and Applications*, pp. 223–78. Cambridge: Cambridge University Press.

——— Touzi, N. (1996). Option hedging and implied volatilities in a stochastic volatility model. *Mathematical Finance* 6, 279–302.

Roberts, G. O. and Stramer, O. (2001). On inference for nonlinear diffusion models using the Hastings–Metropolis algorithms. *Biometrika* 88, 603–21.

Robinson, P. M. (2003). *Time Series with Long Memory*. Oxford: Oxford University Press.

Rogers, L. C. G. and Williams, D. (1996). *Diffusions, Markov Processes and Martingales. Volume 2, Ito Calculus* (2nd edn.). Chichester: Wiley.

Rosenberg, B. (1972). The behaviour of random variables with nonstationary variance and the distribution of security prices. Unpublished paper: Research Program in Finance, Working paper 11, Graduate School of Business Administration, University of California, Berkeley.

Sandmann, G. and Koopman, S. J. (1998). Estimation of stochastic volatility models via Monte Carlo maximum likelihood. *Journal of Econometrics* 87, 271–301.

Schwert, G. W. (1989). Why does stock market volatility change over time? *Journal of Finance* 44, 1115–53.

Scott, L. O. (1987). Options pricing when the variance changes randomly: theory, estimation and an application. *Journal of Financial and Quantitative Analysis* 22, 419–38.

——— (1991). Random-variance option pricing. *Advances in Future and Options Research* 5, 113–35.

Sentana, E. (1998). The relationship between conditionally heteroskedastic factor models and factor GARCH models. *The Econometrics Journal* 1, 1–9.

Shephard, N. (1993). Fitting non-linear time series models, with applications to stochastic variance models. *Journal of Applied Econometrics* 8, S135–S152.

——— (1994). Local scale model: state space alternative to integrated GARCH processes. *Journal of Econometrics* 60, 181–202.

——— Pitt, M. K. (1997). Likelihood analysis of non-Gaussian measurement time series. *Biometrika* 84, 653–67.

Smith, A. A. (1993). Estimating nonlinear time series models using simulated vector autoregressions. *Journal of Applied Econometrics* 8, S63–S84.

Sørensen, M. (2000). Prediction based estimating equations. *The Econometrics Journal* 3, 123–47.

Stein, E. M. and Stein, J. (1991). Stock price distributions with stochastic volatility: an analytic approach. *Review of Financial Studies* 4, 727–52.

Tauchen, G. and Pitts, M. (1983). The price variability–volume relationship on speculative markets. *Econometrica* 51, 485–505.

Taylor, S. J. (1980). Conjectured models for trends in financial prices, tests and forecasts. *Journal of the Royal Statistical Society, Series A* 143, 338–62.

——— (1982). Financial returns modelled by the product of two stochastic processes—a study of daily sugar prices 1961–79. In Anderson, O. D. (ed.), *Time Series Analysis: Theory and Practice, 1* 203–26. Amsterdam: North-Holland.

——— (1986). *Modelling Financial Time Series*. Chichester: John Wiley.

——— (2000). Consequences for option pricing of long memory in volatility. Unpublished paper, Lancaster University.

——— Xu, X. (1997). The incremental volatility information in one million foreign exchange quotations. *Journal of Empirical Finance* 4, 317–40.

Uhlig, H. (1997). Bayesian vector autoregressions with stochastic volatility. *Econometrica* 65, 59–73.

Wiggins, J. B. (1987). Option values under stochastic volatilities. *Journal of Financial Economics* 19, 351–72.

Wong, C. K. (1999). New methods for performing efficient inference for linear and log-normal volatility models. Unpublished M.Phil. Economics Thesis, University of Oxford.

Yu, J. (2003). On leverage in a stochastic volatility. *Journal of Econometrics*, Forthcoming.

Zhang, L., Mykland, P., and Aït-Sahalia, Y. (2003). A tale of two time scales: determining integrated volatility with noisy high-frequency data. Unpublished paper presented at the Realized volatility conference, Montreal, 8 November 2003.

Part I
Model Building

1

A Subordinated Stochastic Process Model with Finite Variance for Speculative Prices*

PETER K. CLARK [1]

S. Bochner's concept of a subordinate stochastic process is proposed as a model for speculative price series. A general class of finite-variance distributions for price changes is described, and a member of this class, the lognormal–normal, is tested against previously proposed distributions for speculative price differences. It is shown with both discrete Bayes' tests and Kolmogorov–Smirnov tests that finite-variance distributions subordinate to the normal fit cotton futures price data better than members of the stable family.

1.1 Introduction

The past seventeen years have seen a large amount of research by academic economists on prices in speculative markets, an area which was formerly studied almost exclusively by financial speculators and their advisors.[2] Considering the time series of prices at short intervals on a speculative market such as that for futures in commodities, or corporation shares, one primary characteristic is evident. If X_t denotes price at time t and $\Delta X_t = X_t - X_{t-1}$, examination of the data suggests that:

$$E(\Delta X_t) = 0 \text{ and } E(\Delta X_t \cdot \Delta X_s) = 0, \quad t \neq s.$$

The increments in the price process are stationary in the mean and uncorrelated; a random walk model

$$X_t = X_{t-1} + \varepsilon_t, \quad E(\varepsilon_t) = 0, \quad E(\varepsilon_t \varepsilon_s) = 0, \quad t \neq s \tag{1}$$

explains these empirical facts well.

Besides empirical realism, the random walk model has a theoretical basis (see Bachelier (1900)). If price changes are correlated, then alert speculators should notice the correlation and trade in the right direction until the relationship

---

* This work was previously published as P. K. Clark (1973), 'A Subordinated Stochastic Process Model with Fixed Variance for Speculative Prices', *Econometrica* 41,1. Copyright © The Econometric Society. Reproduced by kind permission.

[1] Thanks are due to Hendrik Houthakker and Christopher Sims for both encouragement and advice in developing this paper. As usual, all remaining errors are my own. This research was supported by a Harvard Dissertation Fellowship, NSF Grant 33-708, and the Boston College Department of Economics.
[2] See Clark (1970) for a comprehensive bibliography, or Cootner (1964) for a collection of these articles.

is removed. This was first shown by Bachelier in 1900, when he derived the diffusion equation from a condition that speculators should receive no information from past prices. Equation (1) is, of course, a solution to a discrete formulation of the diffusion problem.

It is also empirically evident that the price changes ΔX_t, however independent, are not normally distributed. Instead of having the normal shape, which would be the case if the components in ΔX_t were almost independent and almost identically distributed,[3] ΔX has too many small and too many large observations, as pictured in Figure 1.1.

One way to express this is to say that the distribution of ΔX is leptokurtic, since the sample kurtosis,

$$\widehat{K}_{\Delta X} = \frac{(1/n)\sum_i (\Delta X_i - \overline{\Delta X})^4}{[(1/n)\sum_i (\Delta X_i - \overline{\Delta X})^2]^2},$$

is much greater than 3, the value for a normal population.

It is evident, then, that conditions sufficient for the Central Limit Theorem are not met by the influences which make up ΔX. The violation of these conditions and the reason for the leptokurtic distribution of ΔX is the subject of the present article.

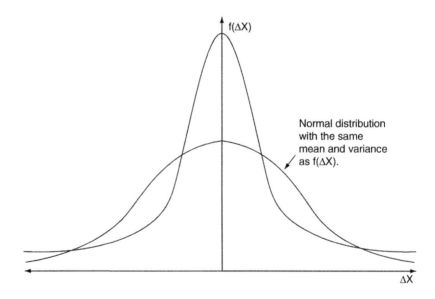

Fig. 1.1. Distribution of ΔX, the daily changes in price.

---

[3] Feller (1966), Gnedenko and Kolmogorov (1954), and Loève (1955) contain good expositions on the conditions under which the Central Limit Theorem is satisfied.

In 1963, Mandelbrot set out to explain this non-normality in price changes that had been observed by Kendall (1953) and many others.[4] The observed distribution of price changes clearly indicates that the Central Limit Theorem does not apply to them. But what condition is being violated? Mandelbrot decided that the individual effects making up a price change did not have finite variance, but were still independent. The distribution of price change should then belong to the stable family of distributions, which were shown by Levy (1925) to be the only possible limit distributions for sums of independent random variables.[5] These stable distributions have an unbounded kurtosis and will usually give high values for any measured sample kurtosis, thus making them good candidates for the distribution of price change.

The opposing hypothesis presented and tested in this paper is that the distribution of price change is subordinate[6] to a normal distribution. The price series for cotton futures evolves at different rates during identical intervals of time. The number of individual effects added together to give the price change during a day is variable and in fact random, making the standard Central Limit Theorem inapplicable.

The different evolution of price series on different days is due to the fact that information is available to traders at a varying rate. On days when no new information is available, trading is slow, and the price process evolves slowly. On days when new information violates old expectations, trading is brisk, and the price process evolves much faster.

1.2 Distributions subordinate to the normal distribution

1.2.1 The Central limit theorem

As we have noted in the last section, empirical evidence shows that the random elements that make up cotton futures price differences do not obey conditions sufficient for the Central Limit Theorem to apply. In the following development, the Central Limit Theorem is generalized in a way that makes the resulting limit distributions applicable to the distribution of cotton futures price differences.

First, one variant of the Central Limit Theorem and two lemmas are stated without proof:[7]

Lemma 1 For $n = 1, 2, \ldots,$ *and* $t > 0,$

$$\left| e^{it} - 1 - it - \frac{(it)^2}{2!} - \cdots - \frac{(it)^{n-1}}{(n-1)!} \right| \leq \frac{t^n}{n!}.$$

That is, the Taylor Series expansion for e^{it} differs from e^{it} by less than the first excluded term.

---

[4] Mandelbrot (1963) lists many references to the problem of non-normality, one as early as 1915.
[5] Gnedenko and Kolmogorov (1954) is the classic exposition in this field.
[6] For a definition and explanation of subordination, see Section 2.
[7] See Feller (1966) for proofs of both lemmas and a slightly modified form of Theorem 1.

Lemma 2 Let $m_n = \int_{-\infty}^{\infty} y^n dF_y$, and $M_n = \int_{-\infty}^{\infty} |y|^n dF_y$, where y is a random variable and F_y is its distribution; m_n and M_n are extended real numbers. If $M_n < \infty$, then the nth derivative of $\Phi = E(e^{iwy})$, the characteristic function of y, exists and is a continuous function given by: $\Phi^{(n)}(w) = i^n \int_{-\infty}^{\infty} e^{iwy} y^n dF_y$.

Corollary If $m_2 < \infty$, then $\Phi'(0) = im_1$, and $\Phi''(0) = -m_2$.

Theorem 1 (Central Limit Theorem): Let $\{Y_i\}$ be a sequence of identically distributed independent random variables with mean 0 and variance 1. Let $S_n = \sum_{i=1}^{n} Y_i$. Then the distribution of $S_n/\sqrt{n}$ tends to the unit normal distribution.

First, we may generalize this theorem to the case where the number of terms, n, in the sum S_n is itself a random variable.

Theorem 2[8] Let $\{N_n\}$ be a sequence of positive integral valued random variables obeying the property $plim_{n\to\infty}(N_n/n) = 1$. Let $\{Y_i\}$ have the same distribution as in Theorem 1, and $S_{N_n} = (\sum_{i=1}^{N_n} Y_i$. Assume $\{N_i\}$ and $\{Y_i\}$ are mutually independent. Then $S_{N_n}/\sqrt{n}$ converges in probability to the unit normal distribution as $n \to \infty$.

Proof It must be shown that $\Phi^{N_n}(w/\sqrt{n})$, the characteristic function of $S_{N_n}/\sqrt{n}$, approaches $e^{-w^2/2}$, the characteristic function of a unit normal variable, as $n \to \infty$.

$$\Phi(w/\sqrt{n}) = \int_{-\infty}^{\infty} e^{i(w/\sqrt{n})y} dF_y.$$

By Lemma 1 and the Corollary to Lemma 2, $\Phi(w/\sqrt{n}) = 1 - (w^2/2n) + o(1/n)$ as $n \to \infty$. Log $\Phi(w/\sqrt{n}) \to -(1/2n)w^2$ as $n \to \infty$, and $\log \Phi^{N_n}(w/\sqrt{n}) \to (N_n/n) \cdot (-w^2/2), n \to \infty$. Since by hypothesis $(N_n/n)_{\overrightarrow{prob}} 1, n\to\infty$, $\Phi^{N_n}(w/\sqrt{n}) \overrightarrow{prob} e^{-w^2/2}$, $n \to \infty$, and the theorem is proved.

This theorem says that if N_n has small variation around n for large n, then $\sum_{i=1}^{N_n} Y_i$, the random sum of random variables, still approaches the normal distribution.

Now suppose that N_n has appreciable variance around n even for large n. This is the case that is relevant for the cotton futures price process. The number of small price changes added up on each day is variable. For instance, let $N_n = [Zn]$ where Z has mean 1 and variance $\Gamma > 0$, where [ ] denotes "largest integer less than". Following the development in Theorem 2, for large n,

$$N_n \log \Phi(w/\sqrt{n}) \sim \frac{[Zn]}{n}\left(-\frac{1}{2}w^2\right), \quad n \to \infty,$$

$$\Phi^{N_n}(w/\sqrt{n}) \sim e^{-Zw^2/2}, \quad n \to \infty.$$

---

[8] The proof of a theorem similar to this was given by Robbins (1948). See also Anscombe (1952), Billingsley (1963), Renyi (1957) and (1960), and Feller (1966) for theorems on limit distributions of random sums of random variables.

This characteristic function may be inverted to find the limit distribution of $S_{N_n}/\sqrt{n}$. This is the characteristic function for a variable with random variance Z; as we shall see, the distribution for such a variable is not normal, and depends on the distribution of Z.

We have just proved the following theorem:

Theorem 3[9] Let $\{Y_i\}$ be distributed as in Theorem 1, and let

$$S_{N_n} = \sum_{i=1}^{N_n} Y_i.$$

Let $N_n = [Zn]$ for large n, where Z is a random variable with mean 1, again independent of $\{Y_i\}$. Then $S_{N_n}/\sqrt{n}$ has $f(u) = (1/\sqrt{2\pi Z})e^{-u^2/2Z}$ as its density.

We now have the limit distribution of S_{N_n} conditional on Z. Over a long period of time, the price changes of cotton futures will be the marginal distribution of S_{N_n} found by taking the expectation of the distribution above with respect to Z. This simple procedure yields the subordinate distributions described below.

1.2.2 Subordinated stochastic processes

Discrete stochastic processes are indexed by a discrete variable, usually time, in a straightforward manner: X_0, X_1, ..., X_t, X_{t+1}, ... This may also be written $X(0)$, $X(1)$, ... $X(t)$, ...; $X(s)$ is the value that a particular realization of the stochastic process assumes at time s. Instead of indexing by the integers 0, 1, 2, ..., the process could be indexed by a set of numbers t_1, t_2, t_3, ..., where these numbers are themselves a realization of a stochastic process (with positive increments, so that $t_1 \leq t_2 \leq t_3 \leq \ldots$).[10] That is, if $T(t)$ is a positive stochastic process, a new process $X(T(t))$ may be formed. This process is said to be *subordinated* to $X(t)$; $T(t)$ is called the *directing process*. The distribution of $\Delta X(T(t))$ is said to be *subordinate* to the distribution of $\Delta X(t)$.

Note that $\Delta X(t)$ will assume the role of the individual effects in the evolution of the price process, while $T(t)$ is a clock measuring the speed of evolution. $X(T(t))$ is, of course, the price process itself.

The following theorem holds for very general classes of subordinated stochastic processes with independent increments. Aside from providing a simple formula for calculating the variance of the increments, it also shows that this variance is finite for processes having increments with finite variance, and directed by a process with increments of finite mean.

[9] See Robbins (1948) for a different result on the limit distribution of a random sum of random variables.
[10] The idea of a subordinated process was originated by Bochner (1960). However, for a simpler exposition, see Feller (1966 pp. 333 ff.).

Theorem 4[11] Let $X(t)$ and $T(t)$ be processes with stationary independent increments; that is,

1 $X(t_{k+1}) - X(t_k)(k = 1, 2, \ldots, n-1)$ are mutually independent for any finite set $t_1 \leq t_2 \leq \ldots \leq t_n$, and similarly for $T(t)$;
2 $X(s+t) - X(s)$ depends on t but not on s for all s, and similarly for $T(t)$.

Let the increments of $X(t)$ be drawn from a distribution with mean 0 and finite variance σ^2; i.e. $E[X(s+1) - X(s)] = 0$, all s, and $E[X(s+1) - X(s)]^2 = \sigma^2$, all s. Let the increments of $T(t)$ be drawn from a positive distribution with mean α, independent of the increments of $X(t)$. That is, $E[T(s+1) - T(s)] = \alpha$, and $[T(s+t) - T(s)] \geq 0$, $t > 0$. Then the subordinated stochastic process $X(T(t))$ has stationary independent increments with mean 0 and variance $\alpha\sigma^2$.

Proof If the steps $\Delta; X(t)$ are independent with mean 0 and variance σ^2, then v steps have mean 0 and variance $v\sigma^2$. Therefore the variance of $\Delta X(T(t))$ conditional on $\Delta T(t)$ is

$$\text{var}(\Delta X(T(t)) | \Delta T(t) = v) = v\sigma^2.$$

The unconditional variance of $\Delta X(T(t))$ is just the expectation of the conditional variance

$$E_{\Delta(T(t))}(v\sigma^2) = \alpha\sigma^2.$$

The expectation of the mean of the steps over the distribution of $\Delta T(t)$ is clearly 0.
    Note that no mention has been made of the variance of the increments of the directing process; this says that if the directing process has a finite mean, then $\Delta X(T(t))$ will have a finite variance unless $\Delta X(t)$ does not. It also indicates that even if the parameters σ^2 and α are specified, a family of distributions with 0 mean and identical variance may be obtained by allowing the variance or other parameters of distribution of $\Delta T(t)$ to change.

Corollary 4.1 If $X(t)$ is normal with stationary independent increments, and $T(t)$ has stationary independent positive increments with finite second moment which are independent of X, then the kurtosis, k, of the increments of $X(T(t))$ is an increasing function of the variance of the increments of $T(t)$.

Proof The kurtosis μ_4/σ^4 for a normal distribution is 3. Therefore conditional on $\Delta T(t) = v$,

$$E(\Delta X(T(t))^4 | \Delta T(t) = v) = 3v^2\sigma^4.$$

The unconditional expectation is

$$E_{\Delta T(t)}(3v^2\sigma^4) = 3\sigma^4(\alpha^2 + \text{var}(v)).$$

---

[11] Robbins (1948) proves this theorem in somewhat less generality.

The unconditional kurtosis is then

$$k_{\Delta X(T(t))} = \frac{3\sigma^4(\alpha^2 + \text{var}(v))}{\alpha^2\sigma^4} = 3\left[\frac{\alpha^2 + \text{var}(v)}{\alpha^2}\right] \tag{2}$$

where α is the mean of v, the random variable which represents the increment of $T(t)$.

Note that this corollary shows that the introduction of any directing process makes the distribution of the increments of $X(T(t))$ only more leptokurtic. The corollary is directly applicable to the limit distributions found in Theorem 3, since we know that the limit distribution of a random sum of random variables which obey the Central Limit Theorem is asymptotically normal with random variance, or in new terminology, subordinate to the normal distribution.

Corollary 4.2 If the condition that the increments of $T(t)$ are stationary and independent is removed, then Theorem 4 still holds, with the exception that the increments of $X(T(t))$ are uncorrelated as opposed to independent.

As has been pointed out by Mandelbrot and Taylor (1967), in certain cases distributions subordinate to a normal distribution have symmetric stable distributions. Feller (1966) shows that if $X(t)$ and $T(t)$ have stationary mutually independent increments, when $\Delta X(t)$ has a symmetric stable distribution with $1 < \alpha_1 \leq 2$[12] and $\Delta T(t)$ has a stable distribution with $0 < \alpha_2 < 1$, then $\Delta X(T(t))$ has a stable distribution with $\alpha = \alpha_1 \cdot \alpha_2$.

Note that this result fits intuitively with Theorem 4. If $\alpha_1 = 2$, and $\Delta X(T(t))$ therefore has a distribution subordinate to a normal distribution, the variance of this distribution is finite if the mean of the distribution of $\Delta T(t)$ is finite, but is infinite in this case, where F_T has no mean.

1.2.3 The Distribution of the lognormal–normal increments
As a special case of the subordinate distributions in the last section, consider a process $X(t)$ whose independent increments $\Delta X(t)$ are normally distributed, directed by a process $T(t)$, whose independent increments are lognormally distributed. By a lognormal distribution, we mean a random variable x whose density is:

$$f(x;\mu, \sigma_1^2) = \frac{1}{2\pi\sigma_1^2 \cdot x}\exp\left(-\frac{(\log x - \mu)^2}{2\sigma_1^2}\right). \tag{3}$$

---

[12] α is a parameter of stable distributions, $0 < \alpha \leq 2$. Stable distributions behave asymptotically as $f(u) \sim |u|^{-(\alpha+1)}$ for large u, so that for $\alpha \leq 1$ they have no mean, and for $\alpha < 2$ they have no variance.

It is named the lognormal distribution because $u = \log x$ is normally distributed with mean μ and variance σ_1^2.[13] As may be easily shown, the mean of x is $\mu_x = e^{\mu + \sigma_1^2/2}$ and the variance of x is

$$\sigma_x^2 = e^{2\mu + \sigma_1^2}[e^{\sigma_1^2} - 1].$$

Theorem 4 now tells us that if $\Delta X(t)$ is distributed normally with mean 0 and variance σ_2^2, the increments $\Delta X(T(t))$ of the lognormal–normal process have mean 0 and variance:

$$\sigma_{\Delta X(T(t))}^2 = \sigma_2^2 \cdot e^{\mu + \sigma_1^2/2}.$$

Corollary 4.1 says that for given $(\mu + \sigma_1^2/2)$ but increasing σ_1^2, the variance of this distribution stays constant while its kurtosis increases as much as desired. Presumably this distribution will fit the observed distribution of cotton price changes much better than the normal distribution, and might do better than the stable distributions.[14]

Theorem 5 A random process subordinated to a normal process with independent increments distributed $N(0, \ \sigma_2^2)$ and directed by a lognormal with independent increments (and parameters μ and σ_1^2) has the following lognormal–normal increments:

$$f_{LNN}(y) = \frac{1}{2\pi\sigma_1^2 \cdot \sigma_2^2} \int_0^\infty v^{-3/2} \cdot \exp\left(\frac{-(\log v - \mu)^2}{2\sigma_1^2}\right) \cdot \exp\left(\frac{-y^2}{2v\sigma_2^2}\right) dv. \qquad (4)$$

Proof As in Theorem 4, the distribution of $\Delta X(T(t))$ is just the expectation of the distribution of $F_x(0, \ t\sigma_2^2)$, the expectation being taken over the increments of $T(t)$. That is:

$$f_{LNN}(y) = E_t[f_N(0, \ t\sigma_2^2)(y)]$$

where t is lognormally distributed. Thus

$$f_{LNN}(y) = \int_0^\infty \left[\frac{1}{2\pi v\sigma_2^2}\exp\left(-\frac{y^2}{2v\sigma_2^2}\right)\right]\left[\frac{1}{2\pi\sigma_1^2 \cdot v}\exp\left(-\frac{(\log v - \mu)^2}{2\sigma_1^2}\right)\right] dv.$$

Simplification yields Formula (4).

---

[13] Aitchison and Brown (1957) have a complete discussion of the properties of the lognormal distribution.

[14] In fact, the lognormal–normal distribution was included because it was found empirically to be the most useful. See Clark (1970) for other distributions subordinate to the normal. It is not clear theoretically why operational time should be lognormally distributed.

This relatively complicated formula may be approximated by numerical integration techniques.

1.3 Tests of the conditional distribution $[\Delta X(T(t))|\Delta T(t)]$ and the distribution of $\Delta T(t)$

At the end of Section 1, it was mentioned that the price process, $X(T(t))$, evolved at different rates on different days. An obvious measure of this speed of evolution is trading volume. In fact, if the price changes on individual trades were uncorrelated, $T(t)$, the directing process, would be the cumulative trading volume up to time t. The distribution of the increments of the price process $\Delta X(T(t))$ would then have a distribution subordinate to that of the price changes on individual trades, and directed by the distribution of trading volume.

The way to test the hypothesis that trading volume in some sense measures the speed of evolution is clear; the relationship between trading volume and price change variance must be examined. If trading volume is not related to the speed of evolution, there should be no correlation between $V(t)$ (trading volume on day t) and $[\Delta X(T(t))]^2$. If trading volume is the directing process, the relationship should be linear, with the proportionality coefficient representing the variance of $\Delta X(t)$.

The first approach was the grouping of the two samples of 1,000 observations each on cotton futures prices into twenty groups of fifty each by increasing volume.[15] The sample variance and kurtosis within each group were calculated. These results are displayed in Table 1.1. Trading volume and price change variance seem to have a curvilinear relationship.

More significantly, note that the kurtosis has been very much reduced when price changes with similar volumes are considered. The variance of the sample kurtosis from a normal population is $24/n$, where n is the sample size. Thus any sample kurtosis that lies between 1.6 and 4.4 is within 2 standard deviations of the true value, 3, expected with a normal parent. The vast majority of sample kurtoses lie within this range for both samples.

The average sample kurtosis is larger than 3 for both samples; but this is just as expected. Each volume class contains a range of volumes; just as in the case of the entire sample, this makes the sample distribution of the daily price changes non-normal. However, since each volume class contains a much smaller range of volumes, this phenomenon is considerably reduced. Note that the last two volume classes in both samples have significantly higher kurtosis than the other classes; this is clearly caused by the larger range of volumes included in these classes. Grouping by volume classes has brought the kurtosis of the price change distribution to within two standard deviations of that expected from a normal parent, while the original kurtosis of the whole sample is 100 standard deviations away.

---

[15] See the Appendix for a description of the data used.

Table 1.1. Price change variance and kurtosis by volume class

Sample One: 17 January 1947 to 31 August 1950				*Sample Two*: 24 March 1951 to 10 February 1955			
Volume range	Volume mean	Sample variance	Sample kurtosis	Volume range	Volume mean	Sample variance	Sample kurtosis
Entire sample				Entire sample			
326–12156	2718.94	584.55	19.45	488–10571	2733.40	501.73	20.49
326–939	718.4	30.51	3.95	488–979	794.7	18.67	2.64
948–1123	1030.7	59.60	3.53	985–1187	1078.4	42.93	3.57
1124–1297	1223.7	48.87	4.64	1202–1336	1271.4	56.56	3.03
1298–1434	1371.0	102.70	5.09	1337–1509	1432.2	59.52	2.73
1435–1556	1493.2	105.46	4.02	1510–1631	1570.0	53.44	2.65
1558–1710	1628.7	73.76	3.21	1634–1766	1699.1	87.41	2.30
1711–1873	1788.4	104.65	2.73	1768–1895	1822.5	89.84	4.04
1874–2032	1955.3	138.53	4.75	1899–2026	1963.8	105.71	3.71
2033–2225	2121.8	173.38	4.18	2029–2190	2110.8	136.25	3.59
2227–2408	2316.2	300.17	4.55	2191–2353	2266.1	178.86	3.57
2408–2595	2504.9	310.99	2.93	2355–2537	2445.7	214.31	4.82
2608–2807	2712.4	240.52	3.47	2538–2705	2615.1	223.56	2.68
2807–2995	2912.5	347.13	3.01	2709–2913	2816.6	283.70	4.82
2998–3279	3146.0	486.91	4.55	2913–3179	3043.7	263.73	2.12
3284–3539	3399.6	352.68	2.95	3180–3434	3294.6	295.70	3.63
3540–3800	3676.2	800.07	2.61	3436–3763	3581.1	520.92	2.98
3803–4194	4013.8	711.67	3.14	3765–4128	3935.4	642.46	1.99
4204–4737	4434.3	785.06	2.07	4160–4795	4509.6	937.33	2.35
4739–5512	5149.3	2716.77	5.14	4800–5754	5238.9	2067.90	8.76
5556–12156	6782.3	3695.87	6.35	5759–10571	7178.2	3659.21	4.41

To investigate the curvilinear relationship between price variance and trading volume, the regressions in Table 1.2 were used. The results indicate that either $\sigma^2 = Ae^{\chi v}$ or $\sigma^2 = Bv^\beta$ are equally good in explaining movement of price variance. The first faces the theoretical objection that $\sigma^2(0) \neq 0$ but is negligibly different from 0 for the size of numbers we are using. The linear specification is clearly worse; the F statistics calculated for linear regressions with a constant term are about 125, with a large negative intercept. The high negative intercept term for the unconstrained regressions indicates that the linear model performs very poorly, as does the low F statistic. Even if all trades on any given day are perfectly correlated, the dependence of price change variance on volume would be only $\sigma^2 \sim v^2$; the data reject even this high dependence as too low.

To see how this curvilinear dependence of price change variance on volume might occur, consider how the futures market actually works. At any time there are a number of traders in the market who have expectations about the price of a given cotton contract. Some will have long positions (holding contracts), some

Table 1.2. Daily price change variance as a function of daily volume[a]

	Sample 1:	
(a) $\log(\Delta X^2) = 1.977 + .0008219v$,		$F = 295.20$,
(.149) (.00004784)		
(b) $\log(\Delta X^2) = -12.71 + 2.181 \log(v)$,		$F = 280.38$,
(1.01) (.1303)		
(c) $\Delta X^2 = .31374v$,		$F = 156.25$
(.02428)		
	Sample 2:	
(a) $\log(\Delta X^2) = 1.968 + .0007334v$,		$F = 236.83$,
(.149) (.00004766)		
(b) $\log(\Delta X^2) = -12.73 + 2.1503 \log(v)$,		$F = 253.69$.
(1.05) (.1350)		
(c) $\Delta X^2 = .25598v$,		$F = 86.24$.
(.02611)		

[a] The numbers in parentheses are standard errors. $F_{.01}(1, 998) = F_{.01}(1, 999) = 6.66$.

will have short positions (having sold contracts), and some may have no net position at all if they are waiting for more favorable conditions. When new information (in the form of data that the traders consider relevant) flows to the market, both prices and traders' price expectations will change. If the information is uncertain (i.e. some traders shift expectations up and others down on the basis of the information), or if only "inside" traders get the information first, then large price changes will be coincident with high volumes. On the other hand, very large price changes will probably be due to information that is perceived by all traders to move the price in one direction. News of widespread insect problems might be an example of this sort of information in the cotton futures market. In this case, all traders would revise their expectations in the same direction, and the price change would have relatively low volume.

Thus the relationship $\text{var}(\Delta X) = Cv^{2.18}$ is seen as a combination of correlation of price changes on individual trades, and a deficiency of volume at high price changes, caused by traders moving their expectations in unison. Trading volume is taken as an instrument for the true operational time, or an "imperfect clock" measuring the speed of evolution of the price change process. The regressions in Table II are taken as the way to adjust the "volume clock" to get the best obtainable estimate of operational time.

It is now natural to use these equations estimating "operational time" to adjust price changes and find the distribution of $\Delta X(t)$. That is, if $\Delta T(t) = f(v(t))$, then $\Delta X(T(t))/\sqrt{f(v(t))}$ should be distributed as $\Delta X(t)$. The results of this adjustment are summarized in Table 1.3.

The distribution of the Kolmogorov–Smirnov statistic under a complex null hypothesis is not known exactly, but the significance level is reduced in the normal case. Although these K–S statistics are very encouraging, the sample

Table 1.3. Distribution of $\Delta X(t)/\sqrt{f(v(t))}$ for $f(v) = Av^\alpha$ and $f(v) = Be^{\beta v}$

	Sample 1	Sample 2
$f(v)$	$e^{-12.71}v^{2.1818}$	$e^{-12.73}v^{2.1503}$
K–S test against normality	.0321 (.26)[a]	.0195 (.84)
Kurtosis	4.55	4.56
$f(v)$	$e^{1.977}e^{.0008219v}$	$e^{1.968}e^{.0007334v}$
K–S test against normality	.0294 (.35)	.0239 (.62)
Kurtosis	4.26	4.18

[a] The numbers in parentheses indicate the probability that the preceding value of the K–S statistic will be exceeded when the null hypothesis is true.

kurtosis is still too high. This is attributable to one of two causes. Either $\Delta T(t) = f(v(t))$ and the estimation procedure in Section 2 has not found the true $f(v)$, or $\Delta T(t) = f(v(t)) \cdot u(t)$ where $u(t) \neq 1$. In either case the transformation $\Delta X(t)/\sqrt{f(v(t))}$ leaves a small deterministic or random element of operational time still in the adjusted series. Since the results in Section 2 tell us that introduction of operational time will always lead to increased kurtosis, either type of error should lead to results like those in Table 1.3.[16] The relative strength of these numbers is seen when the figures in Table 1.3 are compared with those in Table 1.1 for the entire sample. The K–S test statistics against normality are .114 for Sample 1 and .121 for Sample 2, both of which have probability of less than .000001 of occurrence if the sample is drawn from the normal parent. Similarly, the kurtosis has been reduced a very significant amount.

Although the results are far from perfect, they are good enough to conclude that the "imperfect clock" hypothesis is a good approximation to the truth at this level of analysis.

There is, then, a strong case for normality of price change when it is adjusted for operational time. To find the distribution of price change, however, the distribution of $\Delta T(t)$ must be found. Both the gamma and lognormal distributions were fit to the two specifications of $\Delta T(t) = (f(v(t)))$ for operational time. Only the lognormal results are reported in Table 1.4, since the lognormal fit very much better than the gamma.

The easiest way to test for lognormality is to take logarithms of the sample and test for normality; since this is the method used, the kurtosis of the sample after logarithms have been taken is also displayed in Table 1.4. Note that testing the lognormality of $f(v) = Av^\alpha$ is equivalent to testing the lognormality of v, while testing the lognormality of $f(v) = Be^{\beta v}$ is equivalent to testing the normality of v.

[16] Although the introduction of operational time always increases kurtosis, it is easy to think of a statistical adjustment procedure that could make $k < 3$. By making overestimates of variance (or $f(v)$) on very high price changes, but not having them too low on small price changes, it is possible to cut off the tails entirely in the adjusted distribution. Any regression method of estimation will usually have both positive and negative errors on the low and high ends of the volume range. In fact, $f(v)$ in Table 1.2 tends to underestimate on the high end.

Table 1.4 Tests of lognormality of $\Delta T(t) = f(v(t))$ for $f(v) = Av^\alpha$ and $f(v) = Be^{\beta v}$

	Sample 1	Sample 2
$f(v)$	$e^{-12.71}v^{2.1818}$	$e^{-12.73}v^{2.1503}$
K-S statistic against lognormality	.03343 (.21)[a]	.01562 (.97)
Kurtosis of log $(f(v))$	2.929	2.858
$f(v)$	$e^{1.977}e^{.0008219v}$	$e^{1.968}e^{.0007334v}$
K–S statistic against lognormality	.08303 (.00001)	.1114 (.00000)
Kurtosis of log $(f(v))$	6.744	6.115

[a] Again, as in Table 1.3, the numbers in parentheses are the probability of exceeding the given K-S statistic if the null hypothesis were true.

The results in Table 1.4 indicate that v is lognormally distributed as opposed to normally distributed; the model $f(v) = Av^\alpha$ is the better one to use, given both models seem to work equally well as operational time.

All of the results above are very strong evidence in favor of the finite-variance subordination model. They also point out that the marginal distribution (unconditional on operational time) of price changes should be lognormal-normal rather than stable. If $\Delta X(t)$ is normal, then $\Delta T(t)$ must have a stable distribution with a very long tail (no finite mean) in order that $\Delta X(T(t))$ have a stable distribution. If this were the case, the lognormal fit in Table 1.4 should be much worse.

1.4 A direct test of the two competing hypotheses

Two approaches were used to test the lognormal–normal (LN) family against the stable (S) family of distributions as the parent of the observed distribution of price changes for cotton futures.

The first test was a Bayesian one, with discrete prior and posterior distributions over the two hypotheses. The construction of this test, although not completely rigorous, was well motivated by practical considerations. Suppose a decision-maker is trying to decide whether cotton futures price changes have a stable or lognormal–normal distribution, and his initial position before examination of the data is complete ignorance. Then his prior distribution should have $P(S) = P(LN) = .5$, and presumably after the sample information has been examined, these probabilities will change.

Calculation of posterior probabilities could proceed in straightforward fashion if S and LN were not complicated, with an infinite number of parameter values available within each hypothesis. In view of the fact that analytical calculation of likelihoods as functions of parameter values was considered impossible by the author, a second-best approach was used. Twenty-five simple hypotheses (i.e. exactly-specified sets of parameters) within each set of S and LN were chosen, using all the prior information possible about the region in which these parameter points should lie. Such a strategy assumes that the likelihood functions are smooth and do not have high peaks between the selected points in parameter space. It also makes use of the present decision-maker's relative indifference about the exact parameter values.

Once this method is adopted, prior probabilities $\{P_i^A\}_{i=1}^{50}$ may be assigned in such a way that P_i^A are the same for all i, and that $\Sigma_S P_i^A = \Sigma_{LN} P_i^A = .5$. Posterior probabilities $\{P_i^B\}_{i=1}^{50}$ for these hypotheses may be calculated using Bayes' rule:

$$P_i^B = \frac{P_i^A \cdot L(S_m|H_i)}{\Sigma_i L(S_m|H_i)P_i^A}$$

where $L(S_m|H_i)$ is the likelihood of the sample given hypothesis i. Posterior probabilities for S and LN are $\Sigma_S P_i^B$ and $\Sigma_{LN} P_i^B$ respectively. Each simple hypothesis was given a prior probability of 0.02. The parameters which constituted each simple hypothesis were made up by using theoretical considerations to guess what combinations of parameters would maximize the likelihood of the sample.

1.4.1 Lognormal–normal distributions

Let $\Delta T(t) = T(t) - T(t-1)$ be distributed lognormally with parameters μ, σ_1^2. That is, $\log(\Delta T(t))$ is distributed normally with mean μ and variance σ_1^2.

Let $\Delta X(t) = X(t) - X(t-1)$ be distributed normally with mean 0 and variance $\sigma_2^2 \cdot F_T$ has mean $e^{\mu+\sigma_1^2/2}$ and variance $e^{2\mu+\sigma_1^2}(e^{\sigma_1^2}-1)$. Theorem 4 then says that the variance of the distribution of $\Delta X(T(t)) = X(T(t)) - X(T(t-1))$ is $\sigma_2^2 \cdot e^{\mu+\sigma_1^2/2}$.

Since the data are normalized so that the sample variance is 1, one constraint on the parameters for the prior distribution of the lognormal–normal is:

$$\sigma_2^2 \cdot e^{\mu+\sigma_1^2/2} = 1.$$

Corollary 4.1 states that the kurtosis of the lognormal–normal family is

$$k = 3\left[\frac{e^{2\mu+\sigma_1^2} + e^{2\mu+\sigma_1^2}(e^{\sigma_1^2}-1)}{e^{2\mu+\sigma_1^2}}\right] = 3e^{\sigma_1^2}.$$

Thus another constraint on the parameters in the prior distribution is $\sigma_1^2 = \log(k/3)$ where k is the sample kurtosis.

1.4.2 Stable distributions

The characteristic function for this family is $e^{-\gamma|u|^\alpha}$, which converges to $e^{-\sigma^2 u^2/2}$ as $\alpha \to 2$, when the normal distribution is obtained. If $\alpha < 2$, then γ must be smaller than 0.5 to fit a sample with a sample variance of 1, so $1 < \alpha < 2$ and $0 < \gamma < .5$ is the correct region for the prior. Since these restrictions represent far less information than the restrictions on the lognormal–normal, some preliminary calculations of the likelihood were made to narrow down the region for the prior which would present the stable distributions in the most favorable light.

The concepts involved in constructing this test are elementary; the difficult problems are the practical ones. In order to calculate the likelihood of a sample, the density of the distribution of the sample under the null hypothesis must be known. For the case at hand, these densities are:

Stable: $f_S(x;\alpha,\ \gamma) = 1/\pi \int_0^\infty \cos(ux)e^{-\gamma|u|^\alpha} du,$ (5)

and

Lognormal–normal:

$$f_{LN}(x;\mu,\ \sigma_1^2,\ \sigma_2^2) = \frac{1}{2\pi\sigma_1^2\sigma_2^2} \int_0^\infty v^{-3/2} \exp\left(-\frac{(\log v - \mu)^2}{2\sigma_1^2} - \frac{x^2}{2v\sigma_2^2}\right) dv. \quad (6)$$

Expression (5) is a consequence of the fact that the characteristic function of a distribution is its Fourier transform, while expression (6) is the lognormal–normal density derived in Section 2. Since neither of the integrals on the right hand side of these equations may be solved analytically, the problem of finding an approximate likelihood function for any sample reduces to finding values of f_S or f_{LN} for many different values of x, and then interpolating to find the likelihoods for sample values of x.

The density for the stable distributions (5) is by far the easier to approximate accurately; the integral on the right is the Fourier transform of $e^{-\gamma|u|^\alpha}$, and the fast Fourier transform methods that have been recently developed[17] are extremely accurate. For the test at hand, the value of $f_S(x)$ was tabulated for $x \in [0,\ 10]$ at 2048 equal intervals. This range was adequate, for no observations were recorded at more than 10 sample standard deviations from 0.

Calculation of $f_{LN}(x)$ was less accurate and more costly. First, the interval over which the integrand in (6) was greater than 10^{-15} was found. The required integral was then calculated by using Simpson's rule with 601 points after dividing the interval up so that the interpolation points would be closer together when the integrand was changing rapidly. This process was repeated for $x \in [0,\ 10]$ at 101 points. Both distributions required small adjustments so that their numerical integral on $[-10,\ 10]$ equalled 1.

Tables 1.5 and 1.6 give posterior probabilities and likelihoods for the samples, given the parameters in the distributions. Again, all prior probabilities are 0.02.

The posterior probability of S and LN for the two samples are: Sample 1 —$P(S)=.11 \times 10^{-5}, P(LN) = .999999$; and Sample 2 —$P(S)=.0007, P(LN) = .9993$. These results are very convincing evidence that the observed leptokurticity in the price change distribution for cotton futures is caused by the fact that the data are recorded in "clock" time rather than operational time.

---

[17] J. W. Cooley and J. W. Tukey (1965). In fact, these methods are accurate and fast enough to calculate four or five place tables of the stable distributions at relatively small expense, if anyone so desired.

Table 1.5. Posterior probabilities and likelihoods of sample 1

Stable Distribution

α	γ	Likelihood = $A \times 10^{-B}$		Posterior Prob. = $C \times 10^{-D}$	
		A	B	C	D
1.3	.3	.7028	539	.6895	8
1.3	.325	.8671	539	.8507	8
1.35	.275	.4910	539	.4817	8
1.35	.3	.5742	538	.5634	7
1.35	.325	.3453	538	.3388	7
1.35	.35	.2057	539	.2018	8
1.375	.287	.5393	538	.5291	7
1.375	.312	.9776	538	.9788	7
1.375	.337	.1378	538	.1352	7
1.4	.275	.2630	538	.2580	7
1.4	.3	.1476	537	.1449	6
1.4	.325	.5001	538	.4907	7
1.4	.35	.1913	539	.1877	8
1.425	.287	.1139	537	.1117	6
1.425	.312	.1156	537	.1134	6
1.425	.337	.1045	538	.1025	7
1.45	.275	.4439	538	.4355	7
1.45	.30	.1397	537	.1371	6
1.45	.325	.3047	538	.2989	7
1.475	.287	.8759	538	.8594	7
1.475	.312	.5729	538	.5621	7
1.475	.337	.3739	539	.3668	8
1.5	.275	.2698	538	.2647	7
1.5	.3	.5507	538	.5403	7
1.55	.275	.6532	539	.6409	8

Lognormal–Normal Distribution

μ	σ_1^2	σ_2^2	Likelihood = $A \times 10^{-B}$		Posterior Prob. = $C \times 10^{-D}$	
			A	B	C	D
-.5	1.5	.7	.3677	532	.3608	1
-.5	1.5	.25	.3425	537	.3362	6
-.5	2.5	.5	.2418	533	.3272	2
-1.49	1.6	2.0	.5673	537	.5566	6
-1.21	1.6	1.5	.2124	534	.2084	3
-.8	1.6	1.0	.9510	533	.9389	2
-.11	1.6	.5	.4191	532	.4112	1
.59	1.6	.25	.3236	532	.3175	1
-1.31	1.8	1.5	.6728	534	.6601	3
-.90	1.8	1.0	.3198	532	.3138	1
-.21	1.8	.5	.1047	531	.1026	0
.49	1.8	.25	.7619	532	.7475	1
-1.59	2.0	2.0	.1591	537	.1473	6
-1.41	2.0	1.5	.1254	533	.1230	2
-1.0	2.0	1.0	.4798	532	.4707	1
-.31	2.0	.5	.6633	532	.6508	1
.39	2.0	.25	.2920	532	.2865	1
.30	1.8	.30	.1084	531	.1064	0
.13	1.8	.35	.8771	532	.8605	1
.13	1.85	.35	.8512	532	.8356	1
.15	1.85	.35	.8434	532	.8275	1
.11	1.85	.35	.7978	532	.7827	1
-1.10	2.0	1.10	.3919	532	.3845	1
-1.0	2.2	.9	.5261	532	.5162	1
-.9	2.0	1.10	.6026	534	.5912	3

Table 1.6. Posterior probabilities and likelihoods for sample 2

Stable Distribution							Lognormal–Normal Distribution							
		Likelihood = $A \times 10^{-B}$		Posterior Prob. = $C \times 10^{-D}$						Likelihood = $A \times 10^{-B}$		Posterior Prob. = $C \times 10^{-D}$		
α	γ	A	B	C	D		μ	σ_1^2	σ_2^2	A	B	C	D	
1.35	.275	.1806	520	.1617	4		−.26	1.9	.5	.5415	517	.4853	1	
1.35	.3	.2104	520	.1886	4		−1.05	1.9	1.0	.6388	517	.5726	1	
1.40	.275	.5946	520	.5329	4		−.36	1.9	.5	.6319	517	.5664	1	
1.40	.3	.2945	520	.2640	4		−.21	1.8	.5	.3222	517	.2888	1	
1.45	.275	.5909	520	.5296	4		−1.00	2.0	1.0	.3048	517	.2732	1	
1.45	.3	.1407	520	.1261	4		−.31	2.0	.5	.6611	517	.5925	1	
1.50	.275	.1877	520	.1682	4		.39	2.0	.25	.3017	517	.2704	1	
1.45	.25	.8906	521	.7982	5		−.21	2.0	.5	.1772	517	.1588	1	
1.475	.262	.2776	520	.2488	4		.49	2.0	.25	.1086	517	.9733	2	
1.35	.287	.2919	520	.2616	4		−.44	1.9	.6	.5520	517	.4948	1	
1.375	.262	.1151	520	.1032	4		−.15	1.9	.45	.4847	517	.4344	1	
1.375	.275	.3889	520	.3486	4		−.03	1.9	.4	.4376	517	.3922	1	
1.375	.287	.4973	520	.4457	4		−.39	1.8	.6	.3013	517	.2701	1	
1.375	.3	.2881	520	.2582	4		.02	1.8	.4	.2710	517	.2429	1	
1.375	.312	.9115	521	.8170	5		.15	1.8	.35	.2713	517	.2432	1	
1.40	.262	.2303	520	.2063	4		−.49	1.8	.60	.7456	517	.6683	1	
1.40	.287	.6217	520	.2346	4		−.08	1.8	.40	.5358	517	.4797	1	
1.425	.262	.3374	520	.3024	4		.05	1.8	.35	.4721	517	.4231	1	
1.425	.275	.6861	520	.6149	4		−1.49	2.0	.60	.7656	517	.6862	1	
1.425	.287	.5783	520	.5138	4		−.20	2.0	.45	.5707	517	.5115	1	
1.425	.3	.2255	520	.2021	4		−.08	2.0	.40	.4897	517	.4389	1	
1.45	.262	.3558	520	.3189	4		−.59	2.0	.60	.7588	517	.6801	1	
1.45	.287	.4246	520	.3815	4		−.30	2.0	.45	.3874	517	.3472	1	
1.475	.275	.3756	520	.3366	4		−.18	2.0	.40	.3035	517	.2720	1	
1.475	.287	.2316	520	.2076	4		.05	1.9	.40	.1143	517	.1024	1	

Note that the results are independent of the choice of prior distribution as long as at least one of the prior points in the *LN* hypothesis is in the region of high likelihood. This is only another way of saying that the likelihood of a lognormal-normal having generated the sample is very significantly higher than the likelihood for any stable distributions.

One way to see why this is true is to look at the maximum likelihood distributions in each family, as displayed in Table 1.7. The primary difference is that the lognormal-normal distribution is larger at 0 and smaller in the tails; if there were very many observations 8 or 9 sample standard deviations from the mean, then the stable distribution would have fared much better on the tests. Instead, the sample is characterized by a few large observations that would be unlikely if

Table 1.7. Stable and lognormal–normal distributions which maximize the likelihood of the samples

X	$f_{LNN}(x)$ (1)[a]	$f_S(x)$ (2)	$f_{LNN}(x)$ (3)	$f_S(x)$ (4)
	Sample 1		*Sample 2*	
0	.7755	.6856	.7717	.7159
.1	.7356	.6711	.7399	.6999
.2	.6394	.6304	.6566	.6549
.3	.5302	.5696	.5495	.5882
.4	.4340	.4972	.4449	.5092
.5	.3557	.4216	.3569	.4275
.6	.2925	.3494	.2880	.3503
.7	.2414	.2849	.2349	.2822
.8	.2000	.2300	.1935	.2249
.9	.1665	.1849	.1606	.1786
1.0	.1393	.1487	.1342	.1420
1.2	.0989	.0882	.0951	.0822
1.4	.0716	.0605	.0688	.0556
1.6	.0526	.0431	.0507	.0392
1.8	.0393	.0318	.0380	.0287
2.0	.0298	.0277	.0289	.0217
2.5	.0156	.0129	.0153	.0114
3.0	$.870 \times 10^{-2}$	$.891 \times 10^{-2}$	$.869 \times 10^{-2}$	$.720 \times 10^{-2}$
3.5	$.509 \times 10^{-2}$	$.538 \times 10^{-2}$	$.517 \times 10^{-2}$	$.471 \times 10^{-2}$
4.0	$.310 \times 10^{-2}$	$.388 \times 10^{-2}$	$.320 \times 10^{-2}$	$.339 \times 10^{-2}$
4.5	$.196 \times 10^{-2}$	$.284 \times 10^{-2}$	$.206 \times 10^{-2}$	$.247 \times 10^{-2}$
5.0	$.127 \times 10^{-2}$	$.221 \times 10^{-2}$	$.136 \times 10^{-2}$	$.191 \times 10^{-2}$
6.0	$.575 \times 10^{-3}$	$.140 \times 10^{-2}$	$.637 \times 10^{-3}$	$.126 \times 10^{-2}$
7.0	$.282 \times 10^{-3}$	$.954 \times 10^{-3}$	$.323 \times 10^{-3}$	$.820 \times 10^{-3}$
8.0	$.148 \times 10^{-3}$	$.687 \times 10^{-3}$	$.175 \times 10^{-3}$	$.589 \times 10^{-3}$
9.0	$.815 \times 10^{-4}$	$.515 \times 10^{-3}$	$.998 \times 10^{-4}$	$.440 \times 10^{-3}$
10.0	$.466 \times 10^{-4}$	$.399 \times 10^{-3}$	$.598 \times 10^{-4}$	$.340 \times 10^{-3}$

[a] $(1)\mu = .3 \sigma_1^2 = 1.8 \sigma_2^2 = .3; (2)\alpha = 1.4, \ \gamma = .3; (3)\mu = -.49 \sigma_1^2 = 2.0 \sigma_2^2 = .6; (4)\alpha = 1.425, \ \gamma = .275.$

the underlying distribution were normal, but not large enough to make the stable family a likely contender.

The evidence for the lognormal–normal is made stronger by the fact that the parameters derived from the theory for the prior distribution turn out to be the ones which maximize the likelihoods of both samples. Values which did not fit the restrictions gave much lower likelihoods for the samples.

On the other hand, the parameters of the stable distribution in the region of maximum likelihood were quite different from what was expected. Instead of $\alpha = 1.8$ (or close to 2), α is much lower for both samples. This is a standard indication of specification error; the model is a bad approximation to the data, so the estimated parameters turn out to be different from those theoretical considerations indicate.

Estimates of $\alpha = 1.4$ also cast doubt on the graphs of cumulative variance used by Mandelbrot (1963). With an α this low, the sample variance as a function of sample size should have a pronounced upward slope. The relative flatness of these graphs indicates that the underlying population has high probabilities of large changes, but still a finite variance. The lognormal–normal distribution and other subordinate distributions are very suitable for representing this type of behavior.

As a second test of the two hypotheses, the Kolmogorov–Smirnov statistics testing each sample against the maximum likelihood distributions in Table 1.7 were calculated. The results are tabulated in Table 1.8.

Note that the probabilities in parentheses are calculated using asymptotic results, but only a small number of steps is used for the numerical *LNN* distribution, so some "small sample" bias is involved.

Note also that the K–S statistic is better at examining a distribution in the range of high density than in the tails; 20 out of 1,000 observations at 20 standard deviations from the mean would change the likelihood results radically, but would have only a small effect on the K–S results.

It is clear also that a bias in favor of the *LNN* hypothesis exists because of the statutory limits on price movements. However, examination of the data for 10 individual futures over the span 30–250 days until maturity[18] revealed this bias to be extremely small. For all of these 10 futures, the limit (2 cents) was reached on only 3 occasions. Furthermore, the limit was an average of 8 sample standard

Table 1.8. K–S Statistics testing the samples against the maximum likelihood lognormal–normal and stable distributions

Sample 1		Sample 2	
LNN	Stable	*LNN*	Stable
.0856 (.80)[a]	.0374 (.44)	.0955 (.68)	.0438 (.25)

[a] Numbers in parenthesis are the probability that the given value of the K–S statistic will be exceeded if the null hypothesis is true.

[18] This period was chosen so that the market would not be excessively thin.

deviations from 0, thus making it a very weak constraint. It seems clear that the absence of this limitation would not have changed the above results.

In summary, then, the empirical evidence points to acceptance of the finite-variance subordination model. The standard Central Limit Theorem holds only when the number of random variables being added is constant (in probability limit, at least); in the case of speculative markets, this restriction is violated, and the limit distribution of price changes is subordinate to the normal distribution.

Appendix construction of a long time series for cotton futures

The data on price, transactions, and volume for cotton futures is readily available in daily form for the years 1945–1958 in *United States Commodity Exchange Administration, Trade in Cotton Futures*. Considering the care with which the data were gathered, these daily figures potentially give very long and accurate time series. Except for a brief period during the Korean War when trading was suspended[19] due to price controls, these series were recorded daily, and they represent two periods of 1,000 observations each.[20] Such a wealth of data potentially provides ideal circumstances for testing hypotheses about the structure of price movements on speculative markets.

As even the most casual observer of commodity markets knows, however, no contract (or future) has a lifetime that is this long. Contracts are made for delivery of cotton on a particular date (almost always on the fifteenth of March, May, July, October, or December). Trading in any particular contract begins about a year and a half before the delivery date on the contract, and ends on that date. Taken by itself, then, any one contract will yield a time series of only 300 points, many of which are taken when the market is thin and there is very little trading in that particular future (i.e. at the beginning and end of its life).

To remedy this situation, and generate longer time series that always represented prices and volumes on an active market, a continuous time series of prices and volume was constructed. The intent was to define a "contract" that matured a fixed distance in the future, analogous to "90-day futures" that exist in some foreign exchange markets. This fixed distance in the future was taken to be the average time to maturity of all futures in the market. Care was taken to make sure this was the same for all days, thereby avoiding the problem of changing the interest accruing to the seller of the contract.

The most straightforward way of defining this average future is to construct a weight function $W(\tau)$, where τ is the time distance from now that each of the existing contracts mature. Since a few contracts usually come into existence a year and a half before the maturity date, this function was constructed for $\tau = 1, 2, \ldots 510$. Although the time pattern of futures contracts in existence

[19] 26 January, 1951 to 23 March, 1951.
[20] "Sample 1" in the text is from 17 January 1947 to 31 August 1950, while "Sample 2" is from 24 March 1951 to 10 February 1955.

clearly changes over time, the weight function applied to all dates should be the same, so that the "time to maturity" of the weighted average constructed remains relatively fixed in time. The "price" of this constructed cotton future is

$$P_t = \frac{\Sigma_T W(\tau) P_t^\tau}{\Sigma_T W(\tau)}$$

where $T = \{$set of all existing $\tau\}$ and P_t^τ is the price at time t of the contract maturing at time $t + \tau$. Typically, this sum includes eight terms.

To estimate $W(\tau)$, the average time pattern of contracts in existence, the proportion of all contracts was tabulated for all $\tau \in (0,\ 510)$ days in the years 1946 to 1951. This consisted of about 25 proportions for each. These proportions were then averaged, giving the average proportion of open interest for each time distance in the future, for integral numbers of days.

This procedure yields a rough approximation to the $W(\tau)$ function desired, except that the finite amount of data makes it possible for $W(\tau)$ to have many more than one local maximum. Since examination of the data reveals that open interest has only one local maximum on any one day, it is reasonable to require $W(\tau)$ to have this property also. Essentially, what is required is some sort of smoothing operation to remove the small irregularities in $W(\tau)$; a very simple and effective method to accomplish this smoothing is a moving average. In this case, an eleven-period centered moving average sufficed to give $W(\tau)$ the required shape: first rising to a maximum, then monotonically falling, eventually to zero. Figure 1.2 displays $W(\tau)$ graphically.

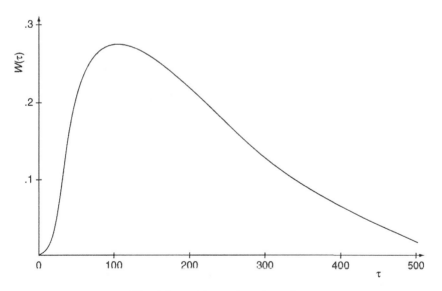

Fig. 1.2. $W(\tau)$ as a function of τ.

Note that "Sample 2" starts when there was still a price ceiling imposed on the May 1951 and July 1951 contracts. Ideally, the sample period should be moved to a later starting point, but the bias involved in starting on 24 March is undoubtedly small. Price changes are constrained to 0 only for the May contract, with the July contract displaying some variability. The price changes used in the analysis are weighted average, which always includes unconstrained contracts; less than 30 per cent of the volume is traded in May and July, 1951 futures. Thus about 1 per cent of the sample is affected by the price controls. The similarity of results for both samples indicates that the bias toward too many small price changes is negligible.

Also, weekends might be a source of error; intermittently throughout both sample periods the markets were open on Saturdays. The spectra for trading volume and price change indicate that the six-day cycle that might be introduced by Saturday trading is nonexistent. Similarly, no five-day cycle is formed by treating weekends the same as overnight periods.

References

Aitchison, J. and Brown, J. A. C. (1957). *The Lognormal Distribution*. Cambridge: Cambridge University Press.

Anscombe, F. J. (1952). Large Sample Theory of Sequential Estimation. *Proceedings of the Cambridge Philosophical Society* 48, 600–7.

Bachelier, L. (1900). *Theory of Speculation*. Paris: Gauthier-Villars.

Billingsley, P. (1963). Limit Theorems for Randomly Selected Partial Sums. *Annals of Mathematical Statistics* 33, 85–92.

Bochner, S. (1960). *Harmonic Analysis and the Theory of Probability*. Berkeley: University of California Press.

Clark, P. K. (1970). A Subordinated Stochastic Process Model of Cotton Futures Prices, unpublished Ph.D. dissertation, Harvard University, May.

Cooley, J. W. and Tukey, J. W. (1965). An Algorithm for the Machine Calculation of Complex Fourier Series. *Mathematics of Computation* 19, 297–301.

Cootner, P. H. (ed.) (1964). *The Random Character of Stock Market Prices*. Cambridge, MA.: M.I.T. Press.

Feller, W. (1966). *An Introduction to Probability Theory and Its Application*, Vol. II. New York: John Wiley and Sons.

Gnednenko, B. V. and Kolmogorov, A. N. (1954). *Limit Distributions for Sums of Independent Random Variables*. Cambridge, MA: Addison-Wesley.

Kendall, M. G. (1953). The Analysis of Economic Time Series: Part I, Prices. *Journal of the Royal Statistical Society* 96, 11–25.

Levy, P. (1925). *Calcul des Probabilités*. Paris: Gauthier-Villars.

Loève, M. M. (1955). *Probability Theory*. New York: Van Nostrand.

Mandelbrot, B. (1963). The Variation of Certain Speculative Prices. *Journal of Business* 36, 394–419.

Mandelbrot, B. and Taylor, H. (1967). On the Distribution of Stock Price Differences, *Operations Research* 15, 1057–62.

Renyi, A. (1957). On the Asymptotic Distribution of a Sum of a Random Number of Independent Random Variables. *Acta Mathematica* (Hungary) 8, 193–9.

—— (1960). On the Central Limit Theorem for a Random Number of Random Variables. *Acta Mathematica* (Hungary) 11, 97–102.

Robbins, H. (1948). The Asymptotic Distribution of the Sum of a Random Number of Random Variables. *Bulletin of the American Mathematical Society* 54, 1151–61.

United States Commodity Exchange Administration. *Trade in Cotton Futures*. Washington, DC: U.S. Government Printing Office.

2

Financial Returns Modelled by the Product of Two Stochastic Processes—A Study of Daily Sugar Prices, 1961–79*

STEPHEN J. TAYLOR

Daily returns from financial assets (stocks, bonds, commodities, currencies) have fluctuating variances and small autocorrelations. Such behaviour, for returns X_t, is modelled by the product process

$$X_t = E(X_t) + V_t U_t,$$

with V_t and U_t independent stochastic processes having $V_t > 0$, $E(U_t) = 0$, $\mathrm{var}(U_t) = 1$.

The realised value of V_t is a conditional standard deviation for X_t and fluctuates with time. It is supposed that $\log(V_t)$ equals an annual constant plus an AR(1) process and that U_t has autocorrelations that can be modelled by an ARMA (1,1) process.

The product process is estimated for 4786 daily prices of London sugar futures, using autocorrelation analyses. Implications for investors and the stability of the parameter estimates over time are discussed.

2.1 Statistical properties of financial returns

Stocks, commodities and currencies are all examples of financial assets whose prices change several times during each market session. Time series analyses of financial prices have been reported for various time scales and this paper considers daily prices, denoted by $\{z_t\}$. Lower-case letters will denote observed values and upper-case letters will denote random variables. Curly brackets {} will denote time series or stochastic processes.

Most researchers apply a logarithmic transformation to prices followed by first differencing to define daily returns,

$$x_t = \log(z_t) - \log(z_{t-1}). \tag{1}$$

Returns, unlike prices, are approximately stationary; they almost equal

$$(z_t - z_{t-1})/z_{t-1},$$

* This work was previously published as S. J. Taylor (1982), 'Financial Returns Modelled by the Product of Two Stochastic Processes: A Study of Daily Sugar Prices, 1961–79' *Time Series Analysis: Theory and Practice 1, Edited by O. D. Anderson* published by North-Holland Publishing Company. Copyright © S. J. Taylor. Reproduced by kind permission.

the proportional price-change, since returns are always small. The logarithmic transformation is the best choice from the power family introduced by Box and Cox (1964), according to a maximum likelihood analysis by Taylor and Kingsman (1979).

This paper defines *non-linear* stochastic processes $\{X_t\}$ possessing all the well-known properties of financial returns and illustrates a method for estimating the process parameters. Four properties of the process generating observed returns are important.

1. The average value of returns is positive for stocks and commodities and exceeds the return obtainable from risk-free investments (Dimson and Brealey, 1978; Merton, 1980; Bodie and Rosansky, 1980).

2. The variance of returns appears to fluctuate. Sample variances calculated from disjoint sets of returns are often significantly different. Examples are given in Section 2.3 and also by Praetz (1969) and Fielitz (1971) for stocks, Labys and Thomas (1975) and Taylor and Kingsman (1979) for commodities, and Levich (1979) for currencies. Variances have been shown to depend on trading volume (Clark, 1973; Westerfield, 1977; Rogalski, 1978), although the parameters of the relationship are time-dependent.

3. Returns have a leptokurtic distribution with fatter tails than a normal distribution. A student's t-distribution, with few degrees-of-freedom, provides a reasonable approximation to the distribution of observed returns (Praetz, 1972; Blattberg and Gonedes, 1974; Taylor and Kingsman, 1979).

4. Any dependence between returns is slight, when measured by autocorrelation coefficients. The random walk hypothesis states that returns are uncorrelated but it has been refuted for U.S. and U.K. commodity markets (Cargill and Rausser, 1975; Taylor, 1980) and for small European stock markets (Jennergren and Korsvold, 1974). Nevertheless, the maximum autocorrelation is generally less than 0.1, if the asset is traded at least once every market day.

Section 2.2 defines non-linear processes having the preceding properties. Methods of parameter estimation are illustrated for nineteen years of sugar prices, described in Section 2.3. The methods are presented in Sections 2.4 to 2.6 and the stability of the parameter values over time is discussed in Section 2.7. Research into the economic consequences of the correlations between commodity returns requires a stochastic process which is both accurate and capable of simulation. Section 2.8 explains how simulation of the recommended process can help to clarify the efficiency of financial markets.

2.2 Product processes

2.2.1 Definitions
A stochastic process, $\{S_t\}$ say, is linear if it equals an MA (∞) process

$$S_t - E(S_t) = \sum_{i=0}^{\infty} \theta_i \varepsilon_{t-1}, \tag{2}$$

with the ε_t both *independent* and identically distributed. Asymptotic results about the sampling distributions of autocorrelation coefficients have been proved for *linear* processes (Anderson and Walker, 1964) and are used for Box–Jenkins time series analysis. The fluctuations in variance exhibited by financial returns are inconsistent with linear processes. Therefore non-linear models are required and standard autocorrelation tests are not valid.

Fluctuations in variance will be observed if $\{X_t\}$ is a non-linear process defined by multiplying two other processes, which might both be linear perhaps after Box–Cox, power transformations.

Suppose,

    (i) $\{V_t\}$ has positive variance and realisations that are always positive at all times,

    (ii) $\{U_t\}$ has zero mean and unit variance,

    (iii) For all s and t, V_s and U_t are independent,

and then define the difference between X_t and its unconditional mean, $\bar{\mu}$, by

$$X_t - \bar{\mu} = V_t U_t. \tag{3}$$

The process $\{X_t\}$ will be called a *product process*. Given a realisation $\{v_t\}$ of $\{V_t\}$, the conditional standard deviations of the X_t are v_t and hence time-dependent. Returns will thus appear to have fluctuating variance if $\{V_t\}$ has high positive autocorrelations and high coefficient-of-variation.

2.2.2 Remarks

Note first that if both $\{V\}$ and $\{U\}$ are stationary processes then the process $\{X\}$ is also stationary. Therefore observed fluctuations in sample variances do not imply non-stationarity, rather they refute all linear models. Secondly, note that if the U_t are independent, then the X_t are uncorrelated but not independent.

Linear, bilinear and state-dependent processes (Granger and Andersen 1978; Priestley 1980) are generated by independent shocks ε_t at a rate one per unit time, but the product process is determined by two (or more) independent shocks per unit time. This is an important distinction. It is suggested that the V-shocks decide the volatility or volume of trading whilst the U-shocks are the impact of unpredictable information about the asset. Although the X_t can have constant variance, their variances conditional on all past shocks to the V- and U-processes are in general not constant but a function of at least v_{t-1}. Most bilinear and all state-dependent models have, conditional on the past shocks, constant variance. These non-linear models, with the possible exception of heterogenous bilinear models (Granger and Andersen, 1978, p. 31), cannot explain observed variance fluctuations. The realisations $\{v_t\}$, $\{u_t\}$, are not observed and product processes are not invertible. Granger and Andersen (1978) regard noninvertibility as a handicap which prevents optimal forecasts. However, Taylor (1980) has shown that useful forecasts can be obtained for product processes.

2.2.3 Special cases considered

This paper presents methods for estimating the unspecified parameters of the product process: the mean of $\{X\}$ (in Section 4), the mean, variance and auto-correlations of $\{V\}$ (in Section 5) and the autocorrelations of $\{U\}$ (in Section 6). Particular attention is given to parameter estimation when $\{\log(V)\}$ minus an annual variable is a Gaussian, linear AR(1) process, and $\{U\}$ is Gaussian and has the ARMA(1, 1) autocorrelations,

$$\rho_{i, U} = Ap^i \text{ with } A > 0 \text{ and } 1 > p > 0.$$

An earlier paper reported empirical results for the unit variance U-process (Taylor, 1980), here attention is focused on the "variance" process $\{V\}$. Deductions about the V-process will follow first from the results:

$$E(|X_t - \bar{\mu}|) = E(V_t)E(|U_t|), \ \text{Var}(X_t) = E(V_t^2), \tag{4}$$

and secondly, by studying the autocorrelations of $(x_t - \bar{x})^2$, a method pioneered by Granger and Andersen (1978).

2.3 Sugar prices

A time series of 4,786 daily returns will be investigated. It is calculated from the daily closing prices of sugar, from January 1961 to November 1979, recorded for December futures contracts traded at the London sugar market. The December 1961 contract provides prices from January 1961 to November 1961 and thereafter successive contracts provide prices for twelve-month periods, from the beginning of December to the end of the following November.

Purchasers of a futures contract, say the December 1979 contract bought in January 1979, expect to receive 50 tonnes of sugar during December 1979; similarly sellers promise to deliver 50 tonnes of sugar during the future month. Most purchasers and sellers, particularly speculators, cancel their commitments by respectively selling and buying contracts before the delivery date. Farmers and manufacturers can control their business risks by trading contracts. Commodity exchanges and trading conditions are described in detail by Teweles, Harlow, and Stone (1974) and in a book edited by Granger (1979).

Figure 2.1 shows the movement of prices, per tonne, over the 19 years considered. They start at £26 and finish at £166, and range from a minimum of £14 in November 1966 to a maximum of £665 in November 1974 (the vertical axis represents the logarithm of the price). Prices for two years are also plotted as Figure 2.2, which clearly demonstrates fluctuations in the variance of returns; in the notation of the product process, the values of v_t for 1963 far exceed those for 1966. Figure 2.2 does not illustrate the most extreme values of the sample

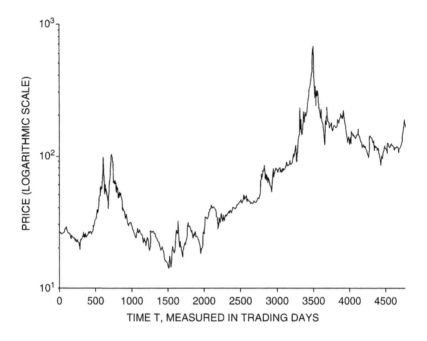

Fig. 2.1. Sugar prices, 1961–79

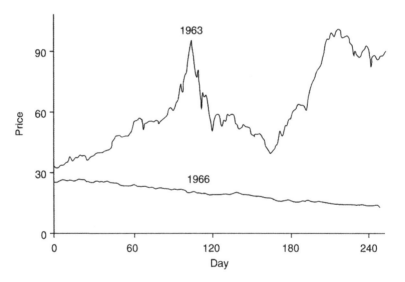

Fig. 2.2. Daily prices for two December sugar contracts

variance—returns in 1974 and 1975 were even more volatile than those in 1963, whilst returns for 1961, 1970 and 1971 varied less than the 1966 returns. Table 2.1 records the annual sample variances of the returns and likelihood-ratio tests have shown the values are, statistically, significantly different. The differences are even more substantial when price-changes ($z_t - z_{t-1}$) are considered (Taylor and Kingsman, 1979).

2.4 An estimate of the average return

It is assumed that the unconditional expected return, $E(X_t)$, is a constant, $\bar{\mu}$. The sample mean $\bar{x}$ is the logical estimate of $\bar{\mu}$ and equals 2.65/10,000 for the sugar returns.

An investor who bought December futures, for the same days and contracts used to define the returns, would have received $\exp(N\bar{x}) = £3.55$ on 1 December, 1979 for every £1 invested on 3 January 1961, ignoring commission costs, with N = 4786 being the number of returns studied. This is equivalent to receiving compound interest at a rate of 6.9% per annum. A slightly better return would have been obtained by risk-free investment in U.K. government securities (cf. Dimson and Brealey, 1978). Estimates of $\bar{\mu}$ are, however, inaccurate even for time series spanning almost two decades, a conclusion emphasised by Merton (1980). Very different annual compound returns would have been estimated if the data had ended in 1969 or 1974, namely −2.5% and 22.6% respectively.

Financial theory claims that $E(X_t)$ always exceeds the time-dependent risk-free rate of return. Ignoring the implied variations of the unconditional expected return has negligible consequences for the subsequent analysis; Taylor (1980) considers the consequences for autocorrelation tests in detail.

2.5 Estimation of the V-process

2.5.1 A class of models

The observed variations in annual sample variances may be caused by either annual or within year effects or by both. A class of models for $\{V_t\}$, combining annual effects $\{C_t\}$ and within year variations $\{D_t\}$, is defined by

$$\log(V_t) = C_t + D_t. \tag{5}$$

By definition, $C_s = C_t$ whenever the times s and t refer to the same annual futures contract. It will be assumed, for analytic convenience, that the C_t are identically distributed Normal random variables, that $\{D_t\}$ is a stationary, linear, Gaussian process having zero mean, and that every pair C_s and D_t are independent. The mean and variance of $\log(V_t)$ are denoted by α and β^2 respectively, so that $\alpha = E(C_t)$ and $\beta^2 = \text{var}(C_t) + \text{var}(D_t)$. The variances of C_t and D_t are denoted by $\kappa\beta^2$ and $(1 - \kappa)\beta^2$, respectively, and the special cases $\kappa = 0$ and $\kappa = 1$, will be discussed.

Assuming V_t to be log–normal has useful consequences, some of which are amplified later. First, the constraints $V_t > 0$, for all t, are automatically satisfied.

Second, convenient analytic results about the autocorrelations of $\{V_t^2\}$ can be obtained. Third, if the U_t are Normal distributed, then the returns X_t have the lognormal–normal distribution suggested by Clark (1973) for cotton futures data. The students-t distribution, proposed for the X_t by Praetz (1972), corresponds to Normal U_t and the right-skewed, inverted-gamma distribution for V_t^2.

It might be thought that the average annual effect, $E(C_t)$, is increasing as the years progress. The rank correlation coefficient between annual variance and time, calculated using Table 2.1, is however 0.08 and insignificant. Alternatively, it might be supposed that prices increase in volatility as contracts approach termination, giving $E(D_{t+i}) > E(D_t)$ when $i > 0$ and the times t and $t + i$ refer to the same contract (Rutledge, 1976). Table 1 gives the sample variances for semi-annual periods. The geometric mean of the ratios of second-half variance to first-half variance equals 1.06 and would be less than 1 if the data ended in 1978. It seems reasonable therefore to assume that $E(D_t)$ is constant.

2.5.2 The mean and variance of V

From the definition of the product process, equation (3), and the independence of the processes $\{V_t\}$ and $\{U_t\}$, it follows that

$$E(V_t) = E|X_t - \bar{\mu}|/E|U_t| \tag{6}$$

$$\text{and } E(V_t^2) = E(X_t - \bar{\mu})^2/\text{var}(U_t) = \text{var}(X_t) \tag{7}$$

Table 2.1. Sample variances for sugar returns

Contract	Returns	Annual Variance $\times 10^4$	Semi-annual variances $\times 10^4$		
			First	Second	Ratio
1961	232	0.82	0.83	0.81	0.97
1962	253	2.27	3.13	1.41	0.45
1963	252	11.81	10.26	13.44	1.31
1964	253	5.73	9.40	2.12	0.23
1965	254	2.43	2.02	2.85	1.41
1966	255	1.76	1.05	2.48	2.38
1967	252	7.54	6.54	8.33	1.27
1968	252	3.23	2.05	4.39	2.14
1969	253	2.75	1.31	4.16	3.18
1970	254	1.08	1.40	0.76	0.55
1971	254	1.05	1.64	0.45	0.27
1972	255	6.35	8.32	4.44	0.53
1973	251	2.23	2.31	2.17	0.94
1974	251	15.17	17.39	13.07	0.75
1975	253	18.90	20.51	17.10	0.83
1976	255	4.36	2.36	6.25	2.64
1977	253	2.15	2.07	2.25	1.09
1978	253	2.08	1.46	2.71	1.86
1979	251	2.43	1.10	3.71	3.37

Let δ denote $E|U_t|$. We assume that U_t has the standard Normal distribution, so $\delta = 0.798$, and will later justify our assumption using empirical evidence. It can be seen that estimates for one of the two processes (here $\{V\}$) are inevitably dependent upon assumptions about *both* $\{V\}$ and $\{U\}$.

For the sugar returns, the sample mean of the numbers $|x_t - \bar{x}|$ is 0.0149, and the returns have sample variance 5.01×10^{-4}. Hence, if $\mu_V = E(V)$ and $\sigma_V^2 = \text{var}(V)$

$$\hat{\mu}_V = 0.0149/0.798 = 0.0187$$
$$\text{and } \hat{\sigma}_V^2 = 5.01(10^{-4}) - (0.0187)^2 = 1.51(10^{-4}).$$

Note that $\hat{\mu}_V/\hat{\sigma}_V = 1.52$, and hence, because V_t must always be positive, its distribution cannot be Normal.

Assuming $\log(V_t) \sim N(\alpha, \beta^2)$, $\mu_V = \exp(\alpha + \frac{1}{2}\beta^2)$, and
$$\sigma_V^2 = \exp(2\alpha + \beta^2)\{\exp(\beta^2) - 1\}$$

and consequently estimates of α and β^2 are calculated as

$$\hat{\alpha} = \log(\hat{\mu}_V^2/\{\hat{\mu}_V + \hat{\sigma}_V^2\}^{\frac{1}{2}}) = -4.156$$
$$\text{and } \hat{\beta}^2 = \log(1 + \hat{\sigma}_V^2/\hat{\mu}_V^2) = 0.356.$$

The estimated median value of V_t equals $\exp(\hat{\alpha}) = 0.0157$, also $\exp(\hat{\alpha} - 1.96\hat{\beta})$ $= 0.0049$ and $\exp(\hat{\alpha} + 1.96\hat{\beta}) = 0.0505$.

2.5.3 Autocorrelation formulae

Information about the autocorrelations of the V-process can be obtained by studying the square-process, $\{S_t\}$, defined by

$$S_t = (X_t - \bar{\mu})^2 = V_t^2 U_t^2. \tag{8}$$

Straightforward algebra, and the assumption that the V- and U-processes are mutually independent, shows that $E(S_t) = E(V_t^2)$ and that the covariances are

$$\text{cov}(S_t, S_{t+i}) = \text{cov}(V_t^2, V_{t+i}^2) + E(V_t^2 V_{t+i}^2)\,\text{cov}(U_t^2, U_{t+i}^2). \tag{9}$$

The general model for $\{V_t\}$, defined by equation (5), is not stationary. However, the correlations between V_t^2 and V_{t+i}^2 will depend on only the time lag i *if* t and $t + i$ are times referring to the same contract. This assumption is made throughout the remainder of this paper and notation such as $\rho_{i,V}^2$ will denote the auto7-correlations of $\{V_t^2\}$ conditional upon identical contracts. Division of equation (9) by var(S_t) and further algebra gives the autocorrelations of the square-process as

$$\rho_{i,S} = \frac{\text{var}(V_t^2)}{\text{var}(S_t)} \left[\rho_{i,V^2} + \{\rho_{i,V^2} + \pi_2\}\rho_{i,U^2}\text{var}(U_t^2)\right], \tag{10}$$

with $\pi_2 = E(V_t^2)^2/\text{var}(V_t^2)$. $\tag{11}$

Equation (10) can be used to estimate ρ_{i,V^2}, from sample estimates of $\rho_{i,S}$ if ρ_{i,V^2} is substantially greater than the second term in the square brackets; it is thus necessary to consider ρ_{i,U^2}, var(U_t^2) and π_2.

For linear and Gaussian $\{U_t\}$, $\rho_{i,U^2} = \rho_{i,U}$ (Granger and Newbold, 1976). This result should give a crude estimate of the autocorrelations of $\{U_t^2\}$ whenever $\{U_t\}$ is approximately linear. As the $\rho_{i,U}$ are always small for financial returns, ρ_{i,U^2} will be extremely small. In Taylor (1980), I fitted a model to sugar prices having $0 < \rho_{i,U} < 0.05$ (all $i > 0$). These correlations are re-estimated in Section 6 with the same conclusions, so ρ_{i,U^2} is probably less than 0.0025. The variance of U_t^2 depends on the kurtosis of U_t, denoted k_U. For our assumption that the U_t are Normal, $k_U = 3$ and the variance of U_t^2 is $k_U - 1 = 2$. When $\log(V_t)$ is normally distributed with variance β^2, the quantity π_2 equals $1/\{\exp(4\beta^2) - 1\}$ which is estimated by replacing β with $\hat{\beta}$ to give 0.32. Thus approximately,

$$\pi_2 \, \rho_{i,U^2} \, \text{var}(U_t^2) \simeq 0.32(0.0025) \, (2) = 0.0016.$$

Therefore it appears acceptable, for financial returns, to write

$$\rho_{i,S} \simeq \lambda\rho_{i,V^2} \tag{12}$$

with $\lambda = \text{var}(V_t^2)/\text{var}(S_t)$. More algebra shows that:

$$\lambda = \frac{1}{(1+\pi_2)\,k_U - \pi_2}. \tag{13}$$

Inserting the estimate $\hat{\pi}_2 = 0.32$ and the assumed value $k_U = 3$ in equation (13) gives an estimate for λ, which is $\hat{\lambda} = 0.27$.

Granger and Newbold (1976) prove that the autocorrelations of $\{V_t^2\}$ are related to those of $\{\log(V_t)\}$ by the formula

$$\rho_{i,V^2} = \frac{\exp(4\beta^2\rho_{i,\log V}) - 1}{\exp(4\beta^2) - 1} \tag{14}$$

here applying the assumption that $\{\log(V_t)\}$ is Gaussian. Remember that all autocorrelations refer to random variables defined for the same contract, so

$$\rho_{i,\,\log V} = \{\mathrm{var}(C_t) + \rho_{i,\,D}\mathrm{var}(D_t)\}/\beta^2. \tag{15}$$

As $\rho_{i,\,D}$ approaches zero for large i, $\rho_{i,\,\log V}$ converges to $\mathrm{var}(C_t)/\beta^2$, which is denoted by κ. Combining equations (12), (14), and (15) gives

$$\rho_{i,\,S} \simeq \lambda \frac{e^{4\beta^2\{\kappa+(1-\kappa)\rho_{i,\,D}\}}-1}{\exp(4\beta^2)-1} \tag{16}$$

2.5.4 Estimates of the autocorrelations of S

Estimates, $r_{i,\,S}$, of the theoretical autocorrelations $\rho_{i,\,S}$, of the square-process, have been calculated from the formulae,

$$s_t = (x_t - \bar{x})^2,$$
$$r_{i,\,S} = \frac{\Sigma(s_t - \bar{s})(s_{t+i} - \bar{s})/(N - n_c i)}{\Sigma(s_t - \bar{s})^2/N} \tag{17}$$

with N and n_c equal to the number of returns and contracts respectively, $\bar{x}$ and $\bar{s}$ are sample means calculated from all N observations and the numerator summation is over those t for which both the times t and $t + i$ refer to the same contract. The multiplier $N/(N - n_c i)$ appears in equation (17) to avoid bias. It would be deleted for tests using the autocorrelations.

Figure 2.3 shows the estimates for time lags from 1 to 50 days, with estimates of the autocorrelations of the returns, denoted $r_{i,\,X}$; they are tabulated in Table 2.2. All the plotted $r_{i,\,S}$ are positive and they decrease fairly smoothly from the first estimate, $r_{l,\,S} = 0.25$.

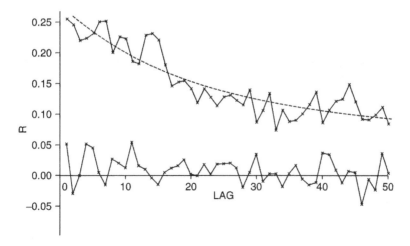

Fig. 2.3. Autocorrelations for processes S squared returns (upper curve) and X returns (lower curve).

Table 2.2. Autocorrelation coefficients

Lag	$r_{i,S}$	$r_{i,X}$	$r_{i,Y}$	Lag	$r_{i,S}$	$r_{i,X}$	$r_{i,Y}$
1	.2547	.0541	.0685	26	.1318	.0208	.0085
2	.2455	−.0299	−.0110	27	.1232	.0132	.0313
3	.2195	−.0001	.0216	28	.1155	−.0196	.0036
4	.2232	.0529	.0537	29	.1400	.0052	.0145
5	.2311	.0466	.0643	30	.0876	.0354	.0236
6	.2502	.0059	−.0019	31	.1056	−.0095	−.0086
7	.2519	−.0152	.0056	32	.1342	.0027	.0060
8	.2000	.0281	.0345	33	.0744	.0036	.0227
9	.2251	.0211	.0430	34	.1069	−.0181	.0120
10	.2224	.0135	.0147	35	.0887	.0032	−.0196
11	.1860	.0556	.0379	36	.0904	.0170	.0029
12	.1821	.0169	.0104	37	.1007	−.0063	.0001
13	.2282	.0114	.0068	38	.1157	−.0154	−.0037
14	.2309	−.0030	.0108	39	.1365	−.0117	.0267
15	.2209	−.0143	.0049	40	.0864	.0375	.0330
16	.1809	.0059	.0278	41	.1063	.0353	.0144
17	.1464	.0134	.0302	42	.1215	.0092	−.0061
18	.1530	.0169	.0203	43	.1250	−.0121	.0135
19	.1550	.0263	.0379	44	.1505	.0072	.0278
20	.1426	.0023	.0157	45	.1212	.0052	−.0105
21	.1194	.0002	.0085	46	.0924	−.0477	−.0247
22	.1416	.0190	.0110	47	.0921	−.0065	.0060
23	.1283	.0018	.0142	48	.0990	−.0240	−.0117
24	.1145	.0194	.0227	49	.1118	.0371	.0314
25	.1282	.0197	.0096	50	.1154	.0035	.0156

Several of the $r_{i,S}$ far exceed $2/\sqrt{N} = 0.029$, thus the hypothesis of independent and identically distributed X_t is immediately refuted. It is also clear that $r_{i,S}$ exceeds $r_{i,X}$ for small time lags which refutes the more general hypothesis that $\{X_t\}$ is linear. Figure 2.3 shows furthermore that the variables D_t must be stochastic. For constant D_t would imply $\kappa = 1$ and then all the $\rho_{i,S}$ are equal, but it is seen that the $\rho_{i,S}$ do depend on the time lag. Simulations conclusively confirm this result.

2.5.5 Estimates of the autocorrelations of V
We note from Figure 2.3 that the $r_{i,S}$ for lags 1 to 7 are approximately equal to the estimate $\hat{\lambda} = 0.27$. Therefore $\rho_{i,D}$ is almost 1 for small i. We can also deduce that $\rho_{i,D}$ is much smaller than 1 for large i, so $\{D\}$ is unlikely to be an integrated process, such as a random walk. Thus the simplest model for the within year variations D_t, consistent with Figure 2.3, is an AR(1) process with autocorrelations $\rho_{i,D} = \phi^i$ with ϕ positive and large. Certainly low order moving-average processes are impossible.

Estimates of ϕ and the remaining parameter of interest, κ, have been obtained by minimising the function:

$$F(\kappa, \phi) = N \sum_{i=1}^{50} (\rho_{i,s} - r_{i,s})^2 \tag{18}$$

with $\rho_{i,s}$ approximated by the right side of equation (16) with $\hat{\beta}$ and $\hat{\lambda}$ substituted for β and λ. Minimising the right-hand-side of equation (18) as a function of λ, κ and ϕ gave less accurate estimates of all the parameters for simulated data, so I prefer to minimise over κ and ϕ alone with λ estimated from equation (13). The maximum lag considered, here 50, is an arbitary choice but higher values give similar estimates.

The least F was obtained for

$$\hat{\kappa} = 0.37, \quad \hat{\phi} = 0.970 \text{ with } F(\hat{\kappa}, \ \hat{\phi}) = 120.5.$$

Estimates of $\rho_{i,s}$ obtained from the above figures are plotted as the dotted line on Figure 2.3. The dotted line fits fairly well but passes above the $r_{i,s}$ at lags 1 to 5 and 17 to 28 and below most of the $r_{i,s}$ at lags 6 to 16. This might be caused by the positive correlation between the sample autocorrelations. Minimum values of F for specific values of κ are plotted as Figure 2.4a and the values of F, when $\kappa = \hat{\kappa}$, for various ϕ are plotted as Figure 2.4b.

As $\hat{\kappa}$ is less than a half, the majority of the fluctuations in returns variance are attributed to within year effects. It is clear from Figure 2.4a that the special case of κ equal to zero is feasible, a possibility discussed further in Section 2.7. When $\kappa = 0$, the best ϕ is 0.986 with $F = 128.1$. The high estimate $\hat{\phi}$ shows however that the variance of returns changes relatively slowly.

2.5.6 Estimation of the realised value of V

An unobservable realisation $\{v_t\}$ of the process $\{V_t\}$ occurs as time progresses. Estimates of the v_t are required, first for inferences about the U-process and secondly, to help investors assess the time-dependent trading risks. An estimation method investigated in detail by Taylor and Kingsman (1979), is summarized here. The main idea is to use past observed returns to estimate the current level of the V-process, working from the result that $E(V_t)$ equals $E|X_t - \bar{\mu}|/\delta$, with $\delta = E|U_t|$. A past return x_{t-i}, $i > 0$, gives the crude estimate $|x_{t-i} - \bar{x}|/\delta$ for v_{t-i}. Exponentially weighted averages of these estimates provide improved estimates of the v_t if the V-process changes slowly. This appears to be correct because of the high estimate for ϕ. Thus consider the estimates

$$\hat{v}_t = \gamma \sum_{i=0}^{\infty} (1 - \gamma)^i |x_{t-i} - \bar{x}|/\delta$$
$$= (1 - \gamma)\hat{v}_{t-1} + \gamma|x_t - \bar{x}|/\delta \tag{19}$$

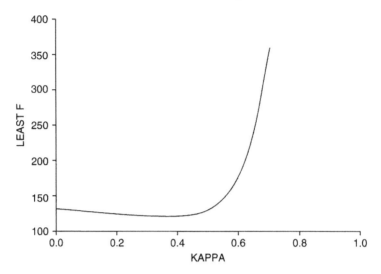

Fig. 2.4a. Least F for various kappa.

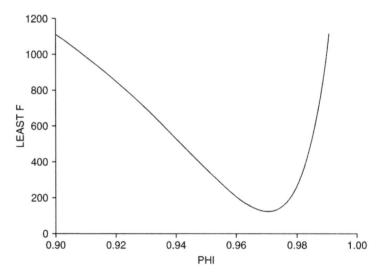

Fig. 2.4b. Least F for various PHI, when kappa $= 0.37$.

Taylor and Kingsman used maximum-likelihood methods to show that the best γ is approximately 0.10, although they left the unimportant term $\bar{x}$ out of their equations.

To implement equation (19), δ is replaced by 0.798 once more and an initial estimate $\hat{v}_{20}$ is calculated from the first twenty returns for 1961, using 0.05 times $\Sigma|x_t - \bar{x}|$. For the 1962 contract an initial value is obtained by averaging $|x_t - \bar{x}|$ for 20 returns recorded for 1962 sugar, over the dates of the final 20 returns studied for the 1961 contract, and similarly for later years. The estimates of v_t for 19 sugar contracts have a right-skewed distribution with, approximately, median equal to 0.0150, 50% of estimates between 0.0105 and 0.0229 and 95% of estimates within 0.006 to 0.0425.

2.6 Estimation of the U-process

A detailed empirical study of the U-process has been published recently, including analysis of the sugar prices from 1961 to 1973 (Taylor, 1980). This section therefore emphasises hitherto unpublished results.

2.6.1 The distribution of U

It has already been noted that the maximum feasible value for the $\rho_{i,S}$, assuming both U and $\log(V)$ are Normal, is $\hat{\lambda} = 0.275$ which is similar to the largest observed $r_{i,S}$. Further evidence about the distribution of U can be obtained by considering the relationship between the kurtoses of X and U, denoted k_X and k_U respectively:

$$k_X = k_U E(V^4)/E(V^2)^2. \tag{20}$$

When $\log(V)$ is Normal, with variance β^2, the kurtosis of X is $k_U \exp(4\beta^2)$. This is equal to 12.5, for Normal U with β replaced by the empirical estimate. The empirical kurtosis of X is 8.9; simulations show that this number is consistent with the assumptions made.

An alternative distribution is Student's t, with v degrees-of-freedom. In Taylor and Kingsman (1979), $v = 9$ was suggested and then $\delta = 0.77$, $\hat{\beta} = 0.534$, $\hat{\lambda} = 0.175$, $k_U = 3 + 6/(v - 4) = 4.2$ and the predicted kurtosis is 13.1. The far lower value for $\hat{\lambda}$, less than $r_{i,S}$ for i from 1 to 16, shows that a Normal distribution for U is more appropriate.

2.6.2 A class of models

Price trends are the popular alternative to the hypothesis that the U_t are uncorrelated. Let $\{T_t\}$ denote a trend component, and let $\{\varepsilon_t\}$ be independent and identically distributed, zero mean variables. Conjectured trend models are characterised by the equations:

$$U_t = T_t + \varepsilon_t, \quad E(T_s\varepsilon_t) = 0 \text{ all } s, t$$
$$\rho_{i,T} = p^i (0 < p < 1). \tag{21}$$

Equation (21) is valid for several processes, including some AR(1) processes and the original model of Taylor and Kingsman (1978), namely $T_t = T_{t-1}$ with probability p, T_t is independent of all $T_s, s < t$, with probability $1 - p$. We denote $\text{var}(T_t)$ by A and then $\text{var}(\varepsilon_t) = 1 - A$. Defining μ_t by $\bar{\mu} + V_t T_t$ and e_t by $V_t \varepsilon_t$ gives $X_t = \mu_t + e_t$, as studied in Taylor (1980), relating X_t to a partially predictable trend μ_t plus unpredictable terms e_t.

2.6.3 Autocorrelation formulae

For trend models, the $\rho_{i,U}$ are identical to the autocorrelations of an ARMA(1,1) process, viz.

$$\rho_{i,U} = Ap^i, A > 0, \ i > 0, \ 1 > p > 0 \tag{22}$$

For all product processes,

$$\rho_{i,X} = \rho_{i,U} \frac{\rho_{i,V} + \pi_1}{1 + \pi_1} \tag{23}$$

with $\pi_1 = \{E(V_t)\}^2/\mathrm{var}(V_t)$. $\tag{24}$

Assuming $\log(V_t)$ is Normal distributed with variance β^2, π_1 is estimated by $1/\{\exp(\hat{\beta}^2) - 1\}$ which is 2.34 for the sugar data. Using the estimates of $\rho_{i,V}$ obtained in Section 5, the ratio $\rho_{i,X}/\rho_{i,U}$ decreases from 0.99 when i is 1 to 0.84 when i equals 50.

2.6.4 Estimates of the autocorrelations of U

Biassed estimates of $\rho_{i,U}$ would be obtained from the sample autocorrelations of the returns, $r_{i,X}$. A far more important defect is $r_{i,X}$ is the failure of the standard large sample result, $\mathrm{var}(R_{i,X}) \simeq 1/N$, because $\{X_t\}$ is non-linear. I intend to write a paper showing that, when the X_t have symmetric distributions and are approximately uncorrelated, the variance of $R_{i,X}$ (defined in the manner of equation 17) can be estimated from data by

$$\mathrm{var}(R_{i,X}) = \left[\frac{N}{N - n_c i}\right]^2 \frac{\sum (x_t - \bar{x})^2(x_{t+i} - \bar{x})^2}{\{\sum (x_t - \bar{x})^2\}^2}. \tag{25}$$

Estimates of N multiplied by $\mathrm{var}(R_{i,X})$ are plotted as the upper set of crosses on Figure 2.5, commencing with $N \, \mathrm{var}(R_{1,X}) \simeq 3.0$. There is, as expected, a very good linear relationship between these estimates and the $r_{i,S}$.

It is clear that autocorrelations estimated from the returns are inefficient, because of the large fluctuations in variance. These can be neutralised by calculating *rescaled returns*,

$$y_t = (x_t - \bar{x})/\hat{v}_{t-1} \simeq (v_t/\hat{v}_{t-1})u_t, \tag{26}$$

which are better approximations to the unobservable u_t than the x_t. In equation (26), $\hat{v}_{t-1}$ is used, rather than $\hat{v}_t$, to avoid dividing x_t by a function of itself.

Rescaling can be justified by considering the variance of the $R_{i,Y}$, here defined for data by

$$r_{i,Y} = \frac{\sum (y_t - \bar{y})(y_{t+i} - \bar{y})/(n - n_c i)}{\sum (y_t - \bar{y})^2/n}$$

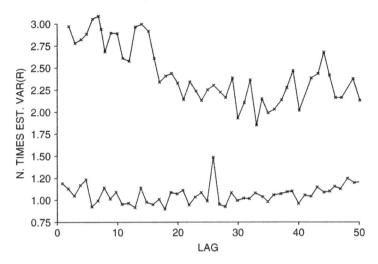

Fig. 2.5. Estimated variances of sample autocorrelations for returns
(upper curve) and rescaled returns (lower).

with $n = N - 20$ and both summations beginning at $t = 21$. Estimates of n
multiplied by var$(R_{i,Y})$, calculated in the manner of equation (25), are the
lower set of crosses on Figure 2.5. It is seen that n var$(R_{i,Y})$ is approximately 1,
unlike Nvar$(R_{i,X})$.

Figure 2.6 shows the recommended autocorrelation estimates, $r_{i,Y}$, and they
are listed in Table 2.2 for comparison with the inefficient estimates, $r_{i,X}$. All the
estimates are small but they differ significantly from zero according to several
tests (cf. Taylor, 1980, 1981). Substantial autocorrelation cannot be induced by
either the rescaling transformation or time-dependent expected returns, $E(X_t)$.

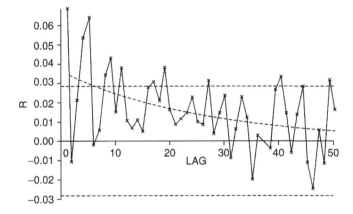

Fig. 2.6. Autocorrelations of the rescaled returns. Dotted curve is the fitted
autocorrelations dashed lines are 95% CI for white noise.

The maximum induced autocorrelation is less than 0.004 (cf. Taylor, 1980). Note that most of the $r_{i, Y}$ are positive, as predicted for price-trend models by equation (22).

2.6.5 Spectral estimates
Price-trend models have theoretical spectra proportional to

$$g(\omega) = 1 + 2 \sum_{i>0} Ap^i \cos(i\omega) = 1 - A + \frac{A(1 - p^2)}{1 + p^2 - 2p \cos(\omega)} . \qquad (28)$$

These spectra decrease monotonically over $0 \leqslant \omega \leqslant \pi$, with $g(0) = 1 + 2Ap/(1 - p)$ so that the peak at $\omega = 0$ will be thin and tall if 1-p is small. The spectrum has been estimated by

$$\hat{g}(\omega) = 1 + 2 \sum_{i=1}^{99} \lambda_i r_{i, Y} \cos(i\omega)$$

with the λ_i equal to Parzen weights $(1 > \lambda_1 > \ldots > \lambda_{99} > 0)$. Correct spectral methodology for financial time series is described by Praetz (1979).

Figure 2.7 shows the estimates $\hat{g}(\omega)$. The peak predicted at $\omega = 0$ occurs. Indeed it refutes the hypothesis of independent and identically distributed U_t, since $\hat{g}(0) = 1 + 2\Sigma\lambda_i r_{i, Y} = 2.26$ and the standardised statistic $\{\hat{g}(0) - 1\}/(4n^{-1}\Sigma\lambda_i^2)^{\frac{1}{2}}$ equals 8.48. It is shown in Taylor (1981) that $\hat{g}(0)$ is a powerful statistic for testing the random walk hypothesis against the price-trend hypothesis defined by equation (22).

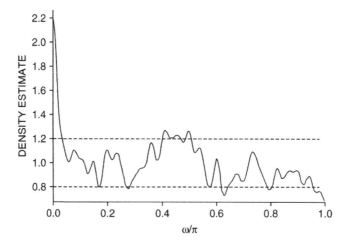

Fig. 2.7. Estimated spectral density note high density when ω small dashed lines are 95% CI for white noise.

2.6.6   Estimates of the trend parameters

The simplest ARMA (k, ℓ) process capable of describing the significant auto-correlations plotted on Figure 2.6 has $k = \ell = 1$, giving

$$(1 - pB)(1 - qB)^{-1} U_t = \text{white noise.} \tag{29}$$

As ARMA(1,1) processes have $\rho_{i+1} = p\rho_i$ for all $i > 0$, price trend models are a feasible and simple description of the observed autocorrelations. Other feasible models must have $k + \ell > 2$ and have not been investigated. To obtain $\rho_{i,U} = Ap^i$, the parameter q must be the solution of both

$$q^2 - q\{1 + (1 - 2A)p^2\}/\{(1 - A)p\} + 1 = 0 \text{ and } q < 1. \tag{30}$$

Estimates of A and p have been obtained, as in Taylor (1980), by minimising

$$S(A, p) = n \sum_{i=1}^{50} (\rho_{i,U} - r_{i,Y})^2. \tag{31}$$

and gave $\hat{A} = 0.0358$, $\hat{p} = 0.962$, $\hat{q} = 0.935$ and $S(\hat{A}, \hat{p}) = 70.6$. The fitted autocorrelations, $\hat{A}\hat{p}^i$, are the curve plotted on Figure 2.6. Increasing the lags considered above 50 gives very similar estimates. The quantity $m = (1 - p)^{-1}$ can be identified with the average duration of trends and here $\hat{m}$ equals 26 trading days. Least values of S for various p are plotted on Figure 2.8.

Assuming the $r_{i,Y}$ to be approximately independent and normal distributed, with variance n^{-1}, the conditional log-likelihood of the autocorrelations is

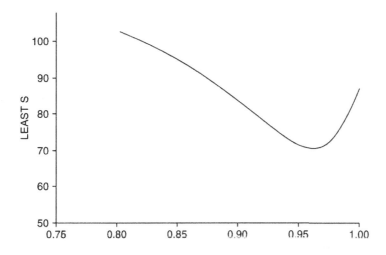

Fig. 2.8. Least S, for various P.

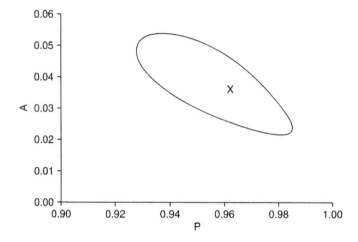

Fig. 2.9. 95% Confidence region for A, P. Point estimates marked by X.

$$\log L(r_1, r_2, \ldots, r_{50} | A, p) \simeq \text{constant} - \frac{1}{2} S(A, p) \tag{32}$$

A very approximate joint 95% confidence region for the two parameters can then be shown to be all pairs (A_0, p_0) for which $S(A_0, p_0) < S(\hat{A}, \hat{p}) + 5.99$ using Prob $(x_2^2 > 5.99) = 0.05$. This region is plotted as Figure 2.9.

2.7 Discussion

Product processes can in theory explain the variations in the annual sample variances of daily returns, linear and state-dependent processes cannot. To assess this theoretical claim, 100 years of returns have been simulated using for parameter values the estimates given previously. Comparison of the cumulative distributions of the empirical and simulated annual variances, by a two-sample Kolmogorov–Smirnov statistic, gives a test value of 0.17 for comparison with the 10% critical value equal to 0.31; the test is probably conservative because estimates have replaced unknown, hypothetical, population parameters in the simulations. These simulations do not refute product processes as an approximation to the 'true' process.

Similar simulations for the special case $\kappa = 0$, corresponding to constant annual effects C_t, gave a test value of 0.28. Using $\kappa > 0$ appears to give a better approximation to the empirical variances, in both tails.

Nineteen years of prices have been simulated, ten times, to obtain some information about the accuracy of the parameter estimates. The range of the ten estimates for λ was from 0.245 to 0.306 compared with a true value of 0.275, for κ from 0 (three times) to 0.57 (true value 0.37), for ϕ from 0.933 to 0.977 (true value 0.97), for A from 0.0124 to 0.0484 (true value 0.036), and for P from 0.950 to 0.986 (true value 0.962).

Table 2.3. Notation summary

Process	Mean	Variance	Autocorrelations	Relationships
C	α	$\kappa\beta^2$	Not specified	
D	0	$(1 - \kappa)\beta^2$	ϕ^i	
ε	0	$1 - A$	Zero if $i \neq 0$	
S	$\exp(2\alpha + 2\beta^2)$	Eqn. 9	Eqn. 10	$S = V^2U^2$
T	0	A	p^i	
U	0	1	Ap^i	$U = T + \varepsilon$
log(V)	α	β^2	Eqn. 15	$\log V = C + D$
X	$\bar{\mu}$	$\exp(2\alpha + 2\beta^2)$	Eqn. 23	$X = \bar{\mu} + UV$
Z	Not stationary			$\log Z = (1 - B)^{-1}X$

Special stochastic processes for $\{V\}$ and $\{U\}$ have been investigated, possessing four and two parameters respectively as summarised in Table 2.3. It would be remarkable if the parameters best approximating the data studied did not change during the two decades. Estimates for the 1960s (1961–9) and 1970s (1970–9) are listed in Table 2.4. There do not appear to be any substantial differences, although perhaps both the mean and variance of the V-process are increasing with time thus increasing the unconditional variance of the returns. Estimates of the trend parameters, A and p, are not accurate even for a decade of returns,

Table 2.4. Parameter estimates

	1961–79	1961–69	Sugar contracts: 1970–79
Expected return			
$\bar{\mu} \times 10^4$	2.6	−1.0	5.9
V-process			
Mean $\times 10^2$	1.873	1.779	1.954
Standard dev. $\times 10^2$	1.225	1.070	1.346
α	−4.156	−4.183	−4.129
β	0.597	0.556	0.623
κ	0.37	0.28	0.42
ϕ	0.971	0.968	0.970
U-process			
A	0.036	0.046	0.026
m	26	21	30
p	0.962	0.952	0.967
q	0.935	0.919	0.947
Both processes			
λ	0.275	0.262	0.283
Least sums-of-squares			
$F(\hat{\kappa}, \hat{\lambda}, \hat{\phi})$	120.7	151.0	111.2
$S_{(A, P)}$	70.6	60.5	56

nevertheless the two confidence regions have a considerable intersection. When p is constrained to be the estimate for the decades combined, the best estimates of A are 0.041 for the 1960s and 0.027 for the 1970s. The difference is not statistically significant at the 5% level.

A referee suggested excluding the three years of exceptional price variation (1963, 1974, 1975) and then modelling behaviour in the more orderly years. It was found, for the remaining 16 years, that the returns are still the output from a non-linear process having substantial within contract changes in the conditional standard deviations $\{v\}$.

Model adequacy has been checked by comparing the first fifty autocorrelation 'errors' (empirical minus model fit) for the 1960s with the corresponding 'errors' for the 1970s. The correlations between the sets of errors are 0.04 for the square series, $\{s\}$, and 0.21 for the rescaled returns, $\{y\}$. These correlations are insignificant. However, both estimates $r_{1,\,Y}$ exceed the fitted values by more than 0.03 and both $r_{2,\,Y}$ are less than the fitted numbers by over 0.04; here the standard deviation of $r_{i,\,Y}$ is about 0.02.

It has been assumed that the magnitude of the trend component $\mu_t = \bar{\mu} + V_t T_t$ is dependent, via V_t, upon the magnitude of the unpredictable component $e_t = V_t \varepsilon_t$. If, however, μ_t *and* e_t are independent, estimates of A should be relatively low when the sample variance of the returns is relatively high. The assumption has been assessed by calculating estimates of A for the four years when the sample variance was below 1.8 and for the four years when it was above 7.5. When p is estimated by the 19-year estimate, the best A estimates for the four-year subset are 0.0325 and 0.0396, for low and high variances respectively, so the assumed common influence upon μ_t *and* e_t (namely V_t) is upheld. This conclusion remains valid when further low and high variance years are considered.

Product processes are probably capable of describing several other time series of financial prices. The special cases investigated here provide a simple model for sugar prices, which may require refinements for other data. My experience suggests that ideally at least 2000 prices should be studied, although the assumption of constant parameter values may then lack credibility. Also, all apparent large price—changes need to be checked because errors will particularly alter the $r_{i,\,s}$.

Studying the autocorrelations of the squared adjusted returns, $(x_t - \bar{x})^2$, is an interesting check for non-linear behaviour irrespective of the relevance of a product process model.

2.8 An efficient market?

Significant correlation between returns does not necessarily refute the efficient market hypothesis. This hypothesis states that all methods of deciding when to buy and sell, over a particular time period and using past prices to evaluate the decisions, are inferior to the strategy of buying at the beginning of the period and selling at its conclusion, after trading costs have been deducted (Fama, 1970; Richards, 1979).

Optimal forecasts of future prices are easy to calculate for the price-trend models of Section 6.2 and are more accurate, empirically, than random walk forecasts (Taylor, 1980). For example, the forecasts recommended for sugar prices after analysing the prices from 1961 to 1973 have been evaluated for the later period, 1974 to 1979, with mean square error reductions (relative to random walk predictions) of 0.6% and 3.5% for horizons of 1 and 10 days respectively.

Small autocorrelations have usually been interpreted as evidence for market efficiency. However, no one has discovered the amount of autocorrelation sufficient to refute efficiency. It would be interesting to know which values of the trend parameters A and p correspond to inefficient markets. Mathematical analysis based upon several assumptions, including the ideal situation of correctly known A and p, is possible and places the sugar estimates in the inefficient region, when commission charges and the bid–ask spread total 1%. In practice, if a trend model generated the U-process, A and p could be estimated but not accurately. Then, given estimates (A, p) and any points (A_0, p_0) in a confidence region for the true trend parameters, it is necessary to decide the economic value of trades based upon A and p when actual returns have autocorrelations fixed by A_0 and P_0. At this point an accurate model of the price's stochastic process must be simulated. This can now be done, using the product process. Preliminary results imply that most of the 95 per cent confidence region, Figure 2.9, corresponds to an inefficient market.

Acknowledgements

I am again grateful to Dr. B. G. Kingsman and L. Balasuriya for supplying the sugar prices and to Mrs. A. Welsby for typing the manuscript.

References

Anderson, T. W. and Walker, A. M. (1964). On the asymptotic distribution of the autocorrelations of a sample from a linear stochastic process. *Annals of Mathematical Statistics* 35, 1296–1303.

Blattberg, R. C. and Gonedes, N. J. (1975). Temporal behaviour in commodity futures markets. *Journal of Business* 47, 244–80.

Bodie, Z and Rosansky, V. I. (1980). Risk and return in commodity futures. *Financial Analysts Journal* May/June issue, 27–39.

Box, G. E. P. and Cox, D. R. (1964). An analysis of transformations. *Journal of the Royal Statistical Society* 26B, 211–252.

Cargill, T. F. and Rausser, G. C., (1975). Temporal price behaviour in commodity futures markets. *Journal of Finance* 30, 1043–53.

Clark, P. K. (1973). A subordinated stochastic process model with finite variance for speculative prices. *Econometrica* 41, 135–55.

Dimson, E. and Brealey, R A (1978). The risk premium on U.K. equities. *Investment Analyst* 52, 14–18.

Fama, E. F. (1970). Efficient capital markets: a review of theory and empirical work. *Journal of Finance* 25, 383–417.

Fielitz, B. D. (1971). Stationarity of random data: some implications for the distributions of stock price changes. *Journal of Financial and Quantitative Analysis* 6, 1025–1034.

Granger, C. W. J. (1979). (ed.) Trading in commodities, 3rd edn (Woodhead-Faulkner, Cambridge, U.K.)

Granger, C. W. J. and Andersen, A. P. (1978). An introduction to bilinear time series models Vandenhoeck and Ruprecht, Gottingen, W. Germany.

Granger, C. W. J. and Newbold, P. (1976). Forecasting transformed series. *Journal of the Royal Statistical Society* 38B, 189–203.

Jennergren, L. P. and Korsvold, P. E. (1974). Price formation in the Norwegian and Swedish stock markets—some random walk tests. *Swedish Journal of Economics* 76, 171–85.

Labys, W. C. and Thomas, H. C. (1975). Speculation, hedging and commodity price behaviour: an international comparison. *Applied Economics* 7, 287–301.

Levich, R. M. (1979). The international money market: an assessment of forecasting techniques and market efficiency (JAI Press, Greenwich, U.S.A.).

Merton, R. C. (1980). On estimating the expected return on the market, an exploratory investigation. *Journal of Financial Economics* 8, 323–61.

Praetz, P. D. (1969). Australian share prices and the random walk hypothesis. *Australian Journal of Statistics* 11, 123–39.

——(1972). The distribution of share price changes. *Journal of Business* 45, 49–55.

——(1979). Testing for a flat spectrum on efficient market price data. *Journal of Finance* 34, 645–58.

Priestley, M. B. (1980). State-dependent models: a general approach to non-linear time series analysis. *Journal of Time Series Analysis* I 47–71.

Richards, P. H. (1979). U.K. and European share price behaviour: the evidence (London, Kogan Page).

Rogalski, R. J. (1978). The dependence of prices and volume. *Review of Economics and Statistics* 60, 268–74.

Rutledge, D. J. S. (1976). A note on the variability of futures prices. *Review of Economics and Statistics* 58, 118–20.

Taylor, S. J. (1980). Conjectured models for trends in financial prices, tests and forecasts. *Journal of the Royal Statistical Society* 143A, 338–62.

——(1981). Tests of the random walk hypothesis against a price–trend hypothesis, submitted for publication.

——Kingsman, B. G. (1979). An analysis of the variance and distribution of commodity price-changes. *Australian Journal of Management* 4, 135–149.

Teweles, F. J., Harlow, C. V., and Stone, H. L. (1974). The commodity futures game New York, McGraw-Hill.

Westerfield, R. (1977). The distribution of common stock price changes: an application of transaction times and subordinated stochastic models. *Journal of Financial and Quantitative Analysis* 12, 743–66.

3

The Behavior of Random Variables with Nonstationary Variance and the Distribution of Security Prices*

BARR ROSENBERG

When the variance of a population of random variables is nonstationary, the population kurtosis is greater than the kurtosis of the probability distribution of the individual random variables. Therefore, the high kurtosis observed in the distribution of security prices can be explained by high kurtosis in the individual price changes, nonstationarity in the variances of the price changes, or any combination of these two causes. For a 100-year series of monthly changes in the Standard & Poor's Composite Index, fluctuations in variance as forecasted by a two-parameter model explain 70 percent of the deviation of the sample kurtosis from normality. The results suggest that increments in the logarithms of security prices obey a normal distribution with predictably fluctuating variance.

3.1 Introduction

In hundreds of economic series the empirical frequency of outlying observations is greater than would be expected from the normal distribution. For example, in Figure 3.1, the frequency distribution of 100 years of monthly changes in the logarithm of the Standard & Poor's Composite Price Index for the New York Stock Exchange is superimposed on a graph of the normal distribution with equal variance. The empirical distribution shows a greater concentration of mass near zero and much more massive tails than the normal distribution. The largest price change is 9.3 standard deviations from the mean. With kurtosis defined as the ratio of the fourth moment to the square of the second moment, the sample kurtosis is 14.79, in contrast to a kurtosis of 3 for the normal distribution. Unimodal leptokurtic distributions similar to this one have been observed in virtually every security or commodity market that has been studied.

As a result, research in finance has been concerned with explaining these empirical distributions and with analyzing their consequences for portfolio management. The first noteworthy innovation in this direction was the suggestion of the class of nonnormal stable distributions by Mandelbrot (1963). This hypothesis

* This work was previously published as B. Rosenberg (1972), 'The Behavior of Random Variables with Nonstationary Variance and the Distribution of Security Prices', Working Paper No. 11, University of California, Berkeley, Institute of Business and Economic Research, Graduate School of Business Administration, Research Programme in Finance. Copyright © Barr Rosenberg 1972. Reproduced by kind permission.

implies that the variance of security price changes is infinite and, hence, has important implications for statistical methodology (summarized recently in Granger and Orr (1972)) and for portfolio management (summarized recently in Fama and Miller (1972, p. 261–275)). Press (1967) later suggested that each price change is the sum of a random number, r, of normally distributed variables, where r obeys the Poisson Distribution. In this model, every price change obeys the same compound distribution equal to a normal distribution with Poisson distributed variance. Praetz (1972) maintained Press's basic formulation but proposed that the variance might follow an inverted gamma distribution, and confirmed that the resulting distribution provided a better fit to some empirical data than any of the previously suggested alternatives.

All of these approaches to the problem coincide in assuming that price changes are identically distributed in all periods, in which case this distribution must be similar to the empirical frequency distribution observed over a large number of periods. Thus, all approaches preserve the basic implication of the very long tails in the empirical frequency distributions: in each and every period the investor is faced with a nonneglible probability of a price change of extraordinary magnitude. This view has been widely accepted by students of finance in the past decade. It has sobering consequences. For instance, the average magnitude of the largest 1 percent of the monthly changes in the S&P Composite Index is nine times as great as the average magnitude of the remaining 99 percent. Apparently the investor will first be lulled by a long series of small changes in security prices drawn from the mass of the probability distribution near zero, and then will be suddenly shocked by an immense change drawn from the tails of the distribution.

Formally, let z_t, $t = 1, , T$ denote a series of price changes. Following the arguments in Alexander (1964, p. 208), Moore (1964), and Osborne (1964), z should be a measure of the proportional change in price. The choice of the particular proportional measure is of minor importance for the purposes of this study, and the traditional choice of $z_t = \log p_{t+1} - \log p_t$ will be made. Then the prevailing view in finance is represented by the null hypothesis:

> The variables z_t, $t = 1, , T$ are serially independent and identically distributed.

The alternative hypothesis offered in this paper is that the variance of z fluctuates in a predictable fashion over time. This hypothesis implies that the investor will not be surprised by extraordinarily large price changes when they occur, but rather will have been forewarned by signs that the forthcoming variance is high. Formally, the alternative hypothesis is the following:

> The random variables z_t are determined by the model $z_t = m_t + v_t^{1/2}\eta_t$, $t = 1, , T$. The η_t are serially independent random variables with identical distribution functions $F(\cdot)$ having mean equal to zero, variance equal to one, and kurtosis equal to γ. The variables v_t, $t = 1, , T$, which are the variances of the price changes, obey a stochastic process that can be forecasted. The η_t are contemporaneously independent of the v_t.

A histogram of the 100-year history of monthly price changes, corrected for forecasted variance fluctuations by the methods developed below, appears in

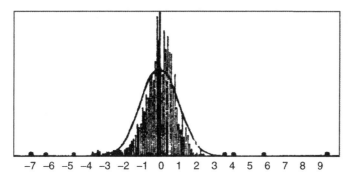

Fig. 3.1. Histogram of standardized monthly price changes[a] compared
to a standard normal distribution

[a] The series $_1y$ as defined in Section 3.4, divided by $\sqrt{\sum_{t=1}^{T} {_1y_t^2}/T}$.

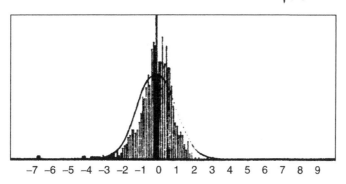

Fig. 3.2. Histogram of monthly price changes corrected for
forecast standard errors[a]

[a] The series $({_1y_t}/\sqrt{\sum_{t=1}^{T} {_1y_t^2}/T})/{_1\hat{s}_t}$, where $_1\hat{s}_t$ is the (standardized) forecast standard deviation, explained in Section 3.5. The histogram is superimposed
on the same standard normal distribution as in Figure 3.1.

Figure 3.2. Notice the reductions in the variance and the kurtosis of the distribution relative to Figure 3.1. The results suggest that the distribution of the η_t may
eventually be shown to be indistinguishable from the normal distribution.

In Section 3.2, below, the relationship between fluctuations in the variance of a
series of random variables and the kurtosis of the series is explored. In Section
3.3, the use of a linear regression model to analyze fluctuations in variance is
explained. In Section 3.4, the stock price series to be analyzed is described and
some necessary adjustments to the series are derived. In Section 3.5, the results of
the experiment are reported. Section 3.6 provides a brief discussion of the
implications of the experiment.

3.2 The Kurtosis of a population with nonconstant variance

3.2.1. Consider the case defined in the alternative hypothesis. Let the random variables $y_t = z_t - m_t$, $t = 1, , T$ be transformed to have mean zero. In studying the properties of the y_t, the first step is to describe their probability distribution on the assumption that the v_t are equal to a set of fixed realized values. Let $E_v(\cdot) \equiv E(\cdot | v_1, \ldots, v_T)$ be the expectation operator which implements this perspective. Then it is an immediate consequence of the independence between v_t and η_t, and of the assumption that η_t has mean zero, variance 1, and kurtosis equal to γ, that

$$\left.\begin{aligned}
E_v(y_t) &= \sqrt{v_t}\, E_v(\eta_t) = 0 \\
E_v(y_t^2) &= v_t E_v(\eta_t^2) = v_t \\
E_v(y_t^4) &= v_t^2 E_v(\eta_t^4) = \gamma v_t^2
\end{aligned}\right\} \tag{3.2.1}$$

$$KURTOSIS_v(y_t) \equiv E_v(y_t^4)/(E_v(y_t^2))^2 = \gamma. \tag{3.2.2}$$

Similarly, the expected values of the sample moments of the series $\{y_1, \ldots, y_T\}$ are

$$\left.\begin{aligned}
E_v(\mu_1) &\equiv E_v(\sum_t y_t/T) = \sum_t (E_v(y_t)/T) = 0 \\
E_v(\mu_2) &\equiv E_v(\sum_t y_t^2/T) = \sum_t (E_v(y_t^2)/T) = \sum_t v_t/T = \bar{v}_1 \\
E_v(\mu_4) &\equiv E_v(\sum_t y_t^4/T) = \sum_t (E_v(y_t^4)/T) = \gamma \sum_t v_t^2/T = \gamma \bar{v}_2
\end{aligned}\right\} \tag{3.2.3}$$

$$KURTOSIS_v(y) \equiv E_v(\mu_4)/(E_v(\mu_2))^2 = \gamma \bar{v}_2/\bar{v}_1^2, \tag{3.2.4}$$

where μ_i is the ith moment about zero of the y sample, and $\bar{v}_i$ is the corresponding moment of the v sample. Let $\bar{v}_i'$ be the ith moment of the v sample about the mean, so that the equality $\bar{v}_2 = \bar{v}_2' + \bar{v}_1^2$ states the familiar fact that the mean square is equal to the variance plus the square of the mean. Furthermore, let $c = \sqrt{\bar{v}_2'/\bar{v}_1^2}$ be the coefficient of variation of the v sample. Then,

$$KURTOSIS_v(y) = ((\bar{v}_2' + \bar{v}_1^2)/\bar{v}_1^2)\gamma = (1 + c^2)\gamma. \tag{3.2.5}$$

Thus, the population kurtosis of y is always greater than the kurtosis of the individual distributions from which the population was compounded, and the increase is determined by the coefficient of variation of v.

Also, under appropriate assumptions concerning the existence of moments for F and the moments of the v sample, it can be shown that the probability limit (plim) of the sample kurtosis (μ_4/μ_2^2) as $T \to \infty$ is equal to the population kurtosis.

3.2.2. The next step is to examine the probability distribution of y on the assumption that the variances $\{v_1, \ldots, v_T\}$ are the realization of a stochastic process V. Let $\bar{V}_i = E[\bar{v}_1]$ and $\sigma_v^2 = E[\bar{v}_2']$ denote the (finite) expected values of the sample mean and sample variance of the realizations of V, and let the pattern of serial dependence in V remain unspecified. (As a special case, V could be a wide-sense stationary stochastic process with mean $\bar{v}$, variance σ_v^2, and arbitrary autocorrelation function.) Let $E(\cdot)$ denote the expectation operator taken over all possible realizations $\{v_1, \ldots, v_T\}$, with the probability distribution of these determined by V. It follows that $E(\cdot) = E[E_v(\cdot)]$. Therefore, the moments of y are found by computing the expectations of (3.2.1) and (3.2.3) with respect to V,

$$\left.\begin{aligned}
E(y_t) &= E[E_v(y_t)] = E(0) = 0 \\
E(y_t^2) &= E[E_v(y_t^2)] = E(v_t) = \bar{V} \\
E(y_t^4) &= E[E_v(y_t^4)] = \gamma E(v_t^2) = \gamma(\bar{V}^{-2} + \sigma_v^2).
\end{aligned}\right\} \tag{3.2.6}$$

Similarly,

$$E(\mu_1) = 0, \quad E(\mu_2) = \bar{V}, \quad E(\mu_4) = \gamma(\bar{v} + \sigma_v^2) \tag{3.2.7}$$

$$KURTOSIS(y) = E[KURTOSIS_v(y)] = \gamma E(1 + c^2). \tag{3.2.8}$$

The expected value of c^2 does not simplify because c^2 is the ratio of the first and second moments of the realization $\{v_1, \ldots, v_T\}$. The distribution of this ratio depends in a complex fashion on the serial dependence in V. However, the plim of the ratio will be the ratio of the corresponding population moments under appropriate assumptions concerning the moments of V.

$$\text{plim} \, (KURTOSIS(y)) = \gamma(1 + \frac{\sigma_v^2}{\bar{V}^2}) \tag{3.2.9}$$

If the autocorrelation of V is predominantly positive, the expected value of the coefficient of variation will be smaller than the population value for small sample sizes. (Heuristically, when v fluctuates slowly, the sample variance of a short series of successive values of v will be reduced, because a long sample is required to exhibit the full tendency of v to vary.) For this same reason, from (3.2.8) it follows that the population kurtosis of y will increase as the sample length grows. Finally, under assumptions on the existence of moments of F and V, the plim of the sample kurtosis of y will again equal the population kurtosis.

$$\text{plim} \, (\mu_4/\mu_2^2) = \gamma(1 + \sigma_v^2/\bar{V}^{-2}) \tag{3.2.10}$$

3.2.3. It is also interesting to examine the behavior of moving sums of the y_t (which correspond, in the model of security prices, to the logarithms of price changes cumulated over several time intervals). Consider the sum of ℓ successively observed y_t, $_\ell y_t \equiv \sum_{s=t}^{t+\ell-1} y_s$. Let $_\ell v_t \equiv \sum_{s=t}^{t+\ell-1} v_s$. Assuming a fixed realization of the v_t,

$$E_v({}_\ell y_t) = 0$$
$$E_v({}_\ell y_t^2) = {}_\ell v_t$$
$$E_v({}_\ell y_t^4) = (\gamma - 3) \sum_{s=t}^{t+\ell-1} v_s^2 + 3{}_\ell v_t^2 \qquad \qquad (3.2.11)$$

$$KURTOSIS_v({}_\ell y_t) = (\gamma - 3)\left(\sum_{s=t}^{t+\ell-1} v_s^2\right)/{}_\ell v_t^2 + 3. \qquad (3.2.12)$$

If successive values of v_s are similar, the first term in (3.2.12) will be similar to $(\gamma - 3)/\ell$, and the kurtosis of the sum will converge toward 3 as ℓ increases.

The next inquiry is into the moments of the ${}_\ell y$ population, again assuming a fixed realization of the v_t. Assume that the intervals of length ℓ over which the variables are summed are nonoverlapping, so that the population in question is the series of variables ${}_\ell y_t = \sum_{s=t}^{t+\ell-1} y_s$, for $t = 1, \ell + 1, 2\ell + 1, \ldots, J\ell - \ell + 1$, or, in more compact notation, the series of variables ${}_\ell y_{j\ell+1}, j = 0, \ldots, J - 1$. For ease of comparison with the results for individual y_t, assume that the length of the entire period is an integral multiple of ℓ, so that $T = J\ell$. Define ${}_\ell \mu_i \equiv \sum_{j=0}^{J-1} {}_\ell y_{j\ell+1}^i/J$ and ${}_\ell v_i \equiv \sum_{j=0}^{J-1} {}_\ell v_{j\ell+1}^i/J$. Since the sums are taken over non-overlapping intervals, the sets of η contributing to the different ${}_\ell y_t$ will be independent of one another. Therefore,

$$E_v({}_\ell \mu_1) = 0, \ E_v({}_\ell \mu_2) = \sum_{j=0}^{J-1}\sum_{s=1}^{\ell} \bar{v}_{j\ell+s}/J ={}_\ell \bar{v}_1 = \ell(\bar{v}_1)$$

$$\qquad \qquad (3.2.13)$$

$$E_v({}_\ell \mu_4) = \frac{(\gamma - 3)}{J}\sum_{j=0}^{J-1}\sum_{s=1}^{\ell} v_{j\ell+s}^2 + \frac{3}{J}\sum_{j=0}^{J-1}\left(\sum_{s=1}^{\ell} v_{j\ell+s}\right)^2 = (\gamma - 3)\ell\bar{v}_2 + 3{}_\ell\bar{v}_2.$$

From these expressions, the population kurtosis can be derived.

$$KURTOSIS_v({}_\ell y) = E_v({}_\ell \mu_4)/(E_v({}_\ell \mu_2))^2 = ((\gamma - 3)\ell\bar{v}_2 + 3{}_\ell\bar{v}_2)/(\ell\bar{v}_1)^2$$
$$= \frac{(\gamma - 3)}{\ell}\frac{\bar{v}_2}{\bar{v}_1^2} + 3\left(\frac{{}_\ell\bar{v}_2}{{}_\ell\bar{v}_1^2}\right) = 3 + \left(\frac{\gamma - 3}{\ell}\right)(1 + c^2) + 3{}_\ell c^2 \qquad (3.2.14)$$

where ${}_\ell c$ is the coefficient of variation of the sample ${}_\ell v_{j\ell+1}, j = 0, \ldots, J - 1$. To facilitate comparison with the preceding case, (3.2.4) can be rewritten

$$KURTOSIS_v(y) = 3 + (\gamma - 3)(1 + c^2) + 3c^2. \qquad (3.2.15)$$

Thus the deviation of the population kurtosis from normality is made up of two terms. The first, which reflects the nonnormality of η, is multiplied by the factor $(1 + c^2)$, but reduced by the factor $1/\ell$. The second term, the contribution of the variation of the ${}_\ell v$, occurs regardless of the kurtosis of the η distribution, and is proportional to ${}_\ell c^2$. The inequality ${}_\ell c^2 \leqslant c^2$ will always hold? At one extreme, if the v_t are constant within each interval, so that all variation occurs between intervals, $_\ell c^2 = c^2$. At another extreme, where successive values of v_t within the same interval are unrelated (so that $\sum_{j=0}^{J-1} (\bar{v}_{j\ell+n_1} - v_1)(\bar{v}_{j\ell+n_2} - v_1) = 0$ for all $n_1 < n_2 \leqslant \ell$), $_\ell c^2 = c^2/\ell$. Where the v_t follow a slowly changing stochastic process, with strong positive serial correlation over small intervals, the situation will lie somewhere between these two extremes and nearer the first. In this case, the contribution of the kurtosis of η is reduced by the factor of $1/\ell$, while the contribution from the variation of v is reduced by the factor $c_\ell^2/c^2 \sim 1$. On the other hand, if the sums of ℓ terms are chosen by random sampling, without replacement, from the series $\{y_1, , y_T\}$, rather than as sequential sums, successive terms appearing in the same sum will be unrelated, so that the second of the two extremes will hold approximately, and

$$KURTOSIS_v(_\ell y) - 3 \sim \frac{KURTOSIS_v(y) - 3}{\ell}. \qquad (3.2.16)$$

3.2.4. Finally, consider the sample moments of $_\ell y$ implied by the stochastic process $\mathcal{V}$. As in Subsection 3.2.2., these moments are just the expected values, with respect to $\mathcal{V}$, of the moments conditional on a fixed realization of $\mathcal{V}$. Thus,

$$E(_\ell y_t) = 0$$
$$E(_\ell y_t^2) = \ell \bar{v}$$
$$E(_\ell y_t^4) = \ell(\gamma - 3)(\bar{v}^2 + \sigma_v^2) + 3E[_\ell v_t^2]$$
$$KURTOSIS(_\ell y_t) = 3 + (\gamma - 3)E\left[\left(\sum_{s=t}^{t+\ell-1} v_s^2\right)\middle/_\ell v_t^2\right]$$
$$E(_\ell\mu_1) = 0$$
$$E(_\ell\mu_2) = \ell\bar{v}$$
$$E(_\ell\mu_4) = \ell(\gamma - 3)(\bar{v}^2 + \sigma_v^2) + 3E[_\ell v_2]$$
$$KURTOSIS(_\ell y) = 3 + \frac{(\gamma - 3)}{\ell}E(1 + c^2) + 3E(_\ell c^2)$$
$$(3.2.17)$$

Where an expectation on the right-hand side has not been simplified, its value depends on the autocorrelation function of $\mathcal{V}$. Again under appropriate assumptions concerning the moments of F and of $\mathcal{V}$, the plims of these expectations will be the corresponding functions of the population moments of v, and, moreover, the plims of the sample moments of $_\ell y$ will equal these population moments of $_\ell y$. Also, as before, the population kurtosis of $_\ell y$ will increase as sample size grows if v fluctuates slowly relative to the length ℓ of the differencing interval.

3.3 The use of a regression model to analyze fluctuations in variance

Consider briefly some of the factors which might influence the variance of price change in a security market. One factor is the elapsed time between successive price measurements. It is reasonable to assume that, other things being equal, the variance will be a linear function of both the number of hours of trading and the number of calendar days $\longrightarrow$ in the interval. However, the variance of price change will also depend on the variance of economic change per unit of time, and upon the amplitude of price response within each hour of trading. It is therefore helpful to divide other influences on price variance into two parts: the determinants of the variance of the economic, financial, social, and other exogenous information reaching the market; and the determinants of the amplitude of the market's response to this information.

Within the first category are such factors as the variability of aggregate economic activity, the rate of technological innovation, the sensitivity of earnings to changes in cost or demand functions, the variance of exogenous changes in the asset positions of market participants, the probability of significant changes in tax legislation, and the degree of sensitivity to international events. Within the second category are such factors as the trading mechanism within the market, the number and character of traders participating in the market, legal restrictions on traders' actions such as margin requirements and restrictions on short sales and options, the schedule of transactions costs, the vulnerability of the market to temporarily self-fulfilling but irrational expectations ("bullish" and "bearish" psychologies), and the traders' expectations as to the normal range of price fluctuations.

There will be a certain degree of feedback from the variance of market prices and from realized price changes to some of these factors, but all of them have an existence independent of contemporaneous events on the market floor. This is not true of the volume of transactions. It is reasonable that large price changes will tend to be accompanied by large volume, and vice versa, and significant relationships have been established between squared price changes and volume (Granger and Morgenstein (1970, Ch. 8)). However, the volume should not be treated as jointly determined with the variance, but rather as being jointly determined with the realized price change, for volume is generated in the trading which produces the realized price change. Factors that tend to increase the *variance* of price change will also tend to increase the *expected* volume, and vice versa. It is the relationship between these factors and the variance of price change that is of primary interest.

A known relationship of this kind would afford the opportunity to forecast price variance and might also lead to constructive recommendations concerning market organization. Moreover, a description of historical fluctuations in price variance would provide a basis for statistical analysis of the historical stock price distribution, as well as a model of heteroscedasticity in historical price changes that would be useful in a variety of other empirical studies.

3.3.1. If the variance of market price change was an observable variable, it would be possible to regress it directly upon explanatory variables representing the influences suggested above. In reality, the variance is not observed, but the observed squared price change is a realization of the underlying distribution with expected value equal to the variance and, accordingly, provides a means to carry out the regression. To clarify this, assume that the true/stochastic process $\mathcal{V}$ determining the variances v_t is of the form

$$v_t = f(\underset{\sim}{x}_t, \underset{\sim}{b}, u_t), \quad t = 1, \ldots, T \tag{3.3.1}$$

where $\underset{\sim}{x}_t$ is a $(k \times 1)$ vector of predetermined variables, $\underset{\sim}{b}$ is a $(k \times 1)$ vector of parameters, and the disturbances u_t are serially independent, identically distributed variables that are contemporaneously uncorrelated with the predetermined variables. The variables η_t, which were previously assumed to be independent of the v_t, are now assumed to be independent of $x_1, \ldots, x_K, \underset{\sim}{b}$, and u_t. Then the equation

$$y_t^2 = f(\underset{\sim}{x}_t, \underset{\sim}{b}, u_t)\eta_t^2, \quad t = 1, \ldots, T \tag{3.3.2}$$

provides the basis for regression analysis.

For example, suppose that the variance is determined by the multiplicative model

$$v_t = x_{1t}^{b_1} x_{2t}^{b_2} \ldots x_{Kt}^{b_K} e^{u_t}, \quad t = 1, \ldots, T \tag{3.3.3}$$

where the u_t have mean zero, variance σ^2, and are independent of $x_1, \ldots, x_K$. Assume further that η_t is bounded away from zero, so that $\log \eta_t^2$ has a finite mean α_1 and a finite variance α_2. Then the logarithm of (3.3.2) is

$$\begin{aligned} \log y_t^2 &= \sum_{i=1}^{K} b_i \log x_{it} + u_t + \log \eta_t^2 \\ &= \alpha_1 + \sum_{i=1}^{K} b_i \log x_{it} + \delta_t \end{aligned} \tag{3.3.4}$$

where $\delta_t = u_t + \log \eta_t^2 - \alpha_1$. This regression equation meets all of the conditions for the Gauss–Markov theorem, since the additive random variables $\delta_t, t = 1,, T$ are identically distributed with mean zero and variance $\sigma^2 + \alpha_2$ and are independent of $x_1, \ldots, x_K$.

As another example, assume that the variance is determined by an additive model

$$v_t = \sum_{i=1}^{K} x_{it} b_i + u_t = \underset{\sim}{x}_t' \underset{\sim}{b} + u_t, t = 1, \ldots, T \tag{3.3.5}$$

where the disturbances u_t are again assumed to be serially independent with mean zero and variance σ^2. Then the regression equation may be written

$$y_t^2 = v_t \eta_t^2 = v_t + v_t(\eta_t^2 - 1)$$
$$= \underset{\sim}{x}_t' \underset{\sim}{b} + u_t + (\underset{\sim}{x}_t' \underset{\sim}{b} + u_t)(\eta_t^2 - 1) \qquad (3.3.6)$$
$$= \underset{\sim}{x}_t' \underset{\sim}{b} + \varepsilon_t, \text{ where } \varepsilon_t = u_t + (\underset{\sim}{x}_t' \underset{\sim}{b} + u_t)(\eta_t^2 - 1).$$

The stochastic properties of the series ε_t, $t = 1, \ldots, T$, are not ideal, but the least squares estimator based on (3.3.6) does provide a consistent estimator of $\underset{\sim}{b}$. To demonstrate this, the relevant moments of the ε_t, taken with respect to the specification of the stochastic process $\mathcal{V}$, must be evaluated. In consistency with the notation of the previous section, let $E(\,\cdot\,) = E(\,\cdot\,|x_1, \ldots, x_K, \underset{\sim}{b}, \sigma^2)$. Then

$$E(\varepsilon_t) = E(u_t) + E(\underset{\sim}{x}_t' \underset{\sim}{b} + u_t)E(\eta_t^2 - 1) = 0 \qquad (3.3.7)$$

since the components of v_t are independent of η_t, and since $E(u_t) = 0$ and $E(\eta_t^2) = \mathrm{VAR}(\eta_t) = 1$. Similarly,

$$\mathrm{VAR}(\varepsilon_t) = E(\varepsilon_t^2) = E[u_t^2] + 2E(u_t(\underset{\sim}{x}_t' \underset{\sim}{b} + u_t))E(\eta_t^2 - 1)$$
$$+ E[(\underset{\sim}{x}_t' \underset{\sim}{b} + u_t)^2]E[(\eta_t^2 - 1)^2] \qquad (3.3.8)$$
$$= \sigma^2 + ((\underset{\sim}{x}_t' \underset{\sim}{b})^2 + \sigma^2)(\gamma - 1).$$

Also, $E(\underset{\sim}{x}_t \varepsilon_t) = \underset{\sim}{0}$, because of the zero correlation between u_t and $\underset{\sim}{x}_t$, and the independence between η_t and x_t. Therefore, with the mild assumption that plim $\left(\sum_{t=1}^{T} \underset{\sim}{x}_t \underset{\sim}{x}_t' / T\right)$ exists and is nonsingular, the probability limit of the least squares estimator $\hat{\underset{\sim}{b}} = \left(\sum_{t=1}^{T} \underset{\sim}{x}_t \underset{\sim}{x}_t'\right)^{-1} \sum_{t=1}^{T} \underset{\sim}{x}_t y_t^2$ is

$$\mathrm{plim}\,\hat{\underset{\sim}{b}} = \mathrm{plim}\left(\sum_{t=1}^{T} \underset{\sim}{x}_t \underset{\sim}{x}_t'\right)^{-1}\left(\sum_{t=1}^{T} \underset{\sim}{x}_t(\underset{\sim}{x}_t' \underset{\sim}{b} + \underset{\sim}{u}_t + (\underset{\sim}{x}_t' \underset{\sim}{b} + u_t)(\eta_t^2 - 1))\right)$$

$$= \underset{\sim}{b} + \mathrm{plim}\left(\frac{\sum_{t=1}^{T} \underset{\sim}{x}_t \underset{\sim}{x}_t'}{T}\right)^{-1}\left(\frac{\sum_{t=1}^{T} \underset{\sim}{x}_t \underset{\sim}{u}_t}{T} + \frac{\sum_{t=1}^{T} x_t(\underset{\sim}{x}_t' \underset{\sim}{b} + u_t)(\eta_t^2 - 1)}{T}\right) = \underset{\sim}{b}.$$

$$(3.3.9)$$

Thus, the random terms ε_t are heteroscedastic and dependent upon the explanatory variables and regression parameters, but the dependence is limited to such a degree that least square regression provides consistent estimators of the regression parameters.

3.3.2. The results of Section 2 concerning the kurtosis of y can be easily applied to a stochastic process $\mathcal{V}$ of form (3.3.1). The details for the linear regression model (3.3.5) will be worked out here. Let $\bar{\underset{\sim}{x}} = \sum_{t=1}^{T} x_t / T$ and let $\underset{\sim}{H} = \sum_{t=1}^{T} (\underset{\sim}{x}_t - \underset{\sim}{x}) (\underset{\sim}{x}_t - \underset{\sim}{x})' / T$. Then the moments of the realization $\{v_1, \ldots, v_T\}$ are

$$\bar{V} = E[v_1] = \underset{\sim}{\bar{x}}{}' \underset{\sim}{b} \tag{3.3.10}$$

$$\bar{V}^2 + \sigma_v^2 = E[v_2] = (\underset{\sim}{\bar{x}}{}' \underset{\sim}{b})^2 + \underset{\sim}{b}{}' \underset{\sim}{H} \underset{\sim}{b} + \sigma^2 \tag{3.3.11}$$

When these expressions are substituted into (3.2.9), the limiting value for the kurtosis of y is found to be

$$\gamma_y \equiv \text{plim}[KURTOSIS(y)] = \gamma \left(1 + \frac{\underset{\sim}{b}{}' \underset{\sim}{H} \underset{\sim}{b} + \sigma^2}{(\underset{\sim}{\bar{x}}{}' \underset{\sim}{b})^2} \right) \tag{3.3.12}$$

The moments of the moving sums of the y_t can be found similarly by substituting (3.3.10) and (3.3.11) into (3.2.17). The terms in (3.2.17) $\Longrightarrow$ that depend on the serial dependence of the v_t are now determined by the behavior over time of the deterministic component $\underset{\sim}{x}{}'_t \underset{\sim}{b}$.

Equation (3.3.12) provides a consistent means of estimating γ. With appropriate assumptions on the existence of higher moments of u and η, the sample kurtosis of y provides a consistent estimator for γ_y, the mean of y_t^2, $t = 1, \ldots, T$, provides a consistent estimator for $\bar{v}$, and the estimator $\hat{\underset{\sim}{b}}$ provides a consistent estimator for $\underset{\sim}{b}{}' \underset{\sim}{H} \underset{\sim}{b}$, namely $\hat{\underset{\sim}{b}}{}' \underset{\sim}{H} \hat{\underset{\sim}{b}}$.

Unfortunately, estimation of σ^2 is somewhat problematic. The difficulty is to distinguish the contribution of σ^2 to the residual variance in the regression (3.3.6) from the contribution of γ. Examining (3.3.8), it is apparent that these two contributions can, in principle, be discriminated, for the error variance contributed by σ^2 is identical for all observations, whereas the variance contributed by γ is a linear function of $\underset{\sim}{x}{}'_t \underset{\sim}{b}$. Thus, using a consistent estimator of $\underset{\sim}{b}$, the linear regression

$$(y_t^2 - \underset{\sim}{x}{}'_t \hat{\underset{\sim}{b}})^2 = \gamma \sigma^2 + (\underset{\sim}{x}{}'_t \underset{\sim}{b})^2 (\gamma - 1) + \zeta_t, \quad t = 1, \ldots, T, \tag{3.3.13}$$

where the left-hand variable is the squared residual in the fitted regression (3.3.6), will yield consistent estimators of γ and σ^2, if the appropriate higher moments of u and η exist. However, this approach is not robust against minor misspecifications in the model. Also, since the dependent variable involves the fourth power of the price change, the outcome will be extremely sensitive to the values of a few realized price changes. Rather than relying upon this approach or upon some analogous but more sophisticated device, it may be preferable to take the conservative stance that σ^2 is zero, which is equivalent to assuming that γ is maximal. This approach yields a consistent upper bound for γ,

$$\gamma = \gamma_y \left(\frac{\bar{v}^2}{\bar{v}^2 + \underset{\sim}{b}{}' \underset{\sim}{H} \underset{\sim}{b} + \sigma^2} \right) \leq \gamma_y \left(\frac{\bar{v}^2}{\bar{v}^2 + \underset{\sim}{b}{}' \underset{\sim}{H} \underset{\sim}{b}} \right) \sim \hat{\gamma}_y \left(\frac{\hat{\bar{v}}^2}{\hat{\bar{v}}^2 + \underset{\sim}{b}{}' \underset{\sim}{H} \underset{\sim}{b}} \right). \tag{3.3.14}$$

To conclude this subsection, note that the consistent estimators for γ and σ^2 provide an estimate of the heteroscedasticity in the residuals in the basic regression (3.3.6). Aitken's Generalized Least Squares can therefore be applied to (3.3.6), using the estimated diagonal variance-covariance matrix (3.3.8), to yield asymptotically more efficient estimators of $\underset{\sim}{b}$.

3.3.3. The remaining task of this section is to examine an interim method of analyzing the variances of security price changes that can be used in the absence of operational measurements of the exogenous factors influencing this variance. The suggested approach is to employ a moving average of realized squared price changes as an estimate of the prevailing variance. The two moving-average regression models which will be used in the experiment, each of which will be estimated separately for values of ℓ from 1 through 6, are:

$$\ell y_t^2 = \alpha + \beta A_t, \tag{3.3.15}$$

where $\qquad A_t = \sum_{s=2}^{11} y_{t-s}^2 / 10, \qquad$ and $\qquad$ (3.3.16)

$$\ell y_t^2 = \alpha + \beta_\ell B_t,$$

where $\qquad \ell B_t = \sum_{s=2}^{11} (y_{t-s}^2 + y_{t+(\ell-1)+s}^2)/20.$

The moving-average approach is a natural one that could stand on its own without any reference to the more general regression model proposed previously. However, the broader perspective in which the variances are viewed as the consequence of identifiable underlying factors allows a much richer interpretation of the results of the moving average model. Suppose that the true model for v is of the form

$$v_t = \underset{\sim}{x}_t' \underset{\sim}{b} + \sum_{s=1}^{S} w_s v_{t-s} + \sum_{r=1}^{R} w_r y_{t-r}^2 + u_t, \qquad t = 1, \ldots, T. \tag{3.3.17}$$

As before, the x variables represent exogenous factors. In addition, an auto-regression on lagged values of the variance is included, since the V process may exhibit inertia or some other internal dynamics. Moreover, a distributed lag on the realized values of the squared price changes is included, since the dispersion of the price changes actually observed in preceding periods may influence traders' expectations as to the magnitude of price change in the present period. Equation (3.3.17) yields the regression relation

$$y_t^2 = \underset{\sim}{x}_t' \underset{\sim}{b} + \sum_{s=1}^{S} w_s v_{t-s} + \sum_{r=1}^{R} w_r y_{t-r}^2 + \varepsilon_t, \qquad t = 1, \ldots, T. \tag{3.3.18}$$

If this is the true regression model, the moving-average regressions are mis-specified, and the results must be interpreted in this light. The contributions of each of the three kinds of predetermined variables in (3.3.17)—the exogenous factors, the lagged variances, and the lagged squared price changes–will be captured in the regression coefficients for the moving average only to the degree that the moving average is a surrogate for (is correlated with) these variables. In discussing the implications of the misspecification, it is sufficient to touch on three important points that are crucial to the interpretation of the results.

First, the moving averages can capture the effects of the exogenous factors only to the degree that these factors are slowly changing over time. Many of the important factors cited earlier in this section do change slowly relative to the one-month recording intervals in the data. However, some factors change too quickly to be captured. In particular, the duration of the month, both in terms of calendar days and in terms of hours of trading, will fluctuate from month to month in response to the calendar and cannot be captured by the moving average. Fortunately, this factor is of minor importance in studying monthly data; the squared coefficient of variation is less than .01, so that from (3.2.8) the contribution to the kurtosis of y is, at most, 1 percent.

Secondly, there is a problem of simultaneity in using the two-sided moving average as an explanatory variable. The average includes future observations, y_{t+s}^2, which depend on future values, v_{t+s}. But according to (3.3.17), v_{t+s} depends on the current value of y_t^2, both directly through the distributed lag and indirectly through the autoregression on v_t. Hence, the regression coefficient for the two-sided moving average will capture not only some of the determinants of v_t, but also part of the reverse effect of v_t and y_t^2 on future values of v. This problem does not arise with the lagged moving average.

Third, in using the lagged moving average of y^2 as a surrogate for the exogenous factors and for the autoregression on v, an interesting "errors in variables" problem arises. To clarify this issue, assume that the exogenous factors change so slowly that $x_t'b$ is highly correlated with v_t, thus permitting these two terms to be merged. Assume further that the weights in the distributed lags in the true model correspond to the lagged moving average so that the true model becomes

$$y_t^2 = \alpha + \phi V_t + \omega A_t + \varepsilon_t, \qquad t = 1, \ldots, T, \tag{3.3.21}$$

where $V_t = \sum_{s=2}^{11} v_{t-s}/10$ and A_t is defined as before. Hence, in the regression model (3.3.15), A_t serves, in part, to capture its own effect and, in part, as a surrogate for V_t. But A_t is related to V_t, for

$$A_t = \sum_{s=2}^{11} y_{t-s}^2/10 = \sum_{s=2}^{11} (v_{t-s} + \varepsilon_{t-s})/10 = V_t + \theta_t, \tag{3.3.22}$$

where $\theta_t = \sum_{s=2}^{11} \varepsilon_{t-s}/10$.

It is useful to distinguish two extreme cases. At one extreme, where $\phi = 0$, (3.3.21) coincides with (3.3.15), the regression model is correctly specified, and the results can accordingly be accepted at face value. At the other extreme, where $\omega = 0$, the true model is

$$y_t^2 = \alpha + \phi V_t + \varepsilon_t, \tag{3.3.23}$$

and (3.3.15), (3.3.22), and (3.3.23) constitute a pure case of the errors-in-variables problem. This is an unusually interesting case, because the appropriate corrections to achieve consistent estimators can be derived. From the specification of the model,

$$E[\theta_t] = E[\varepsilon_t] = E[\theta_t \varepsilon_t] = E[\theta_t V_t] = E[\varepsilon_t V_t] = 0$$

$$\mathrm{VAR}[\varepsilon_t] = (\gamma - 1)v_t + \sigma^2, \quad \mathrm{VAR}[\theta_t] = \sum_{s=2}^{11} \mathrm{VAR}[\varepsilon_{t-s}]/100. \tag{3.3.24}$$

On the assumption that the v_t change slowly over time, $VAR(\theta_t) \simeq VAR(\varepsilon_t)/10$, and the results will be little effected if it is assumed that for all t the individual variances are equal to their average values, $\mathrm{VAR}[\varepsilon_t] = VAR(\varepsilon)$, $VAR(\phi_t) = VAR(\varepsilon)/10$. Then applying the familiar approach to the errors in variables problem (e.g. Johnston (1972, pp. 281–291)), it follows that

$$\mathrm{plim}(\hat{\beta}) = \phi \frac{\mathrm{VAR}(V)}{\mathrm{VAR}(V) + \mathrm{VAR}(\varepsilon)/10} \tag{3.3.25}$$

Also, from (3.3.23),

$$\mathrm{VAR}(y^2) = \phi^2 \mathrm{VAR}(V) + \mathrm{VAR}(\varepsilon). \tag{3.3.26}$$

Finally,

$$\mathrm{VAR}(A) = \mathrm{VAR}(V) + \mathrm{VAR}(\varepsilon)/10. \tag{3.3.27}$$

Since $\hat{\beta}$, $\mathrm{VAR}(y^2)$, and $\mathrm{VAR}(A)$ are computed statistics, these three equations in the three unknowns ϕ, $\mathrm{VAR}(V)$, and $\mathrm{VAR}(\varepsilon)$ may be solved to obtain estimators of ϕ and VAR(V). More generally, if the dependent variable in the regression is the square of the price change cumulated over ℓ periods, so that the assumed true model is

$$\ell y_t^2 = \alpha + \phi V_t + \sum_{s=0}^{\ell-1} \varepsilon_{t+s}, \tag{3.3.28}$$

(3.3.25) and (3.3.27) hold as before and (3.3.26) is modified to

$$\text{VAR}(_{\ell}y^2) = \phi^2\text{VAR}(V) + \ell\text{VAR}(\varepsilon). \tag{3.3.26*}$$

The solutions of (3.3.25), (3.3.26*), and (3.3.27) yield an upper bound for γ, which has been corrected for the errors-in-variables effect,

$$\gamma \leqslant \gamma_{\ell}y\left(\frac{_{\ell}\bar{v}^2}{_{\ell}\bar{v}^2 + \sigma_{\ell}^2 v}\right) \simeq \hat{\gamma}_{\ell}y\left(\frac{\left(\overline{_{\ell}y^2}\right)^2}{\left(\overline{_{\ell}y^2}\right)^2 + \hat{\phi}^2\widehat{\text{VAR}}(V)}\right). \tag{3.3.29}$$

In summary, if the variance of price change is determined by a distributed lag on realized squared price changes, then the approximate upper bound is (3.3.14), which simplifies in the special case (3.3.15) to

$$\gamma \leqslant \gamma_{\ell}y\left(\frac{_{\ell}\bar{v}^2}{_{\ell}\bar{v}^2 + \sigma_{\ell v}^2}\right) \simeq \hat{\gamma}_{\ell}y\left(\frac{\left(\overline{_{\ell}y^2}\right)^2}{\left(\overline{_{\ell}y^2}\right)^2 + \hat{\beta}^2 VAR(A)}\right). \tag{3.3.30}$$

On the other hand, if the variance of price change is determined by an auto-regression perturbed by exogenous factors, the upper bound (3.3.29) is appropriate. If the truth lies somewhere in between, then the correct upper bound will lie between these extremes.

3.4 The data

The price series used in the experiment is the Standard & Poor's Monthly Composite Stock Price Index (the S&P 500). The values of this index and of S&P indexes for many industrial subgroups are readily available for the period from 1871 to the present "Standard and Poor's Trade and Security Statistics: Security Price Index Record," an annual publication from the Standard and Poor's Corporation. The Composite Index is a natural choice for a basic experiment, not only because of its extraordinarily long history, but also because it closely parallels the total value of common stock equity in the United States.

3.4.1. Under the null hypothesis stated in Section 1, the variance of the random increment in the logarithm of price is proportional to the elapsed time over which the increment occurs. Therefore, since the average month contains 4–1/3 weeks, the variance of $_{\ell}z_t$ is approximately 4.333 ℓv_w, where v_w is the variance of the increment between successive Wednesdays. Also, the series of differences of logarithms taken over successive nonover-lapping intervals are serially independent with variances that will be equal except for the minor variations due to the varying number of days in a month.

There are more than 100 years, or 1200 months, of data. Thus, there are 1200+ observations for the case $\ell = 1$, 600+ for $\ell = 2$, 400+ for $\ell = 3$, 300+ for $\ell = 4$, 240+ for $\ell = 5$, *and* 200+ for $\ell = 6$. To insure that the sample size remains large, the maximum differencing interval used is $\ell = 6$. (The apparent sample size could be increased by including all 1200 possible differencing intervals of length ℓ in the same sample, or by studying ℓ distinct but overlapping samples, $i = 1, \ldots, \ell$, each made up of the series of nonoverlapping intervals starting with the ith month in the sample. However, the sampling properties of the results are clearer when nonoverlapping intervals are used, and there are sufficient data in the sample to prove the point of the article in this way.)

Let C_t denote the value of the composite index in month t, and let $_\ell c_t = \log C_{t+\ell} - \log C_t$. It would appear to be entirely natural to use each variable $_\ell c_t$ to operationalize the corresponding variable $_\ell z_t$, since this amounts to using the value of the composite price index as a measure of the price in that month. If the composite index were an instantaneous measure of the level of market prices at some fixed time in the month, $_\ell c_t$ would indeed be a measure of the movement in the logarithm of "market price" from one instantaneous recording moment to another ℓ months later, and it would be entirely appropriate to use it as the variable $_\ell z_t$.

Unfortunately, the Standard & Poor's indexes are not constructed so as to be instantaneous measures of the market price level. The Index is actually a splice of two differently constructed indexes: until December 1917, the monthly price index was a weighted average of individual security "prices," with each price, because of data limitations, defined as the monthly mid-range (the average of the high and low in the month); since January 1918, the monthly price index has been defined as the average, taken over all Wednesdays in the month, of the weighted average of the individual securities' Wednesday closing prices. The reasons for this change in definition and the exact nature of the indexes are explained in detail in Cowles (1939). Each definition yields a "monthly price" which is actually the result of applying some averaging measure to the entire monthly price history. The averaging measures alter the variances of the price changes and destroy the property of serial independence as well. This point is demonstrated elegantly in Daniels (1966) and further discussed in Rosenberg (1971). Following the approaches taken in Daniels (1996), Rosenberg (1970, 1971), the extent of the reduction in variance and the magnitude of the resultant serial correlation can be deduced for each of the averaging measures.

For the mid-range, with the assumption that the null hypothesis holds and, in addition, the assumption that z_t is normally distributed and some simplifying assumptions about the procedure for constructing the mid-range index,

$$\text{VAR}(_\ell c_t) = ((\ell - 1)4.333 + 2.659)v_w = \frac{(\ell - 1) + .6137}{\ell}\text{VAR}(_\ell z_t). \qquad (3.4.1)$$

For the post-1918 period, following the approach sketched in Rosenberg (1971) and with attention to the varying numbers of Wednesdays in successive months,

$$\text{VAR}(_\ell c_t) = ((\ell - 1)4.333 + 2.967)v_w = \frac{(\ell - 1) + .6846}{\ell}\text{VAR}(_\ell z_t). \qquad (3.4.2)$$

The spurious shift in the variance of c_t in January 1918 would be taken as a minor validation of the alternative hypothesis if it were not corrected for. Accordingly, the series of log differences prior to 1917 must be corrected by a multiplicative factor so that, under the null hypothesis, the corrected pre-1917 and post-1918 variances are identical. If the effects of the two averaging measures are exactly as asserted in (3.4.1) and (3.4.2), the factor should be $f_\ell = \sqrt{((\ell - 1) + .6846)/((\ell - 1) + .6137)}$ for differencing intervals of length ℓ.

3.4.2. Next consider the possibility of dependence between two price changes, $_\ell c_s$ and $_m c_t$, for $s < t$. As long as the first interval ends in a month prior to the month in which the second interval begins, the serial independence of the increments in the underlying price process assures that the price changes will be independent of one another. However, if the first interval ends in the same month as the second begins, the two measured changes each involve the same averaging measure C_t taken over the entire month t, and, accordingly, serial dependence enters in. For the case of successive differencing intervals of length ℓ, the spurious serial correlation can be shown to be equal, on the average, to

$$\text{CORR}(_\ell c_{t-\ell},\, _\ell c_t) = (1 - a)/2((\ell - 1) + a), \tag{3.4.3}$$

where $a = \text{VAR}(_1 c)/\text{VAR}(_1 z)$.

In particular, the spurious correlation of successive first differences equals .315 for the pre-1917 period, and .230 for the post-1918 period, if the variance reductions are as given in (3.4.1) and (3.4.2).

Relation (3.4.3) provides a check of the validity of (3.4.1) and (3.4.2), for the spurious reduction in variance is uniquely related to the spurious serial correlation introduced into the series. For the pre-1917 period (558 observations), the actual serial correlation of the series $_1 c_t$ is .315, exactly equal to the predicted spurious serial correlation. For the post-1918 period (635 observations), the actual serial correlation is .291, in contrast to the predicted spurious serial correlation of .230. This difference of .061 is marginally significant, since the asymptotic approximation to the standard error of the estimated correlation coefficient is .036 under the null hypothesis (Kendall and Stuart (1966, p. 432)). It may reflect a somewhat larger variance reduction than predicted in (3.4.2), or positive serial correlation in the increments to the underlying price process, or any combination of these two causes. In fact, the cause may be serial correlation in the underlying price changes, for .061 is in the same range as serial correlations observed for the first differences of various price series over short differencing intervals in the period 1920–1970. In sum, the observed serial correlation of the composite index appears to be largely consistent with the predictions of (3.4.3), and therefore appears to confirm (3.4.1) and (3.4.2).

However, to assure that misspecification of the correction factor did not affect the results in any way, the analyses were run for three cases: no correction factor; the correction factor f_ℓ; and the correction factor lying between these cases, which would be appropriate if all of the serial correlation in the post-1918 period were spurious. The results never differed importantly from one case to the next, so only those results with the correction factor f_ℓ, which are the least favorable to the alternative hypothesis, will be reported.

To facilitate the interpretation of the results, each corrected series $_\ell c_t$ was also multiplied by a constant multiplicative factor $h_\ell = \sqrt{\ell/((\ell-1)+.6846)}$ over the whole history. This correction offsets the variance reductions in (3.4.2), so that under the null hypothesis, the transformed variance is equal to the variance of the underlying $_\ell z_t$. The transformation of scale in no way affects the explanatory power of the regression.

Some additional minor adjustments to the data were needed to deal with the closure of the New York Stock Exchange for four months in 1914—differencing intervals overlapping this period were deleted—and to deal with the discontinuous change in the variance reduction in January 1918. The series $_\ell c$ as corrected were then used in the regressions.

3.4.3. Two problems arise from the spurious serial dependence in the c_t (which is not removed by the multiplicative corrections). First, it is desirable that each dependent variable $_\ell c_t$ be independent, under the null hypothesis, of the moving average used to predict its variance. The averaging measures render $_\ell c_t$ dependent on any price changes which involve prices in month t through $t + \ell$. However, $_\ell c_t$ remains independent of any of the $_1 c_s$ taken over differencing intervals that end prior to t or begin subsequent to $t + \ell$. Accordingly, the moving averages are defined so as to omit the variables $_1 c_{t-1}$ through $_1 c_{t+\ell}$ inclusive, thereby insuring the desired independence under the null hypothesis. Secondly, the $\longrightarrow$ spurious first-order serial correlation of the $_\ell c_t$ induces a spurious serial correlation in successively observed $_\ell c_t^2$ and, hence, in the residuals in the regressions (3.3.15) and (3.3.16). However, it can be shown that the spurious serial correlation in the regression residuals will be less than $.1/\ell$, so that there will be a negligible reduction in the efficiency of the least squares estimators.

One last problem is the effect of the averaging measures upon the kurtosis of the price changes. For the pre-1917 period, where the mid-range was used, if $_1 z_t$ is normally distributed with kurtosis of 3, the kurtosis of $_1 c_t$ is reduced to 2.798 under the null hypothesis (Rosenberg (1970)). Anticipating the results of the experiment, which imply that the distribution of z_t is similar to the normal, it may be hoped that the reduction in kurtosis was of this magnitude. The effect on the kurtosis of the post-1918 averaging measure can be computed directly under the null hypothesis. The effect turns out to be small: KURTOSIS $(_1 c_t) \simeq .95(\ KURTOSIS(_1 z_t) - 3)$ $+3$. Overall, the kurtosis of $_1 c_t$ can be expected to be similar to that of $_1 z_t$, but slightly lower. Whatever difference there is between the two kurtosis decreases sharply as ℓ increases. In summary, the success of the experiment in explaining the kurtosis of the corrected changes in the S&P Composite Index will be strongly indicative of the success that could be achieved in explaining the kurtosis of the underlying price changes, but the two results would not be identical.

3.5 The experiment

The first step in studying the data is to analyze the mean values of the price changes. The mean value constitutes one component of expected return, so it should be relatively small in magnitude and should change slowly over time, but there is no reason to expect it to be zero. However, polynomial distributed lag regressions applied to the series $_1c_t$ (not yet corrected as explained in Section 3.4, since the multiplicative correction factor perturbs the mean if this is nonzero) did not uncover any systematic patterns. Even the mean value of the series, computed separately over the periods 1871–1917 and 1918–1971, is not significantly different from zero at the 99 percent level of confidence in either period. The explanation is not that the true mean is zero, but rather that over differencing intervals of a few months the variance of stock price changes entirely swamps the contribution of the mean. This finding is consistent with other experience Fama (1970, p. 400), all of which seems to show that adjustments for the means of stock price changes have a negligible effect in studies of their probability distributions. Accordingly, rather than make a problematic assumption about the pattern of the mean values over time, the means of the z_t were assumed to be identically zero for all t. Under this assumption, the corrected series $_\ell c_t, \ell = 1, , 6$ will take the role of the series $_\ell y_t$ as defined in Sections 3.2 and 3.3.

It was decided to divide the sample into two parts: one, covering the years 1871–1950, to be used in the regressions; and the other, covering the years 1951–1971, to be reserved to test the predictive ability of the models. When the experiment was begun, the length of the moving average to be used in the regressions had not yet been determined. Lagged moving averages of lengths 10 and 30 were tried, so that the first 32 months of the sample were sacrificed to initialize the explanatory variables. The moving average of length 10 produced a better fit and was therefore selected for the experiment. (No further effort was made to select the length of the moving average so as to maximize goodness of fit, since a search of this kind might cast some doubt on the eventual results.)

Then regressions of the form (3.3.15) and (3.3.16) were run. The results are reported in Tables 3.1 and 3.2. Since the series of dependent variables for each ℓ is based on the same series of underlying price changes, the regression results are jointly dependent. Accordingly, in comparing the null hypothesis with the alternative hypothesis, it is appropriate to rely only upon one of the regressions—specifically, the regression for $\ell = 1$, with the largest number of observations and, hence, the largest amount of information. Under the null hypothesis, the regression coefficient β is equal to zero in all regressions. However, for $\ell = 1$, the t-statistic for $\hat{\beta}$ in the regression on the lagged moving average is 10.06. The 99.99 percent confidence point for the t-distribution is 4.1, so that even allowing for inflation in the tails of the distribution of the t-statistic as a result of heteroscedasticity and high kurtosis in the regression disturbances, the experiment appears to provide conclusive evidence for the existence of *forecastable* fluctuations in variance. Similarly, the t-statistic for $\hat{\beta}$ in the regression on the two-sided moving average is 12.04, providing yet more conclusive evidence for the existence of *systematic* fluctuations in variance.

The estimated $\hat{\beta}$ are also highly significant for $\ell > 1$. The value of $\hat{\beta}$ should increase in direct proportion to ℓ, since the variance of price change should be the sum of its components. However, in regressions on the lagged moving average, the increase is less than in proportion to ℓ. One might first suspect the corrections designed to introduce comparability across different ℓ (explained at the end of Section 3.4.2), but the means of the squared price changes given in the third column of Table 3.1, which are unbiased estimates of the average variances, do increase in proportion to ℓ, so that these corrections are seen to have been successful. Since the adjusted regression coefficients $\hat{\phi}$ are more closely proportional to ℓ, it appears that a part of the difficulty is removed by the errors-in-variables approach. The remaining discrepancies, which show up in the $\hat{\phi}$ and also in the $\hat{\beta}$ estimated for the two-sided moving average, are probably due to the variations in the sample variances of the $_\ell y^2$ as ℓ increases, seen in column 4 of Table 3.1, which are accidental consequences of the timing of the differencing intervals for each ℓ.

At the right-hand side of Table 3.1, consistent upper bounds on γ. (the kurtosis of the individual price changes), are computed for the two cases described in Section 3.3.3. Under the assumption that variance is determined by a distributed lag on realized squared price changes (3.3.30), the upper bounds lie somewhat above the kurtosis of the normal distribution. Under the assumption that the variance is determined by an autoregression perturbed by exogenous factors (3.3.29), the upper bounds fluctuate below the kurtosis of the normal distribution. The arguments of Section 3 suggest that the true upper bound should lie between these two extremes.

The estimated regressions provide rules for predicting the variances of the historically observed price changes, respectively, $_\ell \hat{v}_t = \hat{\alpha} + \hat{\beta} A_t$ and $_\ell \hat{v}_t = \hat{\alpha} + \hat{\beta}_\ell B_t$. Each series $\{_\ell \hat{v}_1, \ldots, _\ell \hat{v}_N\}$ can be standardized so as to have geometric average equal to unity. Let $_\ell \hat{s}_t^2$ denote such a standardized variance prediction. Consider the contrast between the series of variables $\{_\ell y_1, \ldots, _\ell y_N\}$ and the adjusted series $\{_\ell y_1/_\ell \hat{s}_1, \ldots, _\ell y_N/_\ell \hat{s}_N\}$. Under the null hypothesis, the

Table 3.1. Regressions of the form $_\ell y_t^2 = \alpha + \beta A_t$, where $A_t = \sum_{s=21}^{11} y_{t-s}^2/10$ for nonoverlapping intervals of ℓ months from the sample period August 1873–December 1950

ℓ	Sample Size	Moments of $_\ell v^2$		R^2	$\hat{\alpha}$	$\hat{\beta}$	$\hat{\phi}$	Upper bounds on γ	
		Mean $(\times 10^2)$	Variance $(\times 10^4)$		(*t*-Statistics)			From Eq. (3.30)	From Eq. (3.29)
1	923	.31	1.31	.099	.00106 (2.57)	.666 (10.06)	1.067	6.19	4.61
2	461	.66	4.69	.154	.00167 (1.55)	1.578 (9.14)	3.421	4.45	2.57
3	307	.92	4.80	.181	.00406 (3.12)	1.637 (8.21)	2.540	3.28	2.57
4	230	1.15	5.58	.103	.00693 (4.01)	1.477 (5.13)	2.596	3.74	3.04
5	184	1.60	9.79	.119	.00961 (3.80)	2.038 (4.85)	4.291	3.49	2.59
6	153	1.96	18.10	.134	.01078 (2.91)	2.822 (4.84)	7.615	3.61	2.17

Table 3.2. Regressions of the form $_\ell y_t^2 = \alpha + \beta_\ell B_t$, where $_\ell B_t = \sum_{s=2}^{11} (_1 y_{t-s}^2 + _1 y_{t+(\ell-1)+s}^2)/20$ for nonoverlapping intervals of length ℓ from the sample period August 1873–December 1950

ℓ	Sample size	R^2	$\hat{\alpha}$	$\hat{\beta}$
			(t-statistics)	
1	923	.1360	.00030	.913
			(0.70)	(12.04)
2	461	.1955	.00006	2.098
			(0.06)	(10.56)
3	307	.2553	.00185	2.339
			(1.42)	(10.22)
4	230	.3590	.00144	3.260
			(0.94)	(11.30)
5	184	.3895	.00230	4.392
			(1.04)	(10.77)
6	153	.5204	−.00168	6.813
			(−0.57)	(12.79)

former are identically distributed, while the latter are heteroscedastic as a result of the erroneous division by $_\ell \hat{s}_t$. In contrast, under the alternative hypothesis, the former are heteroscedastic, while the latter should be less heteroschedastic as a result of division by the predicted standard deviations. Thus, by comparing the properties of the two series, additional insight into the relative validity of the two hypotheses is obtained.

For one thing, since the predicted variances are standardized to have geometric average equal to one, any reduction in the dispersion of $_\ell y$ achieved by the adjustment should reflect a true explanation of heteroscedasticity. A substantial reduction is achieved: for regression on the lagged moving average, $\sum (_1 y_t/_1 \hat{s}_t)^2 / \sum_1 y_t^2 = .802$; for regression on the two-sided moving average, $\sum (_1 y_t/_1 \hat{s}_t)^2 / \sum_1 y_t^2 = .757$.

Moreover, if the alternative hypothesis holds, division by the predicted standard deviations should remove fluctuations in variance and thereby reduce the kurtosis of the population. Conversely, if the null hypothesis holds, $1/_\ell \hat{s}_t$ and $_\ell y_t$ are independent except for the tenuous link provided by the two estimated regression coefficients. Therefore, according to the results of Section 3.2.1, division by the predicted standard deviations should increase the kurtosis of $_\ell y$. In Figure 3.2, the histogram of the adjusted series $_1 y_t/_1 \hat{s}_t$, where $_1 \hat{s}_t$ is predicted on the basis of the lagged moving average, is superimposed on the same normal distribution as in Figure 3.1. Comparing the two figures, the reduction in both scale and kurtosis achieved by the adjustment is apparent. A quantitative indication of the reduction in kurtosis is given in Tables 3.3 and 3.4. The reduction in kurtosis over the entire sample history, using the regression coefficients estimated from the regression subsample only, is very great.

Table 3.3. Kurtosis of $_1y_t$ before and after division by forecast
standard deviation $_1\hat{s}_t = \sqrt{\hat{\alpha} + \hat{\beta}A_t}$

ℓ	Entire Sample Period August 1873–December 1971				Reserved Subsample January 1951–December 1971		
	Sample Size	Kurtosis of		Percent of Deviation from Normal Explained	Sample Size	Kurtosis of	
		$_1y_t$	$_1y_t/_1\hat{s}_t$			$_1y_t$	$_1y_t/_1\hat{s}_t$
1	1175	14.79	6.50	70.3	252	4.71	5.04
2	587	12.33	5.64	71.7	126	3.80	3.85
3	391	6.78	4.00	73.5	84	3.73	4.07
4	293	5.64	4.19	54.9	63	3.06	3.10
5	234	5.21	4.11	49.7	50	3.53	3.72
6	195	6.01	4.15	61.7	42	3.08	3.07

Table 3.4. Kurtosis of $_1y_t$ before and after division by the
predicted[a] standard deviation $_1\hat{s}_t = \sqrt{\hat{\alpha} + \hat{\beta}_\ell B_t}$

ℓ	Entire sample period August 1873–December 1970/1971				Reserved subsample January 1951–December 1970/1971		
	Sample size	Kurtosis of		Percent of deviation from normal explained	Sample size	Kurtosis of	
		$_1y_t$	$_1y_t/_1\hat{s}_t$			$_1y_t$	$_1y_t/_1\hat{s}_t$
1	1162	14.83	4.61	86.4	239	4.91	4.57
2	581	12.36	3.86	90.8	120	3.94	3.62
3	387	6.79	3.86	77.3	80	3.86	4.14
4	291	5.62	3.95	63.7	61	3.06	2.60
5	232	5.24	3.79	64.7	48	3.64	3.88
6	194	5.98	4.66	44.3	41	3.00	2.85

[a] For $\ell = 6$, where the estimate of α was negative, $\hat{\alpha}$ was set to zero.

However, the change in kurtosis taken over the subsample reserved for predictive testing is disappointing. The prediction based on the lagged moving average reduces the kurtosis in only one case out of six, the prediction based on the two-sided moving average reduces it in four cases out of six. The explanation for this mediocre performance is easily seen in Figure 3.3, where the standardized series $_1y$ is plotted against a standard deviation band predicted by the lagged moving average. It is clear that the variance fluctuated greatly in the period 1920–1950, but very little in the period 1951–1971. Thus, when the lagged moving average is applied over the entire sample, there are major fluctuations in variance to explain; the sample kurtosis, which is originally very high as a result of these

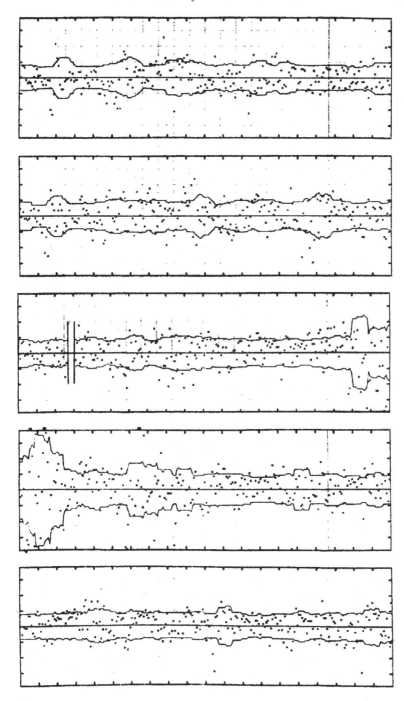

Fig. 3.3. Standardized monthly price changes, 1872–1971, superimposed upon a band of width equal to two forecast standard deviations.

fluctuations, is reduced substantially when they are successfully predicted by the regression. In the reserved subsample, however, there is little fluctuation in variance; as a result, the sample kurtosis is not very high originally, and the corrections implied by the regression model introduce enough noise to offset largely the little true explanatory power that it is possible for them to provide. Thus, the poor reduction in kurtosis is not necessarily to be blamed on a change in the regression parameters from the regression sample to the reserved sample, but rather on the relative stability of variance, for whatever exogenous reason, in the latter period. This interpretation is confirmed by the fact that if the reserved sample is extended backwards by only three years, so as to cover the period 1947–1971 (as was done by mistake in one of the computations), fluctuation in variance is introduced into the sample, the sample kurtosis rises, and the lagged moving average does succeed in substantially reducing the kurtosis.

3.6 Summary and discussion

In Section 2, the kurtosis of a series of random variables was shown to increase in proportion to the square of the coefficient of variation of the variances of the individual random variables. In Section 3.3, many exogenous factors were suggested which can reasonably be expected to influence the variance of stock price changes. As a consequence, it was argued that the correct model to determine the variance of price changes may involve the effects of several exogenous factors, an autoregression on lagged values of the variance, and a distributed lag on the realized squared price changes. A procedure to estimate such a relationship by regression was explained. Since the appropriate explanatory variables to represent the exogenous factors have not yet been constructed, and since the lagged values of the variance are unobservable, the closest one can come to estimating the true model at the present time is to use lagged squared price changes as explanatory variables. A crude version of this approach, the use of a lagged moving average, provides a benchmark, since improved specification of the model can only increase the explanatory power.

This device was applied to a series of monthly price changes in the New York Stock Exchange, as defined in Section 3.4. The results in Section 3.5 establish conclusively the existence of forecastable fluctuations in variance. Indeed, 70 percent of the deviation of the sample kurtosis from normality can be explained by the forecasted variances. The still better results for a two-sided moving average, where 86 percent of the deviation of the kurtosis from normality is explained, and the low values of the consistent upper bounds on the true kurtosis of the random variables (computed for the lagged moving average model, with and without an errors-in-variables adjustment) suggest that better forecasting models for the variance will explain virtually all of the nonnormality in the empirical frequency distribution of NYSE stock price changes.

These results suggest a new way of looking at the probability distribution of stock prices. Previously, the empirical frequency distribution observed over many periods was presumed to be a realization of the distribution prevailing at each instant in history. The long tails in this distribution were explained either by a nonnormal, infinite-variance stable distribution Mandelbrot (1963) or by the hypothesis of fluctuating variance in a normal distribution Praetz (1972) and Press (1967). The suggestion of fluctuating variance is not new; it appeared at least as early as 1961 in a remark by Working (see the edited volume by Cootner (1964, p. 191)). What is new in the present results is the fact that the fluctuations in variance can be modeled and forecasted. Instead of the probability distribution at any one time having the same long tails as the observed empirical frequency distribution, as would be the case if the variance fluctuation were random and unpredictable, the price change actually has a nearly normal distribution at any one time, with a variance which can be forecasted using an appropriate model. The apparent kurtosis of the empirical frequency distribution is the result of mixing distributions with predictably differing variances. Thus, the study of the probability distribution of security price changes must be broken into two parts: (i) modeling the fluctuations in variance in the series, and (ii) analyzing the distribution of price changes net of these predictable variance fluctuations. The outlines for this two-part approach are provided in this article, but much research in this area remains.

The results of the experiment have widespread implications for financial management and the theory of security markets. Some of these are the following: (i) the requirement for forecasts of price variance; (ii) the opening of the study of the determinants of price variance as a field of economic analysis; (iii) the need to respond to fluctuations in variance in portfolio management; (iv) the role of fluctuations in variance, through their effect on the riskiness of investment and, hence, on the appropriate risk premium, as an influence on the price level.

These innovations in finance will be important only to the degree that variance can be expected to exhibit forecastable and significant fluctuations in the future. In the NYSE data, very large forecastable fluctuations occurred in the first half of this century, but the variance of monthly price changes has been relatively stable thus far in the second half. It is important to anticipate the extent of future fluctuations in variance in the NYSE and other financial markets.

References

Alexander, S. S. (1964). Price movements in speculative markets: trends or random walks, in Cootner (1964), 199–218.

Cootner, P. (1964). *The Random Character of Stock Market Prices*, edited volume, Cambridge, Mass: MIT Press.

Cowles, A. (1939) *Common Stock indexes*, 2nd edition, Bloomington, Ind.: Princiepia Press, 1939.

Davids, H. E. (1966) Autocorrelation between first differences of mid-ranges, *Econometrica*, 34, 215–9.

Fama, E. F. (1970) Efficient capital markets: a review of theory and empirical work, *Journal of Finance*, 25, 383–417.

Fama, E. F. and M. H. Miller (1972) *The Theory of Finance*, New York: Holt, Rinehort and Winston.

Granger, C. W. J. and O. Morgenstein (1970) *The Predictability of Stock Market Prices*, Levington, Mass.: Heath Levington Books.

Granger, C. W. J. and D. Orr (1972). 'Infinite Variance' and research strategy in time series analysis, *Journal of the American Statistical Association*, 67, 275–85.

Johnson, J. (1972) *Econometric Methods*, 2nd edition, New York: McGraw Hill.

Kendall, M. G. and A. Stuart (1966). *The Advanced Theory of Statistics*, Volume 3, New York: Hafner Publishing Company.

Mandelbrot, B. (1963). The variation of certain speculative prices. *Journal of Business* 36, 394–419.

Moore, A. B. (1964). Some characteristics of changes in common stock prices, in Cootner (1964), 139–61.

Osborne, M. F. M. (1964). Brownian motion and the stock market, in Cootner (1964), 100–28.

Praetz, P. D. (1972). The distribution of share prices. *Journal of Business* 45, 45–55.

Press, S. J. (1967). A compound events model for security prices. *Journal of Business* 40, 317–35.

Rosenberg, B. (1970) The distribution of the mid-range – a comment, *Econometrica*, 38, 176–7.

Rosenberg, B. (1971) Statistical analysis of price series obscured by averaging measures, *Journal of Financial and Quantitative Analysis*, 6, 1083–94.

4

The Pricing of Options on Assets with Stochastic Volatilities*

JOHN HULL AND ALAN WHITE[†]

Abstract

One option-pricing problem that has hitherto been unsolved is the pricing of a European call on an asset that has a stochastic volatility. This paper examines this problem. The option price is determined in series form for the case in which the stochastic volatility is independent of the stock price. Numerical solutions are also produced for the case in which the volatility is correlated with the stock price. It is found that the Black-Scholes price frequently overprices options and that the degree of overpricing increases with the time to maturity.

One option-pricing problem that has hitherto remained unsolved is the pricing of a European call on a stock that has a stochastic volatility. From the work of Merton (1973), Garman (1976), and Cox, Ingersoll, and Ross (1985), the differential equation that the option must satisfy is known. The solution of this differential equation is independent of risk preferences if (a) the volatility is a traded asset or (b) the volatility is uncorrelated with aggregate consumption. If either of these conditions holds, the risk-neutral valuation arguments of Cox and Ross (1976) can be used in a straightforward way.

This paper produces a solution in series form for the situation in which the stock price is instantaneously uncorrelated with the volatility. We do not assume that the volatility is a traded asset. Also, a constant correlation between the instantaneous rate of change of the volatility and the rate of change of aggregate consumption can be accommodated. The option price is lower than the Black–Scholes (B–S) (1973) price when the option is close to being at the money and higher when it is deep in or deep out of the money. The exercise prices for which overpricing by B–S takes place are within about 10 percent of the security price. This is the range of exercise prices over which most option trading takes place, so we may, in general, expect the B–S price to overprice options. This effect is exaggerated as the time to maturity increases. One of the most surprising implications of this is that, if the B–S equation is used to determine the implied

* This work was previously published as J. Hull and A. White (1987), 'The Pricing of Options on Assets with Stochastic Volatilities', *The Journal of Finance*, XLII, 2 Copyright © Blackwell Publishing. Reproduced by kind permission.

† The authors would like to thank Phelim P. Boyle, Michael Brennan, Herbert Johnson, Stephen Ross, Eduardo Schwartz, and an anonymous referee for helpful comments on earlier drafts of this paper. This research was funded by the Financial Research Foundation of Canada.

volatility of a near-the-money option, the longer the time to maturity the lower the implied volatility. Numerical solutions for the case in which the volatility is correlated with the stock price are also examined.

The stochastic volatility problem has been examined by Merton (1976), Geske (1979), Johnson (1979), Johnson and Shanno (1985), Eisenberg (1985), Wiggins (1985), and Scott (1986). The Merton and Geske papers provide the solution to special types of stochastic volatility problems. Geske examines the case in which the volatility of the firm value is constant so that the volatility of the stock price changes in a systematic way as the stock price rises and falls. Merton examines the case in which the price follows a mixed jump-diffusion process. Johnson (1979) studies the general case in which the instantaneous variance of the stock price follows some stochastic process. However, in order to derive the differential equation that the option price must satisfy, he assumes the existence of an asset with a price that is instantaneously perfectly correlated with the stochastic variance. The existence of such an asset is sufficient to derive the differential equation, but Johnson was unable to solve it to determine the option price. Johnson and Shanno (1985) obtain some numerical results using simulation and produce an argument aimed at explaining the biases observed by Rubinstein (1985). Eisenberg (1985) examines how options should be priced relative to each other using pure arbitrage arguments. Numerical solutions are attempted by Wiggins (1985) and Scott (1986).

Section 4.1 of this paper provides a solution to the stochastic volatility option-pricing problem in series form. Section 4.2 discusses the numerical methods that can be used to examine pricing biases when the conditions necessary for the series solution are not satisfied. Section 4.3 investigates the biases that arise when the volatility is stochastic but when a constant volatility is assumed in determining option prices. Conclusions are in Section 4.4.

4.1 The stochastic volatility problem

Consider a derivative asset f with a price that depends upon some security price, S, and its instantaneous variance, $V = \sigma^2$, which are assumed to obey the following stochastic processes:

$$dS = \phi S \, dt + \sigma S \, dw \tag{1}$$

$$dV = \mu V \, dt + \xi V \, dz. \tag{2}$$

The variable ϕ is a parameter that may depend on S, σ, and t. The variables μ and ξ may depend on σ and t, but it is assumed, for the present, that they do not depend on S. The Wiener processes dz and dw have correlation ρ. The actual process that a stochastic variance follows is probably fairly complex. It cannot take on negative values, so the instantaneous standard deviation must approach zero as σ^2 approaches zero. Since S and σ^2 are the only state variables affecting the price of the derivative security, f, the risk-free rate, which will be denoted by r, must be constant or at least deterministic.

One reason why this problem has not previously been solved is that there is no asset that is clearly instantaneously perfectly correlated with the state variable σ^2. Thus, it does not seem possible to form a hedge portfolio that eliminates all the risk. However, as was shown by Garman (1976), a security f with a price that depends on state variables θ_i must satisfy the differential equation

$$\frac{\partial f}{\partial t} + \frac{1}{2} \sum_{i,j} \rho_{ij} \sigma_i \sigma_j \frac{\partial^2 f}{\partial \theta_i \partial \theta_j} - rf = \sum_i \theta_i \frac{\partial f}{\partial \theta_i} [-\mu_i + \beta_i(\mu^* - r)], \qquad (3)$$

where σ_i is the instantaneous standard deviation of θ_i, ρ_{ij} is the instantaneous correlation between θ_i and θ_j, μ_i is the drift rate of θ_i, β_i is the vector of multiple-regression betas for the regression of the state-variable "returns" $(d\theta/\theta)$ on the market portfolio and the portfolios most closely correlated with the state variables, μ^* is the vector of instantaneous expected returns on the market portfolio and the portfolios most closely correlated with the state variables, and r is the vector with elements that are the risk-free rate r. When variable i is traded, it satisfies the $(N + 1)$-factor CAPM, and the ith element of the right-hand side of (3) is $-r\theta_i \partial f / \partial \theta_i$.

In the problem under consideration, there are two state variables, S and V, of which S is traded. The differential equation (3) thus becomes

$$\frac{\partial f}{\partial t} + \frac{1}{2}\left[\sigma^2 S^2 \frac{\partial^2 f}{\partial S^2} + 2\rho\sigma^3 \xi S \frac{\partial^2 f}{\partial S \partial V} + \xi^2 V^2 \frac{\partial^2 f}{\partial V^2}\right] - rf$$
$$= -rS\frac{\partial f}{\partial S} - [\mu - \beta_v(\mu^* - r)]\sigma^2 \frac{\partial f}{\partial V}, \qquad (4)$$

where ρ is the instantaneous correlation between S and V. The variable β_v is the vector of multiple-regression betas for the regression of the variance "returns" (dV/V) on the market portfolio and the portfolios most closely correlated with the state variables, and μ^* is as defined above. Note that, since these expected returns depend on investor risk preferences, this means that, in general, the option price will depend on investor risk preferences. We shall assume that $\beta_v(\mu^* - r)$ is zero or that the volatility is uncorrelated with aggregate consumption. This is not an unreasonable assumption and means that the volatility has zero systematic risk.[1] The derivative asset must then satisfy:

$$\frac{\partial f}{\partial t} + \frac{1}{2}\left[\sigma^2 S^2 \frac{\partial^2 f}{\partial S^2} + 2\rho\sigma^3 \xi S \frac{\partial^2 f}{\partial S \partial V} + \xi^2 V^2 \frac{\partial^2 f}{\partial V^2}\right] - rf = -rS\frac{\partial f}{\partial S} - \mu\sigma^2 \frac{\partial f}{\partial V}. \qquad (5)$$

---

[1] This assumption can be relaxed to: $\beta_v(\mu^* - r)$ is constant. The solution is then the same as the solution when $\beta)_v(\mu^* - r) = 0$ except that μ is replaced by $\hat{\mu}$, where $\hat{\mu} = \mu - \beta_v(\mu^* - r)$. We are grateful to George Athanassakos, a Ph.D. student at York University, for pointing this out to us.

It will also be assumed that $\rho = 0$, i.e. that the volatility is uncorrelated with the stock price. As the work of Geske (1979) shows, this is equivalent to assuming no leverage and a constant volatility of firm value.

An analytic solution to (5) for a European call option may be derived by using the risk-neutral valuation procedure. Since neither (5) nor the option boundary conditions depend upon risk preferences, we may assume in calculating the option value that risk neutrality prevails. Thus, $f(S, \sigma^2, t)$ must be the present value of the expected terminal value of f discounted at the risk-free rate. The price of the option is therefore

$$f(S_t, \sigma_t^2, t) = e^{-r(T-t)} \int f(S_T, \sigma_T^2, T) p(S_T | S_t, \sigma_t^2) dS_T, \qquad (6)$$

where

$T =$ time at which the option matures;

$S_t =$ security price at time t;

$\sigma_t =$ instantaneous standard deviation at time t;

$p(S_T | S_t, \sigma_t^2) =$ the conditional distribution of S_T given the security price and variance at time t;

$$E(S_\tau | S_t) = S_t e^{r(\tau - t)};$$

and $f(S_T, \sigma_T^2, T)$ is max $[0, S - X]$. The condition imposed on $E(S_\tau | S_t)$ is given to make it clear that, in a risk-neutral world, the expected rate of return on S is the risk-free rate.

The conditional distribution of S_T depends on both the process driving S and the process driving σ^2. Making use of the fact that, for any three related random variables x, y, and z the conditional density functions are related by

$$p(x|y) = \int g(x|z)h(z|y)dz,$$

equation (6) may be greatly simplified. Define $\bar{V}$ as the mean variance over the life of the derivative security defined by the stochastic integral

$$\bar{V} = \frac{1}{T-t} \int_t^T \sigma_\tau^2 d\tau.$$

Using this, the distribution of S_T may be written as

$$p(S_T | \sigma_t^2) = \int g(S_T | \bar{V}) h(\bar{V} | \sigma_t^2) d\bar{V},$$

where the dependence upon S_t is suppressed to simplify the notation. Substituting this into (6) yields

$$f(S_t, \sigma_t^2, t) = e^{-r(T-t)} \int \int f(S_T) g(S_T|\bar{V}) h(\bar{V}|\sigma_t^2) dS_T d\bar{V},$$

which can then be written as

$$f(S_t, \sigma_t^2, t) = \int \left[e^{-r(T-t)} \int f(S_T) g(S_T|\bar{V}) dS_T \right] h(\bar{V}|\sigma_t^2) d\bar{V}. \tag{7}$$

Under the prevailing assumptions ($\rho = 0$, μ and ξ independent of S), the inner term in (7) is the Black–Scholes price for a call option on a security with a mean variance $\bar{V}$, which will be denoted $C(\bar{V})$. To see this we need the following lemma:

Lemma: Suppose that, in a risk-neutral world, a stock price S and its instantaneous variance σ^2 follow the stochastic processes

$$dS = rS\,dt + \sigma S\,d\tilde{z} \tag{a}$$

$$d\sigma^2 = \alpha\sigma^2 dt + \xi\sigma^2 d\tilde{w} \tag{b}$$

where r, the risk-free rate, is assumed constant, α and ξ are independent of S, and $d\tilde{z}$ and $d\tilde{w}$ are independent Wiener processes. Let $\bar{V}$ be the mean variance over some time interval $[0, T]$ defined by

$$\bar{V} = \frac{1}{T} \int_0^T \sigma^2(t) dt. \tag{c}$$

Given (a), (b), and (c), the distribution of $\log\{S(T)/S(0)\}$ conditional upon $\bar{V}$ is normal with mean $rT - \bar{V}T/2$ and variance $\bar{V}T$.

It is important to distinguish between the distributions of $\{S(T)/S(0)|\bar{V}\}$, $\{S(T)/S(0)\}$, and $\bar{V}$. The first is lognormal; the last two are not.

To see that the lemma is true, first let us suppose that σ^2 is deterministic but not constant. In this case, the terminal distribution of $\log\{S(T)/S(0)\}$ is normal with mean $rT - \bar{V}T/2$ and variance $\bar{V}T$. Note that the parameters of the lognormal distribution depend only on the risk-free rate, the initial stock price, the time elapsed, and the mean variance over the period. Thus, any path that σ^2 may follow and that has the same mean variance $\bar{V}$ will produce the same lognormal distribution. If σ^2 is stochastic, there are an infinite number of paths that give the same mean variance $\bar{V}$, but all of these paths produce the same terminal distribution of stock price. From this we may conclude that, even if σ^2 is stochastic, the terminal distribution of the stock price given the mean variance $\bar{V}$ is lognormal.

An alternative way to consider this problem is to assume that the variance changes at only n equally spaced times in the interval from 0 to T. Define S_i as the stock price at the end of the ith period and V_{i-1} as the volatility during the ith period. Thus, $\log(S_i/S_{i-1})$ has a normal distribution with mean

$$\frac{rT}{n} - \frac{V_{i-1}T}{2n}$$

and variance

$$\frac{V_{i-1}T}{n}.$$

If S and V are instantaneously uncorrelated, this is also the probability distribution of $\log(S_i/S_{i-1})$ conditional on V_i. The probability distribution of $\log(S_T/S_0)$ conditional on the path followed by V is therefore normal with mean $rT - \bar{V}T/2$ and variance $\bar{V}T$. This distribution depends only on $\bar{V}$. By letting $n \to \infty$, the lemma is seen to be true.

It is important to realize that the lemma does not hold when S and V are instantaneously correlated. In this case, $\log(S_i/S_{i-1})$ and $\log(V_i/V_{i-1})$ are normal distributions that in the limit have correlation ρ. The density function of $\log(V_i/V_{i-1})$ is normal with mean

$$\frac{\mu T}{n} - \frac{\xi^2 T}{2n}$$

and variance

$$\frac{\xi^2 T}{n},$$

so that $\log(S_i/S_{i-1})$ conditional on V_i is normal with mean

$$\frac{rT}{n} - \frac{V_{i-1}T}{2n} + \rho \frac{\sqrt{V_{i-1}}}{\xi} \left[\log(V_i/V_{i-1}) - \frac{\mu T}{n} + \frac{\xi^2 T}{2n} \right]$$

and variance

$$\frac{V_{i-1}T}{n}(1 - \rho^2).$$

Thus, $\log(S_T/S_0)$ conditional on the path followed by V has a normal distribution with mean

$$rT - \frac{\bar{V}T}{2} + \sum_i \frac{\rho\sqrt{V_{i-1}}}{\xi} \left[\log\left(\frac{V_i}{V_{i-1}}\right) - \frac{\mu T}{n} + \frac{\xi^2 T}{2n} \right]$$

and variance

$$\bar{V}T(1 - \rho^2).$$

This distribution clearly depends on attributes of the path followed by V other than $\bar{V}$.

It is also interesting to note that the lemma does not carry over to a world in which investors are risk averse. In such a world, the drift rate of the stock price depends on σ^2 through the impact of σ^2 on the stock's β. This means that the mean of the terminal stock price distribution depends on the path that a nonconstant σ^2 follows. Different paths for σ^2 that have the same mean variance produce distributions for the log of the terminal stock price that have the same variance but different means. In this case, it is not true that the terminal distribution of the stock price given the mean variance $\bar{V}$ is lognormal.

Since $\log(S_T/S_0)$ conditional on $\bar{V}$ is normally distributed with variance $\bar{V}T$ when S and V are instantaneously uncorrelated, the inner integral in equation (7) produces the Black–Scholes price $C(\bar{V})$, which is

$$C(\bar{V}) = S_t N(d_1) - Xe^{-r(T-t)}N(d_2),$$

where

$$d_1 = \frac{\log(S_t/X) + (r + \bar{V}/2)(T - t)}{\sqrt{\bar{V}(T - t)}d_2 = d_1 - \sqrt{\bar{V}(T - t)}}.$$

Thus, the option value is given by

$$f(S_t, \sigma_t^2) = \int C(\bar{V})h(\bar{V}|\sigma_t^2)d\bar{V}. \tag{8}$$

Equation (8) is always true in a risk-neutral world when the stock price and volatility are instantaneously uncorrelated. If, in addition, the volatility is un-correlated with aggregate consumption, we have shown that the option price is independent of risk preferences and that the equation is true in a risky world as well. Equation (8) states that the option price is the B–S price integrated over the distribution of the mean volatility. It does not seem to be possible to obtain an analytic form for the distribution of $\bar{V}$ for any reasonable set of assumptions about the process driving V. It is, however, possible to calculate all the moments of $\bar{V}$ when μ and ξ are constant. For example, when $\mu \neq 0$,

$$E(\bar{V}) = \frac{e^{\mu T} - 1}{\mu T}V_0$$

$$E(\bar{V}^2) = \left[\frac{2e^{(2\mu + \xi^2)T}}{(\mu + \xi^2)(2\mu + \xi^2)T^2} + \frac{2}{\mu T^2}\left(\frac{1}{2\mu + \xi^2} - \frac{e^{\mu T}}{\mu + \xi^2}\right)\right]V_0^2,$$

and, when $\mu = 0$,

$$E(\bar{V}) = V_0$$

$$E(\bar{V}^2) = \frac{2(e^{\xi^2 T} - \xi^2 T - 1)}{\xi^4 T^2} V_0^2$$

$$E(\bar{V}^3) = \frac{e^{3\xi^2 T} - 9e^{\xi^2 T} + 6\xi^2 T + 8}{3\xi^6 T^3} V_0^3.$$

The proofs of these results are available from the authors on request; they have been produced independently by Boyle and Emanuel (1985).

Expanding $C(\bar{V})$ in a Taylor series about its expected value, $\bar{\bar{V}}$, yields

$$f(S_t, \sigma_t^2) = C(\bar{\bar{V}}) + \frac{1}{2}\frac{\partial^2 C}{\partial \bar{V}^2}\bigg|_{\bar{\bar{V}}} \int (\bar{V} - \bar{\bar{V}})^2 h(\bar{V})d\bar{V} + \cdots$$

$$= C(\bar{\bar{V}}) + \frac{1}{2}\frac{\partial^2 C}{\partial \bar{V}^2}\bigg|_{\bar{\bar{V}}} \mathrm{Var}(\bar{V}) + \frac{1}{6}\frac{\partial^3 C}{\partial \bar{V}^3}\bigg|_{\bar{\bar{V}}} \mathrm{Skew}(\bar{V}) + \cdots,$$

where $\mathrm{Var}(\bar{V})$ and $\mathrm{Skew}(\bar{V})$ are the second and third central moments of $\bar{V}$. For sufficiently small values of $\xi^2(T - t)$, this series converges very quickly. Using the moments for the distribution of $\bar{V}$ given above this series becomes when $\mu = 0$:

$$f(S, \sigma^2) = C(\sigma^2)$$

$$+ \frac{1}{2}\frac{S\sqrt{T-t}N'(d_1)(d_1 d_2 - 1)}{4\sigma^3} \times \left[\frac{2\sigma^4(e^k - k - 1)}{k^2} - \sigma^4\right]$$

$$+ \frac{1}{6}\frac{S\sqrt{T-t}N'(d_1)[(d_1 d_2 - 3)(d_1 d_2 - 1) - (d_1^2 + d_2^2)]}{8\sigma^5} \tag{9}$$

$$\times \sigma^6 \left[\frac{e^{3k} - (9 + 18k)e^k + (8 + 24k + 18k^2 + 6k^3)}{3k^3}\right] + \cdots,$$

where

$$k = \xi^2(T - t)$$

and the t subscript has been dropped to simplify the notation. The choice of $\mu = 0$ is justified on the grounds that, for any nonzero μ, options of different maturities would exhibit markedly different implied volatilities. Since this is never observed empirically, we must conclude that μ is at least close to zero.

When the volatility is stochastic, the B–S price tends to overprice at-the-money options and underprice deep-in-the-money and deep-out-of-the-money options. (We define an at-the-money option as one for which $S = Xe^{-r(T-t)}$.) The easiest way to see this is to note that (8) is just the expected B–S price, the expectation being taken with respect to $\bar{V}$,

$$f = E[C(\bar{V})].$$

When C is a concave function, $E[C(\,\cdot\,)] < C(E[\,\cdot\,])$, while, for a convex function, the reverse is true. The B–S option price $C(\bar{V})$ is convex for low values of $\bar{V}$ and concave for higher values. Thus, at least when ξ is small, we find that the B–S price tends to underprice for low values of $\bar{V}$ and overprice for high values of $\bar{V}$. It seems strange that a stochastic variance can lower the option price below the price it would have if the volatility were nonstochastic. However, this is consistent with the results Merton (1976) derived for the mixed jump-diffusion process. There he showed that, if the option is priced by using the B–S results based on the expected variance (the expectation being formed over both jumps and continuous changes), then the price might be greater or less than the correct price.

To determine the circumstances under which the B–S price is too high or too low, examine the second derivative of $C(\bar{V})$.

$$C''(\bar{V}) = \frac{S\sqrt{T-t}}{4\bar{V}^{3/2}} N'(d_1)(d_1 d_2 - 1),$$

where d_1 and d_2 are as defined above. The curvature of C is determined by the sign of C'', which depends on the sign of $d_1 d_2 - 1$. The point of inflection in $C(\bar{V})$ is given when $d_1 d_2 = 1$, that is, when

$$\bar{V} = \frac{2}{T-t}[\sqrt{1 + [\log(S/X) + r(T-t)]^2} - 1].$$

Denote this value of $\bar{V}$ by I. When $\bar{V} < I$, $C'' > 0$ and C is a convex function of $\bar{V}$. When $\bar{V} > I$, $C'' < 0$ and C is a concave function of $\bar{V}$. If $S = Xe^{-r(T-t)}$, then $I = 0$; this means that C is always a concave function of $\bar{V}$, and, regardless of the distribution of $\bar{V}$, the actual option price will always be lower than the B-S price. As $\log(S/X) \to \pm\infty$, I becomes arbitrarily large, and C is always convex so that the actual option price is always greater than the B-S price. Thus, we find that the B-S price always overprices at-the-money options but underprices options that are sufficiently deeply in or out of the money.

It is clear from this argument that $\partial f/\partial\xi$ may be positive or negative. The comparative statics with respect to the remaining six parameters, S, X, r, σ_t, $T-t$, and μ, are consistent with Merton's (1973) distribution-free theorems. Since μ and ξ are presumed independent of S, the distribution $h(\bar{V})$ is independent of S, X, and r. Thus, with respect to these three parameters, the comparative statics of $f(\,\cdot\,)$ are the same as the comparative statics of $C(\,\cdot\,)$. This follows since $C(\,\cdot\,)$ is monotonic in these three parameters, and h is everywhere non-negative. Thus, we find, as one might expect,

$$\frac{\partial f}{\partial S} = E\left[\frac{\partial C(\bar{V})}{\partial S}\right] > 0$$

$$\frac{\partial f}{\partial X} = E\left[\frac{\partial C(\bar{V})}{\partial X}\right] < 0$$

$$\frac{\partial f}{\partial r} = E\left[\frac{\partial C(\bar{V})}{\partial r}\right] > 0.$$

The remaining three parameters $T - t$, μ, and σ_t affect both $C(\cdot)$ and $h(\cdot)$. The effect of increasing any of them is to increase the option price:

$$\frac{\partial f}{\partial \mu} > 0, \quad \frac{\partial f}{\partial \sigma_t^2} > 0, \quad \frac{\partial f}{\partial T} > 0.$$

To see this, note that $\partial f/\partial T$, $\partial f/\partial \mu$, and $\partial f/\partial \sigma_t^2$ are positive for every possible sample path of σ^2. Thus, they must also be positive when averaged across all possible sample paths.

In this section, it was shown that, if the stochastic volatility is independent of the stock price, the correct option price is the expected Black–Scholes price where the expectation is taken over the distribution of mean variances. This is given in equation (8). If the solution (8) is substituted into the differential equation (5), the equation is separable in h and C. The details of this substitution are available from the authors on request. The density function $h(\bar{V})$ is shown to satisfy the following differential equation:

$$\frac{\partial h}{\partial t} + \frac{\bar{V} - V_t}{T - t}\frac{\partial h}{\partial \bar{V}} + \frac{1}{2}\xi^2 \bar{V}_t^2 \frac{\partial h}{\partial V_t} + \mu V_t \frac{\partial h}{\partial V_t} = 0,$$

where $V_t = \sigma_t^2$. This can, in principle, be solved for the density function of the mean variance.

4.2 Other numerical procedures

We now consider efficient ways in which Monte Carlo simulation can be used to calculate the option price when some of the assumptions necessary for the series solution in (9) are relaxed. For our first result, we continue to assume that $\rho = 0$. However, we allow ξ and μ to depend on σ and t. This means that V can follow a mean-reverting process. One simple such process occurs when

$$\mu = a(\sigma^* - \sigma) \tag{10}$$

and ξ, a, and σ^* are constants.

The result in (8) still holds (i.e., the call price is the B–S price integrated over the distribution of $\bar{V}$). An efficient way of carrying out the Monte Carlo simulation involves dividing the time interval $T - t$ into n equal subintervals. Independent standard normal variates $v_i(1 \le i \le n)$ are sampled and are used to generate the variance V_i at time $t + i(T - t)/n$ using the formula:

$$V_i = V_{i-1}e^{[(\mu-\xi^2/2)\Delta t+v_i\xi\sqrt{\Delta t}]},$$

where $\Delta t = (T - t)/n$ and, if μ and ξ depend on σ, their values are based on $\sigma = \sqrt{V_{i-1}}$. The B–S option price, p_1, is calculated with the volatility set equal to the arithmetic mean of the V_i's ($0 \leq i \leq n$). The procedure is then repeated using the antithetic standard normal variables, $-v_i(0 \leq i \leq n)$, to give a price, p_2, and

$$y = \frac{p_1 + p_2}{2}$$

is calculated. The mean value of y over a large number of simulations gives an excellent estimate of the option price. This can be compared with the B–S price based on V_0 to give the bias.

Note that it is not necessary to simulate both V and S. Also, the antithetic variable technique that is described in Hammersley and Handscomb (1964) considerably improves the efficiency of the procedure. In the mean-reverting model in (10) when $S = X = 1$, $r = 0$, $T = 90$ days, $\sigma_0 = 0.15$, $\xi = 1.0$, $a = 10$, $\sigma^* = 0.15$, and $n = 90$, 1000 simulations gave a value for the option of 0.029 with a standard error of 0.000014. The bias is -0.00038 (with the same standard error). The method can be used to deal with the situation where the conditions for the series solution in (9) hold but where ξ is too large for the series to converge quickly. Table 4.1 compares the values given by this Monte Carlo procedure with the values given by (9) for particular cases.

Table 4.1. Comparison of Monte Carlo procedure and series solution; option parameters: $\sigma_0 = 10\%$, $\xi = 1$, $\mu = 0$, $T - t = 180$ days

S/X	Price		B–S Price bias		
	B–S	Equation 9	Equation 9	Monte Carlo	
			Percent bias	Percent bias	Standard error
0.75	0.0000	0.0000	*******	******	237.85
0.76	0.0000	0.0000	******	******	139.41
0.77	0.0000	0.0000	******	970.57	153.57
0.78	0.0000	0.0000	786.47	787.43	133.70
0.79	0.0000	0.0000	588.78	383.43	44.22
0.80	0.0000	0.0001	436.12	336.43	39.21
0.81	0.0000	0.0001	354.37	330.68	46.90
0.82	0.0000	0.0001	232.00	173.55	21.21
0.83	0.0001	0.0002	164.02	134.14	14.91
0.84	0.0001	0.0003	114.54	102.17	10.67
0.85	0.0002	0.0004	78.32	69.55	8.41
0.86	0.0004	0.0006	52.14	54.55	6.74
0.87	0.0006	0.0008	33.53	37.95	5.43
0.88	0.0009	0.0011	20.55	23.50	3.02
0.89	0.0013	0.0015	11.70	16.46	2.74

Continued

Table 4.1. *Continued*

S/X	Price		B–S Price bias		
	B–S	Equation 9	Equation 9	Monte Carlo	
			Percent bias	Percent bias	Standard error
0.90	0.0019	0.0021	5.83	10.07	1.99
0.91	0.0027	0.0028	2.07	5.53	1.45
0.92	0.0039	0.0039	−0.23	2.49	1.09
0.93	0.0053	0.0052	−1.53	0.22	0.90
0.94	0.0071	0.0069	−2.17	−1.45	0.78
0.95	0.0094	0.0091	−2.40	−2.36	0.58
0.96	0.0119	0.0117	−2.38	−2.53	0.38
0.97	0.0151	0.0148	−2.22	−2.61	0.29
0.98	0.0188	0.0185	−1.98	−2.52	0.25
0.99	0.0231	0.0228	−1.72	−2.32	0.21
0.01	0.0281	0.0276	−1.45	−2.16	0.19
1.01	0.0334	0.0330	−1.20	−1.61	0.16
1.02	0.0394	0.0390	−0.97	−1.24	0.12
1.03	0.0461	0.0456	−0.76	−1.09	0.13
1.04	0.0529	0.0526	−0.58	−0.65	0.10
1.05	0.0603	0.0601	−0.41	−0.35	0.08
1.06	0.0682	0.0681	−0.28	−0.19	0.08
1.07	0.0765	0.0764	−0.16	−0.05	0.07
1.08	0.0850	0.0850	−0.06	0.06	0.06
1.09	0.0939	0.0939	0.01	0.13	0.05
1.10	0.1030	0.1030	0.07	0.17	0.05
1.11	0.1122	0.1124	0.11	0.20	0.04
1.12	0.1216	0.1218	0.13	0.19	0.03
1.13	0.1312	0.1314	0.15	0.19	0.03
1.14	0.1409	0.1411	0.15	0.19	0.03
1.15	0.1506	0.1509	0.15	0.13	0.02
1.16	0.1605	0.1607	0.14	0.14	0.02
1.17	0.1703	0.1706	0.13	0.10	0.01
1.18	0.1802	0.1804	0.11	0.10	0.01
1.19	0.1902	0.1904	0.10	0.08	0.01
1.20	0.2001	0.2003	0.08	0.08	0.01
1.21	0.2101	0.2102	0.07	0.05	0.01
1.22	0.2201	0.2202	0.06	0.05	0.01
1.23	0.2300	0.2301	0.05	0.03	0.00
1.24	0.2400	0.2401	0.04	0.03	0.00

For our second result, we allow ρ to be nonzero and allow μ and ξ to depend on S as well as σ and t. We continue to assume that V is uncorrelated with aggregate consumption so that risk-neutral valuation can be used. In this case, it is necessary to simulate both S and V. The time interval is divided up as before, and two independent normal variates u_i and $v_i (1 \leq i \leq n)$ are sampled and used to generate the stock price S_i and variance V_i at time i in a risk-neutral world using the formulae:

$$S_i = S_{i-1} e^{[(r-V_{i-1}/2)\Delta t + u_i \sqrt{V_{i-1}\Delta t}]}$$

$$V_i = V_{i-1} e^{[(\mu - \xi^2/2)\Delta t + \rho u_i \xi \sqrt{\Delta t} + \sqrt{1-\rho^2} v_i \xi \sqrt{\Delta t}]}. \tag{11}$$

Again, the values of μ and ξ are based on $\sigma^2 = V_{i-1}$ and $S = S_{i-1}$. The value of

$$e^{-r(T-t)} \max[S_n - X, \, 0]$$

is calculated to give one "sample value," p_1, of option price. A second price, p_2, is calculated by replacing u_i with $-u_i(1 \le i \le n)$ and repeating the calculations; p_3 is calculated by replacing v_i with $v_i(1 \le i \le n)$ and repeating the calculations; p_4 is calculated by replacing u_i with $-u_i$ and v_i with $-v_i(1 \le i \le n)$ and repeating the calculations. Finally, two sample values of the B–S price q_1 and q_2 are calculated by simulating S using $\{u_i\}$ and $\{-u_i\}$, respectively, with V kept constant at V_0. This provides the following two estimates of the pricing bias:

$$\frac{p_1 + p_3 - 2q_1}{2} \quad \text{and} \quad \frac{p_2 + p_4 - 2q_2}{2}.$$

These estimates are averaged over a large number of simulations.

This procedure uses the antithetic variable technique (twice) and the control variate technique. Both are described in Hammersley and Handscomb (1964). The principle of the control variate technique is that the difference between the values of the two variables can often be obtained most accurately for a given number of simulations when both are calculated using the same random number streams. Furthermore, this is often true even when the value of one of the variables can be calculated analytically.

This procedure is applicable to a wider range of situations than the first one but is not as efficient. For the mean-reverting model example considered above, the standard error of the pricing bias using $n = 90$ and 1000 simulations was 0.000041 (compared with 0.000014 for the first procedure). Also, approximately three times as much computer time was consumed.

4.3 Properties of the option price

In this section, the properties of the option price given by the series solution in equation (9) and the numerical solutions of Section II are examined. The principal finding is that, when the volatility is uncorrelated with the stock price, the option price is depressed relative to the B–S price for near-the-money options. When the volatility is correlated with the stock price, this at-the-money price depression continues on into the money for positive correlation and out of the money for negative correlation. As might be expected, these effects are exaggerated as the volatility, σ, the volatility of the volatility, ξ, or the time to maturity,

$T - t$, increases. The surprising result of this is that longer term options have lower implied volatilities, as calculated by the B–S equation, than do shorter term options whenever the B–S price overprices the option.

Consider first the case in which the volatility is uncorrelated with the stock price and μ and ξ are constant. Figure 4.1 shows the general relationship between the B–S price and the correct option price. The option being priced has 180 days to maturity; the volatility of the underlying asset is initially fifteen percent per annum; $\mu = 0$ and $\xi = 1$. The B–S price is too low deep in and out of the money and, surprisingly, too high at the money. The largest absolute price differences occur at or near the money. The actual magnitude of the pricing error is quite small and is magnified twenty-five-fold to make it visible in Figure 4.1.

The choice of a value of ξ is not obvious. It is possible to estimate ξ by examining the changes in volatilities implied by option prices. Alternatively, ξ can be estimated from changes in estimates of the actual variance. For currencies and currency options listed on the Philadelphia exchange, Hull and White (1987) found that the estimates of ξ using both methods ranged from 1 to 4. Both of the estimation methods have weaknesses. Using the implied volatilities is at best an indirect procedure for estimating ξ. It is also contaminated by the fact that the changes in implied volatility are, at least to some extent, a result of pricing errors in the options. The problem with using estimates of the actual variance is that it requires very large amounts of data. Because of these weaknesses, the low end of the range for ξ was chosen as a conservative estimate.

In Figure 4.2, the effect of changing σ_t is shown, and, in Figure 4.3, the effect of changing ξ is shown. While the absolute magnitude of the price bias is very small, as a percentage of the B–S price it is quite significant. The principal result of

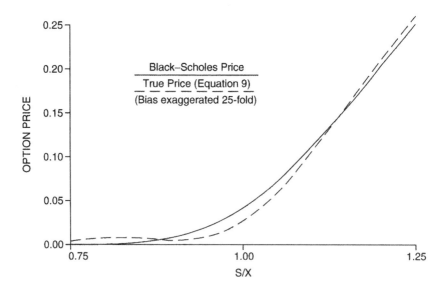

Fig. 4.1. Pricing bias when $\mu = 0$, $r = 0$, $\sigma_t = 15\%$, $\xi = 1$, $T - t = 180$ days.

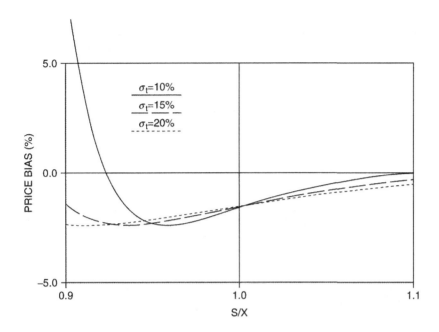

Fig. 4.2. Effect of varying σ_t When $\mu = 0$, $r = 0$, $\xi = 1$, $T - t = 180$ days.

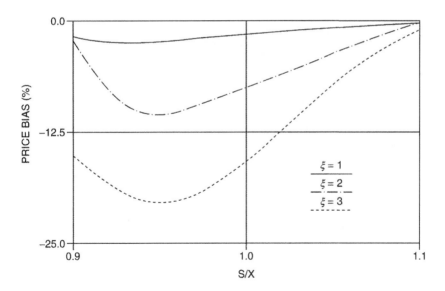

Fig. 4.3. Effect of varying ξ When $\mu = 0$, $r = 0$, $\sigma_t = 15\%$, $T - t = 180$ days.

increasing σ_t^2 is to make the percentage price bias for out-of-the-money (in-the-money) options more positive (negative). When one looks sufficiently far out of the money, this effect is reversed, with higher σ_t^2 causing smaller biases. The effect on at- or in-the-money options is small. The main effect of increasing ξ is to lower the price of (i.e. to make the bias more negative for) near-the-money options. Although not evident from Figure 4.3, it is true that, for sufficiently deep out-of-the-money options, the reverse is true; increasing ξ increases a positive bias.

Figures 4.1 and 4.2 were produced using the series solution in equation (9). For Figure 4.3, when $\xi = 2$ and 3, it was found that the series solution did not converge quickly, and the Monte Carlo simulation approach was used. This was also used to investigate the results for the mean-reverting process in (10). As might be expected, the results for this process show biases that are similar to but less pronounced than those for the case when μ and ξ are constant. The effect of moving to a mean-reverting process from a process where μ and ξ are constant is to reduce the variance of $\bar{V}$. It is similar to the effect of reducing ξ.

The effect of a nonzero ρ when both μ and ξ are constant was investigated using the Monte Carlo simulation approach in equation (11). The results are shown in Table 4.2. When the volatility is positively correlated with the stock price, the option price has a bias relative to the B–S price, which tends to decline as the stock price increases. Out-of-the-money options are priced well above the B–S price, while the price of in-the-money options is below the B–S price. The crossing point, the point at which the B–S price is correct, is slightly below being at the money. When the volatility is negatively correlated with the stock price, the reverse is true. Out-of-the-money options are priced below the B–S price, while in-the-money options have prices above the B–S price. The crossing point is slightly in the money. When ρ is zero, the bias is a combination of these two effects. The price is above the B–S price for in- and out-of-the-money options and below the B–S price at the money. For all values of ρ, the absolute percentage bias tends to zero as S/X tends to infinity. These general observations appear to be true for all maturities.

The intuition behind these effects can be explained by the impact that the correlation has on the terminal distribution of stock prices. First, consider the case in which the volatility is positively correlated with the stock price. High stock prices are associated with high volatilities; as stock prices rise, the probability of large positive changes increases. This means that very high stock prices become more probable than when the volatility is fixed. Low stock prices are associated with low volatilities; if stock prices fall, it becomes less likely that large changes take place. Low stock prices become like absorbing states, and it becomes more likely that the terminal stock price will be low. The net effect is that the terminal stock price distribution is more positively skewed than the lognormal distribution arising from a fixed volatility. When volatility changes are negatively correlated with stock price changes, the reverse is true. Price increases reduce the volatility so that it is unlikely that very high stock prices will result. Price decreases increase volatility, increasing the chance of large positive price changes; very low prices become less likely. The net effect is that the terminal stock price distribution is more peaked than the usual lognormal distribution.

Table 4.2. Price bias as a percentage of the Black–Scholes price for varying values of s/x and correlation, ρ, between the volatility and the stock price; option parameters: $\sigma_0 = 15\%$, $r = 0$, $\xi = 1$, and $\mu = 0$

T (days)	ρ	S/X				
		0.90	0.95	1.00	1.05	1.10
90	−1.0	−66.06	−22.68	−2.13	1.84	1.56
		(1.98)	(0.51)	(0.23)	(0.12)	(0.08)
	−0.5	−31.55	−10.89	−1.62	0.91	0.89
		(1.14)	(0.32)	(0.13)	(0.07)	(0.04)
	0.0	3.72	−0.98	−0.92	−0.25	0.07
		(0.50)	(0.13)	(0.05)	(0.03)	(0.02)
	0.5	39.37	7.70	−0.53	−1.68	−0.85
		(1.12)	(0.28)	(0.12)	(0.07)	(0.04)
	1.0	72.24	15.62	−0.84	−3.12	−1.56
		(2.42)	(0.61)	(0.25)	(0.14)	(0.09)
180	−1.0	−56.22	−22.49	−4.77	0.94	1.79
		(1.23)	(0.55)	(0.31)	(0.21)	(0.15)
	−0.5	−25.96	−11.50	−2.93	0.27	1.29
		(0.80)	(0.35)	(0.20)	(0.13)	(0.09)
	0.0	0.63	−2.25	−1.87	−0.82	−0.09
		(0.42)	(0.17)	(0.09)	(0.06)	(0.04)
	0.5	24.04	5.30	−1.10	−2.57	−1.61
		(0.78)	(0.32)	(0.19)	(0.11)	(0.09)
	1.0	45.99	12.43	−1.11	−4.58	−4.05
		(1.69)	(0.77)	(0.40)	(0.27)	(0.18)
270	−1.0	−53.32	−23.12	−7.53	−0.20	2.01
		(1.11)	(0.58)	(0.39)	(0.28)	(0.21)
	−0.5	−25.33	−12.33	−5.29	−0.44	0.62
		(0.73)	(0.39)	(0.25)	(0.17)	(0.13)
	0.0	−1.88	−3.56	−2.45	−1.37	−0.52
		(0.40)	(0.21)	(0.14)	(0.09)	(0.07)
	0.5	17.87	4.36	−1.77	−2.81	−2.37
		(0.69)	(0.39)	(0.24)	(0.17)	(0.14)
	1.0	33.41	8.94	−1.09	−6.21	−5.07
		(1.64)	(0.87)	(0.55)	(0.34)	(0.26)

One phenomenon arising from these results might be called the time-to-maturity effect. If the time to maturity is increased with all else being held constant, the effect is the same as increasing both σ_t and ξ. Thus, longer term near-the-money options have a price that is lower (relative to the B–S price) than that of shorter term options. Because the B–S price is approximately linear with respect to volatility, these proportional price differences map into equivalent differences in implied volatilities. If the B–S equation is used to calculate implied volatilities, longer term near-the-money options will exhibit lower implied volatilities than shorter term options. This effect occurs whenever the B–S formula overprices the option. Table 4.3 shows the effects of changing terms on the implied volatilities for an option with an expected volatility of 15 percent, $\xi = 1$, $\mu = 0$, and $r = 0$ for different values of ρ and S/X. The time-to-maturity effect is clear. In the worst case, it changes the implied volatility by almost one half of 1 percent. The effect increases as ξ increases and as the initial volatility increases.

This time-to-maturity effect is counterintuitive. One might expect that uncertainty about the volatility would increase uncertainty about the stock price, hence raising the option price, and that longer times to maturity would exacerbate this. The actual result is just the opposite. Wherever the B–S formula overprices the

Table 4.3. Implied volatility calculated by Black–Scholes formula from the option prices given in Table 4.2; actual expected mean volatility 15%; option parameters: $\sigma_0 = 15\%$, $r = 0$, $\xi = 1$, and $\mu = 0$

T (days)	ρ	S/X				
		0.90	0.95	1.00	1.05	1.10
90	−1.0	11.94	13.38	14.68	15.69	16.63
		(0.13)	(0.04)	(0.03)	(0.04)	(0.08)
	−0.5	13.75	14.23	14.76	15.34	15.97
		(0.05)	(0.02)	(0.02)	(0.03)	(0.04)
	0.0	15.13	14.93	14.86	14.91	15.08
		(0.02)	(0.01)	(0.01)	(0.01)	(0.02)
	0.5	16.32	15.53	14.92	14.36	13.98
		(0.03)	(0.02)	(0.02)	(0.03)	(0.05)
	1.0	17.29	16.07	14.87	13.80	13.00
		(0.07)	(0.04)	(0.04)	(0.05)	(0.13)
180	−1.0	11.66	13.04	14.28	15.26	15.99
		(0.09)	(0.05)	(0.05)	(0.06)	(0.08)
	−0.5	13.59	14.01	14.56	15.08	15.72
		(0.05)	(0.03)	(0.03)	(0.04)	(0.05)
	0.0	15.03	14.81	14.72	14.77	14.94
		(0.02)	(0.01)	(0.01)	(0.02)	(0.02)
	0.5	16.20	15.45	14.83	14.27	14.06
		(0.04)	(0.03)	(0.03)	(0.03)	(0.05)
	1.0	17.23	16.05	14.83	13.70	12.50
		(0.08)	(0.06)	(0.06)	(0.08)	(0.13)
270	−1.0	11.38	12.79	13.87	14.95	15.85
		(0.09)	(0.06)	(0.06)	(0.07)	(0.09)
	−0.5	13.38	13.83	14.20	14.89	15.27
		(0.05)	(0.04)	(0.04)	(0.04)	(0.06)
	0.0	14.88	14.66	14.63	14.66	14.77
		(0.02)	(0.02)	(0.02)	(0.02)	(0.02)
	0.5	16.07	15.41	14.73	14.30	13.96
		(0.04)	(0.04)	(0.04)	(0.04)	(0.06)
	1.0	16.97	15.84	14.84	13.44	12.70
		(0.09)	(0.08)	(0.08)	(0.09)	(0.13)

option, it is due to the local concavity of the B–S price with respect to σ. Because of the concavity of the option price with respect to volatility, increases in volatility do not increase the option price as much as decreases in volatility decrease the price. Thus, the average of the B–S prices for a stochastic volatility with a given mean lies below the B–S price for a fixed volatility with the same mean for all near-the-money options. As the time to maturity increases, the variance of the stochastic volatility increases, exacerbating the effect of the curvature of the option price with respect to volatility. Wherever the B–S price underprices the option, the reverse effect is observed.

The implications of these results for empirical tests of option pricing are interesting. Rubinstein (1985) compared implied volatilities of matched pairs of options differing only in exercise price. In the period 1976–1977, he generally found that, as S/X increased, the implied volatility decreased. For the subsequent period 1977–1978, the reverse was true. Rubinstein also compared matched pairs of options differing only in time to maturity. He found that, in the 1976–1977 period, the shorter term options had higher implied volatilities for out-of-the-money options. For at-the-money and in-the-money options, the reverse is true.

In the period 1977–1978, almost all options exhibited the property that shorter term options had higher implied volatilities.

The observed implied volatility patterns in relation to S/X are consistent with a situation in which, during the 1976–1977 period, the volatility was positively correlated with the stock price, while, in the 1977–1978 period, the correlation was negative. However, the results from comparing implied volatilities across different times to maturity are not consistent with this. If the volatility were positively correlated with the stock price, we would expect out-of-the-money options to exhibit increasing implied volatility with increasing time to maturity.

It is difficult to draw direct comparisons between Rubinstein's results and our model. As suggested by equation (9), the key element is the relationship between the stock price and the present value of the exercise price. Thus, when Rubinstein chooses pairs matched on the basis of exercise price, they are not truly matched in the variable of interest, the present value of the exercise price. Figure 4.4 illustrates the price biases for different times to maturity for the case in which volatility is uncorrelated with the stock price and the risk-free rate is not zero. The net effect of the nonzero risk-free rate is to lower the effective exercise price of longer term options. Figure 4.4 shows that increasing the time to maturity raises the implied volatility for almost all options except the very deep in-the-money options, in which case the effect is very small. When the volatility is positively correlated with the stock price, the effect is to enhance the time-to-maturity effect for all but very deep out-of-the-money options. When the correlation is negative, the result is a reduction of the time-to-maturity effect for out-of-the-money options and an enhancement of the tendency to observe higher implied volatilities in long-term in-the-money options. This latter effect is, however, very small. Thus, overall, we might expect the time-to-maturity effect to be strongest for out-of-the-money options and weakest for in-the-money options. This is exactly what Rubinstein found.

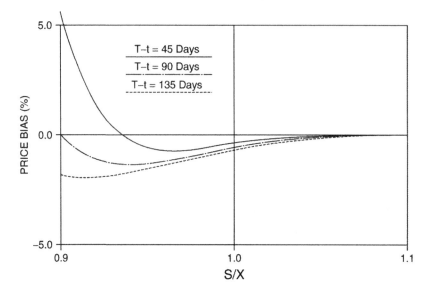

Fig. 4.4. Effect of varying $T - t$ When $\mu = 0$, $r = 10\%$, $\sigma_t = 15\%$, $\xi = 1$.

The results of Rubinstein may not be inconsistent with the model presented in this paper, but neither do they seem to provide strong support. In order for them to support this model, it is necessary to posit that, from one year to the next, the correlation between stock prices and the associated volatility reversed sign. It is difficult to think of a convincing reason why this event should occur. It is tempting to suggest that the observed effect may be a sampling result that can occur if some stocks have positive correlations and some have negative correlations. In this case, by changing the relative numbers of each group in the sample from period to period, we could see the observed result. Unfortunately, Rubinstein found that the result also prevailed on a security-by-security basis.

4.4 Conclusions

The general differential equation of Garman (1976) is used to derive a series solution for the price of a call option on a security with a stochastic volatility that is uncorrelated with the security price. It is shown for such a security that the Black–Scholes price overvalues at-the-money options and undervalues deep in- and out-of-the-money options. The range over which overpricing by the B–S formula takes place is for stock prices within about ten percent of the exercise price. The magnitude of the pricing bias can be up to 5 percent of the B–S price.

The case in which the volatility is correlated with the stock price is examined using numerical methods. When there is a positive correlation between the stock price and its volatility, out-of-the-money options are underpriced by the B–S formula, while in-the-money options are overpriced. When the correlation is negative, the effect is reversed. These results can be used to explain the empirical observations of Rubinstein (1985) but require the questionable assumption that the correlation between volatilities and stock prices reverses from one year to the next.

This paper has concentrated on the pricing of a European call option on a stock subject to a stochastic volatility. The results are directly transferable to European puts through the use of put-call parity. They are also transferable to American calls on non-dividend-paying stocks. This follows from Merton's (1973) results. The pricing of American puts, however, cannot be easily determined.

References

Black, F. and Scholes, M. (1973). The Pricing of Options and Corporate Liabilities. *Journal of Political Economy* 81, 637–59.

Boyle, P. P. and Emanuel, D. (1985). Mean Dependent Options. Working Paper, Accounting Group, University of Waterloo.

Cox, J. C., Ingersoll, J. E., and Ross, S. A. (1985). An Intertemporal General Equilibrium Model of Asset Prices. *Econometrica* 53, 363–84.

Cox, J. C. and Ross, S. A. (1976). The Valuation of Options for Alternative Stochastic Processes. *Journal of Financial Economics* 3, 145–66.

Eisenberg, L. (1985). Relative Pricing from No-Arbitrage Conditions: Random Variance Option Pricing. Working Paper, University of Illinois, Department of Finance.

Garman, M. (1976). A General Theory of Asset Valuation under Diffusion State Processes. Working Paper No. 50, University of California, Berkeley.

Geske, R. (1979). The Valuation of Compound Options. *Journal of Financial Economics* 7, 63–81.

Hammersley, J. M. and Handscomb, D. C. (1964). *Monte Carlo Methods*. London: Methuen.

Hull, J. C. and White, A. (1987). Hedging the Risks from Writing Foreign Currency Options. *Journal of International Money and Finance*, 6, 131–52.

Johnson, H. E. (1979). Option Pricing When the Variance Is Changing. Graduate School of Management Working Paper 11–79, University of California, Los Angeles.

——Shanno, D. (1985). Option Pricing When the Variance is Changing. Graduate School of Administration Working Paper 85–07, University of California, Davis.

Merton, R. C. (1973). The Theory of Rational Option Pricing. *Bell Journal of Economics and Management Science* 4, 141–83.

——(1976). Option Pricing When Underlying Stock Returns Are Discontinuous. *Journal of Financial Economics* 3, 125–44.

Rubinstein, M. (1985). Nonparametric Tests of Alternative Option Pricing Models Using All Reported Trades and Quotes on the 30 Most Active CBOE Option Classes from August 23, 1976 through August 31, 1978. *Journal of Finance* 40, 455–80.

Scott, L. O. (1986). Option Pricing When the Variance Changes Randomly: Theory and an Application. Working Paper, University of Illinois, Department of Finance.

Wiggins, J. B. (1985). Stochastic Variance Option Pricing. Sloan School of Management, Massachusetts Institute of Technology.

5

The Dynamics of Exchange Rate Volatility: A Multivariate Latent Factor Arch Model*

FRANCIS X. DIEBOLD AND
MARC NERLOVE

Summary

We study temporal volatility patterns in seven nominal dollar spot exchange rates, all of which display strong evidence of autoregressive conditional heteroskedasticity (ARCH). We first formulate and estimate univariate models, the results of which are subsequently used to guide specification of a multivariate model. The key element of our multivariate approach is exploitation of factor structure, which facilitates tractable estimation via a substantial reduction in the number of parameters to be estimated. Such a latent-variable model is shown to provide a good description of multivariate exchange rate movements: the ARCH effects capture volatility clustering, and the factor structure captures commonality in volatility movements across exchange rates.

5.1 Introduction

In this paper we specify and estimate a multivariate time-series model with an underlying latent variable whose innovations display autoregressive conditional heteroskedasticity (ARCH). Various aspects of this factor-analytic approach are sketched in Diebold (1986) and Diebold and Nerlove (1987); here we provide a more complete exposition, propose a new estimation procedure, and present a detailed substantive application to movements in seven major dollar spot exchange rates. To guide multivariate specification, we begin with a univariate analysis and relate the results to apparent random walk behaviour, leptokurtic unconditional distributions and convergence to normality under temporal aggregation.

The univariate results point to the need for a multivariate specification, but multivariate ARCH modelling is difficult, due to the large number of parameters which must be estimated. We therefore propose a multivariate latent-variable model in which the common factor displays ARCH. The conditional variance–covariance structure of the observed variables arises from joint dependence on a common factor; this leads to common volatility movements across rates, which are in fact observed.

The plan of the paper is as follows. In Section 5.2 we discuss economic issues related to non-constant exchange rate volatility, and we underscore the importance of subsequent ARCH findings. In Section 5.3 we briefly report the results of univariate analyses, focusing on unit roots and ARCH effects. The multivariate model with factor structure is specified, estimated, and compared to the univariate models in Section 5.4. Section 5.5 concludes.

5.2 Non-constant exchange rate volatility

The difficulty of explaining exchange rate movements during the post-1973 float with purchasing power parity, monetary, or portfolio balance models has become increasingly apparent. Meese and Rogoff (1983*a*, *b*) systematically document the out-of-sample empirical failure of these models, and they find that a simple random-walk model predicts the major rates during the floating period as well as (or better than) any of the alternatives, including a flexible price monetary model (Frenkel, 1976; Bilson, 1979), a sticky price monetary model (Dornbusch, 1976; Frankel, 1979), a sticky price monetary model with current account effects (Hooper and Morton, 1982), six univariate time-series models, a vector autoregressive model, and the forward rate.

In this paper we study seven major dollar spot rates: the Canadian dollar (CD), French franc (FF), Deutschemark (DM), Italian lira (LIR), Japanese yen (YEN), Swiss franc (SF), and British pound (BP). We find that, in the class of linear time-series models, the random walk is a very good approximation to the underlying conditional mean process; therefore we would not expect other linear models to dominate in terms of predictive performance. However, when the class of models under consideration is broadened to allow for possible nonlinearities, we find strong evidence of ARCH (Engle, 1982) in the one step ahead prediction errors, so that the disturbances in the 'random walk' are uncorrelated but not independent.

The finding of ARCH in exchange rates is important. First, ARCH provides a way of formalizing the observation that large changes tend to be followed by large changes (of either sign), and small by small, leading to contiguous periods of volatility and stability. Such temporal clustering of prediction error variances has been well documented in pioneering work on stochastic processes for financial assets, such as Mandelbrot (1963) and Fama (1965), and is visually apparent in exchange rate movements. Second, ARCH effects are consistent with the unconditional leptokurtosis in exchange rate changes documented by Westerfield (1977) and Boothe and Glassman (1987).[1] Finally, under mild regularity conditions, ARCH effects vanish under temporal aggregation as convergence to

---

[1] Detailed characterizations of the conditional and unconditional moment structures of ARCH processes are provided by Engle (1982) and Milhoj (1986).

unconditional normality occurs.[2] This phenomenon has been observed by Fama (1976) and Boothe and Glassman (1987), and cannot be explained by the commonly used return-generating models in the stable family.

We also show that ARCH models may be used to generate statistically and economically meaningful measures of exchange rate volatility. The nature, time pattern, and economic effects of exchange rate volatility are recurrent topics in the literature. Volatility of exchange rates is of importance because of the uncertainty it creates for prices of exports and imports, for the value of international reserves and for open positions in foreign currency, as well as for the domestic currency value of debt payments and workers' remittances, which in turn affect domestic wages, prices, output, and employment. Under risk-aversion, risk premia form a wedge in arbitrage conditions (such as uncovered interest parity) and may therefore influence the determination of spot exchange rates. Such risk premia depend on the dispersion of the distribution of future spot rates, which varies over time. ARCH effects (if present), provide a parsimonious description of such an evolving conditional variance. By estimating an appropriate ARCH model we can solve for the implied time-series of conditional variances, and thus obtain a meaningful measure of volatility for that rate.

Finally, a finding of random walks with ARCH disturbances means that, although a particular exchange rate change cannot be forecast, its changing variance can be forecast. Thus, ARCH may be exploited to obtain time-varying confidence intervals for point forecasts of exchange rate changes (zero for a random-walk model), and hence is naturally suited to the modelling of time-varying risk premia. In periods of high volatility these intervals are large, and in less volatile periods they are smaller. This stands in marked contrast to the standard constant variance random-walk model, which ignores the changing environment in which forecasts are produced and the associated temporal movements in forecast error variances.

5.3 Univariate analysis

We study weekly spot rates from the first week of July 1973 to the second week of August 1985.[3] All data are seasonally unadjusted interbank closing spot prices (bid side), Wednesdays, taken from the *International Monetary Markets Yearbook*. Wednesdays were chosen because very few holidays occur on that day, and there is no problem of weekend effects.

In our sample 632 observations, fewer than eight holidays occurred on a Wednesday; when they did, the observation for the following Thursday was

---

[2] This is shown by Diebold (1988), who obtains the result by applying a central limit theorem for dependent, identically distributed, random variables due to White (1984).

[3] Detailed univariate results are contained in Diebold (1988).

used. The use of point-in-time data avoids the introduction of spurious serial correlation via the Working (1960) effect. Following standard convention, all exchange rates except the pound are measured in units of local currency per dollar. We work with log spot rates; the log specification avoids prediction problems arising from Jensen's inequality (Meese and Rogoff, 1983a) and $(1 - L) \ln S_t$ has the convenient interpretation of approximate percentage change.[4]

We now proceed to consider conditional mean specification. A visual inspection indicated nonstationarity in each of the series. (The DM/\$ rate, which together with the BP/\$ rate will be used for illustration, is shown in Figure 5.1.) The sample autocorrelation functions were calculated for each series up to lag 40, and clearly indicated homogeneous nonstationarity, as evidenced by the fact that all were positive, failed to damp, and had very smooth, persistent movements. Even the YEN, whose autocorrelation function declined the most quickly, had a sample autocorrelation of 0·848 at lag 20.

The sample partial autocorrelation functions were also calculated for each of the seven exchange rates, and the results were qualitatively the same for each series: each had a very large and highly significant value (extremely close to one) at lag 1, while the values at all other lags were insignificantly different from zero. Specifically, the lag 1 sample partial autocorrelations for the CD, FF, DM, LIR,

Fig. 5.1. Log DM/\$ rate.

---

[4] Throughout this paper, the generic notation S_t denotes an exchange rate at time t.

YEN, SF, BP were, respectively, 0·99, 1·00, 1·00, 1·00, 1·00, 1·00, and 0·99. Thus, the distinct cutoff in the sample partial autocorrelation functions after lag 1, the smooth and slowly declining behaviour of the sample autocorrelation functions, and the values of the highly significant first sample partial autocorrelation strongly suggested first-order homogeneous nonstationarity in general, and the random walk in particular, for each series.

This preliminary evidence was supported by a battery of formal unit root tests. Solo's (1984) test is a Lagrange multiplier (LM) test for unit roots in general ARMA models; since it is an LM test, it requires estimates only under the null of a unit root. We therefore began by differencing the series and formulating appropriate models. However, use of model selection procedures such as Akaike's (1974) and Schwarz's (1978) information criteria (AIC and SIC, respectively), as well as visual inspection of the sample autocorrelation functions, revealed no evidence of a moving average component in any of the seven $(1 - L) \ln S_t$ series. The simpler Dickey–Fuller test for unit roots in autoregressive series (Dickey, 1976; Fuller, 1976) was therefore employed, allowing for high-order autoregressive lag operator polynomials, as well as trend under the alternative.[5] The test amounts to regressing $(1 - L) \ln S_t$ on an intercept, trend term, $\ln S_{t-1}$, and lags of $(1 - L) \ln S_t$, and testing the 't-statistic' on $\ln S_{t-1}$ against the appropriate null distribution, tabulated in Fuller (1976) as τ_τ, which is *not* Student's t.

The results of τ_τ tests for unit roots in AR(7) representations are given in Table 5.1. The basic message is clear: we consistently fail to reject the unit root null. In addition, the small magnitude and general statistical insignificance of the coefficients on lagged $\Delta \ln S_t$ values (not shown) indicated very little serial correlation in any of the first-differenced series. The Hasza–Fuller (1979) joint test of the null hypothesis of two unit roots (with trend allowed under the alternative) is also shown in Table 5.1. The results are given in the column labelled 'HF$_\tau$'. We

Table 5.1. Test for unit root in ln S, trend allowed under the alternative

Currency	τ_τ	HF$_\tau$
CD	−2.74	31.40[***]
FF	−1.16	30.90[***]
DM	−1.12	28.34[***]
LIR	−1.47	26.71[***]
YEN	−1.86	22.84[***]
SF	−1.26	24.49[***]
BP	−1.33	23.70[***]

The symbols *, **, and *** respectively denote significance at the 10, 5, and 2 per cent levels. Tests are for unit root(s) in an AR(7) representation, allowing for trend under the alternative, τ_τ is the Dickey–Fuller test for a single unit root, and HF$_\tau$ is the Hasza–Fuller joint test for two unit roots.

---

[5] This class of tests has recently been shown by Schwert (1987*a*, *b*) to perform quite well, even under misspecification of the ARMA representation.

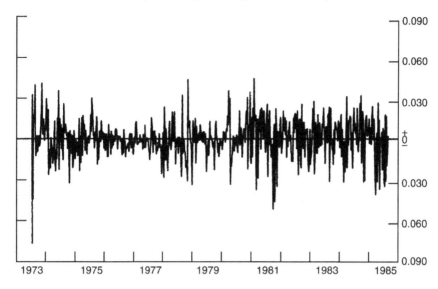

Fig. 5.2. Change in log DM/$ rate.

reject the null conclusively for each rate, confirming the result of one, and only one, unit root in each series.[6]

Visual inspection of the $\Delta \ln S$ series revealed no evidence of serial correlation, although there did seem to be persistence in the conditional variances, as we discuss in detail below. Such effects are evident in the plot of $\Delta \ln S_{DM}$ given in Figure 5.2. The sample autocorrelations were calculated for each $\Delta \ln S$ series up to lag 40, and in each case they strongly indicated white noise, as did the sample partial autocorrelation functions. (Allowance for the possible presence of ARCH only strengthens the conclusions, as shown in Diebold, 1988.) As a conservative safeguard against specification error, however, the models estimated subsequently make use of AR(3) conditional mean representations, in order to account for any weak serial correlation that might be present.

Finally, in order to assess the distributional properties of the $\Delta \ln S$ series, various descriptive statistics are reported in Table 5.2, including mean, variance, standard deviation, skewness, kurtosis, the Kiefer–Salmon (1983) Lagrange multiplier normality test, and a variety of order statistics. Included among the order statistics is the studentized range, which may also be used to test normality. In particular, the hypothesis of normality is rejected for each exchange rate, whether the studentized range test or the Kiefer–Salmon test is used. Further evidence on the nature of deviations from normality may be gleaned from the sample skewness and kurtosis measures. While skewness of each series is always

---

[6] In addition, Pantula (1985) has shown that the asymptotic distribution of the Dickey–Fuller test statistic is invariant to ARCH. This convenient property does not hold for standard tests of stationary serial correlation; see Domowitz and Hakkio (1983) and Diebold (1988).

Table 5.2. Weekly nominal dollar spot rates, test statistics, $\Delta \ln S$

Statistic	CD	FF	DM	LIR	YEN	SF	BP
Mean (μ)	0.00049	0.00126	0.00034	0.00189	-0.00017	-0.00024	-0.00104
t(μ = 0)	2.35**	2.28**	0.61	3.77***	-0.33	-0.37	-1.92*
Variance	0.00003	0.00019	0.00019	0.00016	0.00016	0.00027	0.00018
Std. Dev.	0.00526	0.01390	0.01381	0.01260	0.01276	0.01640	0.01360
Skewness	0.56098	0.26069	-0.08594	0.44196	-0.21592	-0.1072	0.34407
Kurtosis	4.70565	2.53659	1.23452	3.08811	3.26364	1.495	3.2979
KS	633.61***	178.99***	38.97***	1667.12***	280.55***	58.74***	268.34***
KS1	31.90***	6.86***	0.77	18.54***	4.88**	1.20	12.24***
KS2	601.71***	172.13***	38.20***	1648.58***	275.67***	57.54***	256.1***
Maximum	0.03754	0.07478	0.05776	0.09679	0.06980	0.06616	0.07246
Q3	0.00309	0.00788	0.00826	0.00725	0.00641	0.00892	0.00543
Median	0.00067	0.00070	0.00050	0.00061	0.00030	0.00039	-0.00058
Q1	-0.00240	-0.00545	-0.00732	-0.00373	-0.00520	-0.00872	-0.00839
Minimum	-0.01762	-0.04583	-0.04839	-0.07490	-0.05671	-0.05421	-0.05322
Mode	0	0	0	0	0	0	0
SR	10.49***	8.68***	7.69***	13.63***	9.91***	7.34***	9.24***

KS = Kiefer–Salmon normality test, decomposed into KS1 (skewness test) and KS2 (kurtosis test).
Q3 = Third quartile.
Q1 = First quartile.
SR = Studentized range.
Significance levels: * = 10 per cent, ** = 5 per cent, *** = 1 per cent.

very close to zero, the kurtosis is very large, ranging from 1.23 for the DM to 8.09 for the LIR.[7] In addition, the Kiefer–Salmon Lagrange multiplier statistic, distributed as χ_2^2 under the null of normality, may be decomposed into two asymptotically independent χ_1^2 variates, the first being an LM test for normal skewness and the second an LM test for normal kurtosis. These show that most of the non-normality in each series is due to leptokurtosis.

We have seen that the conditional mean of each exchange rate is, to a close approximation, linearly unpredictable; however, this need not be true for the conditional variances. The ARCH model of Engle (1982) is particularly relevant in the time-series context.[8] Suppose that:

$$\varepsilon_t | \varepsilon_{t-1}, \ldots, \varepsilon_{t-p} \sim N(0, \sigma_t^2), \tag{1}$$

$$\sigma_t^2 = f(\varepsilon_{t-1}, \ldots, \varepsilon_{t-p}), \tag{2}$$

where

$$\varepsilon_t = \Delta \ln S_t - \sum_{k=1}^{3} \rho_k \Delta \ln S_{t-k}.$$

Throughout this paper we adopt the following natural parameterization:

$$\sigma_t^2 = \alpha_0 + \sum_{i=1}^{p} \alpha_t \varepsilon_{t-i}^2, \tag{3}$$

where $\alpha_0 > 0$, $\alpha_i \geqslant 0$, $i = 1, \ldots, p$. The conditional variance of ε_t is allowed to vary over time as a linear function of past squared realizations. In the expected value sense, then, today's variability depends linearly on yesterday's variability, so that large changes tend to be followed by large changes, and small by small, or either sign. The ARCH model formalizes this phenomenon and enables us to test for it rigorously.

Estimation and hypothesis testing for the ARCH model have been treated by Engle (1982) and Weiss (1985). The log-likelihood function is:

$$\ln L(\rho, \alpha; \Delta \ln S) = \text{const} - \sum_{t=1}^{T} \ln \sigma_t - \frac{1}{2} \sum_{t=1}^{T} \frac{\varepsilon_t^2}{\sigma_t^2}. \tag{4}$$

The simplicity of $\ln L$ under the null of no ARCH makes the Lagrange multiplier test extremely attractive. Because of the large sample size we used the TR^2 version given in Engle (1982), which indicated strong ARCH effects. Information criteria

---

[7] Throughout this paper, 'kurtosis' refers to excess kurtosis, so that a value of zero corresponds to normality.

[8] See also Hsieh (1988), Bollerslev (1987a) and Milhoj (1987) for variations on this theme, with particular attention to the modelling of asset price movements.

were used to determine appropriate order; in no case did we identify an order greater than twelve. We therefore estimated ARCH(12) models for each series.

In addition, it may be argued on a priori grounds that the α_i, $i = 1, \ldots, p$ should be monotonically decreasing. This follows from the basic intuition of the ARCH model, which is that high volatility 'today' tends to be followed by similar volatility 'tomorrow' and vice-versa. In this spirit it is unreasonable to let a squared innovation from the distant past have a greater effect on current conditional variance than a squared innovation from the recent past. This intuition may be enforced by restricting the α_i, $i = 1, \ldots, p$ to be linearly decreasing:

$$\sigma_t^2 | \Psi_{t-1} = \alpha_0 + \theta[p\varepsilon_{t-1}^2 + (p-1)\varepsilon_{t-2}^2 + \ldots + \varepsilon_{t-p}^2]. \tag{5}$$

$$\Psi_{t-1} = \{\varepsilon_{t-1}, \ldots, \varepsilon_{t-p}\}. \tag{6}$$

The estimates of the linearly constrained ARCH models are given in Table 5.3, along with the maximized log-likelihoods, iterations to convergence, the sum of the $\hat{\alpha}_i$, and the unconditional variance.[9] The estimated models are third-order AR representations (with allowance for a non-zero mean) with twelfth-order linearly constrained ARCH disturbances:

$$(1 - \rho_1 L - \rho_2 L^2 - \rho_3 L^3)\Delta \ln S_t = \mu + \varepsilon_t,$$
$$\varepsilon_t | \varepsilon_{t-1}, \ldots, \varepsilon_{t-12} \sim N(0, \sigma_t^2), \tag{7}$$
$$\sigma_t^2 = \alpha_0 + \theta \sum_{i=1}^{12} (13 - i)\varepsilon_{t-i}^2.$$

As expected, the intercept and AR parameters are often insignificant and always very small, while the ARCH parameters are highly significant and of substantial magnitude. The conditional mean intercept term is insignificant for all exchange rates. All but two of the 21 autoregressive lag coefficients for the seven currencies are positive, all are very small, and most are insignificant, as expected. Convergence was obtained for each exchange rate in no more than 13 iterations of Davidon–Fletcher–Powell, and the log-likelihoods were noticeably single-peaked, leading to the same parameter estimates for a variety of startup values.[10]

The estimated conditional variances are easily obtained. We begin with the estimated disturbances:

$$\hat{\varepsilon}_{jt} = \Delta \ln S_{jt} - \text{const}_j - \hat{\rho}_{1j}\Delta \ln S_{j,t-1} - \hat{\rho}_{2j}\Delta \ln S_{j,t-2} - \hat{\rho}_{3j}\Delta \ln S_{j,t-3}, \tag{8}$$

for $j = $ CD, FF, DM, LIR, YEN, SF, BP. The estimated conditional variance is then given by:

---

[9] For conformity with subsequent results, the reported maximized log-likelihoods are for $1000\Delta \ln S$.

[10] The first 12 observations are used as initial conditions for the conditional variance. The point likelihoods are therefore summed over $t = 13, \ldots, T$ to construct the sample likelihood.

Table 5.3. Weekly nominal dollar spot rates, ARCH model estimates

	CD	FF	DM	LIR	YEN	SF	BP
μ	0.00029	0.00077	-0.00016	0.00065	-0.00021	-0.00023	-0.00088
	(1.48)	(1.61)	(-0.33)	(2.10)*	(-0.46)	(-0.42)	(-1.81)*
ρ_1	0.12436	0.06323	0.09167	0.06318	0.05542	0.06323	0.05452
	(2.81)***	(1.48)	(2.20)**	(1.49)	(1.22)	(1.49)	(1.24)
ρ_2	0.07845	0.09044	0.07200	0.06785	0.07959	0.03115	0.03981
	(1.81)*	(2.11)**	(1.71)*	(1.52)	(1.77)*	(0.72)	(0.90)
ρ_3	-0.02651	0.05090	-0.00239	0.06138	0.08140	0.02060	0.04679
	(-0.60)	(1.21)	(-0.06)	(1.38)	(1.78)*	(0.48)	(1.06)
$\sqrt{\alpha_0}$	0.00364	0.00797	0.00731	0.00367	0.00803	0.00761	0.00800
	(11.90)***	(10.12)***	(8.69)***	(6.27)***	(13.72)***	(7.20)***	(13.65)***
$\sqrt{\theta}$	0.08372	0.09664	0.09912	0.12287	0.09184	0.10505	0.09430
	(10.00)***	(12.97)***	(13.72)***	(20.37)***	(13.89)***	(14.96)***	(15.74)***
iterations	12	12	11	12	11	11	11
ln L	-1310.10	-1887.00	-1880.24	-1765.71	-1845.78	-1976.72	-1871.15
$\Sigma\alpha_i$	0.547	0.728	0.766	1.178	0.658	0.861	0.694
$\alpha_0/(1-\Sigma\alpha_i)$	0.000029	0.000234	0.000228	NA	0.000189	0.000417	0.000209

Significance levels: * = 10 per cent, ** = 5 per cent, *** = 1 per cent.

$$\hat{\sigma}_{jt}^2 = \hat{\alpha}_{0j} + \hat{\theta} \sum_{i=1}^{12} (13 - i)\hat{\varepsilon}_{j,\,t-i}^2, \tag{9}$$

$j = $ CD, FF, DM, LIR, YEN, SF, BP. The estimated DM/\$ and \$/BP conditional standard deviations for linear ARCH(12) models are shown in Figures 5.3 and 5.4, respectively.[11]

While there are substantial 'own-country' effects in the movements of the conditional variances of each of the seven rates, similarities in the qualitative conditional variance movements are apparent. There is a tendency towards high conditional variance in the very early part of the float, perhaps due to the uncertainty created by the 70 per cent increase in the posted price of Arabian crude oil of October 1973, and the additional 100 per cent increase in December 1973. Towards the middle of the 1970s we see generally smaller conditional variances as gloomy economic news translates into relatively smooth dollar depreciation, culminating in the historic lows achieved against the DM, YEN and other major currencies on 29 December 1977. The year 1978, particularly the latter part, brings a return of higher volatility, as large intervention efforts by the Federal Reserve and the Treasury begin to turn the dollar around. Another period of very high conditional variances arises in mid-1981, as interest rates in the 20 per cent range brought the dollar to new highs against the major European currencies. The CD also reached a post-1981 low on 31 July, closing at 80·9 US

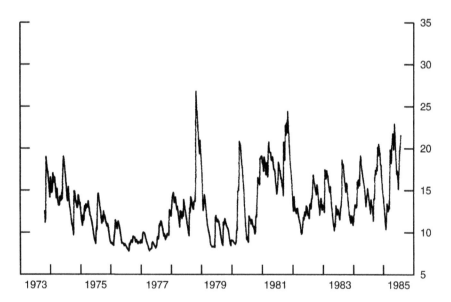

Fig. 5.3. Conditional standard deviation, DM, univariate model.

[11] For conformity with subsequent multivariate results, the conditional standard deviations displayed are those of $1000\,\Delta \ln S_t$.

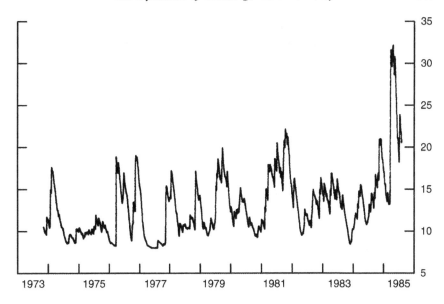

Fig. 5.4. Conditional standard deviation, BP, univariate model.

cents. As inflation subsided, so too did exchange rate volatility, but it did begin to grow again towards the end of the sample.

5.4 A multivariate model with factor structure

While the univariate ARCH models estimated above offer good statistical descriptions of exchange rate movements, they are not satisfying relative to a full multivariate model. They do, however, provide useful guidance for multivariate specification. The move to a multivariate framework is important for a number of reasons. First, non-zero covariances among exchange rate innovations require simultaneous multivariate estimation if full efficiency is to be achieved. In the present case of vector exchange rate modelling, all rates are bilateral dollar rates, which makes zero innovation covariances very unlikely. The portfolio-balance approach to exchange rates implies such covariation, because new information coming to the market (regarding the state of the US economy, for example) affects *all* dollar rates, as agents' asset demands shift and portfolios are rebalanced.

Second, the conditional covariances may not be constant. Specifically, they may display temporal persistence, exactly like the conditional variances. If this is found to be the case, examination of the time-paths of conditional covariances may provide useful information. As noted by Bollerslev (1987*b*), for example, risk premia in asset pricing models depend either on the covariation among asset prices or the covariation among marginal rates of substitution; in general, we do not expect such risk premia to be time-invariant.

Third, further insight into the nature of exchange rate interaction may be gained via multivariate parameterization motivated by latent variable considerations. The role of 'news' in the determination of exchange rate movements (Frenkel, 1981) suggests not only correlation among exchange rate shocks, but also commonality in the conditional variance movements of the shocks (regardless of correlation), as all exchange rates react to the arrival of new information. In such a model, movements in each exchange rate may be ascribed to an underlying factor representing news (common across all rates) upon which country-specific shocks are superimposed. In short, a common factor approach has a strong substantive motivation that simultaneously produces a parsimonious variance–covariance structure.

Consider first the multivariate model of Kraft and Engle (1982), which is a direct generalization of the earlier univariate model, except that the temporal evolution of an entire variance–covariance matrix is now modelled. If Ψ_{t-1} is an information set containing:

$$\{\varepsilon_{j,\ t-1}, \ \ldots, \ \varepsilon_{j,\ t-p}\}, \ j = 1, \ \ldots, \ N, \tag{10}$$

then the N-variate ARCH(p) exchange rate system is given by:

$$\varepsilon_t | \Psi_{t-1} \sim N(0, \ H_t(\Psi_{t-1})), \tag{11}$$

where $\varepsilon_t = (\varepsilon_{1t}, \ \ldots, \ \varepsilon_{Nt})'$. H_t is an $(N \times N)$ symmetric positive definite conditional variance–covariance matrix, where:

$$H_{ij,\ t} = \alpha_{ij,\ 0} + \varepsilon_{t-1}' C_{1,\ ij}\varepsilon_{t-1} + \ldots + \varepsilon_{t-p}' C_{p,\ ij}\varepsilon_{t-p}. \tag{12}$$

Each element of H_t is therefore a sum of quadrature forms in $\varepsilon_{t-1}, \ \ldots, \ \varepsilon_{t-p}$, and depends on the pth-order past histories of all innovation squares and cross-products. The full variance–covariance matrix may then be assembled as:

$$H_t = H_0 + (I \otimes \varepsilon_{t-1})' C_1 (I \otimes \varepsilon_{t-1}) + \ldots + (I \otimes \varepsilon_{t-p})' C_p (I \otimes \varepsilon_{t-p}), \tag{13}$$

where C_k is an $(N^2 \times N^2)$ matrix with $(N \times N)$ blocks $C_{k,\ ij}$. It will be convenient for our purposes to vectorize the lower triangle of H_t and write:

$$h_t = a_0 + A_1 \eta_{t-1} + \ldots + A_p \eta_{t-p}, \tag{14}$$

where:

$$h_t = \text{vec}(\text{LT}(H_t)),$$

$$\dim(h_t) = \dim(a_0) = \dim(\eta_{t-i}) = \frac{N^2 + N}{2}, \ i = 1, \ \ldots, \ p$$

$$\dim(A_t) = \left(\frac{N^2 + N}{2} \times \frac{N^2 + N}{2}\right), \ i = 1, \ \ldots, \ p.$$

The operators 'vec', 'dim', and 'LT' are the vectorization, dimension, and lower triangle operators, respectively, and the vector η_{t-i} contains all squared innovations and innovation cross-products at lag i.

Consistent, asymptotically efficient and normal parameter estimates are obtained by maximizing the log-likelihood, which is a direct multivariate analogue of the univariate case. The point log-likelihoods are given by

$$\ln L_t = -(N/2)\ln 2\pi + 1/2\ln|H_t^{-1}| - \frac{1}{2}\varepsilon_t' H_t^{-1}\varepsilon_t, \tag{15}$$

and the likelihood for the sample is the sum of the point likelihoods.

The model developed thus far has

$$K = \frac{(N^2 + N)}{2} + p\frac{(N^2 + N)^2}{2}$$

parameters to be estimated. For a seven-variable ARCH(12) exchange rate system, $K = 9536$! Our task, then, is to impose various restrictions designed to reduce the number of free parameters, while simultaneously not imposing too much prior information on the data.

The system as written above allows each conditional variance and covariance to depend on p lags of the squared innovations and innovation cross-products of every exchange rate in the system. A more manageable and intuitively reasonable parameterization is obtained by allowing each conditional variance to depend only on own lagged squared innovations and each conditional covariance to depend only on own lagged innovation cross-products. This corresponds to diagonal A matrices, and it reduces the number of parameters by two orders of magnitude, since we now have only

$$K = \frac{N^2 + N}{2} + p\frac{(N^2 + N)}{2}$$

parameters to estimate. For $N = 7$ and $p = 12$, $K = 364$, which is still too large a number to handle.

Fortunately, however, we may use the results of section 3, in which we argued for a linearly decreasing ARCH lag weight structure, to provide further parametric economy. We retain $A_i = \text{diag}$, $i = 1, \ldots, p$, but we now require that A_i be a scalar matrix with diagonal elements $(p - i + 1)$, $i = 1, \ldots, p$, and we write:

$$h_t = a_0 + M(A_1\eta_{t-1} + \ldots + A_p\eta_{t-p}), \tag{16}$$

where M is an

$$\left(\frac{N^2 + N}{2} \times \frac{N^2 + N}{2}\right)$$

diagonal matrix. Rewrite the system as:

$$h_t = a_0 + M \sum_{i=1}^{p} (p - i + 1)\eta_{t-i}. \tag{17}$$

This leads to $K = (N^2 + N)$ parameters to be estimated, which for our seven-variate ARCH(12) exchange rate system is 56. This is still a very large number of parameters; in addition, such a specification cannot account for the fact that substantial commonality appears to exist in exchange rate volatility movements.

A factor analytic approach enables us to simultaneously address both problems. Consider the seven-variate system:

$$\begin{array}{cccc} \varepsilon_t & \lambda & F_t & e_t \\ (7 \times 1) & = (7 \times 1)(1 \times 1) & + (7 \times 1), \end{array} \tag{18}$$

where:

$$E(F_t) = E(e_{jt}) = 0, \text{ for all } j \text{ and } t,$$
$$E(F_t F_t') = 0, \ t \text{ not equal to } t',$$
$$E(F_t e_{jt'}) = 0 \text{ for all } j, \ t, \ t',$$
$$E(e_{jt} e_{kt'}) = \begin{bmatrix} \gamma_j, & \text{if } j = k, \ t = t' \\ 0 & \text{otherwise} \end{bmatrix}$$

(All expectations are understood to be conditional.) If in addition:

$$F_t / F_{t-1}, \ \ldots, \ F_{t-12} \sim N(0, \ \sigma_t^2), \tag{19}$$

$$\sigma_t^2 = \alpha_0 + \theta \sum_{i=1}^{12} (13 - i) F_{t-i}^2, \tag{20}$$

then it follows that:

$$H_t = \sigma_t^2 \lambda \lambda' + \Gamma, \tag{21}$$

where $\Gamma = \text{cov}(e_t)$. Thus, the jth time-t conditional variance is given by:

$$H_{jjt} = (\lambda_j^2 \alpha_0 + \gamma_J) + \lambda_j^2 \theta \sum_{i=1}^{12} (13 - i) F_{t-i}^2, \tag{22}$$

and the jkth time-t conditional covariance is:

$$H_{jkt} = (\lambda_j \lambda_k \alpha_0) + \lambda_j \lambda_k \theta \sum_{i=1}^{12} (13 - i) F_{t-i}^2. \tag{23}$$

The intuitive motivation of such a model is strong. The common factor F represents general influences which tend to affect all exchange rates. The impact of the common factor on exchange rate j is reflected in the value λ_j. The 'unique factors', represented by the e_j, reflect uncorrelated country-specific shocks. The conditional variance–covariance structure (H_t) of the observed variables arises from their joint dependence on the common factor F. All conditional variance and covariance functions depend on the common movements of F. The parameters of those functions are different, however, depending on the λ and γ values.

Before beginning the empirical analysis, all data are multiplied by 1000, to help avoid the formation of non-positive definite point conditional covariance matrices (H_t) while iterating. It is of interest to note that such rescaling changes only the intercept parameters in the ARCH variance and covariance equations. In particular, multiplying all data by a constant K multiplies all intercepts by K^2. This result enables judicious choice of start-up values for multivariate ARCH estimation. In addition, we take:

$$\varepsilon_{jt} = \Delta \ln S_{jt} - \text{const}_j - \hat{\rho}_{1j}\Delta \ln S_{j,t-1} - \cdots - \hat{\rho}_{3j}\Delta \ln S_{J,t-3}, \qquad (24)$$

$j = \text{CD}, \ldots, \text{BP}$, where the parameter estimates are as given in Table 5.3. Such conditioning on the univariate ARCH conditional mean parameter estimates is necessary for numerical tractability.

We begin by discussing a preliminary two-step estimation and testing procedure, and then we discuss simultaneous parameter estimation using a Kalman filter. In the first step of the two-step procedure we factor the unconditional covariance matrix and extract a time series of latent factor values $\{\hat{F}_t\}$. In the second step we test for and model ARCH effects in the extracted factor. In this way preliminary estimates of the model parameters λ_j, γ_j, $(j = \text{CD}, \ldots, \text{BP})$, as well as α_0 and θ, are obtained, which are subsequently used as start-up values for simultaneous estimation.

First, we factor the unconditional covariance matrix, which we denote by H. Without loss of generality, we set the unconditional variance (denoted σ^2) of the common factor to unity, to establish the factor's scale. Then:

Table 5.4.

	CD	FF	DM	LIR	YEN	SF	BP
CD	1.00000	—	—	—	—	—	—
FF	0.27662	1.00000	—	—	—	—	—
DM	0.25856	0.81059	1.00000	—	—	—	—
LIR	0.19834	0.65705	0.64533	1.00000	—	—	—
YEN	0.09878	0.49253	0.52593	0.41756	1.00000	—	—
SF	0.22164	0.70914	0.82814	0.55323	0.53976	1.00000	—
BP	−0.24631	−0.59277	−0.60461	−0.47431	−0.37155	−0.53196	1.00000

$$H = \lambda\lambda' + \Gamma. \tag{25}$$

There are 14 parameters to be estimated (7λ and 7γ) from 28 independent covariance equations. This is necessary, but not sufficient, for identification. The Joreskog (1979) sufficient conditions for identification are also satisfied, however, since $\sigma^2 = 1$ and Γ is diagonal. We next obtain estimates of the λ and γ values, as well as an extracted time series of factor values $\{\hat{F}_t\}$.[12] The correlation matrix of the ε vector is as shown in table 5.4, which indicates strong cross-equation interaction. The eigenvalues of this matrix are 4·06, 0·94, 0·62, 0·53, 0·46, 0·26, 0·14, indicating the presence of one strong common factor, corresponding to the large maximum eigenvalue of 4·06. The estimated (λ_j, γ_j) pairs are (1·47, 25·14), (11·70, 47·87), (12·84, 19·48), (8·66, 80·44), (7·27, 107·47), (13·94, 69·59), ($-8·82$, 106·96), for the CD, FF, DM, LIR, YEN, SF, and BP, respectively.[13]

Second, we test for the model ARCH effects in $\{\hat{F}_t\}$. The Lagrange multiplier test statistic for white noise against an ARCH(12) alternative has a value of 53·01, which is highly significant. We therefore replace σ^2 with:

$$\sigma_t^2 = \alpha_0 + \theta \sum_{t=1}^{12} (13 - i)\hat{F}_{t-i}^2. \tag{26}$$

The unconditional variance is still normalized to unity, by imposing the restriction $\theta = (1 - \alpha_0)/78$. We then obtain the second-step estimates of α_0 and θ, as with the earlier univariate estimates, conditional upon the extracted factor $\{\hat{F}_t\}$. Convergence is obtained in four iterations of Davidon–Fletcher–Powell, yielding $\hat{\alpha}_0 = 0 \cdot 027$, which implies a θ estimate of 0·012. Given that we now have preliminary estimates of all model parameters and the common factor, it is of interest to evaluate the multivariate log likelihood obtained by summing (15) and to compare it to the sum of the univariate log likelihoods, in order to get a rough feel for the improvement yielded by the multivariate factor approach. This multivariate log likelihood takes a value of $-11,640\cdot45$, which is substantially greater than the sum of $-12,536\cdot70$ for the seven independent univariate ARCH models.

Having established the likely presence of a common factor displaying ARCH effects, we now turn to simultaneous parameter estimation, which is done by casting the model in state-space form, using the Kalman filter to obtain the innovation vectors and their covariance matrices, and constructing the multivariate log likelihood via a prediction error decomposition. Such an approach is

[12] First-step estimates of factor loadings (λ) and country-specific shock variances (γ), as well as the extracted time-series of latent factor values, are obtained using SAS procedure FACTOR. Alternatively, one could estimate the parameters by maximizing a likelihood constructed with a Kalman filter, and extract the factor with a Kalman smoother, as in Watson and Engle (1983).

[13] The negative BP correlations with other currencies are expected because of the reciprocal units in which the BP is measured. The negative λ value for BP is similarly expected.

closely related to the DYMIMIC model of Watson and Engle (1983). The state-space form of the model is given by

$$F_t = v_t, \qquad \text{(transition equation)} \tag{27}$$

$$\varepsilon_t = \lambda F_t + e_t, \qquad \text{(observation equation)} \tag{28}$$

where:

$$v_t | v_{t-1}, \ldots, v_{t-12} \sim N(0, \sigma_t^2), \tag{29}$$

$$\sigma_t^2 = \alpha_0 + \theta \sum_{i=1}^{12} (13 - i) F_{t-i}^2, \tag{30}$$

and $e_t \sim N(0, \Gamma)$, $E(v_t e_s) = 0$, $E(e_t F_0) = 0$ for all s, t. To estimate the model we must take account of the fact that σ_t^2 is not measurable with respect to observable factor extractions. We therefore replace (30) with

$$\sigma_t^2 = \alpha_0 + \theta \sum_{i=1}^{13} (13 - i) \overset{*}{F}_{t-i}^2, \tag{31}$$

where the $\overset{*}{F}_{t-i}$ are Kalman-filter-based state vector estimates, to be defined shortly. The log likelihood which we construct is therefore best viewed as an approximation. To identify the model, we again normalize the unconditional variance of the latent factor to unity. The Kalman filter is used to obtain the time series of (7×1) innovation vectors ε_t and their conditional covariance matrices H_t. The log likelihood is then formed as:

$$\ln L = \text{const} - 1/2 \sum_{t=1}^{T} (\ln |H_t| + \varepsilon_t' H_t^{-1} \varepsilon_t). \tag{32}$$

The prediction equations for the state vector F (which in this case is a scalar) and its covariance matrix Ω (which in this case is just a scalar variance) are very simple:

$$\overset{*}{F}_{t/t-1} = 0 \tag{33}$$

$$\overset{*}{\Omega}_{t/t-1} = \sigma_t^2, \tag{34}$$

where

$$\sigma_t^2 = \alpha_0 + (1 - \alpha_0)/78 \sum_{i-1}^{12} (13 - i) \overset{*}{F}_{t-i}^2.$$

Similarly, the updating recursions have the simple form:

$$\overset{*}{F}_t = \overset{*}{\Omega}_{t/t-1} \lambda' H_t^{-1} \varepsilon_t, \tag{35}$$

$$\overset{*}{\Omega}_t = \overset{*}{\Omega}_{t/t-1} - \overset{*}{\Omega}_{t/t-1} \lambda' H_t^{-1} \lambda \overset{*}{\Omega}_{t/t-1}, \tag{36}$$

where the innovation ε_t has covariance matrix:

$$H_t = \lambda \overset{*}{\Omega}_{t/t-1} \lambda' + \Gamma, \tag{37}$$

$$= \sigma_t^2 \lambda \lambda' + \Gamma. \tag{38}$$

In order to maintain conformity with the univariate analyses, the likelihood function is constructed over observations 13–632, using as $\overset{*}{F}_1, \ldots, \overset{*}{F}_{12}$ the values of $\hat{F}_1, \ldots, \hat{F}_{12}$ obtained from the first step of the two-step estimation procedure.

A few observations are in order. First, note that due to the degenerate Markov nature of the state vector $F_t = v_t$, the updating recursion for Ω_t is never used. In the fully dynamic case in which:

$$F_t = \phi F_{t-1} + v_t, \tag{39}$$

we would have:

$$\overset{*}{\Omega}_{t/t-1} = \phi^2 \overset{*}{\Omega}_{t-1} + \sigma_t^2, \tag{40}$$

evaluation of which requires $\overset{*}{\Omega}_{t-1}$ and hence the updating recursion. The lack of serial correlation in the exchange rate innovation vector ε_t makes this unnecessary. Second, the innovation covariance matrix (38) delivered by the Kalman filter is similar in structure to the one used in the two-step estimation procedure. The Kalman filter, however, produces real-time extractions of F_t, as opposed to the two-step procedure which conditions on first-step extractions. Finally, again due to the lack of serial correlation in the transition equation, the smoothed (at end of sample) estimates of the state vector are simply the real-time updated values $(\overset{*}{F}_t)$; this is very convenient.

Parameter estimates are shown in Table 5.5, together with their asymptotic standard errors. Convergence was obtained in 44 iterations of Davidon–Fletcher–Powell, using the two-step estimates as start-up values. All factor loadings are highly significant. The European currencies FF, DM, LIR, SF and BP load most heavily on the factor; the YEN loads less heavily, and the CD loads substantially less heavily.[14] This categorization is reasonable in light of the highly

[14] The small factor loading for the CD, however, should not be interpreted as indicating 'no ARCH'. The significant dependence of the CD on the common factor indicates that it should be conditionally heteroskedastic, although we expect the ARCH effects to be less pronounced than those of the other currencies, due to the small loading. This is consistent with the results of Table 5.3, in which the estimated ARCH parameter θ is smallest for the CD.

Table 5.5. Common factor loadings and unique factor standard deviations

	CD	FF	DM	LIR	YEN	SF	BP
$\hat{\lambda} =$	1.60	11.96	13.07	9.18	7.71	14.24	−9.33
	(0.57)	(4.11)	(4.51)	(3.14)	(2.69)	(4.89)	(3.23)
$\hat{\gamma} =$	5.20	6.74	4.52	8.83	10.33	8.38	10.23
	(0.14)	(0.23)	(0.24)	(0.27)	(0.31)	(0.28)	(0.30)

integrated nature of the European economies, particularly France, Germany and Switzerland. In addition, Germany, France and Italy are members of the European Monetary System (EMS), founded in March 1979, before which they participated in the 'snake. The parity bands for the LIR established under the EMS are wider than those for other currencies, which may provide some insight into the slightly smaller common-factor loading and larger specific-factor variance for the LIR.[15]

Examination of the percentage of exchange rate innovation variance explained by the common factor enables us to assess the balance achieved between common-factor-induced commonality and specific-factor-induced divergence in volatility movements. The common factor explains 9, 77, 93, 54, 37, 77, and 47 per cent of variation in the CD, FF, DM, LIR, YEN, SF and BP, respectively. Thus, the currencies with small factor loadings do not, in general, have fully counterbalancing small specific factor variances. In fact, the LIR, YEN and BP, currencies with relatively lower loadings, have the largest specific shock variances. The rankings of percentage variation explained are therefore similar to those of the absolute factor loadings.

The estimated ARCH effects in the common factor are quite strong. We obtain an estimate of $0·16$ for $\sqrt{\alpha_0}$, with an asymptotic standard error of $0·06$, which (due to the unit unconditional variance constraint) implies a θ estimate of $0·012$. The associated sum of the ARCH lag weights, given by $78\hat{\theta}$, is therefore $0·975$, which is quite close to the unit circle, and somewhat greater than most of the univariate θ estimates. Presumably, the volatility persistence associated with the common factor reflects an effort to accommodate the high volatility persistence found earlier for the LIR. The time series of extracted common factor values is shown in Figure 5.5. The temporal behaviour of the factor is similar to that of the DM, which reflects the DM's central role in the international monetary system and is consistent with the large percentage of DM variation explained by the common factor. Finally, the maximized log likelihood is $−11604·29$, which exceeds the sum of the maximized univariate log likelihoods by more than 900.

The estimated conditional standard deviations for the factor model are obtained by substituting all multivariate estimates into the square root of (22).

---

[15] While this discussion is meant to be suggestive, it is certainly not exhaustive. Member countries adhere to parity bands set for *intra*-EMS exchange rates (e.g. FF/DM and LIR/DM), while, the rates studied here are all *dollar* rates. The effect of the EMS on volatility of intra-EMS exchange rates is examined in greater detail in Diebold and Pauly (1988*b*) and Bollerslev (1987*b*).

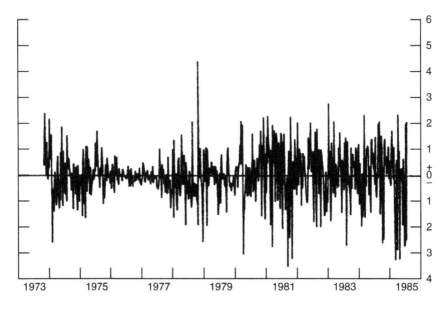

Fig. 5.5. Estimated common factor.

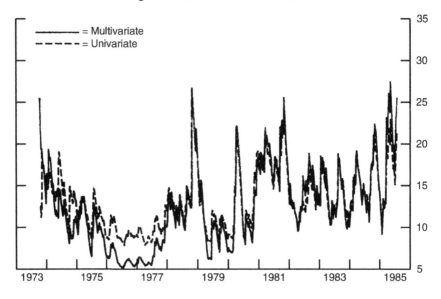

Fig. 5.6. Conditional standard deviations, DM, univariate
and multivariate models.

The univariate and multivariate results for the DM are compared in Figure 5.6.
The two estimates display high coherence, particularly during the latter half of
the sample, reflecting the high percentage of DM variation explained by the
common factor. Some notable divergences do occur, however, such as that of

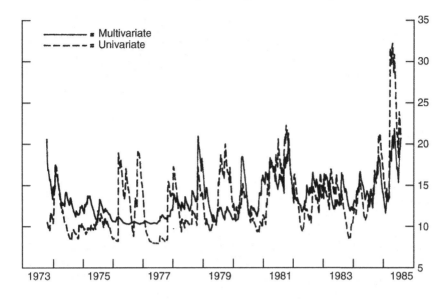

Fig. 5.7. Conditional standard deviations, BP, univariate and
multivariate models.

1976–1977, in which the multivariate estimate of conditional volatility is lower,
and the corresponding multivariate conditional confidence interval becomes
tighter. For contrast, we display in Figure 5.7 the univariate and multivariate
conditional standard deviation estimates for the BP, a currency for which the
common factor explains relatively *little* variation. The divergence between the
two volatility estimates is greater than for the DM. As expected, the movements
in univariate volatility estimates are generally more pronounced than those
associated with the factor model, and some univariate conditional volatility
movements, such as those of 1975–1976 and late 1979, have no counterpart in
the multivariate volatility estimates.

5.5 Conclusions

We argue that nominal dollar spot rates during the post-1973 float are well
described by an approximate vector random walk with ARCH innovations,
and we show that the comovements have a factor structure that can be exploited
for tractable parameter estimation. More precisely, we identify a particular type
of martingale that appears to provide a useful description of exchange rate
movements. We hope that our results will facilitate multivariate generalizations
of existing univariate empirical studies such as Domowitz and Hakkio (1985),
McCurdy and Morgan (1985), Engle, Lillien and Robbins (1987) and Diebold
and Pauly (1988*a*), as well as extensions of existing multivariate studies such as
Engle, Granger and Kraft (1984) and Bollerslev, Engle and Wooldridge (1988).

In addition, we hope that our results will stimulate additional theoretical research on the conditional moment structure of equilibrium asset price fluctuations. While the conditional volatility movements which we document are *consistent* with recent general-equilibrium asset-pricing models of exchange rate determination, such as Manuelli and Peck (1986), they do not arise as explicit *predictions* of such models. In this sense, perhaps, measurement is currently ahead of theory.

Several refinements would be desirable in future work. First, the statistical properties of the estimates produced by our two-step procedure merit further investigation, perhaps along the lines of Pagan (1984, 1986). In particular, while we can obtain a minimum-variance unbiased first-step extraction of $\{F_t\}$, we can never extract it with certainty, even with an infinitely large sample. Second, while we modify the model associated with our simultaneous estimation procedure to accommodate the fact that F_t is never observed, it would be preferable (but much harder) to preserve the original model and instead appropriately modify the Kalman filter recursions. Third, the high persistence which we find in the conditional variance of the common factor points to the potential usefulness of models with integrated common-factor conditional variance. Finally, it would be of interest to investigate the possible presence of ARCH (or GARCH, as in Bollerslev, 1986 and Engle and Bollerslev, 1986) in the country-specific factors.

The finding that movements in the major rates can be well approximated by a multivariate random walk with ARCH is certainly consistent with market efficiency: prices adjust rapidly and fully reflect all available information. But what precisely is the significance of ARCH? One explanation runs as follows. In an efficient exchange market, traders respond nearly instantaneously to incoming information; the supply of, and demand for, each currency is always in balance at each moment. But, of course, there must be differences of opinion about the significance of the information for any trades to take place. New information coming into the market affects supply and demand; old information is already incorporated in these schedules and thus in the previous equilibria. Most interpretations of market efficiency involve the idea that what is 'new' is not predictable from what is 'old', but predictability is usually interpreted in a linear sense; hence the conclusion that price changes should be serially uncorrelated. Linearity is quite restrictive, however. It is well known that a time-series may be predictable in terms of other variables or its own past in a nonlinear way, yet appear to be uncorrelated serially or with other variables if the relationship is nonlinear. This could be why we find evidence of ARCH, which is a form of nonlinear serial dependence. An alternative explanation is related to the nature of incoming information, which is of different kinds. For some kinds there is more disagreement and uncertainty about the significance or relevance of the information. When signals are relatively clear (i.e. easily and unambiguously interpretable) then, conditional upon those signals, exchange rate volatility is likely to be low. When there is disagreement about the meaning of incoming information, or when clearly relevant and significant information is scarce, we would expect greater market volatility. Our hypothesis, then, is that the quality of new information coming into the market is serially correlated.[16] A (conditionally) volatile 'world' is associated with news of dubious relevance or significance. Conversely, when the 'world' is tranquil, signals are clear and easily interpreted. The 'state of the world' is a serially correlated thing; hence, we find ARCH.

Acknowledgements

This research was partially supported by a grant from the National Science Foundation to the University of Pennsylvania. The comments of two anonymous referees and an associate editor proved very valuable. We are also indebted to T. Bollerslev, W. A. Brock, C. de Vries, R. F. Engle, W. Gaab, H. Garbers, L. R. Klein, H. Koenig, J. H. McCulloch, P. Pauly, J. Peck, A. Rose, P. Spindt, J. H. Stock, P. A. V. B. Swamy, P. Tinsley, M. Watson, and participants in the 1985 and 1986 NBER/NSF Time-Series Analysis Conferences, for helpful comments. The views expressed herein are those of the authors and do not necessarily reflect those of the Federal Reserve System or its staff. All errors are ours.

References

Akaike, H. (1974). A new look at the statistical model identification. *IEEE Transactions on Automatic Control*, AC-19, 716–23.

Bilson, J. F. O. (1979). The DM/$ rate: a monetary analysis, in Brunner, K. and Meltzer, A. (eds), *Policies For Employment, Prices, and Exchange Rates*, Carnegie-Rochester Conference 11. North Holland, Amsterdam.

Bollerslev, T. (1986). Generalized ARCH. *Journal of Econometrics* 31, 307–27.

—— (1987a). A conditional heteroskedastic time series model for speculative prices and rates of return. *Review of Economics and Statistics* 69, 542–7.

—— (1987b). A multivariate GARCH model with constant conditional correlations for a set of exchange rates. Manuscript, Northwestern University.

—— Engle, R. F., and Wooldridge, J. M. (1988). A capital asset pricing model with time varying covariances. *Journal of Political Economy* 95, 116–31.

Boothe, P. and Glassman, D. (1987). The statistical distribution of exchange rates. *Journal of International Economics* 22, 297–319.

Dickey, D. A. (1976). Hypothesis testing for nonstationary time series. Ph.D. Dissertation, Iowa State University, Ames, Iowa.

Diebold, F. X. (1986). Modeling persistence in conditional variances: a comment. *Econometric Reviews* 5, 51–6.

—— (1988). *Empirical Modeling of Exchange Rate Dynamics*. Springer-Verlag. New York, Heidelberg and Tokyo (*Lecture Notes in Economics and Mathematical Systems*, No. 303.)

—— and Nerlove, M. (1987). Factor structure in a multivariate ARCH model of exchange rate fluctuations, in Tarmo Pukkila and Simo Puntanen (eds), *Proceedings of the Second International Tampere Conference in Statistics*, pp. 429–38. Department of Mathematical Sciences/Statistics, University of Tampere, Tampere, Finland.

---

[16] The quantity of information coming to the market per unit of calendar time may also be serially correlated, which may lead to movements in conditional volatility in calendar time. See, for example, Stock (1987).

——Pauly, P. (1988*a*). Endogenous risk in a rational-expectations portfolio-balance model of the DM/$ rate. *European Economic Review* 32, 27–54.

—— —— (1988*b*), Has the EMS reduced member-country exchange rate volatility?. *Empirical Economics* 13, 81–102.

Domowitz, I. and Hakkio, C. S. (1983). Testing for serial correlation in the presence of heteroskedasticity with applications to exchange rate models, Manuscript, Northwestern University.

—— ——(1985). Conditional variance and the risk premium in the foreign exchange market. *Journal of International Economics* 19, 47–66.

Dornbusch, R. (1976). Expectations and exchange rate dynamics. *Journal of Political Economy* 84, 1161–76.

Engle, R. F. (1982). Autoregressive conditional heteroskedasticity with estimates of the variance of U.K. inflation. *Econometrica* 50, 987–1008.

——Bollerslev, T. (1986). Measuring the persistence in conditional variances. *Econometric Reviews* 5, 1–50.

——Granger, C. W. J., and Kraft, D. F. (1984). Combining competing forecasts of inflation using a bivariate ARCH model. *Journal of Economic Dynamics and Control* 8, 151–65.

——Lillien, D. M., and Robins, R. P. (1987). Estimating time-varying risk premia in the term structure: the ARCH-M model. *Econometrica* 55, 391–408.

Fama, E. F. (1965). The behavior of stock market prices. *Journal of Business* 38, 34–105.

——— (1976). *Foundations of Finance.* Basic Books, New York.

Frankel, J. A. (1979). On the mark: a theory of floating exchange rates based on real interest differentials. *American Economic Review* 69, 610–22.

——(1976). A monetary approach to the exchange rate: doctrinal aspects and empirical evidence. *Scandinavian Journal of Economics* 78, 200–24.

——(1981). Flexible exchange rates, prices and the role of news: lessons from the 1970's. *Journal of Political Economy* 89, 665–705.

Fuller, W. A. (1976). *Introduction to Statistical Time Series.* John Wiley and Sons, New York.

Hasza, D. P. and Fuller, W. A. (1979). Estimation for autoregressive processes with unit roots. *Annals of Statistics* 7, 1106–20.

Hooper, P. and Morton, J. E. (1982). Fluctuations in the dollar: a model of nominal and real exchange rate determination. *Journal of International Money and Finance* 1, 39–56.

Hsieh, D. A. (1988). The statistical properties of daily foreign exchange rates: 1974–1983. *Journal of International Economics* 24, 129–45.

Joreskog, K. G. (1979). Author's Addendum to: A general approach to confirmatory maximum likelihood factor analysis, in Joreskog, K. G. and Sorbom, D. (eds), *Advances in Factor Analysis and Structural Equation Models.* Abt Books, Cambridge, Mass.

Kiefer, N. M. and Salmon, M. (1983). Testing normality in econometric models. *Economic Letters* 11, 123–7.

Kraft, D. F. and Engle, R. F. (1982). ARCH in multiple time-series models. UCSD Discussion Paper 82–23.

Mandelbrot, B. (1963). The variation of certain speculative prices. *Journal of Business* 36, 394–419.

Manuelli, R. and Peck, J. (1986). Exchange rate volatility in an equilibrium asset pricing model, Manuscript, Northwestern University.

McCurdy, T. and Morgan, G. I. (1985). Testing the martingale hypothesis in the DM/$ futures and spot markets, Queen's University Discussion Paper 639.

Meese, R. A. and Rogoff, K. (1983*a*). Empirical exchange rate models of the seventies: do they fit out of sample?. *Journal of International Economics* 14, 3–24.

Meese, R. A. and Rogoff, K. (1983*b*). The out of sample failure of empirical exchange rate models: sampling error or misspecification?, in Frenkel, J. (ed.), *Exchange Rates and International Economics*. University of Chicago Press, Chicago, Ill.

Milhoj, A. (1986). The moment structure of ARCH processes. *Scandinavian Journal of Statistics* 12, 281–292.

—— (1987). A conditional variance model for daily deviations of an exchange rate. *Journal of Business and Economic Statistics* 5, 99–103.

Pagan, A. R. (1984). Econometric issues in the analysis of regressions with generated regressors. *International Economic Review* 25, 221–47.

—— (1986). Two-stage and related estimators and their applications. Working Paper 183, Australian National University.

Pantula, S. G. (1985). Estimation of autoregressive models with ARCH errors. Working Paper, Department of Statistics, North Carolina State University.

Schwarz, G. (1978). Estimating the dimension of a model. *Annals of Statistics* 6, 461–4.

Schwert, G. W. (1987*a*). Effects of model misspecification on tests for unit roots in macroeconomic data. *Journal of Monetary Economics* 20, 73–103.

—— (1987*b*). Tests for unit roots: a Monte Carlo investigation. Manuscript, University of Rochester.

Solo, V. (1984). The order of differencing in ARIMA models. *Journal of The American Statistical Association* 79, 916–21.

Stock, J. H. (1987). Measuring business-cycle time. *Journal of Political Economy* 95, 1240–61.

Watson, M. W. and Engle, R. F. (1983). Alternative algorithms for the estimation of dynamic factor, MIMIC, and time-varying coefficient models. *Journal of Econometrics* 15, 385–400.

Weiss, A. A. (1985). Asymptotic theory for ARCH models: stability, estimation, and testing. *Econometric Theory* 2, 107–31.

Westerfield, J. M. (1977). An examination of foreign exchange risk under fixed and floating rate regimes. *Journal of International Economics* 7, 181–200.

White, H. (1984). *Asymptotic Theory for Econometricians*. Academic Press, New York.

Working, H. (1960). A note on the correlation of first differences in a random chain. *Econometrica* 28, 916–18.

6

Multivariate Stochastic Variance Models*

ANDREW HARVEY, ESTHER RUIZ
AND
NEIL SHEPHARD

Changes in variance, or volatility, over time can be modelled using the approach based on autoregressive conditional heteroscedasticity (ARCH). However, the generalizations to multivariate series can be difficult to estimate and interpret. Another approach is to model variance as an unobserved stochastic process. Although it is not easy to obtain the exact likelihood function for such stochastic variance models, they tie in closely with developments in finance theory and have certain statistical attractions. This article sets up a multivariate model, discusses its statistical treatment and shows how it can be modified to capture common movements in volatility in a very natural way. The model is then fitted to daily observations on exchange rates.

6.1 Introduction

Many financial time series, such as stock returns and exchange rates, exhibit changes in volatility over time. These changes tend to be serially correlated and in the *generalized autoregressive conditional heteroscedasticity*, or GARCH model, developed by Engle (1982) and Bollerslev (1986), such effects are captured by letting the conditional variance be a function of the squares of previous observations and past variances. Since the model is formulated in terms of the distribution of the one-step ahead prediction error, maximum likelihood estimation is straightforward. A wide range of GARCH models have now appeared in the econometric literature; see the recent survey by Bollerslev et al. (1992).

An alternative approach is to set up a model containing an unobserved variance component, the logarithm of which is modelled directly as a linear stochastic process, such as an autoregression. Models of this kind are called *stochastic volatility models* or *stochastic variance (SV) models*. They are the natural discrete-time versions of the continuous-time models upon which much of modern finance theory, including generalizations of the Black-Scholes result on option pricing, has been developed; see, for example, Hull and White (1987) and Taylor (1994). Their principal disadvantage is that they are difficult

* This work was previously published as A. C. Harvey, E. Ruiz, and N. Shephard (1994), 'Multivariate Stochastic Variance Models', *Review of Economic Studies*, 61. Copyright © Review of Economic Studies Ltd. Published by Blackwell Publishing. Reproduced by kind permission.

to estimate by maximum likelihood. However they do have other compensating statistical attractions; for example their properties are easily obtained from the properties of the process generating the variance component. Furthermore, they generalize to multivariate series in a very natural way. The main aim of this article is to show how multivariate stochastic variance models can be handled statistically and to explore how well they fit real data.

Section 6.2 reviews some of the basic ideas of univariate GARCH and SV models and compares their properties. The estimation of SV models by a quasi-maximum likelihood procedure is then discussed. In Section 6.3 it is shown how multivariate SV models can be formulated, and how they compare with multivariate GARCH models. The way in which they can handle common movements in volatility in different series is described in Section 6.4 and this is related to ideas of co-integration in variance. Section 6.5 presents an example in which the model is fitted to four sets of exchange rates, and Section 6.6 generalizes the methods so as to handle heavy tailed distributions. The conclusions are given in Section 6.7.

6.2 Univariate models

Let the series of interest be made up of a Gaussian white noise process, with unit variance, multiplied by a factor σ_t, the standard deviation, that is

$$y_t = \sigma_t \varepsilon_t, \quad t = 1, \ldots, T, \quad \varepsilon_t \sim \text{NID}(0, 1). \tag{1}$$

In the GARCH(1, 1) model,

$$\sigma_t^2 = \gamma + \alpha y_{t-1}^2 + \beta \sigma_{t-1}^2, \quad \gamma > 0, \quad \alpha + \beta < 1. \tag{2}$$

This may be generalized by adding more lags of both the squared observations and the variance. All GARCH models are martingale differences, and if the sum of the α and β coefficients is less then one, they have constant finite variance and so are white noise. However, obtaining the general conditions under which σ_t^2 is positive and y_t is stationary is not straightforward; see, for example, Nelson and Cao (1992) and Bollerslev and Engle (1993). Similarly, although it can be shown that y_t exhibits excess kurtosis, the necessary restrictions for fourth moments to exist are not easy to derive.

The dynamics of a GARCH model show up in the autocorrelation function (ACF) of the squared observations. In the GARCH(1, 1) case, the ACF is like that of an ARMA(1, 1) process. If the sum of α and β is close to one, the ACF will decay quite slowly, indicating a relatively slowly changing conditional variance. This has often been observed to happen in practice, and GARCH(1, 1) models with $\alpha + \beta$ close to unity are quite common with real data.

If $\alpha + \beta$ is set to one in the GARCH(1, 1) model, it is no longer weakly stationary since it does not have finite variance. However, Δy_t^2 is stationary and has an ACF like that of an MA(1) process, indicating an analogy with the

ARIMA(0, 1, 1) process. This model is called *integrated GARCH*, or *IGARCH*; see Engle and Bollerslev (1986). It does not follow, though, that y_t^2 will behave like an integrated process in all respects, and, in fact, Nelson (1990) has shown that σ_t^2 is strictly stationary.

The IGARCH model is still a martingale difference, and so forecasts of all future observations are zero. If γ is positive, the predicted variances increase with the lead time. On the other hand, if γ is set to zero, Nelson (1990) shows that the IGARCH process has the rather strange property that, no matter what the starting point, σ_t^2 tends towards zero for most parameter values, so that the series effectively disappears. This leads him to suggest a model in which $\log \sigma_t^2$ has the characteristics of a random walk; see Nelson (1991). This is an example of an *exponential ARCH*, or *EGARCH*, model. Such models have the additional attraction that they can be shown to be a discrete-time approximation to some of the continuous-time models of finance theory.

In a stochastic variance model for (1), the logarithm of σ_t^2, denoted h_t, is modelled as a stochastic process. As with EGARCH, working in logarithms ensures that σ_t^2 is always positive, but the difference is that it is not directly observable. A simple model for h_t is the AR(1) process

$$h_t = \gamma + \varphi h_{t-1} + \eta_t, \quad \eta_t \sim \text{NID}(0, \ \sigma_\eta^2), \tag{3}$$

with η_t generated independently of ε_s for all t, s. Equation (3) is the natural discrete-time approximation to the continuous-time Ornstein–Uhlenbeck process used in finance theory. Dassios (1992) has shown that (1) and (3) is a better discrete-time approximation to the model used in Hull and White (1987) than an EGARCH model. More specifically, if δ denotes the distance between observations, he shows that the density of the variance process converges to the density of the continuous-time variance process at rate δ, whereas in the case of EGARCH the convergence is at rate $\delta^{1/2}$. Similar convergence results hold for the joint moments of the observations.

If $|\varphi| < 1$, we know from standard theory that h_t is strictly stationary, with mean $\gamma_h = \gamma/(1 - \varphi)$ and variance $\sigma_h^2 = \sigma_\eta^2/(1 - \varphi^2)$. Since y_t is the product of two strictly stationary processes, it must also be strictly stationary. Thus the restrictions needed to ensure stationarity of y_t, both in the strict and weak sense, are just the standard restrictions needed to ensure stationarity of the process generating h_t.

The fact that y_t is white noise follows almost immediately when the two disturbance terms are mutually independent. The odd moments of y_t are all zero because ε_t is symmetric. The even moments can be obtained by making use of a standard result for the lognormal distribution, which in the present context tells us that since $\exp(h_t)$ is lognormal, its j-th moment about the origin is $\exp\{j\gamma_h + \frac{1}{2}j^2\sigma_h^2\}$. It follows almost immediately that the variance of y_t is $\exp\{\gamma_h + \frac{1}{2}\sigma_h^2\}$. Similarly the kurtosis is $3\exp\{\sigma_h^2\}$, which is greater than three when σ_h^2 is positive; see Taylor (1986, Chapter 3). Unlike a GARCH model, the fourth moment always exists when h_t is stationary.

The dynamic properties of the model appear most clearly in $\log y_t^2$. Since $y_t = \varepsilon_t \exp(\frac{1}{2} h_t)$,

$$\log y_t^2 = h_t + \log \varepsilon_t^2, \quad t = 1, \ldots, T. \tag{4}$$

The mean and variance of $\log \varepsilon_t^2$ are known to be -1.27 and $\pi^2/2 = 4.93$, respectively; see Abramovitz and Stegun (1970, p. 943). Thus $\log y_t^2$ is the sum of an AR(1) component and white noise and so its ACF is equivalent to that of an ARMA(1, 1). Its properties are therefore similar to those of GARCH(1, 1). Indeed, if σ_η^2 is small and/or φ is close to one, y_t^2 behaves approximately as an ARMA(1, 1) process; see Taylor (1986, p. 74–5, 1993).

The model can be generalised so that h_t follows any stationary ARMA process, in which case y_t is also stationary and its properties can be deduced from the properties of h_t. Alternatively h_t can be allowed to follow a random walk

$$h_t = h_{t-1} + \eta_t, \quad \eta_t \sim \text{NID}(0, \sigma_\eta^2). \tag{5}$$

In this case $\log y_t^2$ is a random walk plus noise, and the best linear predictor of the current value of h_t is an exponentially weighted moving average (EWMA) of past values of $\log y_t^2$. Thus there is a parallel with the IGARCH model where the conditional variance is also an EWMA. The crucial difference is that while the IGARCH conditional variance is known exactly, the variance generated by (5) is an unobserved component, and a better estimator can be obtained by making use of subsequent observations.

The SV model with h_t following a random walk is clearly non-stationary, with $\log y_t^2$ being stationary after differencing. It is quite close to an EGARCH model in this respect. There is no need to introduce a constant term to prevent the kind of behaviour demonstrated for IGARCH by Nelson. As a result the model contains only one unknown parameter.

The estimation of SV models has usually been carried out by variants of the method of moments; see, for example, Scott (1987), Chesney and Scott (1989), Melino and Turnbull (1990) and the references in Taylor (1993). The approach proposed here is a quasi-maximum likelihood method, computed using the Kalman filter. It was put forward independently by Nelson (1988).

In order to estimate the parameters, φ, γ and σ_η^2, consider the following state-space model obtained from (3) and (4):

$$\log y_t^2 = -1.27 + h_t + \xi_t \tag{6a}$$

$$h_t = \gamma + \varphi h_{t-1} + \eta_t \tag{6b}$$

where, $\xi_t = \log \varepsilon_t^2 + 1.27$ and $\text{Var}(\xi_t) = \pi^2/2$. The general form of the model allows for the possibility of the original disturbances in (1) and (3) being correlated. Nevertheless in (6), ξ_t and η_t are uncorrelated; see Appendix A. The question of taking account of any correlation between the original disturbances is to be examined in a later paper.

Although the Kalman filter can be applied to (6), it will only yield minimum mean square *linear* estimators (MMSLEs) of the state and future observations rather than MMSEs. Furthermore, since the model is not conditionally Gaussian, the exact likelihood cannot be obtained from the resulting prediction errors. Nevertheless estimates can be obtained by treating ξ_t as though it were NID $(0, \pi^2/2)$ and maximizing the resulting quasi-likelihood function. Asymptotic standard errors, which take account of the specific form of the non-normality in ξ_t, can be computed using the results established by Dunsmuir (1979, p. 502). The experiments reported in Ruiz (1994) suggest that his QML method works well for the sample sizes typically encountered in financial economics and is usually to be preferred to the corresponding method of moments estimator. A further attraction of applying QML to SV models is that the assumption of normality for ε_t can be relaxed, in which case σ_ξ^2 is estimated unrestrictedly; see Section 6.6.

The Kalman filter approach is still valid when φ is one. The only difference is that the first observation is used to initialize the Kalman filter, whereas when $|\varphi| < 1$ the unconditional distribution of h_t is available at $t = 0$. Once the parameters have been estimated, predictions of future volatility can be made from the predictions of log y_t^2. A smoother can be used to estimate volatility within the sample period; this is also done by Melino and Turnbull (1990) and Scott (1987).

6.3 Multivariate models

The multivariate GARCH model, set out in Bollerslev, Engle and Wooldridge (1988), can, in principle, be estimated efficiently by maximum likelihood. However, the number of parameters can be very large, so it is usually necessary to impose restrictions. For example, Bollerslev (1990) proposes a representation in which the conditional correlations are assumed to be constant. This assumption considerably simplifies estimation and inference, and, according to the evidence in Baillie and Bollerslev (1990) and Schwert and Seguin (1990), it is often empirically reasonable.

Stochastic variance models generalize to multivariate series as follows. Let y_t be an $N \times 1$ vector, with elements

$$y_{it} = \varepsilon_{it}(\exp\{h_{it}\})^{1/2}, \quad i = 1, \ldots, N, \quad t = 1, \ldots, T, \quad (7)$$

where y_{it} is the observation at time t of series i, and $\varepsilon_t = (\varepsilon_{1t}, \ldots, \varepsilon_{Nt})'$ is a multivariate normal vector with zero mean and a covariance matrix, $\sum_\varepsilon$, in which the elements on the leading diagonal are unity and the off-diagonal elements are denoted as ρ_{ij}. Following (3), the variances may be generated by AR(1) processes

$$h_{it} = \gamma_i + \varphi_i h_{it-1} + \eta_{it}, \quad i = 1, \ldots, N, \quad (8)$$

where $\eta_t = (\eta_{1t}, \ldots, \eta_{Nt})'$ is multivariate normal with zero mean and covariance matrix $\sum_\eta$. The model in (7) does not allow the covariances to evolve over time independently of the variances. Thus it is restricted in a similar way to the constant conditional correlation GARCH model.[1]

Model (8) could be generalized so that the $N \times 1$ vector h_t is a multivariate AR(1) process or even an ARMA process. Although the properties of such models could be derived relatively easily, generalizations of this kind are probably not necessary in practice. We will instead focus attention on the special case when h_t is a multivariate random walk. Transforming as in (6) gives

$$w_t = -1.27\iota + h_t + \xi_t \tag{9a}$$

$$h_t = h_{t-1} + \eta_t \tag{9b}$$

where w_t and ξ_t are $N \times 1$ vectors with elements $w_{it} = \log y_{it}^2$ and $\xi_{it} = \log \varepsilon_{it}^2 + 1.27$, $i = 1, \ldots, N$, respectively, and ι is an $N \times 1$ vector of ones; compare the seemingly unrelated time series equation (SUTSE) models described in Harvey (1989, Chapter 8). Treating (9) as a Gaussian state-space model, QML estimators may be obtained by means of the Kalman filter. As in the univariate model, ξ_t and η_t are uncorrelated even if the original disturbances are correlated.

It is shown in Appendix B that the ij-th element of the covariance matrix of ξ_t, denoted Σ_ξ, is given by $(\pi^2/2)\rho_{ij}^*$, where $\rho_{ii}^* = 1$ and

$$\rho_{ij}^* = \frac{2}{\pi^2} \sum_{n=1}^{\infty} \frac{(n-1)!}{(1/2)_n n} \rho_{ij}^{2n}, \quad i \neq j, \ i, j = 1, \ldots, N, \tag{10}$$

where $(x)_n = x(x+1)\ldots(x+n-1)$. Thus the absolute values of the unknown parameters in Σ_ξ, namely the ρ_{ij}'s, the cross-correlations between different ε_{it}'s, may be estimated, but their signs may not, because the relevant information is lost when the observations are squared. However, estimates of the signs may be obtained by returning to the untransformed observations and noting that the sign of each of the pairs $\varepsilon_i \varepsilon_j$, $i, j = 1, \ldots, N$, will be the same as the corresponding pair of observed values $y_i y_j$. Thus the sign of ρ_{ij} is estimated as positive if more than one-half of the pairs $y_i y_j$ are positive.

6.4 Common factors

In the K-factor GARCH model proposed by Engle (1987) the conditional covariance matrix depends on the conditional variances of K orthogonal linear combinations of y_t. Although the model can, in principle, be estimated by maximum

---

[1] If the state space form for the log y_{it}^2's were Gaussian, the conditional covariance between any two observations, y_{it} and y_{jt}, at time $t - 1$, divided by their conditional standard deviations, would give the conditional correlation $\rho_{ij} \exp\{(2p_{ij,\,t|t-1} - p_{ii,\,t|t-1})/8\}$, provided the ε_{it}'s and η_{it}'s are mutually independent. The terms $p_{ij,\,t|t-1}$ denote the ij-th elements of the covariance matrix of the filtered estimators of the h_{it}'s at time t, and since these are constant in the steady state, the conditional correlations are also constant.

likelihood, researchers often encounter computational difficulty with a large number of parameters. Engle, Ng and Rothschild (1990) suggest a simpler two-stage procedure. Bollerslev and Engle (1993) give conditions for covariance stationarity of K-factor GARCH models and show how multivariate IGARCH models allow for the possibility of co-persistence in variance. However, as in the univariate case, there is some ambiguity about what constitutes persistence.

An alternative multivariate model, which is not nested within multivariate GARCH, is the latent factor model of Diebold and Nerlove (1989). The model is a relatively parsimonious one in which the common movements in volatility are ascribed to a single unobserved latent factor subject to ARCH effects. However, this latent factor gives rise to similar common movements in the levels and for many purposes the levels and volatility effects need to be modelled separately.

Common factors can be incorporated in multivariate stochastic variance models very easily by following the literature on common factors in unobserved components time-series models; see Harvey (1989, chapter 8, section 5) for a review and Harvey and Stock (1988) for an application to U.S. data on income and consumption. We will concentrate on the case where there are persistent movements in volatility, modelled by a multivariate random walk. Thus (9) becomes

$$w_t = -1.27\iota + \theta h_t + \bar{h} + \xi_t, \tag{11a}$$

$$h_t = h_{t-1} + \eta_t, \quad \mathrm{Var}(\eta_t) = \Sigma_\eta, \tag{11b}$$

where θ is an $N \times k$ matrix of coefficients with $k \overset{\leq}{=} N$, h_t and η_t are $k \times 1$ vectors, $\sum_\eta$ is a $k \times k$ positive definite matrix and $\bar{h}$ is a $N \times 1$ vector in which the first k elements are zeroes while the last $N - k$ elements are unconstrained. The logarithm of variance for the i-th series is the i-th element of $\theta h_t + \bar{h}$. If $k < N$, the w_t's are co-integrated in the sense of Engle and Granger (1987). In the context of (11) this implies that there are $N - k$ linear combinations of the w_t's which are white noise.

As it stands model (11) is not identifiable. An identifiable model may be set up by requiring that the elements of θ are such that $\theta_{ij} = 0$ for $j > i$, $i = 1, \ldots, N$, $j = 1, \ldots, k$, while Σ_η is an identity matrix. These restrictions are easily imposed, and the model may be estimated by QML using the Kalman filter to compute the prediction errors. Once this has been done, it may be worthwhile considering a rotation of the common factors to get a model with a more useful interpretation. If R is a $k \times k$ orthogonal matrix, the factors $h_t^* = Rh_t$ are still driven by mutually uncorrelated disturbances with unit variances, while the factor loading matrix becomes $\theta^* = \theta R'$.

The finite-sample properties of the QML estimator of model (11) have been studied by carrying out several Monte Carlo experiments. These are reported in Ruiz (1992) and confirm that the method works well for moderate sample sizes. The number of unknown parameters in θ is $(N - k)k + \frac{1}{2}k(k + 1)$, while there are a further $\frac{1}{2}N(N - 1)$ in Σ_ε. Numerical optimization must be carried out with respect to these unknown parameters. We used the quasi-Newton algorithm, EO4 AZF, in the NAG library.

6.5 Empirical application: daily exchange rates

In this section, the stochastic variance model is fitted to four exchange rates: Pound/Dollar, Deutschmark/Dollar, Yen/Dollar and Swiss-Franc/Dollar. The data consist of daily observations of weekdays close exchange rates from 1/10/81 to 28/6/85. The sample size is $T = 946$. Table 6.1 shows Box–Ljung statistics for several transformations of the exchange rates. The chi-square 5% critical value for ten degrees of freedom is 18.3. With the possible exception of the Swiss Franc, the logarithms of the exchange rates appear to be random walks. The important point is that there is strong evidence of nonlinearity in the statistics for the squared differences and their logarithms.

Univariate models were fitted to the differences of the logarithms of each of the exchange rates, with the mean subtracted, that is

$$y_{it} = \Delta \log p_{it} - (\Sigma \Delta \log p_{it})/T, \quad i = 1, \ldots, N, \quad t = 1, \ldots, T.$$

Subtracting the mean ensures that there are no y_{it}'s identically equal to zero; this could create difficulties when logarithms of y_t^2 are taken. The QML estimates of the parameters φ and σ_η^2 in the stationary AR(1) volatility model, (3), are shown in Table 6.2. The estimates of φ are all close to one and the random walk specification, (5), fits almost as well. Asymptotic standard errors, based on Dunsmuir (1979, p. 502), are shown in parentheses, though it should be noted that they cannot be used to test whether σ_η^2 is significantly different from zero; see Harvey (1989, pp. 212–3). The Box–Ljung Q-statistics give no indication of residual serial correlation. Figure 6.1 shows the absolute values, $|y_t|$, for the Pound/Dollar series, together with the estimated standard deviation, exp $(\frac{1}{2}\tilde{h}_{t|T})$, where $\tilde{h}_{t|T}$ is the MMSLE of the volatility level, h_t, as given by a smoothing algorithm.

The augmented Dickey–Fuller test applied to log y_t^2, with nine lags and a constant included, rejects the hypothesis of a unit root at the 1% level for all the series; see Table 6.3. The significance point, for 500 observations, is -3.43 and so the rejection is quite decisive; using a smaller number of lags gave test statistics

Table 6.1. Box–Ljung Q-statistics, based on ten lags, for daily exchange rates, p_t, of various currencies against the dollar

	$\Delta \log p_t$	$(\Delta \log p_t)^2$	$\log (\Delta \log p_t)^2$
Pound	11.19	128.25	45.47
DM	10.03	67.79	64.20
Yen	16.92	109.79	64.67
Swiss Franc	32.67	343.09	57.94

Table 6.2. Estimation results for univariate stochastic volatility models:
(a) AR(1); (b) random walk

		\$/Pound	\$/DM	\$/Yen	\$/SF
(a)	$\hat{\varphi}$	0.9912	0.9646	0.9948	0.9575
		(0.0069)	(0.0206)	(0.0046)	(0.0024)
	$\hat{\sigma}_\eta^2$	0.0069	0.0312	0.0048	0.0459
		(0.0050)	(0.0219)	0.0034)	(0.0291)
	γ	−0.0879	−0. 3556	−0.0551	−0.4239
	$\log L$	−1212.82	−1232.26	−1272.64	−1288.51
(b)	$\hat{\sigma}_\eta^2$	0.0042	0.0161	0.0034	0.0194
		(0.0023)	(0.0063)	(0.0019)	(0.0072)
	$\log L$	−1214.02	−1237.58	−1273.46	−1294.22
	$Q(10)$	3.52	11.41	8.45	8.68

Table 6.3. Augmented Dickey–Fuller test statistics for the logarithms of squared
differences of logarithms of daily exchange rates

	\$/Pound	\$/DM	\$/Yen	\$/SF
't-start'	−7.42	−7.50	−7.63	−7.44

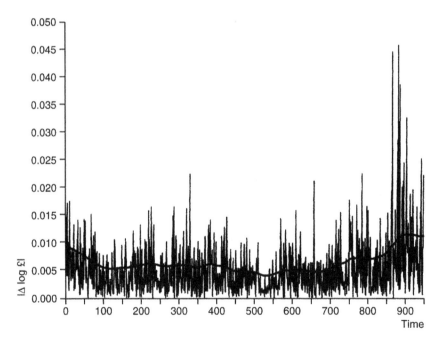

Fig. 6.1. Absolute values of first differences of logged dollar-pound exchange
rate and smooth estimates of standard deviation.

even further from the critical value. However, the reliability of unit root tests in this situation is questionable. The reason is that the reduced form of (6) is

$$\log(y_t^2) = \gamma^* + \varphi \log(y_{t-1}^2) + v_t - \theta v_{t-1}, \tag{12}$$

where v_t is white noise and $\gamma^* = (\gamma - 1.27)/(1 - \varphi)$. Since the variance of ξ_t typically dominates the variance of η_t, the parameter θ will be close to unity for values of φ close to one. For example for the dollar-pound exchange rate, where the estimated φ value is 0.99, the implied θ is -0.97. As shown in Pantula (1991) and Schwert (1989), when the moving-average parameter is very close to one, unit root tests reject the null hypothesis of a unit root too often since the model is difficult to distinguish from white noise.

Since unit root tests based on autoregressive approximations are unreliable in the present context, there is little point in trying to determine the number of common trends on the basis of co-integration tests such as the one described in Johansen (1988). Instead we estimate the unrestructed multivariated local level model, (9), and make a judgement as to the number of possible common trends on the basis of a principal component analysis of the estimate of Σ_η.

QML estimation of (9), with the diagonal elements of the matrix Σ_ξ set to $\pi^2/2$, gives:

$$\hat{\Sigma}_\xi = \frac{\pi^2}{2} \begin{bmatrix} 1.00 & 0.404 & 0.278 & 0.347 \\ & 1.000 & 0.400 & 0.541 \\ & & 1.000 & 0.362 \\ & & & 1.000 \end{bmatrix}$$

and

$$\hat{\Sigma}_\eta = 10^{-3} \begin{bmatrix} 9.65 & 11.42 & 3.97 & 12.07 \\ & 20.43 & 5.44 & 21.09 \\ & & 5.45 & 7.08 \\ & & & 22.31 \end{bmatrix}$$

the value of the maximized quasi-log-likelihood for the multivariate model, -4621.64, is substantially greater than the sum of -4963.06 for the four univariate models. The number of additional parameters in the multivariate model is 12, and so the value of 682·8 taken by the (quasi-) likelihood ratio test statistic, is highly significant if judged against a χ_{12}^2 distribution.

From (10), the implied covariance (correlation) matrix for ε_t is

$$\hat{\Sigma}_\varepsilon = \begin{bmatrix} 1.00 & 0.84 & 0.74 & 0.80 \\ & 1.00 & 0.84 & 0.92 \\ & & 1.00 & 0.81 \\ & & & 1.00 \end{bmatrix}$$

Estimating the signs of the cross correlations in Σ_ε from the signs of pairs of y_t's indicated they were all positive. The correlation matrix corresponding to the estimate of Σ_η is

$$
\text{Corr}(\hat{\eta}) = \begin{bmatrix} 1.00 & 0.81 & 0.55 & 0.82 \\ & 1.00 & 0.51 & 0.99 \\ & & 1.00 & 0.64 \\ & & & 1.00 \end{bmatrix}
$$

It is interesting to note that the correlations between the elements of ε_t are uniformly high for all four exchange rates, while for η_t the correlations involving the Yen are much lower than the European currencies.

The results of a principal components analysis of Σ_η and its correlation matrix appear in Table 6.4. The units of measurement are not relevant since logarithms have been taken, but differences appear in the results for the covariance and correlation matrices, primarily because the Yen shows much less variation than the other three exchange rates. The two first components account for 94% or 95% of the total variance of the disturbance η_{it}, $i = 1, 2, 3, 4$. The second component is relatively more important when the correlation matrix is analysed, with a fairly high loading on the Yen. Table 6.5 shows the first two eigenvectors multiplied by the square roots of the corresponding eigenvalues. For the analysis of the correlation matrix these figures give the correlations between the principal components and the disturbances η_{it}, $i = 1, 2, 3, 4$. In this case, the first component can perhaps be interpreted as a general underlying factor, strongly correlated with the European exchange rates, but less so with the Yen, while the second component is correlated most strongly with the Yen. The loadings for the first component in the analysis of the covariance matrix invite a similar interpretation, but the Yen is not dominant in the second component.

Table 6.4. Principal components analysis of (a) $\hat{\Sigma}_\eta$ and (b) corresponding correlation matrix

(a)	Eigenvalues	0.0515	0.0037	0.0027	1.4281×10^{-6}
	Eigenvectors	0.3781	−0.1443	0.9144	−0.0139
		0.6205	0.3749	−0.1873	0.6629
		0.2066	−0.9156	−0.2260	0.2605
		0.6553	0.0170	−0.2789	−0.7018
	Percentage of variance	88.98	6.43	4.58	0.00
(2b)	Eigenvalues	3.1933	0.5703	0.2363	7.02×10^{-5}
	Eigenvectors	0.5033	0.2102	0.8381	−0.0095
		0.5290	0.3476	−0.3973	0.6644
		0.4097	−0.9020	−0.0182	0.1348
		0.5468	0.1460	−0.3733	−0.7350
	Percentage of variance	79.83	14.26	5.91	0.00

Table 6.5. Principal components analysis: First two eigenvectors multiplied by square roots of corresponding eigenvalues for (a) correlation matrix, and (b) covariance matrix

Series	(a)		(b)	
1	0.8994	0.1587	0.0858	−0.0088
2	0.9453	0.2625	0.1408	0.0229
3	0.7321	−0.6812	0.0469	−0.0558
4	0.9771	0.1103	0.1487	0.0010

In principal components analysis, the covariance matrix is decomposed as $\hat{\Sigma}_\eta = EDE'$, where E is the matrix of eigenvectors and D is a diagonal matrix of eigenvalues. The principal components, $E'w_t$, have covariance matrix D. Noting that $ED^{1/2}D^{-1/2}E'$ is an identity matrix, the model in (9) may be written as

$$w_t = -1.27i + \theta h_t^* + \xi_t \tag{13a}$$

$$h_t^* = h_{t-1}^* + \eta_t^*, \quad \text{Var}(\eta_t^*) = I \tag{13b}$$

where $h_t^* = D^{-1/2}E'h_t$ and $\theta = ED^{1/2}$. This provides a useful link with model (11) when $k = N$, the necessary restrictions on θ coming from the properties of standardised eigenvectors rather than by setting elements above the leading diagonal to zero. If the estimate of Σ_η were of rank k, then θ would be an $N \times k$ matrix. Note that in the present application, the first two columns of θ are given by the entries in Table 6.5.

The principal components analysis suggests that two factors might be enough to account for the movements in volatility. Estimating (11) with $k = 2$, and the restrictions $\theta_{12} = 0$ and $\Sigma_\eta = I$ gives:

$$\log(\hat{y}_{1t}^2) = -1.27 + 0.108\hat{h}_{1t}$$
$$\log(\hat{y}_{2t}^2) = -1.27 + 0.102\hat{h}_{1t} + 0.014\hat{h}_{2t}$$
$$\log(\hat{y}_{3t}^2) = -1.27 + 0.016\hat{h}_{1t} + 0.054\hat{h}_{2t} - 7.42$$
$$\log(\hat{y}_{4t}^2) = -1.27 + 0.095\hat{h}_{1t} + 0.023\hat{h}_{2t} - 1.38$$

and

$$\hat{\Sigma}_\xi = \frac{\pi^2}{2}\begin{bmatrix} 1.00 & 0.382 & 0.271 & 0.334 \\ & 1.00 & 0.390 & 0.539 \\ & & 1.00 & 0.358 \\ & & & 1.00 \end{bmatrix}$$

with a quasi-log-likelihood of −4626.48. The implied correlation matrix for ε_t is

$$\hat{\Sigma}_\varepsilon = \begin{bmatrix} 1.00 & 0.83 & 0.73 & 0.79 \\ & 1.00 & 0.83 & 0.92 \\ & & 1.00 & 0.81 \\ & & & 1.00 \end{bmatrix}.$$

Again, estimating the signs of the cross-correlations in Σ_ε from the signs of pairs of y_t's indicates that they are all positive.

Factor rotation was carried out using the orthogonal matrix

$$R = \begin{bmatrix} \cos\lambda & -\sin\lambda \\ \sin\lambda & \cos\lambda \end{bmatrix}$$

and a graphical method; see Schuessler (1971). For clockwise rotation, setting the angle, λ, to 16·23° gives a loading of zero for the first factor on the third series, the Yen; see Figure 6.2 and Table 6.6. Setting the angle to 352·48° gives a loading of zero for this second factor on the DM and very small loadings on the other two European currencies. The first rotation therefore has the dominant factor, the

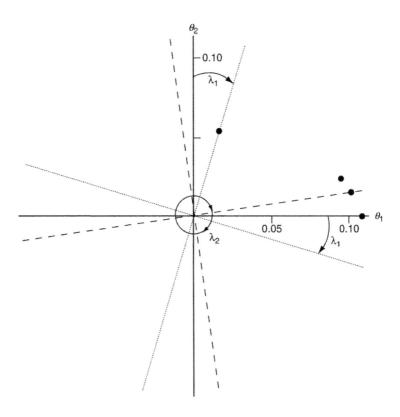

Fig. 6.2. Factor rotation.

Table 6.6. Loadings after rotations

	$\lambda = 16.23°$		$\lambda = 352.48°$	
Pound/Dollar	0.103	0.030	0.107	−0.014
DM/Dollar	0.095	0.042	0.103	0
Yen/Dollar	0	0.056	0.023	0.051
SF/Dollar	0.085	0.048	0.097	0.010

first common trend h_{1t}, related only to the European exchange rates, while the second common trend, h_{2t}, is a general trend which underlies the volatility of all the exchange rates including the Yen. In the second rotation, which is actually quite close to the original when the movement is in an anti-clockwise direction, the first common trend affects the European exchange rates to a similar extent, but leads to smaller movements in the Yen. The second common trend has its effect almost exclusively on the Yen; compare the results for the principal components analysis of the correlation matrix as given in Table 6.4. The message in the two rotations is essentially the same and which one is adopted is really a matter of taste. The standard deviations implied by the two common trends for the second rotation, $\exp(\frac{1}{2}\tilde{h}_{jt|T})$, $j = 1, 2$, are plotted in Figure 6.3. The standard

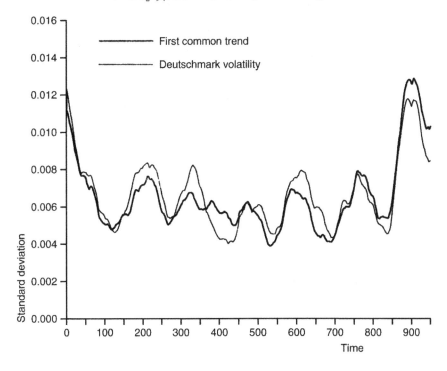

Fig. 6.3a. Smooth estimates of standard deviation for the first common trend with the corresponding estimates for the Deutschmark.

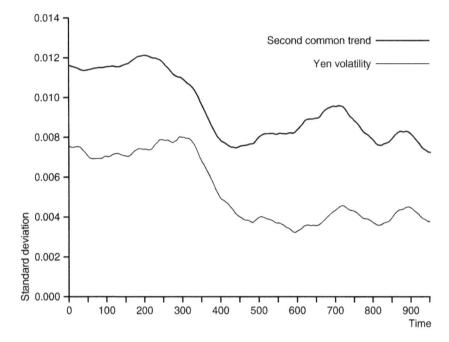

Fig. 6.3b. Smooth estimates of standard deviation for the second common trend
with the corresponding estimates for the Yen.

deviations estimated from the univariate models for the Deutschmark and Yen
are shown for comparison.

6.6 Heavy-tailed distributions

The GARCH model may be generalized by letting ε_t have a Student t-distribu-
tion; see Bollerslev (1987). This is important because the kurtosis in many
financial series is greater than the kurtosis which results from incorporating
conditional heteroscedasticity into a Gaussian process. A similar generalization
is possible for the SV model. Once again it can be shown that when h_t is
stationary, y_t is white noise and it follows immediately from the properties of
the t-distribution that the formula for the unconditional variance generalizes to
$\{v/(v-2)\} \exp(\gamma_h + \frac{1}{2}\sigma_h^2)$.

Let ε_t in (1) be a t-variable written as

$$\varepsilon_t = \zeta_t/\kappa_t^{1/2}, \quad t = 1, \ldots, T, \tag{14}$$

where ζ_t is a standard normal variate and $v\kappa_t$ is distributed, independently of ζ_t,
as a χ^2 with v degrees of freedom. Thus

$$\log \varepsilon_t^2 = \log \zeta_t^2 - \log \kappa_t, \tag{15}$$

and it follows from Abramovitz and Stegun (1970, p. 943) that the mean and variance of $\log \kappa_t$ are $\psi'(v/2) - \log(v/2)$ and $\psi'(v/2)$ respectively, where $\psi(.)$ and $\psi'(.)$ are the digamma and trigamma functions respectively. The ACF of $\log y_t^2$ has the same form as before.

The state-space model corresponding to (6) can be estimated for a given value of v. Alternatively the variance of $\log \varepsilon_t^2$ can be treated as an additional unknown parameter. In both cases the asymptotic theory in Dunsmuir (1979, p. 502) applies since the required moments of $\log \varepsilon_t^2$ exist even when v is one. Leaving the distribution of ε_t unspecified means that γ_h is not identified since the expected value of $\log \varepsilon_t^2$ is unknown. Similarly, when h_t follows a random walk its estimated values will include the expectation of $\log \varepsilon_t^2$. Thus the level of volatility is not determined. However, if ε_t is assumed to have a t-distribution, the estimated variance of $\log \varepsilon_t^2$ implies a value of v when set to $4.93 + \psi'(v/2)$, and this in turn enables the expectation of $\log \varepsilon_t^2$ to be calculated. In the exchange rate application, the unrestricted estimates of the variance of $\log \varepsilon_t^2$ imply that the distribution of ε_t is normal for the Pound and Deutschmark, that is v is infinity, while for the Yen and Swiss Franc v is approximately six.

The generalization to the multivariate model can be made by assuming that (14) holds for $i = 1, \ldots, N$ with the ζ_{it}'s following a multivariate normal distribution, with a correlation matrix as specified for ε_t in (7), but with the κ_{it}'s mutually independent. The covariance matrix of the vector of $\log \varepsilon_{it}^2$ variables, Σ_ξ, is the sum of the covariance matrix of the $\log \zeta_{it}^2$ variables, defined as in (10), and a diagonal matrix in which the i-th diagonal element is the variance of $\log \kappa_{it}$. Each diagonal element in the covariance matrix of ε_t, Σ_ε, is equal to the variance of the corresponding t-distribution, that is Var $(\varepsilon_{it}) = v_i/(v_i - 2)$ for $v_i > 2$ and $i = 1, \ldots, N$. As regards the off diagonal elements

$$E(\varepsilon_{it}\varepsilon_{jt}) = E(\kappa_i^{-1/2})E(\kappa_j^{-1/2})E(\zeta_i\zeta_j), \quad i \neq j, \quad i,j = 1, \ldots, N.$$

The last term is obtained from the corresponding covariance of $\log \zeta_i^2$ and $\log \zeta_j^2$ using (10), while

$$E(\kappa_i^{-1/2}) = v_i^{1/2}2^{-1/2}\Gamma\{(v_i - 1)/2)\}/\Gamma(v_i/2), \quad i = 1, \ldots, N.$$

Fitting the above multivariate model gave the following results

$$\hat{\Sigma}_\xi = \frac{\pi^2}{2}\begin{bmatrix} 1.00 & 0.411 & 0.303 & 0.380 \\ & 1.00 & 0.434 & 0.586 \\ & & 1.00 & 0.419 \\ & & & 1.000 \end{bmatrix} + \begin{bmatrix} 0.000 & & & \\ & 0.000 & & \\ & & 0.406 & \\ & & & 0.510 \end{bmatrix}$$

and

$$\hat{\Sigma}_\eta = 10^{-3} \begin{bmatrix} 8.69 & 10.25 & 2.92 & 10.24 \\ & 19.16 & 4.07 & 18.82 \\ & & 4.02 & 5.21 \\ & & & 18.96 \end{bmatrix}$$

The maximized quasi-log-likelihood, -4618.06, is slightly higher than for the Gaussian model reported in Section 5. The implied degrees of freedom for the Yen and Swiss Franc are 5.86 and 4.84 respectively.

The correlation matrix for ε_t is

$$\Sigma_\varepsilon = \begin{bmatrix} 1.00 & 0.85 & 0.88 & 0.99 \\ & 1.00 & 0.99 & 1.12 \\ & & 1.52 & 1.18 \\ & & & 1.70 \end{bmatrix}.$$

The covariance matrix of η_t is not very different from the one reported for the Gaussian model, and the same is true of the correlation matrix

$$\text{Corr}(\hat{\eta}) = \begin{bmatrix} 1.00 & 0.79 & 0.49 & 0.80 \\ & 1.00 & 0.46 & 0.99 \\ & & 1.00 & 0.60 \\ & & & 1.00 \end{bmatrix}.$$

As a result the common trends, and the implied groupings of exchange rates, are similar.

6.7 Conclusion

The multivariate stochastic variance model has a natural interpretation and is relatively parsimonious. The parameters can be estimated without too much difficulty by a quasi-maximum likelihood approach, and the movements in variance can be estimated by smoothing. The extension to heavier tailed distributions can be carried out very easily using the t-distribution.[2] The model fits well to exchange rates, and is able to capture common movements in volatility. The volatility in the three European exchange rates depends primarily on one factor. This factor affects the Yen to a much lesser extent, and the Yen is primarily affected by a second factor. Other rotations offer a slightly different interpretation but the special behaviour of the Yen is always apparent.

---

[2] The STAMP package can be used to carry out estimation by QML for univariate models. A multivariate version is currently being developed. Further information can be obtained by writing to the first author at LSE.

Appendix A. Uncorrelatedness of variables after transformation

Consider two random variables, ε and η, which may be dependent. Assume $E(\eta) = 0$ and let $h(.)$ be an even function such that $E[h(\varepsilon)]$ exists. If the covariance between η and $h(\varepsilon)$ exists, it is zero under the following conditions:

A.1 The density of ε, $f(\varepsilon)$, is symmetric.

A.2 $E(\eta|\varepsilon)$ is an odd function of ε.

The result follows because

$$\text{Cov}(\eta,\ h(\varepsilon)) = E[\eta(h(\varepsilon) - E[h(\varepsilon)])] = E[\eta h(\varepsilon)] = E[E(\eta|\varepsilon)h(\varepsilon)].$$

and, under A.2, $E[E(\eta|\varepsilon)h(\varepsilon)]$ is an odd function of ε, and so given A.1 its expected value is zero.

In the application here, $h(\varepsilon) = \log \varepsilon^2$ is an even function, and if ε and η are zero mean bivariate normal, conditions A.1 and A.2 are satisfied, and so

$$\text{Cov}(\eta,\ \log \varepsilon^2) = 0.$$

When ε has a Student t-distribution with v degrees of freedom, it can be written as $\varepsilon = \zeta \kappa^{-1/2}$, where $v\kappa$ is distributed independently of ζ as χ_v^2. If ζ and η are bivariate normal, then

$$E(\eta \log \varepsilon^2) = E[\eta(\log \zeta^2 - \log \kappa)] = E[\eta \log \zeta^2] - E(\eta)E(\log \kappa) = 0$$

and so η and $\log \varepsilon^2$ are again uncorrelated. Note that the result holds even if ε is Cauchy distributed ($v = 1$), since although the mean of ε does not exist in this case, $E[\log \varepsilon^2]$ does exist and in fact is zero.

Conditions A.1 and A.2 are satisfied if the joint distribution of ε and η satisfies the symmetry condition:

A.3 $g(\varepsilon,\ \eta) = g(-\varepsilon,\ -\eta)$.

This follows because A.3 implies A.1 since

$$f(\varepsilon) = \int_{-\infty}^{\infty} g(\varepsilon,\ \eta)d\eta = \int_{-\infty}^{\infty} g(-\varepsilon,\ -\eta)d\eta = \int_{-\infty}^{\infty} g(-\varepsilon,\ \eta)d\eta = f(-\varepsilon).$$

while A.3 implies A.2 because

$$E(\eta|\varepsilon) = \int_{-\infty}^{\infty} \eta \frac{g(\varepsilon,\ \eta)}{f(\varepsilon)} d\eta = \frac{1}{f(\varepsilon)} \int_{-\infty}^{\infty} \eta g(-\varepsilon,\ -\eta)d\eta$$
$$= \frac{-1}{f(-\varepsilon)} \int_{-\infty}^{\infty} \eta g(-\varepsilon,\ \eta)d\eta = -E(\eta|-\varepsilon).$$

Appendix B. Correlations between transformations of standard normal variables

In this appendix we derive the expression for Corr ($\log \varepsilon_1^2$, $\log \varepsilon_2^2$) where ε_1 and ε_2 are bivariate standard normal variables with correlation coefficient ρ.

Define $u = (\varepsilon_1^2)^{1/2}$ and $v = (\varepsilon_2^2)^{1/2}$. Johnson and Kotz (1972) give the following expression for the moments of u and v

$$E(u^r v^s) = \frac{1}{(\Gamma(1/2))^2} \left[2^{(r+s)/2} \Gamma\left(\frac{1+r}{2}\right) \Gamma\left(\frac{1+s}{2}\right) F\left(\frac{r}{2}, \frac{2}{2}; \frac{1}{2}; \rho^2\right) \right] \quad \text{(B.1)}$$

where $F(a, b; c; z)$ is the hypergeometric function given by

$$F(a, b; c; z) = \sum_{n=0}^{\infty} \frac{(a)_n (b)_n}{(c)_n} \frac{z^n}{n!} = 1 + \frac{ab}{\gamma} z + \frac{a(a+1)b(b+1)}{2!\gamma(\gamma+1)} z^2 + .s \quad \text{(B.2)}$$

where $(a)_n = \Gamma(a+n)/\Gamma(a)$.

The moment generating function of $\log \varepsilon_1^2$ and $\log \varepsilon_2^2$ is given by

$$m(t_1, t_2) = E[\exp\{t_1 \log \varepsilon_1^2 + t_2 \log \varepsilon_2^2\}] = E[\varepsilon_1^{2t_1} \varepsilon_2^{2t_2}]. \quad \text{(B.3)}$$

Using (B.1) in (B.3) and taking logarithms yields

$$\log m(t_1, t_2) = (t_1 + t_2)\log(2) + \log \Gamma((1/2) + t_1) + \log \Gamma((1/2) + t_2) \\ + \log F(-t_1, -t_2; 1/2; \rho^2) - 2 \log \Gamma(1/2) \quad \text{(B.4)}$$

and, therefore,

$$\frac{\partial^2 \log m(t_1, t_2)}{\partial t_1 \partial t_2} = \frac{1}{F} \frac{\partial^2 F}{\partial t_1 \partial t_2} - \frac{1}{F^2} \frac{\partial F}{\partial t_1} \frac{\partial F}{\partial t_2}. \quad \text{(B.5)}$$

To find the covariance between $\log \varepsilon_1^2$ and $\log \varepsilon_2^2$, expression (B.5) has to be evaluated at $t_1 = t_2 = 0$. Given the expression for the hypergeometric function in (B.2), it is easy to see that at $t_1 = t_2 = 0$

$$F(0, 0; 1/2; \rho^2) = 1 \quad \text{(B.6)}$$

$$\frac{\partial F}{\partial t_1} = \frac{\partial F}{\partial t_2} = 0 \quad \text{(B.7)}$$

and

$$\frac{\partial^2 F}{\partial t_1 \partial t_2} = \sum_{n=1}^{\infty} \frac{((n-1)!)^2 \rho^{2n}}{(1/2)_n n!} = \sum_{n=1}^{\infty} \frac{(n-1)!}{(1/2)_n n} \rho^{2n}. \quad \text{(B.8)}$$

Substituting (B.6), (B.7) and (B.8) into (B.5), we get

$$\text{Cov}(\log \varepsilon_1^2, \ \log \varepsilon_2^2) = \sum_{n=1}^{\infty} \frac{(n-1)!}{(1/2)_n n} \rho^{2n} \qquad \text{(B.9)}$$

The variance of $\log \varepsilon_i^2$ is given by $\pi^2/2$ for $i = 1, \ 2$ and therefore the correlation is as in expression (10) in the text.

Acknowledgements

A preliminary version of this paper was presented at the EC^2 conference in Rotterdam in December, 1991, and at seminars at LSE, Oxford, INSEE, Florence, Bilbao, Bank of Spain, Pompeu Fabra, Princeton, Harvard–MIT and Warwick. We are grateful to the participants, and to Javier Hidalgo, Alain Monfort, Enrique Sentana and Stephen Taylor for helpful comments. The referees also made a number of helpful comments and suggestions. All errors are our responsibility.

Support from the ESRC, as part of the project "Estimation and Diagnostic Testing of Unobserved Components Models", grant No. R000 23 3574, is gratefully acknowledged.

References

Abramowitz, M. and Stegun, N. C. (1970). *Handbook of Mathematical Functions* (New York: Dover Publications Inc.).

Baillie, R. T. and Bollerslev, T. (1990). A Multivariate Generalized ARCH Approach to Modeling Risk Premia in Forward Foreign Exchange Rate Markets. *Journal of International Money and Finance* 9, 309–24.

Bollerslev, T. (1986). Generalized Autoregressive Conditional Heteroskedasticity. *Journal of Econometrics* 51, 307–27.

—— (1987). A Conditional Heteroskedastic Time Series Model for Speculative Prices and Rates of Return. *Review of Economics and Statistics* 69, 542–7.

—— (1990). Modelling the Coherence in Short-Run Nominal Exchange Rates: A Multivariate Generalized ARCH Approach. *Review of Economics and Statistics* 72, 498–505.

—— Engle, R. F. (1993). Common Persistence in Conditional Variances. *Econometrica* 61, 167–86.

—— —— Wooldridge, J. M. (1988). A Capital Asset Pricing Model with Time Varying Covariances. *Journal of Political Economy* 96, 116–31.

—— Chou, R. Y., and Kroner, K. F. (1992). ARCH Modeling in Finance: A Review of the Theory and Empirical Evidence. *Journal of Econometrics* 52, 5–59.

Chesney, M. and Scott, L. (1989). Pricing European Currency Options: A Comparison of the Modified Black–Scholes Model and a Random Variance Model. *Journal of Financial and Quantitative Analysis* 24, 267–84.

Dassios, A. (1992). Asymptotic Approximations to Stochastic Variance Models (mimeo, LSE).

Diebold, F. X. and Nerlove, M. (1989). The Dynamics of Exchange Rate Volatility: A Multivariate Latent ARCH Model. *Journal of Applied Econometrics* 4, 1–21.

Dunsmuir, W. (1979). A Central Limit Theorem for Parameter Estimation in Stationary Vector Time Series and Its Applications to Models for a Signal Observed with Noise. *Annals of Statistics* 7, 490–506.

Engle, R. F. (1982). Autoregressive Conditional Heteroscedasticity with Estimates of the Variance of United Kingdom Inflation. *Econometrica* 50, 987–1007.

——(1987), Multivariate GARCH with Factor Structures–Cointegration in Variance (unpublished paper, UCSD).

—— and Bollerslev, T. (1986). Modelling the Persistence of Conditional Variances. *Econometric Reviews* 5, 1–50.

—— and Granger, C. W. J. (1987). Co-integration and Error Correction: Representation, Estimation and Testing. *Econometrica* 55, 251–76.

—— Ng, V. K. and Rothschild, M. (1990). Asset Pricing with a Factor ARCH Covariance Structure: Empirical Estimates for Treasury Bills. *Journal of Econometrics* 45, 213–38.

Harvey, A. C. (1989). *Forecasting, Structural Time Series Models and the Kalman Filter* (Cambridge: Cambridge University Press).

—— and Stock, J. H. (1988). Continuous Time Autoregressive Models with Common Stochastic Trends. *Journal of Economic Dynamics and Control* 12, 365–84.

Hull, J. and White, A. (1987). Hedging the Risks from Writing Foreign Currency Options. *Journal of International Money and Finance* 6, 131–52.

Johansen, S. (1988). Statistical Analysis of Cointegration Vectors. *Journal of Economic Dynamics and Control* 12, 231–54.

Johnson, N. L. and Kotz, S. (1972). *Distributions in Statistics: Continuous Multivariate Distributions* (New York: John Wiley and Sons Inc.).

Melino, A. and Turnbull, S. M. (1990). Pricing Foreign Currency Options with Stochastic Volatility. *Journal of Econometrics* 45, 239–65.

Nelson, D. B. (1988). The Time Series Behaviour of Stock Market Volatility and Returns (Unpublished Ph.D. Dissertation, Massachusetts Institute of Technology).

——(1990). Stationarity and Persistence in the GARCH(1, 1) Model. *Econometric Theory* 6, 318–34.

——(1991). Conditional Heteroscedasticity in Asset Returns: A New Approach. *Econometrica* 59, 347–70.

—— Cao, C. Q. (1992). Inequality Constraints in the Univariate GARCH Model. *Journal of Business and Economic Statistics* 10, 229–35.

Pantula, S. G. (1991). Asymptotic Distributions of Unit-Root Tests when the Process is Nearly Stationary. *Journal of Business and Economic Statistics* 9, 63–71.

Ruiz, E. (1992). Heteroscedasticity in Financial Time Series (Unpublished Ph.D. Dissertation, University of London).

——(1994). Quasi-Maximum Likelihood Estimation of Stochastic Volatility Models. *Journal of Econometrics* (forthcoming).

Schuessler, K. (1971). *Analysing Social Data: A Statistical Orientation* (Boston: Houghton Mifflin Company).

Schwert, G. W. (1989). Tests for Unit Roots: A Monte Carlo Investigation. *Journal of Business and Economic Statistics* 7, 147–60.

—— Seguin, P. J. (1990). Heteroskedasticity in Stock Returns. *Journal of Finance* 45, 1129–55.

Scott, L. O. (1987). Option Pricing when the Variance Changes Randomly. Theory, Estimation and an Application. *Journal of Financial and Quantitative Analysis* 22, 419–38.

Taylor, S. J. (1986). *Modelling Financial Time Series* (Chichester: John Wiley).

——(1994). Modelling Stochastic Volatility. *Mathematical Finance* 4, 183–204.

7

Stochastic Autoregressive Volatility:
A Framework for Volatility Modeling*

TORBEN G. ANDERSEN[1]

This paper introduces a general class of stochastic volatility models that can serve as a basis for modeling and estimating simultaneous equation systems involving multivariate volatility processes. The class consists of processes obtained as monotone polynomial transformations of so-called stochastic autoregressive volatility (SARV) models. The class permits a flexible modeling of volatility and avoids strong distributional assumptions. Most of the standard stochastic volatility models are incorporated in the framework, including the lognormal autoregressive model and stochastic volatility generalizations of GARCH and EGARCH. General conditions for strict stationarity, ergodicity, and the existence of finite lower-order unconditional moments for SARV are established. Closed-form expressions for the lower-order moments constitute the basis for the proposed generalized method of moments estimation procedure. As an illustration we consider an information-driven model of the return volatility–trading volume system for financial assets. Parameters with structural interpretation are estimated and an extended Kalman-filter procedure allows for the construction of volatility forecasts based on the bivariate return-volume series. Empirical results are based on daily NYSE data for IBM over 1973–1991.

Keywords: stochastic volatility, GARCH, return volatility, trading volume, mixture of distributions hypothesis, generalized method of moments

7.1 Introduction

Modeling and estimating the volatility of financial return series has been high on the agenda of financial economists over the last decade. The early developments were spurred by the introduction of autoregressive conditional heteroskedasticity (ARCH) (Engle, 1982) and generalized ARCH (GARCH) (Bollerslev, 1986), and these models still provide the backbone of much current research (Bollerslev, Chou, and Kroner, 1992). However, a plethora

* This work was previously published as T. G. Andersen (1994), 'Stochastic Autoregressive Volatility: A Framework for Volatility Modelling', *Mathematical Finance*, 4,2. Copyright © Blackwell Publishing. Reproduced by kind permission.

[1] The paper develops ideas originally put forth in my Ph.D. dissertation at Yale University. I am grateful to the members of my dissertation committee, Peter Phillips, Steve Ross, and Steve Heston, for advice. In addition, I thank an anonymous referee, Stan Pliska, and in particular Stephen Taylor for numerous comments which helped sharpen the focus of the paper. Naturally, all errors remain my own responsibility.

of alternative models, many in the so-called stochastic volatility category, have emerged in recent years. This development is in part a response to the success of ARCH. The qualitative features of financial return series that ARCH capture are so well documented that attention has shifted to the question: Which forces in the economic system are responsible for the generation of ARCH patterns? Multivariate structural models attempting to identify the forces behind conditional heteroskedasticity in volatility, the interaction between volatility and other economic variables, and the comovements of volatility across assets are now commonplace. In this context the ARCH assumption that volatility is driven by prior observable variables can become a constraint. Moreover, the proliferation of parameters in multivariate ARCH models is a serious problem. Consequently, a number of multivariate stochastic volatility models have been introduced. However, the proposed class of stochastic volatility models remains limited, consisting mainly of linear factor volatility models with distributional assumptions drawn from the conditional normal class, and typically excluding simultaneously determined nonreturn variables. Although some general procedures have been proposed, they do not allow consistent parameter estimation for a broad range of interesting alternative distributional assumptions and functional forms for the observable endogenous variables and volatility processes.

This paper introduces a general class of stochastic volatility models that can serve as a basis for modeling and estimation of simultaneous equation systems involving multivariate volatility processes and related (nonreturn) variables. The models consist of monotone polynomial transformations of so-called stochastic autoregressive volatility (SARV) processes and permit a flexible modeling of volatility. For example, the quadratic SARV and the exponential SARV are direct stochastic volatility generalizations of the empirically successful GARCH(1,1) and EGARCH(1,1) models. In fact, SARV encompasses most of the specifications in popular use in the literature, e.g. the standard EGARCH, lognormal stochastic volatility, and factor volatility models. The stochastic volatility models are generally less tractable than ARCH models and maximum likelihood estimation is usually not feasible. However, we demonstrate that the class of models in the SARV category possesses desirable properties. In particular, the polynomial SARV is shown to be strictly stationary and ergodic, have finite lower-order unconditional moments, and be asymptotically independent of a random initial value under a wide range of parameter constellations. The result is valid under weak distributional assumption and allows us to explore stochastic volatility processes that are not conditionally normal. We show that estimation of the models by GMM techniques is feasible subject to standard regularity and identification conditions. Exact expressions for the unconditional lower-order integer moments of SARV processes are derived for the purpose of facilitating identification, estimation, and specification testing. Identification of parameters is potentially a thorny issue for SARV models. We provide some sufficient conditions for identification in SARV, and these results are typically applicable to a much wider range of (polynomial) SARV models.

An important feature of the stochastic volatility framework is the ability to incorporate systems of equations involving nonreturn variables and contemporaneous mixtures of distributions. A leading example is provided by the mixture of distributions theory of the joint return-volume relation in financial markets, in which an observed information arrival process is posited as a common driving force behind the observables. For illustration, a version of this return volatility–trading volume model is estimated, taking full advantage of the framework developed in the paper. The mixture model is important in its own right, with implications for the modeling of financial markets in general and the return generating process and volatility estimation in particular. For example, the model enables us to utilize the joint observations on returns and trading volume in the construction of historical volatility series and volatility forecasts. At present, consistent and practical alternatives to the GMM estimation strategy proposed here do not exist for the functional forms and distributional assumptions given in this application. The only feasible alternative strategy is the related method of simulated moments (SM). This method can potentially handle even more general specifications for which the analytic expressions for the unconditional moments cannot be obtained in closed form. Nonetheless, whenever feasible, the GMM procedure is more efficient than SM, and given the evidence on the performance of GMM estimators in these settings, this may be a serious concern (Andersen and Sørensen, 1993). Consequently, the exact GMM procedure is also an important benchmark for the performance of the SM procedures (Duffie and Singleton, 1989).

The exposition proceeds as follows. Section 7.2.1 discusses the distinctive features of conditionally heteroskedastic and stochastic volatility processes. Section 7.2.2 introduces the concept of SARV processes and polynomial SARV models, while Section 7.2.3 provides some important examples. Section 7.2.4 establishes basic statistical properties of SARV, such as general conditions for strict stationarity, ergodicity, and the existence of finite unconditional moments. Section 7.3 reviews the econometric methodology. The GMM estimation is described and specific conditions for parameter identification are provided. Section 7.4 provides an empirical application, an investigation of the daily return and volume data for IBM common stock. Parameter estimates with structural interpretation are obtained. Moreover, an extended Kalman-filter procedure allows for the construction of volatility forecasts based on the bivariate return-volume series. Section 7.5 concludes. All proofs are collected in the appendix.

7.2 Stochastic autoregressive volatility

7.2.1 The general framework

A common feature of the economic systems investigated in this paper is the presence of univariate volatility processes of the general form

$$x_t = \mu_t + \sigma_t Z_t, \tag{2.1}$$

where $\mu_t = \mu(y_{t-1})$ is a measurable function of prior observables, i.e., $y_{t-1} \in I_{t-1}$, where I_{t-1} denotes the observable information set at time $t-1$. The $\{Z_t\}$ process is independently and identically distributed, mean zero, unit variance, and independent of all prior and contemporanous variables in the system. Finally, σ_t is a strictly positive volatility process which remains to be specified.

Equation (2.1) is not very restrictive. The main requirement is that the temporal dependency of x_t can be described fully by the first- and second-order conditional moments. This is typical of any volatility model.[2] It implies the existence of standardized residuals with distributions that are invariant to the evolution of the system

$$Z_t = (x_t - \mu_t)/\sigma_t. \tag{2.2}$$

Since x_t and μ_t are known at time t, Z_t is directly observable if we know σ_t. Hence, whether σ_t is observable or not is arguably the *key* feature of any volatility model. It is exactly what separates conditional heteroskedastic volatility models such as ARCH from stochastic volatility models.[3]

The simplest models have deterministic volatility, allowing only for predictable variation in volatility, e.g., seasonal effects. Formally, $\sigma_t = \sigma_0(t)$ for a function $\sigma_0(t) \in I_0$. The orthogonality of $Z_t = (x_t - \mu_t)/\sigma_0(t)$ can be exploited directly, and under distributional assumptions on Z_t maximum likelihood estimation (MLE) is straightforward. However, these models are inadequate when the data display conditional heteroskedasticity. In *conditionally heteroskedastic volatility models*, volatility varies over time in response to developments in the system

$$\sigma_t = \sigma(z_{t-1}), \tag{2.3}$$

where $z_{t-1} \in I_{t-1}$. The latter condition ensures that the error Z_t in (2.2) is observable under the null of correct model specification, and standard MLE procedures are again available.

For illustration and ease of reference we list a couple of the popular ARCH volatility specifications from the literature. GARCH(1,1) (Bollerslev, 1986; Taylor, 1986) takes the form

$$\sigma_t^2 = \omega + \beta\sigma_{t-1}^2 + \alpha\sigma_{t-1}^2 Z_{t-1}^2, \quad \omega, \ \beta, \ \alpha \geq 0, \tag{2.4}$$

with Z_t assumed, e.g., normal, student $t(v)$, or generalized error (GED$_w$) distributed (Nelson 1991).

---

[2] See Andersen (1992*b*) for a general definition of volatility. The chief constraint imposed on (2.1) is that μ_t equals the conditional mean w.r.t. prior observable variables. This can be relaxed at some cost in notational complexity.

[3] Technically, the question is one of measurability of σ_t w.r.t. to the σ-field generated by prior observable information. This condition is only meaningful, however, if we avoid certain ambiguities in the assignment of contemporaneous i.d. noise to σ_t and Z_t. These considerations are not central to the current exposition so we simply assume the volatility representation to be genuine, i.e., all contemporaneous noise is incorporated in Z_t. This is usually the case in practice (Andersen, 1992*b*).

Alternatively, the exponential ARCH or EGARCH(p, q) has (Nelson, 1991)

$$\ln \sigma_t^2 = \omega_0 + \sum_{i=1}^{p} \beta_i \ln \sigma_{t-i}^2 + \sum_{j=1}^{q} \gamma_j(\theta_0 \, Z_{t-j} + \gamma_0[|Z_{t-j}| - E|Z_t|]). \tag{2.5}$$

Stochastic volatility models do not allow σ_t to be written in the form (2.3). This may be due to dependency on prior unobserved variables or the presence of a separate contemporaneous shock to the volatility process. Instead, the general specification takes the form

$$\sigma_t = g(K_t), \tag{2.6}$$

where K_t is an unobserved, latent process driving the volatility process, and g is an increasing mapping from the support of K_t to $(0, \infty)$. Complete characterization of the model requires specification of the functional form for g and the dynamics of the K_t process.

The fact that K_t is not measurable w.r.t. I_{t-1} complicates estimation and specification testing. Even under specific distributional assumptions on K_t, standard MLE is usually infeasible. Exceptions arise when K_t is i.i.d. (Tauchen and Pitts, 1983), or K_t is restricted to a few discrete values (regimes) (Hamilton, 1988; Hamilton and Susmel, 1992; Cai, 1993).

The most widely used stochastic volatility model is the lognormal.[4] It provides a discrete time approximation to a diffusion which is popular in the option pricing literature. It takes the form

$$\ln \sigma_t = \xi + \phi[\ln \sigma_{t-1} - \xi] + \gamma\eta_t, \tag{2.7}$$

where Z_t and η_t are i.i.d. standard normal random variables with corr $(Z_t, \eta_t) = \delta$.[5] It fits our basic framework for $K_t = \ln \sigma_t$ and $g(K_t) = \exp(K_t)$.

This lognormal model has been estimated in a variety of ways including simple moment matching (MM) (Taylor 1986), generalized method of moments (GMM) (Melino and Turnbull, 1990), quasimaximum likelihood (QMLE) (Harvey, Ruiz, and Shephard, 1992), various simulated method of moment (SM) procedures (Duffie and Singleton, 1989; Gallant and Tauchen, 1992), Bayesian Markov Chain Monte Carlo analysis (MCMC) (Jacquier, Polson, and Rossi, 1993, hereafter, JPR), and simulation-based MLE (Danielsson and Richard, 1993;

---

[4] The model was introduced by Taylor (1980, 1982, 1986), who also refers to it as the autoregressive random variance model (Taylor, 1994). We call it lognormal stochastic volatility in order to emphasize our distinction between stochastic volatility and ARCH models. Identical or closely related models were employed by, among others, Scott (1987), Melino and Turnbull (1987), Wiggins (1987), Hull and White (1987), Johnson and Shanno (1987), Chesney and Scott (1989), and Heston (1993).

[5] A comparison of (2.5) and (2.7) suggests that EGARCH(1,1) and lognormal stochastic volatility possess a rather similar structure. The semblence is more than superficial. Continuous record asymptotics demonstrate that they have identical diffusion limits, i.e. provide a discrete time approximation to the same diffusion process (Nelson and Foster, 1991).

Danielsson, 1993). Apart from MM, GMM, and QML, the approaches are computationally intensive. In addition, the Monte Carlo evidence in JPR suggests that GMM and QML have poor finite sample performance in terms of bias and root-mean-square error (RMSE) of the estimated parameters.[6] They document superior performance of the likelihood-based MCMC, although the MCMC bias and RMSE remain high relative to similar measures for standard ARCH models.

The discussion points to weaknesses of the lognormal stochastic volatility model. It is subject to specific distributional assumptions that are critical to the estimation procedures and even under the maintained assumptions the parameters can be hard to estimate with precision in samples of usual size, in particular when standard versions of estimation procedures such as MM, GMM, and QML are used. The next section introduces a class of volatility models that is empirically manageable, includes the lognormal model as a special case, generalizes the popular GARCH(1,1), and can be estimated directly by GMM. The models provide flexibility in terms of distributional assumptions and functional forms which is required for consistent estimation in an array of interesting economic systems. Moreover, they simplify comparisons to ARCH models, and the proposed GMM procedure may possess better finite sample properties for some of these alternative models than it does for the lognormal model.

7.2.2 Stochastic autoregressive volatility

We focus on models that incorporate volatility processes from the following class.

Definition 2.1 The univariate process x_t is a *polynomial stochastic autoregressive volatility (SARV) model* if

(i) $x_t = \mu_t + \sigma_t Z_t$ is a genuine volatility representation for x_t.
(ii) $\sigma_t^q = g(K_t); q = 1, 2; g: D_K \to D_\sigma \subseteq (0, \infty)$ is an increasing function.
(iii) $K_t = h(K_{t-1}, u_t) = \omega + \beta K_{t-1} + [\gamma + \alpha K_{t-1}]u_t; \ h: D_K x D_u \to D_k \subseteq (-\infty, \infty);$
      $\alpha, \ \beta, \ \gamma \geq 0; \alpha + \beta > 0; \alpha + \gamma > 0.$ If $\omega = \gamma = 0$, then $K_t = 0$ for all t.
(iv) $g(K) = \sum_{j=0}^{\infty} \eta_j K^j; \ J = \sup_j \{j | \eta_j \neq 0\}.$
(v) u_t is i.i.d. $(1, \sigma_u^2); \sigma_u^2 > 0; u_t \in D_u \subseteq (-\beta/\alpha, \infty).$
(vi) Z_t is independent of $u_{t-j}, \ j \geq 0.$

Conditions (i) and (ii) mirror (2.1) and (2.6). The main restriction is the first-order Markov structure imposed on the driving process, K_t, in condition (iii). We refer to K_t as a SARV process. The exclusion of a longer lag structure does not reflect theoretical necessity but the practical need for parsimony. Moreover, a first-order autoregressive process appears adequate in most empirical applications. The

[6] Andersen and Sørensen (1993) document that the JPR simulations exaggerate the weakness of GMM due to the inclusion of an excessive number of sample moments and the choice of estimator of the GMM weighting matrix. Moreover, the results are sensitive to the choice of 500 observations in the simulations rather than, e.g. 1500, the size of the original data set. However, the Bayesian MCMC still dominates the improved GMM procedure in terms of RMSE.

polynomial transformation, g, in (iv) allows for a flexible functional form and enables us, in conjunction with the choice of $q = 1$ or $q = 2$, to accommodate models such as the lognormal stochastic volatility model and stochastic volatility extensions of GARCH(1,1). We consider $q = 1$ the leading case, and for this case we term $g(K_t)$ the *polynomial SARV process* generating the *polynomial SARV model*, x_t. For $q = 2$, we obtain a polynomial SARV process for σ_t^2 rather than σ_t. Hence, we refer to the volatility process as a *square root* (SR) *polynomial SARV process*. Finally, conditions (v) and (vi) impose restrictions on the innovation processes in the system. Condition (v) normalizes the contemporaneous shock to the volatility process to have unit mean, be nondegenerate, and only take on values that ensures $\beta + \alpha u_t > 0$ (with probability 1). Condition (vi) requires the i.i.d. error process Z_t to be independent of the prior shocks to the volatility process, so Z_t represents a purely random disturbance to the returns process.

The parameterization is promising for several reasons. First, it generalizes GARCH(1,1) and exponential ARCH(1,1), or EGARCH, which have been remarkably successful empirically. Second, the Markov structure is an intuitively appealing restriction on volatility processes governed by information arrivals. This interpretation is popular in the context of the normal-mixture distribution theory of returns (Clark, 1973; Tauchen and Pitts, 1983; Taylor, 1994). Third, Nelson, (1990*a*) proves stationarity and ergodicity of the GARCH(1,1) process and provides conditions for existence of higher-order moments. This result can be extended to SARV processes and serve as a basis for estimation and specification testing. In sum, SARV constitutes a convenient starting point for stochastic volatility generalizations. We consider some interesting special cases.

7.2.3 Examples of polynomial SARV models

The SR-SARV is obtained for $g(K) = K^{1/2}$, or equivalently $\sigma_t^2 = K_t$. We have

$$\sigma_t^2 = \omega + \beta\sigma_{t-1}^2 + [\gamma + \alpha\sigma_{t-1}^2]u_t, \quad \omega, \ \beta, \ \alpha > 0, \ \gamma \geq 0. \tag{2.8}$$

This provides a direct stochastic volatility generalization of GARCH(1,1), which is obtained by specifying $\gamma = 0$ and $u_t = Z_{t-1}^2$.

Similarly, letting $g(K) = K$, the identity mapping, the SARV process generalizes a (SD-) GARCH(1,1) specification for the conditional standard deviation of x_t:

$$\sigma_t = \omega + \beta\sigma_{t-1} + [\gamma + \alpha\sigma_{t-1}]u_t, \quad \omega, \ \beta, \ \alpha > 0, \ \gamma \geq 0. \tag{2.9}$$

SD-GARCH(1,1) follows from $\gamma = 0$ and $u_t = c|Z_{t-1}|$ with c chosen to ensure a mean of 1.

As a last example of stochastic volatility generalizations of ARCH models, consider the EGARCH(1,1), i.e., (2.5) with $p = q = 1$. It is a special case of exponential SARV:

$$\ln(\sigma_t) = \omega + \beta \ln \sigma_{t-1} + (\gamma + \alpha \ln \sigma_{t-1})u_t. \qquad (2.10)$$

EGARCH(1,1) is obtained from $\alpha = 0, g(K) = \exp(K)$, $\gamma = \gamma_1/2$, $\omega = (\omega_0 - \gamma_1)/2$, and $u_t = 1 + \theta_0 Z_{t-1} + \gamma_0[|Z_{t-1}| - E|Z_t|]$. Specific distributional assumptions concerning the error innovations u_t and Z_t are not required.[7] Notice, furthermore, that $g(K)$ is a monotone polynomial transformation, since $\exp(K) = \sum_{j=0}^{\infty} K^j/j!$.

In our final example we verify that the *lognormal stochastic volatility model* is, indeed, a SARV model. This is not entirely obvious since condition (vi) of Definition 2.1 requires independence between the two contemporaneous shocks Z_t and u_t while the two disturbance terms generally are correlated in the lognormal volatility model. However, rewrite (2.7) as

$$\ln \sigma_t = \omega + \beta \ln \sigma_{t-1} + \gamma u_t,$$

where $\omega = \xi(1 - \phi) - \gamma$, $\beta = \phi$, and $u_t = 1 + \eta_t \sim$ i.i.d. $N(1,1)$. Next, notice

$$\varepsilon_t = \sigma_t Z_t = \exp(\omega + \beta \ln \sigma_{t-1})[\exp(\gamma u_t)Z_t] = \tilde{\sigma}_t \tilde{Z}_t$$

for $\tilde{\sigma}_t = \exp(K_t)$, $K_t = \omega + \beta \ln \sigma_{t-1}$, and $\tilde{Z}_t = \exp(\gamma u_t)Z_t$ with $\mathrm{var}(\tilde{Z}_t) = 1$ via appropriate rescaling of ω.

The equation $\varepsilon_t = \tilde{\sigma}_t \tilde{Z}_t$ is the lognormal SARV version of (2.1) with $\varepsilon_t = x_t - \mu_t$. Furthermore, $\tilde{\sigma}_t = g(K_t) = \exp(K_t)$ and the SARV equation is

$$K_t = \ln \tilde{\sigma}_t = \omega + \beta K_{t-1} + \beta \gamma u_{t-1} = \omega + \beta K_{t-1} + \tilde{\gamma} \tilde{u}_t,$$

where $\tilde{\gamma} = \beta \gamma$ and $\tilde{u}_t = u_{t-1}$.

It is straightforward to verify that all conditions of Definition 2.1 are satisfied with $\alpha = 0$. This specification merges the contemporaneous shocks into a lognormal-normal mixture, $\tilde{Z}_t$, while current volatility, $\tilde{\sigma}_t$, is a function of the prior unobserved state variable K_{t-1} and a (prior) volatility shock $\tilde{u}_t$.[8]

7.2.4 Basic properties of the SARV process

This section establishes necessary and sufficient conditions for stationarity and ergodicity of the SARV process. These properties are indispensible for our estimation strategy. In addition, the impact of conditioning on an initial distribution for the SARV process at $t = 0$ is explored. Finally, analytic expressions for the lower-order unconditional moments of the process are developed. The

---

[7] Practical identification issues may necessitate the imposition of additional restrictions during estimation.

[8] It shows that the lognormal SARV has conditional rather than contemporaneous stochastic volatility. In fact, the representation in (2.7) is nongenuine, while the present is genuine (Andersen, 1992b).

SARV moment expressions enable us to utilize method of moment based estimation procedures for a wide class of (polynomial) SARV models. We emphasize these procedures because classical MLE procedures generally are infeasible for genuine stochastic volatility models.[9]

We distinguish between an unconditional and a conditional version of the SARV process. The latter conditions on a possibly random starting value K_0 for the process. By substituting repeatedly $(t-1$ times) in equation (iii) of Definition 2.1 we obtain

$$_cK_t = \sum_{j=0}^{t-1} \prod_{i=0}^{j-1} (\beta + \alpha u_{t-i})(\omega + \gamma u_{t-j}) + K_0 \prod_{i=0}^{t-1} (\beta + \alpha u_{t-i}), \qquad (2.11)$$

where $_cK_t$ denotes the SARV process conditional on the random starting value K_0.[10]

The initial condition is assigned a given, potentially degenerate, probability distribution which is finite with probability 1 and independent of u_t and Z_t for $t \geq 0$. Extending Definition 2.1, condition (iii) with such initial conditions generates a *conditional SARV process*.

If, instead, the SARV process extends back indefinitely we have

$$K_t = \sum_{j=0}^{\infty} \prod_{i=0}^{j-1} (\beta + \alpha u_{t-i})(\omega + \gamma u_{t-j}), \qquad (2.12)$$

where again $K_t \equiv 0$ if $\omega = 0$ and $\gamma = 0$. This is simply a restatement of the process from Definition 2.1 (without initial conditions) and constitutes the standard (*unconditional*) *SARV process*. The most significant properties of SARV are collected in Theorem 2.1, while corresponding results for the polynomial SARV are provided in the following corollary.

Theorem 2.1 Let a conditional SARV process, $_cK_t$, be given, and let the associated (unconditional) SARV process, if it exists, be denoted K_t. If the restrictions, $E[\ln(\beta + \alpha u_t)] < 0$, and $0 < p < \infty$ are valid, then

(i) K_t is strictly stationary, ergodic, and has a well-defined probability measure on $(-\infty, \infty)$. If $\omega \neq 0$ or $\gamma > 0$ the measure is nondegenerate.
(ii) $K_t -_c K_t \to 0$ a.s.
(iii) $|E(K_t^p)| < \infty$ if and only if $E[(\beta + \alpha u_t)^p] < 1$ and $E[u_t^p] < \infty$.
(iv) *If* $|E(K_0^p)| < \infty$ then $\lim_{t\to\infty} E(_cK_t^p) = E(K_t^p)$.

---

[9] An alternative is estimation by simulation. Duffie and Singleton (1993) extend the original work of McFadden (1989) and Pakes and Pollard (1989) to a time-series context. However, the regularity conditions can be hard to verify for the general SARV model, and practical applications have been limited to the univariate lognormal SARV, so the empirical performance of the estimators in higher dimensions remains largely unknown.

[10] We use the conventions (i) $\prod_{i=0}^{-1}(\cdot) \equiv 1$ and (ii) $K_t \equiv 0$ if $\omega = \gamma = 0$.

On the other hand, if $E[\ln(\beta + \alpha u_t)] \geq 0$, $\omega \neq 0$ or $\gamma > 0$, $\alpha > 0$, and $\omega\alpha + \gamma(1 - \beta) \neq 0$, then $|_c K_t| \to \infty$ a.s. and K_t is not well defined.

If $E[\ln(\beta + \alpha u_t)] \geq 0$, $\omega \neq 0$ or $\gamma > 0$, and $\omega\alpha + \gamma(1 - \beta) = 0$ or $\alpha = 0$, then $_c K_t$ is akin to a random walk with or without drift, and again K_t is not well defined.

Property (i) guarantees that SARV processes are well behaved. Property (iii) is a general condition for finiteness of the unconditional moments in SARV. Finally, properties (ii) and (iv) suggest that concentrating on the simpler unconditional version of the process is not critical since, asymptotically, the two versions of SARV are indistinguishable. The conditions for stationarity are less stringent than those for existence of finite unconditional moments of SARV, and the distinction is nontrivial. By Jensen's inequality, we have $E[\ln(\beta + \alpha u_t)]$ $< \ln(E[\beta + \alpha u_t]) = \ln(\beta + \alpha)$. Hence, from (iii), the first-order moment of K_t does not exist for $\alpha + \beta = 1$, but, from (i), the process is nevertheless strictly stationary. This generalizes results in Nelson (1991) for IGARCH(1,1) (GARCH(1,1) with $\alpha + \beta = 1$). The point is further illustrated by considering the expectation of the conditional volatility process. From (2.11) we find, conditional on a starting value, K_0,

$$E[_c K_t] = \sum_{j=0}^{t-1} (\beta + \alpha)^j (\omega + \gamma) + K_0(\beta + \alpha)^t.$$

For $\alpha + \beta = 1$, a volatility shock persists indefinitely (in L^1 or mean), even for $\omega = \gamma = 0$. If (i) $\alpha + \beta > 1$, or (ii) $\alpha + \beta = 1$ and either ω or γ is positive, then the conditional volatility process is "mean explosive"; i.e., shocks are exacerbated over time and expected future values grow beyond any bound in finite time.[11] However, the process may still be strictly stationary, in which case the absence of finite moments reflects the "fat tails" in the underlying stationary distribution.

The stochastic volatility IGARCH(1,1) model exemplifies all of the points nicely. It implies $E[_c K_t] = (\omega + \gamma)t + K_0$, so for $\omega = \gamma = 0$ the conditional expectation behaves like a random walk without drift, and shocks to K_0 persist forever (in mean). Nevertheless, from (ii) and Definition 2.1, the process converges almost surely to zero! Thus, it displays properties that are rather unintuitive for a conditional variance process. Moreover, the empirical evidence favors $\omega > 0$ over $\omega = 0$. But when $\omega + \gamma > 0$ the conditional expectation behaves like a random walk *with drift* and is explosive, in spite of the fact that the process is strictly stationary and ergodic. This case mirrors the behavior of the stationary SARV model with $\alpha + \beta > 1$. Thus, the null hypothesis of $\alpha + \beta = 1$ has no special implications.[12] The proper focus is rather on the hypothesis of

---

[11] It is possible to define a string of different "persistence" concepts in the spirit of Nelson (1990a). The one considered in the text corresponds to his "persistence of z_t in L^1 in $_u \sigma_t^2$," which in my notation would be "persistence of u_t in L^1 in K_t." Results analogous to his Theorem 5 on these various measures of persistence may be derived in the present context.

[12] Nelson (1990b) provides an interesting perspective. He shows that $\alpha + \beta$ converges to one in the diffusion limit of GARCH(1, 1) as the sampling interval shrinks. The intuition is straightfor-

$\alpha + \beta < 1$ versus $\alpha + \beta \geq 1$. These distinct subsets of the parameter space separate SARV processes with finite unconditional means from those without. Finiteness of the unconditional moments are, of course, required for any method-of-moments-type estimation.[13]

The following corollary is a simple consequence of Theorem 2.1 and Definition 2.1

Corollary 2.1 Let a Jth-order polynomial SARV process, $\sigma_t = g(K_t)$, be given. If $E[\ln(\beta + \alpha u_t)] < 0$, then

   (i) σ_t is strictly stationary, ergodic, and has a well-defined probability measure on $(0, \infty)$. If $\omega \neq 0$ or $\gamma > 0$ the measure is nondegenerate.

   (ii) For J finite: $E(\sigma_t) < \infty$ if and only if $E[(\beta + \alpha u_t)^J] < 1$.

   (iii) For J finite: $E(\sigma_t^2) < \infty$ if and only if $E[(\beta + \alpha u_t)^{2J}] < 1$.

   (iv) For $J = \infty$: $E(\sigma_t) < \infty$ if and only if $\sum_{j=0}^{\infty} \eta_j E[K_t^j] < \infty$.

   (v) If $|E(\sigma_0)| < \infty$, then $\lim_{t \to \infty} E(_c\sigma_t) = E(\sigma_t)$, where $_c\sigma_t = g(_cK_t)$.

The corollary provides the main properties necessary for practical applications of polynomial SARV models. Property (i) ensures strict stationarity and ergodicity while (ii) and (iii) characterize the conditions for finite unconditional means and variance in finite-order polynomial SARV models. Condition (iv) provides the corresponding result for infinite-order polynomial SARV models. Finally, (v) assures us that, asymptotically, the conditional process suffices for the calculation of unconditional expectations.

Unconditional integer moments of SARV can be calculated directly. Theorem 2.2 provides all the first-, second-, and third-order moments plus, for brevity, only a few fourth-order moments. These results are also useful for computation of low-order moments in a variety of polynomial SARV models.

Theorem 2.2 The volatility process, K_t, in the unconditional stationary and ergodic SARV model satisfying $E[\ln(\beta + \alpha u_t)] < 0$, has the following unconditional moments for integers $i, j \geq 0$, $k > 0$.
The first-order moment exists if $E[\beta + \alpha u_t] = \alpha + \beta < 1$, and

$$E(K_t) = (\omega + \gamma)/(1 - \alpha - \beta) = \kappa. \tag{2.13}$$

The second-order moments exist if $E[(\beta + \alpha u_t)^2] = (\alpha + \beta)^2 + \alpha^2 \sigma_u^2 < 1$, and

$$\text{var}(K_t) = \frac{(\gamma + \alpha \kappa)^2}{1 - (\alpha + \beta)^2 - \alpha^2 \sigma_u^2} \sigma_u^2, \tag{2.14}$$

ward. The diffusion assumption requires the conditional variance to change "slowly," but then the process must, on average, remain virtually constant over short intervals, which requires $\alpha + \beta$ to approach 1 (from below). This does not imply that unconditional second moments explode.

[13] In addition, absence of finite moments complicate the proofs of standard asymptotically based inference procedures, although Lumsdaine (1990) demonstrates validity of standard asymptotic theory in the presence of IGARCH effects.

$$\text{cov}(K_t, \ K_{t-j}) = (\alpha + \beta)^j \text{var}(K_t).$$

The third-order moments exist if

$$E[(\beta + \alpha u_t)^3] = (\alpha + \beta)^3 + 3(\alpha + \beta)\alpha^2\sigma_u^2 + \alpha^3 E[(u_t - 1)^3] < 1,$$

and

$$E[K_t - \kappa]^3 = \frac{D_0\sigma_u^2 + D_1 E[u_t - 1]^3}{1 - E[\beta + \alpha u_t]^3}, \tag{2.16}$$

where $D_0 = 6(\alpha + \beta)\alpha(\gamma + \alpha\kappa) \text{var}(K_t)$ and $D_1 = (\gamma + \alpha\kappa)^3 + 3\alpha^2(\gamma + \alpha\kappa) \text{var}(K_t)$.

$$E[(K_t - \kappa)^2(K_{t-k} - \kappa)] = C_0 E[(K_t - \kappa)^2(K_{t-k+1} - \kappa)] + C_1(\alpha + \beta)^{k-1} \tag{2.17}$$

where $C_0 = (\alpha + \beta)^2 + \alpha^2\sigma_u^2$, $C_1 = 2\alpha(\gamma + \alpha\kappa)\sigma_u^2 \text{var}(K_t)$, and

$$E[(K_t - \kappa)(K_{t-j} - \kappa)^2] = (\alpha + \beta)^j E[(K_t - \kappa)^3], \tag{2.18}$$

$$E[(K_t - \kappa)(K_{t-i} - \kappa)(K_{t-i-j} - \kappa)] = (\alpha + \beta)^i E[(K_t - \kappa)^2(K_{t-j} - \kappa)]. \tag{2.19}$$

Fourth-order moments exist if

$$E[\beta + \alpha u_t]^4 = (\alpha + \beta)^4 + 6(\alpha + \beta)^2\alpha^2\sigma_u^2 + 4(\alpha + \beta)\alpha^3 E[u_t - 1]^3 + \alpha^4 E[u_t - 1]^4 < 1,$$

and

$$E(K_t - \kappa)^4 = \frac{G_0\sigma_u^2 + G_1 E[u_t - 1]^3 + G_2 E[u_t - 1]^4}{1 - E[\beta + \alpha u_t]^4} \tag{2.20}$$

where $G_0 = 6(\gamma + \alpha\kappa)(\alpha + \beta)^2[(\gamma + \alpha\kappa) \text{var}(K_t) + 2\alpha E[K_t - \kappa]^3]$,

$\qquad G_1 = 12(\gamma + \alpha\kappa)(\alpha + \beta)\alpha[(\gamma + \alpha\kappa) \text{var}(K_t) + \alpha E[K_t - \kappa]^3]$,

$\qquad G_2 = (\gamma + \alpha\kappa)[(\gamma + \alpha\kappa)^3 + 6(\gamma + \alpha\kappa)\alpha^2 \text{var}(K_t) + 4\alpha^3 E[K_t - \kappa]^3]$,

and

$$E[(K_t - \kappa)^2(K_{t-k} - \kappa)^2] = C_0' E[(K_t - \kappa)^2(K_{t-k+1} - \kappa)^2] + C_1'(\alpha + \beta)^{k-1}, \tag{2.21}$$

with $C_0' = C_0$ *and* $C_1' = 2\alpha(\gamma + \alpha\kappa)\sigma_u^2 E(K_t - \kappa)^3$. When the inequality condition associated with a given moment is violated, the moment is infinite.

Similar results can be obtained for any positive integer moment but the expressions grow fairly involved and the conditions for finite moments become increasingly stringent as the order of the moment increases. Whether such higher-order moments are needed for estimation depends on the model specification. Finally, note that calculation of a given moment requires the existence of corresponding and lower-order moments of u_t. In this context, distributional assumptions amount to restrictions on the relationship between the moments of u_t. Absent such restrictions, the number of parameters grows one for one with the number of higher-order moments, and parsimony dictates the inclusion of a minimal amount.

The geometrically decaying covariances in (2.15) indicate that $\alpha + \beta$ is a measure of persistence in the SARV model, just as it is in GARCH(1,1). This feature is brought out more clearly by the following respecification of the SARV model.

$$K_t = (\omega + \gamma) + (\alpha + \beta)K_{t-1} + (\gamma + \alpha K_{t-1})\tilde{u}_t, \qquad (2.22)$$

where $\tilde{u}_t = u_t - 1$ is i.i.d. $(0, \sigma_u^2)$. Hence, the dependence of expected future volatility on the current state is governed primarily by $\alpha + \beta$, although nonlinear transformations of K_t make the last term above important as well. Notice furthermore the dual roles of γ and α. They impact expected future volatility via the first two terms, and they affect the variability of future volatility through the conditional variance of the innovation. From (2.22) it is apparent that separate identification of α and β, as well as ω and γ, hinges on higher-order return moments, which then involves higher-order moments of K_t and u_t. The next section deals with estimation under these circumstances.

We conclude this section by considering some well-known results for the lognormal SARV in light of our present results. The lognormal SARV is a special case of the infinite-order SARV process that we termed the exponential SARV. Some additional restrictions are generally required to obtain closed-form solutions for the unconditional moments in this model. For the lognormal SARV they take the form of distributional assumptions. We also note that, given those distributional assumptions, the conditions for strict stationarity and finiteness of all moments coincide in this model.

Example 2.1 The lognormal SARV process takes the form

$$K_t = \kappa + \beta(K_{t-1} - \kappa) + \theta u_t, \quad u_t \text{ i.i.d. } N(0, 1),$$

$$\sigma_t = \exp(K_t) = \sum_{j=0}^{\infty} \frac{K_t^j}{j!}.$$

This is a special case of exponential SARV, (2.10), with $\alpha = 0$. Exponential SARV is strictly stationary and ergodic with well-defined probability measure on $(0, \infty)$ for $E[\ln(\beta + \alpha u_t)] = \ln \beta < 0$ (Corollary 2.1, (i)) which implies $\beta < 1$.

Moreover, a necessary condition for $E|K_t^p| < \infty$ is (Theorem 2.1, (iii)) $E[(\beta + \alpha u_t)^p] = \beta^p < 1$ or, again, $\beta < 1$, and $E[u_t^p] < \infty$. Thus, moments of arbitrarily high order must exist for u_t. However, this condition, as well as the stronger necessary and sufficient condition [Corollary 2.1, (iv)]: $E[\exp(K_t)] < \infty$, generally require the imposition of additional restrictions, if closed-form solutions for the integer moments are needed. The lognormal SARV accomplishes this by assuming u_t is standard normal. For completeness, we list the unconditional moments for σ_t. Denoting the unconditional mean and variance of K_t by κ and var(K), we obtain

$$E(\sigma_t^m) = \exp[m\kappa + m^2 \text{var}(K)/2],$$
$$\text{cov}(K_t, \ K_{t-j}) = \beta^j \text{var}(K),$$
$$E(\sigma_t^m \sigma_{t-j}^n) = E(\sigma_t^m)E(\sigma_t^n)\exp(mn \ \text{cov}(K_t, \ K_{i-j})),$$

where j is a nonnegative integer, and m, n are positive constants.

7.3 Econometric specifications and methodology

7.3.1 System of equations involving stochastic volatility
An important feature of polynomial SARV processes is that they are well suited as building blocks for systems of equations involving both returns and other economic series as endogenous variables. In this section we outline a framework for GMM estimation of such systems.

We consider a general system of equations of the following form ($t = 1, \ldots, T$):

$$\varepsilon_t(\theta) = x_t - \mu_t(\theta) = b\sigma_t Z_t + v_t, \tag{3.1a}$$

$$Y_t = H(\sigma_t, \ \ldots, \ \sigma_{t-j}, \ v_t, \ \ldots, \ v_{t-L}, \ X_t, \ \ldots, \ X_{t-M}; \ \theta; \ \upsilon_t). \tag{3.1b}$$

In this system, ε_t is an $N \times 1$ vector of innovations, θ is the vector of parameters, b is the $N \times 1$ vector of factor loadings, σ_t is a polynomial SARV process, and v_t and υ_t are mutually independent vectors with i.i.d.(0,1) random components that are independent of all current and prior variables. Finally, Y_t is an $N_1 \times 1$ vector of nonreturn variables that are determined jointly with ε_t by a known function H of a finite set of endogenous variables and observable exogenous vectors $\{X_{t-j}\}_{j \geq 0}$.

The models in Section 7.2.3 are special cases of this framework (with $N_1 = 0$). The examples below illustrate the usefulness of allowing for additional equations in the system.

Example 3.1 In Andersen (1993) the following SARV return volatility–trading volume system is obtained:

$$R_t | \sigma_t \sim N(r, \ \sigma_t^2), \tag{3.2}$$

$$V_t | \sigma_t \sim c \cdot \mathrm{Po}(m_0 + m_1 \sigma_t^2), \quad c > 0, \tag{3.3}$$

$$\sigma_t = \omega + \beta \sigma_{t-1} + (\gamma + \alpha \sigma_{t-1}) u_t, \quad u_t \text{ is positive, i.i.d.}(1, \ \sigma_u^2), \tag{3.4}$$

where R_t, the asset return, conditional on a volatility process σ_t representing an information arrival process, is Gaussian; V_t, the standardized trading volume is Poisson distributed conditional on σ_t; the disturbances of the conditional distributions in (3.2) and (3.3) are mutually independent and orthogonal of the error process in the SARV process (3.4), $\{u_t\}$; the parameter vector is $\theta = (r, \ c, \ m_0, \ m_1, \ \omega, \ \beta, \ \alpha, \ \gamma, \ \sigma_u^2)$, and all variables are scalars.

The system is inspired by an explicit microstructure model, and related to the specifications of Clark (1973), Tauchen and Pitts (1983), Gallant, Hsieh, and Tauchen (1991), and Foster and Viswanathan (1993). The theory is consistent with vector generalizations, including asset-specific volatility processes along with common volatility processes. The functional form and the Poisson distribution for volume are novel. This reflects the limiting distribution of a binomial variable governing the trading process and distinguishes it from the usual conditional Gaussian specification (Harris, 1986, 1987). An additional advantage is that the present model explicitly imposes nonnegativity on the volume series.

Example 3.2 An SR-Factor SARV model for returns, $R_t = (R_{it})_{i=1}^N$, with one common factor is given by

$$R_{it} = r_i + b_i \sigma_t Z_t + v_{it}, \quad i = 0, \ 1, \ \ldots, \ N, \tag{3.5}$$

where σ_t and Z_t are random variables, their product constituting the common factor, b_t is the loading of the ith asset return on the common factor with $b_0 \equiv 1$ providing a normalization of the factor, $\{v_{it}\}$ is the idiosyncratic noise process of the ith asset return, and r_i is the mean return on the ith asset.

Example 3.2 is closely related to the factor models in Diebold and Nerlove (1989) and Laux and Ng (1990). The common factor volatility process is assumed to evolve according to the SR-SARV specification in (2.8). Likewise, v_{it} is allowed to follow an SR-SARV process, which is independent of K_t, Z_t, and $\{v_{jt}\}$ for $j \neq i$. Finally, Z_t is assumed i.i.d. $N(0,1)$.

7.3.2 GMM Estimation

GMM estimation of the system (3.1) exploits the convergence of selected sample moments to their unconditionally expected values. Typically, population moments of the type $E(\varepsilon_{it}^n \varepsilon_{j, \ t-k}^s)$, $E(\varepsilon_{it}^n Y_{j, \ t-k}^s)$ and $E(Y_{it}^n Y_{j, \ t-k}^s)$ are chosen for low positive integer values of n, s, and k. The corresponding sample moments at t are denoted $m_t(\theta) = (m_{1t}(\theta), \ \ldots, \ m_{Qt}(\theta))$, where the number of moments, Q, exceeds the dimension of θ, say n. The true parameter vector is denoted θ_0, and the sample moments are $M_T(\theta) = (M_{1T}(\theta), \ldots, M_{QT}(\theta))$.[14] Finally, the corresponding vector of analytical moments is $A(\theta)$. The GMM estimator, $\hat{\theta}_T$, minimizes the distance between $A(\theta)$ and $M_T(\theta)$ over the parameter space Ξ in the quadratic form

$$\hat{\theta}_T = \arg_{\theta \in \Xi} \min \left(A(\theta) - M_T(\theta) \right)' \Gamma_T^{-1} \left(A(\theta) - M_T(\theta) \right). \qquad (3.6)$$

The specific metric is determined by the choice of the positive definite and possibly random weighting matrix, Γ_T. Under suitable regularity conditions $\hat{\theta}_T$ is consistent and asymptotically normal:

$$T^{1/2} \Omega_T^{-1/2} (\hat{\theta}_T - \theta_0) \sim N(0, \ I_n).$$

The optimal weighting matrix, Γ_T^{-1}, minimizes the asymptotic covariance matrix, $\lim_{T \to \infty} \Omega_T$.[15] Using an appropriate weighting matrix is important. The sample moments may be highly correlated and strongly serially dependent. If this is ignored, say by letting $\Gamma_T = I_Q$, the result may be a serious loss of efficiency (Hansen 1982). It has become customary to employ a consistent nonparametric estimate of Γ_T.[16] A popular choice is the NW (Newey and West 1987) heteroskedasticity and autocorrelation consistent (HAC) co-variance matrix estimator, but other choices are feasible, such as the quadratic spectral (QS) estimator (Andrews, 1991).

7.3.3 Identification
The previous section outlines a general procedure for GMM estimation of SARV systems. However, in any particular application regularity conditions should be checked (Hansen, 1982; Andrews, 1991). An important concern is parameter identification. If the data generating mechanism is system (3.1) with true parameter θ_0, the asymptotic behavior of the sample moments, which generally are a function of $\theta \in \Xi$, depends on θ_0. Assuming a law of large numbers applies, we write

$$\lim_{T \to \infty} M_T(\theta; \ \theta_0) = E[m_t(\theta, \ \theta_0)] = c(\theta; \ \theta_0).$$

A prerequisite for identification is that the equation $A(\theta) = c(\theta; \theta_0)$ has a unique solution, θ_0, among all $\theta \in \Xi$.

---

[14] By definition $M_{1T}(\theta) = \sum_{t=k+1}^{T} m_{it}(\theta)/(T-k)$ for $i = 1, \ldots, Q$.

[15] It is given by the inverse of $\Gamma_T = E[(1/T) \sum_{t=1}^{T} \sum_{r=1}^{T} (m_t - A(\theta))(m_r - A(\theta))']$.

[16] In principle, we can calculate all elements of Γ_T as functions of the parameters, but there is a large number of entries in the matrix each consisting of a large number of lags, and at each lag the expressions are lengthy, involving covariances of the moments we evaluated in Theorem 2.2. Moreover, the issue of how to best utilize this information during variance-covariance matrix estimation remains an open question. Hence, traditional non-parametric estimation appears appropriate.

Usually, the SARV parameters must be derived exclusively from the unconditional moments of the volatility process because the volatility parameters do not
appear in equations involving observables, such as (3.1a) and (3.1b), except
indirectly through σ_t. Theorem 3.1 provides conditions for identification of the
volatility parameters from low-order moments of the volatility process. The
conditions get weaker as more higher-order moments are included which reflects
the use of additional information. However, asymptotic normality of the estimates hinges on the variance-covariance matrix of the sample moments being
finite, e.g., including fourth-order moments implies assuming finite eight-order
unconditional moments when estimating the weighting matrix. Thus, there
are good reasons for considering identification from the lowest-order moments
possible.

For convenience, we rewrite the SARV process in (2.17) as

$$K_t = \kappa + \rho(K_{t-1} - \kappa) + (\delta + K_{t-1})U_t, \qquad (3.7)$$

where $\kappa = (\omega + \gamma)/(1 - \alpha - \beta)$, $\rho = \alpha + \beta$, $\delta = \gamma/\alpha$, $U_t = \alpha(u_t - 1)$.

If moments up to order L, $L > 1$, are included, $E(U_t^j)$ for $j = 2, \ldots, L$ are
additional parameters.

Theorem 3.1 (1) If a SARV process has finite Lth-order unconditional moments,
$L \geq 3$, then the parameters $(\kappa, \rho, \delta, \sigma_u^2, E(U_t^3))$ are identified from the first
three unconditional moments of K_t, and each additional higher-order moment
of U_t can be identified from the same and lower moments in K_t.

The original parameter vector $\theta = (\omega, \gamma, \beta, \alpha, \sigma_u^2, E[u_t - 1]^3)$ is identified if
we impose one of the following restrictions:

(i) $\omega = c_0 < \kappa(1 - \rho)$, or $\gamma = c_1 > 0$, or $\beta = c_2$, where $c_i, i = 0, 1, 2$ are known
constants.

(ii) $E[U_t^j] = m_j(\eta)$, with η a parameter vector such that the equation system
$\alpha^j E[u_t - 1]^j = m_j(\eta)$, $j = 2, \ldots, L$, has a unique solution in (α, η).

(2) If only finiteness of the second-order moments of K_t is ensured, i.e. $L = 2$,
then κ and ρ are the only parameters identified by the moments
$E(K_t)$, $E(K_t K_{t-j})$, $j = 0, 1 \ldots$. If, in addition, the restriction $\gamma = 0$ is imposed,
then the entire set of parameters in (3.1), $(\rho, \delta, \kappa(U_t), E[U_t^3])$, is identified.
However, α, β, and σ_u^2 are not identified. Finally, all parameters, i.e.
$(\omega, \gamma, \beta, \alpha, \sigma_u^2)$ as well as $(\rho, \delta, \kappa, (U_t), E[U_t^3])$ are identified if two of the
following three restrictions are satisfied:

(a) $\omega = m_0$ or $\gamma = m_1$ or $\gamma = m_2 \cdot \omega$,
(b) $\beta = m_3$ or $\alpha = m_4$ or $\beta = m_5 \cdot \alpha$,
(c) $\sigma_u^2 = m_6$, for example via a distributional assumption on u_t,

where m_i, $i = 0, 1, \ldots, 6$, are known constants.

The distributional assumptions in Theorem 3.1 may appear abstract. An
example that fits condition (c) is for u_t to be χ_1^2-distributed. Then, of course,

$\sigma_u^2 = 2$. An illustration of condition (ii) is slightly more involved, and is provided by the following example.

Example 3.3 Assume u_t is lognormal, $\log N(\mu, \sigma_n^2)$. The imposed mean of unity implies $\mu = -\sigma_n^2/2$. The equation system in condition (ii) becomes (C_2, C_3 are known, strictly positive constants)

$$\alpha^2(\exp(\sigma_n^2 - 1)) = C_2 \quad \text{and} \quad \alpha^3(\exp(3\sigma_n^2) - 3\exp(\sigma_n^2) + 2) = C_3.$$

Noting $\exp(3\sigma_n^2) - 3\exp(\sigma_n^2) + 2 = (\exp(\sigma_n^2) - 1)^2(\exp(\sigma_n^2) + 2)$, we get ($C = C_2^3/C_3^2 > 0$)

$$\alpha = \frac{C_3}{C_2(\exp(\sigma_n^2) - 1)(\exp(\sigma_n^2) + 2)} \quad \text{and} \quad C(\exp(\sigma_n^2) - 1)(\exp(\sigma_n^2) + 2)^2 = 1.$$

Analyzing this system, one finds a unique solution for $\exp(\sigma_n^2)$ in the interval $(1, \infty)$. Thus, the implied solution for σ_n^2 is strictly positive. This implies a unique solution for α as well.

An important implication of Theorem 3.1 is that identification of all original parameters requires additional restrictions. They can be given in the form of parameter restrictions (case (i)), or moment restrictions derived from, e.g., distributional assumptions (case (ii)). The identification problem is due to parameters in the general SARV specification that serve closely related roles. In particular, the constant, ω, and the "stochastic" constant, $\gamma \cdot u_t$, may be difficult to distinguish empirically. Both parameters are included in the general model in order to incorporate a variety of models in a unified framework. SARV models with a priori restrictions such as $\omega = 0$ or $\gamma = 0$ are parsimonious representations of stochastic volatility and retain a large degree of generality and flexibility.[17] Similar considerations surround the separate identification of the α and β parameters. As noted earlier, $\alpha + \beta$ is an important gauge on the persistence of shocks to volatility. This sum is readily estimated from second-order unconditional moments. However, separate identification of α and β is interesting for several reasons, e.g., comparisons to GARCH models, and requires additional restrictions. Not surprisingly, imposing specific distributional assumptions on u_t suffices. Then higher-order moments, if finite, can be used to disentangle α and σ_u^2. An alternative is the parameter restriction $\omega = 0$, but $\gamma \neq 0$, which generalizes GARCH models with a "stochastic constant" term.

We conclude this section by discussing the identification of the parameters in the return volatility–trading volume system, Example 3.1.[18] It serves to illustrate

[17] One advantage of having the various specifications nested within a general framework is that the imposed restrictions may be assessed in related models. For example, an informal evaluation of the hypothesis, $\omega = 0$, is conducted by adopting a distributional assumption allowing for estimation of the general model, and testing the hypothesis in this setting.

[18] Identification of the factor SARV model in Example 3.2 proceeds similarly (Andersen, 1992*a*).

a general approach: (i) verify the identification of the parameters of the system not associated with the volatility process and the identification of the moments of the stochastic volatility process, K_t, from observable sample moments; (ii) refer back to Theorem 3.1 in order to resolve the remaining identification issues.[19]

Example 3.4 Consider the system (3.2)–(3.4). Write (3.2) as

$$R_t = r + \sigma_t Z_t, \quad Z_t \sim \text{i.i.d. } N(0, 1).$$

The verification of identification can now be performed sequentially:

(i) $E(R_t) = r$ identifies the mean return parameter.

(ii) $E|R_t - r| = E|Z_t|E(\sigma_t) = (2/\pi)^{1/2}E(\sigma_t)$ determines $E(\sigma_t)$.

(iii) $E(R_t^2) = r^2 + E(\sigma_t^2)$ and $E|R_t - r||R_{t-j} - r| = (2/\pi)E(\sigma_t\sigma_{t-j})$ can be solved for the second-order moments of $\sigma_t(\sigma_t = K_t)$, using (2.15).

(iv) $E[(R_t - r)^2|R_{t-j} - r|] = (2/\pi)^{1/2}E(\sigma_t^2\sigma_{t-j})$ and analogous expressions provide the requisite third-order moments for Theorem 3.1.

(v) $E[V_t] = c(m_0 + m_1E[\sigma_t^2])$, with $E[\sigma_t^2]$ known, and $E[V_t^2] = E[V_t]^2 + c^2(m_0 + m_1E[\sigma_t^2])$ can easily be solved for c.

(vi) $E[(V_t - E(V_t))|R_{t-j} - r|] = (2/\pi)^{1/2}cm_1[E(\sigma_t^2\sigma_{t-j}) - E(\sigma_t^2)E(\sigma_t)]$. Given c, this determines m_1, and the expression in (v) for $E[V_t]$ then identifies m_0.

The above identifies all parameters in (3.2) and (3.3) plus the unconditional lower-order moments of σ_t. Identification of all parameters in SARV requires one additional constraint on u_t. Below, we estimate this system imposing restrictions of type (ii) from Theorem 3.1.

7.4 An empirical application

7.4.1 The Data

Continuously compounded daily returns on the IBM common stock over the period 1 January 1973, to 31 December 1991, adjusted for dividends and stock splits, were obtained from CRSP. Summary statistics for the full sample and six equally sized subsamples are provided in Table 7.1. The series displays the usual

Table 7.1. Percentage return series: summary statistics

Sample	Full	1	2	3	4	5	6
10^2 *Mean	1.51	−4.61	4.52	−2.08	11.94	1.07	−.94
St. Dev.	1.46	1.76	1.02	1.46	1.36	1.72	1.32
Skewness	−1.04	.32	.64	.61	.35	−4.56	−.65
Kurtosis	27.8	5.61	5.49	5.34	3.86	75.41	8.76

[19] All the moments need not be used in the estimation procedure if the objectives of the empirical investigation are consistent with some of the strong assumptions of Theorem 3.1 or the less ambitious parameterization in (3.7).

characteristics of financial returns: the average daily return is tiny, the standard deviation of returns, 1.46%, is almost 100 times the sample mean, the returns are slightly skewed to the left and have excess kurtosis relative to the normal distribution. Moreover, the autocorrelations for the absolute returns series at lags 1 through 25 were found to be positive and highly significant. Thus, the series displays the usual dependency in the higher-order return moments. The daily IBM trading volume is from the S&P's Daily Stock Price Guide. Table 7.2 gives annual growth rates over subsamples. The most striking feature is the strong but erratic trend. On average, the growth in shares traded is about 13% a year. Moreover, there is a seasonal effect: volume drops between Christmas and New Year. Consequently, we delete all observations from December 23 to the first trading day of the following year. This leaves 4703 observations in each series. Finally, we calculated cross-correlations between return volatility and volume over annual samples. The short samples were used to minimize the effect of the trend in volume. Not surprisingly, we found a strong positive relation between the series, consistent with prior research (Karpoff 1987).

A serious practical problem is that our theory is built on the assumption of stationarity, while the volume series is strongly trending. We present results obtained by detrending volume by a nonparametric regression procedure based on a normal kernel.[20] Table 7.3 presents summary statistics for the detrended volume series. The mean is, due to the scaling, near unity, while the skewness is positive in all subsamples, and it displays excess kurtosis. In addition, we found that the autocorrelations for the derived volume series displays a smooth, regular

Table 7.2. Annual percentage growth rate in trading volume: measured from one subsample to the next

Between Sample	1–2	2–3	3–4	4–5	5–6
Growth Rate	17.8	7.8	22.3	17.8	−.01

Table 7.3. Normalized volume series: summary statistics

Sample	Full	1	2	3	4	5	6
Mean	.993	.974	1.02	.948	1.02	1.03	.977
St. Dev.	.413	.486	.428	.366	.397	.402	.391
Skewness	2.10	3.28	1.60	1.60	1.26	1.74	2.06
Kurtosis	13.0	23.9	7.00	7.18	5.05	9.49	11.2
Maximum	5.93	5.93	3.40	3.13	2.88	3.86	3.73
Minimum	.222	.292	.222	.331	.332	.285	.276

[20] The method provides a long-run weighted moving average termed "normal volume," and the detrended series is then constructed by dividing each actual trading figure by the corresponding "normal" volume for the day. The approach is motivated by approximate stationarity of the log-differences of volume which suggests that percentage deviations from trend are stationary. The results are robust w.r.t. alternative procedures, such as detrending by a moving mean or median.

decline from significantly positive values at low lags to about zero at lags beyond 30.[21] In sum, the detrended volume series appears stationary and displays the properties we expect from theory.

7.4.2 Empirical results

We illustrate the type of results obtained from estimation of the return-volume system. First, identification must be assured. In accord with Theorem 3.1, we impose restrictions on higher-order moments of u_t. For brevity we only report results for the case where u_t equals the absolute value of a standardized GED_w variable. Referring to Example 3.4 and following the strategy of Example 3.3 one may, indeed, verify that the parameter vector is identified. Alternative identifying restrictions have been explored but the qualitative implications of the findings are quite robust.

The estimation procedure requires the inclusion of lagged variables in the moments. We decided to rely on lower-order moments up to lag 20. This led us to the following type of moments: $E(R_t)$, $E(R_t^2)$, $E(|R_t - r|)$, $E(R_t^4)$, $E(V_t)$, $E(V_t^2)$, $E(V_t R_t^2)$, $E(|R_t - r||R_{t-i} - r|)$, $E(R_t^2 R_{t-i}^2)$, $E(V_t V_{t-i})$, $E(V_{t-i}|R_t - r|)$, $|i| > 0$. However, from simulation evidence (Andersen and Sørensen 1993, henceforth AS], it is not appropriate to include all 20 lags for each moment in the estimation procedure since it results in an excessive number of moments relative to sample size. Hence, we included a rather arbitrary selection of lags for each of the "dynamic" moments, except for the criteria that (i) a majority are lower-order moments (more precisely estimated than higher-order moments); (ii) we avoid having all dynamic moments be included at the same lag (to reduce the multi-collinearity in the inverse of the weighting matrix); (iii) the total number of moments does not exceed 24 in the subsamples (consistent with the findings in AS).

The system was estimated over the full sample and three equally sized sub-samples (1568 daily pairs). The results are summarized in Table 7.4.[22] The last row reports the p-values for the standard χ^2-test of goodness of fit. None of the statistics indicate rejection of the model at standard significance levels.[23] More-over, the point estimates all appear reasonable and fall within the theoretical bounds that are consistent with the assumptions underlying the estimation procedure. The estimated daily mean returns are small, and vary across subsamples, although most are not significantly different from zero. The daily return standard deviation, $\bar{\sigma}$, is very uniform across the three subsamples with estimates ranging from 1.24 to 1.31%. Perhaps most significantly, the estimates of the persistence measure, $\alpha + \beta$, are much smaller than the ones usually obtained from daily

---

[21] Our findings are consistent with an observation by Harris (1987) that trading volume should display a higher degree of autocorrelation in the normal-mixture model than in the squared returns series.

[22] The estimates were obtained using the NW weighting matrix, but with Andrews' (1991) data-dependent choice of bandwidth. Estimating the system with the QS weighting matrix did not alter the results in a qualitatively significant manner.

[23] This is encouraging, but perhaps also surprising in the case of the model estimated over the entire sample, as one may expect some structural breaks, particularly in the trading processes, over the 20-year period which would render our stationarity assumptions invalid.

Table 7.4. Return volatility–volume system: sarv-ged(w),
30 moments, nw var-cov matrix estimation, standard volume series,
data-dependent lag length

Sample	Full[a]	1[b]	2	3
r	.012	−.037	.032	.013
	$(.020)^c$	(.035)	(.031)	(.032)
$\bar{\sigma} = E(K_t^{1/2})$	1.31	1.31	1.30	1.24
	(.017)	(.044)	(.027)	(.024)
$\beta + \alpha$	.756	.787	.710	.834
	(.050)	(.044)	(.079)	(.068)
α	.239	.327	.156	.135
	(.060)	(.089)	(.080)	(.062)
$c \cdot m_0$	.650	.650	.371	.747
	(.044)	(.029)	(.097)	(.051)
$c \cdot m_1$	.171	.157	.329	.139
	(.025)	(.017)	(.058)	(.033)
c	.041	.054	.021	.050
	(.010)	(.011)	(.015)	(.011)
w	1.13	2.26	.932	.575
	(.377)	(1.35)	(.693)	(.186)
χ^2 (p-val.)[d]	.66	.38	.77	.99

[a] Estimation based on the following moments: $E(R_t)$, $E(R_t^2)$, $E(|R_t - r|)$, $E(R_t^4)$, $E(V_t)$, $E(V_t^2)$, $E(V_t R_t^2)$, $E(|R_t - r||R_{t-j} - r|)$,
  $j = 1, 3, 6, 10, 13; 16, 19; E(R_t^2 R_{t-i}^2)$, $i = 2, 4, 7; E(V_t V_{t-j})$, $j = 1, 4, 8, 11, 14, 17, 20;$
  $E(V_{t-|i|}|R_t - r|)$, $i = \pm 1, 5, 9, 12, 15, 18$.
[b] For the subsamples estimation is based on 24 of the above moments.
[c] Asymptotic standard errors are reported below parameter estimates.
[d] Standard χ^2-test for goodness of fit; p-value reported.

returns using standard GARCH models. This is consistent with the results in Foster and Viswanathan (1993) and parallels some of the findings by Gallant, Rossi, and Tauchen (1992, 1993) concerning the impact of expanding a dynamic model of return volatility into a joint bivariate system by incorporating volume observations. However, the latter rely on a very differently detrended volume series as well as seminonparametric estimation techniques, which allows them to investigate qualitative aspects of the system but renders structural interpretation difficult.

The parameter cm_0 corresponds roughly to the fraction of the daily trading volume, which is independent of the information flow since the average volume by normalization is close to unity. In this interpretation between 50% and 60% of the daily volume is unrelated to the arrival of news, while the information-sensitive components of trade, reflected in the coefficient cm_1, accounts for the remainder. The scaling constant c is a nuisance parameter, but appears to be estimated with a great deal of precision. Finally, the GED parameter, w, which characterizes the tail behavior of the conditional volatility process, is poorly estimated.[24] The large standard deviations are due to the erratic higher-order moments, which are critical for estimation of this parameter. Nonetheless, the evidence clearly favors the hypothesis of thick tails in the volatility innovations ($w < 2$).

Our results provide indirect support for a modified version of the mixture of distributions hypothesis and are also relevant to parts of the microstructure literature. Moreover, they set the stage for volatility estimation and forecasting exploiting information from both the return and volume series. The highly non-linear structure of the system complicates the task of obtaining reliable estimates of the time series of information arrivals (volatility). However, taking the parameter estimates as given, it is feasible to apply an approximate, extended Kalman filter procedure.[25] This allows for within-sample volatility estimates and out-of-sample forecasts. Andersen (1992a) compares SARV-based Kalman-filtered volatility estimates and volatility forecasts to the corresponding series from a (SD-) GARCH model. The findings were mixed, with no one model consistently dominating the other over the different subsamples. These findings do not prove that SARV-based volatility estimates consistently can compete with GARCH estimates. The robustness of the results must clearly be investigated further, and the selected criteria for comparison must be scrutinized. However, the results do suggest that some form of volatility estimates derived from a bivariate modeling of the return-volume relation may be useful as supplements to GARCH estimates of return volatility.[26]

7.5 Conclusion

This paper develops a framework for the modeling and estimation of systems of equations involving volatility processes from the class of polynomial stochastic autoregressive volatility. A rather exhaustive treatment of identification and estimation procedures for volatility processes in this class is given. It provides a guideline for estimation of a wide array of stochastic volatility systems, including stochastic volatility generalizations of SD-GARCH(1,1), GARCH(1,1), and EGARCH(1,1), termed respectively the standard SARV, the quadratic SARV, and the exponential SARV models (including the lognormal stochastic volatility model). But most significantly, it allows for more general functional forms and distributional assumptions relative to the alternative estimation methods such as QMLE or simulated MLE. The return-volume system estimated in the paper is but one theoretically motivated example. For instance, multivariate volatility factors may be associated with a host of different economic variables besides volume, which intrinsically do not obey the standard assumptions used in the stochastic

[24] Recall that the tails of the GED become fatter as w approaches zero, and for $w < 2$ the distribution displays excess kurtosis relative to the normal distribution.

[25] For an introduction to the Kalman filter and a discussion of the approximate and extended versions of the filter, see Harvey (1989, chap. 3). In this setting Kalman filter estimates are no longer optimal. Instead, the performance will, among other things, depend on the degree of nonlinearity over the range of values attained by the state vector.

[26] For additional evidence and a more detailed discussion, see Andersen (1993).

volatility literature. Analysis of these systems requires methods similar to those explored here. When closed-form expressions for the unconditional moments are not available, the method of simulated moments may still be feasible. However, the small sample properties of these estimators are largely unknown in this setting and may be found lacking. In any case, the exact GMM procedures will provide important benchmarks for the performance of these models. The available Monte Carlo evidence suggests that concerns about the efficiency of GMM and simulation estimators are justified.

Avenues for future research include further exploration of simultaneous equation systems of the type described, the analysis of the finite sample performance of the proposed GMM procedures in these settings, and the development of alternative estimation methods which can perform efficient inference and volatility series extraction simultaneously in one step for a broad class of stochastic volatility models.

Appendix

Proof of Theorem 1 (i) To prove that K_t is finite under the stated assumptions, we show that the terms of the sum in (2.12) are $O(\exp(-\lambda j))$ for some $\lambda > 0$ with probability 1. For $\alpha > 0$, we use the fact that $\omega + \gamma u_{t-j} = (\omega - \gamma \beta/\alpha) + \gamma/\alpha(\beta + \alpha u_{t-j})$ to rewrite the sum as

$$K_t = \frac{\omega - \beta \gamma}{\alpha} + \left(\omega + \frac{\gamma(1-\beta)}{\alpha}\right) \sum_{j=0}^{\infty} \prod_{i=0}^{j} (\beta + \alpha u_{t-i}). \tag{A.1}$$

Hence, we only need to deal with the product of the terms $\beta + \alpha u_{t-i}$. We proceed as in Nelson (1990a, Theorem 2.2). However, a number of the details are different from his case, so, for completeness, we provide an outline of the proof. Let $\delta = E[\ln(\beta + \alpha u_t)]$ and notice $\delta < 0$. By the strong law of large numbers for i.i.d. random variables there exists, with probability 1, a random positive $M < \infty$ such that, for all $j > M$,

$$\left| j^{-1} \sum_{i=0}^{j-1} \ln(\beta + \alpha u_{t-i}) - \delta \right| < \frac{|\delta|}{2}.$$

Consequently, for all $j > M$,

$$\sum_{i=0}^{j-1} \ln(\beta + \alpha u_{t-i}) < \frac{j\delta}{2}$$

and hence

$$\prod_{i=0}^{j-1} (\beta + \alpha u_{t-i}) < \exp(j\delta/2) = O(\exp(-\lambda j)),$$

where $\lambda = -\delta/2 > 0$, so the series converges a.s. For $\alpha = 0$, $K_t = \sum_{j=0}^{\infty} \beta^j (\omega + \gamma u_{t-j}) = \omega/(1 - \beta) + \gamma \sum_{j=0}^{\infty} \beta^j u_{t-j}$. Moreover, in this case $\delta < 0$ implies $\beta < 1$, so this sum is clearly convergent.

In order to establish strict stationarity and ergodicity it is sufficient to verify that the mapping $k: (u_t, u_{t-1}, \ldots) \to (-\infty, \infty)$ that defines K_t, i.e., $K_t = k(u_t, u_{t-1}, \ldots)$, is measurable (Stout 1974, Theorem 3.5.8), because $\{u_{t-i}\}_{i\geq 0}$ itself is, trivially, strictly stationary and ergodic. Again, from the above arguments, it is enough to consider the sum of products of the form $(\beta + \alpha u_{t-i})$, $i \geq 0$. Since a finite number of sums and products of measurable functions is measurable, the functions $f_n = \sum_{j=0, \ldots, n} \prod_{i=0, \ldots, j} (\beta + \alpha u_{t-i})$ are measurable for any finite n. Moreover, f_n is increasing in n, so $\sup_n f_n = \sum_{j=0, \ldots, \infty} \prod_{i=0, \ldots, j} (\beta + \alpha u_{t-i})$ and this function is measurable (Royden 1968, chap. 3, Theorem 20). $K_t = k(u_t, u_{t-1}, \ldots)$ is an affine transformation of such a function and thus measurable.

Finally, we show that the probability measure of K_t is nondegenerate for all t if $\omega \neq 0$ or $\gamma > 0$. Assume K_t has a degenerate distribution. Then, for some constant c, it follows from the SARV specification that $\text{Prob}[c = \omega + \beta c + (\gamma + \alpha c)u_t] = 1$, which is a contradiction since u_t is assumed nondegenerate ($\sigma_u^2 > 0$).

(ii) From (2.11) and (2.12) we have for $\omega \neq 0$ or $\gamma > 0$

$$_c K_t - K_t = -\sum_{j=t}^{\infty} \prod_{i=0}^{j-1} (\beta + \alpha u_{t-i})(\omega + \gamma u_{t-j}) + K_0 \prod_{i=0}^{t-1} (\beta + \alpha u_{t-i}). \tag{A.2}$$

From the proof of (i) we know that the first term on the right-hand side is the tail of a convergent series and, consequently, vanishes for $t \to \infty$. The second term may be written as

$$K_0 \exp\left[\sum_{i=0}^{t-1} \ln(\beta + \alpha u_{t-i})\right] = K_0 \exp\left[\sum_{i=0}^{t-i} Y_t\right],$$

where $Y_i = \ln(\beta + \alpha u_{t-i})$ is an i.i.d. sequence with $E[Y_i] < 0$. Hence, from the strong law of large numbers, $\sum_i Y_i \to -\infty$, and the term will converge to zero as $t \to \infty$. For $\omega = \gamma = 0$, the first term in (2.11) is zero, and the second converges to zero as above. This is consistent with the definition of K_t as identically zero for this case.

(iii) Let $E[(\beta + \alpha u_t)^p] = \zeta$. From (A.1), for $\alpha > 0$ we need only show $E[(\sum_{j=0, \ldots, \infty} \prod_{i=0, \ldots, j} (\beta + \alpha u_{t-i}))^p] < \infty$. Let $X_j = \prod_{i=0, \ldots, j} (\beta + \alpha u_{t-i})$. Then we must prove $E[K_t^p] = E[(\sum_{j=0, \ldots, \infty} X_j)^p] < \infty$. Now, $X_j > 0$ with probability 1, for all j, and $E[X_j^p] = \zeta^{j+1}$. We have the following inequalities:

$$\sum_j E(X_j^p) \leq E\left[\left(\sum_j X_j\right)^p\right] \leq \left[\sum_j (E[X_j^p])^{1/p}\right]^p, \quad \text{for } 1 \leq p, \tag{A.3}$$

$$\left[\sum_j (E[X_j^p])^{1/p}\right]^p \leq E\left[\left(\sum_j X_j\right)^p\right] \leq \sum_j E(X_j^p), \quad \text{for } 0 < p < 1. \quad (A.4)$$

The right inequality in (A.3) is Minkowski's integral inequality while the left inequality is a companion (Hardy, Littlewood, and Polya, 1991, Theorems 198, 199, and extensions, Section 6.17). The inequalities are reversed for $p < 1$, as displayed in (A.4). In the current context they imply

$$\sum_j \zeta^{j+1} \leq E\left[\left(\sum_j X_j\right)^p\right] \leq \left[\sum_j \zeta^{(j+1)/p}\right]^p, \quad \text{for } 1 \leq p,$$

$$\left[\sum_j \zeta^{(j+1)/p}\right]^p \leq E\left[\left(\sum_j X_j\right)^p\right] \leq \sum_j \zeta^{j+1}, \quad \text{for } 0 < p < 1.$$

Clearly, all the terms involving power series of ζ are convergent for $\zeta < 1$ and divergent to infinity for $\zeta \geq 1$. Hence, $|E[K_t^p]| < \infty$ for $\zeta < 1$. Note also $|E[K_t^p]| = \infty$ if $\zeta \geq 1$. Finally, the condition $E[u_t^p] < \infty$ is clearly a necessary condition for $E[(\beta + \alpha u_t)^p] < 1$.

For $\alpha = 0$, $K_t = \omega/(1-\beta) + \gamma \sum_{j=0}^{\infty} \beta^j u_{t-j}$, and $E[u_t^p] < \infty$ is necessary and sufficient for $|E[K_t^p]| < \infty$.

(iv) Define the usual L^p-norm by $\|X\|_p = E[|X|^p]$ for $0 < p \leq 1$, and $\|X\|_p = (E|X|^p)^{1/p}$ for $p > 1$. From standard arguments we have

$$\left|\ \|K_t\|_p - \|_c K_t\|_p \right| \leq \|_c K_t - K_t\|_p,$$

which implies $E[_c K_t^p] - E[K_t^p] \to 0$ if $E|K_t -_c K_t|^p \to 0$.

Again letting $X_j = \prod_{i=0,\dots,j}(\beta + \alpha u_{t-i})$ and hence $E[X_j^p] = \zeta^{j+1}$, and using $\omega + \gamma u_{t-j} = (\omega - \gamma\beta/\alpha) + \gamma/\alpha(\beta + \alpha u_{t-j})$ we may rewrite (A.2) as

$$_c K_t - K_t = K_0 X_{t-1} - \left(\omega - \frac{\beta\gamma}{\alpha}\right)\sum_{j=t}^{\infty} X_{j-1} - \frac{\gamma}{\alpha}\sum_{j=t}^{\infty} X_j \quad (A.5)$$

for $\alpha > 0$. Using the upper inequalities in (A.3) and (A.4) on the terms in (A.5) yields

$$E|_c K_t - K_t|^p \leq \left[E[K_0^p]^{1/p}\zeta^{t/p} + \left|\omega + \frac{\beta\gamma}{\alpha}\right|\sum_{j=t,\dots,\infty}\zeta^{j/p} + \frac{\gamma}{\alpha}\sum_{j=t,\dots,\infty}\zeta^{(j+1)/p}\right]^p, \quad 1 < p,$$

$$E|_c K_t - K_t|^p \leq E[K_0^p]\zeta^t + \left|\omega + \frac{\beta\gamma}{\alpha}\right|^p\sum_{j=t,\dots,\infty}\zeta^j + \frac{\gamma}{\alpha}\sum_{j=t,\dots,\infty}\zeta^{j+1}, \quad 0 < p \leq 1.$$

The upper bounds collapse to zero as $t \to \infty$ if $E[K_0^p] < \infty$ and (from (iii)) $\zeta < 1$. For $\alpha = 0$, (A.2) simplifies and the proof above applies in straightforward fashion.

Finally, we must demonstrate that the conditional process, $_cK_t$, diverges a.s. when $E[\ln(\beta + \alpha u_t)] = \delta \geq 0$ and $\omega\alpha + \gamma(1 - \beta) \neq 0$. If this is true then $|K_t|$ is clearly not well defined (or infinite) from (ii)). For $\alpha > 0$, the proof follows from the following restatement of (2.11):

$$_cK_t + \frac{\gamma}{\alpha} = \left[\omega + \frac{\gamma(1 - \beta)}{\alpha}\right] \sum_{j=0}^{t-1} \prod_{i=0}^{j-1} (\beta + \alpha u_{t-i}) + \left(K_0 + \frac{\gamma}{\alpha}\right) \prod_{j=0}^{t-1} (\beta + \alpha u_{t-j}). \quad \text{(A.6)}$$

The last term on the right-hand side is $(K_0 + \gamma/\alpha)X_{t-1}$, where X_{t-1} is strictly positive. Thus, we may rewrite the right-hand side as

$$_cK_t + \frac{\gamma}{\alpha} = X_{t-1}\left[\left(K_0 + \frac{\gamma}{\alpha}\right) + \left(\omega + \frac{\gamma + (1 - \beta)}{\alpha}\right)\sum_{j=0}^{t-1}\frac{X_{j-1}}{X_{t-1}}\right]. \quad \text{(A.7)}$$

For $\delta > 0$, the sum of the ratios X_{j-1}/X_{t-i} will converge. To see this, note

$$\sum_{j=0}^{t-1}\frac{X_{j-1}}{X_{t-1}} = \sum_{j=1}^{t-1}\exp\left(\sum_{i=0}^{j-1} -\ln(\beta + \alpha u_{j+i})\right).$$

Since $E[-\ln(\beta + \alpha u_{j+i})] = -\delta < 0$, the situation is entirely analogous to the one analyzed under (i) below (A.1) and the same proof applies. Thus, the term in brackets in (A.7) converges to a nondegenerate random variable, while the X_{t-i} term multiplying it diverges to infinity. This follows, since in the notation below (A.2) we have $X_{t-1} = \exp(\sum_{i=0}^{t-1} Y_i)$, where Y_i is an i.i.d. sequence with $E[Y_i] > 0$, and $\sum_i Y_i \to \infty$ by the strong law of large numbers. Hence, $|_cK_t| \to \infty$ a.s. in this case.

For $\delta = 0$, the ratio $X_{j-1}/X_{t-i} = \exp(\sum_{i=0}^{j-1} -\ln(\beta + \alpha u_{j+i}))$ is a strictly positive and increasing function of a random walk without drift, and since u_t is nondegenerate it follows that both limes superior and limes inferior of the sum is infinite (Stout 1974, Theorem 6.1.4 and Corollary 6.1.1), i.e.

$$\ln\left[\frac{\sum_{j=0}^{t-1} X_{j-i}}{X_{t-1}}\right] \geq \sup_{1 \leq j \leq t-1}\left\{\sum_{i=0}^{j-1} -\ln(\beta + \alpha u_{j+i})\right\}$$

and the right-hand side diverges to infinity. Hence, in this case the term in brackets of (A.7) diverges, and $_cK_t$ becomes a product of a strictly positive and increasing transformation of a random walk and a divergent term. Thus, $|_cK_t| \to \infty$ a.s.

For $\omega\alpha + \gamma(1 - \beta) = 0$, the recursion simplifies. Equation (A.6) becomes

$$_cK_t + \frac{\gamma}{\alpha} = K_0 + \frac{\gamma}{\alpha}\exp\left[\sum_{j=0}^{t-1}\ln(\beta + \alpha u_{t-j})\right] = \left(K_0 + \frac{\gamma}{\alpha}\right)\exp[X_{t-1}]. \quad \text{(A.8)}$$

Again, if $\delta > 0$ or $\delta = 0$, X_i is a random walk with a positive drift or a random walk without a drift, respectively. In the former case, $|_cK_t| \to \infty$, and in the latter it is a transformation of a random walk which will wander indefinitely over the full range $(0, \infty)$. In either case, the sum defining K_t will not converge, and K_t does not exist.

For $\alpha = 0$: $_cK_{t+1} = \sum_{j=0}^{t} \beta^j(\omega + \gamma u_{t-j}) + \beta^t K_0$. Here, $\delta \geq 0$ is equivalent to $\beta \geq 1$, so random walk $(\beta = 1)$ and divergence $(\beta > 1)$ is readily established. Clearly, K_t cannot be defined.

Proof of Theorem 2.2 The conditions for finiteness of the unconditional moments, given in Theorem 2.1, (iii), are readily calculated as functions of the parameters, when $p = 1, \ldots, 4$, and correspond to the expressions given in the theorem. The mean of K_t is derived by taking expected values of both sides of (2.9) with $K_t = \sigma_t$ and rearranging. Next, solving (2.13) for ω yields $\omega = (1 - \alpha - \beta)\kappa - \gamma$. Substituting back into the definition of SARV and rearranging gives

$$K_t - \kappa = (\alpha + \beta)(K_{t-1} - \kappa) + (\gamma + \alpha K_{t-1})(u_t - 1).$$

The moments are now determined by plugging this expression in for the leading term of the appropriate moment, calculating, and rearranging. The method is similar in all cases, and we only indicate the nature of the calculations for one of the more involved cases, the third-order central moment. One finds, remembering $u_t - 1$ is independent of the rest of the terms:

$$\begin{aligned} E[(K_t - \kappa)^3] &= E[(\alpha + \beta)(K_{t-1} - \kappa) + (\gamma + \alpha K_{t-1})(u_t - 1)]^3 \\ &= (\alpha + \beta)^3 E[(K_t - \kappa)^3] + 3(\alpha + \beta)\sigma_u^2 E[(\gamma + \alpha K_t)^2(K_t - \kappa)] . \\ &\quad + E[(\gamma + \alpha K_t)^3]E[(u_t - 1)^3] \end{aligned}$$

Separate calculations reveal

$$E[(\gamma + \alpha K_t)^2(K_t - \kappa)] = 2\alpha(\gamma + \alpha\kappa)\mathrm{var}(K_t) + \alpha^2 E[(K_t - \kappa)^3],$$
$$E[(\gamma + \alpha K_t)^3] = (\gamma + \alpha\kappa)^3 + 3\alpha^2(\gamma + \alpha\kappa)\mathrm{var}(K_t) + \alpha^3 E[(K_t - \kappa)^3].$$

Substituting these terms back into the original equation, collecting the terms involving $E[(K_t - \kappa)^3]$, and rearranging yields the result reported in Theorem 2.2.

Proof of Theorem 3.1 The proof consists of tedious manipulations of the system of equations. We verify identification in the case of finite third-order moments. The remaining results are obtained in similar fashion.

We have $E(K_t) = \kappa = (\omega + \gamma)/(1 - \alpha - \beta)$, implying $\omega = \kappa(1 - \alpha - \beta) - \gamma$. Hence, given κ, ω is identified only when $(\alpha + \beta)$ and γ are identified. Next, from (K_t) we observe ((2.14))

$$\text{var}(K_t) = (\gamma^2 + 2\gamma\alpha\kappa + \alpha^2\kappa^2)\sigma_u^2/(1 - (\alpha + \beta)^2 - \alpha^2\sigma_u^2).$$

But then $\text{cov}(K_t, K_{t-1}) = (\alpha + \beta)\text{var}(K_t)$ identifies $\rho = (\alpha + \beta)$.
Now, let $X_j = E[(K_t - \kappa)^2(K_{t-j} - \kappa)]$, so X_j is known for $j = 1, 2, 3$.
From (2.17) we find $X_j = C_0 X_{j-1} + C_1(\alpha + \beta)^{j-1}$ and derive

$$C_0 = (X_3 - (\alpha + \beta)X_2)/(X_2 - (\alpha + \beta)X_1) = (\alpha + \beta)^2 + \alpha^2\sigma_u^2.$$

Since $\alpha + \beta$ is identified, we determine $\text{var}(U_t) = \alpha^2\sigma_u^2$ from the above relation. Furthermore, the identification of C_0 leads to determination of C_1. But $C_1 = 2\,\text{var}(K_t)(\alpha\gamma\sigma_u^2) + 2\kappa\,\text{var}(K_t)(\alpha^2\sigma_u^2)$, and all components of the last term in the sum are known which means that the unknown component of the first term, i.e., $\alpha\gamma\sigma_u^2$, is identified. In passing, note also that $X_0 = E(K_t^3)$ can be derived from the above expression for X_1. Now, return to $\text{var}(K_t)$. Given the terms we have determined by now, the relation identifies $\gamma^2\sigma_u^2 + 2\kappa\alpha\gamma\sigma_u^2$. This yields the value of $\gamma^2\sigma_u^2$, and combined with $\alpha \cdot \gamma \cdot \sigma_u^2$ it identifies $\delta = \gamma/\alpha$. Finally, observe that the constants in (2.16) may be written

$$D_0 = 6\rho(\delta + \kappa)\,\text{var}(U_t)\,\text{var}(K_t) \text{ and}$$

$$D_1 = \alpha^3[(\delta + \kappa)^3 + 3(\delta + \kappa)\,\text{var}(K_t)] = \alpha^3 D_2.$$

D_0 and D_2 are identified, so substituting D_1 back into (2.16) one may solve for $\alpha^3 E[(u_t - 1)^3] = E[U_t^3]$. This completes the demonstration that $(\rho, \delta, \kappa, \text{var}(U_t), E[U_t^3])$ is identified from the first three moments of K_t. Next, notice that any of the conditions in assumption (i) will allow the calculation of α from the knowledge of $(\rho, \delta, \kappa, \text{var}(U_t), E[U_t^3])$, and the rest of the original parameters are then derived in straightforward fashion. If, instead, assumption (ii) is valid, then the equations $\alpha^2\sigma_u^2(\eta) = E(U_t^2)$ and $\alpha^3 E[(u_t - 1)^3](\eta) = E(U_t)^3]$ can be solved for a unique value of α, and the rest of the parameters are determined easily.

References

Andersen, T. G. (1992a). Return Volatility and Trading Volume in Financial Markets: An Information Flow Interpretation of Stochastic Volatility, unpublished Ph.D. dissertation, Yale University.

——(1992b). Volatility, Working Paper #144, Department of Finance, J. L. Kellogg Graduate School of Management, Northwestern University.

——(1993). Return Volatility and Trading Volume: An Information Flow Interpretation of Stochastic Volatility, Northwestern University, forthcoming.

——Sørensen, B. E. (1993). GMM Estimation of a Stochastic Volatility Model: A Monte Carlo Study, working paper, Department of Finance, J. L. Kellogg Graduate School of Management, Northwestern University.

Andrews, D. W. K. (1991). Heteroskedasticity and Autocorrelation Consistent Covariance Matrix Estimation. *Econometrica* 59, 817–58.

Bollerslev, T. (1986). Generalized Autoregressive Conditional Heteroskedasticity. *Journal Econometrics* 31, 307–27.

—— Chou, and Kroner, K. F. (1992). ARCH Modeling in Finance. *Journal of Econometrics* 52, 5–59.

Cai, J. (1993). A Markov Model of Unconditional Variance in ARCH, working paper, J. L. Kellogg Graduate School of Management, Northwestern University.

Chesney, M. and Scott, L. O. (1989). Pricing European Currency Options: A Comparison of the Modified Black-Scholes Model and a Random Variance Model. *Journal of Financial Quantative Analysis* 24, 267–84.

Clark, P. K. (1973). A Subordinated Stochastic Process Model with Finite Variance for Speculative Prices. *Econometrica* 41, 135–55.

Danielsson, J. (1993). Stochastic Volatility in Asset Prices: Estimation with Simulated Maximum Likelihood. *Journal of Econometrics*.

—— Richard, J.-F. (1993). Accelerated Gaussian Importance Sampler with Application to Dynamic Latent Variable Models, working paper, University of Iceland and University of Pittsburgh.

Diebold, F. X. and Nerlove, M. (1989). The Dynamics of Exchange Rate Volatility: A Multivariate Latent Factor ARCH Model. *Journal of Applied Econometrics* 4, 1–21.

Duffie, D. and Singleton, K. J. (1989). Simulated Moments Estimation of Markov Models of Asset Prices, working paper, Graduate School of Business, Stanford University.

—— —— (1993). Simulated Moments Estimation of Markov Models of Asset Prices. *Econometrica* 61, 929–52.

Engle, R. F. (1982). Autoregressive Conditional Heteroskedasticity with Estimates of the Variance of United Kingdom Inflation. *Econometrica* 50, 987–1007.

Foster, F. D. and Viswanathan, S. (1993). Can Speculative Trading Explain the Volume-Volatility Relation? working paper, Duke University.

Gallant, A. R., Hsieh, D. A., and Tauchen, G. E. (1991). On Fitting a Recalcitrant Series: The Pound/Dollar Exchange Rate, 1974–83, in *Nonparametric and Semiparametric Methods of Econometrics and Statistics, Proceedings of the Fifth International Symposium in Economic Theory and Econometrics,* (eds.) Barnett, W. A., Powell, J., and G. E. Tauchen. London: Cambridge University Press, 199–240.

—— Rossi, P. E., and Tauchen, G. E. (1992). Stock Prices and Volume. *Review of Financial Studies* 5, 199–242.

—— —— —— (1993). Nonlinear Dynamic Structures. *Econometrica* 61, 871–908.

—— and Tauchen, G. E. (1992). Which Moments to Match? working paper, Duke University.

Hamilton, J. D. (1988). Rational Expectations Econometric Analysis of Changes in Regime: An Investigation of the Term Structure of Interest Rates. *Journal of Economic Dynamics and Control* 12, 385–423.

—— Susmel, R. (1992). Autoregressive Conditional Heteroskedasticity and Changes in Regime, working paper, University of California, San Diego.

Hansen, L. P. (1982). Large Sample Properties of Generalized Methods of Moments Estimators. *Econometrica* 50, 1029–54.

Hardy, G. H., Littlewood, J. E., and Polya, G. (1991). *Inequalities.* London: Cambridge University Press.

Harris, L. (1986). Cross-Security Tests of the Mixture of Distributions Hypothesis. *Journal of Financial Quantative Analysis* 21, 39–46.

—— (1987). Transaction Data Tests of the Mixture of Distributions Hypothesis. *Journal of Financial Quantative Analysis* 22, 127–41.

Harvey, A. C. (1989). *Forecasting, Structural Time Series Models and the Kalman Filter.* New York: Cambridge University Press.

—— Ruiz, E. and Shephard, N. (1992). Multivariate Stochastic Variance Models, working paper, London School of Economics.

Heston, S. L. (1993). A Closed-Form Solution for Options with Stochastic Volatility, with Application to Bond and Currency Options. *Review of Financial Studies* 6, 327–43.

Hull, J. and White, A. (1987). The Pricing of Options on Assets with Stochastic Volatilities. *Journal of Finance* 42, 281–300.

Jacquier, E., Polson, N. G. and Rossi, P. E. (1993). Bayesian Analysis of Stochastic Volatility Models, working paper, Chicago Graduate School of Business.

Johnson, H. and Shanno, D. (1987). Option Pricing When the Variance Is Changing. *Journal of Financial Quantative Analysis* 22, 143–52.

Karpoff, J. M. (1987). The Relation between Price Changes and Trading Volume: A Survey. *Journal of Financial Quantative Analysis* 22, 109–26.

Laux, P. and Ng, L. K. (1991). Intraday Heteroskedasticity and Comovements in the Foreign Currency Futures Market, working paper, Department of Finance, University of Texas at Austin.

Lumsdaine, R. L. (1990). Asymptotic Properties of the Maximum Likelihood Estimator in GARCH(1,1) and IGARCH(1,1) Models, unpublished manuscript, Department of Economics, Harvard University.

McFadden, D. L. (1989). A Method of Simulated Moments for Estimation of Discrete Response Models without Numerical Integration. *Econometrica* 57, 995–1026.

Melino, A. and Turnbull, S. M. (1990). Pricing Foreign Currency Options with Stochastic Volatility. *Journal of Econometrics* 45, 239–265.

Nelson, D. B. (1990a). Stationarity and Persistence in the GARCH(1,1) Model. *Econometric Theory* 6, 318–34.

—— (1990b). ARCH Models as Diffusion Approximations. *Journal of Econometrics* 45, 7–38.

—— (1991). Conditional Heteroskedasticity in Asset Returns: A New Approach. *Econometrica* 59, 347–70.

—— Foster, D. P. (1991). Filtering and Forecasting with Misspecified ARCH Models. II: Making the Right Forecast with the Wrong Model, working paper, University of Chicago.

Newey, W. K. and West, K. D. (1987). A Simple, Positive Semi-definite, Heteroskedasticity Consistent Covariance Matrix. *Econometrica* 55, 703–8.

Pakes, A. and Pollard, D. (1989). Simulation and the Asymptotics of Optimization Estimators. *Econometrica* 57, 1027–57.

Royden, H. L. (1968). *Real Analysis* 2nd edn. New York: Macmillan.

Scott, L. O. (1987). Option Pricing When the Variance Changes Randomly: Theory, Estimation and an Application. *Journal of Quantative Analysis* 22, 419–38.

Stout, W. F. (1974). *Almost Sure Convergence.* New York: Academic Press.

Tauchen, G. and Pitts, M. (1983). The Price Variability–Volume Relationship on Speculative Markets. *Econometrica* 51, 485–505.

Taylor, S. J. (1980). Conjectured Models for Trends in Financial Prices, Tests and Forecasts. *Journal of the Royal Statistical Society* A 143, 338–62.

—— (1982). Financial Returns Modelled by the Product of Two Stochastic Processes—A Study of the Daily Sugar Prices 1961–79, in *Time Series Analysis: Theory and Practice.* 1, (ed.) O. D. Anderson. Amsterdam: North-Holland.

—— (1986). *Modelling Financial Time Series* Chichester: Wiley.

—— (1994). Modeling Stochastic Volatility. *Math. Finance* 4(2), 183–204.

Wiggins, J. B. (1987). Option Values under Stochastic Volatility: Theory and Empirical Estimates. *Journal of Financial Economics* 19, 351–72.

8

Long Memory in Continuous-time Stochastic Volatility Models*

FABIENNE COMTE AND ERIC RENAULT

This paper studies a classical extension of the Black and Scholes model for option pricing, often known as the Hull and White model. Our specification is that the volatility process is assumed not only to be stochastic, but also to have long-memory features and properties. We study here the implications of this con-tinuous-time long-memory model, both for the volatility process itself as well as for the global asset price process. We also compare our model with some discrete time approximations. Then the issue of option pricing is addressed by looking at theor-etical formulas and properties of the implicit volatilities as well as statistical infer-ence tractability. Lastly, we provide a few simulation experiments to illustrate our results.

Keywords: continuous-time option pricing model, stochastic volatility, volatility smile, volatility persistence, long memory

8.1 Introduction

If option prices in the market were conformable with the Black–Scholes (1973) formula, all the Black–Scholes implied volatilities corresponding to various options written on the same asset would coincide with the volatility parameter σ of the underlying asset. In reality this is not the case, and the Black–Scholes (BS) implied volatility $\sigma_{t,\,T}^{imp}$ heavily depends on the calendar time t, the time to maturity $T - t$, and the moneyness of the option. This may produce various biases in option pricing or hedging when BS implied volatilities are used to evaluate new options or hedging ratios. These price distortions, well known to practitioners, are usually documented in the empirical literature under the ter-minology of the smile effect, where the so-called "smile" refers to the U-shaped pattern of implied volatilities across different strike prices.

It is widely believed that volatility smiles can be explained to a great extent by a modeling of stochastic volatility, which could take into account not only the so-called volatility clustering (i.e. bunching of high and low volatility episodes) but also the volatility effects of exogenous arrivals of

* This work was previously published as F. Comte and E. Renault (1998), 'Long Memory in Continuous Time Stochastic Volatility Models' *Mathematical Finance* 8, 4. Copyright © Black-well Publishing. Reproduced by kind permission.
A previous version of this paper has benefitted from helpful comments from S. Pliska, L. C. G. Rogers, M. Taqqu, and two anonymous referees. All remaining errors are ours.

information. This is why Hull and White (1987), Scott (1987), and Melino and Turnbull (1990) have proposed an option pricing model in which the volatility of the underlying asset appears not only time-varying but also associated with a specific risk according to the "stochastic volatility" (SV) paradigm

$$\begin{cases} \frac{dS(t)}{S(t)} = \mu(t,\ S(t))dt + \sigma(t)dw^1(t) \\ d(\ln \sigma(t)) = k(\theta - \ln \sigma(t))dt + \gamma dw^2(t), \end{cases} \tag{1.1}$$

where $S(t)$ denotes the price of the underlying asset, $\sigma(t)$ is its instantaneous volatility, and $(w^1(t),\ w^2(t))$ is a nondegenerate bivariate Brownian process. The nondegenerate feature of $(w^1,\ w^2)$ is characteristic of the SV paradigm, in contrast to continuous-time ARCH-type models where the volatility process is a deterministic function of past values of the underlying asset price.

The logarithm of the volatility is assumed to follow an Ornstein–Uhlenbeck process, which ensures that the instantaneous volatility process is stationary, a natural way to generalize the constant-volatility Black and Scholes model. Indeed, any positive-valued stationary process could be used as a model of the stochastic instantaneous volatility (see Ghysels, Harvey and Renault (1996) for a review). Of course, the choice of a given statistical model for the volatility process heavily influences the deduced option pricing formula. More precisely, Hull and White (1987) show that, under specific assumptions, the price at time t of a European option of exercise date T is the expectation of the Black and Scholes option pricing formula where the constant volatility σ is replaced by its quadratic average over the period:

$$\sigma^2_{t,\ T} = \frac{1}{T-t} \int_t^T \sigma^2(u)\, du, \tag{1.2}$$

and where the expectation is computed with respect to the conditional probability distribution of $\sigma^2_{t,\ T}$ given $\sigma(t)$. In other words, the square of implied Black–Scholes volatility $\sigma^{imp}_{t,\ T}$ appears to be a forecast of the temporal aggregation $\sigma^2_{t,\ T}$ of the instantaneous volatility viewed as a flow variable.

It is now well known that such a model is able to reproduce some empirical stylized facts regarding derivative securities and implied volatilities. A symmetric smile is well explained by this option pricing model with the additional assumption of independence between w^1 and w^2 (see Renault and Touzi (1996)). Skewness may explain the correlation of the volatility process with the price process innovations, the so-called leverage effect (see Hull and White, 1987). Moreover, a striking empirical regularity that emerges from numerous studies is the decreasing amplitude of the smile being a function of time to maturity; for short maturities the smile effect is very pronounced (BS implied volatilities for synchronous option prices may vary between 15% and 25%), but it almost completely disappears for longer maturities. This is conformable to a formula like (1.2) because it shows that, when time to maturity is increased, temporal aggregation of volatilities erases conditional heteroskedasticity, which decreases the smile phenomenon.

The main goal of the present paper is to extend the SV option pricing model in order to capture well-documented evidence of **volatility persistence** and particularly occurrence of fairly pronounced smile effects even for rather long maturity options. In practice, the decrease of the smile amplitude when time to maturity increases turns out to be much slower than it goes according to the standard SV option pricing model in the setting (1.1). This evidence is clearly related to the so-called volatility persistence, which implies that temporal aggregation (1.2) is not able to fully erase conditional heteroskedasticity.

Generally speaking, there is widespread evidence that volatility is highly persistent. Particularly for high frequency data one finds evidence of near unit root behavior of the conditional variance process. In the ARCH literature, numerous estimates of GARCH models for stock market, commodities, foreign exchange, and other asset price series are consistent with an IGARCH specification. Likewise, estimation of stochastic volatility models show similar patterns of persistence (see, e.g. Jacquier, Polson, and Rossi, 1994). These findings have led to a debate regarding modeling persistence in the conditional variance process either via a unit root or a long memory-process. The latter approach has been suggested both for ARCH and SV models; see Baillie, Bollerslev, and Mikkelsen (1996), Breidt, Crato, and De Lima (1993), and Harvey (1993). This allows one to consider **mean-reverting** processes of stochastic volatility rather than the extreme behavior of the IGARCH process which, as noticed by Baillie et al. (1996), has low attractiveness for asset pricing since "the occurrence of a shock to the IGARCH volatility process will persist for an infinite prediction horizon."

The main contribution of the present paper is to introduce long-memory mean reverting volatility processes in the continuous time Hull and White setting. This is particularly attractive for option pricing and hedging through the so-called **term structure of BS implied volatilities** (see Heynen, Kemna, and Vorst, 1994). More precisely, the long-memory feature allows one to capture the well-documented evidence of persistence of the stochastic feature of BS implied volatilities, when time to maturity increases. Since, according to (1.2), BS implied volatilities are seen as an average of expected instantaneous volatilities in the same way that long-term interest rates are seen as average of expected short rates, the type of phenomenon we study here is analogous to the studies by Backus and Zin (1993) and Comte and Renault (1996) who capture persistence of the stochastic feature of long-term interest rates by using long-memory models of short-term interest rates.

Indeed, we are able to extend Hull and White option pricing to a continuous-time long-memory model of stochastic volatility by replacing the Wiener process

w^2 in (1.1) by a fractional Brownian motion w_α^2, with α restricted to $0 \le \alpha < \frac{1}{2}$ (instead of $|\alpha| < \frac{1}{2}$ allowed by the general definition because long memory occurs on that range only). Note that the Wiener case corresponds to $\alpha = 0$. Of course, for nonzero α, w_α^2 is no longer a semimartingale (see Rogers 1995), and thus usual stochastic integration theory is not available. But, following Comte and Renault (1996), we only need L^2 theory of integration for Gaussian processes and we obtain option prices that, although they are functions of the underlying volatility processes, do ensure the semimartingale property as a maintained hypothesis for asset price processes (including options).[1] This semimartingale property is all the more important for asset prices processes because stochastic processes that are not semimartingales do not admit equivalent martingale measures. Indeed we know from Delbaen and Schachermayer (1994) that an asset price process admits an equivalent martingale measure if and only if the NFLVR (no free lunch with vanishing risk) condition holds. As stressed by Rogers (1995), when this condition fails, "this does not of itself imply the existence of arbitrage, though in any meaningful economic sense it is just as bad as that." In that event, Rogers (1995) provides a direct construction of arbitrage with fractional Brownian motion. As long as the volatility itself is not a traded asset, all asset price processes that we consider here (underlying asset and options written on it) are conformable to the NFLVR. Note that we have nevertheless the same usual problem as in all models of that kind: the nonuniqueness of the neutral-risk equivalent measure.

The paper is organized as follows. We study in Section 8.2 the probabilistic properties of our Fractional Stochastic Volatility (FSV) model in continuous time, obtained by replacing the Wiener process w^2 in (1.1) by the following process that may be seen as a truncated version of the general fractional Brownian motion[2]:

$$w_\alpha^2(t) = \int_0^t \frac{(t-s)^\alpha}{\Gamma(1+\alpha)} dw^2(s), \qquad 0 < \alpha < \frac{1}{2}.$$

We explain why a high degree of fractional differencing α allows one to take into account the apparent widespread finding of integrated volatility for high frequency data. Section 8.3 gives the basis for more empirical studies of our FSV model through discrete time approximations. We stress the advantages of continuous-time modeling of long memory with respect to the usual ARFIMA à la Geweke and Porter-Hudak (1983) or their FIGARCH analogue in the ARCH literature. The main point is that only a continuous-time definition of

---

[1] We are very grateful to L. C. G. Rogers to have helped us, in a private communication, to check this point. The semimartingale property of an option price C_t comes from the fact that it is computed as a conditional expectation of a (nonlinear) function of $\int_t^T \sigma^2(u)du$. This integration reestablishes the semimartingale property that was lost by the volatility process itself.

[2] This process is a tool for easy L^2 definitions of integrals w.r.t. the Fractional Brownian Motion (FBM), but can be replaced by the true FBM $\int_{-\infty}^0 ((t-s)^\alpha - (-s)^\alpha)dw^2(s) + w_\alpha^2(t)$.

the parameters of interest allows one to clearly disentangle long-memory parameters from short-memory ones.

Section 8.4 is devoted to the issue of option pricing and the study of the properties and features of implied volatilities. Since the first equation of (1.1) has remained invariant by our long-memory generalization of the Hull and White (1987) option pricing model, their argument can be extended in order to set an option pricing formula. The only change is the law of motion of the instantaneous volatility, whose long-memory feature modifies the orders of conditional heteroskedasticity (forecasted, temporally aggregated, ...) and of kurtosis coefficients with respect to time to maturity. We derive some formulas about these orders which extend those of Drost and Werker (1996) and thus "close the FIGARCH gap."

The statistical inference issue is addressed in Section 8.5. Of course, if the instantaneous volatility $\sigma(t)$ were observed, Comte and Renault's (1996) work about the estimation of continuous-time long-memory models could be used. But instantaneous volatilities are not directly observed and can only be filtered, either by an extension to FIGARCH models of Nelson and Foster's (1994) methodology or by using option prices as Pastorello, Renault, and Touzi (1993) do in the Hull and White context. Note that for $\alpha \neq 0$ the volatility process is no longer Markovian, so this may make awkward the practical use of the Hull and White option pricing formula. Nevertheless, it is shown how one could extend the Pastorello et al. (1993) methodology to the present framework. The alternative methodology we suggest in the present paper is to use approximate discretizations of the $S(t)$ stock price process in order to obtain some proxies of instantaneous volatilities and work with approximate likelihoods.

The discretizations found in Section 8.3 are used in Section 8.6 to perform some simulation experiments about continuous-time FSV models. A descriptive study of the resulting paths can then be obtained. The estimation procedures are compared through these Monte Carlo experiments. The misspecification bias introduced by a FIGARCH approximation of our continuous-time models is documented.

8.2 The fractional stochastic volatility model

8.2.1 A simple fractional long-memory process

Comte and Renault (1996) used fractional processes to generalize the notion of Stochastic Differential Equation (SDE) of order p. We consider here only the first-order fractional SDE:

$$dx(t) = -kx(t)dt + \sigma dw_\alpha(t), \qquad x(0) = 0,\ k > 0,\ 0 < \alpha < \frac{1}{2}. \qquad (2.1)$$

The solution can be written (see Comte and Renault, 1996) as $x(t) = \int_0^t e^{-k(t-s)}\sigma dw_\alpha(s)$. Integration with respect to w_α is defined only in the

Wiener L^2 sense and for the integration of deterministic functions only. We thus obtain families of Gaussian processes. The process $x(t)$ also can be written as $\int_0^t a(t-s)\,dw(s)$ with

$$
\begin{aligned}
a(x) &= \frac{\sigma}{\Gamma(1+\alpha)} \frac{d}{dx} \int_0^x e^{-ku}(x-u)^\alpha du \\
&= \frac{\sigma}{\Gamma(1+\alpha)} \left(x^\alpha - ke^{-kx} \int_0^x e^{ku}u^\alpha du \right).
\end{aligned}
\tag{2.2}
$$

We denote by $y(t)$ the "stationary version" of $x(t)$, $y(t) = \int_{-\infty}^t a(t-s)dw(s)$. Therefore, the solution x of the fractional SDE is given by

$$
x(t) = \int_0^t \frac{(t-s)^\alpha}{\Gamma(1+\alpha)} dx^{(\alpha)}(s),
\tag{2.3}
$$

where its derivative of order α is the solution

$$
x^{(\alpha)}(t) = \frac{d}{dt} \int_0^t \frac{(t-s)^{-\alpha}}{\Gamma(1-\alpha)} = \int_0^t e^{-k(t-s)}\sigma\,dw(s)
\tag{2.4}
$$

of the associated standard SDE.

We can also give the general (continuous-time) spectral density of processes that are solutions of (2.1):

$$
f^c(\lambda) = \frac{\sigma^2}{\Gamma(1+\alpha)^2\lambda^{2\alpha}} \frac{1}{\lambda^2+k^2}.
\tag{2.5}
$$

Lastly, it seems interesting to note that long-memory fractional processes as considered in Comte and Renault (1996) and solutions of (2.1) in particular have the following properties proved in Comte (1996):

    i. The covariance function $\gamma = \gamma_y$ associated with x satisfies for $h \to 0$ and ψ constant:

$$
\gamma(h) = \gamma(0) + \frac{1}{2}\psi.|h|^{2\alpha+1} + o(|h|^{2\alpha+1}).
\tag{2.6}
$$

    ii. x is ergodic in the L^2 sense: $\frac{1}{T}\int_0^T x(s)ds \xrightarrow[T\to\infty]{m.s.} 0$.

    iii. There is a process $z(t)$ equivalent[3] to $x(t)$ and such that the sample function of z satisfies a Lipschitz condition of order β, $\forall \beta \in (0, \alpha+\frac{1}{2})$, a.s.

Thus the greater the value of α, the smoother the path of the process.

---

[3] Two processes are called equivalent if they coincide almost surely.

8.2.2 Properties of the Volatility in the FSV Model

The basic idea of our modeling strategy (see (1.1)) is to assume that the logarithm $x(t) = \ln \sigma(t)$ of the stochastic volatility is a solution of the first-order SDE (2.1). For the sake of simplicity, we assume $\theta = 0$ since it does not change the probabilistic properties of the process. Thus the volatility process $\sigma(t)$ is asymptotically equivalent (in quadratic mean) to the stationary process:

$$\tilde{\sigma}(t) = \exp\left(\int_{-\infty}^{t} e^{-k(t-s)} \gamma dw_{\alpha}^2(s) \right), \qquad k > 0, \ 0 < \alpha < \frac{1}{2}. \tag{2.7}$$

As in usual diffusion models of stochastic volatility, the volatility process is assumed to be asymptotically stationary and nowhere differentiable. This is the reason we do not use an SDE (even fractional) of higher order. Nevertheless, the fractional exponent α provides some degree of freedom in the order of regularity. Indeed, it is possible to show for $\sigma(t)$ the same type of regularity property as for the fractional process $x(t) = \ln \sigma(t)$.

Proposition 2.1 Let $r_{\sigma}(h) = \text{cov}(\tilde{\sigma}(t+h), \ \tilde{\sigma}(t))$, where $\tilde{\sigma}$ is given by (2.7). Then, for $h \to 0$, $r_{\sigma}(h) = r_{\sigma}(0) + \eta.|h|^{2\alpha+1} + o(|h|^{2\alpha+1})$, where η is a given constant.

(See Appendix A for all proofs.)

Roughly speaking, the autocorrelation function of the stationary process σ fulfills the regularity condition that ensures the Lipschitz feature of the sample paths. The greater α is, the smoother the path of the volatility process is. Therefore, a high degree of fractional differencing α allows one to take into account the apparent widespread finding of integrated volatility for high frequency data (see the simulation in Section 8.6.2). As a matter of fact, we can see that

$$\alpha > 0 \Rightarrow \frac{r_{\sigma}(h) - r_{\sigma}(0)}{h} \xrightarrow[h \to 0]{} 0,$$

which could be interpreted as a near-integrated behavior

$$\frac{r_{\sigma}(h) - r_{\sigma}(0)}{h} = \frac{\rho^h - 1}{h} \xrightarrow[h \to 0]{} \ln \rho \xrightarrow[\rho \to 1]{} 0$$

if $\sigma(t)$ is considered as a continuous-time AR(1) process with a correlation coefficient ρ near 1.

This analogy between a unit root hypothesis and its fractional alternatives has already been used for unit root tests by Robinson (1993). Robinson's methodology could be a useful tool for testing integrated volatility against long memory in stochastic volatility behavior.

The concept of persistence that we advance thanks to the fractional framework is that of long memory instead of indefinite persistence of shocks as in the IGARCH framework. Indeed, we can prove the following result:

Proposition 2.2 In the context of Proposition 2.1, we have

(i) $r_\sigma(h)$ is of order $O(|h|^{2\alpha-1})$ for $h \to +\infty$.

(ii) $\lim_{\lambda \to 0} \lambda^{2\alpha} f_\sigma(\lambda) = c \in \mathbb{R}^+$, where $f_\sigma(\lambda) = \int_\mathbb{R} r_\sigma(h) e^{i\lambda h}\, dh$ is the spectral density of $\tilde\sigma$.

Proposition 2.2 illustrates that the volatility process itself (and not only its logarithm) does entail the long-memory properties (generally summarized as in (i) and (ii) by the behavior of the covariance function near infinity and of the spectral density near zero) we could expect in the FSV model.

8.3 Discrete approximations of the FSV model

8.3.1 The volatility process

The volatility process dynamics are characterized by the fact that $x(t) = \ln \sigma(t)$ is a solution of the fractional SDE (2.1). So we know two integral expressions for $x(t)$ (with the notations of Section 2.1):

$$x(t) = \int_0^t \frac{(t-s)^\alpha}{\Gamma(1+\alpha)} dx^{(\alpha)}(s) = \int_0^t a(t-s)\, dw^2(s),$$

where $a(t-s)$ is given by (2.2).

A discrete time approximation of the volatility process is a formula to numerically evaluate these integrals using only the values of the involved processes $x^{(\alpha)}(s)$ and $w^2(s)$ on a discrete partition of $[0,\ t]$: j/n, $j = 0, 1, \ldots, [nt]$.[4] A natural way to obtain such approximations (see Comte, 1996) is to approximate the integrands by step functions:

$$x_{n,\,1}(t) = \int_0^t \frac{\left(t - \frac{[ns]}{n}\right)^\alpha}{\Gamma(1+\alpha)} dx^{(\alpha)}(s) \quad \text{and} \quad x_{n,\,2}(t) = \int_0^t a\left(t - \frac{[ns]}{n}\right) dw^2(s), \quad (3.1)$$

which gives, neglecting the last terms for large values of n,

$$\hat{x}_n(t) = \sum_{j=1}^{[nt]} \frac{\left(t - \frac{j-1}{n}\right)^\alpha}{\Gamma(1+\alpha)} \Delta x^{(\alpha)}\left(\frac{j}{n}\right) \quad \text{and}$$

$$\tilde{x}_n(t) = \sum_{j=1}^{[nt]} a\left(t - \frac{j-1}{n}\right) \Delta w^2\left(\frac{j}{n}\right), \tag{3.2}$$

where we use the following notations: $\Delta x^{(\alpha)}(\frac{j}{n}) = x^{(\alpha)}(\frac{j}{n}) - x^{(\alpha)}(\frac{j-1}{n})$ and $\Delta w^2(\frac{j}{n}) = w^2(\frac{j}{n}) - w^2(\frac{j-1}{n})$.

Indeed, all these approximations converge toward the x process in distribution in the sense of convergence in distribution for stochastic processes as defined in

---

[4] $[z]$ is the integer k such that $k \le z < k+1$.

Billingsley (1968); this convergence is denoted by $\overset{\mathcal{D}}{\Rightarrow}$. This result is proved in Comte (1996).

Proposition 3.1 $x_{n,1} \overset{\mathcal{D}}{\Rightarrow} x$, $x_{n,2} \overset{\mathcal{D}}{\Rightarrow} x$, $\hat{x}_n \overset{\mathcal{D}}{\Rightarrow} x$, and $\tilde{x}_n \overset{\mathcal{D}}{\Rightarrow} x$ when n goes to infinity.

The proxy $\hat{x}_n$ is the most useful for comparing our FSV model with the standard discrete time models of conditional heteroskedasticity, whereas the most tractable for mathematical work is $\tilde{x}_n$.

8.3.2 FSV versus FIGARCH

Expression (3.2) provides a proxy $\hat{x}_n$ of x in function of the process $x^{(\alpha)}(\frac{j}{n})$, $j = 0, 1, \ldots, [nt]$, which is an AR(1) process associated with an innovation process $u(\frac{j}{n})$, $j = 0, 1, \ldots, [nt]$. Let us denote by

$$(1 - \rho_n L_n) x^{(\alpha)}\left(\frac{j}{n}\right) = u\left(\frac{j}{n}\right) \tag{3.3}$$

the representation of this process, where L_n is the lag operator corresponding to the sampling scheme $\frac{j}{n}$, $j = 0, 1, \ldots$, $L_n Y(\frac{j}{n}) = Y(\frac{j-1}{n})$, and $\rho_n = e^{-k/n}$ is the correlation coefficient for the time interval $\frac{1}{n}$.

Since the process $x^{(\alpha)}$ is asymptotically stationary, we can assume without loss of generality that its initial value is zero, $x^{(\alpha)}(\frac{j}{n}) = 0$ for $j \leq 0$, which of course implies $u(\frac{j}{n}) = 0$ for $j \leq 0$. Then we can write

$$\hat{x}_n\left(\frac{j}{n}\right) = \sum_{i=1}^{j} \frac{(j-i+1)^\alpha}{n^\alpha \Gamma(1+\alpha)} \left[x^{(\alpha)}\left(\frac{i}{n}\right) - x^{(\alpha)}\left(\frac{i-1}{n}\right) \right]$$

$$= \left[\sum_{i=0}^{j-1} \frac{(i+1)^\alpha - i^\alpha}{n^\alpha \Gamma(1+\alpha)} L_n^i \right] x^{(\alpha)}\left(\frac{j}{n}\right).$$

Thus,

$$\hat{x}_n\left(\frac{j}{n}\right) = \left[\sum_{i=0}^{j-1} \frac{(i+1)^\alpha - i^\alpha}{n^\alpha \Gamma(1+\alpha)} L_n^i \right] (1 - \rho_n L_n)^{-1} u\left(\frac{j}{n}\right). \tag{3.4}$$

Expression (3.4) gives a parameterization of the volatility dynamics in two parts: a long-memory part that corresponds to the filter $\sum_{i=0}^{+\infty} a_i L_n^i / n^\alpha$ with $a_i = ((i+1)^\alpha - i^\alpha)/\Gamma(1+\alpha)$ and a short-memory part that is characterized by the AR(1) process: $(1 - \rho_n L_n)^{-1} u(\frac{j}{n})$.

We can show that the long-memory filter is "long-term equivalent" to the usual discrete time long-memory filter $(1 - L)^{-\alpha} = \sum_{i=0}^{+\infty} b_i L^i$, where $b_i = \Gamma(i+\alpha)/(\Gamma(i+1)\Gamma(\alpha))$, in the sense that there is a long-term relationship (a cointegration relation) between the two types of processes. Indeed, we can show (see Comte 1996) that the two long-memory processes, $Y_t = \sum_{i=0}^{+\infty} a_i u_{t-i}$ and $Z_t = \sum_{i=0}^{+\infty} b_i u_{t-i}$, where a_i and b_i are defined previously and u_t is any short-term memory stationary process, are cointegrated: $Y_t - Z_t$ is short memory and $\sum_{i=0}^{+\infty} |a_i - b_i| < +\infty$, whereas $\sum_{i=0}^{+\infty} a_i = \sum_{i=0}^{+\infty} b_i = +\infty$.

But this long-term equivalence between our long-memory filter and the usual discrete time one $(1 - L)^{-\alpha}$ does not imply that the standard parameterization ARFIMA $(1, \alpha, 0)$ is well suited in our framework. Indeed, short-memory characteristics may be hidden by the short-term difference between the two filters. In other words, not only $(1 - \rho_n L_n)(n(1 - L_n))^\alpha \hat{x}_n(\frac{i}{n})$ is not in general a white noise,[5] but we are not even sure that $(n(1 - L_n))^\alpha \hat{x}_n(\frac{i}{n})$ is an AR(1) process (even though we know that it is a short-memory stationary process). The usual discrete time filter $(1 - L)^\alpha$ introduces some mixing between long- and short-term characteristics (see Comte, 1996 and Section 8.6.3 for illustration).

This is the first reason why we believe that the FSV model is more relevant for high-frequency data than the FIGARCH model since the latter is based on an ARFIMA modeling of the squared innovations (see Baillie et al., 1996). The second reason is that the FSV model represents the log-volatility as an "AR(1) long-memory" process with a specific risk (in the particular case $\alpha = 0$, (3.4) corresponds to the stochastic variance model of Harvey, Ruiz, and Shephard, 1994), but the GARCH type modeling does not introduce an exogenous risk of volatility and, by the way, does not explain why option markets are useful to hedge a specific risk.

8.3.3 The global filtering model

In order to obtain a complete discrete time approximation of our FSV model, we have to discretize not only the volatility process, but also the associated asset price process $S(t)$ according to (1.1). Since it is not difficult to compute some discretizations of the trend part of an SDE, we can assume in this subsection, for the sake of notational simplicity, that $\ln S(t)$ is a martingale. Not only are we always able to perform a preliminary centering of the price process in order to be in this case, but also it is well known that the martingale hypothesis is often directly accepted, for exchange rates for example. So, with $Y(t) = \ln S(t)$ we are interested in the following dynamics:

$$\begin{cases} dY(t) = \sigma(t)dw^1(t) \\ d(\ln \sigma(t)) = -k \ln \sigma(t)dt + \gamma dw_\alpha^2(t). \end{cases} \tag{3.5}$$

For a known process σ, a discretized approximation Y_n of the process Y can directly be obtained by a way similar to (3.1):

$$Y_n(t) = \int_0^t \sigma\left(\frac{[ns]}{n}\right) dw^1(s)$$

$$= \sum_{j=1}^{[nt]} \sigma\left(\frac{j-1}{n}\right) \Delta w^1\left(\frac{j}{n}\right) + \sigma\left(\frac{[nt]}{n}\right)\left(w^1(t) - w^1\left(\frac{[nt]}{n}\right)\right).$$

---

[5] The fractional differencing operator $(1 - L)^\alpha$ has to be modified into $(n(1 - L_n))^\alpha$ in order to correctly normalize the unit root with respect to the unit period of time.

And by a remark of the same type as (3.2), we can also consider $\hat{Y}_n(t) = \sum_{j=1}^{[nt]} \sigma(\frac{i-1}{n})\Delta w^1(\frac{i}{n})$. It can be proved that:

Lemma 3.1 $Y_n \overset{D}{\Rightarrow} Y$ and $\hat{Y}_n \overset{D}{\Rightarrow} Y$, when n grows to infinity.

But from a practical viewpoint, the discretizations Y_n and $\hat{Y}_n$ are not very useful because they are based on the values of the process σ, which cannot be computed without some other errors of discretization. Thus we are more interested in the following joint discretization:

$$
\tilde{\sigma}_n(t) = \exp\left[\sum_{j=1}^{[nt]} a\left(t - \frac{j-1}{n}\right)\Delta w^2\left(\frac{j}{n}\right)\right],
$$

$$
\tilde{Y}_n(t) = \sum_{j=1}^{[nt]} \tilde{\sigma}_n\left(\frac{j-1}{n}\right)\Delta w^1\left(\frac{j}{n}\right).
$$

(3.6)

We can then prove the following proposition.

Proposition 3.2

$$
\begin{pmatrix} \tilde{Y}_n \\ \tilde{\sigma}_n \end{pmatrix} \overset{D}{\Rightarrow} \begin{pmatrix} Y \\ \sigma \end{pmatrix} \quad \text{and thus} \quad \begin{pmatrix} \tilde{S}_n = \ln \tilde{Y}_n \\ \tilde{\sigma}_n \end{pmatrix} \overset{D}{\Rightarrow} \begin{pmatrix} S \\ \sigma \end{pmatrix} \quad \text{when } n \to \infty.
$$

Another parameterization can be obtained by using $\hat{\sigma}_n(t) = \exp(\hat{x}_n(t))$ rather than $\tilde{\sigma}_n(t) = \exp(\tilde{x}_n(t))$; the previous section has shown how this parameterization is given by α and ρ_n.

We have something like a discrete time stochastic variance model à la Harvey et al. (1994) which converges toward our FSV model when the sampling interval $\frac{1}{n}$ converges toward zero. The only difference is that, when $\alpha \neq 0$, $\ln \tilde{\sigma}_n(t)$ is not an AR(1) process but a long-memory stationary process. Such a generalization has in fact been considered in discrete time by Harvey (1993) in a recent working paper. He works with $y_t = \sigma_t \varepsilon_t$, $\varepsilon_t \sim IID(0, 1)$, $t = 1, \ldots, T$, $\sigma_t^2 = \sigma^2 \exp(h_t)$, $(1 - L)^d h_t = \eta_t$, $\eta_t \sim IID(0, \sigma_\eta^2)$, $0 \le d \le 1$. The analogy with (3.6) is then obvious, with the remaining problem being the choice of the right approximation of the fractional derivation studied in the previous subsection. Moreover, our case is a little different from the one studied by Harvey in that we have in mind a volatility process of the type ARFIMA (1, α, 0) where he has an ARFIMA (0, d, 0). But such discrete time models may be also useful for statistical inference.

8.4 Option pricing and implied volatilities

8.4.1 Option pricing

The maintained assumption of our option pricing model is characterized by the price model (1.2), where $(w^1(t), w^2(t))$ is a standard Brownian motion. Let $(\Omega, \mathscr{F}, \mathbb{P})$ be the fundamental probability space. $(\mathscr{F}_t)_{t \in [0, T]}$ denotes the

$\mathbb{P}$-augmentation of the filtration generated by $(w^1(\tau),\ w^2(\tau))$, $\tau \leq t$. It coincides with the filtration generated by $(S(\tau),\ \sigma(\tau))$, $\tau \leq t$ or $(S(\tau),\ x^{(\alpha)}(\tau))$, $\tau \leq t$, with $x(t) = \ln \sigma(t)$.

We look here for the call option premium C_t, which is the price at time $t \leq T$ of a European call option on the financial asset of price S_t at t, with strike K and maturing at time T. The asset is assumed not to pay dividends, and there are no transaction costs.

Let us assume that the instantaneous interest rate at time t, $r(t)$, is deterministic, so that the price at time t of a zero coupon bond of maturity T is $B(t,\ T) = \exp(-\int_t^T r(u)\,du)$.

We know from Harrison and Kreps (1981) that the no free lunch assumption is equivalent to the existence of a probability distribution $\mathbf{Q}$ on $(\Omega,\ \mathscr{F})$, equivalent to $\mathbb{P}$, under which the discounted *price processes* are martingales. We emphasize that no change of probability of the Girsanov type could have transformed the volatility process into a martingale, but there is no such problem for the price process $S(t)$. This stresses the interest of such models where the nonstandard fractional properties are set on $\sigma(t)$ and not directly on $S(t)$. This avoids any of the possible problems of stochastic integration with respect to a fractional process, which does not admit any standard decomposition. Indeed, the σ process appears only as a predictible and even L^2 continuous integrand.

Then we can use the standard arguments. An equivalent measure $\mathbf{Q}$ is characterized by a continuous version of the density process of $\mathbf{Q}$ with respect to $\mathbb{P}$ (see Karatzas and Shreve, 1991, p. 184):

$$M(t) = \exp\left(-\int_0^t \lambda(u)'dW(u) - \frac{1}{2}\int_0^t \lambda(u)'\lambda(u)\,du\right),$$

where $W = (w^1,\ w^2)'$ and $\lambda = (\lambda_1,\ \lambda_2)'$ is adapted to $\{\mathscr{F}_t\}$ and satisfies the integrability condition $\int_0^T \lambda(u)'\lambda(u)du < \infty$ a.s. The processes λ_1 and λ_2 can be considered as risk premia relative to the two sources of risk w^1 and w^2. Moreover, the martingale property under $\mathbf{Q}$ of the discounted asset prices implies that: $\lambda_1(t)\sigma(t) = \mu(t,\ S(t)) - r(t)$.

As the market is incomplete, as is usual in such a context (two sources of risk and only one risky asset traded), there is no such relation fixing the volatility risk premium λ_2 and, indeed, the martingale probability $\mathbf{Q}$ is not unique.

We need to restrict the set of equivalent martingale probabilities by assuming that the process $\lambda_2(t)$ is a deterministic function $\bar{\lambda}_2$ of the two arguments t and $\sigma(t)$:

$$\textbf{(A)} \qquad \lambda_2(t) = \bar{\lambda}_2(t,\ \sigma(t)), \quad \forall t \in [0,\ T],$$

which is a common assumption.

Girsanov's theorem leads to a characterization of the distribution under $\mathbf{Q}$ of the underlying asset. Let:

$$\tilde{w}^1(t) = w^1(t) + \int_0^t \lambda_1(u)\,du \qquad \text{and} \qquad \tilde{w}^2(t) = w^2(t) + \int_0^t \lambda_2(u)\,du.$$

Then $(\tilde{w}^1, \tilde{w}^2) = \tilde{w}'$ is a two-dimensional standard $\mathbf{Q}$-Wiener process adapted to $\{\mathscr{F}_t\}$. In particular, $\tilde{w}^1$ and $\tilde{w}_2$ are independent under $\mathbf{Q}$ by construction. Moreover σ is the solution to an equation depending only on w^2 that can be rewritten as a stochastic differential equation in $\tilde{w}^2$ (depending also on λ_2). Thus the processes $\tilde{w}^1$ and σ are still independent under $\mathbf{Q}$. With $\mathbf{Q}$ defined as previously, the call option price is given by

$$C_t = B(t, T)\mathbb{E}^{\mathbf{Q}}[\text{Max}(0, S_T - K)\,|\,\mathscr{F}_t], \qquad (8.4.1)$$

where $\mathbb{E}^{\mathbf{Q}}(.\,|\,\mathscr{F}_t)$ is the conditional expectation operator, given $\mathscr{F}_t$, when the price dynamics is governed by $\mathbf{Q}$. Since $\tilde{w}^1$ and σ are independent under $\mathbf{Q}$, the $\mathbf{Q}$ distribution of $\ln(S_T/S_t)$ given by $d\ln S_t = (r(t) - (\sigma(t)^2/2)dt + \sigma(t)d\tilde{w}^1(t)$ conditionally on both $\mathscr{F}_t$ and the whole volatility path $(\sigma(t))_{t\in[0,\ T]}$ is Gaussian with mean $\int_t^T r(u)du - \frac{1}{2}\int_t^T \sigma(u)^2 du$ and variance $\int_t^T \sigma(u)^2 du$. Therefore, computing the expectation (8.4.1) conditionally on the volatility path gives:

$$C_t = S(t)\left\{\mathbb{E}_t^{\mathbf{Q}}\left[\Phi\left(\frac{m_t}{U_{t,T}} + \frac{U_{t,T}}{2}\right)|\mathscr{F}_t\right] - e^{-m_t}\mathbb{E}_t^{\mathbf{Q}}\left[\Phi\left(\frac{m_t}{U_{t,T}} - \frac{U_{t,T}}{2}\right)|\mathscr{F}_t\right]\right\}, \qquad (8.4.2)$$

where $m_t = \ln\left(\frac{S(t)}{KB(t,T)}\right)$, $U_{t,T} = \sqrt{\int_t^T \sigma(u)^2 du}$, and $\Phi(u) = \frac{1}{\sqrt{2\pi}}\int_{-\infty}^u e^{-t^2/2}dt$.

The dynamics of σ are now given by

$$\ln\frac{\sigma(t)}{\sigma(0)} = \left(-k\int_0^t \ln\sigma(u)\,du - \gamma\int_0^t \frac{(t-s)^\alpha}{\Gamma(1+\alpha)}\lambda_2(s)ds\right) + \gamma\tilde{w}_\alpha^2(t),$$

where

$$\tilde{w}_\alpha^2(t) = \int_0^t \frac{(t-s)^\alpha}{\Gamma(1+\alpha)}d\tilde{w}^2(s).$$

Then differentiating $x(t) = \ln\sigma(t)$ with fractional order α gives:

$$dx^{(\alpha)}(t) = (-kx^{(\alpha)}(t) + \gamma\lambda_2(t))dt + \gamma d\tilde{w}^2(t), \qquad (8.4.3)$$

where

$$x^{(\alpha)}(t) = \frac{d}{dt}\int_0^t \frac{(t-s)^{-\alpha}}{\Gamma(1-\alpha)}x(s)ds$$

is the derivative of (fractional) order α of x.

We can give the general solution of (4.3):

$$x^{(\alpha)}(t) = \left(c + \int_0^t \gamma e^{ks}\lambda_2(s)ds + \int_0^t \gamma e^{ks}d\tilde{w}^2(s)\right)e^{-kt}$$

and deduce x by fractional integration.

As usual, when one wants to perform statistical inference using arbitrage pricing models, two approaches can be imagined: either specify a given parametric form of the risk premium or assume that the associated risk is not compensated. When trading of volatility is observed it might be relevant to assume a risk premium on it. But we choose here, for the sake of simplicity (see, e.g., Engle and Mustafa, 1992 or Pastorello et al., 1993 for similar strategies in short-memory settings) to assume that the volatility risk is not compensated, i.e., that $\lambda_2 = 0$. Under this simplifying assumption, which has some micro-economics foundations (see Pham and Touzi, 1996), the probability distributions of $U_{t, T}$ are the same under $\mathbb{P}$ and under $\mathbf{Q}$. In other words the expectation operator in the option pricing formula (8.4.2) can be considered with respect to $\mathbb{P}$.

8.4.2 Implied volatilities
Practitioners are used to computing the so-called Black–Scholes implicit volatility by inversion of the Black–Scholes option pricing formula on the observed option prices. If we assume that these option prices are given by (4.2) and that the volatility risk is not compensated, the Black–Scholes implicit volatility appears to be a forecast of the average volatility $\sigma_{t, T}$ on the lifetime of the option $(\sigma_{t, T}^2 = (T - t)^{-1} U_{t, T}^2)$. If we consider the proxy of the option price (4.2) deduced from a first-order Taylor expansion (around $(T - t)^{-1} \mathbb{E} U_{t, T}^2$) of the Black–Scholes formula considered as a function of $\sigma_{t, T}^2$, the Black–Scholes implicit volatility dynamics would be directly related to the dynamics of

$$\sigma_{imp, T}^2(t) = \frac{1}{T - t} \int_t^T \mathbb{E}(\sigma^2(u)|\mathcal{F}_t)du.$$

To describe the dynamics of this "implicit volatility" we start by analyzing the conditional laws and moments of σ:

$$\mathbb{E}(\sigma(t + h)\,|\,\mathcal{F}_t) = \exp\left(g(t + h) + \int_0^t a(t + h - s)dw^2(s) + \frac{1}{2}\int_0^h a^2(x)dx \right)$$

for $x(t) = \ln \sigma(t) = g(t) + \int_0^t a(t - s)dw^2(s)$, $g(t) = x(0) + (1 - e^{-kt})\theta$, and $a(x)$ as usual. Or, if we work with the stationary version of σ:

$$\mathbb{E}(\sigma(t + h)\,|\,\mathcal{F}_t) = \exp\left(\int_{-\infty}^t a(t + h - s)dw^{(2)}(s) + \frac{1}{2}\int_0^h a^2(x)dx \right).$$

To have an idea of the behavior of the implicit volatility, we can prove:

Proposition 4.1 $y_t = \mathbb{E}(\sigma^2(t + 1)|\mathcal{F}_t)$ is a long-memory process in the sense that $\mathrm{cov}(y_t, y_{t+h})$ is of order $O(|h|^{2\alpha-1})$ for $h \to +\infty$ and $\alpha \in\,]0,\ 1/2[$.
$\mathrm{Var}(\mathbb{E}(\sigma(t + h)|\mathcal{F}_t))$ is of order $O(|h|^{2\alpha-1})$ for $h \to +\infty$ if $\alpha \in\,]0, 1/2[$ and of order $e^{-k|h|}$ if $\alpha = 0$.

Proposition 4.1 shows that, thanks to the long-memory property of the instantaneous volatility process, the stochastic feature of forecasted volatility does not vanish at the very high exponential rate but at the lower hyperbolic rate. This rate of convergence explains the stochastic feature of implicit volatilities, even for fairly long maturity options.

Since $T > t$, we can set $T = t + \tau$. We take $\tau = 1$ for simplicity and study the long-memory properties of the stationary (if we work with the stationary version of σ) process which is now defined by

$$\sigma_{imp}^2(t) = \int_0^1 \mathbb{E}(\sigma^2(t + u)|\mathscr{F}_t)du.$$

Proposition 4.2 $z_t := \sigma_{imp}^2(t)$ is a long-memory process in the sense that $\text{cov}(z_t, z_{t+h})$ is of order $O(|h|^{2\alpha - 1})$ for $h \to +\infty$ and $\alpha \in]0, 1/2[$.

We have already documented (see Section 6.5) some empirical evidence to confirm the theoretical result of Proposition 4.2. Indeed, when we use daily data on CAC40 and option prices on CAC40 (of the Paris Stock Exchange) and we try to estimate a long-memory parameter by regression on the log-periodogram (see Robinson, 1996), we find that the stock price process S is a short-memory process and the B.S. implicit volatility process is a long-memory one.

Finally, the dynamics of conditional heteroskedasticity of the stock price process S can be described through the marginal kurtosis. We are not only able to prove a convergence property like Corollary 3.2 of Drost and Werker (1996) but also to measure the effect of the long-memory parameter on the speed of convergence:

Proposition 4.3 Let $\varphi(h) = \mathbb{E}|Y(h) - \mathbb{E}Y(h)|^4 = \mathbb{E}Z(h)^4$ denote the fourth centered moment of the rate of return $Y(h) = \ln\frac{S(h)}{S(0)}$ on $[0, h]$, with $Z(t) = \int_0^t \sigma(u)dw^1(u)$. Then $\varphi(h)/h^2$ is bounded on $\mathbb{R}$.

Moreover, let $kurt_Y(h) = \varphi(h)/(\text{Var}\,Y(h))^2$ denote the kurtosis coefficient of $Y(h)$. Then

$$\lim_{h \to 0} kurt_Y(h) = 3\frac{\mathbb{E}(\sigma^4)}{(\mathbb{E}(\sigma^2))^2} > 3, \quad \text{for} \quad \alpha \in \left[0, \frac{1}{2}\right]$$

at rate $h^{2\alpha+1}$ (continuity in $\alpha = 0$),[6] and $\lim_{h \to +\infty} kurt_Y(h) = 3$ for $\alpha \in [0, \frac{1}{2}[$ at rate $h^{2\alpha - 1}$ if $\alpha \in]0, \frac{1}{2}[$,[7] and at rate $e^{-(k/2)h}$ if $\alpha = 0$.

The discontinuity in 0 of the speed of convergence of $\lim_{h \to +\infty} kurt_Y(h)$ with respect to α is additional evidence of the persistence in volatility introduced by the

---

[6] That is, $kurt_Y(h) - 3[\mathbb{E}(\sigma^4)/(\mathbb{E}(\sigma^2))^2]$ is of order $h^{2\alpha+1}$ for $h \to 0$.

[7] That is, $kurt_Y(h) - 3$ is of order $h^{2\alpha-1}$ for $h \to +\infty$.

α parameter. When there is long memory ($\alpha > 0$) the leptokurtic feature due to conditional heteroskedasticity vanishes with temporal aggregation at a slow hyperbolic rate, while with a usual short-memory volatility process it vanishes at an exponential rate.

Note that the limit for h going to 0 of $kurt_Y(h)$ is close to 3 (and thus the log-return Y is close to Gaussian) if and only if $Var\sigma^2$ is close to 0, that is, if σ is close to deterministic (small value of the diffusion coefficient γ); this leads us back to the standard Black–Scholes world.

8.5 Statistical inference in the FSV model

8.5.1 Statistical inference from stock prices

Several methods are provided in Comte and Renault (1996) and Comte (1996) to estimate the parameters of an "Ornstein–Uhlenbeck long-memory" process, which here is the set of parameters (α, k, θ, γ) implied by the first-order equation fulfilled by the log-volatility process. Those methods of course are all based on a discrete time sample of observations of one path of $\ln\sigma$. Such a path is not available here.

The idea then is to find approximations of the path deduced from the observed $S(t_i)$ and to replace the true observations usually used by their approximations in the estimation procedure. Let us recall briefly that those procedures are as follows:

- either we find α by log-periodogram regression using the semiparametric results of Robinson (1996) and (k, θ, γ) by estimating an AR(1) process after fractional differentiation at the estimated order,

- or all parameters are estimated by minimizing the Whittle-type criterium approximating the likelihood in the frequency domain, as studied by Fox and Taqqu (1986) and Dahlhaus (1989).

The natural idea for approximating σ is then based on the quadratic covariation of $Y(t) = \ln(S(t))$. Indeed, $\langle Y \rangle_t = \int_0^t \sigma^2(s)\,ds$ and, if $\{t_1, \ldots, t_m\}$ is a partition of $[0, t]$ and $t_0 = 0$, then

$$\lim_{step \to 0} \sum_{k=1}^m (Y_{t_k} - Y_{t_{k-1}})^2 = \langle Y \rangle_t \text{ in probability, where step} = \max_{1 \le i \le m} \{|t_i - t_{i-1}|\}.$$

Then as $(\langle Y \rangle_t - \langle Y \rangle_{t-h})/h \xrightarrow[h \to 0]{} \sigma^2(t)$ a.s. and provided that high-frequency data are available, we can think of cumulating the two limits by considering a partition of the partition to obtain estimates of the derivative of the quadratic variation.

Let $[0, T]$ be the interval of observation, let $t_k = kT/N$, $N = np$, be the dates of observations, and let Y_{t_k}, $k = 0, \ldots, N$, be the sample of observations of the log-prices. Then we have n blocks of length p and we set: $\langle \hat{Y} \rangle_t^{(N)}$ $= \sum_{k=0}^{[(tN)/T]=[nt]} (Y_{t_k} - Y_{t_{k-1}})^2$ so that $((\langle \hat{Y} \rangle_t^{(N)} - \langle \hat{Y} \rangle_{t-h}^{(N)}/h)$ is computed from the underlying blocks with $h = T/n$. In other words,

$$\hat{\sigma}_{n,p}^2(t) = \frac{n}{T} \sum_{k=[\frac{tN}{T}]-p+1}^{[\frac{tN}{T}]} (Y_{t_k} - Y_{t_{k-1}})^2$$

because $[((t - (T/n)N)/T] = [tN/T - p]$. Then we have:

Proposition 5.1 Let $Y(t) = \int_0^t \sigma(s)dw^1(s)$ and $\sigma(t) = \tilde{\sigma}(t)$ with $\tilde{\sigma}$ given by formula (2.7). Then $\forall \varepsilon > 0$,

$$\lim_{\substack{n \to \infty \\ p \to \infty}} \sup_{t \in [0, T]} p^{1-\varepsilon} \mathbb{E} \left(\hat{\sigma}_{n,p}^2(t) - \sigma^2(t) \right)^2 = 0.$$

Thus p must be as large as possible for the rate of convergence to be optimal. On the other hand we are interested in large sizes n of the sample of deduced volatilities. This is the reason there is a trade-off between n and p, taking into account the constraint $N = np$. A possible choice could be to choose n and p of order $\sqrt{N}$.

Then we have to estimate μ, supposed to be a constant, and we notice that the finite variation terms that have been omitted in Y are known to have no weight in the quadratic covariation. The estimate of μ can be chosen here as usual (see Renault and Touzi, 1996): $e^{\hat{\mu}_{np}\Delta t} = \frac{1}{np}\sum_{k=1}^{np} \frac{S_{t_k}}{S_{t_{k-1}}}$, $\Delta t = \frac{T}{np}$, $t_k = \frac{kT}{np}$, or sometimes: $\tilde{\mu}_{np} = \frac{np}{T} \frac{1}{np} \sum_{k=1}^{np} \frac{S_{t_k} - S_{t_{k-1}}}{S_{t_{k-1}}}$, which completes the estimation procedure.

8.5.2 Statistical inference from option prices

Another way to estimate the volatility parameters could be the use of the informational content of option prices and associated implied volatilities in the spirit of Engle and Mustafa (1992) or Pastorello et al. (1993) (assuming that the volatility risk is not compensated). Unfortunately, the non-Markovian feature of the long-memory process implies that the Hull and White option pricing formula is not so simple to invert to recover latent instantaneous volatilities as in the usual case. Nevertheless, if sufficiently high frequency data are available to approximate integrals by finite sums, we are able to generalize the Pastorello et al. (1993) procedure thanks to a first-stage estimate of the long-memory parameter α. To see this point, let us assume for instance that we observe at times t_i, $i = 0$, 1, $\ldots$, n, option prices C_{t_i} for options of exercise dates $t_i + \Delta$ (for a fixed Δ), that are at the money in the generalized sense: $S_{t_i} = K_{t_i}B(t_i, t_i + \Delta)$, where K_{t_i} is the exercise price of an option traded at date t_i. In this case, we know from (4.2) that:

$$C_{t_i} = S_{t_i} \left(2\mathbb{E}^{\mathbb{P}} \left(\Phi \left(\frac{U_{t_i, t_i+\Delta}}{2} \right) \right) - 1 \,\Big|\, \mathscr{F}_{t_i} \right). \tag{5.1}$$

The information set $\mathscr{F}_{t_i}$ in the above expectation is defined as the sigma-field generated by $(w^1(\tau), \sigma(\tau), \tau \leq t_i)$. But since the two processes w^1 and σ are independent and $U_{t_i, t_i+\Delta}$ is depending on σ only, the information provided by

$w^1(\tau)$, $\tau \leq t_i$ is irrelevant in the expectation (5.1). Moreover, thanks to (2.4) and (2.3), we know that the sigma-field generated by $x(\tau) = \ln \sigma(\tau)$, $\tau \leq t_i$, coincides with the sigma-field generated by the short-memory process $x^{(\alpha)}(\tau), \tau \leq t_i$. On the other hand, thanks to (2.3), $U_{t_i, t_i+\Delta}$ appears like a complicated function (see Appendix B) of $x^{(\alpha)}(\tau)$, $\tau \leq t_i + \Delta$.

In other words, (5.1) gives the option price as a function of:

- first, the past values $x^{(\alpha)}(\tau)$, $\tau \leq t_i$, which define the deterministic part of $U_{t_i, t_i+\Delta}$,

- second, the Ornstein–Uhlenbeck parameters (k, θ, γ), which characterize the conditional probability distribution of $x^{(\alpha)}(\tau)$, $\tau > t_i$, given the available information $\mathscr{F}_{t_i}$ summarized by $x^{(\alpha)}(t_i)$,

- third, the long-memory parameter α, which defines the functional relationship between $U_{t_i, t_i+\Delta}$ and the process $x^{(\alpha)}$.

The Black–Scholes implicit volatility $\sigma_{imp}^{BS}(t_i)$ is by definition related to the option price C_{t_i} in a one-to-one fashion by

$$C_{t_i} = S_{t_i}\left[2\Phi\left(\frac{\sqrt{\Delta}\sigma_{imp}^{BS}(t_i)}{2}\right) - 1\right]. \tag{5.2}$$

The comparison of (5.1) and (5.2) shows that the dynamics of $\sigma_{imp}^{BS}(t_i)$ are determined not only by the dynamics of the Ornstein–Uhlenbeck process $x^{(\alpha)}$ but also by the complicated functional relationship between $U_{t_i, t_i+\Delta}$ and the past values of $x^{(\alpha)}$. This is why the BS implicit volatility is itself a long-memory process whose dynamics cannot analytically be related to the dynamics of the instantaneous latent volatility. Nevertheless, the relationship between $U_{t_i, t_i+\Delta}$ and $x^{(\alpha)}$ can be approximated by (see Appendix B):

$$U_{t_i, t_i+\Delta}^2 = \int_{t_i}^{t_i+\Delta} \exp\left(2\sum_{t<t_i}\frac{(u-\tau)^\alpha}{\Gamma(1+\alpha)}\Delta(x^{(\alpha)}(\tau))\right) \times \exp\left(f(x^{(\alpha)}(t_i); Z(u, t_i, \alpha))\right)du,$$

$$\tag{5.3}$$

where f is a deterministic function and $Z(u, t_i, \alpha)$ is a process independent of $\mathscr{F}_{t_i}$.

Thanks to Proposition 4.2, we can estimate α in a first step by a log-periodogram regression on the implicit volatilities. In a second stage, we shall assume that α is known (the lack of accuracy due to estimated α will not be considered here) and we propose the following scheme for an indirect inference procedure, in the spirit of Pastorello et al. (1993):

$$\theta \xrightarrow{\text{simulation of}} x^{(\alpha)}(t; \theta) \to \tilde{C}_t(\theta) \xrightarrow{BS^{-1}+\alpha\text{-filter}} (\ln \tilde{\sigma})_{imp}^{(\alpha)}(\theta) \to \tilde{\beta}(\theta)$$

$$C_t \xrightarrow{BS^{-1}+\alpha\text{-filter}} (\ln \sigma)_{imp}^{(\alpha)} \to \hat{\beta}.$$

The meaning of this scheme is the following: for a given value θ of the parameters of the Ornstein–Uhlenbeck process $x^{(\alpha)}$, we are able to simulate a sample path $x^{(\alpha)}(t; \theta)$; then thanks to (5.3) and (5.1), we can get simulated values $\tilde{C}_t(\theta)$ conformable to the Hull–White pricing. Of course, this procedure is computer intensive since the expectation (5.1) itself has to be computed by Monte Carlo simulations. Nevertheless, as soon as option prices $\tilde{C}_t(\theta)$ are available, the associated Black–Scholes implicit volatilities $\tilde{\sigma}_{imp}(\theta)$ are easy to compute, and finally, through the fractional differential operator, we obtain a process $(\ln \tilde{\sigma}_{imp})^{(\alpha)}(t; \theta)$ whose dynamics should mimic the dynamics of the Ornstein–Uhlenbeck process $x^{(\alpha)}$.

This proxy of the instantaneous volatility dynamics provides the basis of our indirect inference procedure. More precisely, $\tilde{\beta}(\theta)$ (respectively, $\hat{\beta}$) denotes the pseudomaximum likelihood estimator of the parameters of the simulated process $(\ln \tilde{\sigma}_{imp})^{(\alpha)}(t; \theta)$ (respectively, the observed process $(\ln \sigma_{imp})^{(\alpha)}(t)$ when the pseudolikelihood is defined by an Ornstein–Uhlenbeck modeling of these processes.

The basic idea of the indirect inference procedure is to compute a consistent estimator of the structural parameters θ by solving in θ the equations $\tilde{\beta}(\theta) = \hat{\beta}$.

It is clear that the consistency proof of Gourieroux, Monfort, and Renault (1993) can be easily extended to this setting thanks to the ergodicity property of the processes; on the other hand, the asymptotic probability distributions have to be reconsidered to take into account the long-memory features.

8.6 Simulation and experiments

8.6.1 Simulation of the path of a fractional stochastic volatility price

First, we illustrate in Figure 8.1 the general behavior of the sample path of $Y = \ln S$ generated by small step discretization, $h(= 1/n) = 0.02$ and $\mu = \theta = 0$, $(\alpha, k, \gamma) = (0.3, 1, 0.01)$. We can see that we obtain paths that are very similar to what is observed for exchange rates. Compare this for instance with the graph given by Baillie et al. (1996) for DM–US dollar exchange rate. In both cases, there seems to be a "long memory" of the main pick that seems to appear again after its occurrence, even if attenuated.

8.6.2 An apparent unit root

Another comparison can be made with Baillie et al.'s (1996) work. Indeed, they argue that their discrete time fractional model gives another representation of persistence that can remain stationary, contrary to usual unit roots models.

Here, we want to show that our model may exhibit an apparent unit root if a wrong parameterization is assumed for estimation. For that purpose, we look at what is obtained if the model is estimated as if it were a GARCH(1,1) process:

$$\begin{cases} \varepsilon_t = \ln S_t = \sigma_t z_t, \\ \sigma_t^2 = \omega + a\varepsilon_{t-1}^2 + b\sigma_{t-1}^2. \end{cases} \qquad \mathbb{E}_{t-1}z_t = 0, \operatorname{Var}_{t-1}z_t = 1$$

In other words, $(1 - \phi L)\varepsilon_t^2 = \omega + (1 - bL)v_t$ where $\phi = a + b$ and v is a white noise.

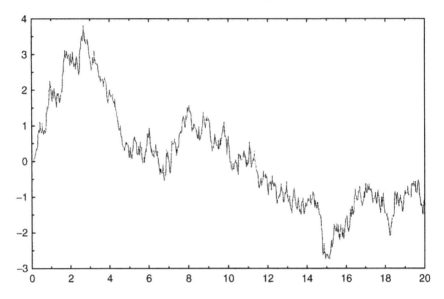

Fig. 8.1. Simulated path of log-stock price in the long-memory FSV model;
$N = 1000$, $h = 0.02$, $(\alpha, k, \gamma) = (0.3, 1, 0.01)$.

Table 8.1. An apparent unit root for φ. a garch(1,1) is estimated instead of the true fsv simulated. 140 samples generated

	Empirical mean	Empirical std. dev.
ω	1.5843	1.3145
φ	1.0453	0.1109
b	−0.1935	0.3821

We estimate parameter (ω, ϕ, b) through minimizing $l(\theta, \varepsilon_1, \ldots, \varepsilon_T)$ $= \sum_{t=1}^{T} (\ln \sigma_t^2 + \varepsilon_t^2 \sigma_t^{-2})$. The results are reported in Table 8.1 and Figure 8.2. One hundred forty samples have been generated, starting with 5,000 points (with a step $hh = 0.1$) and with one point out of ten (i.e. 500 points), kept for the estimation procedure with a step $h = 1$ and $(\alpha, k, \gamma) = (0.3, 2, 1)$. We find also an apparent unit root for φ, and the empirical distribution of ϕ clearly appears to be centered at 1. We can see that φ is the more stable of the estimated coefficients and is always very near 1. Other tries have been made with other parameters for the continuous time model with the same kinds of results. Thus, continuous-time fractional models are good representations of apparent persistence.

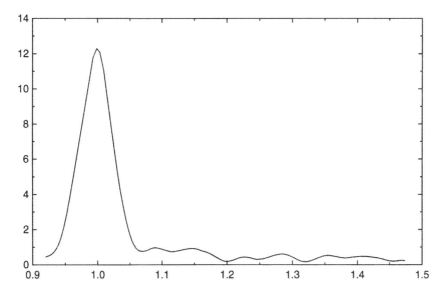

Fig. 8.2. Empirical distribution of φ when the FSV model is estimated as a
GARCH (1,1) process; $\varepsilon_t = \sigma_t z_t$, $\sigma_t^2 = \omega + a\varepsilon_{t-1}^2 + b\omega_{t-1}^2$,
$\varphi = a + b$; 140 samples generated.

8.6.3 Comparison of the filters

Now we give an illustration of the quality of the continuous-time filter defined by
$a_i = ((i + 1)^\alpha - i^\alpha)$ (see Section 8.3.2) as compared with the usual discrete time one
$(1 - L)^{-\alpha}$.

We generated N observations at step $hh = 0.01$ of the AR(1) process $x^{(\alpha)}$ as
given in formula (3.3) with $(\alpha, k, \gamma) = (0.3, 3, 1)$, which gave an N-sample of x
as given by (3.2). Then we kept $n = N/10$ observations of the true AR(1), $x^{(\alpha)}$,
and of the x process. We applied the continuous-time filter at step $h = 10hh = 0.1$
to the n-sample x, which gave observations of a process $x_1^{(\alpha)}$; we applied the
discrete time filter at step $h = 10hh$ to the same n-sample x, which gave observa-
tions of a process $x_2^{(\alpha)}$. The paths of $x^{(\alpha)}$, $x_1^{(\alpha)}$, and $x_2^{(\alpha)}$ can be compared. It appears
that the continuous-time filter is better than the discrete time one.

We generated 100 such samples of $x^{(\alpha)}$, $x_1^{(\alpha)}$, and $x_2^{(\alpha)}$ and computed L^1 and L^2
distances between $x^{(\alpha)}$ and $x_i^{(\alpha)}$, $i = 1$, 2; that is,

$$d_{L^1}(x^{(\alpha)}, x_i^{(\alpha)}) = \frac{1}{n} \sum_{j=1}^{n} |x^{(\alpha)}(j) - x_i^{(\alpha)}(j)|,$$

$$d_{L^2}(x^{(\alpha)}, x_i^{(\alpha)}) = \frac{1}{n} \sum_{j-1}^{n} (x^{(\alpha)}(j) - x_i^{(\alpha)}(j))^2, \; i = 1, \; 2.$$

Table 8.2. L^1 and L^2 Distances between the original paths and the
filtered paths with the two filters. Filter 1 is the continuous-time
filter, filter 2 the discrete time one

	$x^{(\alpha)}, x_1^{(\alpha)}$	$x^{(\alpha)}, x_2^{(\alpha)}$
d_{L^1}	0.1048	0.2135
d_{L^2}	0.1359	0.3607

The results are reported in Table 8.2. Even if the numbers do not have any
meaning in themselves, the comparison leads clearly to the conclusion that the
first filter is significantly better. For a convincing comparison of the twelve first
partial autocorrelations of the three samples, see Comte (1996).

8.6.4 Estimation of α by log-periodogram regression in three models

Lastly, we compared the estimations of α obtained by regression of $\ln I(\lambda)$ on $\ln \lambda$,
where $I(\lambda)$ is the periodogram (see Geweke and Porter-Hudak, 1983 for the idea,
Robinson, 1996 for the proof of the convergence and asymptotic normality of the
estimator, and Comte, 1996 to check the assumptions given by Robinson).

We used 100 samples with length 400, where 4000 points were generated for the
continuous-time models with a step 0.1 and one point out of ten was kept for the
estimation. We had $(\alpha, k, \gamma) = (0.3, 3, 1)$, in particular $\alpha = 0.3$ in all cases.

But we compared two ways of estimating α: either working directly on the log-
periodogram of the process $x(t) = \ln \sigma(t)$ (which exactly corresponds to our
fractional Ornstein–Uhlenbeck model) or working on $\sigma(t) = \exp(x(t))$, since it
fulfills the same long-memory properties (see Proposition 2.2).

As a benchmark for this estimation of α, we considered a third estimation
through the following procedure. Assuming that the observed path would be
associated with $\tilde{x}(t) = (1 - L)^{-\alpha} x^{(\alpha)}(t)$ (with a sampling frequency $h = 1$) instead
of $x(t)$, we could then estimate α by a log-periodogram regression on the path
$\tilde{x}(t)$, which is referred to below as the ARFIMA method. The three methods
should provide consistent estimators of the same value for α. The results are
reported in Table 8.3: they are better with x than with an ARFIMA model or
with $\exp x$, and the recommendation is to work with x instead of $\exp x$. Let us
nevertheless notice that the bad result for the ARFIMA model could be explained

Table 8.3. Estimation of α with log-periodogram regression for
three models. 100 samples, length 400. true value: $\alpha = 0.3$

	Empirical mean	Empirical std. dev.
x	0.2877	0.0629
$\exp x$	0.2568	0.0823
ARFIMA	0.3447	0.0864

by the fact that the discrete time filter $(1 - L)^{-\alpha}$ had been applied to the low frequency path $x^{(\alpha)}(t)$ with step $h = 1$.

8.6.5 Estimation with real data

We carried out log-periodogram regressions on real stock prices and implicit volatilities associated with options on CAC40 of the Paris Stock Exchange. First, for the log-prices, we found from our 775 daily data that $\alpha_{\text{price}} = 0.0035$. This is near $\alpha = 0$ and confirms the short-memory feature of prices. On the contrary, we found for a sequence $|\sigma_{t+1} - \sigma_t|$ that $\alpha_{\text{volat}} = 0.2505$, which illustrates the long-memory feature of the volatilities. We emphasize that we have to take absolute values of the increments of the implicit volatilities (see Ding, Granger, and Engle, 1993), since we otherwise have:

	$\ln(\sigma_{t+1}/\sigma_t)$	$\sigma_{t+1} - \sigma_t$	σ_t	$(\sigma_{t+1} - \sigma_t)^2$
α	-0.30493	-0.37589	0.67034	0.21490

so that squaring is also possible. Missing values are replaced by the global mean.

Two preliminary conclusions can be derived from the previous empirical evidence. First, it appears that the volatility is not stationary and must be differenced. Secondly, the long-memory phenomenom is stronger when we consider absolute values (or squared values) of the differenced volatility. This seems to indicate some asymmetric feature in the volatility dynamics, as observed in asset prices by Ding et al. (1993).

These two points lead us to modify our long-memory diffusion equation on $\sigma(t)$. This work is still in progress. Nevertheless, the previous empirical evidence has to be interpreted cautiously, because if we take into account small sample biases, it is clear that an autoregressive operator $(1 - \rho L)$ with ρ close to one is empirically difficult to identify against a fractional differentiation $(1 - L)^{\alpha}$.

Appendix A: Proofs

Proof of proposition 2.1 We are going to use the result given in equation (2.6) (see Comte 1996) which gives for $\tilde{x} = \ln(\tilde{\sigma})$ and $h \to 0 : r_{\tilde{x}}(h) = r_{\tilde{x}}(0) + \psi.|h|^{2\alpha+1} + o(|h|^{2\alpha+1})$ with, for $h \geq 0$:

$$V(\tilde{x}(t + h) - \tilde{x}(t)) = 2(r_{\tilde{x}}(0) - r_{\tilde{x}}(h)) = 2\left(\int_0^{+\infty} a^2(x)dx - \int_0^\infty a(x)a(x + h)dx\right),$$

and the fact that if $X \rightsquigarrow \mathcal{N}(0, s^2)$ then $\mathbb{E}(\exp X) = e^{s^2/2}$. Then, still for $h \geq 0$ (and $r_\sigma(-h) = r_\sigma(h)$):

$$r_\sigma(h) = \mathbb{E}(\exp(\tilde{x}(t + h) \times \exp(\tilde{x}(t)) - \mathbb{E}(\exp(\tilde{x}(t + h)) \times \mathbb{E}(\exp(\tilde{x}(t)))$$

$$r_\sigma(h) = \mathbb{E}\left(\exp\left(\int_{-\infty}^{t} (a(t+h-s)+a(t-s))\,dw^2(s)\right)\right.$$
$$\left.\times \exp\left(\int_{t}^{t+h} a(t+h-s)\,dw^2(s)\right)\right)$$
$$- \mathbb{E}\left(\exp\left(\int_{-\infty}^{t+h} a(t+h-s)\,dw^2(s)\right)\right) \times \mathbb{E}\left(\exp\left(\int_{-\infty}^{t} a(t-s)\,dw^2(s)\right)\right)$$

This yields, for $h \geq 0$, with the second point, to

$$r_\sigma(h) = \exp\left(\int_0^{+\infty} a^2(x)\,dx\right)\left(\exp\left(\int_0^{+\infty} a(x+h)a(x)\,dx\right) - 1\right).$$

Then, for $h \geq 0$:

$$r_\sigma(h) - r_\sigma(0) = \exp\left(\int_0^{+\infty} a^2(x)\,dx\right)$$
$$\times \left(\exp\left(\int_0^{+\infty} a(x+h)a(x)\,dx\right) - \exp\left(\int_0^{+\infty} a^2(x)\,dx\right)\right),$$

and factorizing the first right-hand term again:

$$r_\sigma(h) - r_\sigma(0) = \exp\left(2\int_0^{+\infty} a^2(x)\,dx\right)(\exp(r_{\tilde{x}}(h) - r_{\tilde{x}}(0)) - 1).$$

Then for $h \to 0$, $K = \exp(\int_0^{+\infty} a^2(x)\,dx)$, we have:

$$r_\sigma(h) - r_\sigma(0) = K^2(\exp(\psi.|h|^{2\alpha+1} + o(|h|^{2\alpha+1})) - 1) = K^2\psi|h|^{2\alpha+1} + o(|h|^{2\alpha+1})$$

which gives the announced result. $\square$

Proof of Proposition 2.2 (i) The previous computations give, with the same K as above: $r_\sigma(h) = K(\exp(r_{\tilde{x}}(h)) - 1)$ and it has been proved in Comte (1996) that $r_{\tilde{x}}(h) = \mu|h|^{2\alpha-1} + o(|h|^{2\alpha-1})$ for $h \to +\infty$, where μ is a constant. This implies straightforwardly that $r_\sigma(h) = K\mu|h|^{2\alpha-1} + o(|h|^{2\alpha-1})$, which gives (i). $\square$

(ii) $\int_0^{+\infty} r_\sigma(h)\cos(\lambda h)dh = \int_0^A r_\sigma(h)\cos(\lambda h)dh + \frac{1}{\lambda}\int_{\lambda A}^{+\infty} r_\sigma(\frac{u}{\lambda})\cos u du$. Now for A chosen great enough, the development of r_σ near $+\infty$ implies $\lambda^{2\alpha}f_\sigma(\lambda) = \lambda^{2\alpha}\int_0^A r_\sigma(h)\cos(\lambda h)dh + \int_{\lambda A}^{+\infty} u^{2\alpha-1}\cos u du + o(1)$, and consequently $\lim_{\lambda\to 0} \lambda^{2\alpha}f_\sigma(\lambda) = \int_0^{+\infty} u^{2\alpha-1}\cos u du$ where the integral is convergent near 0 because $2\alpha > 0$ and near $+\infty$ because: $\int_1^{+\infty} u^{2\alpha-1}\cos u du = [u^{2\alpha-1}\sin u]_1^{+\infty} - (2\alpha-1)\int_1^{+\infty} u^{2\alpha-2}\sin u du$ where all terms are obviously finite. $\square$

Proof of Lemma 3.1 For the proof of the first convergence: $Y_n \overset{\mathcal{D}}{\Rightarrow} Y$ on a compact set $[0, T]$, we check the L^2 pointwise convergence of $Y_n(t)$ toward $Y(t)$, and then a tightness criterion as given by Billingsley (1968, Th. 12.3): $\mathbb{E}|Y_n(t_2) - Y_n(t_1)|^p \leq C.|t_2 - t_1|^q$ with $p > 0$, $q > 1$, and C a constant.

The L^2 convergence is ensured by computing:

$$\mathbb{E}(Y_n(t) - Y(t))^2 = \mathbb{E}\left(\int_0^t \left(\sigma\left(\frac{[ns]}{n}\right) - \sigma(s)\right) dw^1(s)\right)^2$$

$$= \mathbb{E}\left(\int_0^t \left(\sigma\left(\frac{[ns]}{n}\right) - \sigma(s)\right)^2 ds\right)$$

$$= \int_0^t \mathbb{E}\left(\sigma\left(\frac{[ns]}{n}\right) - \sigma(s)\right)^2 ds \text{ with Fubini.}$$

Then the L^2 convergence is obviously given by an inequality: $\mathbb{E}(\sigma(t_2) - \sigma(t_1))^2 \leq \tilde{C}.|t_2 - t_1|^\gamma$ for a positive γ and a constant $\tilde{C}$.

As usual, let $x(t) = \int_0^t a(t-s) dw^2(s)$ and let $t_1 \leq t_2$.

$$\mathbb{E}(\sigma(t_2) - \sigma(t_1))^2 = \mathbb{E}(\exp(x((t_2))) - \exp(x(t_1)))^2 = \mathbb{E}(e^{2x(t_2)} + e^{2x(t_1)} - 2e^{x(t_1)+x(t_2)})$$

$$= e^{2\int_0^{t_1} a^2(x)dx} + e^{2\int_0^{t_2} a^2(x)dx}$$

$$- 2e^{\frac{1}{2}\int_0^{t_1} a^2(x)dx + \frac{1}{2}\int_0^{t_2} a^2(x)dx + \int_0^{t_1} a(x)a(t_2-t_1+x)dx}$$

$$= e^{2\int_0^{t_2} a^2(x)dx}$$

$$\times \left(1 + e^{-2\int_{t_1}^{t_2} a^2(x)dx} - 2e^{-\frac{3}{2}\int_{t_1}^{t_2} a^2(x)dx - \int_0^{t_1} a(x)(a(x)-a(t_2-t_1+x))dx}\right)$$

$$\leq 2e^{2\int_0^{t_2} a^2(x)dx}\left(1 - e^{-\frac{3}{2}\int_{t_1}^{t_2} a^2(x)dx - \int_0^{t_1} a(x)(a(x)-a(t_2-t_1+x))dx}\right).$$

The term inside the last parentheses being necessarily nonnegative, the term in the last great exponential is nonpositive. Moreover $|\int_{t_1}^{t_2} a^2(x)dx| \leq M_1^2|t_2 - t_1|$ with $M_1 = \sup_{x\in[0, T]} |a(x)|$, and since a is α-Hölder,

$$\left|\int_0^{t_1} a(x)(a(x) - a(t_2 - t_1 + x))dx\right| \leq C_\alpha|t_2 - t_1|^\alpha \int_0^{t_1} |a(x)|dx \leq C_\alpha|t_2 - t_1|^\alpha M_1 T,$$

which implies $|\int_{t_1}^{t_2} a^2(x)dx + \int_0^{t_1} a(x)(a(x) - a(t_2 - t_1 + x))dx| \leq M_2|t_2 - t_1|^\alpha$, with $M_2 = M_2(T)$. Then using that $\forall u \leq 0$, $0 \leq 1 - e^u \leq |u|$, we have $\mathbb{E}(\sigma(t_2) - \sigma(t_1))^2 \leq 2K^2 M_2|t_2 - t_1|^\alpha$, $\alpha \in]0, \frac{1}{2}[$ where $K = \exp(\int_0^{+\infty} a^2(x)dx)$ as previously. Then, $\mathbb{E}(\sigma([ns]/n) - \sigma(s))^2 \leq 2K^2 M_2(\frac{1}{n})^\alpha$ gives:

$$\mathbb{E}(Y_n(t) - Y(t))^2 \leq \frac{2K^2 M_2 T}{n^\alpha} \qquad \forall t \in [0, T],$$

which ensures the L^2 convergence.

We use a straightforward version of Burkholder's inequality (see Protter, 1992, p. 174), $\mathbb{E}|M_t|^p \le C_p \mathbb{E}\langle M \rangle_t^{p/2}$, where C_p is a constant and M_t a continuous local martingale, $M_0 = 0$, to write (with an immediate adaptation of the proof on $[t_1, t_2]$ instead of $[0, t]$):

$$\mathbb{E}|Y_n(t_2) - Y_n(t_1)|^p = \mathbb{E}\left|\int_{t_1}^{t_2} \sigma\left(\frac{[ns]}{n}\right) dw^1(s)\right|^p \le C_p \mathbb{E}\left|\int_{t_1}^{t_2} \sigma^2\left(\frac{[ns]}{n}\right) ds\right|^{p/2}.$$

Let us choose $p = 4$:

$$
\begin{aligned}
\mathbb{E}|Y_n(t_2) - Y_n(t_1)|^4 &\le C_4 \mathbb{E}\left|\int_{t_1}^{t_2} \sigma^2\left(\frac{[ns]}{n}\right) ds\right|^2 \\
&= C_4 \int\int_{[t_1, t_2]^2} \mathbb{E}\left(\sigma^2\left(\frac{[nu]}{n}\right)\sigma^2\left(\frac{[nv]}{n}\right)\right) du\, dv \\
&\le C_4 \int\int_{[t_1, t_2]^2} \sqrt{\mathbb{E}\tilde{\sigma}^4 \times \mathbb{E}\tilde{\sigma}^4} du\, dv \quad (\tilde{\sigma} \text{ given by } (2.7)) \\
&= C_4 \mathbb{E}\tilde{\sigma}^4 (t_2 - t_1)^2, \quad \mathbb{E}\tilde{\sigma}^4 = \exp\left(8 \int_0^{+\infty} a^2(x) ds\right).
\end{aligned}
$$

This gives the tightness and thus the convergence.

The second convergence is deduced from the first one, the decomposition: $Y_n(t) = \hat{Y}_n(t) + u_n(t)$, with $u_n(t) = \sigma(\frac{[nt]}{n})(w^1(t) - w^1(\frac{[nt]}{n}))$, and Theorem 4.1 of Billingsley (1968): $(X_n \overset{D}{\Rightarrow} X$ and $\rho(X_n, Z_n) \overset{P}{\to} 0) \Rightarrow (Z_n \overset{D}{\Rightarrow} X)$, where $\rho(x, y) = \sup_{t\in[0, T]}|x(t) - y(t)|$. Here $\rho(Y_n, \hat{Y}_n) = \sup|u_n(t)|$ and $u_n(t) = M([nt]/n)$ is a martingale so that Doob's inequality (see Protter, 1992, p. 12, Th. 20) gives:

$$\mathbb{E}\left(\sup_{t\in[0, T]}|u_n(t)|\right)^2 \le 4 \sup_{t\in[0, T]} \mathbb{E}(u_n(t)^2).$$

Then,

$$
\begin{aligned}
\mathbb{E}u_n(t)^2 &= \mathbb{E}\left(\sigma^2\left(\frac{[nt]}{n}\right)\left(w^1(t) - w^1\left(\frac{[nt]}{n}\right)\right)^2\right) \\
&= \mathbb{E}\left(\sigma^2\left(\frac{[nt]}{n}\right)\right)\mathbb{E}\left(w^1(t) - w^1\left(\frac{[nt]}{n}\right)\right)^2 \\
&= \left(t - \frac{[nt]}{n}\right)\mathbb{E}\left(\sigma^2\left(\frac{[nt]}{n}\right)\right) \le \frac{1}{n}\mathbb{E}(\tilde{\sigma}^2),
\end{aligned}
$$

which achieves the proof. $\square$

Proof of Proposition 3.2
  • First we prove the following implication:

$$\begin{cases} \tilde{Y}_n \overset{D}{\Rightarrow} Y & \text{or tight} \\ \tilde{\sigma}_n \overset{D}{\Rightarrow} \sigma & \text{or tight} \end{cases} \text{and} \begin{pmatrix} \tilde{Y}_n(t) \\ \tilde{\sigma}_n(t) \end{pmatrix} \overset{L^2}{\longrightarrow} \begin{pmatrix} Y(t) \\ \sigma(t) \end{pmatrix} \text{imply} \begin{pmatrix} \tilde{Y}_n \\ \tilde{\sigma}_n \end{pmatrix} \overset{D}{\Rightarrow} \begin{pmatrix} Y \\ \sigma \end{pmatrix}.$$

Indeed, the functional convergences of both sequences imply their tightness and thus the tightness of the joint process. This can be seen from the very definition of tightness as given in Billingsley (1968), that can be written for $\tilde{Y}_n: \forall \varepsilon, \exists K_n$ (compact set) so that $\mathbb{P}(\tilde{Y}_n \in K_n) > 1 - (\varepsilon/2)$ and then, for this ε, we have for $\tilde{\sigma}_n: \exists K'_n$ (compact set) so that $\mathbb{P}(\tilde{\sigma}_n \in K'_n) > 1 - \frac{\varepsilon}{2}$. Then:

$$\begin{aligned} \mathbb{P}((\tilde{Y}_n, \tilde{\sigma}_n) \in K_n \times K'_n) &= 1 - \mathbb{P}(\tilde{Y}_n \notin K_n \text{ or } \tilde{\sigma}_n \notin K'_n) \\ &\geq 1 - \mathbb{P}(\tilde{Y}_n \notin K_n) - \mathbb{P}(\tilde{\sigma}_n \notin K'_n) \\ &= \mathbb{P}(\tilde{Y}_n \in K_n) + \mathbb{P}(\tilde{\sigma}_n \in K'_n) - 1 \\ &\geq 1 - \varepsilon. \end{aligned}$$

Now, the tightness and the pointwise L^2 convergence of the couple imply the convergence of the joint process.

- Let us check the pointwise L^2 convergence of $\tilde{Y}_n$:

$$\begin{aligned} \mathbb{E}(\tilde{Y}_n(t) - Y(t))^2 &= \mathbb{E}\left(\int_0^{[nt]/n} \left(\tilde{\sigma}_n\left(\frac{[ns]}{n}\right) - \sigma(s) \right) dw^1(s) + \int_{\frac{[nt]}{n}}^t \sigma(s) dw^1(s) \right)^2 \\ &= \int_0^{[nt]/n} \mathbb{E}\left(\left(\tilde{\sigma}_n\left(\frac{[ns]}{n}\right) - \sigma(s) \right)^2 \right) ds + \int_{[nt]/n}^t \mathbb{E}(\sigma^2(s)) ds. \end{aligned}$$

The last right-hand term is less than $\frac{1}{n}\mathbb{E}(\tilde{\sigma}^2)$ and goes to zero when n grows to infinity and the first right-hand term can be written, for the part under the integral, as

$$\begin{aligned} \mathbb{E}\left(\tilde{\sigma}_n\left(\frac{[ns]}{n}\right) - \sigma(s) \right)^2 \right) &= \mathbb{E}\left(\exp\left(\int_0^{[nt]/n} a\left(t - \frac{[ns]}{n}\right) dw^2(s) \right) \right. \\ &\quad \left. - \exp\left(\int_0^t a(t - s) dw^2(s) \right) \right)^2. \end{aligned}$$

Now, for X_n and X following $\mathcal{N}(0, \mathbb{E}X_n^2)$ and $\mathcal{N}(0, \mathbb{E}X^2)$ respectively, $\mathbb{E}(e^{X_n} - e^X)^2 = e^{2\mathbb{E}X_n^2} + e^{2\mathbb{E}X^2} - 2e^{\mathbb{E}(X_n+X)^2/2}$, which goes to zero when n grows to infinity if $\mathbb{E}X_n^2 \underset{n \to +\infty}{\longrightarrow} \mathbb{E}X^2$ and $\mathbb{E}(X_n + X)^2 \underset{n \to +\infty}{\longrightarrow} 4\mathbb{E}X^2$.

This can be checked quite straightforwardly here with $X = \int_0^t a(t - s) dw^2(s)$ and $X_n = \int_0^{[nt]/n} a(t - \frac{[ns]}{n}) dw^2(s)$, so that:

$$\mathbb{E}X_n^2 = \int_0^{[nt]/n} a^2\left(t - \frac{[ns]}{n}\right) ds_{n \to +\infty} \int_0^t a^2(t - s)ds = \mathbb{E}X^2,$$

$$\mathbb{E}(X_n + X)^2 = \int_0^{[nt]/n} a^2\left(t - \frac{[ns]}{n}\right) ds + \int_0^t a^2(t - s)ds$$

$$+ 2\int_0^{[nt]/n} a\left(t - \frac{[ns]}{n}\right) a(t - s)ds \ {}_{n \to +\infty} \ 4\mathbb{E}X^2.$$

This result gives in fact both L^2 convergences of $\tilde{Y}_n(t)$ and of $\tilde{\sigma}_n(t)$.

- The tightness of $\tilde{\sigma}_n$ is then known from Comte (1996) and the tightness of $\tilde{Y}_n$ can be deduced from the proof of Lemma 3.1 with $\mathbb{E}\tilde{\sigma}_n^4(t)$ instead of $\mathbb{E}\tilde{\sigma}^4$, which is still bounded.

Proof of Proposition 4.1 We work with $\sigma(t) = \exp\left(\int_{-\infty}^t a(t - s)dw^2(s)\right)$, but the results would obviously still be valid with the only asymptotically stationary version of σ. We use here and for the proof of Proposition (4.2), the following result:

$$\forall \eta \geq 0, \quad \lim_{h \to +\infty} h^{1-2\alpha}\left(\int_\eta^{+\infty} a(x)a(x + h)dx\right) = C, \qquad (A.1)$$

where C is a constant. This result can be straightforwardly deduced from Comte and Renault (1996) through rewriting the proof of the result about the long-memory property of the autocovariance function (extended here to the case $\eta \neq 0$).

- We know that $y_t = \mathbb{E}(\sigma^2(t + 1) \mid \mathscr{F}_t) = \exp(2\int_0^1 a^2(x)dx) \exp(2\int_{-\infty}^t a(t + 1 - s) dw^2(s))$. Then:

$$cov(y_{t+h}, \ y_t) = \mathbb{E}(y_{t+h}y_t) - \mathbb{E}(y_{t+h})\mathbb{E}(y_t)$$

$$= \exp\left(4\int_0^1 a^2(x)dx\right)$$

$$\times \mathbb{E}\left(\exp\left(2\int_{-\infty}^{t+h} a(t + h + 1 - s) dw^2(s)\right.\right.$$

$$\left.\left. + 2\int_{-\infty}^t a(t + h - s) dw^2(s)\right)\right)$$

$$- \exp\left(4\int_0^1 a^2(x)dx\right) \times \exp\left(4\int_0^{+\infty} a^2(x + 1)dx\right)$$

$$= \exp\left(4\int_0^{+\infty} a^2(x)dx\right)\left(\exp\left(4\int_1^{+\infty} a(x + h)a(x)dx\right) - 1\right).$$

This proves the stationarity of the y process, and, with (A.1), which gives the order of the term inside the exponential, implies the announced order $h^{2\alpha-1}$.

- $\mathbb{E}(\sigma(t+h)|\mathscr{F}_t)$, still with the stationary version of σ, is given by

$$\exp\left(\int_{-\infty}^{t} a(t+h-s)\,dw^2(s)\right) \times \exp\left(\frac{1}{2}\int_{t}^{t+h} a^2(t+h-s)\,ds\right).$$

Then, as $(\mathbb{E}(\mathbb{E}(\sigma(t+h\mid\mathscr{F}_t)))^2 = (\mathbb{E}\sigma(t+h))^2$, we have:

$$\mathrm{Var}(\mathbb{E}(\sigma(t+h)|\mathscr{F}_t)) = \exp\left(\int_{0}^{h} a^2(x)dx\right) \times \exp\left(2\int_{0}^{+\infty} a^2(x+h)dx\right)$$
$$- \exp\left(\int_{0}^{+\infty} a^2(x)dx\right)$$
$$= \exp\left(\int_{0}^{+\infty} a^2(x)dx\right)\left(\exp\left(\int_{h}^{+\infty} a^2(x)dx\right) - 1\right).$$

As $a(x) = x^\alpha \tilde{a}(x) = x^{\alpha-1}.x\tilde{a}(x) = O(x^{\alpha-1})$ for $x \to +\infty$ since we know that $\lim_{x\to+\infty} x\tilde{a}(x) = a_\infty$. Then, for $h \to +\infty$,

$$\int_{h}^{+\infty} (x^{\alpha-1})^2(x\tilde{a}(x))^2 dx = O\left(a_\infty^2 \int_{h}^{+\infty} x^{2\alpha-2}dx\right) = O(h^{2\alpha-1}).$$

Developing again the exponential of this term for great h gives the order $h^{2\alpha-1}$, and even the limit of the variance divided by $h^{2\alpha-1}$ for $h \to +\infty$, which is $K(a_\infty^2/1 - 2\alpha)$ with $K = \exp(\int_{0}^{+\infty} a^2(x)dx)$.
For $\alpha = 0$, $a(x) = e^{-kx}$ gives obviously for the variance an order Ce^{-kh}. □

Proof of Proposition 4.2 We have to compute $\mathrm{cov}(z_t, z_{t+h})$.

$$\mathbb{E}(z_{t+h}z_t) = \mathbb{E}\left(\int_{0}^{1} \mathbb{E}(\sigma^2(t+h+u)|\mathscr{F}_{t+h})du \times \int_{0}^{1} \mathbb{E}(\sigma^2(t+v)|\mathscr{F}_t)dv\right)$$
$$= \int_{0}^{1}\int_{0}^{1} \left[\mathbb{E}\left(e^{(2\int_{0}^{u} a^2(x)\,dx)}e^{(2\int_{-\infty}^{t+h} a(t+h+u-s)\,dw^2(s))}e^{(2\int_{0}^{v} a^2(x)\,dx)}e^{(2\int_{-\infty}^{t} a(t+v-s)\,dw^2(s))}\right)\right] du\,dv$$
$$= \int_{0}^{1}\int_{0}^{1} \left[e^{(2\int_{0}^{u} a^2(x)dx + 2\int_{0}^{v} a^2(x)dx)}e^{(2\int_{-\infty}^{t} (a(t+h+u-s)+a(t+v-s))^2 ds)}e^{(2\int_{t}^{t+h} a^{2(t+h+u-s)ds})}\right] du\,dv$$
$$= \int_{0}^{1}\int_{0}^{1} e^{(4\int_{0}^{+\infty} a^2(x)dx + 4\int_{0}^{+\infty} a(x+h+u)a(x)dx)} du\,dv.$$

Moreover, with the same kind of computations we have $\mathbb{E}(z_{t+h})\mathbb{E}(z_t) = \exp(4\int_{0}^{+\infty} a^2(x)dx)$ so that:

$$\mathrm{cov}(z_t, z_{t+h}) = \exp\left(4\int_{0}^{+\infty} a^2(x)dx\right)$$
$$\times \left[\int_{0}^{1}\int_{0}^{1}\left(\exp\left(4\int_{v}^{+\infty} a(x+h+u-v)a(x)\,dx\right) - 1\right)du\,dv\right].$$

Then z is stationary and another use of (A.1) gives the order $h^{2\alpha-1}$ for $h \to +\infty$.   □

Proof of Proposition 4.3 Let $Z(t) = \int_0^t \sigma(u)dw^1(u)$. Then we know (see Protter 1992 p. 174, for $p = 4$) that $\mathbb{E}Z(t)^4 = \frac{4(4-1)}{2}\mathbb{E}\int_0^t Z^2(s)d\langle Z \rangle_s$. As $\langle Z \rangle_s = \int_0^s \sigma^2(u)du$, we find: $\mathbb{E}Z(t)^4 = 6\mathbb{E}(\int_0^t Z^2(s)\sigma^2(s)\,ds) = 6\int_0^t \mathbb{E}(Z^2(s)\sigma^2(s))\,ds$, with Fubini's theorem. Then $\mathbb{E}(Z^2(t)\sigma^2(t)) = \mathbb{E}(\int_0^t (\sigma(t)\sigma(u))\,dw^1(u))^2 = \mathbb{E}\int_0^t (\sigma^2(t)\sigma^2(u))\,du$ (σ and w^1 are independent). This yields

$$\mathbb{E}Z(t)^4 = 6\int_0^t \int_0^s (r_{\sigma^2}(|s-u|) + (\mathbb{E}\sigma^2)^2)du\,ds,$$

where r is the autocovariance function, and, lastly, $\varphi(h) = 3h^2(\mathbb{E}\sigma^2)^2 + 3\int\int_{[0,\,h]^2} r_{\sigma^2}(|s-u|)du\,ds$.

- Near zero, the autocovariance function of σ^2 is of the same kind as the one of σ, with a replaced by $2a$, since $\sigma = \exp(x)$. Then we know from Proposition 2.1 that, for $h \to 0$: $r_{\sigma^2}(h) = r_{\sigma^2}(0) + Ch^{2\alpha+1} + o(h^{2\alpha+1})$, where C is a constant and $\alpha \in]0, \frac{1}{2}[$. Then replacing in $\varphi(h)$ gives

$$\varphi(h) = 3h^2((\mathbb{E}\sigma^2)^2 + r_{\sigma^2}(0)) + \frac{3C}{(2\alpha+2)(2\alpha+3)}h^{2\alpha+3} + o(h^{2\alpha+3}).$$

For $\alpha = 0$, $a(x) = \exp(-kx)$ gives $r_{\sigma^2}(h) = e^{2/k}(\exp(\frac{2}{k}e^{kh}) - 1)$ which leads to: $r_{\sigma^2}(h) = r_{\sigma^2}(0) - 2e^{4/k}h + o(h)$, for $h \to 0$. This implies the continuity for $\alpha = 0$. Now, $\mathbb{E}(Y(h) - \mathbb{E}Y(h))^2 = \mathbb{E}(\int_0^h \sigma(u)dw^1(u))^2 = \mathbb{E}\int_0^h \sigma^2(u)\,du = h\mathbb{E}\sigma^2$ implies that

$$\lim_{h \to 0} kurt_Y(h) = 3\frac{\mathbb{E}\sigma^4}{(\mathbb{E}\sigma^2)^2} > 3.$$

- From Proposition 2.2, we know that, for $\alpha \in]0, \frac{1}{2}[$ and $h \to +\infty$,

$$\int\int_{[0,\,h]^2} r_{\sigma^2}(|s-u|)du\,ds = O\left(\int\int_{[1,\,h]^2} u^{2\alpha-1}du\,ds\right) = O(h^{2\alpha+1}),$$

but for $\alpha = 0$, $r_{\sigma^2}(h) = e^{2/k}(\frac{2}{k}e^{-kh} + o(e^{-kh}))$. This gives the result and the exponential rate for $\alpha = 0$.

Proof of Proposition 5.1 Let $m = [Nt/T]$, then

$$\mathbb{E}\hat{\sigma}^2_{n,p}(t) = \frac{n}{T}\sum_{k=m-p+1}^{m} \mathbb{E}\left(\int_{t_{k-1}}^{t_k} \sigma(s)dw^1(s)\right)^2 = \frac{n}{T}\sum_{k=m-p+1}^{m} \mathbb{E}\left(\int_{t_{k-1}}^{t_k} \sigma^2(s)ds\right)$$

$$= \frac{n}{T}\mathbb{E}\left(\int_{t_{m-p}}^{t_m} \sigma^2(s)ds\right) = \frac{n}{T}\mathbb{E}(\sigma^2)(t_m - t_{m-p}) = \frac{n}{T}p \times \frac{T}{np}\mathbb{E}\sigma^2, = \mathbb{E}\sigma^2,$$

where $\mathbb{E}\sigma^2 = \exp\left(\frac{1}{2}\int_0^{+\infty} a^2(x)dx\right)$. This ensures the L^1 convergence of the sequence, uniformly in t.

Before computing the mean square, let:

$$f(z) = f(|z|) = \mathbb{E}\sigma^2(u)\sigma^2(u + |z|)$$
$$= \exp\left(4\int_0^{+\infty} a^2(x)dx + 4\int_0^{+\infty} a(x)a(x + |z|)dx\right).$$

Then

$$\mathbb{E}[\hat{\sigma}_{n,p}^2(t) - \sigma^2(t)]^2 = \mathbb{E}\left[\frac{n}{T}\sum_{k=m-p+1}^{m}(Y_{t_k} - Y_{t_{k-1}})^2 - \sigma^2(t)\right]^2$$

$$= \frac{n^2}{T^2}\mathbb{E}\left[\sum_{k=m-p+1}^{m}(Y_{t_k} - Y_{t_{k-1}})^2\right]^2$$

$$+ \mathbb{E}\sigma^4(t) - 2\frac{n}{T}\mathbb{E}\left[\sum_{k=m-p+1}^{m}\sigma^2(t)(Y_{t_k} - Y_{t_{k-1}})^2\right]^2.$$

We consider separately the different terms.

$$\mathbb{E}[\sigma^2(t)(Y_{t_k} - Y_{t_{k-1}})^2]^2 = \mathbb{E}\left[\int_{t_{k-1}}^{t_k}\sigma(t)\sigma(s)dw^1(s)\right]^2 = \mathbb{E}\left[\int_{t_{k-1}}^{t_k}\sigma^2(t)\sigma^2(s)ds\right]$$

$$= \int_{t_{k-1}}^{t_k} f(t - s)ds$$

as σ and w^1 are independent. As in a previous proof, we have:

$$\mathbb{E}\left[\int_{t_{k-1}}^{t_k}\sigma(s)dw^1(s)\right]^4 = 3\iint_{[t_{k-1},\,t_k]^2} f(u - v)\,du\,dv,$$

and for $j \neq k$: $\mathbb{E}[(Y_{t_k} - Y_{t_{k-1}})^2(Y_{t_j} - Y_{t_{j-1}})^2] = \mathbb{E}(\int_{t_{k-1}}^{t_k}\sigma^2(s)ds \times \int_{t_{j-1}}^{t_j}\sigma^2(s)ds)$. This gives:

$$\mathbb{E}\left[\sum_{k=m-p+1}^{m}(Y_{t_k} - Y_{t_{k-1}})^2\right]^2 = 2\sum_{k=m-p+1}^{m}\iint_{[t_{k-1},\,t_k]^2} f(u - v)\,du\,dv$$

$$+ \iint_{[t_{m-p},\,t_m]^2} f(u - v)\,du\,dv.$$

Now with all the terms:

$$\mathbb{E}[\hat{\sigma}_{n,p}^2(t) - \sigma^2(t)] = \frac{n^2}{T^2}\left(2\sum_{k=m-p+1}^{m}\int\int_{[t_{k-1},\ t_k]^2}f(u-v)\,du\,dv\right.$$

$$\left.+\int\int_{[t_{m-p},\ t_m]^2}f(u-v)\,du\,dv\right)$$

$$+\mathbb{E}\sigma^4(t)-\frac{2n}{T}\int_{[t_{m-p},\ t_m]}f(t-s)ds$$

$$=\frac{2n^2}{T^2}\sum_{k=m-p+1}^{m}\int\int_{[t_{k-1},\ t_k]^2}(f(u-v)-f(0))\,du\,dv$$

$$+\frac{n^2}{T^2}\int\int_{[t_{m-p},\ t_m]^2}(f(u-v)-f(0))\,du\,dv$$

$$-\frac{2n}{T}\int_{[t_{m-p},\ t_m]^2}(f(t-s)-f(0))\,ds+2\frac{\mathbb{E}\sigma^4}{p}.$$

Let $K_1 = \exp(8\int_0^{+\infty}a^2(s)ds)$. Then $f(h) = K_1 r_\sigma(h)$ where r_σ is as in Proposition 2.1. Proposition 2.1 then implies $|f(h) - f(0)| \le K_1 C|h|^{2\alpha+1}$, where C is a positive constant.

This implies that: $\forall \varepsilon > 0$, $\exists \eta > 0$, so that $|v-u| < \eta \Rightarrow |f(v-u) - f(0)| < \varepsilon$. Let then $\varepsilon = 1/p$, then $\eta = \eta(\varepsilon)$ is fixed and

$$\mathbb{E}[\hat{\sigma}_{n,p}^2(t) - \sigma^2(t)]^2 \le \frac{2n^2}{T^2}\times p \times \left(\frac{T}{np}\right)^2 \times \frac{1}{p} + \frac{n^2}{T^2}\times\left(\frac{T}{n}\right)^2\times\frac{1}{p}+\frac{2n}{T}\times p\frac{T}{T}\times\frac{1}{p}+2\frac{\mathbb{E}\sigma}{p}$$

if $|t_m - t_{m-p}| = \frac{T}{n} < \eta$, which implies $|t_k - t_{k-1}| = \frac{T}{np} < \eta$. Then

$$\mathbb{E}[\hat{\sigma}_{n,p}^2(t) - \sigma^2(t)]^2 \le \left(\frac{2}{p}+1+2+2\mathbb{E}\sigma^2\right)\times\frac{1}{p}=\left(\frac{2}{p}+3+2\mathbb{E}\sigma^2\right)\times\frac{1}{p}.$$

Then $\forall a > 0$, $n > T/\eta \Rightarrow p^{1-a}.\mathbb{E}[\hat{\sigma}_{n,p}^2(t) - \sigma^2(t)]^2 \le \frac{C}{pa}$, where $C = 5 + 2\mathbb{E}\sigma^2$.

The stationarity implies that the result is uniform in t, so that
$$\lim_{n,\ p\rightarrow+\infty}\sup_{t\in[0,T]} p^{1-a}\mathbb{E}[\hat{\sigma}_{n,p}^2(t) - \sigma^2(t)]^2 = 0. \qquad \square$$

Appendix B

We suppose here $r = 0$ and $\lambda_2 = 0$, so that $x^{(\alpha)}(t) = (\ln \sigma)^{(\alpha)}(t)$ can be written:

$$x^{(\alpha)}(t) = e^{-kt}\left(x^{(\alpha)}(0) + \int_0^t e_{ks}\gamma d\tilde{w}^2(s)\right).$$

Then $U_{t,T}^2 = \int_t^T \sigma^2(u)du$ can be written:

$$U_{t,T}^2 = \int_t^T \exp\left(2\int_0^t \frac{(u-s)^\alpha}{\Gamma(1+\alpha)}dx^{(\alpha)}(s)\right) \times \exp\left(2\int_t^u \frac{(u-s)^\alpha}{\Gamma(1+\alpha)}dx^{(\alpha)}(s)\right)du.$$

Then the first part, $\exp(2\int_0^t \frac{(u-s)^\alpha}{\Gamma(1+\alpha)}dx^{(\alpha)}(S))$, is "deterministic" knowing $\mathscr{F}_t$. For the second part, since we have for $s > t$ that $x^{(\alpha)}(S) = e^{-k(s-t)}x^\alpha(t) + \int_t^s e^{-k(s-x)}\gamma d\tilde{w}^2(x)$, we find that

$$x^{(\alpha)}(s) = e^{-k(t-s)}x^{(\alpha)}(t) + \int_s^t e^{k(s-x)}\gamma d\tilde{w}^2(x),$$

$$\int_t^u \frac{(u-s)^\alpha}{\Gamma(1+\alpha)}dx^{(\alpha)}(s) = x^{(\alpha)}(t) \times \left(-k\int_t^u \frac{(u-s)^\alpha}{\Gamma(1+\alpha)}e^{-k(s-t)}ds\right)$$
$$-k\int_t^u \frac{(u-s)^\alpha}{\Gamma(1+\alpha)}\int_t^s e^{k(s-x)}\gamma d\tilde{w}_2(x)$$
$$+\gamma\int_t^u \frac{(u-s)^\alpha}{\Gamma(1+\alpha)}d\tilde{w}^2(s).$$

This term depends then only on $(x^{(\alpha)}(t))$ and on **future** increments of the Brownian motion $\tilde{w}^2$; those increments are independent of $\mathscr{F}_t$. This is the reason we can write

$$\exp\left(2\int_t^u \frac{(u-s)^\alpha}{\Gamma(1+\alpha)}dx^{(\alpha)}(s)\right) = f(x^{(\alpha)}(t); Z(u,\ t,\ \alpha)).$$

At time $t = t_i$, this gives the announced formula, with $\ln[f(x^{(\alpha)}(t);Z(u,\ t,\ \alpha))] = x^{(\alpha)}(t)\varphi(t,\ u) + Z(u,\ t,\ \alpha)$; $\varphi(t,\ u)$ is a deterministic function, $Z(u,\ t,\ \alpha)$ is a process independent of $\mathscr{F}_t$:

$$Z(t,\ u,\ \alpha) = -k\int_t^u \frac{(u-s)^\alpha}{\Gamma(1+\alpha)}\int_t^s e^{k(s-x)}\gamma d\tilde{w}^2(x) + \gamma\int_t^u \frac{(u-s)^\alpha}{\Gamma(1+\alpha)}d\tilde{w}^2(s).$$

References

Backus, D. K. and Zin, S. E. (1993). Long-Memory Inflation Uncertainty: Evidence from the Term Structure of Interest Rates. *Journal of Money, Credit, Banking* 3, 681–700.

Baillie, R. T., Bollerslev, T., and Mikkelsen, H. O., (1996). Fractionally Integrated Generalized Autoregressive Conditional Heteroskedasticity. *Journal of Econometrics* 74, 3–30.

Billingsley, P. (1968). *Convergence of Probability Measures*. New York: Wiley.

Black, F. and Scholes, M. (1973). The Pricing of Options and Corporate Liabilities. *Journal of Political Economy* 3, 637–54.

Breidt, F. J., Crato, N., and De Lima, P. (1993). Modeling Long-Memory Stochastic Volatility, discussion paper, Iowa State University.

Comte, F. (1996). Simulation and Estimation of Long Memory Continuous Time Models. *Journal of Time Series Analysis* 17, 19–36.

—— Renault, E. (1996). Long Memory Continuous Time Models. *Journal of Econometrics* 73, 101–49.

Dalhuas, R. (1989). Efficient Parameter Estimation for Self-Similar Processes. *Annals of Statistics* 17, 1749–66.

Delbaen, F. and Schachermayer, W. (1994). A General Version of the Fundamental Theorem of Asset Pricing. *Mathematical Analysis* 300, 463–520.

Ding, Z. C., Granger, C. W. J., and Engle, R. F. (1993). A Long Memory Property of Stock Market Returns and a New Model. *Journal of Empirical Finance* 1, 83–106.

Drost, F. C. and Werker, B. J. M. (1996). Closing the GARCH Gap: Continuous Time GARCH Modeling. *Journal of Econometrics* 74, 31–58.

Engle, R. F. and Mustafa, C. (1992). Implied ARCH Models from Options Prices. *Journal of Econometrics* 52, 289–331.

Fox, R. and Taqqu, M. S. (1986). Large Sample Properties of Parameter Estimates for Strongly Dependent Time Series. *Annals of Statistics* 14, 517–32.

Geweke, J. and S. Porter-Hudak (1983). The Estimation and Application of Long Memory Time Series Models. *Journal of Time Series Analysis* 4, 221–38.

Ghysels, Harvey, E. A., and Renault, E. (1996). Stochastic Volatility; In *Handbook of Statistics*, Vol. 14. *Statistical Methods in Finance*, Maddala, G. S., (ed.). Amsterdam: North Holland, Ch. 5, 119–91.

Gourieroux, C., Monfort, A., and Renault, E. (1993). Indirect Inference. *Journal of Applied Econometrics* 8, S85–S118.

Harrison, J. M. and Kreps, D. M. (1981). Martingale and Arbitrage in Multiperiods Securities Markets. *Journal of Economic Theory* 20, 381–408.

Harvey, A. C. (1993). Long Memory in Stochastic Volatility, London School of Economics, working paper.

—— Ruiz, E., and Shephard, N. (1994). Multivariate Stochastic Variance Models. *Review of Economic Studies* 61, 247–64.

Heynen, R., Kemna, A., and Vorst, T. (1994). Analysis of the Term Structure of Implied Volatilities. *Journal of Financial Quantitative Analysis* 29, 31–56.

Hull, J. and White, A. (1987). The Pricing of Options on Assets with Stochastic Volatilities. *Journal of Finance* 3, 281–300.

Jacquier, E., Polson, N. G., and Rossi, P. E. (1994). Bayesian Analysis of Stochastic Volatility Models (with discussion). *Journal of Business and Economic Statistics* 12, 371–417.

Karatzas, I. and Shreve, S. E. (1991). *Brownian Motion and Stochastic Calculus* 2nd ed. New York: Springer-Verlag.

Mandelbrot, B. B. and Van Ness (1968). Fractional Brownian Motions, Fractional Noises and Applications. *SIAM Review* 10, 422–37.

Melino, A. and Turnbull, S. M. (1990). Pricing Foreign Currency Options with Stochastic Volatility. *Journal of Econometrics* 45, 239–65.

Merton, R. C. (1973). The Theory of Rational Option Pricing. *Bell Journal of Economic Management Science* 4, 141–83.

Nelson, D. B. and Foster, D. P. (1994). Asymptotic Filtering Theory for ARCH Models. *Econometrica* 1, 1–41.

Pastorello, S., Renault, E., and Touzi, N. (1993). Statistical Inference for Random Variance Option Pricing. *Southern European Economics Discussion Series*.

Pham, H. and Touzi, N. (1996). Intertemporal Equilibrium Risk Premia in a Stochastic Volatility Model. *Mathematical Finance* 6, 215–36.

Protter, P. E. (1992). *Stochastic Integration and Differential Equations.* New York: Springer-Verlag.

Renault, E. and Touzi, N. (1996). Option Hedging and Implicit Volatilities in a Stochastic Volatility Model. *Mathematical Finance* 6, 279–302.

Robinson, P. M. (1993). Efficient Tests for Nonstationary Hypotheses, Working paper, London School of Economics.

——(1996). Semiparametric Analysis of Long-Memory Time Series. *Annals of Statistics* 22, 515–39.

Rogers, L. C. G. (1995). Arbitrage with Fractional Brownian Motion, University of Bath, discussion paper.

Rozanov, Yu. A. (1968). *Stationary Random Processes.* San Francisco: Holden-Day.

Scott, L. O. (1987). Option Pricing when the Variance Changes Randomly: Estimation and an Application. *Journal of Financial and Quantitative Analysis* 22, 419–38.

Part II
Inference

9

Bayesian Analysis of Stochastic
Volatility Models*

ERIC JACQUIER,
NICHOLAS G. POLSON AND PETER E. ROSSI

New techniques for the analysis of stochastic volatility models in which the logarithm of conditional variance follows an autoregressive model are developed.
A cyclic Metropolis algorithm is used to construct a Markov-chain simulation
tool. Simulations from this Markov chain converge in distribution to draws from
the posterior distribution enabling exact finite-sample inference. The exact solution
to the filtering/smoothing problem of inferring about the unobserved variance states
is a by-product of our Markov-chain method. In addition, multistep-ahead predictive densities can be constructed that reflect both inherent model variability and
parameter uncertainty. We illustrate our method by analyzing both daily
and weekly data on stock returns and exchange rates. Sampling experiments are
conducted to compare the performance of Bayes estimators to method of moments
and quasi-maximum likelihood estimators proposed in the literature. In both
parameter estimation and filtering, the Bayes estimators outperform these other
approaches.

Keywords: Bayesian inference; Markov-chain Monte Carlo; Method of moments;
Nonlinear filtering; Quasi-maximum likelihood; Stochastic volatility.

Interest in models with stochastic volatility dates at least to the work of Clark
(1973), who proposed an iid mixture model for the distribution of stock-price
changes. Unobservable information flow produces a random volume of trade in
the Clark approach. Tauchen and Pitts (1983) and Gallant, Hsieh, and Tauchen
(1991) noted that if the information flows are autocorrelated, then a stochastic
volatility model with time-varying and autocorrelated conditional variance might
be appropriate for price-change series. Stochastic volatility models also arise as
discrete approximations to various diffusion processes of interest in the continuous-time asset-pricing literature (Hull and White, 1987; Melino and Turnbull,
1990; Wiggins, 1987).

The purpose of this article is to develop new methods for inference and
prediction in a simple class of stochastic volatility models in which logarithm of
conditional volatility follows an autoregressive (AR) times series model. Unlike
the autoregressive conditional heteroscedasticity (ARCH) and generalized

* This work was previously published as E. Jacquier, N. G. Polson, and P. E. Rossi (1994),
'Bayesian Analysis of Stochastic Volatility Models (with Discussion)', *Journal of Business and
Economic Statistics* 12, 4. Copyright © 1994 American Statistical Association. Reproduced by
kind permission.

ARCH (GARCH) models (see Bollerslev, Chou, and Kroner (1992) for a survey of ARCH modeling), both the mean and log-volatility equations have separate error terms. The ease of evaluating the ARCH likelihood function and the ability of the ARCH specification to accommodate the time-varying volatility found in many economic time series has fostered an explosion in the use of ARCH models. On the other hand, the likelihood function for stochastic volatility models is difficult to evaluate, and hence these models have had limited empirical application.

The current literature on inference and prediction for stochastic volatility models is brief. Rather than pursuing a likelihood-based approach, Taylor (1986), Melino and Turnbull (1990), and Vetzal (1992) relied on the method of moments (MM) to avoid the integration problems associated with evaluating the likelihood directly. As is well known, the MM may be inefficient relative to a likelihood-based method of inference. This problem is particularly severe in the case of stochastic volatility models because the score function cannot be computed to suggest which moments should be used for MM estimation. Nelson (1988), Harvey, Ruiz, and Shephard (1994), and Ruiz (1994) employed approximate linear filtering methods to produce a quasi-maximum likelihood (QML) estimator. As Harvey et al. (1994) and Ruiz (in press) pointed out, the accuracy of the normality approximation used in the filtering approach will depend on where the true parameters lie in the parameter space. Specifically, the approximation will worsen as the volatility equation variance decreases. Finally, Danielsson (in press) and Danielsson and Richard (1992) developed new methods for approximating the integral used in evaluating the likelihood function. Without a direct and "error-free" method for evaluating the likelihood, it is difficult to gauge the accuracy of the integral approximations proposed in these articles.

In applications of stochastic volatility models to financial data, prediction and filtering as well as parameter estimation are major goals of the analysis. The literature only offers approximate filtering solutions to the problem of inferring about the unobservable volatilities and predicting future volatility. Furthermore parameter estimates are routinely "plugged in" to multistep-ahead prediction formulas, and often the contribution of parameter uncertainty to forecast variability is not accounted for. Finally, all of the techniques discussed in the stochastic volatility literature rely on asymptotic approximations to conduct inference.

We propose a new Bayesian approach in which the latent volatility structure is directly exploited to conduct finite-sample inference and calculate predictive distributions. We augment the stochastic volatility parameters with the time series of volatilities and construct a Markov chain that can be used to draw directly from the joint posterior distribution of the model parameters and unobservable volatilities. Our algorithm combines the idea of data augmentation as advanced by Tanner and Wong (1987) with a hybrid Metropolis independence chain (see Tierney, 1991). In less than one half-hour of workstation central processing unit (CPU) time, we compute simulation-based estimates of posterior quantities of interest to a very high degree of accuracy.

The rest of the article is outlined as follows. Section 9.1 describes our algorithm and discusses its theoretical properties. Section 9.2 discusses the problem of smoothing and developing predictive distributions of future variances. Section 9.3 applies the method to analysis of stock-return data. Section 9.4 reports sampling experiments that compare the performance of our likelihood-based Bayes estimator with both MM and QML procedures. Section 9.5 provides results on filtering performance.

9.1 The model and Markov-chain Monte Carlo approach

The general stochastic volatility model views the time series of the data, y, as a vector generated from a probability model, $p(y|h)$, where h is a vector of volatilities. Each data point y_t has variance h_t, which is time dependent. The volatilities h are unobserved and are assumed to be generated by the probability mechanism, $p(h|\omega)$. The density of the data is a mixture over the h distribution, $p(y|\omega) = \int p(y|h)p(h|\omega)dh$.

Carlin, Polson, and Stoffer (1992) used a Gibbs sampling procedure for analysis of nonlinear state-space models, allowing for nonnormal error densities but with a time invariant scale h. Our focus here is on modeling variation in h over time rather than elaborations of the process governing the mean. McCulloch and Tsay (1993) considered a class of priors for variance changes in which the ratios of volatilities have a random-walk component based on an inverse gamma innovation. Their focus was more on the filtering problem with the process parameters specified a priori. In our approach, we wish to consider prediction and filtering with a hierarchical structure in which we infer about the volatility equation parameters rather than just fixing them to implement a filtering procedure.

Uhlig (1991) introduced a different volatility model in which the ratio of volatilities has a Beta distribution. Uhlig also provided a multivariate model in which the covariance structures have a generalized multivariate Beta distribution. In Uhlig's models, the range of possible variance ratios is restricted to a finite interval and has a complicated interaction with the variance of the volatility. The advantage of Uhlig's approach is that it provides exact expressions for the marginal likelihood. One must rely on high-dimensional numerical integration, however, to provide a solution to the problem of inferring about the Beta distribution range parameters as well as solving the prediction and filtering problem.

9.1.1 Simple stochastic volatility models and comparisons to arch approaches

To focus discussion on the key aspects of modeling and estimating stochastic volatility models, we will start with a simple model in which the conditional variance of a series $\{y_t\}$ follows a log-AR(1) process. Jacquier, Polson, and Rossi (1993) considered priors and methods for the general multivariate case:

$y_t = \sqrt{h_t} u_t$, $\ln h_t = \alpha + \delta \ln h_{t-1} + \sigma_v v_t$, and $(u_t, v_t) \sim$ independent $N(0, 1)$. Here $\omega' = (\alpha, \delta, \sigma_v)$. In our Bayesian simulation framework, it will be a simple matter to introduce exogenous regressors into the mean equation as well as to accommodate an AR(p) process for the log variance.

Although the preceding model is quite parsimonious, it is capable of exhibiting a wide range of behavior. Like ARCH/GARCH models, the model can give rise to a high persistence in volatility (sometimes referred to as "volatility clustering"). Even if $\delta = 0$, the model is a variance mixture that will give rise to excess kurtosis in the marginal distribution of the data. In ARCH/GARCH models with normal errors, the degree of kurtosis is tied to the roots of the variance equation; as the variances become more autocorrelated, the degree of mixing also increases. In the ARCH/GARCH literature, it has become common (e.g. see Nelson 1991) to use nonnormal innovation densities to accommodate the high kurtosis of various financial time series. In the stochastic volatility model, the σ_v parameter governs the degree of mixing independently of the degree of smoothness in the variance evolution.

Jacquier et al. (1993) demonstrated how to accommodate correlation between the mean and variance equations errors, which will introduce an asymmetry into the conditional variance function of the sort documented in the EGARCH literature. Although adding correlation is an interesting extension, not all economic time series display a "leverage" effect. Evidence from the EGARCH literature suggests that the leverage effect is small for interest-rate and exchange-rate series. Vetzal (1992) found a small and insignificant correlation in his analysis of the treasury bill (T-bill) series. Gallant, Rossi, and Tauchen (1992) found that the leverage effect in a stock index series is sensitive to conditioning arguments and outliers.

There are important differences between likelihood functions for the standard GARCH and stochastic volatility models. To illustrate this point, we fit GARCH and stochastic volatility models to weekly returns on a portfolio formed of the smallest decile of listed New York Stock Exchange (NYSE) stocks (see Section 9.3 for a complete analysis of other portfolios and individual stocks). Based on the Schwarz criterion, we select a GARCH(1, 1) model that was fitted by maximum likelihood. The stochastic volatility model is fitted using the Bayes estimators developed in this article (see Table 9.1, Section 9.3, for the estimates). Figure 9.1 compares the autocorrelation of the squared returns with the implied theoretical autocorrelations of the fitted stochastic volatility model (see Appendix A for the expression) and the GARCH model [see Bollerslev (1986) for derivation of GARCH autocorrelation function (acf)]. The stochastic volatility and GARCH acf's are computed by inserting the Bayes or maximum likelihood estimators (MLE's) in the theoretical expressions. The fitted GARCH and stochastic volatility models have very different implied acf's with the stochastic volatility model in closer conformance with the data. This serves to illustrate that the likelihood functions for the GARCH and stochastic volatility models put different weights on various moments functions. This point of view is further corroborated by Hsieh's (1991) findings that ARCH/GARCH/EGARCH filters

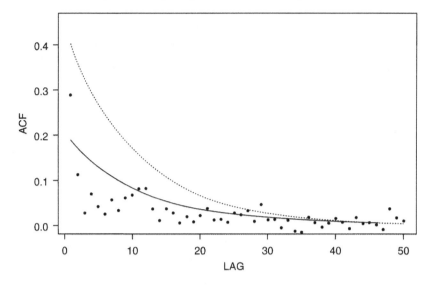

Fig. 9.1. ACF of squared returns, fitted GARCH, and SVOL models, weekly decile 1 portfolio: squared returns, points; GARCH (1, 1), Dotted Line; SVOL, Solid Line.

do not remove all nonlinear dependencies in the series as measured by a battery of BDS-inspired statistics. On the other hand, Hsieh found that when an autoregressive stochastic volatility filter is applied to the data, no remaining nonlinear dependencies are found. Danielsson (in press) also provided some goodness-of-fit evidence that the stochastic volatility model may perform better than some variants of ARCH models including the EGARCH model.

Our goal in this article is to provide a practical method for analysis of stochastic volatility models and not to resolve the controversy over whether ARCH or stochastic volatility models provide a better approximation to the data-generating process for economic and financial data. Practical difficulties have kept investigators from using the stochastic volatility model even though it offers a natural alternative to ARCH and has some advantages in the smoothing and prediction of unobserved variances. It is our view that the limited evidence available at this time suggests that stochastic volatility models are a promising alternative to various ARCH variants.

9.1.2 The marginal likelihood dilemma

As noted by many authors, the fundamental problem with even the simplest stochastic volatility specification is that the marginal likelihood over the parameters of the stochastic volatility process is defined by a T-dimensional integral $\ell(\omega) = \int p(y \mid h)p(h \mid \omega)dh$, where $\omega' = (\alpha, \delta, \sigma_v, \rho), y' = (y_1, \ldots, y_T)$ and $h' = (h_1, \ldots, h_T)$. The stochastic volatility model can be thought of as specifying a prior over the sequence of $\{h_t\}$. Our prior consists of the view that the volatilities evolve smoothly (for large positive δ) according to the AR process. A naive strategy for approximating ℓ would be to simulate from the "prior" $p(h|\omega)$ and average the conditional likelihood, $p(y\,|\,h)$, over these draws, $\hat{\ell}(\omega) = \Sigma\, p(y\,|\,h_i)/H$, where h_i $(i = 1, \ldots, H)$ are simulation draws from the $p(h\,|\,\omega)$ model. In more than a few dimensions, it is well known that this sort of integration strategy will not work. Because we do not know where the likelihood has mass, we are drawing from the prior to compute the expectation of the conditional likelihood, $p(y\,|\,h)$. The prior may be centered far away from the conditional likelihood. As we see in Section 9.1.3, one important advantage of our Markov-chain simulation approach is that draws are made from the posterior rather than prior distribution of $h\,|\,\omega$.

Inspired by the ideas of importance sampling, Danielsson and Richard (1992) proposed a more accurate integration strategy to calculate $\ell(\omega)$. They approximated ℓ and then used these approximations along with a derivative-free optimizer to produce estimates. Although they were able to assess the accuracy of their method in evaluating the likelihood for $\delta = 0$ (this is the iid mixing model), the unavailability of the likelihood for any other value of the parameters makes it difficult to evaluate the accuracy of their methods for any other value of δ. Even if it is possible to evaluate the marginal likelihood with low error, asymptotic theory must be used to approximate the sampling distribution of the approximate MLE. Another alternative would be to use the Danielsson and Richard strategy to evaluate the likelihood in a more standard Bayesian analysis. Monte Carlo methods of numerical integration could be used to compute posterior expectations of functions of interest such as posterior means. In effect, this strategy would nest the Danielsson and Richard integration strategy inside of a standard importance sampling approach to conducting posterior analysis. Because thousands of likelihood evaluations would be required to set up the importance function and perform the Monte Carlo integration, however, a Bayesian analysis based on the Danielsson–Richard simulated likelihood method is not yet computationally feasible, based on the timing estimates for likelihood evaluation given by Danielsson (in press; 1993 personal communication).

9.1.3 Bayesian analysis and Markov-Chain Monte Carlo

We view the specification of the stochastic volatility model as a hierarchical structure of conditional distributions. The hierarchy is specified by a sequence of three distributions, the conditional distribution of $y|h$, the conditional distribution of $h|\omega$, and the marginal or prior distribution of ω. In this view, the stochastic volatility equation, governed by $p(h|\omega)$, is a prior with hyperparameters ω. The joint posterior distribution of h and ω is proportional to the product of these three distributions. In this sense, we have augmented the parameters, ω, with h to form a large parameter vector, $(\omega, h) \in \Omega \times H$. This idea is termed data augmentation and was pioneered in Markov-chain Monte Carlo (MCMC) by Tanner and Wong (1987). The joint posterior is given by Bayes theorem $\pi(h, \omega\,|\,y) \propto p(y\,|\,h)p(h\,|\,\omega)p(\omega)$. From this joint posterior, the marginal $\pi(\omega|y)$ can be used to make inferences about the stochastic volatility parameters, and the marginal $\pi(h|y)$ provides the solution to the "smoothing" problem of inferring about the unobserved volatilities. To compute these marginal distributions, we construct a Markov chain with invariant distribution π. Extremely long samples are computable in short order on any workstation, enabling us to construct very precise simulation-based estimates of any posterior quantity. Mueller (1991) developed Markov-chain algorithms for analysis of factor ARCH and other dynamic models for which the marginal likelihood is easily computed. Mueller's methods do not extend to the stochastic volatility case.

Breaking the joint posterior into various conditional distributions is the key to constructing the appropriate Markov-chain sampler. For example, conditional on h, the posterior distribution of $\omega, p(\omega \,|\, y, h)$, is simple to compute from standard Bayesian treatment of linear models. If it were also possible to sample directly from $p(h\,|\,\omega, y)$, then we could easily construct a Markov chain by alternating back and forth between drawing from $p(h\,|\,\omega, y)$ and $p(\omega\,|\,h, y)$. This process of alternating between conditional distributions produces a cyclic chain, a special case of which is the Gibbs sampler (see Gelfand and Smith, 1990).

In the case of the stochastic volatility model, it is not possible to sample directly from $p(h\,|\,\omega, y)$ at low cost. Instead, we decompose the joint distribution, $p(h\,|\,\omega, y)$ further into the set of conditionals $p(h_t\,|\,h_{-t}, \omega, y)$, where h_{-t} denotes the rest of the h vector other than h_t. In our case, it is difficult to sample from these univariate conditional distributions. Instead, our approach is to construct a hybrid method that uses a series of Metropolis accept/reject independence chains which do not directly sample from the conditionals $p(h_t|h_{-t}, \omega, y)$ but nonetheless provide the posterior as the stationary distribution of the chain. Our algorithm is known as a cyclic independence Metropolis chain. We now give the details on how to implement such a Markov chain.

9.1.4 The algorithm

To construct the chain, we first sample from $p(\omega|h, y)$ and then sample indirectly from $p(h|\omega, y)$. We specify a standard natural conjugate prior for $(\beta, \sigma_v), \beta' = (\alpha, \delta), p(\beta, \sigma) = p(\beta|\sigma)\, p(\sigma)$, where $\beta|\sigma \sim N(\overline{\beta}, \sigma^2 A^{-1}), \sigma \sim IG(v_0, s_0^2)$. The posterior for $\omega|h$ is available from standard linear-models theory. We can easily draw the ω vector at one time by drawing from the appropriate multivariate normal and gamma random variables. Clearly, we can extend the AR(1) model for the volatilities to include higher-order returns, keeping the standard linear-models framework. One obvious advantage of the Bayesian approach for the general AR (p) model is that we can put on "smoothness" or "damping" priors on the AR coefficients to deal with the problem of excessive sampling variability caused by the addition of more model parameters.

To draw from $h|\omega, y$ requires more effort. We can easily exploit the Markovian structure of the stochastic volatility model to break down the joint posterior of the entire h vector by considering the series of univariate conditional densities, $p(h_t|h_{t-1}, h_{t+1}, \omega, y_t), t = 1, \ldots, T$. If it were possible to draw directly from these univariate densities, our algorithm would reduce to a Gibbs sampler in which we would draw successively from $p(\omega|h, y)$ and then each of the T univariate conditionals in turn to form one step in the Markov-chain. Because T draws from these univariate conditional densities are required for one step in the chain and then the chain has to be iterated for several thousand steps, however, it is imperative that the univariate sampling methods be highly efficient.

The univariate conditional densities have an unusual form, which is produced by the normal form for the conditional sampling density and the lognormal forms for the volatility equations,

$$(^*) \qquad p(h_t|h_{t-1}, h_{t+1}, \omega, y_t)$$
$$\propto p(y_t|h_t)p(h_t|h_{t-1})p(h_{t+1}|h_t)$$
$$\propto h_t^{-.5} \exp \{ -.5y_t^2/h_t\}1/h_t$$
$$\exp \{ -(\ln h_t - \mu_t)^2/(2\sigma^2)\},$$

where $\mu_t = (\alpha(1 - \delta) + \delta(\ln h_{t+1} + \ln h_{t-1}))/(1 + \delta^2)$ and $\sigma^2 = \sigma_v^2/(1 + \delta^2)$. Here we have combined both of the log-normal terms and completed the square on $\ln h_t$. In these cases, when the density is not of a standard form, it is natural to consider an accept/reject sampling method. An ideal accept/reject density, $q(x)$, is a density for which there exists a constant such that $p(x) \leq cq(x)$ for all x and for which the ratio $p(x)/q(x)$ is relatively constant over the range of x in which p has most of its mass. In this application, the fact that there is no analytic expression for the normalizing constant of the conditional density further complicates matters. The normalizing constant is a function of the conditioning arguments, which will vary as the sampler progresses. Thus, even with a valid accept/reject density that truly dominates p, we would have to find the constant c required to raise q over p for each time period, which could involve an optimization problem at each draw. The solution commonly taken in the random-number-generation literature (e.g. see Ripley, 1987, ch. 3) is to develop customized bounding procedures for each special case. These ideas do not adapt well to simulating from conditional densities with unknown and changing normalizing constants. Furthermore, even if the blanketing constant could be found at low computational cost, it may be difficult to find a valid accept/reject density that would be efficient in the sense of accepting a high percentage of the draws.

Our solution is to modify the Markov chain by allowing repeats of points in the sample sequence producing what is called a Metropolis chain. It should be emphasized that although the Metropolis chain repeats points in the draw sequence the invariant distribution of the chain is absolutely continuous. First, we choose a candidate simulation density, q, which is cheap to sample from and closely mimics the shape of the univariate conditional density, p. We do not actually have to guarantee dominance, however. Second, we introduce a Metropolis independence chain to handle situations in which the sample points from q are such that dominance fails (see Tierney (1991) for a discussion of independence Metropolis chains). Shephard (1993) used a Metropolis chain to implement the E step of a simulated EM algorithm for the random-walk special case of the stochastic volatility models considered here. To implement the simulated EM approach, a decision rule must be established that determines the number of steps that the Metropolis algorithm is iterated at each E step. Because there is no theoretical guidance in selection of this rule, it must be established that a proposed rule provides a large enough number of Metropolis steps to endow the simulated EM with adequate sampling properties for all relevant regions of the sampling space.

We choose a candidate simulation density to be the kernel of the independence chains by exploiting the special form of the conditional density function. The first term in the density expression (*) is the density of the inverse of a gamma-distributed random variable (this is to be distinguished from the inverted gamma density): $X \sim 1/Z, Z \sim \text{gamma}(\phi, 1/\lambda); P_x(x) = \lambda^\phi/\Gamma(\phi)x^{-(\phi+1)}\exp(-\lambda/x)$. We approximate the lognormal term by matching the first and second moments of the lognormal to the moments of the inverse gamma. The two inverse gamma density forms can then be combined to form one inverse gamma with parameters, $\phi = (1 - 2\exp(\sigma^2))/(1 - \exp(\sigma^2)) + .5; \lambda = (\phi - 1)(\exp(\mu_t + .5\sigma^2)) + .5y_t^2$. The inverse gamma is a good choice for a simulation "blanketing" density because its right tail is algebraic, allowing it to dominate the lognormal density on the right. Our experiments with a lognormal blanketing density have shown the danger of choosing a blanketing density that does not dominate in the right tail.

The only remaining problem is to devise a method for choosing c. Because we no longer require that c be chosen so that cq dominates p, we choose c so as to trade off too frequent rejection from high c values with too frequent "staying" from the Metropolis mechanism. We compute the ratio of the unnormalized p density and normalized q density at the three points centered on the mode of the inverse gamma distribution. The median of these ratios is used to calculate c. We find that we accept between 70% and 80% of all draws when they are constructed in this manner and "stay" less than 5% of the time. This indicates that the inverse gamma density is a good approximation to the conditional density.

To construct the Markov chain on the full state space, $(h, \omega) \in H \times \Omega$, we piece together T Metropolis independence accept/reject chains to handle each coordinate in the h vector and the generation from $p(\omega|h, y)$. Each chain samples from the accept/reject density at each step and modifies one h_t coordinate. We construct a chain that moves from the point (h, ω) to (h', ω') by cycling through T Metropolis chains to update h to h' and then draw $w|h', y$ to update ω to ω'. We now establish that this hybrid chain has invariant distribution π, the joint posterior of (h, ω).

9.1.5 Convergence of the cyclic metropolis chain
The basic idea behind MCMC is to specify a Markov chain, with transition kernel P that is ergodic (irreducible and aperiodic) with π as its stationary distribution. Two widely used chains are the Gibbs sampler (Geman and Geman, 1984) and the Metropolis algorithm (see Tierney, 1991 for a general discussion). The desired distribution π can be simulated by picking an arbitrary initial state X_0 and then applying the transition kernel of the chain giving rise to the sequence $\{X_t\}$. The general Metropolis algorithm works as follows. Let $Q(x, y)$ be the Metropolis transition kernel. Suppose that the chain is currently at $X_t = x$. Then generate a

candidate point as the new point, X_{t-1}. We accept this new point, y, with probability $\alpha(x, y)$, where $\alpha(x, y) = \min\{(p(y)Q(x, y))/(p(x)Q(y, x)), 1\}$. Here we only need to know π up to a proportionality constant, $\pi(x) \propto p(x)$. A Metropolis independence chain is fashioned by sampling candidate steps, Y, from a fixed density that does not depend on x (hence the term "independence" chain). For the independence chain, with transition kernel $Q(x, y) = f(y)$, the acceptance probability is given by $\alpha(x, y) = \min\{w(y)/w(x), 1\}$, where $w(z) = p(z)/f(z)$. If rejection sampling is used, then $f(x) \propto \min\{p(x), cq(x)\}$, where q is the accept/reject density.

If $cq(x)$ were to dominate for all x, then this chain would simply "pass through" iid accept/reject draws and provide an iid sampling method. If, however, cq does not dominate p, then there is the chance that the chain will simulate an ordinate at which $w(y)/w(x)$ will be less than 1. In these circumstances, the chain may actually choose to stay at a point for more than one draw. The intuition behind the working of the Metropolis chain is that, although accept/reject sampling works by rejecting draws so as to reduce the sampling density at points where cq is much larger than p, the Metropolis builds up mass at points where p dominates cq by repeating values.

To implement a Metropolis independence chain on the whole state space $(H \times \Omega)$ would be inadvisable because, although we can calculate the joint posterior of h and ω up to a constant of proportionality, accept/reject sampling in high dimensions can be very inefficient. Our solution is to define the transition kernel as the product of T kernels for each of the T elements of the h vector along with the conditional distribution of $\omega|h$, $P: P_1 P_2 \cdots P_T P_{\omega|h}$, where P_t updates $h_t|\omega$ and $P_{\omega|h}$ updates ω. Although each of the P_t chains is reducible because they only update one coordinate at a time), the product has a transition kernel that is positive everywhere and is therefore irreducible and aperiodic (see Tierney 1991, p. 5). It only remains to check that the posterior, π, is the invariant distribution. Standard arguments involving the time reversibility of the general Metropolis chain (see Tierney, 1991, p. 3) can be used to verify that the posterior, π, is the unique invariant distribution of the chain.

Although it is easily verified that our chain is ergodic and converges to the correct stationary distribution, in practice we must be satisfied that the draws are coming from a distribution close to the stationary distribution. This amounts to determining how long the chain must be run to dissipate the effects of the initial state, X_0. Analysis of the second eigenvalues of the chain (Applegate, Kannan, and Polson, 1991) can provide exact information on the run length required to ensure that the chain is within a given tolerance of the invariant distribution. For most models, however, these eigenvalues cannot be calculated. A body of current research seeks to obtain tight bounds on these eigenvalues. For our problem, these bounds are not sufficiently tight to be useful. Therefore, we must rely on simulation experience to assess the speed of convergence.

One common practice, which we follow in our empirical applications, is to discard the first T^* draws under the assumption that the chain will have converged to within a very close tolerance to the invariant distribution. In practice, T^* must be chosen by experience with simulated data. We simulate data from a known stochastic volatility model and verify that the sampler converges in distribution after a specified number of draws. After extensive experimentation, we find that the sampler converges very rapidly to the stationary distribution. The excellent sampling performance of the Bayes estimator reported in Section 4 provides an indirect confirmation that the sampler has converged quickly.

Another issue that has received some attention (see Geweke, 1992; McCulloch and Rossi, in press) is the information content of a given draw sequence. We use the empirical distribution of the draws to estimate posterior quantities of interest (it is also possible to average the conditional distributions as suggested by Gelfand and Smith (1990)). It is important to ensure that these posterior estimates are sufficiently precise for the purpose at hand. In the case of stochastic volatility models, however, a vast number of draws (exceeding 50,000) can be drawn in a matter of hours on even a slow workstation, rendering these considerations less important.

In summary, it is important to remember that these sorts of Markov-chain samplers converge to the required posterior distribution under only mild and verifiable conditions. Furthermore, allocation of more computer time to the simulation will unambiguously increase the amount of information regarding the posterior and provide better inferences. No amount of additional computing resources, however, can improve the quality of inference obtained from asymptotic procedures.

9.2 Smoothing and forecasting

One important use of stochastic volatility models is to infer about values of unobservable conditional volatility both within the sample (smoothing) and out of sample (prediction). For example, option-pricing applications often require some sort of estimates of conditional volatility, and "event"-style studies may wish to relate specific events to changes in volatility. To provide a solution to the smoothing problem, we must compute the conditional distribution of $h_t|y$, where $y' = (y_1, \ldots, y_T)$ is the whole data vector. If this distribution were available, we could simply use $E[h_t|y]$ as the smoothed estimate of h_t. This density also summarizes our uncertainty about the unobservable h_t. An analytical expression for $p(h_t|y)$ is unavailable, even conditional on the volatility parameters ω. We will see, however, that a Monte Carlo estimate of this density is available using our draws from the joint posterior, $\pi(h, \omega)$.

When an investigator uses the MM or simulated likelihood approach to produce parameter estimates, a nonlinear filtering problem has to be solved after the estimation to produce smoothed estimates of h_t. For example, Melino and Turnbull (1990) used approximate Gaussian filtering methods to extract smoothed estimates conditional on MM parameter estimates. These approximate Gaussian filtering methods do not necessarily provide the optimal nonlinear filter. In a related approach, Foster and Nelson (1992) constructed an approximate nonlinear filter based on the EGARCH model.

Our method avoids any asymptotic approximations and provides draws that can be used to solve the smoothing problem as a natural by-product of the simulation process (see Carlin et al. (1992) and McCulloch and Tsay (1993) for related approaches). Our Monte Carlo (MC) sampler has invariant distribution, which is the joint posterior of (h, ω). The solution to the smoothing problem is the marginal posterior of $h_t, p(h_t \mid y)$. We simply use the draws of the h vector to form estimates of these marginals for all T observations. These draws must be made to construct the chain so that they are available at no additional computational cost. Furthermore this marginal distribution directly accounts for parameter uncertainty because $p(h \mid y) = \int p(h \mid \omega, y)p(\omega \mid y)d\omega$. The solution to the non-linear filtering problem is simply $E[h_t \mid y]$, which we can approximate to any desired degree of accuracy by using the draws from the marginal distribution, $p(h_t \mid y)$.

Our MC sampling framework can be extended to include forecasting up to an arbitrary step ahead. The goal of any forecasting exercise is to compute the predictive distribution of a future vector of observations given the past observations. In the case of volatility forecasting, our goal is to compute the predictive density of a vector of future volatilities given the sample data, $p(h_f \mid y)$, where $h'_f = (h_{T+1}, \ldots, h_{T+k})$. Our approach is to compute the joint posterior distribution of the h vector including both sample and future h's and simply marginalize on the future h's, which will be the predictive distribution. Define $y'_f = (y_{T+1}, \ldots, y_{T+k+1})$, $h^{*'} = (h', h'_f)$, and $y^* = (y', y'_f)$. The key insight is that, given y^*, we have already shown how to draw from $p(h^* \mid y^*, \omega)$ and that $p(y_f \mid y, h^*, \omega)$ is simple to draw from. We now piece together three collections of conditional distributions to construct the following chain:

1. $y_f \mid y, h^*, \omega$ (iid normal draws)
2. $h^* \mid y^*, \omega$
3. $\omega \mid h^*$

The second and third conditionals are sampled using the cyclic Metropolis approach outlined in Section 1.

To make forecasts using a standard filtering framework, estimates of h_T are formed using filtering methods, and then estimated parameters are used in conjunction with the model to forecast future variances. There are now two sources of error that must be considered, error in the filtering estimates of h_T and parameter estimation error. Even if the sampling variability in the parameter estimates were negligible, uncertainty in the level of h_T must be reckoned with. There is no reason to believe that asymptotic normal approximations would result in accurate prediction intervals, especially for multistep-ahead forecasts that will involve nonlinearities in the estimate of the persistence parameter, $\hat{\delta}$.

9.3 Analysis of selected stocks and portfolios

To illustrate our Markov-chain simulation method and to compare findings from the stochastic volatility models with findings in the ARCH/GARCH literature, we analyze 15 data sets on a variety of stock portfolios, selected individual stocks, and exchange rates. For the stock data, we rely on weekly stock returns constructed by compounding daily returns from the Center for Research in Security Prices (CRSP) daily NYSE stock files. Weekly returns were used to minimize the asynchronous trading and bid–ask bounce problems in daily data. In addition, there are variance shifts due to weekends, holidays, and day-of-the-week effects that are tangential to the main point of the analysis. By using weekly returns, we hope to minimize these problems while still retaining much of the information on short-term volatility shifts that is present in the daily data.

We first prefilter the returns series to take out an AR(1) term and monthly systematic shifts in the mean returns, $R_t^* = R_t - a - bR_{t-1} - \Sigma d_i Mnth(i)_t$. These residuals are then analyzed via the Markov-chain algorithm outlined in Section 1. If desired, one could accommodate these systematic shifts in the mean of the series in the Markov-chain method by allowing $y_t = x_t'\gamma + \sqrt{h_t}\varepsilon_t$ and conducting an analysis of the joint posterior of $p(\gamma, h, \omega|y)$. This is easily achieved by introducing the conditional posterior distribution of $\gamma|h, \omega$, and y, which can be computed from the standard theory of linear models, although it is straightforward to allow a linear mean function, we expect that information about the mean is approximately independent of information regarding the variance parameters.

Table 9.1 presents estimates of the stochastic volatility parameters for the standard CRSP equal-weighted (EW) and value-weighted (VW) indices of NYSE stocks as well as three decile portfolios corresponding to the 1, 5, and 10 deciles of stock as measured by market capitalization. The posterior mean of δ lies between .91 and .95, exhibiting a high persistence in conditional variances typical of estimates in the ARCH literature. Below the posterior mean and standard deviation is the 95% Bayesian credibility interval that is constructed from the .025 and .975 percentiles of the simulated posterior distribution. It is hard to directly interpret the posterior distribution of σ_v. A parameter that is more interpretable is the coefficient of variation (we use the square) of the volatility process, $\text{var}(h)/E[h]^2 = \exp(\sigma_v/(1 - \delta^2)) - 1$. Since the MC sampler provides draws of the parameters, it is a straightforward computational task to compute the posterior distribution of any function of the parameters. We do not have to rely on delta-method asymptotics. Examination of the posterior distribution of the coefficient of variation suggests that the small stocks (which drive the EW index) have greater variability in the stochastic volatility equation than for the high-capitalization stocks that greatly influence the VW index.

Analysis of the posterior distribution of model parameters for stocks selected from the 1st and 5th decile is given in Table 9.2. As might be expected, the individual stocks have greater variation in the level of persistence as measured by widely varying posterior distributions of δ and σ_v. For this small sample of stocks, there seems to be a relationship between the level of market capitalization and the level of predictability in the stochastic variance equation. All three middle-decile stocks have posterior distributions massed on higher levels of the coefficient of variation than the high-cap stocks. One interesting measure is the half-life of a shock to volatility, $\log(.5)/\log(\delta)$, the posterior moments of which

Table 9.1. Posterior analysis for selected portfolios

Parameter	Posterior means (standard deviation)				
	EW	VW	D1	D5	D10[a]
α	−.69	−.39	−.56	−.71	−.56
	(.12)	(.11)	(.12)	(.36)	(.18)
δ	−.91	−.95	−.93	−.91	−.93
	(.015)	(.013)	(.016)	(.046)	(.022)
	[.88, .94][b]	[.92, .97]	[.89, .96]	[.81, .96]	[.89, .97]
σ_v	.39	.23	.32	.32	.29
	(.025)	(.026)	(.032)	(.095)	(.056)
V_h/E_h^2	1.61	.80	1.1	.92	.93
	(.38)	(.24)	(.28)	(.27)	(.25)
Shock half-life	7.8	14.	9.6	9.4	11.
	(1.4)	(4.3)	(2.3)	(4.5)	(4.5)

Note: Weekly returns, 7/62–12/91. $T = 1,540$. All returns are prefiltered to remove AR (1) + monthly seasonals from mean equation.

[a] EW ≡ equal-weighted NYSE; VW ≡ value-weighted; Dx is decile x portfolio. D1 is the decile of smallest stocks.

[b] Brackets denote 95% Bayes probability interval.

Table 9.2. Posterior analysis for selected stocks

Parameter	Posterior means (standard deviation)					
	IBM	GM	TEX	Broad	Commetco	Bearings[a]
α	−1.2	−.22	−.38	−.39	−.78	−.12
	(.20)	(.079)	(.10)	(.093)	(.13)	(.16)
δ	.83	.97	.95	.93	.87	.81
	(.028)	(.011)	(.014)	(.017)	(.021)	(.024)
	[.77, .88][b]	[.94, .99]	[.92, .97]	[.89, .96]	[.83, .91]	[.76, .86]
σ_v	.40	.14	.23	.25	.43	.53
	(.025)	(.023)	(.028)	(.029)	(.027)	(.028)
V_h/E_h^2	.67	.43	.73	.56	1.3	1.35
	(.12)	(.52)	(.21)	(.15)	(.26)	(.22)
Shock half-life	3.8	26.0	14.	9.7	5.3	3.4
	(.69)	(15.)	(4.1)	(2.5)	(1.0)	(.49)

Note: Weekly returns, 7/62–12/91. $T = 1540$. All returns are prefiltered to remove AR(1) and monthly seasonals from the mean equation.

[a] Tex ≡ Texaco; Broad ≡ Broad Inc.; Commetco ≡ Commercial Metals Company; Bearings ≡ Bearing Inc. Stocks are listed from largest to smallest capitalization in terms of 1991 market value. The 1991 market capitalizations are $50.8 billion, $17.8 billion, $15.8 billion, $621 million, $230 million, and $137.8 million, respectively.

[b] Brackets denote 95% Bayes probability Interval.

are presented in the last row of the table. These measures vary widely from about 3 weeks to over 26 weeks. It is also interesting to observe that, although the posterior distribution of δ is tightly massed, the posterior distribution of the half-life is very diffuse.

The adequacy of asymptotic normal approximations to the posterior is addressed in Figure 9.2, which shows the marginal posteriors of δ, $(h)/E[h]^2$, and the half-life for the EW index and Texaco. All of these distributions show pronounced skewness. This casts some doubt on the usefulness of asymptotic approximations for conducting either Bayesian or frequentist inference.

We computed MM estimates of the model parameters using the set of moments outlined in Section 4. We do not report the MM estimates; instead we summarize the qualitative differences. Some of the MM estimates of δ are very different from the Bayes estimates; for example, the MM estimate of δ for IBM is .996 (compare with .83 from the MC sampler). In most cases, the asymptotic standard errors computed for the MM estimates are larger than the posterior standard deviations reported in Tables 9.1 and 9.2. Although the posterior standard deviations and MM asymptotic errors are not strictly comparable, this does suggest that there is important information missing in the set of moments used in computing the MM estimates. We also found evidence of multiple interior local optima in the MM criterion surface. For example, in the analysis of the Commetco data, we found two interior optima, one at $(\hat{\alpha} = -5.5, \hat{\delta} = .12, \hat{\sigma}_v = .83)$ with an MM criterion value of 20.4 and another at the point $(-.129, .98, .119)$ with value 19.3.

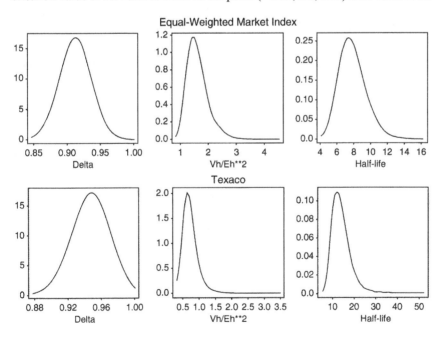

Fig. 9.2. Posterior distributions of selected parameters.

Table 9.3. Posterior analysis for selected daily financial series

Parameter	Posterior means (standard deviation)			
	S&P 500	£/$	DM/$	CD$/$
$\propto$	−.002	−.36	−.56	−.61
	(.004)	(.12)	(.012)	(.12)
δ	.97	.96	.95	.95
	(.008)	(.012)	(.013)	(.009)
	[.96, .99]*	[.94, .98]	[.92, .97]	[.93, .97]
σ_v	.15	.17	.13	.26
	(.017)	(.03)	(.03)	(.025)
V_h/E_h^2	.56	.52	.69	1.1
	(.19)	(.12)	(.14)	(.23)
Shock half-life	29.0	21.6	13.	14.4
	(10.0)	(8.8)	(3.5)	(3.0)

Note: S&P 500-daily change in log (S&P 500) index, filtered to remove calendar effects as documented by Gallant, Rossi, and Tauchen (1992); 1/2/80–12/30/87; $T = 2,023$. £/$, DM/$-daily noon spot rates from the Board of Governors of the Federal Reserve System, supplied by David Hsieh; 1/2/80–5/31/90; $T = 2,614$. CD$/$-daily noon interbank market spot rates from Bank of Canada, supplied by Melino and Turnbull (1990): 1/2/75–12/10 86, $T = 3,011$.
* [,] denotes 95% Bayes probability interval.

In Table 9.3, we present a Bayesian analysis of daily time series that have received attention in the stochastic volatility literature. We examine the daily changes in the log of the S&P 500 stock-price index studied by Gallant, Rossi, and Tauchen (1992) and daily spot exchange rates for the £/$, DM/$, and CD/$ series. The S&P 500 series is prefiltered to remove systematic components from the mean and variance as discussed by Gallant et al. (1992). The £/$ and DM/$ series are noon spot prices from the Board of Governors of the Federal Reserve System, supplied by David Hsieh. The CD/$ series was obtained from Melino and Turnbull (1990). The Bayes estimates of δ for the CD/$ exchange rate agree closely with MM estimates computed by Melino and Turnbull. Our estimates of the coefficient of variation, however, are 10 times larger (1.12 vs. .14). For the DM/$ and £/$ rates, Harvey et al. (1994) found much higher δ values for the £/$ series. It should be pointed out that the Harvey et al. study was conducted on a subperiod of our sample and with data from a different source. The exchange-rate data exhibit a high degree of persistence in volatility although the posterior is massed well away from the unit-root case. Some care should be exercised in interpreting these persistence findings because level shifts in these series brought about by calendar effects and central bank interventions [especially for the U.K. series; see Gallant et al. (1991)] can easily lead to spurious unit-root findings. Our analysis of the S&P series finds a higher level of persistence for the daily series as compared to the weekly stock portfolios, a fact frequently noted in the ARCH literature. The posterior distribution of δ, however, is massed well away from 1 (the posterior probability that $\delta > .99 = .005$).

Taken as a whole, these findings suggest that there may be important differences in the sampling properties of Bayes and other estimation procedures. For this reason, we designed and carried out a set of simulation experiments comparing the sampling performance of the posterior means as Bayes estimators as compared to MM estimators and estimators based on the QML filtering approach of Nelson (1988) and Harvey et al. (1994). These sampling experiments are reported in Section 9.4.

9.4 Sampling experiments

To compare our Bayes estimator to other procedures, we devised a series of simulation experiments designed to gauge performance over a fairly wide range of relevant parameter values. Table 9.4 summarizes the six sets of parameter settings used in the experiments. As discussed previously we have found it most convenient to parameterize the model in terms of the coefficient of variation of h. Our empirical analysis of stock data and exchange-rate data suggests that δ values between .9 and .98 are relevant and that the coefficient of variation fluctuates between .5 and 1.0. To examine the sensitivity of the methods to the size of the stochastic component in the volatility equation, we consider cells symmetrically positioned around the central $\text{var}(h)/E[h]^2 = 1.0$ cell. All experiments are calibrated so that $E[h] = .0009$. If we think of the simulated data as weekly returns, this implies an approximately 20% annual standard deviation, which is typical of many stocks. We consider sample sizes of $T = 500$ for all six cells, and we run one set of simulations at $T = 2,000$ for the central cells to confirm that our findings are consistent across sample sizes. The same set of simulated data sets are used for all three estimators considered.

A review of the findings in the stochastic volatility literature supports our choice of parameter values. All studies find a coefficient of variation of less than 1.0 with δ ranging from around .8 to .995. Melino and Turnbull (1990) analyzed the CD/\$ exchange rate ($T = 3,011$, daily from 1975–1986) and

Table 9.4. Sampling experiment parameter values

$\text{Var}(h)/E[h]^2$		δ		
		.9	.95	.98
10	α	−.821	−.4106	−.1642
	σ_v	.675	.4835	.3082
1	α	−.736	−.368	−.1472
	σ_v	.3629	.26	.1657
.1	α	−.7061	−.353	−.1412
	σ_v	.135	.0964	.0614

Note: All of the models are calibrated so that $E_h = .0009$—that is, about 22% annual standard deviation for weekly data.

reported $\hat{\delta} = .91$ and $V_h/E_h^2 = .14$. Danielsson (in press) studied the daily S&P 500 ($T = 2,202$, 1980–1987) and reported $\hat{\delta} = .96$ and $V_h/E_h^2 = .34$. Vetzal (1992) used weekly T-bill data and got $\hat{\delta} = .94$ and $V_h/E_h^2 = .53$. Harvey et al. (1994) studied daily exchange rates from 1981 to 1985 ($T = 946$) and reported δ estimates from .958 to .995 with V_h/E_h^2 ranging from .47 to .74.

Two methods that have received prominent attention in the literature on estimating stochastic volatility models are the MM and the quasi-likelihood Kalman filtering (QML) approach. Both the MM and QML methods are non-likelihood-based methods that are less efficient than our likelihood-based Bayes method. The purpose of the simulation experiments is to measure the extent of this inefficiency. In the recent generalized MM (GMM) literature, there has been considerable discussion of an efficiency/robustness trade-off in which one might be willing to use inefficient methods in exchange for robustness with respect to departures from the distributional assumptions used in formulating the likelihood. The MM approach considered here, however, uses higher-order moment conditions that depend critically on normality assumptions.

We do not consider the simulated likelihood method (QAM) of Danielsson and Richard (1992) in our simulation experiments for practical computational reasons. Using the number of draws reported by Danielsson (in press), we conservatively estimate that it would take at least three Sparc 2 workstation CPU years to run our full set of simulation experiments. Further refinements of the Danielsson and Richard method may make a full-blown simulation study feasible, and we leave this for future study.

The simulation studies allow for comparison of various methods not only in parameter estimation but also in producing "smoothed" estimates of the unobserved variances. Although our MCMC Bayes procedure yields solutions to the smoothing problem as a natural by-product of the method, the MM, QML, and QAM approaches offer no direct solution to the filtering problem. In the non-Bayesian approach, a method of parameter estimation must be coupled with a nonlinear filtering method to solve the smoothing problem. In the simulation experiments, standard approximate Kalman-filtering methods are compared to the Bayes solution to the filtering problem.

9.4.1 Method of moments

For simple stochastic volatility models such as the one considered here, analytic expressions are available for a large collection of different moments. For more complicated models in which analytic moment expressions are not available, a simulated MM methodology could be employed. The real problem in implementing an MM approach is the choice of moments. Although many collections of these moments are sufficient to identify the stochastic volatility parameters, there is always the question of efficiency loss due to excluding information in the likelihood. The score function of the loglikelihood should suggest which moments should be used. Since the score is not available for these problems, we must guess which set of moments is "sensible." For extremely large samples, we might specify moments from some set of basis functions, which would, one hopes, approximate any score function. A very large number of basis functions and lags might be required, however.

We select the same basic set of moments considered by Melino and Turnbull (1990). We use $\{E[|y_t|^k], k = 1, \ldots, K\}$, $\{E[|y_t y_{t-k}|], k = 1, \ldots, L_a\}$, and $\{E[y_t^2 y_{t-k}^2],$ $k = 1, \ldots, L\}$. The moments of marginal distribution of y_t primarily serve to identify the mean of h, and the autocovariances of the squares and absolute values help to identify δ. As will be discussed, we experimented with the number of lags in the moments of the autocovariance type. Appendix A presents the well-known analytic expressions for these moments as well as the derivatives of the moment expressions with respect to the stochastic volatility parameters. These derivatives are used in optimization problems as well as in the computation of the asymptotic covariance matrix of the method of moments estimator.

The MM estimator is based on the classical MM approach, except that the non-iid character of the moment discrepancies is taken into account in forming the weighting matrix, as in the work of Hansen (1982). Using the notation in Appendix A, define $m_{ij} = \sum f_{ijt}(y)/T$, where m_{ij} indicates moment of type i and power/order j. For example, $m_{11} = \sum |y_t|/T$ with $f_{ijt}(y) = |y_t|$. Let $m_{ij}(\omega)$ be the population moment expression. The MM estimator is defined as $\hat{\omega}_{MM} = \arg \min g'(\omega) W g(\omega)$, where g is the vector of moment deviations and $g = \sum g_t/T, g_t = [m_{ijt} - m_{ij}(\omega)]$, an $m \times 1$ vector, where m is the number of moments used. W is the weighting matrix standard in the GMM literature, $\hat{W}^{-1} = 1/T \sum_k \sum_t w(k, L) g_t g'_{t+k}$, and $w(k, L)$ are the Bartlett weights for up to order K. The MM estimates are based on the first four moments of $|y_t|$, 10 lags of $E[y_t^2 y_{t-k}^2]$, and 10 lags of $E[|y_t|y_{t-k}|]$. Although there is some correlation among the 24 moment discrepancies, there is no evidence of singularity in the weighting matrix.

It is common practice to iterate the computation of the weighting matrix by starting with the identity matrix and then computing new weighting matrices based on the current parameter estimates. Some iterate this process until it has converged in the sense of producing small changes in the criterion function and parameter estimates from iteration to iteration. We found that estimates converge after only a few iterations of the weighting matrix so that weighting matrix issues are less important for this class of problems. In forming the MM estimator, we used five iterations of the weight matrix for $T = 500$ and four for $T = 2,000$.

As is standard in this literature, the asymptotic variance matrix of $\hat{\omega}_{MM}$ is computed as $(D'W^{-1}D)^{-1}$. D is the $3 \times m$ Jacobian matrix of the moment expressions. For the simple stochastic volatility model, it should be possible to calculate W exactly rather than using the standard consistent estimator, although this would be a tedious calculation. More important, we would have to evaluate the exact expression for W at the MM estimates. It is not clear which of these consistent variance estimators should be superior, the standard spectral estimation approach or evaluating the exact W at $\hat{\omega}_{MM}$.

To compute the MM estimates, we employ a state-of-the-art optimizer specifically designed for a sum-of-squares objective function. We use the NPSOL routine from Stanford Optimization Laboratory as implemented in NAG library routine E04UPF. Analytic derivatives are used throughout. Inspection of the moment expressions (derived under the assumption of stationarity) immediately suggests that numerical problems can occur for values of delta close to 1 as well as for large values of σ_v (the moments contain the expression $\exp\{\sigma_v^2/(1-\delta^2)\}$). Furthermore it is well known that σ_v is an absorbing state in the sense that once $\sigma_v = 0$ the MM estimation procedure will just try to match the mean volatility. Our approach to this problem is to place bounds on the parameter space to keep δ from approaching too close to 1 and to keep sigma from getting near 0. Since our optimizer is based on a sequence of quadratic programs that approximate the augmented Lagrangian problem, it is a simple matter to add bounds constraints. Typically, we require $|\hat{\delta}_{MM}| < .995$ and $\hat{\sigma}_v > .001$. These bounds are very far from the parameter values used in the simulations. Another possible solution to this problem would be to work with moments of the log series such as $\log|y_t|$ and $\log(|y_t y_{t-k}|)$. Although this strategy will reduce the overflow problems, it will not eliminate them.

For many simulated data sets, the configuration of sample moments implies a minimum to the MM criterion at a point outside the stationary region. In our procedure, the optimizer will hit the bounds imposed on the problem. There is a serious problem with corner solutions for any sample size in cells with high δ and low coefficient of variation. At $T = 500$, over half of the simulated samples result in corner solutions for $\delta = .95$ or $.98$ and $\mathrm{var}(h)/E[h]^2 = .1$. Both δ and σ_v bounds may be binding, although never at the same time. Even for the middle row of the design, $\mathrm{var}(h)/E[h]^2 = 1.0$, there are larger numbers of δ estimates at the bounds. Obviously, this problem will only worsen for data generated with models showing higher persistence. These problems with corner solutions are less severe but still persist in samples of size 2,000, but they eventually disappear if we examine extremely large samples of 32,000.

Given the large number of corner solutions, it is all the more important to examine the sensitivity of the MM estimates to the starting point for the optimizer. For all simulated samples in the experiment, we started from the true parameter vector. One view is that this gives the MM the "best chance" to find the optimum that we expected to be fairly close to the true parameter values. This argument only holds if there is very little sampling variability. It is possible that the MM criterion surface has multiple local minima. To check this, we took a few samples of 2,000 observations and defined a fine grid over the bounded Ω parameter space. The optimizer was then started from every point on this grid. We could find no evidence of more than one interior minimum. From some starting points, however, the optimizer would stop at the bounds with valid Kuhn–Tucker conditions. From still other starting points and for the same data set, the optimizer would converge at an interior optimum with lower criterion value. Finally, for some data sets, we find the minimum of the criterion at the bounds. Thus our experience to date does not rule out the possibility of either a nonconvex criterion surface or the presence of global optima outside the stationary region.

Table 9.5 shows the absolute sampling performance of the MM estimator for $T = 500$. The table shows the mean and root mean squared error (RMSE) for each of the six cells. The MM estimator exhibits substantial bias, especially for the estimates of σ_v. In addition, there is very substantial sampling variability that results in RMSE's as large as the true parameter value for both δ and σ_v. It should be emphasized that the actual MM estimator investigated in Table 9.4 uses the strong prior information in the assumption of stationarity to attenuate the sampling variability by imposing stationarity bounds.

To assess the adequacy of the standard asymptotic approximations to the sampling distribution of the MM estimator, we computed standardized values of the MM estimates—for example, $(\hat{\delta}_{MM} - \delta)/\hat{\sigma}$, where $\hat{\sigma}$ is the asymptotic standard error. Figure 9.3 shows the sampling distribution of the standardized MM estimates of δ and σ_v along with the $N(0, 1)$ asymptotic distribution. For $T = 500$, there is a substantial difference between the asymptotic and exact sampling distributions. For σ_v, the substantial bias of the MM estimate is evident even for $T = 2,000$.

It is also useful to look at the correlations between the parameter estimates. For all cells, $\hat{\alpha}$ and $\hat{\delta}$ are extremely highly correlated (over .99), for high δ and low variability, there can also be high ($\approx -.95$) correlations between $\hat{\sigma}_v$ and $\hat{\delta}$. Although α and δ are separately identified, the high correlation indicates that, in practice, these parameters are underidentified. It is possible that this high correlation induces a ridge (actually a valley) in the MM criterion surface that could cause problems for the optimizer. In an effort to regularize the surface, we experimented with reparameterizing to $(\alpha/(1 - \delta), \delta, \sigma_v)$. Although this new parameterization eliminates much of the correlation between the parameters, the sampling distribution of $\hat{\delta}$ computed from this parameterization is indistinguishable from the distribution resulting from the standard $(\alpha, \delta, \sigma_v)$ parameterization.

Some might suggest that the poor performance of the MM estimator might be due to inclusion of insufficient lags in the autocovariance-type moments. We used

Table 9.5. Mean and root mean squared error of the MM estimator

$Var(h)/E[h]^2$	α	δ	σ_v	α	δ	σ_v	α	δ	σ_v
10	*−.821*	*.9*	*.675*	*−.4106*	*.95*	*.4835*	*−.1642*	*.98*	*.308*
	−1.47	.83	.59	−.72	.916	.42	−.09	.99	.19
	(1.46)	(.17)	(.23)	(.61)	(.07)	(.18)	(.18)	(.02)	(.14)
1	*−.736*	*.9*	*.363*	*−.368*	*.95*	*.26*	*−.1472*	*.98*	*.1657*
	−1.0	.87	.24	−.51	.93	.16	−.128	.982	.104
	(1.25)	(.17)	(.19)	(.83)	(.11)	(.16)	(.26)	(.036)	(.11)
.1	*−.706*	*.9*	*.135*	*−.353*	*.95*	*.0964*	*−.1412*	*.98*	*.0614*
	−5.0	.30	.06	−4.7	.34	.05	−2.25	.65	.063
	(6.3)	(.88)	(.12)	(6.5)	(.9)	(.09)	(4.7)	(.67)	(.090)

Note: The statistics in this table are based on 500 simulated samples, each consisting of a time series of length 500. For each cell, the top row (italics) shows the true value of the parameters. The following two rows show the mean and root mean squared error (in parentheses).

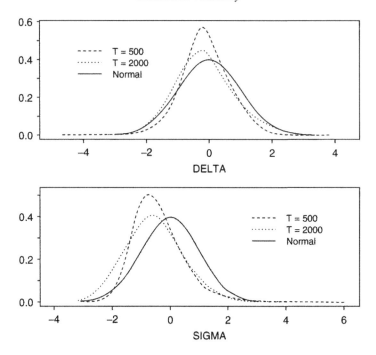

Fig. 9.3. Standardized MM parameter estimates $\mathrm{var}(h)/E[h]^{**2} = 1$, delta $= .9$:-----, $T = 500$; ·······, $T = 2,000$; ——, Normal.

10 lags of both the autocorrelations in the squares and absolute values. Experimentation with a larger number of lags did not affect the sampling performance. It appears that the problem with the MM is the selection of the form of the moments and not the number of lags.

9.4.2 The quasi-maximum likelihood estimator

Nelson (1988) and Harvey et al. (1994) suggested a QML method that is based on a Kalman-filtering approach. The basic stochastic volatility model can be written as a system of two linear equations:

$$\log(y_t^2) = \log(h_t) + \log(\varepsilon_t^2)$$
$$\log(h_t) = \alpha + \delta \log(h_{t-1}) + \sigma_v v_t,$$
$$(\varepsilon_t, v_t) \sim \text{independent } N(0, 1).$$

This is a linear dynamic model in the standard-measurement-equation/state-evolution-equation form. If $\eta_t = \log(\varepsilon_t^2)$ were normally distributed, standard linear filtering theory could be used to evaluate the likelihood and solve the prediction/smoothing problem (see Appendix B for a complete discussion and review of the filtering approach). Since η_t is not normally distributed, linear filtering methods can only approximate the results of the true nonlinear optimal filter. As Harvey et al. (1994) and Ruiz (1994) pointed out, the adequacy of the approximation depends critically on the value of σ_v. For large values of σ_v, the systematic component $[\log(h_t)]$ in the measurement equation will dominate the η_t error term, the normality approximation may be adequate, and the linear filtering approach will be close to optimal. For small values of σ_v, however, the normality approximate will break down, and a linear filtering approach may produce estimates with poor sampling properties relative to a likelihood-based procedure. The real advantage of the QML approach is its speed and adaptibility to many situations. The very fact that we are able to conduct large-scale sampling experiments with our Bayesian methods suggests that computational speed is not an important advantage for the QML procedure in this context.

Table 9.6 presents the sampling performance of the QML estimator for our experimental design. The sampling experiment confirms our intuition that the performance of the QML estimator is best for large values of σ_v. For a coefficient of variation of 10, the QML estimator exhibits little bias and small variability. For smaller values of the coefficient of variation, however, the performance of both of the QML and MM estimators deteriorates rapidly.

It is interesting to compare the relative performance of the MM and QML estimators. The overall impression is that the QML and MM estimators have similar performance with the QML dominating the MM estimator only for the high volatility cells ($\text{var}(h)/E[h]^2 = 10.0$). Ruiz (in press) compared the MM and QML approach on the basis of relative *asymptotic* efficiency and found that the QML approach has very high relative efficiency as compared to the MM estimator for large σ_v values. For smaller σ_v values, the QML is dominated by the MM as measured by asymptotic relative efficiency. Our finite-sample results suggest that the performance of QML for high σ_v cells is only marginally superior

Table 9.6. Mean and root mean squared error of the QML estimator

$\text{Var}(h)/E[h]^2$	α	δ	σ_v	α	δ	σ_v	α	δ	σ_v
10	−.821	.9	.675	−.4106	.95	.4835	−.1642	.98	.308
	−.99	.88	.70	−.55	.93	.51	−.11	.99	.33
	(.48)	(.06)	(.16)	(.32)	(.04)	(.12)	(.09)	(.01)	(.07)
1	−.736	.9	.363	−.368	.95	.26	−.1472	.98	.1657
	−1.4	.81	.45	−1.0	.86	.35	−.20	.97	.22
	(1.6)	(.22)	(.27)	(1.7)	(.23)	(.25)	(.54)	(.08)	(.15)
.1	−.706	.9	.135	−.353	.95	.0964	−.1412	.98	.0614
	−5.5	.23	.33	−5.5	.22	.31	−3.5	.49	.35
	(5.6)	(.79)	(.39)	(6.0)	(.85)	(.41)	(4.6)	(.67)	(.46)

Note: The statistics in this table are based on 500 simulated samples, each consisting of a time series of length 500. For each cell, the top row (italics) shows the true value of the parameters. The following two rows show the mean and root mean squared error (in parentheses).

to the MM. It should be emphasized that we do not consider exactly the same set of parameter values. Ruiz considered values of $\sigma_v = 1$ that imply coefficients of variation still higher than ours. We know of no estimates from a stochastic volatility model with a coefficient of variation even as high as 10, as considered in our high-volatility cells. Most studies, including our own, find coefficients of variation between .1 and 2 or so. Finally, Ruiz pointed out that the asymptotic variance estimates dramatically understate the true sampling variability. This suggests that there may be large differences between actual sampling perform-ance and asymptotic relative efficiency. In addition, the asymptotic relative efficiency measure does not consider the substantial biases that we find for both the MM and QML estimators.

9.4.3 Bayes estimators
Table 9.7 presents the sampling performance of the Bayes estimator. The Bayes estimator is constructed using a draw sequence of length 4,000 from the Markov chain constructed according to the algorithm outlined in Section 1. To assure convergence to the stationary distribution, the first 1,500 draws are discarded, leaving a sequence of length 2,500 to compute an estimate of the posterior mean. To simulate a sequence of this length takes approximately 14 minutes of Sparc 10 CPU time.

In the literature on MCMC (e.g., see McCulloch and Rossi, in press), there is extensive discussion of the dependence of results on initial conditions. We experi-mented with different starting points [the pair (ω, h)] and found no discernible differences between starting points. Examination of draw sequences from the Markov chain shows that the effect of initial conditions is rapidly dissipated in the first hundred or fewer draws. In all of the simulation experiments, we start from the point ($\omega = (- .5, .5, .1)$, and $h_t = y_t^2$). We employ extremely diffuse but

Table 9.7. Mean and root mean squared error of the Bayes estimator

$\text{Var}(h)/E[h]^2$	α	δ	σ_v	α	δ	σ_v	α	δ	σ_v
10	−.821	.9	.675	−.4106	.95	.4835	−.1642	.98	.308
	−.679	.916	.562	−.464	.94	.46	−.19	.98	.35
	(.22)	(.026)	(.12)	(.16)	(.02)	(.055)	(.08)	(.01)	(.06)
1	−.736	.9	.363	−.368	.95	.26	−.1472	.98	.166
	−.87	.88	.35	−.56	.92	.28	−.22	.97	.23
	(.34)	(.046)	(.067)	(.34)	(.046)	(.065)	(.14)	(.02)	(.08)
.1	−.706	.9	.135	−.353	.95	.0964	−.141	.98	.0614
	−1.54	.78	.15	−1.12	.84	.12	−.66	.91	.14
	(1.35)	(.19)	(.082)	(1.15)	(.16)	(.074)	(.83)	(.12)	(.099)

Note: The statistics in this table are based on 500 simulated samples, each consisting of a time series of length 500. For each cell, the top row (italics) shows the true value of the parameters. The following two rows show the mean and root mean squared error (in parentheses).

proper priors centered over the starting point for ω. Our prior standard deviations exceed the posterior standard deviations by a factor of at least 100.

The sampling performance of the Bayes estimator is dramatically superior to that of either the MM or QML estimators. In each of the six cells, both the bias and sampling variance of the Bayes estimator is smaller than either the MM or QML estimator. To summarize the relative performance of the Bayes estimator across experimental cells, we describe the distribution of the ratio of RMSE in Table 9.8. These summary statistics show that, for the parameter settings considered in the sampling experiments, the Bayes estimator dominates both the MM and QML procedures with RMSE's of less than one-half of these other procedures. This superior sampling performance also demonstrates that the convergence of our Markov chain is rapid and reliable.

The only cell in which the QML has a sampling performance near to the Bayes estimator is the $\delta = .98$ and $V_h/E_h^2 = 10$ cell and, in this cell, only for estimation of α and δ. We know of no data set that appears to have come from this region of the parameter space. The MM estimator never comes near to the performance of the Bayes estimator for α and δ, but it does perform slightly better in the estimation of σ_v for the high persistence, very low-volatility cell ($\delta = .98$, $V_h/E_h^2 = .1$). This performance may be somewhat deceptive, however, because over two-thirds of the samples in this cell have an MM surface that gives an optimum at the lower bound for $\sigma_v(.001)$. In effect, this winsorizes the MM estimator to a very favorable, in terms of RMSE, parameter estimate. If all MM estimates were truncated at the lower bound, the RMSE would be .06, even lower than the actual performance.

Figures 9.4 and 9.5 present the sampling distribution of MM, QML, and Bayes estimators for two cells in the experimental design. The substantial biases in the MM estimates of σ_v are evident in both figures. In addition, the Bayes estimator shows a much tighter (but nonnormal with substantial skewness) sampling distribution than either the QML or MM estimators. Figure 9.5 illustrates how dramatically the performance of both the MM and QML estimators degrades in situations with high persistence and low volatility in the variance equation. This situation is typical in financial data that display highly predictable short-term volatility.

Table 9.8. The distribution of the ratio of RMSE

Parameter	Relative RMSE	Median	Range
α	MM: Bayes	3.8	[1.9, 6.6]
	QML: Bayes	4.1	[1.1, 5.5]
δ	MM: Bayes	3.7	[1.8, 6.5]
	QML: Bayes	4.1	[1.1, 5.6]
σ_v	MM: Bayes	1.9	[.95, 3.3]
	QML: Bayes	3.8	[1.2, 5.5]

Stochastic Volatility

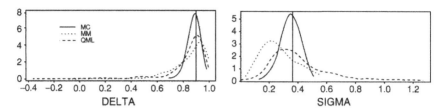

Fig. 9.4. Density of MC posterior means, QML, and MM estimates, $T = 500$, $\text{Var}(h)/E[h]^{**} = 1$, delta = .9: ———, Bayes; ·······, MM; -----, QML.

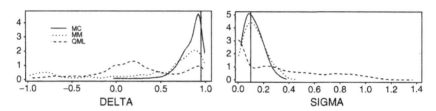

Fig. 9.5. Density of MC posterior means, QML, and MM estimates, $T = 500$, $\text{Var}(h)/E[h]^{**2} = 1$, delta = .95: ———, Bayes; ·······, MM; -----, QML.

Table 9.9 examines one of the central cells in the design for $T = 2,000$. As should be expected, the relative performance of the Bayes estimator is similar to that in the small sample with $T = 500$. For $T = 2,000$, there is little bias for any of the estimators; the superiority of the Bayes estimator ($\frac{1}{3}$ of RMSE of others) is achieved by dramatically lower sampling variability.

9.4.4 Refinements of the MM and QML approaches
Some recent developments in the MM literature hold some promise of improving the performance of the MM estimator considered here. Andersen and Sorensen

Table 9.9. Comparison of method of moments, QML, and Bayes estimators

Method	α	δ	σ_v
	$-.736$	.9	.363
MM	$-.86$	.88	.31
	(.42)	(.06)	(.10)
QML	$-.853$	.88	.383
	(.46)	(.06)	(.11)
Bayes	$-.762$	.896	.359
	(.15)	(.02)	(.034)

Note: The statistics in this table are based on 500 simulated samples. The table shows the mean and the root mean squared error (in parentheses). The true parameter values are in italics, $T = 2,000, \text{var}(h)/E[h]^2 = 1.0$.

(1993) made two refinements of the basic MM procedure: (1) They employed a penalty function to avoid nonstationary parameter estimates, and (2) they used a slightly modified weighting matrix using the weights proposed by Andrews (1991). Andersen and Sorensen replicated a portion of our sampling experiment design, facilitating direct comparison with our results. They achieved about a 25% reduction in RMSE over the numbers reported here, which still puts an MM procedure at a disadvantage relative to Bayes procedure for all except the $\delta = .98$, $V_h/E_h^2 = .1$ cell. In this cell, the Andersen and Sorensen procedure could result in a modest improvement over our current Bayes procedure.[^1]

Gallant and Tauchen (1992) suggested ways of using both parametric and nonparametric procedures to suggest which moments are important in evaluating the score function for the stochastic volatility model. Their procedure involves simulating from the stochastic volatility model at a given parameter setting and using semiparametric methods to approximate the score. Although the Gallant and Tauchen approach has some appealing asymptotic properties, its value in the estimation of stochastic volatility models remains to be determined from a thorough simulation analysis. Finally, this sort of approach may help in parameter estimation but does not help solve the nonlinear filtering and prediction problem.

Our implementation of the QML procedure assumes that it is known that the mean equation error is normal. We view this as giving the maximum possible advantage to QML procedure. It is possible, however, to make σ_η^2 an unknown parameter. Because the linear filter is an approximate method, it might be the case that by freeing this variance parameter we could achieve a better approximation. For this reason, we reran the QML sampling experiments with this parameter free in the algorithm. Overall, the results did not change much at all, with modest improvements in parameter estimation in some cells and some degradation of performance in others. Over all nine cells in the design, including σ_η^2 as a free parameter changed the RMSE for parameter estimation by no more than 15%.

9.5 Smoothing performance

As noted previously, one of the unique advantages of our method is that it provides an exact solution to the smoothing problem of estimating the unobserved variances. The smoothing problem is the problem of computing the posterior distribution of h_t given y, $p(h_t|y)$. A natural smoothed estimate would be $\hat{h}_t = E[h_t|y]$, which can be computed directly (up to simulation error) using the sequence of Markov-chain draws. In the stochastic volatility literature, approximate Kalman-filtering methods are used to approximate this solution to the smoothing problem. To evaluate the smoothing performance of various procedures, we compare our Bayesian MCMC solution to the smoothing problem to approximate Kalman-filtering methods. We consider approximate Kalman-filtering (see Appendix B for details) conditional on the true parameters, MM estimates, and the QML estimates.

Table 9.10 summarizes the smoothing performance. To evaluate the smoothing performance, we compute the grand RMSE $= [(1/NT) \sum_i \sum_t (h_t - \hat{h}_t)^2]^{.5}$ over

Table 9.10. RMSE smoothing performance of approximate Kalman filtering versus Bayes solution

Var$(h)/E[h]^2$	Method	δ		
		.9	.95	.98
10	Approx. Kalman			
	True parameters	24.2	21.1	13.5
	MM estimate	25.4	22.7	16.4
	QML estimate	23.6	22.0	13.9
	Bayes solution	21.1	17.0	12.2
1	Approx. Kalman			
	True parameters	6.74	6.04	5.60
	MM estimate	7.74	7.08	6.52
	QML estimate	7.14	6.64	6.19
	Bayes solution	5.9	5.26	5.04
.1	Approx. Kalman			
	True parameters	2.6	2.5	2.28
	MM estimate	3.0	2.9	2.55
	QML estimate	3.5	3.7	4.83
	Bayes solution	2.58	2.46	2.27

Note: The statistics in this table are based on 500 simulated samples, each consisting of a time series with $T = 500$. RMSE $\times$ 10,000 is displayed.

Table 9.11. Filtering performance

Relative RMSE	Median	Range
Approx. K filter given true parameters: Bayes	1.11	[1.004, 1.24]
Approx. K filter given MM estimates: Bayes	1.29	[1.12, 1.35]
Approx. K filter given QML estimates: Bayes	1.26	[1.12, 2.13]

all $N = 500$ samples for $t = 100, \ldots, 400$. Again we can use relative RMSE as a performance criterion for smoothing; see Table 9.11. It is remarkable that the Bayes smoothing solution dominates not only approximate Kalman filtering based on the MM and QML estimates but also the approximate Kalman-filtering solution using the true parameters.

As outlined in Section 4.4, we also considered the variant of QML, in which σ_η^2 is left as a free parameter. Freeing σ_η^2 unambiguously worsened the filtering performance. For high persistence and low volatility cells, use of the free σ_η^2 parameter can result in a very substantial degradation in filtering performance of up to a 400% increase in RMSE (for the $\delta = .98$, $V_h/E_h^2 = .1$ cell).

Finally, it should be emphasized that we can obtain estimates of the entire posterior distribution of $h_t|y$ rather than just the mean. This distribution can be used to characterize the full level of uncertainty in the smoothing estimates rather than resorting to asymptotic "plug-in" computations in which the estimation error in the parameter estimates is ignored and an asymptotic normal approximation is used.

Acknowledgements

Support from the Johnson Graduate School of Management, Cornell University, the Q Group Research Fund, and Graduate School of Business, University of Chicago, is gratefully acknowledged. We received useful comments from Torben Andersen, Orazio Attanasio, Phil Braun, Peter Carr, Rob Engle, Dan Nelson, Rob McCulloch, George Tauchen, and Mike West. We thank David Hsieh and Angelo Melino for supplying us with exchange-rate data. We thank Ken Vetzal for supplying his moment calculations, which we used to check our derivations.

Appendix A: Moments of the Stochastic log-volatility model

The model is

$$y_t = \sqrt{h_t}\, e_t = \sigma_t e_t, \quad e_t \sim N(0, 1)$$
$$\log h_t = \alpha + \delta \log h_{t-1} + \sigma_v v_t, \quad v_t \sim N(0, 1).$$

Then,

$$\log h_t \sim N\left(\frac{\alpha}{1 - \delta}, \frac{\sigma_v^2}{1 - \delta^2}\right) \sim N(\mu_h, \sigma_h^2).$$

The model in this appendix does not have mean parameters. Moreover, the correlation between e_t and v_t is assumed to be 0. For each type of moment, we write its expectation (m) and the derivative of a discrepancy function (g) with respect to each parameter. The discrepancy function is the difference between the sample moment ($\hat{m}$) and the expected value of the moment.

$E(y_t^m)$

We first compute the expectations of the moments for several values of m:

$$m_{1i} = E(y_t^i) = 0: \text{ no parameter information for } i \text{ odd}$$
$$m_{12} = E(y_t^2) = E(h_t e_t^2) = E(h_t)E(e_t^2) = e^{\mu_h + 1/2\sigma_h^2}$$
$$m_{14} = E(y_t^4) = E(h_t^2 e_t^4) = E(h_t^2)E(e_t^4) = 3e^{2\mu_h + 2\sigma_h^2}$$
$$m_{16} = E(y_t^6) = E(h_t^3 e_t^6) = E(h_t^3)E(e_t^6) = 15e^{3\mu_h + 9/2\sigma_h^2}.$$

Now compute the derivatives of the discrepancy functions:

$$g_{12} = \frac{1}{T}\sum y_t^2 - e^{\mu_h + 1/2\sigma_h^2} \equiv \hat{m}_{12} - m_{12}$$

$$\frac{\partial g_{12}}{\partial \alpha} = -m_{12}\frac{1}{1-\delta}$$

$$\frac{\partial g_{12}}{\partial \delta} = -m_{12}\left(\frac{\alpha}{(1-\delta)^2} + \frac{\delta\sigma_v^2}{(1-\delta^2)^2}\right)$$

$$= -m_{12}\left(\frac{\mu_h}{1-\delta} + \frac{\delta\sigma_h^2}{1-\delta^2}\right)$$

$$\frac{\partial g_{12}}{\partial \sigma_v} = -m_{12}\frac{\sigma_v}{1-\delta^2};$$

$$g_{14} = \frac{1}{T}\sum y_t^4 - 3e^{2\mu_h + 2\sigma_h^2} \equiv \hat{m}_{14} - m_{14}$$

$$\frac{\partial g_{14}}{\partial \alpha} = -m_{14}\frac{2}{1-\delta}$$

$$\frac{\partial g_{14}}{\partial \delta} = -m_{14}\left(\frac{2\alpha}{(1-\delta)^2} + \frac{4\delta\sigma_v^2}{(1-\delta^2)^2}\right)$$

$$= -m_{14}\left(2\mu_h 1 - \delta + \frac{4\delta\sigma_h^2}{1-\delta^2}\right)$$

$$\frac{\partial g_{14}}{\partial \sigma_v} = -m_{14}\frac{4\sigma_v}{1-\delta^2};$$

$$g_{16} = \frac{1}{T}\sum y_t^2 - 15e^{3\mu_h + 9/2\sigma_h^2} \equiv \hat{m}_{16} - m_1,$$

$$\frac{\partial g_{16}}{\partial \alpha} = -m_{16}\frac{3}{1-\delta}$$

$$\frac{\partial g_{16}}{\partial \delta} = -m_{16}\left(\frac{3\alpha}{(1-\delta)^2} + \frac{9\delta\sigma_v^2}{(1-\delta^2)^2}\right).$$

$$\frac{\partial g_{16}}{\partial \sigma_v} = -m_{16}\frac{9\sigma_v}{1-\delta^2}$$

$E(|y_t^m|)$

$$m_{21} = E(|y_t|) = E(\sigma_t|e_t|) = E(\sigma_t)E(|e_t|)$$

$$= \sqrt{\frac{2}{\pi}}e^{1/2\mu_h + 1/8\sigma_h^2}$$

$$m_{23} = E(|y_t|^3) = E(\sigma_t^3|e_t^3|) = E(\sigma_t^3)E(|e_t|^3)$$

$$= 2\sqrt{\frac{2}{\pi}}e^{3/2\mu_h + 9/8\sigma_h^2};$$

$$g_{21} = \frac{1}{T}\sum |y_t| - m_{21}$$

$$\frac{\partial g_{21}}{\partial \alpha} = -m_{21} \frac{1}{2(1-\delta)}$$

$$\frac{\partial g_{21}}{\partial \delta} = -m_{21} \left(\frac{\alpha}{2(1-\delta)^2} + \frac{\delta \sigma_v^2}{4(1-\delta^2)^2} \right)$$

$$= -m_{21} \left(\frac{\mu_h}{2(1-\delta)} + \frac{\delta \sigma_h^2}{4(1-\delta^2)} \right)$$

$$\frac{\partial g_{21}}{\partial \sigma_v} = -m_{21} \frac{\sigma_v}{4(1-\delta^2)};$$

$$g_{23} = \frac{1}{T} \sum |y_t|^3 - m_{23}$$

$$\frac{\partial g_{23}}{\partial \alpha} = -m_{23} \frac{3}{2(1-\delta)}$$

$$\frac{\partial g_{23}}{\partial \delta} = -m_{23} \left(3\alpha 2(1-\delta)^2 + \frac{9\delta \sigma_v^2}{4(1-\delta^2)^2} \right)$$

$$= -m_{21} \left(\frac{3\mu_h}{2(1-\delta)} + \frac{9\delta \sigma_h^2}{4(1-\delta^2)} \right)$$

$$\frac{\partial g_{23}}{\partial \sigma_v} = -m_{23} \frac{9\sigma_v}{4(1-\delta^2)}.$$

$E(y_t^2 y_{t-i}^2)$

$$E(y_t^2 y_{t-i}^2) = E(h_t e_t^2 h_{t-i} e_{t-i}^2)$$
$$= E(h_t h_{t-i}) E(e_t^2) E(e_{t-i}^2) = E(h_t h_{t-i}).$$

Note that

$$\log h_t = \delta^i \log h_{t-i} + \sum_{\tau=0}^{i-1} (\alpha + \sigma_v v_{t-\tau}) \delta^\tau$$

and

$$E(y_t^2 y_{t-i}^2) = E\left[h_{t-i}^{\delta^i+1} \exp\left\{ \sum_{\tau=0}^{i-1} (\alpha + \sigma_v v_{t-\tau}) \delta^\tau \right\} \right]$$

$$= E\left(h_{t-i}^{\delta^i+1} \right) E\left[\exp\left\{ \sum_{\tau=0}^{i-1} (\alpha + \sigma_v v_{t-\tau} \delta^\tau) \right\} \right]$$

$$= \exp\left\{ (1-\delta^i)\mu_h + \frac{1}{2}(1+\delta^i)^2 \sigma_h^2 + \sum_{\tau=0}^{i-1} \left(\alpha\delta^\tau + \frac{1}{2}\sigma_v^2 \delta^2 \tau \right) \right\}$$

$$= \exp\left\{ (1+\delta^i)\mu_h + \frac{1}{2}(1+\delta^i)^2 \sigma_h^2 + \alpha\frac{1-\delta^i}{1-\delta} + \frac{1}{2}\sigma_v^2 \frac{1-\delta^{2i}}{1 \quad \delta^2} \right\}$$

$$= \exp\{ 2\mu_h + \sigma_h^2(1+\delta^i) \} = m_{4,i}.$$

The derivatives are

$$\frac{\partial g_{4i}}{\partial \alpha} = -m_{4i}\frac{2}{1-\delta}$$

$$\frac{\partial g_{4i}}{\partial \delta} = -m_{4i}\left(\frac{2\mu_h}{1-\delta} + \frac{\sigma_h^2}{1-\delta^2}(i\delta^{i-1} - i\delta^{i+1} + 2\delta + 2\delta^{i+1})\right)$$

$$\frac{\partial g_{4i}}{\partial \sigma_v} = -m_{4i}2\sigma_v\frac{1+\delta^i}{1-\delta^2}.$$

$E(|y_t y_{t-i}|)$

$$\begin{aligned}
E(|y_t y_{t-i}|) &= E(\sigma_t|e_t|\sigma_{t-i}|e_{t-i}|) \\
&= E(\sigma_t\sigma_{t-i})E|e_t|E|e_{t-i}| \\
&= \frac{2}{\pi}E(\sigma_t\sigma_{t-i}).
\end{aligned}$$

Note that

$$\log\sigma_t = \delta^i\log\sigma_{t-i} + \sum_{\tau=0}^{i-1}\left(\frac{\alpha}{2} + \frac{\sigma_v}{2}v_{t-\tau}\right)\delta^\tau$$

and

$$\begin{aligned}
E|y_t y_{t-i}| &= \frac{2}{\pi}E\left[\sigma_{t-i}^{\delta^i+1}e\sum_\tau^{i-1}(\alpha + \sigma_v v_{t-\tau})\frac{\delta^\tau}{2}\right] \\
&= \frac{2}{\pi}E(\sigma_{t-i}^{\delta^i+1})E\left[\exp\left\{\sum_\tau^{i-1}(\alpha + \sigma_v v_{t-\tau})\frac{\delta^\tau}{2}\right\}\right] \\
&= \frac{2}{\pi}\exp\left\{(1+\delta^i)\frac{\mu_h}{2} + (1+\delta^i)^2\frac{\sigma_h^2}{8} + \sum_{\tau=0}^{i-1}\left(\frac{\alpha\delta^\tau}{2} + \frac{\sigma_v^2\delta^2\tau}{8}\right)\right\} \\
&= \frac{2}{\pi}\exp\left\{(1+\delta^i)\frac{\mu_h}{2} + (1+\delta^i)^2\frac{\sigma_h^2}{8} + \frac{\alpha}{2}\frac{1-\delta^i}{1-\delta} + \frac{\sigma_v^2}{8}\frac{1-\delta^{2i}}{1-\delta^2}\right\} \\
&= \frac{2}{\pi}\exp\left\{\mu_h + \frac{\sigma_h^2}{4}(1+\delta^i)\right\} \equiv m_{5i}.
\end{aligned}$$

The derivatives are

$$\frac{\partial g_{5i}}{\partial \alpha} = -m_{5i}\frac{1}{1-\delta}$$

$$\frac{\partial g_{5i}}{\partial \delta} = -m_{5i}\left(\frac{\mu_h}{1-\delta} + \frac{\sigma_h^2}{4(1-\delta^2)}(i\delta^{i-1} - i\delta^{i+1} + 2\delta + 2\delta^{i+1})\right)$$

$$\frac{\partial g_{5i}}{\partial \sigma_v} = -m_{5i}\sigma_v\frac{1+\delta^i}{2(1-\delta^2)}.$$

Corr (y_t^2, y_{t-i}^2)

$$\rho_i = \text{corr}(y_t^2, y_{t-i}^2) = (\exp\{\sigma_h^2\delta^i\} - 1)/(3\exp\{\sigma_h^2\} - 1).$$

Appendix B: Approximate Kalman filtering and QML estimation

B.1 The Kalman filter

The stochastic volatility model,

$$y_t = (h_t)^{.5}\varepsilon_t, \varepsilon_t \sim N(0, 1),$$

and

$$\log h_t = \alpha + \delta \log h_{t-1} + \sigma_v v_t, \quad v_t \sim N(0, 1),$$

can be rewritten as

$$\log(y_t^2) = -1.27 + \log h_t + \eta_t, \qquad E[\eta_t] = 0, \text{var}(\eta_t) = \pi^2/2,$$

and

$$\log h_t = \alpha + \delta \log h_{t-1} + \sigma_v v_t, \quad v_t \sim N(0, 1).$$

If the distribution of η_t is approximated by a normal distribution the preceding system becomes a standard dynamic linear model, to which the Kalman filter can be applied. The Kalman filter requires three sets of equations—a prediction and updating set which are run forward through the data, and smoothing equations, which are run backward through the data. We follow the standard notation of Anderson and Moore (1979). Let $\overline{\log h}_{t|t-1}$ be the prediction of $\log h_t$ based on the information available at time $t-1$. $\Omega_{t|t-1}$ is the variance of the prediction. Let $\overline{\log h}_{t|t}$ be the update that uses the information at time t and Ω_t the variance of the update. The equations that recursively compute the predictions and updatings are given by

$$\overline{\log h_{t \mid t-1}} = \alpha + \delta \overline{\log h_{t-1 \mid t-1}},$$
$$\Omega_{t \mid t-1} = \delta^2 \Omega_{t-1 \mid t-1} + \sigma_v^2,$$

and

$$\overline{\log h_{t \mid t}} = \overline{\log h_{t \mid t-1}}$$
$$+ \frac{\Omega_{t \mid t-1}}{f_t} \left[\log(y_t^2) + 1.27 - \overline{\log h_{t \mid t-1}} \right]$$
$$\Omega_{t \mid t} = \Omega_{t \mid t-1} \left(1 - \Omega_{t \mid t-1}/f_t \right),$$

where $f_t = \Omega_{t \mid t-1} + \pi^2/2$. Once the predictions and updates are computed for $t = 1, \ldots, T$, we can obtain the smoothed estimates, $\overline{\log h_{t \mid T}}$, which is the estimate of $\log h_t$ given all information in the sample. $\Omega_{t \mid T}$ denotes the variance of $\overline{\log h_{t \mid T}}$. The smoothing equations are

$$\overline{\log h_{t \mid T}} = \overline{\log h_{t \mid t}} + P_t \left[\overline{\log h_{t+1 \mid T}} - \overline{\log h_{t+1 \mid t}} \right]$$
$$\Omega_{t \mid T} = \Omega_{t \mid t} + P_t^2 (\Omega_{t+1 \mid T} - \Omega_{t+1 \mid t})$$

where $P_t = \delta \Omega_{t \mid t}/\Omega_{t+1 \mid t}$. The system is initialized at the unconditional values, $\Omega_0 = \sigma_v^2/(1 - \delta^2)$ and $\overline{\log h_0} = \alpha/(1 - \delta)$

The prediction, updating, and smoothing estimates of h_t are computed using standard properties of the lognormal distribution.

As discussed in Section 4.4, it is possible to refine the QML to make σ_η^2 a free parameter and avoid an assumption that η is normally distributed.

B.2 QML estimation with the Kalman filter

The quasi-likelihood is defined and computed using the predictive error decomposition (see Harvey, 1981) $\ell(\alpha, \delta, \sigma_v) \propto -1/2 \Sigma \log f_t - 1/2 \Sigma e_t^2/f_t$, where f_t is the prediction error variance just defined and e_t is the one-step-ahead prediction error, $e_t = \log(y_t^2) + 1.27 - \overline{\log h_{t \mid t-1}}$.

References

Andersen, T. G. and Sørensen, B. E. (1993). GMM Estimation of a Stochastic Volatility Model: A Monte Carlo Study, working paper, Northwestern University, J. L. Kellogg Graduate School of Management.

Anderson, B. O. and Moore, J. B. (1979). *Optimal Filtering*, Englewood Cliffs, NJ: Prentice-Hall.

Andrews, D. W. K. (1991). Heteroskedasticity and Autocorrelation Consistent Covariance Matrix Estimation. *Econometrica* 59, 817–58.

Applegate, D., Kannan, R., and Polson, N. G. (1991). Random Polynomial Time Algorithms for Sampling From Joint Distributions, working paper, Carnegie Mellon University, Statistics Dept.

Bollerslev, T. (1986). Generalized Autoregressive Conditional Heteroskedasticity. *Journal of Econometrics* 31, 307–27.

—— Chou, R. Y., and Kroner, K. F. (1992). ARCH Modeling in Finance. *Journal of Econometrics* 52, 5–59.

Carlin, B., Polson, N. G., and Stoffer, D. (1992). A Monte Carlo Approach to Non-normal and Nonlinear State-Space Modelling. *Journal of the American Statistical Association* 87, 493–500.

Clark, P. K. (1973). A Subordinated Stochastic Process Model With Finite Variances for Speculative Prices. *Econometrica* 41, 135–56.

Danielsson, J. (in press), Stochastic Volatility in Asset Prices: Estimation With Simulated Maximum Likelihood. *Journal of Econometrics* 54.

—— Richard, J.-F. (1992). Quadratic Acceleration for Monte Carlo Likelihood Evaluation, unpublished manuscript, University of Iceland, Dept. of Economics.

Foster, D. P. and Nelson, D. B. (1992). Asymptotic Filtering Theory for Univariate ARCH Models, Technical Reports, University of Chicago, Statistics Research Center, Graduate School of Business.

Gallant, A. R., Hsieh, D. A., and Tauchen, G. (1991). On Fitting a Recalcitrant Series: The Pound/Dollar Exchange Rates, 1974–83, in *Nonparametric and Semiparametric Methods in Econometrics and Statistics, Proceedings of the Fifth International Symposium in Economic Theory and Econometrics,* (eds.) Barnett, W. A., Powell, J., and Tauchen, G., Cambridge, U.K.: Cambridge University Press.

—— Rossi, P. E., and Tauchen, G. (1992). Stock Prices and Volume. *The Review of Financial Studies* 5, 199–242.

—— Tauchen G. (1992). Which Moments to Match, unpublished manuscript, University of North Carolina, Dept. of Economics.

Gelfand, A. and Smith, A. F. M. (1990). Sampling-Based Approaches to Calculating Marginal Densities. *Journal of the American Statistical Association* 85, 398–409.

Geman, S. and Geman, D. (1984). Stochastic Relaxation, Gibbs Distributions and the Bayesian Restoration of Images. *IEEE Transactions on Pattern Analysis and Machine Intelligence* 6, 721–41.

Geweke, J. (1992). Evaluating the Accuracy of Sampling-Based Approaches to the Calculation of Posterior Moments, in *Bayesian Statistics 4,* (eds.) Bernardo, J. M. et al., Oxford.: Oxford University Press, pp. 169–93.

Hansen, L. P. (1982). Large Sample Properties of Generalized Method of Moments Estimators. *Econometrica* 50, 1029–54.

Harvey, A. C. (1981). *Time Series Models,* New York: John Wiley.

—— Ruiz, E., and Shephard, N. (1994). Multivariate Stochastic Variance Models. *Review of Economic Studies* 61, 247–64.

Hsieh, D. A. (1991). Chaos and Nonlinear Dynamics: Applications to Financial Markets. *Journal of Finance* 46, 1839–77.

Hull, J. and White, A. (1987). The Pricing of Options on Assets With Stochastic Volatilities. *Journal of Finance* 42, 281–300.

Jacquier, E., Polson, N. G., and Rossi, P. E. (1993). Priors and Models for Multivariate Stochastic Volatility, unpublished manuscript, University of Chicago, Graduate School of Business.

McCulloch, R. E. and Rossi, P. E. (in press). An Exact Likelihood Analysis of the Multinomial Probit Model. *Journal of Econometrics* 54.

—— Tsay, R. S. (1993). Bayesian Inference and Prediction for Mean and Variance Shifts in Autoregressive Time Series. *Journal of the American Statistical Association* 88, 968–78.

Melino, A. and Turnbull, S. M. (1990). Pricing Foreign Currency Options With Stochastic Volatility. *Journal of Econometrics* 45, 7–39.

Muller, P. (1991). A Dynamic Vector ARCH Model for Exchange Rate Data, unpublished manuscript, Duke University, Institute for Statistics and Decision Sciences.

Nelson, D. B. (1988). Time Series Behavior of Stock Market Volatility and Returns, unpublished Ph.D. dissertation, Massachusetts Institute of Technology, Economics Dept.

—— (1991). Conditional Heteroskedasticity in Asset Returns: A New Approach. *Econometrica* 59, 347–70.

Ripley, B. D. (1987). *Stochastic Simulation*, New York: John Wiley.

Ruiz, E. (1994). Quasi-Maximum Likelihood Estimation of Stochastic Variance Models. *Journal of Econometrics* 63, 284–306.

Shephard, N. (1993). Fitting Nonlinear Time Series Models With Applications to Stochastic Variance Models. *Journal of Applied Econometrics* 8, S135–S152.

Tanner, M. A. and Wong, W. H. (1987). The Calculation of Posterior Distributions By Data Augmentation. *Journal of the American Statistical Association* 82, 528–49.

Tauchen, G. and Pitts, M. (1983). The Price Variability–Volume Relationship on Speculative Markets. *Econometrica* 51, 485–505.

Taylor, S. J. (1986). *Modelling Financial Time Series*, New York: John Wiley.

Tierney, L. (1991). Markov Chains for Exploring Posterior Distributions, Technical Report 560, University of Minnesota, School of Statistics.

Vetzal, K. (1992). Stochastic Short Rate Volatility and the Pricing of Bonds and Bond Options, unpublished Ph.D. thesis, University of Toronto, Dept. of Economics.

Wiggins, J. B. (1987). Options Values Under Stochastic Volatility: Theory and Empirical Evidence. *Journal of Financial Economics* 19, 351–72.

Uhlig, H. (1991). BVARTEC—Bayesian Vector Autoregressions With Time Varying Error Covariances, working paper, Princeton University, Dept. of Economics.

10

Stochastic Volatility: Likelihood Inference and Comparison with ARCH Models*

SANGJOON KIM, NEIL SHEPHARD

AND

SIDDHARTHA CHIB

In this paper, Markov chain Monte Carlo sampling methods are exploited to provide a unified, practical likelihood-based framework for the analysis of stochastic volatility models. A highly effective method is developed that samples all the unobserved volatilities at once using an approximating offset mixture model, followed by an importance reweighting procedure. This approach is compared with several alternative methods using real data. The paper also develops simulation-based methods for filtering, likelihood evaluation and model failure diagnostics. The issue of model choice using non-nested likelihood ratios and Bayes factors is also investigated. These methods are used to compare the fit of stochastic volatility and GARCH models. All the procedures are illustrated in detail.

10.1 Introduction

The variance of returns on assets tends to change over time. One way of modelling this feature of the data is to let the conditional variance be a function of the squares of previous observations and past variances. This leads to the autoregressive conditional heteroscedasticity (ARCH) based models developed by Engle (1982) and surveyed in Bollerslev, Engle and Nelson (1994).

An alternative to the ARCH framework is a model in which the variance is specified to follow some latent stochastic process. Such models, referred to as stochastic volatility (SV) models, appear in the theoretical finance literature on option pricing (see, for example, Hull and White (1987) in their work generalizing the Black–Scholes option pricing formula to allow for stochastic volatility). Empirical versions of the SV model are typically formulated in discrete time. The canonical model in this class for regularly spaced data is

$$y_t = \beta e^{h_t/2} \varepsilon_t, \qquad t \geq 1,$$
$$h_{t+1} = \mu + \phi(h_t - \mu) + \sigma_\eta \eta_t,$$
$$h_1 \sim \mathcal{N}\left(\mu, \frac{\sigma^2}{1 - \phi^2}\right), \tag{1}$$

* This work was previously published as S. Kim, N. Shephard, and S. Chib (1998), 'Stochastic Volatility: Likelihood Inference and Comparison with ARCH models' *Review of Economic Studies*, 65. Copyright © The Review of Economic Studies Ltd. Published by Blackwell Publishing. Reproduced by kind permission.

where y_t is the mean corrected return on holding the asset at time t, h_t is the log volatility at time t which is assumed to follow a stationary process ($|\phi| < 1$) with h_1 drawn from the stationary distribution, ε_t and η_t are uncorrelated standard normal white noise shocks and $\mathcal{N}(.,.)$ is the normal distribution. The parameter β or $\exp(\mu/2)$ plays the role of the constant scaling factor and can be thought of as the modal instantaneous volatility, ϕ as the persistence in the volatility, and σ_η the volatility of the log-volatility. For indentifiability reasons either β must be set to one or μ to zero. We show later that the parameterization with β equal to one is preferable and so we shall leave μ unrestricted when we estimate the model but report results for $\beta = \exp(\mu/2)$ as this parameter has more economic interpretation.

This model has been used as an approximation to the stochastic volatility diffusion by Hull and White (1987) and Chesney and Scott (1989). Its basic econometric properties are discussed in Taylor (1986), the review papers by Taylor (1994), Shephard (1996) and Ghysels, Harvey and Renault (1996) and the paper by Jacquier, Polson and Rossi (1994). These papers also review the existing literature on the estimation of SV models.

In this paper we make advances in a number of different directions and provide the first complete Markov chain Monte Carlo simulation-based analysis of the SV model (1) that covers efficient methods for Bayesian inference, likelihood evaluation, computation of filtered volatility estimates, diagnostics for model failure, and computation of statistics for comparing non-nested volatility models. Our study reports on several interesting findings. We consider a very simple Bayesian method for estimating the SV model (based on one-at-a-time updating of the volatilities). This sampler is shown to be quite inefficient from a simulation perspective. An improved (multi-move) method that relies on an offset mixture of normals approximation to a log-chi-square distribution coupled with an importance reweighting procedure is shown to be strikingly more effective. Additional refinements of the latter method are developed to reduce the number of blocks in the Markov chain sampling. We report on useful plots and diagnostics for detecting model failure in a dynamic (filtering) context. The paper also develops formal tools for comparing the basic SV and Gaussian and t-GARCH models. We find that the simple SV model typically fits the data as well as more heavily parameterized GARCH models. Finally, we consider a number of extensions of the SV model that can be fitted using our methodology.

The outline of this paper is as follows. Section 10.2 contains preliminaries. Section 10.3 details the new algorithms for fitting the SV model. Section 10.4 contains methods for simulation-based filtering, diagnostics and likelihood evaluations. The issue of comparing the SV and GARCH models is considered in Section 10.5. Section 10.6 provides extensions while Section 10.7 concludes. A description of software for fitting these models that is available through the internet is provided in Section 10.8. Two algorithms used in the paper are provided in the Appendix.

10.2 Preliminaries

10.2.1 Quasi-likelihood method

A key feature of the basic SV model in (1) is that it can be transformed into a linear model by taking the logarithm of the squares of observations

$$\log y_t^2 = h_t + \log \varepsilon_t^2, \tag{2}$$

where $E(\log \varepsilon_t^2) = -1.2704$ and $\text{Var}(\log \varepsilon_t^2) = 4.93$. Harvey, Ruiz, and Shephard (1994) have employed Kalman filtering to estimate the parameters $\theta = (\phi, \sigma_\eta^2, \mu) \in (-1, 1) \times \Re_+ \times \Re$ by maximizing the quasi likelihood

$$\log L_Q(y|\theta) = -\frac{n}{2}\log 2\pi - \frac{1}{2}\sum_{t=1}^{n}\log F_t - \frac{1}{2}\sum_{t=1}^{n} v_t^2/F_t,$$

where $y = (y_1, \ldots, y_n)$, v_t is the one-step-ahead prediction error for the best linear estimator of $\log y_t^2$ and F_t is the corresponding mean square error.[1] It turns out that this quasi-likelihood estimator is consistent and asymptotically normally distributed but is suboptimal in finite samples because $\log \varepsilon_t^2$ is poorly approximated by the normal distribution, as shown in Figure 10.1. As a consequence, the quasi-likelihood estimator under the assumption that $\log \varepsilon_t^2$ is normal has poor small sample properties, even though the usual quasi-likelihood asymptotic theory is correct.

10.2.2 Markov chain Monte Carlo

An alternative, exact approach to inference in the SV model is based on Markov chain Monte Carlo (MCMC) methods, namely the Metropolis–Hastings and Gibbs sampling algorithms. These methods have had a widespread influence on the theory and practice of Bayesian inference. Early work on these methods appears in Metropolis, Rosenbluth, Rosenbluth, Teller and Teller (1953), Hastings (1970), Ripley (1977) and Geman and Geman (1984) while some of the more recent developments, spurred by Tanner and Wong (1987) and Gelfand and Smith (1990), are included in Chib and Greenberg (1996), Gilks, Richardson and Spiegelhalter (1996) and Tanner (1996, ch. 6). Chib and Greenberg (1995) provide a detailed exposition of the Metropolis–Hastings algorithm and include a derivation of the algorithm from the logic of reversibility.

The idea behind MCMC methods is to produce variates from a given multivariate density (the posterior density in Bayesian applications) by repeatedly sampling a Markov chain whose invariant distribution is the target density of interest. There are typically many different ways of constructing a Markov chain with this property and one goal of this paper is to isolate those that are simulation–efficient

---

[1] The Kalman filter algorithms for computing v_t and F_t are given in the Appendix.

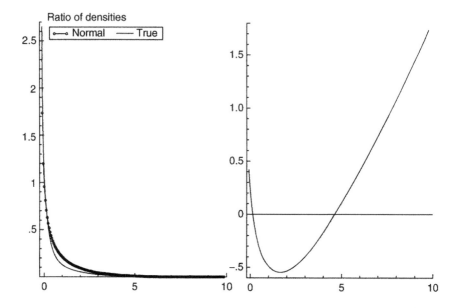

Fig. 10.1. Log-normal approximation to χ^2_1 density. Left is the χ^2_1 density and the log-normal approximation which is used in the quasi-likelihood approach. Right is the log of the ratio of the χ^2_1 density to the approximation.

in the context of SV models. In our problem, one key issue is that the likelihood function $f(y|\theta) = \int f(y|h, \theta)f(h|\theta)dh$ is intractable. This precludes the direct analysis of the posterior density MCMC methods. This problem can be overcome by focusing instead on the density $\pi(\theta, h/y)$, where $h = (h_1, \ldots, h_n)$ is the vector of n latent volatilities. Markov chain Monte Carlo procedures can be developed to sample this density without computation of the likelihood function $f(y|\theta)$. It should be kept in mind that sample variates from a MCMC algorithm are a high-dimensional (correlated) sample from the target density of interest. These draws can be used as the basis for making inferences by appealing to suitable ergodic theorems for Markov chains. For example, posterior moments and marginal densities can be estimated (simulation consistently) by averaging the relevant function of interest over the sampled variates. The posterior mean of θ is simply estimated by the sample mean of the simulated θ values. These estimates can be made arbitrarily accurate by increasing the simulation sample size. The accuracy of the resulting estimates (the so called numerical standard error) can be assessed by standard time series methods that correct for the serial correlation in the draws. The serial correlation can be quite high for badly behaved algorithms.

10.2.2.1 An initial Gibbs sampling algorithm for the SV model
For the problem of simulating a multivariate density $\pi(\psi|y)$, the Gibbs sampler is defined by a blocking scheme $\psi = (\psi_1, \ldots, \psi_d)$ and the associated full

conditional distributions $\psi_i | \psi_{\backslash i}$, where $\psi_{\backslash i}$ denotes ψ excluding the block ψ_i. The algorithm proceeds by sampling each block from the full conditional distributions where the most recent values of the conditioning blocks are used in the simulation. One cycle of the algorithm is called a sweep or a scan. Under regularity conditions, as the sampler is repeatedly swept, the draws from the sampler converge to draws from the target density at a geometric rate. For the SV model the ψ vector becomes (h, θ). To sample ψ from the posterior density, one possibility (suggested by Jacquier, Polson and Rossi (1994) and Shephard (1993)) is to update each of the elements of the ψ vector one at a time.

1. Initialize h and θ.
2. Sample h_t from $h_t | h_{\backslash t}, y, \theta, t = 1, \dots, n$.
3. Sample $\sigma_\eta^2 | y, h, \phi, \mu, \beta$.
4. Sample $\phi | h, \mu, \beta, \sigma_\eta^2$.
5. Sample $\mu | h, \phi, \sigma_\eta^2$.
6. Goto 2.

Cycling through 2 to 5 is a complete sweep of this (single move) sampler. The Gibbs sampler will require us to perform many thousands of sweeps to generate samples from $\theta, h | y$.

The most difficult part of this sampler is to effectively sample from $h_t | h_{\backslash t}, y_t, \theta$ as this operation has to be carried out n times for each sweep. However,

$$f(h_t | h_{\backslash t}, \theta, y) \propto f(h_t | h_{\backslash t}, \theta) f(y_t | h_t, \theta), \qquad t = 1, \dots, n.$$

We sample this density by developing a simple accept/reject procedure.[2] Let $f_N(t | a, b)$ denote the normal density function with mean a and variance b. It can be shown (ignoring end conditions to save space) that

$$f(h_t | h_{\backslash t}, \theta) = f(h_t | h_{t-1}, h_{t+1}, \theta) = f_N(h_t | h_t^*, v^2),$$

---

[2] Other MCMC algorithms for simulating from $h_t | h_{t-1}, h_{t+1}, y_t; \theta$ have been given in the literature by Shephard (1993), Jacquier, Polson and Rossi (1994), Shephard and Kim (1994), Geweke (1994) and Shephard and Pitt (1997). The closest to our suggestion is Geweke (1994) who also bounded $\log f^*$, but by $-0.5 h_t$. This suffers from the property of having a high rejection rate for slightly unusual observations (for example, 0·9 for $|y_t| / \beta \exp(h_t/2) > 3$). Shephard and Pitt (1997), on the other hand, used a quadratic expansion of $\log f^*$ about h_t^*. This increases the generality of the procedure but it involves a Metropolis rejection step and so is more involved. Shephard (1993) approximated f^* by a normal distribution with the same moments as $\log \varepsilon_t^2$.

Geweke (1994) and Shephard and Kim (1994) independently suggested the use of the Gilks and Wild (1992) procedure for sampling from log concave densities such as $\log f(h_t | h_{\backslash t}, \theta, y)$. This is generalizable to non-log-concave densities using the Gilks, Best and Tan (1995) sampler. Typically these routines need about 10 to 12 evaluations of $\log f(h_t | h_{\backslash t}, \theta, y)$ to draw a single random variable. Hence they are about 10 times less efficient than the simple accept/reject algorithm given above.

Jacquier, Polson and Rossi (1994)'s Metropolis algorithm uses a very different approach. They approximate the density of $h_t | h_{\backslash t}$ and so use a non-Gaussian proposal based on f^*. Typically this procedure is considerably slower than the use of the Gilks and Wild (1992) methods suggested above.

where

$$h_t^* = \mu + \frac{\phi\{(h_{t-1} - \mu) + (h_{t+1} - \mu)\}}{(1 + \phi^2)}$$

and

$$v^2 = \frac{\sigma_\eta^2}{1 + \phi^2}.$$

Next we note that $\exp(-h_t)$ is a convex function and can be bounded by a function linear in h_t. Let $\log f(y_t|h_t, \theta) = \text{const} + \log f^*(y_t, h_t, \theta)$. Then

$$\begin{aligned}
\log f^*(y_t, h_t, \theta) &= -\frac{1}{2}h_t - \frac{y_t^2}{2}\{\exp(-h_t)\} \\
&\leq -\frac{1}{2}h_t - \frac{y_t^2}{2}\{\exp(-h_t^*)(1 + h_t^*) - h_t\exp(-h_t^*)\} \\
&= \log g^*(y_t, h_t, \theta, h_t^*).
\end{aligned}$$

Hence

$$f(h_t|h_{\backslash t}, \theta)f^*(y_t, h_t, \theta) \leq f_N(h_t|h_t^*, v^2)g^*(y_t, h_t, \theta, h_t^*).$$

The terms on the right-hand side can be combined and shown to be proportional to $f_N(h_t|\mu_t, v^2)$ where

$$\mu_t = h_t^* + \frac{v^2}{2}[y_t^2 \exp(-h_t^*) - 1]. \tag{3}$$

With these results, the accept–reject procedure (Ripley (1987)) to sample h_t from $f(h_t|h_{\backslash t}, \theta, y)$ can now be implemented. First, propose a value h_t from $f_N(h_t|\mu_t, v^2)$. Second, accept this value with probability f^*/g^*; if rejected return to the first step and make a new proposal.[3]

Sampling σ_η^2 and ϕ Sampling the σ_η^2 and ϕ one at a time is straightforward. If we assume a conjugate prior $\sigma_\eta^2|\phi, \mu \sim \mathscr{IG}(\sigma_r/2, S_\sigma/2)$, then σ_η^2 is sampled from

$$\sigma_\eta^2|y, h, \phi, \mu \sim \mathscr{IG}\left\{\frac{n + \sigma_r}{2}, \frac{S_\sigma + (h_1 - \mu)^2(1 - \phi^2) + \sum_{t=1}^{n-1}((h_{t+1} - \mu) - \phi(h_t - \mu))^2}{2}\right\}, \tag{4}$$

[3] This proposal has an average acceptance rate of approximately $1 - y_t^2\exp(-h_t^*)v_t^2/(4\beta^2)$. A typical situation is where $v_t^2 = 0\cdot01$. Usually $y_t^2\exp(-h_t^*)v_t^2/\beta^2$ will not be very large as h_t^* is the smoothed log-volatility of y_t and so reflects the variation in y_t. An extreme case is where $y_t^2\exp(-h_t^*)\sigma_t^2/\beta^2 = 100$, which leads to an average acceptance rate of approximately $0\cdot75$. In our experience an average acceptance rate of over $0\cdot995$ seems usual for real financial datasets.

where $\mathscr{IG}$ denotes the inverse-gamma distribution. Throughout we set $\sigma_r = 5$ and $S_\sigma = 0.01 \times \sigma_r$.

For ϕ, sampling from the full conditional density is also easy. Let $\phi = 2\phi^* - 1$ where ϕ^* is distributed as Beta with parameters $(\phi^{(1)}, \phi^{(2)})$. Hence, our prior on ϕ is

$$
\pi(\phi) \propto \left\{ \frac{(1+\phi)}{2} \right\}^{\phi^{(1)}-1} \left\{ \frac{(1-\phi)}{2} \right\}^{\phi^{(2)}-1}, \quad \phi^{(1)}, \phi^{(2)} > \frac{1}{2}, \tag{5}
$$

and has support on the interval $(-1, 1)$ with a prior mean of $\{2\phi^{(1)}/ (\phi^{(1)} + \phi^{(2)}) - 1\}$. In our work we will select $\phi^{(1)} = 20$ and $\phi^{(2)} = 1.5$, implying a prior mean of 0.86. Alternative priors could also be used. For example, the flat prior $\pi(\phi) \propto 1$ is attractive in that it leads to an analytically tractable full conditional density. But this prior can cause problems when the data are close to being non-stationary (Phillips (1991) and Schotman and Van Dijk (1991)). Chib and Greenberg (1994) and Marriott and Smith (1992) discuss other priors (restricted to the stationary region) for autoregressive models. We feel that it is important from a data-analytic view to impose stationarity in the SV model. Further, if $\phi = 1$ then the μ terms cancel in (1) and so μ becomes unidentified from the data. The prior we select avoids these two problems rather well.

Under the specified prior, the full conditional density of ϕ is proportional to

$$
\pi(\phi) f(h|\mu, \phi, \sigma_\eta^2),
$$

where

$$
\log f(h|\mu, \phi, \sigma_\eta^2) \propto -\frac{(h_1 - \mu)^2 (1 - \phi^2)}{2\sigma_\eta^2} + \frac{1}{2} \log(1 - \phi^2) \\
- \frac{\sum_{t=1}^{n-1} \{(h_{t+1} - \mu) - \phi(h_t - \mu)\}^2}{2\sigma_\eta^2}, \tag{6}
$$

This function is concave in ϕ for all values of $\phi^{(1)}, \phi^{(2)}$. This means that ϕ can be sampled using an acceptance algorithm. Employ a first order Taylor expansion of the prior about

$$
\hat{\phi} = \sum_{t=1}^{n-1} (h_{t+1} - \mu)(h_t - \mu) / \sum_{t=1}^{n-1} (h_t - \mu)^2,
$$

and combine with $f(h|\mu, \phi, \sigma^2)$. The resulting density provides a good suggestion density. Alternatively, one can specialize the method of Chib and Greenberg (1994) (which is based on the Metropolis–Hastings algorithm). Given the current value $\phi^{(i-1)}$ at the $(i-1)$-st iteration, sample a proposal value ϕ^* from $N(\hat{\phi}, V_\phi)$ where $V_\phi = \sigma_\eta^2 \{\sum_{t=1}^{n-1} (h_t - \mu)^2\}^{-1}$. Then, provided ϕ^* is in the stationary region, accept this proposal value as $\phi^{(i)}$ with probability $\exp\{g(\phi^*) - g(\phi^{(i-1)})\}$ where

$$g(\phi) = \log \pi(\phi) - \frac{(h_1 - \mu)^2(1 - \phi^2)}{2\sigma_\eta^2} + \frac{1}{2}\log(1 - \phi^2).$$

If the proposal value is rejected, set $\phi^{(i)}$ to equal $\phi^{(i-1)}$. Both these approaches can be used with alternative priors on ϕ.

Sampling μ Suppose we work with a diffuse prior[4] on μ, then μ is sampled from the full conditional density

$$\mu | h, \phi, \sigma_\eta^2 \sim \mathcal{N}(\hat{\mu}, \sigma_\mu^2), \tag{7}$$

where

$$\hat{\mu} = \sigma_\mu^2 \left\{ \frac{(1 - \phi^2)}{\sigma_\eta^2} h_1 + \frac{(1 - \phi)}{\sigma_\eta^2} \sum_{t=1}^{n-1} (h_{t+1} - \phi h_t) \right\},$$

and

$$\sigma_\mu^2 = \sigma_\eta^2 \{(n - 1)(1 - \phi)^2 + (1 - \phi^2)\}^{-1}.$$

In our work we sample μ and record the value $\beta = \exp(\mu/2)$.

Illustration To illustrate this algorithm we analyse the daily observations of weekday close exchange rates for the U.K. Sterling/U.S. Dollar exchange rate from 1/10/81 to 28/6/85. The sample size is $n = 946$. Later in the paper we will also use the corresponding series for the German Deutschmark (DM), Japanese Yen and Swiss Franc (SwizF), all against the U.S. Dollar. This data set has been previously analysed using quasi-likelihood methods in Harvey, Ruiz and Shephard (1994). The mean-corrected returns will be computed as

$$y_t = 100 \times \left\{ (\log r_t - \log r_{t-1}) - \frac{1}{n} \sum_{i=1}^{n} (\log r_i - \log r_{i-1}) \right\}, \tag{8}$$

where r_t denotes the exchange rate at time t. The MCMC sampler was initialized by setting all the $h_t = 0$ and $\phi = 0.95, \sigma_\eta^2 = 0.02$ and $\mu = 0$. We iterated the algorithm on the log-volatilities for 1000 iterations and then the parameters and log-volatilities for 50,000 more iterations, before recording the draws from

---

[4] Occasionally, for technical reasons, we take a slightly informative prior such as $\mu \sim N(0, 10)$. In this paper, this prior was used for the computation of Bayes factors.

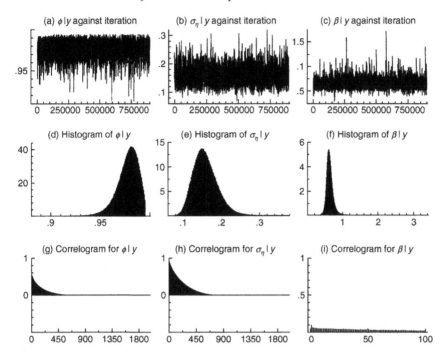

Fig. 10.2. Single move Gibbs sampler for the Sterling series. Graphs (a)–(c): simulations against iteration. Graphs (d)–(f): histograms of marginal distribution. Graphs (g)–(i): corresponding correlograms for simulation. In total 1,000,000 iterations were drawn, discarding the first 50,000.

a subsequent 1,000,000 sweeps. The burn-in period is thus much larger than what is customary in the literature and is intended to ensure that the effect of the starting values becomes insignificant. As a result, there is likely to be no additional information from running multiple chains from dispersed starting values. The complete 1,000,000 iterations[5] are graphed in Figure 10.2 and summarized in Table 10.1.[6]

The summary statistics of Table 10.1 report the *simulation inefficiency* factors of the sampler. These are estimated as the variance of the sample mean from the MCMC sampling scheme (the square of the numerical standard error) divided by

---

[5] We have employed a 32 bit version of the modified Park and Miller (1988) uniform random number as the basis of all our random numbers. This has a period of $2^{31} - 1$, which allows us to draw around 2.1 billion random numbers. In these experiments we are drawing approximately $n \times 2 \times 1.05$ random numbers per sweep of the sampler, where 5% is a very conservative estimate of the overall rejection rate. For this dataset this is 1984 draws per sweep. Given that we employ 1,000,000 sweeps, we are close, but not beyond, the period of our random number generator.

[6] Timings will be given for all the computations given in this paper. These are made using the authors C++ code which has been linked to Ox. The single move algorithm is optimized to this special case and so is about as fast as it is possible to make it. The latter algorithms are much more general and so it is not completely fair to compare the computed time reported here to their times.

Table 10.1. Daily returns for Sterling: summaries of Figure 10.2. The Monte
Carlo S.E. of simulation is computed using a bandwidth, B_M, of 2000, 4000
and 2000 respectively. Italics are correlations rather than covariances of the
posterior. Computer time is seconds on a Pentium Pro/200. The other time
is the number of seconds to perform 100 sweeps of the sampler

	Mean	MC S.E.	Inefficiency	Covariance and correlation		
$\phi\|y$	0.97762	0.00013754	163.55	0.00011062	−0.684	*0.203*
$\sigma_\eta\|y$	0.15820	0.00063273	386.80	−0.00022570	0.00098303	−0.129
$\beta\|y$	0.64884	0.00036464	12.764	0.00021196	−0.00040183	0.0098569
Time	3829.5	0.58295				

the variance of the sample mean from a hypothetical sampler which draws
independent random variables from the posterior (the variance divided by the
number of iterations). We think that the simulation inefficiency statistic is a
useful diagnostic (but by no means the only one) for measuring how well the
chain mixes. The numerical standard error of the sample mean is estimated by
time series methods (to account for the serial correlation in the draws) as

$$\hat{R}_{B_M} = 1 + \frac{2B_M}{B_M - 1} \sum_{i=1}^{B_M} K\left(\frac{i}{B_M}\right) \hat{\rho}(i),$$

where $\hat{\rho}(i)$ is an estimate of the autocorrelation at lag i of the MCMC sampler,
B_M represents the bandwidth and K the Parzen kernel (see, for example, Priestley
(1981, ch. 6)) given by

$$K(z) = 1 - 6z^2 + 6z^3, \quad z \in [0, \frac{1}{2}],$$
$$= 2(1 - z)^3, \quad z \in [\frac{1}{2}, 1],$$
$$= 0, \quad \text{elsewhere.}$$

The correlogram (autocorrelation function) indicates important autocorrelations for ϕ and σ_η at large lag lengths. If we require the Monte Carlo error in
estimating the mean of the posterior to be no more than one percentage
of the variation of the error due to the data, then this Gibb sampler would
have to be run for around 40,000 iterations. This seems a reasonably typical
result: see Table 10.2.

Parameterization An alternative to this sampler is to replace the draw for
$\mu|h, \phi, \sigma_\eta^2$ with that resulting from the alternative parameterization $\beta|y, h$. Such
a move would be a mistake. Table 10.3 reports the inefficiency factor for this

Table 10.2.   Bandwidth B_M was 2000, 4000 and 2000, respectively for the parameters, for all series. In all cases 1,000,000 sweeps were used

Series	$\phi \mid y$		$\sigma_\eta \mid y$		$\beta \mid y$	
	Mean	Inefficiency	Mean	Inefficiency	Mean	Inefficiency
DM	0.96496	122.77	1.15906	292.81	0.65041	15.762
Yen	0.98010	313.03	0.12412	676.35	0.53597	14.192
SwizF	0.95294	145.48	0.20728	231.15	0.70693	13.700

Table 10.3.   Bandwidth B_M was 4000, 4000 and 15,000, respectively for the parameters. 1,000,000 sweeps were used

Series	$\phi \mid y$		$\sigma_\eta \mid y$		$\beta \mid y$	
	Mean	Inefficiency	Mean	Inefficiency	Mean	Inefficiency
Sterling	0.97793	465.30	0.15744	439.73	0.64280	5079.6

sampler using 1,000,000 draws of this sampler. There is a small deterioration in the sampler for $\phi \mid y$ and a very significant reduction in efficiency for $\beta \mid y$. The theoretical explanation for the inadequacies of the β parameterization is provided by Pitt and Shephard (1998).

Reason for slow convergence   The intuition for the slow convergence reported in Table 10.1 is that the components of $h \mid y, \theta$ are highly correlated and in such cases sampling each component from the full conditional distribution produces little movement in the draws, and hence slowly decaying autocorrelations (Chib and Greenberg (1996)). For analytical results, one can think of the Gaussian equivalent of this problem. Under the Gaussian assumption and the linear approximation (2) and (1), the sampler in the simulation of h from $h \mid y, \theta$ has an analytic convergence rate of (Pitt and Shephard (1998, Theorem 1))

$$4\phi^2/\{1 + \phi^2 + \sigma_\eta^2/\mathrm{Var}(\log \varepsilon_t^2)\}^2,$$

where θ is taken as fixed at the expected values given in the results for the Sterling series. If $\mathrm{Var}(\log \varepsilon_t^2)$ is set equal to 4.93, then this result implies a geometric convergence rate of $\rho_A = 0.9943$ and an inefficiency factor of $(1 + \rho_A)/(1 - \rho_A)$ = 350 which is in the range reported in Table 10.1.

   In order to improve the above sampler it is necessary to try to sample the log-volatilities in a different way. One method is to sample groups of consecutive log volatilities using a Metropolis algorithm. This is investigated in Shephard and Pitt (1997). In this paper we detail a more ambitious model specific approach. This approach is described next.

10.3 Improved MCMC algorithms

In this section we design an offset mixture of normals distribution (defined below) to accurately approximate the exact likelihood. This approximation helps in the production of an efficient (adapted Gibbs sampler) Monte Carlo procedure that allows us to sample all the log-volatilities at once. We then show how one can make the analysis exact by correcting for the (minor) approximation error by reweighting the posterior output.

10.3.1 Offset mixture representation

Our approximating parametric model for the linear approximation (2) will be an offset mixture time series model

$$y_t^* = h_t + z_t, \tag{9}$$

where $y_t^* = \log(y_t^2 + c)$ and

$$f(z_t) = \sum_{i=1}^{K} q_i f_N(z_t | m_i - 1.2704, v_i^2),$$

is a mixture of K normal densities f_N with component probabilities q_i, means $m_i - 1.2704$, and variances v_i^2. The constants $\{q_i, m_i, v_i^2\}$ are selected to closely approximate the exact density of $\log \varepsilon_t^2$. The "offset" c was introduced into the SV literature by Fuller (1996, pp. 494–497) in order to robustify the QML estimator of the SV model to y_t^2 being very small. Throughout we will set $c = 0.001$ (although it is possible to let c depend on the actual value taken by y_t^2). It should be noted that the mixture density can also be written in terms of a component indicator variable s_t such that

$$
\begin{aligned}
z_t | s_t = i &\sim \mathcal{N}(m_i - 1.2704, v_i^2), \\
\Pr(s_t = i) &= q_i.
\end{aligned}
\tag{10}
$$

This representation will be used below in the MCMC formulation.

We are now in a position to select K and $\{m_i, q_i, v_i^2\}(i \leq K)$ to make the mixture approximation "sufficiently good". In our work, following for instance Titterington, Smith, and Makov (1985, p. 133), we matched the first four moments of $f_{\exp(z)}(r)$ (the implied log-normal distribution) and $f(z_t)$ to those of a χ_1^2 and $\log \chi_1^2$ random variable respectively, and required that the approximating densities lie within a small distance of the true density. This was carried out by using a non-linear least squares program to move the weights, means and variances around until the answers were satisfactory. It is worth noting that this nonlinear optimization incurs only a one-time cost, as there are no model-dependent parameters involved. We found what we judged to be satisfactory answers by setting $K = 7$. The implied weights, means and variances are given in Table 10.4, while the approximating and the true density are drawn in Figure 10.3. It would be easy

Table 10.4. Selection of the mixing distribution to be $\log \chi_1^2$

ω	$\Pr(\omega = i)$	m_i	σ_i^2
1	0.00730	−10.12999	5.79596
2	0.10556	−3.97281	2.61369
3	0.00002	−8.56686	5.17950
4	0.04395	2.77786	0.16735
5	0.34001	0.61942	0.64009
6	0.24566	1.79518	0.34023
7	0.25750	−1.08819	1.26261

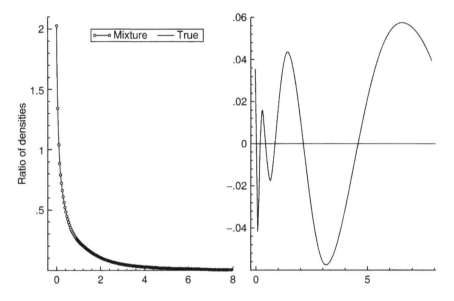

Fig. 10.3. Mixture approximation to χ_1^2 density. Left: χ_1^2 density and mixture approximation. Right: the log of the ratio of the χ_1^2 density to the mixture approximation.

to improve the fit by increasing the value of K, however further experiments that we have conducted suggest that increasing K has little discernible effect on our main results.

10.3.2 Mixture simulator

In the MCMC context, mixture models are best estimated by exploiting the representation in (10). The general algorithm for state space models was suggested independently by Shephard (1994) and Carter and Kohn (1994). The posterior density of interest is $\pi(s, h, \phi, \sigma_\eta^2, \mu | y^*)$, where $s = (s_1, \ldots, s_n)$. In this case, both h and s can be sampled separately in one block and the sampler takes the form:

1. Initialize s, ϕ, σ_η^2 and μ.
2. Sample h from $h|y^*, s, \phi, \sigma_\eta^2, \mu$.
3. Sample s from $s|y^*, h$.
4. Update ϕ, σ_η^2, μ according to (6), (4) and (7).
5. Goto 2.

Note that we are using $y^* = \{\log(y_1^2 + c), \ldots, \log(y_T^2 + c)\}$ in the conditioning set above as a *pointer* to the mixture model. The vectors y^* and y, of course, contain the same information.

The important improvement over the methods in Section 2 is that it is now possible to efficiently sample from the highly multivariate Gaussian distribution $h|y^*, s, \phi, \sigma_\eta, \mu$ because $y^*|s, \phi, \sigma_\eta, \mu$ is a Gaussian time series which can be placed into the state-space form associated with the Kalman filter. The time series literature calls such models partially non-Gaussian or conditionally Gaussian. This particular model structure means we can sample from the entire $h|y^*$, $s, \phi, \sigma_\eta, \mu$ using the Gaussian simulation signal smoother detailed in the Appendix. As for the sampling of s from $s|y^*, h$, this is done by independently sampling each s_t using the probability mass function

$$\Pr(s_t = i|y_t^*, h_t) \propto q_i f_N(y_t^*| h_t + m_i - 1.2704, v_i^2), \quad i \stackrel{<}{=} K.$$

The results from 750,000 sweeps of this mixture sampler are given in Table 10.5 and Figure 10.4. This sampler has less correlation than the single move sampler and suggests that generating 20,000 simulations from this sampler would probably be sufficient for inferential purposes.

10.3.3 Integrating out the log-volatilities

Although this mixture sampler improves the correlation behaviour of the simulations, the gain is not very big as there is a great deal of correlation between the volatilities and parameters. However, we can use the Gaussian structure of $y^*|s, \phi, \sigma_\eta^2$ to overcome this. We can sample the joint distribution $\pi(\phi, \sigma_\eta^2, h, \mu|y^*, s)$ by sampling (ϕ, σ_η^2) from $\pi(\phi, \sigma_\eta^2|y^*, s) \propto f(y^*|s, \phi, \sigma_\eta^2)\pi(\phi, \sigma_\eta^2)$, and

Table 10.5. Daily returns for Sterling against Dollar. Summaries of Figure 10.2. The Monte Carlo S.E. of simulation is computed using a bandwidth, B_M, of 2000, 2000 and 100 respectively. Italics are correlations rather than covariances of the posterior. Computer time is seconds on a Pentium Pro/200. The other time is the number of seconds to perform 100 complete passes of the sampler

	Mean	MC S.E.	Inefficiency	Covariance and correlation		
$\phi \mid y$	0.97779	6.6811e–005	29.776	0.00011093	−0.690	*0.203*
$\sigma_\eta \mid y$	0.15850	0.00046128	155.42	−0.00023141	0.0010131	*−0.127*
$\beta \mid y$	0.64733	0.00024217	4.3264	0.00021441	−0.00040659	0.010031
Time	15,374	2.0498				

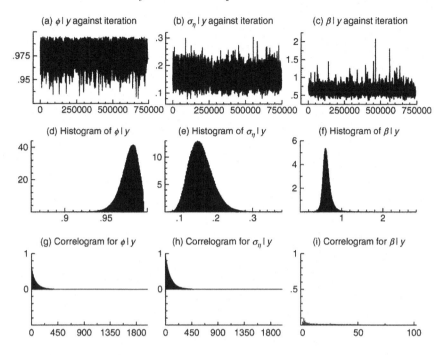

Fig. 10.4. Mixture sampler for Sterling series. Graphs (a)–(c): simulations against iteration. Graphs (d)–(f): histograms of marginal distribution. Graphs (g)–(i): corresponding correlograms for simulation. In total 750,000 iterations were drawn, discarding the first 10,000.

then sampling (h, μ) from $\pi(h, \mu | y^*, s, \phi, \sigma_\eta^2)$ We are able to sample the former distribution because the density $f(y^* | s, \phi, \sigma_\eta^2)$ can be evaluated using an augmented version of the Kalman filter (analytically integrating out μ and h).[7] Then, writing $\mu | y^*, s, \phi, \sigma_\eta^2 \sim \mathcal{N}(\tilde{\mu}, \sigma_{\tilde{\mu}}^2)$ we have that

$$\pi(\phi, \sigma_\eta^2 | y^*, s) \propto \pi(\phi)\pi(\sigma_\eta^2)f(y^* | s, \phi, \sigma_\eta^2) = \pi(\phi)\pi(\sigma_\eta^2)\frac{f(y^* | s, \phi, \sigma_\eta^2, \mu = 0)\pi(\mu = 0)}{\pi(\mu = 0 | y^*, s, \phi, \sigma_\eta^2)}$$

$$\propto \pi(\phi)\pi(\sigma_\eta^2)\prod_{t=1}^{n}F_t^{-1/2}\exp\left(-\frac{1}{2}\sum_{t=1}^{n}v_t^2/F_t\right)\exp\left(\frac{1}{2\sigma_{\tilde{\mu}}^2\tilde{\mu}^2}\tilde{\mu}^2\right)\sigma_{\tilde{\mu}},$$

where v_t is the one-step-ahead prediction error for the best mean square estimator of y_t^*, and F_t is the corresponding mean square error. The quantities $v_t, F_t, \tilde{\mu}, \sigma_{\tilde{\mu}}^2$ are computed from the augmented Kalman filter provided in the Appendix, conditional on s.

---

[7] Augmented Kalman filters and simulation smoothers are discussed in the Appendix.

This implies that we can sample from $\phi, \sigma_\eta^2 | y^*$, s directly by making the proposal $\{\phi^{(i)}, \sigma_\eta^{2(i)}\}$, given the current value $\{\phi^{(i-1)}, \sigma_\eta^{2(i-1)}\}$, by drawing from some density $g(\phi, \sigma_\eta^2)$ and then accepting them using the Metropolis–Hastings probability of move

$$\min\left\{1, \frac{\pi(\phi^{(i)}, \sigma_\eta^{2(i)} | y^*, s)}{\pi(\phi^{(i-1)}, \sigma_\eta^{2(i-1)} | y^*, s)} \frac{g((\phi^{(i-1)}, \sigma_\eta^{2(i-1)}))}{g(\phi^{(i)}, \sigma_\eta^{2(i)})}\right\}. \tag{11}$$

If the proposal value is rejected, we then set $\{\phi^{(i)}, \sigma_\eta^{2(i)}\} = \{\phi^{(i-1)}, \sigma_\eta^{2(i-1)}\}$. We call this an "integration sampler" as it integrates out the log-volatilities.

The structure of the integration sampler is then generically:

1. Initialize $(s, \phi, \sigma_\eta, \mu)$.
2. Sample (ϕ, σ_η^2) from $\pi(\phi, \sigma_\eta^2 | y^*, s)$ using a Metropolis–Hastings suggestion based on $g(\sigma_\eta^2, \phi)$, accepting with probability (11).
3. Sample $h, \mu | y^*, s, \phi, \sigma_\eta^2$ using the augmented simulation smoother given in the Appendix.
4. Sample $s | y^*, h$ as in the previous algorithm.
5. Goto 2.

An important characteristic of this sampler is that the simulation smoother can jointly draw h and μ. The scheme allows a free choice of the proposal density $g(\phi, \sigma_\eta^2)$. We have employed a composite method which first draws 200 samples (discarding the first ten samples) from the posterior density $\pi(\phi, \sigma_\eta^2 | y)$ using a Metropolis–Hastings sampler based on Gilks, Best and Tan (1995) which only requires the coding of the function $y^* | s, \phi, \sigma_\eta^2$ and the prior. These 200 draws are used to estimate the posterior mean and covariance. The mean and twice the covariance are then used to form a Gaussian proposal density $g(\phi, \sigma_\eta^2)$ for the Metropolis–Hastings algorithm in (11). As an alternative, one could also use a multivariate Student t proposal distribution instead of the Gaussian. See Chib and Greenberg (1995) for further discussion on the issues involved in choosing a proposal density for the Metropolis–Hastings algorithm.

The output from the resulting sampler is reported in Figure 10.5 and Table 10.6. These suggest that 2000 samples from this generator would be sufficient for this problem. This result seems reasonably robust to the data set.

10.3.4 Reweighting

The approach based on our (very accurate) offset mixture approximation provides a neat connection to conditionally Gaussian state space models and leads to elegant and efficient sampling procedures, as shown above. We now show that it is possible to correct for the minor approximation error by appending a straightforward reweighting step at the conclusion of the above procedures. This step then provides a sample from the exact posterior density of the parameters and volatilities. The principle we describe is quite general and may be used in other simulation problems as well.

Table 10.6. Daily returns for Sterling against Dollar. Summaries of Figure 10.5. The Monte Carlo S.E. of simulation is computed using a bandwidth, B_M, of 100, 100 and 100 respectively. Italics are correlations rather than covariances of the posterior. Computer time is seconds on a Pentium Pro/200. The other time is the number of seconds to perform 100 complete passes of the sampler

	Mean	MC S.E.	Inefficiency	Covariance and correlation		
$\phi\|y$	0.97780	6.7031e −005	9.9396	0.00011297	− *0.699*	*0.205*
$\sigma_\eta\|y$	0.15832	0.00025965	16.160	−0.00023990	0.0010426	*−0.131*
$\beta\|y$	0.64767	0.00023753	1.4072	0.00021840	−0.00042465	0.010020
Time	8635.2	3.4541				

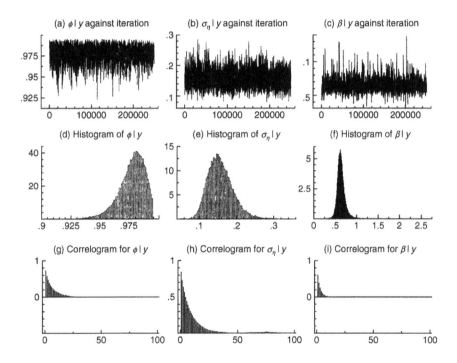

Fig. 10.5. The integration sampler for Sterling series. Graphs (a)–(c): simulations against iteration. Graphs (d)–(f): histograms of marginal distribution. Graphs (g)–(i): corresponding correlograms for simulation. In total 250,000 iterations were drawn, discarding the first 250.

First, write the mixture approximation as making draws from $k(\theta, h|y^*)$, and then define

$$w(\theta, h) = \log f(\theta, h|y) - \log k(\theta, h|y) = \text{const} + \log f(y|h) - \log k(y^*|h),$$

where

$$f(y|h) = \prod_{t=1}^{n} f_N\{y_t|0, \exp(h_t)\},$$

and

$$k(y^*|h) = \prod_{t=1}^{n}\sum_{i=1}^{K} q_i f_N(y_t^*|h_t + m_i - 1.2704, v_i^2).$$

Both these functions involve Gaussian densities and are straightforward to evaluate for any value of h. Then,

$$\mathbf{E}g(\theta)|y = \int g(\theta)f(\theta|y)d\theta$$

$$= \int g(\theta)\exp\{w(\theta, h)\}k(\theta, h|y^*)\,d\theta\,dh \bigg/ \int \exp\{w(\theta, h)\}k(\theta, h|y^*)\,d\theta\,dh.$$

Thus we can estimate functionals of the posterior by reweighting the MCMC draws according to

$$\mathbf{E}g(\hat{\theta})|y = \sum_{j} g(\theta^j)c^j,$$

where the weights are

$$c^j = \exp\{w(\theta^j, h^j)\} \bigg/ \sum_{i}\exp\{w(\theta^i, h^i)\}. \qquad (12)$$

As the mixture approximation is very good, we would expect that the weights c^j would have a small variance.

To see the dispersion of the weights, we recorded the weights from the sampler which generated Figure 10.5 and plotted the resulting log-weights in Figure 10.6. The log-weights are close to being normally distributed with a standard deviation of around one.

To see the effect of the weights on the parameters estimates, we reweighted the 250,000 samples displayed in Figure 10.5. This produced the estimates which are given in Table 10.7. These Monte Carlo estimates of the posterior means are statistically insignificantly different from Monte Carlo estimated values given in Table 10.1. However, the Monte Carlo precision has improved dramatically. Further, the Monte Carlo standard errors indicate that this data set could be routinely analysed using around 1500 sweeps.

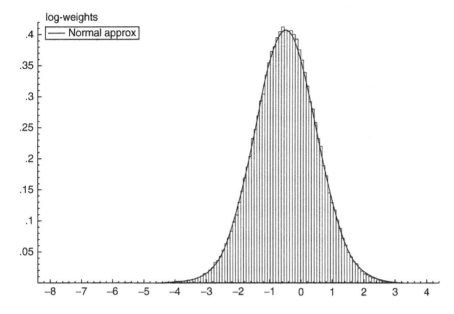

Fig. 10.6. Histogram of the log of the $M \times c^j$ for 250,000 sweeps for the integration sampler and a corresponding approximating normal density with fitted mean and standard deviation. All the weights around zero would indicate a perfect sampler.

This conclusion seems to hold up for some other exchange rate series. Table 10.8 reports the estimates of the parameters and simulation inefficiency measures for the DM, Yen and Swiss Franc series. This table is the exact analog of Table 10.2 for the single move algorithm.

Table 10.7. Daily returns for Sterling against Dollar. Summaries of reweighted sample of 250,000 sweeps of the integration sampler. The Monte Carlo S.E. of simulation is computed using a block one tenth of the size of the simulation. Italics are correlations rather than covariances of the posterior. Computer time is seconds on a Pentium Pro/200. The other time is the number of seconds to perform 100 complete passes of the sampler

	Mean	MC S.E.	Inefficiency	Covariance and correlation		
$\phi\|y$	0.97752	7.0324e −005	11.20	0.00010973	*−0.685*	*0.204*
$\sigma_\eta\|y$	0.15815	0.00024573	14.81	−0.00022232	0.00096037	*−0.129*
$\beta\|y$	0.64909	0.00025713	1.64	0.00021181	−0.00039768	0.0098312
Time	10,105	4.0423				

Table 10.8. Bandwidth, B_M, for each parameter was 100 on all series. In all cases 250,000 sweepes were used

Series	$\phi\|y$		$\sigma_\eta\|y$		$\beta\|y$	
	Mean	Inefficiency	Mean	Inefficiency	Mean	Inefficiency
DM	0.96529	8.31	0.15812	11.99	0.65071	9.73
Yen	0.97998	23.10	0.12503	35.66	0.53534	2.71
SwizF	0.95276	13.52	0.20738	15.33	0.70675	8.38

10.4 Filtering, diagnostics and likelihood evaluation

10.4.1 Introduction

There has been considerable recent work on the development of simulation based methods to perform filtering, that is computing features of $h_t|Y_t, \theta$, for each value of $Y_t = (y_1, \ldots, y_t)$. Leading papers in this field include Gordon, Salmond and Smith (1993), Kitagawa (1996), Isard and Blake (1996), Berzuini, Best, Gilks and Larizza (1997), West (1993) and Muller (1991). We work with a simple approach which is a special case of a suggestion made by Pitt and Shephard (1997). Throughout we will assume θ is known. In practice θ will be set to some estimated value, such as the maximum likelihood estimator or the Monte Carlo estimator of the posterior mean.

The objective is to obtain a sample of draws from $h_t|Y_t, \theta$ given a sample of draws $h_{t-1}^1, \ldots, h_{t-1}^M$ from $h_{t-1}|Y_{t-1}, \theta$. Such an algorithm is called a particle filter in the literature. We now show how this may be done. From Bayes theorem,

$$f(h_t|Y_t, \theta) \propto f(y_t|h_t, \theta)f(h_t|Y_{t-1}, \theta), \tag{13}$$

where

$$f(h_t|Y_{t-1}, \theta) = \int f(h_t|h_{t-1}, \theta)f(h_{t-1}|Y_{t-1}, \theta)dh_{t-1},$$

and $f(h_t|h_{t-1}, \theta) = f_N(h_t|\mu + \phi(h_{t-1} - \mu), \sigma_\eta^2)$ is the normal evolution density. The latter integral can be estimated from the sample $h_{t-1}^1, \ldots, h_{t-1}^M$ leading to the approximations

$$f(h_t|Y_{t-1}, \theta) \simeq \frac{1}{M}\sum_{j=1}^{M}f(h_t \mid h_{t-1}^j, \theta),$$

and

$$f(h_t|Y_t, \theta) \propto f(y_t|h_t, \theta)\frac{1}{M}\sum_{j=1}^{M}f(h_t \mid h_{t-1}^j, \theta). \tag{14}$$

The question now is to sample h_t from the latter density. The obvious importance sampling procedure of producing a sample $\{h_t^j\}$ from $f(h_t|h_{t-1}^j, \theta)$ and then resampling these draws with weights proportional to $\{f(y_t|h_t^j, \theta)\}$ is not efficient. An improved procedure runs as follows. Let $h_{t|t-1} = \mu + \phi(M^{-1}\sum h_{t-1}^j - \mu)$ and $\log f(y_t|h_t, \theta) = \text{const} + \log f^*(y_t, h_t, \theta)$. Now expand $\log f^*(y_t, h_t, \theta)$ in a Taylor series around the point $h_{t|t-1}$ as

$$\log f^*(y_t, h_t, \theta) = -\frac{1}{2}h_t - \frac{y_t^2}{2}\{\exp(-h_t)\}$$
$$\doteq -\frac{1}{2}h_t - \frac{y_t^2}{2}\{\exp(-h_{t|t-1})(1 + h_{t|t-1}) - h_t\exp(-h_{t|t-1})\}$$
$$= \log g^*(h_t, h_{t|t-1}, \theta).$$

Also, after some algebra it can be shown that

$$g^*(h_t, h_{t|t-1}, \theta)\, f(h_t|h_{t-1}^j, \theta) \propto \pi_j\, f_N(h_t|h_{t|t-1}^j, \sigma_\eta^2), \qquad (15)$$

where

$$\pi_j = \exp\left\langle -\frac{1}{2\sigma_\eta^2}[\{\mu + \phi(h_{t-1}^j - \mu)\}^2 - h_{t|t-1}^{j2}]\right\rangle$$

and

$$h_{t|t-1}^j = \mu + \phi(h_{t-1}^j - \mu) + \frac{\sigma_\eta^2}{2}\{y_t^2\exp(-h_{t|t-1}) - 1\}.$$

Hence, the kernel of the target density in (14) can be bounded as

$$f^*(y_t, h_t, \theta)\frac{1}{M}\sum_{j=1}^{M} f(h_t\,|\,h_{t-1}^j, \theta) \doteq g^*(h_t, h_{t|t-1}, \theta)\frac{1}{M}\sum_{j=1}^{M} f(h_t\,|\,h_{t-1}^j, \theta),$$

where the right-hand side terms are proportional to $1/M\sum_{j=1}^{M}\pi_j f_N(h_t\,|\,h_{t|t-1}^j, \sigma_\eta^2)$ due to (15).

These results suggest a simple accept–reject procedure for drawing h_t. First, we draw a proposal value h_t from the mixture density $\sum_{j=1}^{M}\pi_j^* f_N(h_t|h_{t|t-1}^j, \sigma_\eta^2)$, where $\pi_j^* = \pi_j/\sum_j \pi_j$. Second, we accept this value with probability $f^*(y_t, h_t, \theta)/g^*(h_t, h_{t|t-1}, \theta)$. If the value is rejected, we return to the first step and draw a new proposal.

By selecting a large M this filtering sampler will become arbitrarily accurate.

10.4.1.1 Application

To illustrate this, we apply these methods to the Sterling/Dollar series, filtering the volatility. Throughout we will employ $M = 2500$. Similar results were obtained when M fell to 1000, although reducing M below that figure created important biases. The results are made conditional of the estimated parameters, which are taken from Table 10.9 and based on 2500 sweeps of the integration sampler.

The resulting filtered and smoothed estimates of the volatility are given in Figure 10.7, together with a graph of the absolute values of the returns. The graph shows the expected feature of the filtered volatility lagging the smoothed

Table 10.9. Daily returns for Sterling series. Summaries of reweighted sample of 2500 sweeps of the integration sampler. The Monte Carlo S.E. of simulation is computed using a block one-tenth of the size of the simulation. Italics are correlations rather than covariances of the posterior. Computer time is seconds on a Pentium Pro/200. The other time is the number of seconds to perform 100 complete passes of the sampler

	Mean	MC S.E.	Inefficiency	Covariance and correlation		
$\phi\|y$	0.97611	0.0018015	11.636	0.00014783	-0.765	*0.277*
$\sigma_\eta\|y$	0.16571	0.0065029	17.657	-0.00033148	0.0012693	*−0.232*
$\beta\|y$	0.64979	0.0047495	1.4563	0.00030503	-0.00074971	0.008209
Time	97.230	3.8892				

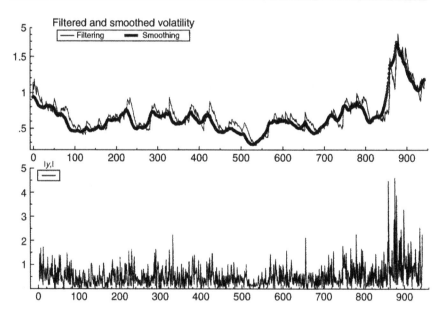

Fig. 10.7. Top: filtered and smoothed estimate of the volatility $\exp(h_t/2)$, computed using $M = 2000$. Bottom: $|y_t|$, the absolute values of the returns.

volatility. Throughout the sample, the filtered volatility is slightly higher than the smoothed values due to the gradual fall in volatility observed for these series during this period.

10.4.2 Diagnostics

Having designed a filtering algorithm it is a simple matter to sample from the one-step-ahead prediction density and distribution function. By definition the prediction density is

$$f(y_{t+1}|Y_t, \theta) = \int f(y_{t+1}|Y_t, h_{t+1}, \theta)f(h_{t+1}|Y_t, h_t, \theta)f(h_t|Y_t, \theta)dh_{t+1}dh_t,$$

which can be sampled by the method of composition as follows. For each value $h_t^j (j = 1, 2, \ldots, M)$ from the filtering algorithm, one samples h_{t+1}^j from

$$h_{t+1}^j|h_t^j \sim \mathcal{N}\{\mu + \phi(h_t^j - \mu), \sigma_\eta^2\}.$$

Based on these M draws on h_{t+1} from the prediction density, we can estimate the probability that y_{t+1}^2 will be less than the observed y_{t+1}^{o2}

$$\text{Pr } (y_{t+1}^2 \leqslant y_{t+1}^{o2}|Y_t, \theta) \cong u_{t+1}^M = \frac{1}{M}\sum_{j=1}^{M} \text{Pr } (y_{t+1}^2 \leqslant y_{t+1}^{o2}|h_{t+1}^j, \theta). \tag{16}$$

For each $t = 1, \ldots, n$, under the null of a correctly specified model u_t^M converges in distribution to independent and identically distributed uniform random variables as $M \to \infty$ (Rosenblatt (1952)). This provides a valid basis for diagnostic checking. These variables can be mapped into the normal distribution, by using the inverse of the normal distribution function $n_t^M = F^{-1}(u_t^M)$ to give a standard sequence of independent and identically distributed normal variables, which are then transformed one-step-ahead forecasts normed by their correct standard errors. These can be used to cary out Box–Ljung, normality, and heteroscedasticity tests, among others.

The computed forecast uniforms and resulting correlograms and *QQ* plots are given in Figure 10.8. The results suggest that the model performs quite well, although it reveals some outliers. However, closer inspection shows that the outliers correspond to small values of y_t^2. This suggests that the SV model fails to accommodate some of the data values that have limited daily movements. On the other hand it appears to perform well when the movements in the data are large. This will be made more formal in the next subsection.

10.4.2.1 Likelihood estimation

The one-step-ahead predictions can also be used to estimate the likelihood function since the one-step-ahead prediction density, $f(y_{t+1}|Y_t)$, can be estimated as

$$\frac{1}{M}\sum_{j=1}^{M} f(y_{t+1}|h_{t+1}^j), \qquad h_{t+1}^j|h_t^j \sim \mathcal{N}\{\mu + \phi(h_t^j - \mu), \sigma_\eta^2\}, \tag{17}$$

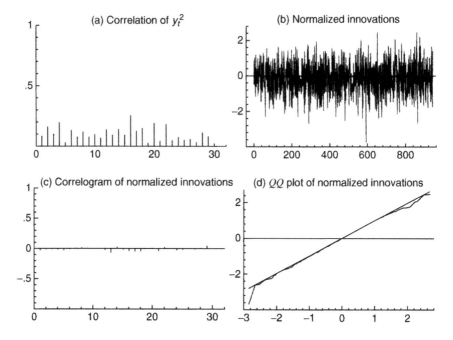

Fig. 10.8. Diagnostic checks. Graph (a): correlogram of y_t^2. Graph (b):
normalized innovations. Graph (c): the corresponding correlogram.
Graph (d): associated QQ-plot.

using drawings from the filtering simulator. The same argument gives a filtered
estimate of h_{t+1} using the information up to time t.

Table 10.10 shows the results from some standard diagnostic checks on the
$n_1^M, \ldots, n_n^M$ produced by the fitted model. Under the correctness of the model, the
diagnostics should indicate that the variables are Gaussian white noise. We
report the skewness and kurtosis coefficients,

Table 10.10. Diagnostics of the SV model using $M = 2500$. BL(l) denotes a Box–
Ljung statistic on l lags. The figures in brackets are simulation standard errors
using 10 replications. The two other models are fitted using ML. The estimated
degrees of the Student t model is given in brackets

	Skew	Kurtosis	Normality	BL (30)	Log-lik
SV	1.4509	0.54221	2.3992	18.555	−918.56
	(0.057)	(0.083)	(0.295)	(0.120)	(0.558)
NID	11.505	21.640	600.65	401.20	−1018.2
tID (4.87)	1.2537	1.2156	3.0494	700.62	−964.56

$$\text{Skew} = \frac{nb_3}{6}, \quad \text{Kurtosis} = \frac{n(b_4 - 3)^2}{24},$$

where b_3 and b_4 denote the standardized estimators of the third and fourth moment of $\{n_t^M\}$ about the mean, an overall Bowman and Shenton (1975) normality statistic which combines these two measures and the Box–Ljung statistic using 30 lags. The table also gives the simulation standard error for these statistics, based on repeating the simulation ten times with different random draws but with the data fixed. Finally, for comparison the table gives the same diagnostics for the $\mathcal{N}(0, \sigma^2)$ and scaled Student t *iid* models. The results suggest that there are no straightforward failures in the way the model has been fitted.

10.5 Comparison of non-nested models via simulation

10.5.1 GARCH model

In this section we compare the fit of basic SV models with the GARCH models commonly used in the literature. Two approaches are used in this non-nested model comparison—one based on likelihood ratios and another based on ratios of marginal likelihoods resulting in what are called Bayes factors.

The notation we use for the Gaussian GARCH(1, 1) model is

$$y_t | Y_{t-1} \sim \mathcal{N}(0, \sigma_t^2), \quad \text{where } \sigma_t^2 = \alpha_0 + \alpha_1 y_{t-1}^2 + \alpha_2 \sigma_{t-1}^2. \tag{18}$$

while the equivalent Student-t model introduced by Bollerslev (1987) is denoted as t-GARCH with v as the notation for the positive degrees of freedom.

The diagnostic statistics given in Table 10.11 suggest that the Gaussian GARCH model does not fit the data very well, suffering from positive skewness and excess kurtosis. This suggests that the model cannot accommodate the extreme positive observations in the data. The t-GARCH model is better, with much better distributional behaviour. Again its diagnostics for serial dependence are satisfactory. The fitted likelihood is very slightly better than the SV model, although it has one more parameter.

Table 10.11. Diagnostics of the ML estimators of the Gaussian and Student t distributed GARCH models. BL(l) denotes a Box–Ljung statistic on l lags. Above the line are the answers of the real data, the ones below are the corrected observations. Figures in brackets for the t-GARCH model are the estimated degrees of freedom

	α_0	$\alpha_1 + \alpha_2$	Skew	Kurt	Normality	BL (30)	Log-lik
GARCH	0.0086817	0.98878	4.5399	4.3553	39.580	16.183	−928.13
t-GARCH (8.44)	0.00058463	0.99359	0.56281	0.31972	0.41897	22.515	−917.22

10.5.2 Likelihood ratio statistics

There is an extensive literature on the statistical comparison of non-nested models based on likelihood ratio statistics. Much of the econometric literature on this topic is reviewed in Gourieroux and Monfort (1994). The approach we suggest here relies on simulation and is based on Atkinson (1986). Related ideas appear in, for instance, Pesaran and Pesaran (1993) and Hinde (1992).

Let $\mathcal{M}_1$ denote the SV model and $\mathcal{M}_0$ the GARCH model. Then, the likelihood ratio test statistic for comparative fit that is investigated here is given by

$$LR_y = 2\{\log \hat{f}(y \mid \mathcal{M}_1, \hat{\theta}_1) - \log f(y \mid \mathcal{M}_0, \tilde{\theta}_0)\},$$

where $\log \hat{f}(y \mid \mathcal{M}_1, \hat{\theta}_1)$ and $\log f(y \mid \mathcal{M}_0, \tilde{\theta}_0)$ denote the respective estimates of the log likelihoods, the former estimated by simulation as described above,[8] $\hat{\theta}_1$ is the estimated posterior mean of SV model parameters and $\tilde{\theta}_0$ the MLE of the GARCH model parameters. The sampling variation of LR_y under the hypothesis that the SV model is true or under the alternative that the GARCH model is true is approximated by simulation, following Atkinson (1986). Clearly, analytical derivations of the sampling distribution are difficult given the unconventional estimators of the log-likelihood.

Under the assumption that the SV model is true and the true values of its parameters are $\theta_1^{(0)}$, we generate simulations $y^i, i = 1, \ldots, M$ from the true model. For each simulated series we estimate the parameters of the GARCH and SV models and record the value of LR_y, which we denote as LR_y^i. The resulting scatter of values $LR_y^1, \ldots, LR_y^M$ are a sample from the exact distribution of LR_y under the SV null. The fact that we estimated the likelihood and the parameters of the SV model for each y^i does not alter this result. Hence we could use these simulations LR_y^i as inputs into a trivial Monte Carlo test (see, for example, Ripley (1987, pp. 171–174)) of the hypothesis that the GARCH model is true. Unfortunately $\theta_1^{(0)}$ is unknown and so it is estimated from the data and chosen to be $\hat{\theta}_1$. This introduces an additional approximation error into the sampling calculation which falls as the sample size $n \to \infty$.

The estimated approximate sampling distributions of LR_y under each hypothesis based on 99 simulations plus the realization from the data are given in Figure 10.9. This figure shows that if the null of the SV model is true, then LR_y can be expected to be positive when the alternative is a Gaussian GARCH, while it is expected to be around zero when the alternative is a t-GARCH.

For the Sterling series the observed LR_y is 19.14 for the SV model against GARCH and -2.68 for the SV model against t-GARCH. This suggests that the SV model fits the data better than the GARCH model but slightly worse than the t-GARCH model (which has one more parameter). These results are confirmed by looking at the simulated LR_y. Table 10.12 records the ranking of the observed LR_y amongst the 99 simulations conducted under the assumption that the SV

---

[8] The GARCH process has to be initialized by setting σ_0^2. The choice of this term effects the likelihood function. In our calculations we set $\sigma_0^2 = \alpha_0/(1 - \alpha_1 - \alpha_2)$.

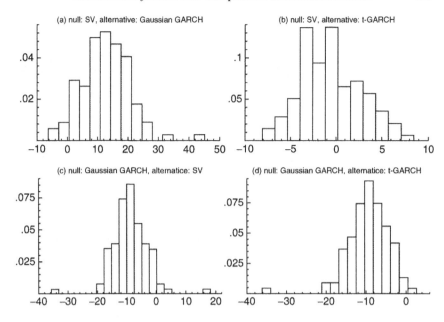

Fig. 10.9. Non-nested testing. Graphs (a)–(b) LR_y computed when SV is true. Graph (a): SV against a GARCH model. Graph (b): SV against a t-GARCH. The observed values are 19·14 and −2·68 respectively, which are 80th and 29th out of the 100 samples. Graphs (c)–(d): LR_y computed when GARCH model is true. Graph (c): GARCH against SV. Graph (d): GARCH against t-GARCH. The observed values are 19·14 and −2·68 respectively, which ranks them 100th and 79th out of the 100 samples.

model is true. Hence if the observed LR_y is the 96th largest, then it is ranked as being 96th. If the ranking is either close to zero or 100 then this would provide evidence against the SV model.

The recorded rankings under the SV hypothesis are not very extreme, with about 20% of the simulations generating LR tests against the GARCH model which are higher than that observed, while 30% of the simulations were lower than that observed for the t-GARCH LR test. Although suggestive, neither of these tests are formally significant. This implies that they are both consistent with the SV model being true.

A more decisive picture is generated when the Gaussian GARCH model is the null hypothesis. No value is as extreme as the observed LR test against the SV model, rejecting the Gaussian GARCH model for these data. The evidence of the test against the t-GARCH model is less strong.

In summary, the observed non-nested LR_y tests give strong evidence against the use of Gaussian GARCH models. The two remaining models are the t-GARCH and SV models. The statistics show a slight preference for the t-GARCH model, but this model is less parsimonious than the SV model and

Table 10.12. Non-nested LR tests of the SV model against the ARCH models. In each case the 99 simulations were added to the observed LR_y to form the histograms. The reported r-th rankings are the r-th largest of the observed LR test out of the 100 LR_y tests conducted under SV or GARCH model

	SV versus GARCH			SV against t-GARCH		
Series	Observed	Rank SV	Rank GARCH	Observed	Rank SV	Rank GARCH
Sterling	19.14	81st	100th	−2.68	29th	79th
DM	11.00	61st	100th	−3.84	9th	87th
Yen	19.84	99th	100th	−30.50	1st	1st
SwizF	53.12	100th	100th	−3.62	20th	98th

so it would be fairer to argue for the statement that they fit the data more or less equally well. These results carry over to the other three exchange rates. The results from the non-nested tests are given in Table 10.12, although there is a considerable evidence that the t-GARCH model is preferable to the SV model for the Yen series.

10.5.3 Bayes factors
An alternative to likelihood ratio statistics is the use of Bayes factors, which are symmetric in the models and extremely easy to interpret. The approach adopted here for the computation of Bayes factors relies on the method developed by Chib (1995). From the basic marginal likelihood identity in Chib (1995), the log of the Bayes factor can be written as

$$\log f(y|\mathcal{M}_1) - \log f(y|\mathcal{M}_0)$$
$$= \{ \log f(y|\mathcal{M}_1, \theta_1^*) + \log f(\theta_1^*|\mathcal{M}_1) - \log f(\theta_1^*|\mathcal{M}_1, y) \}$$
$$- \{ \log f(y|\mathcal{M}_0, \theta_0^*) + \log f(\theta_0^*) - \log f(\theta_0^*|\mathcal{M}_0, y) \},$$

for any values of θ_0^* and θ_1^*. Here $f(\theta_0^*)$ is the GARCH prior density, while $f(\theta_1^*|\mathcal{M}_1)$ is the prior for the SV parameters. The likelihood for the GARCH model is known, while that of the SV model is estimated via simulation as described above. Next, the posterior densities $f(\theta_0^*|\mathcal{M}_0, y)$ and $f(\theta_1^*|\mathcal{M}_1, y)$ are estimated at the single points θ_0^* and θ_1^* using a Gaussian kernel applied to the posterior sample of the parameters. We follow the suggestion in Chib (1995) and use the posterior means of the parameters as θ_0^* and θ_1^* since the choice of these points is arbitrary.

To perform a Bayes estimation of the GARCH model we have to write down some priors for the GARCH parameters. This is most easily done by representing the model in its ARMA(1, 1) form for squared data

$$y_t^2 = \alpha_0 + (\alpha_1 + \alpha_2)y_{t-1}^2 + v_t - \alpha_2 v_{t-1}, \quad v_t = (\varepsilon_t^2 - 1)\sigma_t^2.$$

Hence $\alpha_1 + \alpha_2$ is the persistence parameter, α_2 (which has to be positive) is the negative of the moving average coefficient, while $\alpha_0/(1 - \alpha_1 - \alpha_2)$ is the unconditional expected value of y_t^2. We will place the same prior on $\alpha_1 + \alpha_2$ as was placed on the persistence parameter ϕ in the SV model (see (5)). This will force the GARCH process to be covariance stationary. The prior specification is completed by assuming that $\alpha_2/(\alpha_1 + \alpha_2)|\alpha_1 + \alpha_2 = r_\alpha$ follows a Beta distribution with

$$
\begin{aligned}
&\log f\{\alpha_2/(\alpha_1 + \alpha_2)|\alpha_1 + \alpha_2 = r_\alpha\} \\
&= \text{const} + \{\phi^{(1)} - 1\} \log\left\{\frac{\alpha_2}{r_\alpha}\right\} + \{\phi^{(2)} - 1\} \log\left\{\frac{r_\alpha - \alpha_2}{r_\alpha}\right\}.
\end{aligned} \tag{19}
$$

Since we would expect that $\alpha_2/(\alpha_1 + \alpha_2)$ to be closer to one than zero, we will take $\phi^{(1)} = 45$ and let $\phi^{(2)} = 2$. This gives a mean of 0.957. The scale parameter $\alpha_0/(1 - \alpha_1 - \alpha_2)|\alpha_1, \alpha_2$ are given a standard diffuse inverse chi-squared prior distribution. Finally, for the t-GARCH model, $v - 2$ was given in chi-squared prior with a mean of ten.

In order to carry out the MCMC sampling we used the Gilks, Best, and Tan (1995) procedure which just requires the programming of the priors and the GARCH likelihood.

The results of the calculations are given in Table 10.13. They are very much in line with the likelihood ratio analysis given in Table 10.12. Again the SV model dominates the Gaussian GARCH model, while it suffers in comparison with the t-GARCH model, especially for the Yen data series. It should be mentioned, however, that these conclusions are in relation to the simplest possible SV model. The performance of the SV model can be improved by considering other versions of the model, for example, one that relaxes the Gaussian assumption. We discuss this and other extensions next.

10.6 Extensions

10.6.1 More complicated dynamics

This paper has suggested three ways of performing Bayesian analysis of the SV model: single move, offset mixture and integration sampling. All three extend to

Table 10.13. Estimated Bayes factors for SV model against GARCH model and t-GARCH. All the densities were evaluated at the estimated posterior mean

Series	GARCH			t-GARCH			
	$\alpha_1 + \alpha_2$	$\log f_{\text{GARCH}}$	Log Bayes	$\alpha_1 + \alpha_2$	u	$\log f_{\text{GARCH}}$	Log Bayes
Sterling	0.9802	-928.64	9.14	0.9822	9.71	-918.13	-3.512
DM	0.9634	-952.88	6.52	0.9712	12.82	-945.63	-2.688
Yen	0.9850	-798.79	13.22	0.9939	6.86	774.8	11.28
SwizF	0.9153	-1067.2	27.86	0.9538	7.57	-1039.0	-0.84

the problem where the volatility follows a more complicated stochastic process than an AR(1). A useful framework is

$$h_t = c_t + Z_t \gamma_t, \quad \text{where} \quad \gamma_{t+1} = d_t + T_t \gamma_t + H_t u_t,$$

where $u_t \overset{iid}{\sim} \mathcal{N}(0, I)$, c_t and d_t are assumed to be strictly exogenous, and Z_t, T_t and H_t are selected to represent the log-volatility appropriately. With this framework the log volatility process can be specified to follow an ARMA process.

In the single move Gibbs algorithm, it is tempting to work with the γ_t as

$$f(\gamma_t \mid y_t, \gamma_{t-1}, \gamma_{t+1}) \propto f(y_t \mid c_t + Z_t \gamma_t) f(\gamma_t \mid \gamma_{t-1}) f(\gamma_{t+1} \mid \gamma_t), \tag{20}$$

has a simple structure. However, this would suffer from the problems of large MCMC simulation inefficiency documented above especially if γ_t is high dimensional or if the $\{\gamma_t\}$ process displayed considerable memory (akin to the example given in Carter and Kohn (1994)). Alternatively, one could sample h_t using

$$f(h_t \mid h_{\backslash t}, y) \propto f(y_t \mid h_t) f(h_t \mid h_{\backslash t}),$$

as we can evaluate $h_t \mid h_{\backslash t}$ using the de Jong (1998) scan sampler. This is uniformly superior to the algorithms built using (20). Neither of these choices would be competitive, however, with versions of the multi-move and integration sampler which rely on the state space form and can thus be trivially extended to cover these models.

More sophisticated dynamics for the volatility could be modelled by exploiting factor type models. An example of this is

$$h_t = h_{1t} + h_{2t}, \quad h_{1t+1} = \phi_1 h_{1t} + \eta_{1t}, \quad h_{2t+1} = \phi_2 h_{2t} + \eta_{2t}.$$

where $\phi_1 > \phi_2$ and η_{1t}, η_{2t} are independent Gaussian white noise processes. Here h_{1t} and h_{2t} would represent the longer-term and shorter-term fluctuations in log-volatility. The introduction of such components, appropriately parameterized, produce volatility versions of the long memory models advocated by Cox (1991).

10.6.2 Missing observations

The framework described above can also be extended to handle missing data. Suppose that the exchange rate r_{34} at time 34 is missing. Then the returns y_{34} and y_{35} would be missing. We could complete the data by adding in r_{34} to the list of unknowns in the sampling. Given r_{34} we could generate y and then sweep $h, \theta | y$. Having carried this out we could update r_{34} by drawing it given h, θ and y. Iterating this procedure gives a valid MCMC algorithm and so would efficiently estimate θ from the non-missing data.

This argument generalizes to any amount of missing data. Hence this argument also generalizes to the experiment where we think of the SV model (1) holding at a much finer discretization than the observed data. Think of the model holding at intervals of 1/d-th of a day, while suppose that the exchange rate r_t is available daily. Then we can augment the "missing" intra-daily data $\tilde{r}_t = (r_{t_1}, \ldots, r_{t_{d-1}})$ to the volatilities $\tilde{h}_t = (h_{t_1}, \ldots, h_{t_{d-1}}, h_t)$ and design a simple MCMC algorithm to sample from

$$\tilde{r}_1, \ldots, \tilde{r}_n, \tilde{h}_1, \ldots, \tilde{h}_n, \theta | r_0, \ldots, r_n.$$

This will again allow efficient estimation of θ from the "coarse" daily data even though the model is true at the intra-daily level. This type of argument is reminiscent of the indirect inference methods which have recently been developed for diffusions by Gourieroux, Monfort and Renault (1993) and Gallant and Tauchen (1996), however our approach has the advantage of not depending on the ad hoc choice of an auxiliary model and is automatically fully efficient.

10.6.3 Heavy-tailed SV models

The discrete time SV model can be extended to allow ε_t in (1) to be more heavy-tailed than the normal distribution. This would help in overcoming the comparative lack of fit indicated by Table 10.12 for the Yen series. One approach, suggested in Harvey, Ruiz and Shephard (1994) amongst others, is to use an *ad hoc* scaled Student t distribution, so that

$$\varepsilon_t = \sqrt{\frac{v-2}{v}} \zeta_t \bigg/ \sqrt{\chi^2_{t,v}/v}, \quad \text{where} \quad \zeta_t \overset{iid}{\sim} \mathcal{N}(0,1), \chi^2_{t,v} \overset{iid}{\sim} \chi^2_v,$$

and the ζ_t and $\chi^2_{t,v}$ are independent of one another. The single move and offset mixture algorithms immediately carry over to this problem if we design a Gibbs sampler for $\chi^2_{1,v}, \ldots, \chi^2_{n,v}, h, \theta | y$ or $\chi^2_{1,v}, \ldots, \chi^2_{n,v}, h, \theta, \omega | y$ respectively.

An alternative to this, which can be carried out in the single move algorithm, would be to directly integrate out the $\chi^2_{t,v}$, which would mean $f(y_t | h_t, \theta)$ would be a scaled Student t distribution. This has the advantage of reducing the dimension of the resulting simulation. However, the conditional sampling becomes more difficult. This is because $f(y_t | h_t, \theta)$ is no longer log-concave in h_t and the simple accept/reject algorithm will no longer work. However, one could adopt the pseudo-dominating accept/reject procedure that is discussed in Tierney (1994) and Chib and Greenberg (1995). This version of the algorithm incorporates a Metropolis step in the accept/reject method and does not require a bounding function. The same ideas can also be extended for multivariate models and models with correlated ε_t, η_t errors.

10.6.4 Semi-parametric SV

The offset mixture representation of the SV model naturally leads to a semi-parametric version of the SV model. Suppose we select the "parameters" $m_1, \ldots, m_K, v_1^2, \ldots, v_K^2, q_1, \ldots, q_K$ freely from the data. Then, this procedure is tantamount to the estimation of the density of the shocks ε_t. The constraint that Var $(\varepsilon_t) = 1$ is automatically imposed if μ is incorporated into these mixture weights.

This generic approach to semi-parametric density estimation along with MCMC type algorithms for the updating of the mixture parameters has been suggested by Escobar and West (1995) and Richardson and Green (1997). Mahieu and Schotman (1997) use a simulated EM approach to estimate a small number of mixtures inside an SV model.

10.6.5 Prior sensitivity

The methods developed above can be easily modified to assess the consequences of changing the prior. Instead of rerunning the entire samplers with the alternative prior, one can reweight the simulation output so that it corresponds to the new prior—in much the same way as the simulation was reweighted to overcome the bias caused by the offset mixture. Since the posterior is

$$f(\theta, h \mid y) \propto f(y \mid h, \theta) f(h \mid \theta) f(\theta) = f(y \mid h, \theta) f(h/\theta) f^*(\theta) \frac{f(\theta)}{f^*(\theta)} ,$$

where $f(\theta)$ denotes the new prior and $f^*(\theta)$ the prior used in the simulations, the reweighting follows the form of (12) where $w = \log f(\theta^j) - \log f^*(\theta^j)$. This is particularly attractive as the reweighting is a smooth function of the difference between the old prior f^* and the new prior f. Rerunning the sampler will not have this property.

10.6.6 Multivariate factor SV models

The basis of the N dimensional factor SV model will be

$$y_t = Bf_t + \varepsilon_t,$$

where

$$\binom{\varepsilon_t}{f_t} \sim \mathcal{N}\langle 0, \text{diag} \{ \exp(h_{1t}), \ldots, \exp(h_{Nt}), \exp(h_{N+1t}), \ldots, \exp(h_{N+Kt})\}\rangle,$$

where f_t is K dimensional and

$$(h_{t+1} - \mu) = \begin{pmatrix} \phi_\varepsilon & 0 \\ 0 & \phi_f \end{pmatrix}(h_t - \mu) + \eta_t, \quad \eta_t \sim \mathcal{N}\left\{0, \begin{pmatrix} \Sigma_{\varepsilon\eta} & 0 \\ 0 & \Sigma_{f\eta} \end{pmatrix}\right\}.$$

As it stands the model is highly overparameterized. This basic structure was suggested in the factor ARCH models analysed[9] by Diebold and Nerlove (1989) and refined by King, Sentana and Wadhwani (1994), but replaces the unobserved ARCH process for f_t by SV processes. It was mentioned as a possible multivariate model by Shephard (1996) and discussed by Jacquier, Polson and Rossi (1995).

---

[9] Using approximate likelihood methods. Exact likelihood methods are very difficult to construct for factor ARCH models.

Jacquier, Polson and Rossi (1995) discussed using MCMC methods on a simplified version[10] of this model, by exploiting the conditional independence structure of the model to allow the repeated use of univariate MCMC methods to analyse the multivariate model. This method requires the diagonality of $\phi_\varepsilon, \phi_f, \Sigma_{\varepsilon\eta}$ and $\Sigma_{f\eta}$ to be successful. However, their argument can be generalized in the following way for our offset mixture approach.

Augment the unknown h, θ with the factors f, for then $h|f, y, \theta$ has a very simple structure. In our case we can transform each f_{jt} using

$$\log(f_{jt}^2 + c) = h_{N+jt} + z_{jt}, \quad z_{jt}|s_{jt} = i \sim \mathcal{N}(m_i - 1.2704, v_i^2),$$

noting that given the mixtures the z_{jt} are independent over j as well as t. Hence we can draw from all at once $h|f, s, y, \theta$. This can then be added to routines which draw from $f|y, h, \theta$ and $\theta|y, h, f$ to complete the sampler.

10.7 Conclusion

In this paper we have described a variety of new simulation-based strategies for estimating general specifications of stochastic volatility models. The single move accept/reject algorithm is a natural extension of the previous work in the literature. It is very simple to implement, reliable and is easily generalizable. However, it can have poor convergence properties which has prompted us to develop other samplers which exploit the time series structure of the model.

The key element of our preferred sampler is the linearization made possible by a log-square transformation of the measurement equation and the approximation of a $\log \chi^2$ random variable by a mixture of normal variables. This, coupled with the Bayesian reweighting procedure to correct for the linearization error, enables the analysis of complex models using the well-established methods for working with conditionally Gaussian state-space models. The simulation conducted in this paper shows that our proposed methods can achieve significant efficiency gains over previously proposed methods for estimating stochastic volatility models. Furthermore, this approach will continue to perform reliably as we move to models with more complicated dynamics.

The paper also discusses the computation of the likelihood function of SV models which is required in the computation of likelihood ratio statistics and Bayes factors. A formal comparison of the SV model in relation to the popular heavy tailed version of GARCH model is also provided for the first time. An interesting set of methods for filtering the volatilities and obtaining diagnostics for model adequacy are also developed. The question of missing data is also taken up in the analysis. The results in this paper, therefore, provide a unified set of tools for a complete analysis of SV models that includes estimation, likelihood

---

[10] Their model sets $\Sigma_t \sim \text{NID}(0, \Sigma_\varepsilon)$, rather than allowing the elements to be stochastic volatility models.

evaluation, filtering, diagnostics for model failure, and computation of statistics for comparing non-nested models. Work continues to refine these results, with the fitting of ever more sophisticated stochastic volatility models.

10.8 Available software

All the software used in this paper can be downloaded from the World Wide Web at the URL:

http://www.nuff.ox.ac.uk/users/shephard/ox/

The software is fully documented. We have linked raw C++ code to the graphics and matrix programming language Ox of Doornik (1996) so that these procedures can be easily used by non-experts.

In the case of the single move Gibbs sampler and the diagnostics routines the software is unfortunately specialized to the SV model with AR(1) log-volatility. However, the other procedures for sampling $h|y, s, \theta$ and the resampling weights are general.

Appendix

This appendix contains various algorithms which allow the efficient computations of some of the quantities required in the paper.

1 Basic Gaussian state-space results
We discuss general filtering and simulation smoothing results which are useful for a general Gaussian state-space model. We analyse the multivariate model

$$y_t = c_t + Z_t \gamma_t + G_t u_t,$$

$$\gamma_{t+1} = d_t + T_t \gamma_t + H_t u_t, \quad u_t \overset{iid}{\sim} \mathcal{N}(0, I). \tag{10.21}$$

$$\gamma_1 | Y_0 \sim N(a_{1|0}, P_{1|0}).$$

For simplicity we assume that $G_t H_t' = 0$ and we write the non-zero rows of H_t as M_t, $G_t G_t' = \Sigma_t$ and $H_t H_t' = \Sigma_{\eta t}$. Throughout c_t and d_t are assumed known.

In the context of our paper we have mostly worked with the simplest of models where, putting $\beta = 1$ and letting r_t^d *denote* daily returns computed as (8),

$$\log(r_t^{d2} + \text{const}) = h_t + \varepsilon_t,$$

and

$$h_{t+1} = \mu(1 - \phi) + \phi h_t + \eta_t,$$

where we condition on the mixture s_t such that

$$\varepsilon_t | s_t = i \sim \mathcal{N}(m_i, v_t^2)$$

and

$$\eta_t \sim \mathcal{N}(0, \sigma_\eta^2).$$

So this puts $y_t = \log(r_t^{d2} + \text{const})$, $c_t = m_i$, $G_t = (\sigma_i, 0)$, $\gamma_t = h_t$ and $Z_t = 1$. Likewise $d_t = \mu(1 - \phi)$, $T_t = \phi$ and $H_t = (0, \sigma_\eta)$. Finally, for a stationary initial condition, $a_{1|0} = \mu$ and $P_{1|0} = \sigma_\eta^2/(1 - \phi^2)$. This means that $\varepsilon_t = G_t u_t$, $\eta_t = H_t u_t$ and u_t is a bivariate standard normal.

The Kalman filter is run for $t = 1, \ldots, n$,

$$\gamma_{t+1|t} = d_t + T_t \gamma_{t|t-1} + K_t v_t, \quad P_{t+1|t} = T_t P_{t|t-1} L_t' + \Sigma_{\eta t}, \quad v_t = y_t - Z_t \gamma_{t|t-1} - c_t,$$
$$F_t = Z_t P_{t|t-1} Z_t' + \Sigma_t, \qquad K_t = T_t P_{t|t-1} Z_t' F_t^{-1}, \qquad L_t = T_t - K_t Z_t. \tag{22}$$

Here $\gamma_{t+1|t} = \mathbf{E}(\gamma_{t+1}|y_1, \ldots, y_t)$ while $P_{t+1|t}$ is the corresponding mean square error. More detailed discussion of the state space form and the Kalman filter is given in Harvey (1989).

The simulation signal smoother (de Jong and Shephard (1995)) draws from the multivariate normal posterior

$$(c_1 + Z_1\gamma_1, \ldots, c_n + Z_n\gamma_n)|y, \theta,$$

where θ denotes the parameters of the model. Setting $r_n = 0$ and $N_n = 0$, and writing $D_t = F_t^{-1} + K_t' N_t K_t$, $n_t = F_t^{-1} v_t - K_t' r_t$, we run for $t = n, \ldots, 1$,

$$C_t = \Sigma_t - \Sigma_t D_t \Sigma_t, \qquad\qquad \kappa_t \sim \mathcal{N}(0, C_t),$$
$$r_{t-1} = Z_t' F_t^{-1} v_t + L_t' r_t - V_t' C_t^{-1} \kappa_t, \qquad V_t = \sum_t (D_t Z_t - K_t' N_t T_t), \tag{23}$$
$$N_{t-1} = Z_t' F_t^{-1} Z_t + L_t' N_t L_t + V_t' C_t^{-1} V_t.$$

Then $y_t - \Sigma_t n_t - \kappa_t$ is a draw from the signal $c_t + Z_t\gamma_t|y, \theta, c_{t+1} + Z_{t+1}\gamma_{t+1}, \ldots, c_n + Z_n\gamma_n$.

The freeware package SSFPack, due to Koopman, Shephard and Doornik (1996), provides easy to use functions which perform Kalman filtering and the simulation signal smoothing for an arbitrary state space model.

2 Augmented state-space
Suppose that we write

$$c_t = X_t\beta, \quad d_t = W_t\beta, \quad \beta \sim \mathcal{N}(0, \Lambda),$$

where β is independent of the u_t process. Then we can estimate the states and the regression parameter β at the same time using the augmented Kalman filter and simulation smoother. The first of these ideas is due to de Jong (1991), the second to de Jong and Shephard (1995).

The augmented Kalman filter adds two equations to the Kalman filter (22) which is run with $c_t = 0, d_t = 0$, additionally computing

$$V_t^a = -Z_t \gamma_{t|t-1}^a - X_t, \quad \gamma_{t+1|t}^a = W_t + T_t \gamma_{t|t-1}^a + K_t V_t^a,$$

where $\gamma_{1|0}^a = W_1$. Here V_t^a is a dim$(y_t) \times$ dim(β) matrix. The augmented innovations V_t^a are the innovations resulting from running $-X_t$ through the Kalman filter (22) with $d_t = W_t$. Hence we can compute the posterior of $\beta|y$ by looking at the weighted least squares regression of v_t on $V_t^a \beta$ with prior information $\beta \sim \mathcal{N}(0, \Lambda)$ and variances F_t. If we set $S_1 = \Lambda^{-1}$ and $s_1 = 0$ (the notation of s_t is local to this discussion) then recursively calculating

$$s_{t+1} = s_t + V_t^{a'} F_t^{-1} v_t \text{ and } S_{t+1} = S_t + V_t^{a'} F_t^{-1} V_t^a,$$

we have that $\beta|y, \theta \sim \mathcal{N}(-S_n^{-1} s_n, S_n^{-1})$, where θ now denotes the remaining parameters in the model.

The random regression effect β can be analytically integrated out of the joint density of y and β (given θ) as

$$\begin{aligned} f(y|\theta) = \int f(y|\beta, \theta)\pi(\beta)d\beta &= \frac{f(y|\beta = 0, \theta)\pi(\beta = 0)}{\pi(\beta = 0|y, \theta)} \\ &\propto \prod_{t=1}^{n} F_t^{-1/2} \exp\left(-\frac{1}{2}\sum_{t=1}^{n} v_t^2/F_t\right) |\Lambda|^{-1/2} \exp\left(\frac{1}{2} s_n' S_n^{-1} s_n\right) |S_n^{-1}|^{1/2}, \end{aligned} \tag{24}$$

using the terms from the augmented Kalman filter. This result is due to de Jong (1991).

If we draw from $b \sim \beta|y, \theta$ we can calculate a new set of innovations $v_t^s = v_t + V_t^a b$, which are the innovations from running the Kalman filter on a state space with known $\beta = b$. Hence we can use the simulation signal smoother which draws $c_1 + Z_1\gamma_1, \ldots, c_n + Z_n\gamma_n|y, \beta = b, \theta$ using the simulation signal smoother (23) just by plugging in the v_t^s instead of the v_t. By using both of these draws we are actually sampling directly from the distribution of

$$(\beta, c_1 + Z_1\gamma_1, \ldots, c_n + Z_n\gamma_n) \mid y, \theta.$$

Acknowledgements

This paper is an extensively revised version of a paper with the same title by Sangjoon Kim and Neil Shephard. That version of the paper did not have the section on the use of the reweighting which corrects for the mixture approximation, nor the formal non-nested testing procedures for comparison with GARCH models. Neil Shephard would like to thank the ESRC for their financial support through the project "Estimation via Simulation in Econometrics" and some computational help from Michael K. Pitt and Jurgen A. Doornik. All the authors would like to thank the referees for their comments on the previous version of the paper.

Sangjoon Kim's work was carried out while he was a Ph.D. student at Department of Economics, Princeton University, under the supervision of John Campbell. Sangjoon Kim would like to thank Princeton University for their financial support. The comments of the participants of the "Stochastic volatility" conference of October 1994, held at HEC (Université de Montreal), are gratefully acknowledged. Finally, Neil Shephard would like to thank A. C. Atkinson and D. R. Cox for various helpful conversations on non-nested likelihood ratio testing.

References

Atkinson, A. C. (1986). Monte-Carlo tests of separate families of hypotheses (Unpublished paper, Imperial College, London).

Berzuini, C., Best, N. G., Gilks, W. R., and Larizza, C. (1997). Dynamic graphical models and Markov chain Monte Carlo methods. *Journal of the American Statistical Association* 92, 1403–12.

Bollerslev, T. (1987). A conditional heteroskedastic time series model for speculative prices and rates of return. *Review of Economics and Statistics* 69, 542–7.

——Engle, R. F., and Nelson, D. B. (1994). ARCH models, in Engle, R. F. and D. McFadden (eds.). *The Handbook of Econometrics, Volume 4* (Amsterdam: North–Holland), 2959–3038.

Bowman, K. O. and Shenton, L. R. (1975). Omnibus test contours for departures from normality based on $\sqrt{b_1}$ and b_2. *Biometrika* 62, 243–50.

Carter, C. K. and Kohn, R. (1994). On Gibbs sampling for state space models. *Biometrika* 81, 541–53.

Chesney, M. and Scott, L. O. (1989). Pricing European options: a comparison of the modified Black–Scholes model and a random variance model. *Journal of Financial and Qualitative Analysis* 24, 267–84.

Chib, S. (1995). Marginal likelihood from Gibbs output. *Journal of the American Statistical Association* 90, 1313–21.

——and Greenberg, E. (1994). Bayes inference for regression models with ARMA (p, q) errors. *Journal of Econometrics* 64, 183–206.

————(1995). Understanding the Metropolis–Hastings algorithm. *The American Statistican* 49, 327–35.

————(1996). Markov chain Monte Carlo simulation methods in econometrics. *Econometric Theory* 12, 409–31.

Cox, D. R. (1991). Long-range dependence, non-linearity and time irreversibility. *Journal of Time Series Analysis* 12, 329–35.

De Jong, P. (1991). The diffuse Kalman filter. *Annals of Statistics* 19, 1073–83.

——(1997). The scan sampler. *Biometrika* 84, 929–37.

——Shephard, N. (1995). The simulation smoother for time series models. *Biometrika* 82, 339–50.

Diebold, F. X. and Nerlove, M. (1989). The dynamics of exchange rate volatility: a multivariate latent factor ARCH model. *Journal of Applied Econometrics* 4, 1–21.

Doornik, J. A. (1996). *Ox: Object Oriented Matrix Programming. 1.10* (London: Chapman & Hall).

Engle, R. F. (1982). Autoregressive conditional heteroskedasticity with estimates of the variance of the United Kingdom inflation. *Econometrica* 50, 987–1007.

Escobar, M. and West, M. (1995). Bayesian density estimation and inference using mixtures. *Journal of the American Statistical Association* 90, 577–88.

Fuller, W. A. (1996). *Introduction to Time Series* (2nd ed.) (New York: John Wiley).

Gallant, A. R. and Tauchen, G. (1996). Which moments to match. *Econometric Theory* 12, 657–81.

Gelfand, A. and Smith, A. F. M. (1990). Sampling-based approaches to calculating marginal densities. *Journal of the American Statistical Association* 85, 398–409.

Geman, S. and Geman, D. (1984). Stochastic relaxation, Gibbs distribution and the Bayesian restoration of images. *IEEE Transactions, PAMI* 6, 721–41.

Geweke, J. (1994). Comment on Bayesian analysis of stochastic volatility models. *Journal of Business and Economic Statistics* 12, 397–99.

Ghysels, E., Harvey, A. C., and Renault, E. (1996). Stochastic volatility, in Rao, C. R. and Maddala, G. S. (eds.). *Statistical Methods in Finance* (Amsterdam: North–Holland), 119–91.

Gilks, W. R., Richardson, S., and Spiegelhalter, D. J. (1996). *Markov Chain Monte Carlo in Practice* (London: Chapman & Hall).

Gilks, W. R., Best, N. G., and Tan, K. K. C. (1995). Adaptive rejection Metropolis sampling within Gibbs sampling. *Applied Statistics* 44, 155–73.

—— Wild, P. (1992). Adaptive rejection sampling for Gibbs sampling. *Applied Statistics* 41, 337–48.

Gordon, N. J., Salmond, D. J., and Smith, A. F. M. (1993). A novel approach to non-linear and non-Gaussian Bayesian state estimation. *IEE-Proceedings F* 140, 107–33.

Gourieroux, C. and Monfort, A. (1994). Testing non-nested hypotheses, in Engle, R. F. and D. McFadden (eds.). *The Handbook of Econometrics, Volume 4*, (Amsterdam: North–Holland), 2583–2637.

—— —— Renault, E. (1993). Indirect inference. *Journal of Applied Econometrics* 8, S85–S118.

Harvey, A. C. (1989). *Forecasting, Structural Time Series Models and the Kalman Filter* (Cambridge: Cambridge University Press).

—— Ruiz, E., and Shephard, N. (1994). Multivariate stochastic variance models. *Review of Economic Studies* 61, 247–64.

Hastings, W. K. (1970). Monte-Carlo sampling methods using Markov chains and their applications. *Biometrika* 57, 97–109.

Hinde, J. (1992). Choosing between non-nested models: a simulation approach, in Fahrmeir, L., Francis, B., Gilchrist, R. and Tutz, G. (eds.). *Advances in GLIM and Statistical Modelling, Proceedings of the GLIM92 Conference and the 7th International Workshop on Statistical Modelling, Munich 13–17 July 1992* (New York: Springer-Verlag), 119–24.

Hull, J. and White, A. (1987). The pricing of options on assets with stochastic volatilities. *Journal of Finance* 42, 281–300.

Isard, M. and Blake, A. (1996). Contour tracking by stochastic propagation of conditional density. *Proceedings of the European Conference on Computer Vision, Cambridge* 1, 343–56.

Jacquier, E., Polson, N. G., and Rossi, P. E. (1994). Bayesian analysis of stochastic volatility models (with discussion). *Journal of Business and Economic Statistics* 12, 371–417.

———————— (1995). Models and prior distributions for multivariate stochastic volatility (Unpublished paper, Graduate School of Business, University of Chicago).

King, M., Sentana, E., and Wadhwani, S. (1994). Volatility and links between national stock markets. *Econometrica* 62, 901–33.

Kitagawa, G. (1996). Monte Carlo filter and smoother for non-Gaussian non-linear state space models. *Journal of Computational and Graphical Statistics* 5, 1–25.

Koopman, S. J., Shephard, N., and Doornik, J. A. (1996). SSFPack 1.1: filtering, smoothing and simulation algorithms for state space models in Ox (Unpublished paper and software), available at http://www.nuff.ox.ac.uk/users/shephard/ox/.

Mahieu, R. and Schotman, P. C. (1997). Stochastic volatility and the distribution of exchange rate news. *Journal of Applied Econometrics* 15 (forthcoming).

Marriott, J. M. and Smith, A. F. M. (1992). Reparameterization aspects of numerical Bayesian methodology for autoregressive moving-average models. *Journal of Time Series Analysis* 13, 327–43.

Metropolis, N., Rosenbluth, A. W., Rosenbluth, M. N., Teller, A. H., and Teller, E. (1953). Equations of state calculations by fast computing machines. *Journal of Chemical Physics* 21, 1087–92.

Muller, P. (1991). Numerical integration in general dynamic models. *Contemporary Mathematics* 115, 145–63.

Park, S. and Miller, K. (1988). Random number generators: good ones are hard to find. *Communications of the ACM* 31, 1192–201.

Pesaran, M. H. and Pesaran, B. (1993). A simulation approach to the problem of computing Cox's statistic for testing nonnested models. *Journal of Econometrics* 57, 377–92.

Phillips, P. C. B. (1991). To criticise the critics: an objective Bayesian analysis of stochastic trends. *Journal of Applied Econometrics* 6, 333–64.

Pitt, M. K. and Shephard, N. (1997). Filtering via simulation: an auxiliary variable approach (Working paper, Nuffield College, Oxford).

Pitt, M. K. and Shephard, N. (1998). Analytic convergence rates and parameterisation issues for the Gibbs sampler applied to state space models. *Journal of Time Series Analysis* 19 (forthcoming).

Priestley, M. B. (1981). (London: Academic Press). *Spectral Analysis and Time Series*.

Richardson, S. and Green, P. (1997). On Bayesian analysis of mixtures with unknown number of components. *Journal of the Royal Statistical Society B* 59, 731–92.

Ripley, B. D. (1977). Modelling spatial patterns (with discussion). *Journal of the Royal Statistical Society B* 39, 172–212.

——(1987). *Stochastic Simulation* (New York: Wiley).

Rosenblatt, M. (1952). Remarks on a multivariate transformation. *Annals of Mathematical Statistics* 23, 470–2.

Schotman, P. C. and Van Dijk, H. K. (1991). A Bayesian analysis of the unit root in real exchange rates. *Journal of Econometrics* 49, 195–238.

Shephard, N. (1993). Fitting non-linear time series models, with applications to stochastic variance models. *Journal of Applied Econometrics* 8, S135–S152.

——(1994). Partial non-Gaussian state space. *Biometrika* 81, 115–31.

——(1996). Statistical aspects of ARCH and stochastic volatility, in Cox, D. R., Barndorff-Nielson, O. E., and Hinkley, D. V. (eds.). *Time Series Models in Econometrics, Finance and Other Fields* (London: Chapman & Hall), 1–67.

Kim, S. (1994). Comment on 'Bayesian analysis of stochastic volatility models' by Jacquier, Polson and Rossi. *Journal of Business and Economic Statistics* 11, 406–10.

Shephard, N. and Pitt, M. K. (1997). Likelihood analysis of non-Gaussian measurement time series. *Biometrika* 84, 653–67.

Tanner, M. A. (1996). *Tools for Statistical Inference: methods for exploration of posterior distributions and likelihood functions* (3 edn.) (New York: Springer-Verlag).

—— Wong, W. H. (1987). The calculation of posterior distributions by data augmentation (with discussion). *Journal of the American Statistical Association* 82, 528–50.

Taylor, S. J. (1986). *Modelling Financial Time Series* (Chichester: John Wiley).

—— (1994). Modelling stochastic volatility. *Mathematical Finance* 4, 183–204.

Tierney, L. (1994). Markov Chains for exploring posterior distributions (with discussion). *Annals of Statistics* 21, 1701–62.

Titterington, D. M., Smith, A. F. M., and Makov, U. E. (1985). *Statistical Analysis of Finite Mixture Distributions* (Chichester: John Wiley).

West, M. (1993). Approximating posterior distributions by mixtures. *Journal of the Royal Statistical Society B* 55, 409–42.

11

Estimation of Stochastic Volatility Models with Diagnostics*

A. RONALD GALLANT, DAVID HSIEH AND
GEORGE TAUCHEN

Abstract

Efficient method of moments (EMM) is used to fit the standard stochastic volatility model and various extensions to several daily financial time series. EMM matches to the score of a model determined by data analysis called the score generator. Discrepancies reveal characteristics of data that stochastic volatility models cannot approximate. The two score generators employed here are 'semi-parametric ARCH' and 'nonlinear nonparametric'. With the first, the standard model is rejected, although some extensions are accepted. With the second, all versions are rejected. The extensions required for an adequate fit are so elaborate that nonparametric specifications are probably more convenient.

Keywords: Stochastic volatility; Efficient method of moments (EMM); Diagnostics

11.1 Introduction

The stochastic volatility model has been proposed as a description of data from financial markets by Clark (1973), Tauchen and Pitts (1983), Taylor (1986, 1994), and others. The appeal of the model is that it provides a simple specification for speculative price movements that accounts, in qualitative terms, for broad general features of data from financial markets such as leptokurtosis and persistent volatility. Also, it is related to diffusion processes used in derivatives pricing theory in finance; see Mathieu and Schotman (1994) and references therein. The standard form as set forth, for instance, in Harvey et al. (1994), Jacquier, et al. (1994), and Danielsson (1994), takes the form of an autoregression whose innovations are scaled by an unobservable volatility process, usually distributed as a log-normal autoregression.

Estimation of the stochastic volatility model presents intriguing challenges, and a variety of procedures have been proposed for fitting the model. Extant methods include method of moments (Duffie and Singleton, 1993; Andersen and Sorensen, 1996), Bayesian methods (Jacquier et al. 1994; Geweke, 1994),

* Reprinted from *Journal of Econometrics* 81, A. R. Gallant, D. Hsieh, and G. Tauchen, 'Estimation of Stochastic Volatility Models with Diagnostics', pp 159–192, Copyright © 1997, with permission from Elsevier.

simulated likelihood (Danielsson, 1994), and Kalman filtering methods (Harvey et al. 1994; Kim and Shephard, 1994). Two excellent recent surveys are Ghysels et al. (1995) and Shephard (1995).

Here, we employ the efficient method of moments (EMM) proposed by Bansal et al. (1993, 1995) and developed in Gallant and Tauchen (1996) to estimate and test the stochastic volatility model. EMM is a simulation-based moment matching procedure with certain advantages. The moments that get matched are the scores of an auxiliary model called the 'score generator'. If the score generator approximates the distribution of the data well, then estimates of the parameters of the stochastic volatility model are as efficient as if maximum likelihood had been employed (Tauchen, 1997a; Gallant and Long, 1997). Failure to match these moments can be used as a statistical specification test and, more importantly, can be used to indicate features of data that the stochastic volatility model cannot accommodate (Tauchen, 1997a).

The objective is to report and interpret the EMM objective function surface across a comprehensive set of specifications of the stochastic volatility model. We start with the standard, and widely used setup, with Gaussian errors and short lag lengths, and we proceed to more complicated specifications with long lag lengths. The effort is aimed at generating a comprehensive accounting of how well the model and its extensions accommodate features of the data. An advantage of the EMM procedure is that it is computationally tractable enough to permit this exhaustive specification analysis. Our approach differs from typical practice in the stochastic volatility literature, which is to fit the standard setup and perhaps a single extension in one direction. Since various studies use different specifications, estimation methods, and data sets, it is difficult to reach firm conclusions on the plausibility of the stochastic volatility model. By using EMM, we can confront all of the various extensions, individually and jointly, to a judiciously chosen set of moments determined by a nonparametric specification search for the score generator. Other estimation methods are incapable of investigating the empirical plausibility of such an extended set of specifications for stochastic volatility on the large data sets used here.

We fit the univariate stochastic volatility model to a long time series comprised of 16,127 daily observations on adjusted movements of the Standard and Poor's Composite Price Index, 1928–87. We use such a long series because, among other things, we are interested in the long-term persistence properties of stock volatility.

For this estimation, we use two score generators based on the specification analysis of Gallant et al. (1992). The first is an ARCH model with a homogeneous innovation distribution that is given a nonparametric representation. The specific specification is determined by a standard model selection procedure based on the BIC criterion and specification tests. This model is similar to the most widely used models in the ARCH family. Its score is termed the 'semi-parametric ARCH score'. The second score generator is a fully nonparametric estimator of the distribution of a nonlinear process. It both nests the first and relaxes its homogeneity assumption. The specific specification is determined using the same model selection procedure as above. The corresponding score is termed the 'nonlinear nonparametric score'. These two score generators, determined independently of the stochastic volatility model, are similar to models that are commonly fit to high-frequency financial data.

We undertake a similar exercise for a trivariate stochastic volatility model applied to 4,044 daily observations on adjusted movements of the Standard and Poor's Composite Price Index, adjusted movements of the $/DM spot exchange rate, and the adjusted 90-day Euro-Dollar interest rate, 1977–92.

11.2 The stochastic volatility model

11.2.1 Setup and notation

Let y_t denote the first difference (either simple or logarithmic) over a short time interval, a day for instance, of the price of a financial asset traded on active speculative markets. The basic stochastic volatility for y_t is

$$y_t - \mu_y = \sum_{j=1}^{L_y} c_j(y_{t-j} - \mu_y) + \exp(w_t) r_y z_t,$$

$$w_t - \mu_w = \sum_{j=1}^{L_w} a_j(w_{t-j} - \mu_w) + r_w \tilde{z}_t,$$

where $\mu_y, \{c_j\}_{j=1}^{L_y}, r_y, \mu_w, \{a_j\}_{j=1}^{L_w}$, and r_w are the parameters of the two equations, called the mean and volatility equations, respectively. The processes $\{z_t\}$ and $\{\tilde{z}_t\}$ are mutually independent iid random variables with mean zero and unit variance. Whenever they exist, unconditional expectations are taken with respect to the joint distribution of the processes $\{z_t\}$ and $\{\tilde{z}_t\}$. The first two moments of the z_t and $\tilde{z}_t$ are not separately identified from the other parameters – hence the restriction to $\mathscr{E}(z_t) = \mathscr{E}(\tilde{z}_t) = 0$ and $\text{Var}(z_t) = \text{Var}(\tilde{z}_t) = 1$. Likewise, μ_w is not separately identified; we find numerically the best normalization is simply $\mu_w = 0$. A common assumption in the literature is that both z_t and $\tilde{z}_t$ are independent $N(0, 1)$ random variables and that the lag lengths are short. Typically, $L_w = 1$ and $L_y = 1$, or $L_y = 0$. Below, we entertain other distributional assumptions and search over a broad set of lag lengths. The model implies restrictions on the serial covariance properties of $|y_t|^c, c > 0$, which are worked out in exhaustive detail in Ghysels et al. (1995).

One interpretation of the process w_t, which has its origins in Clark (1973) and is refined in Tauchen and Pitts (1983), is that stochastic volatility reflects the random and uneven flow of new information to the financial market. Over the time period $t - 1$ to t, a random number of individual pieces of information impinge the market. Each piece triggers an independent price movement drawn from a time-homogeneous parent distribution. If $I_t = [\exp(w_t)]^2$ individual pieces impinge on the market then, conditional on I_t, the studentized innovation

$$[y_t - \mu_{t-1,t}]/\sqrt{I_t},$$

where

$$\mu_{t-1,t} = \mu_y + \sum_{j=1}^{L_y} c_j(y_{t-j} - \mu_y),$$

would follow a parent distribution, typically Gaussian. The process I_t is called the mixing process. It is unobservable and presumable serially correlated, which motivates the stochastic volatility specification given above.

11.2.2 Data generator

The stochastic volatility model defines a strictly stationary and Markov process $\{s_t\}$, where $s_t = (y_t, w_t)'$. The process is Markovian of order $L_s = \max(L_y, L_w)$ with conditional density $p_s(s_t|s_{t-L_s}, \ldots, s_{t-1}, \rho)$ given by the stochastic volatility model, where

$$\rho = (\mu_y, c_1, \ldots, c_{L_y}, r_y, a_1, \ldots, a_{L_w}, r_w)'$$

is a vector that contains the free parameters of the stochastic volatility model.

The process $\{y_t\}$ is observed whereas $\{w_t\}$ is regarded as latent. Write $p_{y,J}(y_{t-J}, \ldots, y_t|\rho)$ for the implied joint density under the model of a stretch $y_{t-J}, \ldots, y_t$. Most integrals appearing in formulas in subsequent sections fail to admit closed form solutions. In practice, they must be approximated by quadrature or Monte Carlo integration, although likelihoods can sometimes be computed efficiently using the Kalman filter (Kim and Shephard, 1994). As will be seen, we need to compute expectations under the model of a variety of nonlinear functions. Monte Carlo integration is most convenient, and is effected by averaging over a long realization from the stochastic volatility model. For a general nonlinear function $g(y_{t-J}, y_{t-J+1}, \ldots, y_t)$, integrals of the form

$$\int \cdots \int g(y_{t-J}, y_{t-J+1}, \ldots, y_t) p_{y,J}(y_{t-J}, y_{t-J+1}, \ldots, y_t|\rho) \prod_{k=0}^{J} dy_{t-k}$$

are approximated by

$$\frac{1}{N} \sum_{\tau=J+1}^{N} g(\hat{y}_{\tau-J}, \hat{y}_{\tau-J+1}, \ldots, \hat{y}_\tau),$$

where $\{\hat{y}_\tau\}_{\tau=1}^{N}$ is a long simulated realization from the stochastic volatility model given a value ρ. This is accomplished by simulating $\{\hat{s}_\tau\}_{\tau=1}^{N}$, which is straightforward, and retaining the element $\hat{y}_\tau$ from $\hat{s}_\tau = (\hat{y}_\tau, \hat{w}_\tau)$.

Here, computations are based on realizations of length 50,000–100,000, with the choice having no substantive effect on inferences. To let transients die off, first the volatility equation (which displays substantial persistence) runs for 10,000 periods; next, both the mean equation (which displays minor persistence) and the variance equations run together for another 100 periods, which are discarded; then both equations continue to run together to generate a realization of the desired length.

11.3 The EMM estimator

In Sections 4 and 5 below we employ the efficient method of moments (EMM) methodology as described in Gallant and Tauchen (1996) to estimate and test the stochastic volatility model. The title of the paper is suggestive, 'Which Moments to Match?', and the answer is simple and intuitive: Use the score vector of an auxiliary model that fits the data well to define a GMM criterion function. The EMM method has some computational advantages relative to indirect inference (Gourieroux et al., 1993) as it circumvents the need to refit the score generator to each simulated realization (compute the binding function) and it bypasses a Hessian computation. The ideas behind EMM are as follows.

We observe the data $\{\tilde{y}_t\}_{t=1}^n$, which is presumed to have been generated by the stochastic volatility model for some value $\rho^0 \in R \subset \Re^{\ell_p}$, where ℓ_p is the length of ρ^0. The task is to estimate ρ^0 and test the specification of the model.

Suppose that a probability model for the stochastic process $\{y_t\}_{t=-\infty}^\infty$ defined by the conditional density

$$f(y_t|y_{t-L}, y_{t-L+1}, \ldots, y_{t-1}, \theta), \quad \theta \in \Theta \subset \Re^{\ell_\theta},$$

fits the data $\{\tilde{y}_t\}_{t=1}^n$ reasonably well. Fits well means that when its parameters are estimated by quasi-maximum likelihood

$$\tilde{\theta}_n = \arg \max_{\theta \in \Theta} \sum_{t=L+1}^n \log[f(\tilde{y}_t|\tilde{y}_{t-L}, \ldots, \tilde{y}_{t-1}, \theta)],$$

the model does reasonably well on statistical specification tests and the fit appears sensible from an economic perspective. The functional form of $f(y_t|x_{t-1}, \theta)$ need not have any direct connection to that of the true conditional distribution of y_t given $x_{t-1} = (y_{t-L}, y_{t-L+1}, \ldots, y_{t-1})$, which is

$$\frac{p_{y,L}(y_{t-L}, y_{t-L+1}, \ldots, y_t|\rho^0)}{p_{y,L-1}(y_{t-L}, y_{t-L+1}, \ldots, y_{t-1}|\rho^0)}.$$

It should provide a good approximation, though, for the EMM estimator to be nearly fully efficient (Tauchen, 1997a; Gallant and Long, 1997).

The EMM estimator brings the information in $f(y|x, \tilde{\theta}_n)$ to bear on the task of estimating and testing the stochastic volatility model as follows. Define the criterion

$$m(\rho, \theta) = \int \cdots \int \frac{\partial}{\partial \theta} \log [f(y_t|y_{t-L}, \ldots, y_{t-1}, \theta)]\, p_{y,L}(y_{t-L}, \ldots, y_t \,|\, \rho) \times \prod_{k=0}^{L} dy_{t-k},$$

which is the expected score of the $f(y|x, \theta)$ model under the stochastic volatility model. Hence, $f(y|x, \theta)$ is called the 'score generator'. The induced parameter that $\tilde{\theta}_n$ estimates is that value θ^0 for which $m(\rho^0, \theta) = 0$ (Gallant, 1987, chapter 7, Theorem 8). This fact provides the motivation for the EMM estimator. One expects $m(\rho, \tilde{\theta}_n)$ to be near zero for values of ρ close to ρ^0.

The EMM estimator is

$$\hat{\rho}_n = \arg \min_{\rho \in R} m'(\rho, \tilde{\theta}_n)(\mathscr{I}_n)^{-1} m(\rho, \tilde{\theta}_n),$$

where

$$\tilde{\mathscr{I}}_n = \frac{1}{n} \sum_{t=L+1}^{n} \left[\frac{\partial}{\partial \theta} \log f(\tilde{y}_t|\tilde{x}_{t-1}, \tilde{\theta}_n) \right] \left[\frac{\partial}{\partial \theta} \log f(\tilde{y}_t|\tilde{x}_{t-1}, \tilde{\theta}_n) \right]'.$$

and

$$\tilde{x}_{t-1} = (\tilde{y}_{t-L}, \tilde{y}_{t-L+1}, \ldots, \tilde{y}_{t-1})'.$$

In computing $\hat{\rho}_n$, we do not need to impose restrictions that the parameter space R contains only those ρ for which the model generates stationary data, as such restrictions are automatically enforced on the computation (Tauchen, 1997b). Also, as noted in Gallant and Tauchen (1996), one should, strictly speaking, use a weighted covariance estimator of

$$\mathscr{I}^0 = \text{Var}\left[\frac{1}{\sqrt{n}} \sum_{t=L+1}^{n} \frac{\partial}{\partial \theta} \log f(y_t|y_{t-L}, y_{t-L+1}, \ldots, y_{t-1}, \theta^0) \right]$$

rather than $\tilde{\mathscr{I}}_n$, and formulas are given therein. However, it is unlikely that this generality will be necessary in practice because the use of a weighted covariance estimator means that one thinks that the score generator is a poor statistical approximation to the data generating process. A poor statistical approximation is unlikely because the score generator is, conceptually, a reduced form model, not a structural model, and is usually easy to modify by adding a few parameters so that it fits the data well.

Under regularity conditions stated in Gallant and Tauchen (1996), which are standard regularity conditions such that the maximum likelihood estimator of ρ

in $p(y|x, \rho)$ is consistent and asymptotic normal and such that the quasi-max-imum likelihood estimator of θ in $f(y|x, \theta)$ is asymptotic normal, we have that $\hat{\rho}_n$ is consistent and

$$\sqrt{n}(\hat{\rho}_n - \rho^0) \xrightarrow{\mathcal{J}} N\{0, [(M^0)'(\mathcal{J}^0)^{-1}(M^0)]^{-1}\},$$

where $M^0 = M(\rho^0, \theta^0)$ and $M(\rho, \theta) = (\partial/\partial\rho')m(\rho, \theta)$. M^0 can be estimated con-sistently by $\hat{M}_n = M_n(\hat{\rho}_n, \tilde{\theta}_n)$. The order condition (necessary condition) for identification is $\ell_\rho \leqslant \ell_\theta$; sufficient conditions are discussed in Gallant and Tau-chen (1996). The better the score generator approximates the conditional distri-bution of the data, then the closer is the asymptotic covariance matrix to that of maximum likelihood (Tauchen, 1997a; Gallant and Long, 1997). If the score generator actually nests the true conditional distribution, then full efficiency obtains (Gallant and Tauchen, 1996).

$M_n(\rho, \theta)$ must be computed numerically in order to use the asymptotic distri-bution to get standard errors for setting confidence intervals on the elements of ρ^0. Alternatively, one can avoid computation of $\hat{M}_n$ by using the criterion difference statistic to set confidence intervals (Gallant, 1987, chapter 7, Theorem 15). The latter approach is to be preferred in most time-series applica-tions because it will exclude values of ρ that imply an explosive process from the confidence interval (Tauchen, 1997b).

For specification testing, which is the focus of this paper, we have that

$$nm'(\hat{\rho}_n, \tilde{\theta}_n)(\tilde{\mathcal{J}}_n)^{-1}m(\hat{\rho}_n, \tilde{\theta}_n) \xrightarrow{\mathcal{L}} \chi^2(df)$$

with $df = \ell_\theta - \ell_\rho$ under the null hypothesis that the maintained model $p_{y, L}(y_{t-L}, \ldots, y_t, \rho)$ is correct.

When a model fails a diagnostic test, one would like some suggestions as to what is wrong. Inspection of the quasi-t-ratios

$$\hat{T}_n = S_n^{-1}\sqrt{n}m(\hat{\rho}_n, \tilde{\theta}_n),$$

where $S_n = [\text{diag}(\tilde{\mathcal{J}}_n)]^{1/2}$ can suggest reasons for model failure. As seen in Section 4, different elements of the score vector correspond to different features of the fit. Large quasi-t-ratios reveal the features of the data that the maintained model cannot approximate.

The elements of $\hat{T}_n$ are biased downward in absolute value because the stand-ard errors S_n are too large due to the fact that

$$\sqrt{n}m(\hat{\rho}_n, \tilde{\theta}_n) \xrightarrow{\mathcal{L}} N\{0, \mathcal{J}^0 - (M^0)[(M^0)'(\mathcal{J}^0)^{-1}(M^0)]^{-1}(M^0)'\}.$$

The downward bias can be corrected by computing $\hat{M}_n$ numerically and putting $S_n = (\text{diag}\{\tilde{\mathcal{J}}_n - (\hat{M}_n)[(\hat{M}_n)'(\tilde{\mathcal{J}}_n)^{-1}(\hat{M}_n)]^{-1}(\hat{M}_n)'\})^{1/2}$ in the formula for $\hat{T}_n$.

We have not corrected the bias in this paper because we believe the correction to be unnecessary for two reasons. First, $\mathcal{I}^0 - (M^0)[(M^0)'(\mathcal{I}^0)^{-1}(M^0)]^{-1}(M^0)'$ is the familiar formula for the variance of GLS residuals and experience with GLS regressions suggests that the difference between $\mathcal{I}^0 - (M^0)[(M^0)'(\mathcal{I}^0)^{-1}(M^0)]^{-1}$ $(M^0)'$ and $\mathcal{I}^0$ is negligible in most applications. Secondly, we do not rely on the quasi-t-ratios for inference, we only rely on them for suggestions as to how the stochastic volatility model might be enhanced. When we act upon a suggestion, we check it with the χ^2 statistic. This methodological approach is similar to the well-established F-produced t-test methodology as employed in the statistical Analysis of Variance.

11.4 Univariate empirical results

11.4.1 Data

The data to which we fit the univariate stochastic volatility model is a long time series comprised of 16,127 daily observations, $\{\tilde{y}_t\}_{t=1}^{16,127}$, on adjusted movements of the Standard and Poor's Composite Price Index, 1928–87. This series is the univariate stock series used in Gallant et al. (1992, 1993). The raw series is the Standard and Poor's Composite Price Index (SP), daily, 1928–87. We use a long time series, because, among other things, we want to investigate the long-term properties of stock market volatility. As described in Gallant et al. (1992), the raw series is converted to a price movements series, $100[\log(\mathrm{SP}_t)$ $- \log(\mathrm{SP}_{t-1})]$, and then adjusted for systematic calendar effects in location and scale. Financial data are known to exhibit calendar effects, that is, systematic shifts in location and scale due to different trading patterns across days of the week, holidays, and year-end tax trading. Calendar effects comprise a very small portion of the total variation in the series, although they should still be accounted for in order not to adversely affect subsequent analysis. The raw and adjusted data are plotted in Fig. 11.1. Though long time series sometimes exhibit structural regime switches, there is no such shift apparent in the figure.

11.4.2 Score generators

To implement the EMM estimator we require a score generator $f(y|x, \theta)$ that fits these data well. As documented in Gallant et al. (1992, 1993) the semi-nonparametric (SNP) density proposed by Gallant and Tauchen (1989) does so. Moreover, when refitted to subperiods, estimates are stable.

The SNP density is a member of a class of parameterized conditional densities

$$\mathcal{H}_K = \{f_K(y|x, \theta): \theta = (\theta_1, \theta_2, \ldots, \theta_{\ell_K})\},$$

which expands $\mathcal{H}_1 \subset \mathcal{H}_2 \subset \cdots$ as K increases. It has two desirable properties from the perspective of EMM estimation: (1) The union $\mathcal{H} = \bigcup_{K=1}^{\infty} \mathcal{H}_K$ is quite rich and it is reasonable to assume that the true density $p(y|x)$ of stationary data from a financial market is contained in $\mathcal{H}$. (2) If θ is estimated by quasi-maximum likelihood, viz.

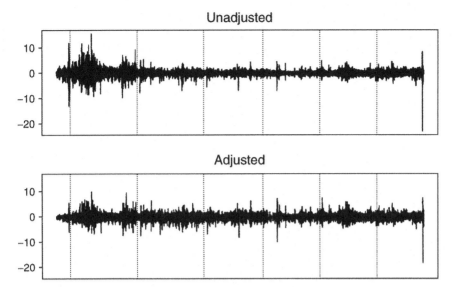

Fig. 11.1. Time series of unadjusted and adjusted stock price movements. The top panel shows a time series plot of the daily unadjusted price movement series, $100(\log P_t - \log P_{t-1})$. The data are daily from 1928 to 1987, 16,127 observations. The bottom panel shows the adjusted price movement series. The adjustments remove calendar effects and long-term trend on the basis of least squares regressions. The adjusted series can reasonably be taken as stationary, which is required for use of the SNP estimator. See section 1 of Gallant et al. (1992) for a description of the adjustment procedure.

$$\tilde{\theta}_n = \arg \max_{\theta \in R^{i_R} K} \frac{1}{n} \sum_{t=L+1}^{n} \log [f_K(\tilde{y}_t | \tilde{y}_{t-L}, \ldots, \tilde{y}_{t-1}, \theta)],$$

and if K grows with sample size n [either adaptively as a random variable $\tilde{K}_n$ or deterministically as a function $K(n)$], then

$$\tilde{p}_n(y|x) = f_K(y|x, \tilde{\theta}_n)$$

is a consistent (Gallant and Nychka, 1987) and efficient (Fenton and Gallant, 1996a; Gallant and Long, 1997) nonparametric estimator of $p(y|x)$ with desirable qualitative features (Fenton and Gallant, 1996b).

A standard method of describing a conditional density $f(y|x, \theta)$ is to set forth a location function μ_x and a scale function R_x that reduces the process $\{y_t\}_{t=-\infty}^{\infty}$ to an innovation process $\{z_t\}_{t=-\infty}^{\infty}$ via the transformation

$$z_t = r_{x_{t-1}}^{-1}(y_t - \mu_{x_{t-1}}).$$

The description is completed by setting forth a conditional density $h(z|x)$ for the innovation process. We follow this recipe in describing $f_K(y|x, \theta) \in \mathcal{H}_K$.

The location function μ_x is affine in x

$$\mu_{x_{t-1}} = b_0 + b'x_{t-1}.$$

It is presumed to depend on $L_\mu \leq L$ lags which is accomplished by putting leading elements of b to zero as required. Note that were one to put r_x to a constant and eliminate the dependence of the innovation density on x by writing $h(z)$ instead of $h(z|x)$ then $\{y_t\}_{t=-\infty}^{\infty}$ would be a vector autoregression (VAR).

The scale function r_x is affine in the absolute values of x

$$r_{x_{t-1}} = \rho_0 + \rho'|x_{t-1}|.$$

It is presumed to depend on $L_R \leq L$ lags which is accomplished by putting leading elements of ρ to zero as required. Note that were one to eliminate the dependence of the innovation density on x by writing $h(z)$ instead of $h(z|x)$ then $\{y_t\}_{t=-\infty}^{\infty}$ would be an ARCH-type process akin to that proposed by Nelson (1991).

For a vector $\zeta = (\zeta_1, \ldots, \zeta_\ell)$ with real elements and a vector $\lambda = (\lambda_1, \ldots, \lambda_\ell)$ with integer elements, let ζ^λ denote the monomial $\prod_{i=1}^{\ell} \zeta_i^{\lambda_i}$ of degree $|\lambda| = \sum_{i=1}^{\ell} |\lambda_i|$ and consider

$$h_K(z|x) = \frac{[P_K(z, x)]^2 \phi(z)}{\int [P_K(u, x)]^2 \phi(u)\, du}$$

formed from the polynomial

$$P_K(z, x) = \sum_{\alpha=0}^{K_z} \left(\sum_{|\beta|=0}^{K_x} a_{\alpha\beta} x^\beta \right) z^\alpha$$

where $\phi(z) = (2\pi)^{-1/2} e^{-z'z/2}$. $P_K(z, x)$ is a polynomial of degree K_z in z whose coefficients are, in turn, polynomials of degree K_x in x. The product $[P_K(z, x)]^2 \phi(z)$ is a Hermite polynomial in z with positivity enforced whose coefficients depend on x. The shape of the innovation density $h_K(z_t|x_{t-1})$ varies with x_{t-1} which permits $h_K(z_t|x_{t-1})$ to exhibit general, conditional shape heterogeneity. By putting selected elements of the matrix $A = [a_{\alpha\beta}]$ to zero, $P_K(z, x)$ can be made to depend on only $L_p \leq L$ lags from x. One may note that if K_z is put to zero, then the innovation density $h_K(z|x)$ is Gaussian. If $K_z > 0$ and $K_x = 0$, then the density can assume arbitrary shape but innovations are homogeneous.

The change of variables $y_t = r_{x_{t-1}} z_t + \mu_{x_{t-1}}$ to obtain the density

$$f_K(y_t|x_{t-1}, \theta) = \frac{\{P_K[r_{x_{t-1}}^{-1}(y_t - \mu_{x_{t-1}}), x_{t-1}]\}^2 \phi[r_{x_{t-1}}^{-1}(y_t - \mu_{x_{t-1}})]}{|r_{x_{t-1}}|^{1/2} \int [P_K(u, x_{t-1})]^2 \phi(u)\, du}.$$

completes the description of the SNP density. The vector θ contains the coefficients $A = [a_{\alpha\beta}]$ of the Hermite polynomial, the coefficients $[b_0, b]$ of the location function, and the coefficients $[\rho_0, \rho]$ of the scale function. To achieve identification, the coefficient $a_{0,0}$ is set to 1. The tuning parameters are L_u, L_r, L_p, K_z, and K_x, which determine the dimension $\ell_K (= \ell_\theta)$ of θ.

When data are heavy tailed, as is typical for data from financial markets, numerical stability can be enhanced without affecting theoretical results by forming the vector of lags x_{t-1} from a series $\{y_t^*\}$ consisting of $\{y_t\}$ that have been centered by subtracting the sample mean, scaled by dividing by the sample standard error, and transformed by the logistic map that takes the interval $(-\infty, \infty)$ into the interval $(-4, 4)$. That has been done both here and in the results reported for this series by Gallant et al. (1992, 1993). Note that it is only the lagged-dependent variables x_{t-1} that are logistic transformed; the contemporaneous y_t is not.

We selected the tuning parameters L_u, L_r, L_p, K_z, and K_x following the protocol that is described in detail in Bansal et al. (1995). Briefly, the model is expanded sequentially according to the BIC (Schwarz, 1978) model selection criterion. It is then expanded further if a battery of statistical specification tests indicate that the BIC specification is inadequate. Following this protocol, we selected the model $L_u = 2, L_r = 18$, and $K_z = 4$ with 26 free parameters, when innovations are constrained to be homogenous (that is, $K_x = 0$, and $L_p = 1$ imposed). This is a semiparametric density with a parametric part comprised of an AR(2)-ARCH(18) model with unconstrained lag coefficients and a nonparametric error density, which is analogous to the model proposed by Engle and Gonzales-Rivera (1991). We term the score from this fit the 'semiparametric ARCH score' in legends for figures and tables. When the homogeneity constraint is dropped, and we follow the same protocol, we select the model $L_u = 2$, $L_r = 18, L_p = 2, K_z = 4$, and $K_x = 1$ with 36 free parameters; this specification does better under BIC than the model with homogeneous errors. This fitted model differs in only minor respects from the preferred SNP specification reported in Gallant et al. (1992). (The differences are due to minor enhancements to the computer program.) We term the score from this fit the 'nonlinear nonparametric score'.

We emerge from this exercise with two sets of scores with which to confront the stochastic volatility model. The first, the semiparametric ARCH score, is defined by a score generator that is very similar to models widely employed in the ARCH literature, though a bit more flexibly parameterized. The second, the nonlinear nonparametric score, is defined by a score generator determined via a complete specification search that accounts for the full complexity of the data.

11.4.3 Fit to the semiparametric ARCH score
Table 11.1 shows the optimized values of the EMM objective function scaled to follow a chi square, as described in Section 11.3. Table 11.2 shows the parameter estimates for the various specifications reported in Table 11.1. From the top panel of Table 11.1, labeled Gaussian, it is seen that the standard stochastic

Table 11.1. Univariate price change series; optimized value of the criterion for
the semiparametric ARCH score generator

Score generator (SNP)						SV model			Objective function		
L_u	L_r	L_p	K_z	K_x	ℓ_θ	L_y	L_w	ℓ_p	χ^2	df	p-val
Gaussian											
2	18	1	4	0	26	2	1	6	86.432	20	<0.0001
2	18	1	4	0	26	2	2	7	79.001	19	<0.0001
2	18	1	4	0	26	2	3	8	72.672	18	<0.0001
2	18	1	4	0	26	2	4	9	69.188	17	<0.0001
2	18	1	4	0	26	2	5	10	67.823	16	<0.0001
2	18	1	4	0	26	2	6	11	61.093	15	<0.0001
$t(v)$, $v = 10, 15, 20, 25$											
2	18	1	4	0	26	2	2	8	78.186	18	<0.0001
2	18	1	4	0	26	2	2	8	68.931	18	<0.0001
2	18	1	4	0	26	2	2	8	69.111	18	<0.0001
2	18	1	4	0	26	2	2	8	69.898	18	<0.0001
Spline											
2	18	1	4	0	26	2	1	8	41.920	18	0.0011
2	18	1	4	0	26	2	2	9	41.351	17	0.0008
2	18	1	4	0	26	2	3	10	37.700	16	0.0016
2	18	1	4	0	26	2	4	11	36.107	15	0.0017
2	18	1	4	0	26	2	4	12	33.768	14	0.0022
2	18	1	4	0	26	2	6	13	18.638	13	0.1348
Gaussian & long-memory											
2	18	1	4	0	26	2	0	6	67.691	20	<0.0001
2	18	1	4	0	26	2	1	7	67.061	19	<0.0001
2	18	1	4	0	26	2	2	8	65.463	18	<0.0001
Spline & long-memory											
2	18	1	4	0	26	2	0	8	34.923	18	0.0097
2	18	1	4	0	26	2	1	9	26.718	17	0.0623
2	18	1	4	0	26	2	2	10	21.781	16	0.1504

L_u is the number of lags in the linear part of the SNP model; L_r is the number of lags in the ARCH part;
L_p the number of lags in the polynomial part, $P(z, x)$. The polynomial $P(z, x)$ is of degree K_z in z and K_x
in x; by convention, $L_p = 1$ if $K_x = 0$. ℓ_θ is the number of free parameters associated with the SNP
model. L_y is the number of lags in the linear conditional mean specification of the stochastic volatility
model, and L_w is the number of lags in the volatility specification. ℓ_p is the number of free parameters of
the stochastic volatility model. χ^2 is the EMM objective function scaled to be distributed $\chi^2(df)$ under
the maintained assumption of correct specification of the stochastic volatility model. Some relevant
quantiles are $\chi^2_{0.99}(20) = 37.566, \chi^2_{0.99}(15) = 30.578$.

volatility model fails to approximate the distribution of the data adequately; it is
overwhelmingly rejected. However, as seen from the objective function surface
laid out across the various panels of the table, certain extensions of the standard
stochastic volatility model fit the data better.

Table 11.2. Univariate price change series: fitted parameter values for the semiparametric ARCH score generator

μ_y	r_y	c_1	c_2	b_{z0}	b_{z1}	b_{z2}	b_{z3}	r_w	a_1	a_2	a_3	a_4	a_5	a_6	d
Gaussian															
0.038	0.927	0.105	0.066		1.000			0.095	0.976						
0.037	0.918	0.105	0.066		1.000			0.155	0.961	−0.662					
0.036	0.909	0.103	0.068		1.000			0.149	0.964	0.010	−0.641				
0.036	0.906	0.103	0.068		1.000			0.172	0.959	−0.209	−0.267	−0.547			
0.037	0.916	0.104	0.068		1.000			0.116	0.972	0.156	−0.185	−0.616	0.304		
0.036	0.909	0.102	0.069		1.000			0.144	0.965	−0.067	−0.592	−0.002	−0.485	0.397	
t															
0.034	0.935	0.103	0.066		$\nu = 10$			0.031	0.993	0.561					
0.036	0.937	0.104	0.066		$\nu = 15$			0.049	0.989	0.378					
0.035	0.928	0.104	0.066		$\nu = 20$			0.124	0.971	−0.521					
0.036	0.926	0.104	0.066		$\nu = 25$			0.132	0.969	−0.580					
Spline															
0.023	0.942	0.110	0.063	0.030	0.921	−0.079	0.097	0.083	0.980						
0.022	0.939	0.109	0.063	0.030	0.933	−0.072	0.083	0.129	0.969	−0.537					
0.022	0.931	0.109	0.064	0.032	0.960	−0.056	0.049	0.138	0.966	0.036	−0.623				
0.021	0.923	0.108	0.064	0.032	0.988	−0.039	0.014	0.212	0.947	−0.558	−0.479	−0.356			
0.022	0.935	0.109	0.063	0.029	0.928	−0.073	0.089	0.029	0.993	1.634	−1.853	1.078	−0.247		
0.023	0.947	0.109	0.064	0.029	0.942	0.064	0.071	0.012	0.998	2.005	−1.970	0.939	0.220	−0.378	
Gaussian & long memory															
0.036	0.908	0.104	0.067		1.000			0.224	−0.159						0.540
0.035	0.904	0.103	0.067		1.000			0.242	0.039	−0.192					0.550
0.034	0.908	0.104	0.066		1.000			0.221							0.539
Spline & long memory															
0.022	0.922	0.111	0.062	0.033	1.046	−0.003	−0.059	0.259	−0.268						0.515
0.021	0.887	0.110	0.060	0.038	1.208	0.095	−0.267	0.369	−0.419	0.128					0.493
0.020	0.863	0.109	0.061	0.044	1.355	0.187	−0.463	0.429							0.486

The rows of Table 11.2 correspond to the rows of Table 11.1. Due to identification restrictions across parameters, the number of parameters in a row do not necessarily correspond to the number of free parameters shown in Table 11.1.

We describe these extensions and seek to determine which features of the data they seem to approximate well and which features poorly. Guided by the objective function, we inspect the EMM quasi-t-ratios $\hat{T}_n$. The elements of $\hat{T}_n$ provide suggestive diagnostics, as pointed out in Section 11.3.

Fig. 11.2 shows these EMM quasi-t-ratios as a bar chart for the case $L_y = 2$, $L_w = 2$, and Gaussian z's. This is the standard stochastic volatility specification

$$y_t - \mu_y = c_1(y_{t-1} - \mu_y) + c_2(y_{t-2} - \mu_y) + \exp(w_t)r_y z_t,$$
$$w_t - \mu_w = a_1(w_{t-1} - \mu_w) + a_2(w_{t-2} - \mu_w) + r_w \tilde{z}_t.$$

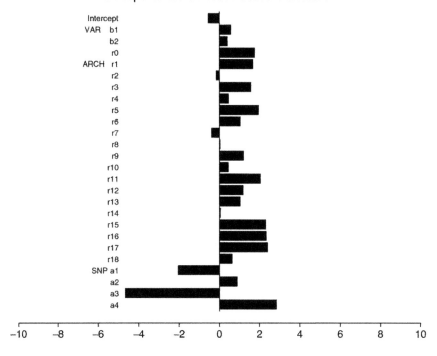

T-Ratios of Mean Score, Lw=2
Semiparametric ARCH Score Generator

Fig. 11.2. EMM quasi-t-ratios for the stochastic volatility model matched to the semiparametric ARCH score. The semiparametric ARCH score is an SNP specification with $L_u = 2, L_r = 18, L_p = 1, K_z = 4, I_z = 0, K_x = 0$, and $I_x = 0$. The VAR t-ratios and ARCH t-ratios shown in the plot correspond to the equations $\mu_x = b_a + b'x$ and $r_x = \rho_o + \rho'x$ of the SNP specification, respectively. The SNP t-ratios correspond to the coefficients of the polynomial $P(z, x)$ of the SNP specification where the subscript indicates degree. The stochastic volatility specification is
$$y_t - \mu_y = c_1(y_{t-1} - \mu_y) + c_2(y_{t-2} - \mu_y)$$
$$+ \exp(w_t)r_y z_t, \; w_t - \mu_w = a_1(w_{t-1} - \mu_w) + a_2(w_{t-2} - \mu_w) + r_w \tilde{z}_t.$$

The source of the rejection of this model is failure to match the features defined by the polynomial part of the SNP score. Either $\exp(w_t)$ is not the correct transformation of the latent variance process or z_t is not Gaussian.

11.4.3.1 Modified exponential

To explore the first possibility, consider the model

$$y_t - \mu_y = c_1(y_{t-1} - \mu_y) + c_2(y_{t-2} - \mu_y) + T_e(w_t)r_y z_t,$$

$$T_e(w_t) = \exp(b_{e0} + b_{e1}w_t) + b_{e2}w_t^2 + b_{e3}I + (w_t)w_t^2,$$

$$w_t - \mu_w = a_1(w_{t-1} - \mu_w) + a_2(w_{t-2} - \mu_w) + r_w \tilde{z}_t,$$

where $I_+(w)$ is 1 if w is positive and is 0 otherwise. The idea is to modify the Taylor expansion of $\exp(\cdot)$ by replacing the quadratic term with a differentiable quadratic spline that has one knot at zero. Inspection of the bar chart (not shown) indicates failure. The fit is improved by better matching the VAR and ARCH scores at the expense of further mismatch to the polynomial part of the SNP score. The exponential transformation appears not to be a problem, so we consider non-Gaussian densities for z_t.

11.4.3.2 t-Errors

A natural way to relax the Gaussian assumption is to use t-errors. Consider the model

$$y_t - \mu_y = c_1(y_{t-1} - \mu_y) + c_2(y_{t-2} - \mu_y) + \exp(w_t)r_y \tau_{vt},$$

$$w_t - \mu_w = a_1(w_{t-1} - \mu_w) + a_2(w_{t-2} - \mu_w) + r_w \tilde{z}_t,$$

where $\{\tau_{vt}\}$ is iid Student-t with v degrees of freedom. The objective function is so flat for values of the degrees of freedom parameter $v \in (10, 20)$ that the optimizer gets stuck and makes no progress when it sees v as free parameter along with the rest. Thus, in the second panel of Table 11.1 we report the value of the objective function for $v = 10, 15, 20, 25$. The specification with t errors helps, but still the model does not fit the data. Fig. 11.3 shows the bar chart for the case $v = 15$; the stochastic volatility model fails to fit the score of the SNP polynomial for the cubic term, suggesting a failure to generate skewness.

11.4.3.3 Spline error transformation

More flexibility than with the t is available from a spline transformation to the Gaussian innovation. Consider

$$y_t - \mu_y = c_1(y_{t-1} - \mu_y) + c_2(y_{t-2} - \mu_y) + \exp(w_t)r_y T_z(z_t),$$
$$T_z(z_t) = b_{z0} + b_{z1}z_t + b_{z2}z_t^2 + b_{z3}I + (z_t)z_t^2,$$
$$w_t - \mu_w = a_1(w_{t-1} - \mu_w) + a_2(w_{t-2} - \mu_w) + r_w \tilde{z}_t.$$

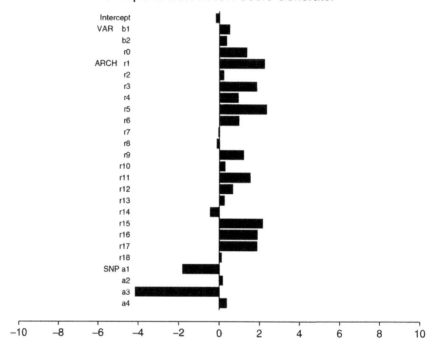

Fig. 11.3. EMM quasi-t-ratios for the t-innovations stochastic volatility model matched to the semiparametric ARCH score. The semiparametric ARCH score is an SNP specification with $L_u = 2, L_r = 18, L_p = 1, K_z = 4, I_z = 0, K_x = 0$, and $I_x = 0$. The VAR t-ratios and ARCH t-ratios shown in the plot correspond to the equations $\mu_x = b_o + b'x$ and $r_x = \rho_o + \rho'x$ of the SNP specification, respectively. The SNP t-ratios correspond to the coefficients of the polynomial $P(z, x)$ of the SNP specification where the subscript indicates degree. The stochastic volatility specification is
$$y_t - \mu_y = c_1(y_{t-1} - \mu_y) + c_2(y_{t-2} - \mu_y)$$
$$+ \exp(w_t) r_y \tau_{15,t}, \ w_t - \mu_w = a_1(w_{t-1} - \mu_w) + a_2(w_{t-2} - \mu_w) + r_w \tilde{z}_t, \text{ where } \tau_{15,t}$$
follows the t-distribution on 15 degrees freedom.

The idea is to allow a deviation from the Gaussian specification by transforming z_t through a differentiable quadratic spline that has one knot at zero. To achieve identification, the constraints $(2\pi)^{-1/2} \int T_z(v) \exp(-v^2/2) dv = 0$ and $(2\pi)^{-1/2} \int T_z^2(v) \exp(-v^2/2) dv = 1$ are imposed on the b_{zj}. From Table 11.1 it is seen that the added flexibility of the spline transform sharply reduces the objective function value. The EMM quasi-t-ratios for this 'spline-transform' fit are shown in Fig. 11.4. The transform works; the moments of the polynomial part of the semiparametric ARCH score are adequately matched.

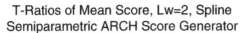

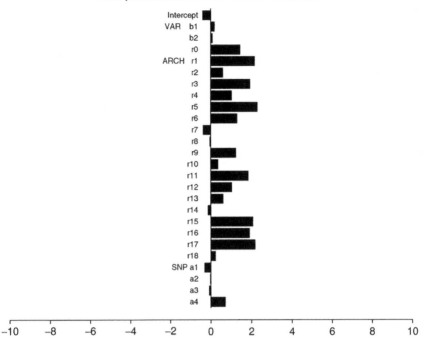

Fig. 11.4. EMM quasi-*t*-ratios for the spline-transform stochastic volatility model matched to the semiparametric ARCH score. The semiparametric ARCH score is an SNP specification with $L_u = 2, L_r = 18, L_p = 1, K_z = 4,$ $I_z = 0, K_x = 0,$ and $I_x = 0$. The VAR *t*-ratios and ARCH *t*-ratios shown in the plot correspond to the equations $\mu_x = b_o + b'x$ and $r_x = \rho_o + \rho'x$ of the SNP specification, respectively. The SNP *t*-ratios correspond to the coefficients of the polynomial $P(z, x)$ of the SNP specification where the subscript indicates degree. The stochastic volatility specification is $y_t - \mu_y = c_1(y_{t-1} - \mu_y) + c_2(y_{t-2} - \mu_y)$
$$+ \exp(w_t)r_y T_z(z_t), T_z(z_t) = b_{z0} + b_{z1}z_t + b_{z2}z_t^2 + b_{z3}I_+(z_t)z_t^2, w_t - \mu_w$$
$$= a_1(w_{t-1} - \mu_w) + a_2(w_{t-2} - \mu_w) + r_w \tilde{z}_t.$$

The effects of the spline are to fatten the tails and introduce an asymmetry as seen in Fig. 11.5. The solid line in the upper left panel is a plot of the spline T_z. This plot can also be interpreted as a plot of the quantiles of the distribution of the random variable $T_z(z_t)$ on the vertical axis against the quantiles of the standard normal distribution on the horizontal axis. If a distribution is Gaussian, then its quantile–quantile plot is a 45° line. A comparison with the 45° line in the upper left panel of Fig. 11.5 indicates heavy tails, because the solid line plots below the 45° line on the left and above on the right, and an asymmetry, because

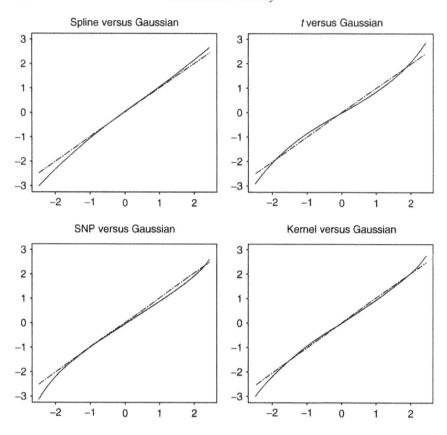

Fig. 11.5. Quantile–quantile plots. The solid line in the upper left panel shows the
spline transform of Fig. 11.4 which can also be interpreted as a plot of the
quantiles of the distribution of the random variable $T_z(z_t)$ on the vertical axis
against the quantiles of the standard normal distribution on the horizontal axis.
The dashed is a plot of the quantiles of the standard normal against the quantiles
of the standard normal. The solid line in the upper right panel is a quantile–
quantile plot of the five degree freedom Student t-distribution. The solid line in
the lower left panel is a quantile–quantile plot of the innovation distribution of
the semiparametric ARCH score generator. The solid line in the lower right panel
is a quantile–quantile plot of a kernel density estimate from ARCH residuals.

the solid line deviates more from the 45° line on the left than on the right. The
asymmetry is also apparent from a comparison with the solid line in the upper
right panel of Fig. 11.5 which shows a quantile-quantile plot of the six-degrees-of-
freedom Student t-distribution. The asymmetry and heavy tails are features of the
data that have been captured by the semiparametric ARCH score as can be seen
in the lower left panel of Fig. 11.5. The EMM moment matching procedure has
transferred these characteristics to the spline-transform stochastic volatility

model. The asymmetry and heavy tails are real features of the data, not artifacts of the SNP fit, as can be seen from the solid line in the lower right panel of Fig. 11.5 which is a quantile–quantile plot of a kernel density estimate from ARCH residuals.

11.4.3.4 Chaotic volatility

Interestingly, one can do as well with a deterministic variance process. EMM quasi-t-ratios (not shown) that result when the variance equation of the model

$$y_t - \mu_y = c_1(y_{t-1} - \mu_y) + c_2(y_{t-2} - \mu_y) + T_w(w_t)r_y T_z(z_t),$$
$$T_w(w_t) = b_{w0} + b_{w1}w_t + b_{w2}w_t^2 + b_{w3}I_+(w_t)w_t^2,$$
$$T_z(z_t) = b_{z0} + b_{z1}z_t + b_{z2}z_t^2 + b_{z3}I_+(z_t)z_t^2,$$

is a moving average in 40 lags

$$w_t = \sum_{j=0}^{40} \frac{40 - j}{40} v_{t-j}$$

from a chaotic Mackey–Glass sequence

$$v_t = v_{t-1} + 10.5\left(\frac{0.2v_{t-5}}{1 + v_{t-5}^{10}} - 0.1v_{t-1}\right)$$

are similar to those shown in Fig. 11.4. This Mackey–Glass variant on the spline-transform stochastic volatility model does slightly better on the SNP scores and slightly worse on the ARCH scores.

11.4.3.5 Long memory

Fig. 11.4 suggests the standard stochastic volatility model has some trouble matching the scores of the flexibly parameterized ARCH model, and somewhat more so at the longer ARCH lags. Bollerslev and Mikkelsen (1996), Ding et al. (1993), and Breidt et al. (1994) present evidence that long-memory models like those of Granger and Joyeux (1980) might be needed to account for the high degree of persistence in financial volatility. Harvey (1993) contains an extensive discussion of the properties of long memory in stochastic volatility models. We thus explore if inclusion of both short- and long-memory helps in fitting the stochastic volatility model.

The long-memory stochastic volatility model is

$$y_t - \mu_y = c_1(y_{t-1} - \mu_y) + c_2(y_{t-2} - \mu_y) + \exp(w_t^*)r_y z_t,$$
$$w_t^* - \mu_w = (1 - \mathscr{L})^{-d} z_{wt},$$
$$z_{wt} = \sum_{j=1}^{L_w} a_j z_{w,\,t-j} + r_w \tilde{z}_t,$$

where $\{z_t\}$ and $\{\tilde{z}_t\}$ are iid Gaussian, $(1 - \mathscr{L})^{-d} = \sum_{k=0}^{\infty} \psi_k(d)\mathscr{L}^k$, and the coefficients $\psi_k(d)$ are obtained from the series expansion of $f(x) = (1 - x)^{-d}$, valid for $|d| < 1$, as described in Sowell (1990). Motivating this specification is the fact that for $|d| < 1/2$, $(1 - \mathscr{L})^d v_t = \varepsilon_t, \{\varepsilon_t\}$ iid with finite variance, defines a strictly stationary process whose moving average representation is $v_t = (1 - \mathscr{L})^{-d}\varepsilon_t = \sum_{k=1}^{\infty} \psi_k(d)\varepsilon_{t-k}$; the autocovariance function of v_t decays arithmetically to zero, instead of exponentially to zero as in the case of an autoregression of finite lag length. For $\frac{1}{2} \le d < 1$, $(1 - \mathscr{L})^d v_t = \varepsilon_t$, defines a nonstationary process. $\{w_t^*\}$ is thus obtained by passing the autoregressive process $\{z_{wt}\}$ through the long-memory moving average filter. For $d = 0$, this generates exactly the same auto-regressive volatility process as earlier, while for $0 < |d| < \frac{1}{2}$, it defines a strictly stationary volatility process with both short- and long-memory components.

Since we need very long realizations for Monte Carlo integration, it is impractical to simulate exactly from this model by, say, computing the Cholesky factorization of the covariance matrix of w_t and proceeding in the usual manner. Instead, we follow Bollerslev and Mikkelsen (1996) and use a method that truncates the moving average filter and lets the process run for a long while to attenuate the effects of transients. Their calculations suggest that truncation at 1000 suffices, so we use the moving average filter $\sum_{k=0}^{1000} \psi_k(d)\mathscr{L}^k$. (Because of the truncation, this method technically generates a stationary process for all $|d| < 1$.) They trim off the first 7000 realizations; we trim off the first 10,000. Some would argue that this method does not actually generate realizations from a long-memory volatility process. The point is well taken but, nonetheless, the Bollerslev–Mikkelsen approach still defines a volatility process $\{w_t^*\}$ with extremely high persistence.

The bottom part of Table 11.1 shows the optimized objective function when the long-memory parameter, d, is estimated jointly with the other parameters of the model subject to a normalization on μ_w for identification. We only estimate the long-memory version for $L_w = 1$ and $L_w = 2$, since the job of the long-memory specification is to take care of longer lags. For the block labeled 'Gaussian & Long Memory' the mean equation is

$$y_t - \mu_y = c_1(y_{t-1} - \mu_y) + c_2(y_{t-2} - \mu_y) + \exp(w_t^*)r_y z_t$$

while for the block labeled 'Spline & Long Memory', the mean equation is

$$y_t - \mu_y = c_1(y_{t-1} - \mu_y) + c_2(y_{t-2} - \mu_y) + \exp(w_t^*)r_y T_z(z_t)$$

where the two-parameter quadratic spline $T_z(\cdot)$ is as defined above.

As seen from Table 11.1, long memory helps, but the Gaussian stochastic volatility model cannot accommodate all of the structure implicit in the semi-parametric ARCH model. With the spline transform, it can. Fig. 11.6 shows the bar chart for the case $L_w = 2$. The impact on the objective function value of long memory is similar to that of introducing two or three extra freely parameterized

T-Ratios of Mean Score, Lw=2, Spline, Long Memory
Semiparametric ARCH Score Generator

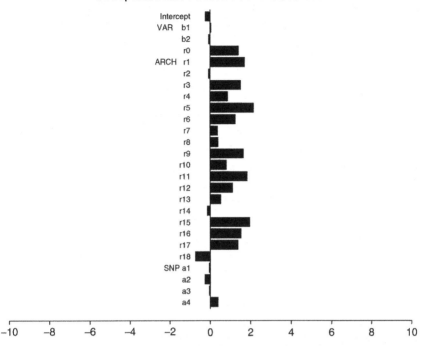

Fig. 11.6. EMM quasi-t-ratios for the spline-transform stochastic volatility model with a long-memory variance equation matched to the semiparametric ARCH score. The semiparametric ARCH score is an SNP specification with $L_u = 2, L_r = 18, L_p = 1, K_z = 4, I_z = 0, K_x = 0$, and $I_x = 0$. The VAR t-ratios and ARCH t-ratios shown in the plot correspond to the equations $\mu_x = b_o + b'_x$ and $r_x = \rho_o + \rho'_x$ of the SNP specification, respectively. The SNP t-ratios correspond to the coefficients of the polynomial $P(z, x)$ of the SNP specification where the subscript indicates degree. The stochastic volatility specification is

$$y_t - \mu_y = c_1(y_{t-1} - \mu_y) + c_2(y_{t-2} - \mu_y)$$
$$+ \exp{(w_t^*)}r_y T_z(z_t), T_z(z_t) = b_{z0} + b_{z1}z_t + b_{z2}z_t^2 + b_{z3}I + (z_t)z_t^2, w_t^* - \mu_w$$
$$= (1 - \mathcal{L})^{-d}z_{wt}, z_{wt} = a_1 z_{w, t-1} + a_2 z_{w, t-2} + r_w \tilde{z}_t.$$

lags into the volatility equation. Overall, long-memory helps about as much as introducing six free lags into the volatility specification.

11.4.4 Fit to the nonlinear semiparametric score
Table 11.3 displays the objective function surface for versions of the stochastic volatility model against the nonlinear nonparametric score; Table 11.4 shows the estimated parameter values. From Table 11.3, the standard model is overwhelmingly rejected. The various extensions provide much improvement over the

Table 11.3. Univariate price change series: optimized value of the criterion for
the nonlinear nonparametric score generator

Score generator (SNP)						SV model			Objective function		
L_u	L_r	L_p	K_z	K_x	ℓ_0	L_y	L_w	ℓ_p	χ^2	df	p-val
Gaussian											
2	18	2	4	1	36	2	1	6	173.361	30	<0.0001
2	18	2	4	1	36	2	2	7	164.337	29	<0.0001
2	18	2	4	1	36	2	3	8	155.449	28	<0.0001
2	18	2	4	1	36	2	4	9	151.243	27	<0.0001
2	18	2	4	1	36	2	5	10	149.350	26	<0.0001
2	18	2	4	1	36	2	4	11	147.984	25	<0.0001
Spline											
2	18	2	4	1	36	2	1	8	151.290	28	<0.0001
2	18	2	4	1	36	2	2	9	150.765	27	<0.0001
2	18	2	4	1	36	2	3	10	144.411	26	<0.0001
2	18	2	4	1	36	2	4	11	143.310	25	<0.0001
2	18	2	4	1	36	2	5	12	143.310	24	<0.0001
2	18	2	4	1	36	2	6	13	142.461	23	<0.0001
Gaussian-asymmetric											
2	18	2	4	1	36	2	1	7	111.497	29	<0.0001
2	18	2	4	1	36	2	2	8	111.487	28	<0.0001
2	18	2	4	1	36	2	3	9	97.536	27	<0.0001
2	18	2	4	1	36	2	4	10	93.969	26	<0.0001
2	18	2	4	1	36	2	5	11	91.075	25	<0.0001
2	18	2	4	1	36	2	6	12	85.711	24	<0.0001
Spline-asymmetric											
2	18	2	4	1	36	2	1	9	78.972	27	<0.0001
2	18	2	4	1	36	2	2	10	78.197	26	<0.0001
2	18	2	4	1	36	2	3	11	75.483	25	<0.0001
2	18	2	4	1	36	2	4	12	70.109	24	<0.0001
2	18	2	4	1	36	2	5	13	69.881	23	<0.0001
2	18	2	4	1	36	2	6	14	69.645	22	<0.0001
Spline & long memory											
2	18	2	4	1	36	2	0	8	152.654	28	<0.0001
2	18	2	4	1	36	2	1	9	146.479	27	<0.0001
2	18	2	4	1	36	2	2	10	143.477	26	<0.0001
Spline-asymmetric & long memory											
2	18	2	4	1	36	2	0	9	94.678	27	<0.0001
2	18	2	4	1	36	2	1	10	72.049	26	<0.0001
2	18	2	4	1	36	2	2	11	71.609	25	<0.0001

L_u is the number of lags in the linear part of the SNP model; L_r is the number of lags in the ARCH part;
L_p the number of lags in the polynomial part, $P(z, x)$. The polynomial $P(z, x)$ is of degree K_z in z and K_x
in x; by convention, $L_p = 1$ if $K_x = 0$. ℓ_θ is the number of free parameters associated with the SNP
model. L_y is the number of lags in the linear conditional mean specification of the stochastic volatility
model, and L_w is the number of lags in the volatility specification. ℓ_ρ is the number of free parameters of
the stochastic volatility model. χ^2 is the EMM objective function scaled to be distributed χ^2 (df) under
the maintained assumption of correct specification of the stochastic volatility model. Some relevant
quantiles are $\chi^2_{0.99}(30) = 50.892$, $\chi^2_{0.99}(25) = 44.314$, $\chi^2_{0.99}(20) = 37.566$.

standard Gaussian model, but nothing comes as close as the spline variants
against the Semiparametric ARCH Score. We now examine the performance of
the extensions in more detail.

μ_y	r_y	c_1	c_2	g	b_{z0}	b_{z1}	b_{z2}	b_{z3}	r_w	a_1	a_2	a_3	a_4	a_5	a_6	d
Gaussian																
0.052	0.767	0.114	0.052						0.092	0.966						
0.051	0.762	0.114	0.051						0.152	0.944	−0.712					
0.050	0.756	0.111	0.052						0.195	0.930	−0.826	−0.510				
0.050	0.748	0.109	0.054						0.223	0.920	−0.746	−0.625	−0.404			
0.050	0.746	0.108	0.054						0.229	0.919	−0.642	−0.733	−0.318	−0.284		
0.050	0.745	0.109	0.054						0.229	0.919	−0.642	−0.732	−0.318	−0.284	−0.009	
Spline																
0.046	0.769	0.114	0.052		0.010	0.905	−0.068	0.117	0.072	0.974						
0.047	0.770	0.114	0.052		0.010	0.901	−0.071	0.123	0.038	0.986	0.475					
0.047	0.770	0.115	0.052		0.009	0.914	−0.062	0.106	0.010	0.997	1.651	−0.802				
0.047	0.771	0.115	0.051		0.009	0.915	−0.061	0.105	0.019	0.994	0.670	0.834	−0.799			
0.047	0.771	0.115	0.051		0.009	0.915	−0.061	0.105	0.019	0.994	0.670	0.834	−0.799			
0.047	0.772	0.115	0.051		0.009	0.914	−0.063	0.107	0.046	0.986	−0.146	0.549	0.575	0.000	−0.695	
Gaussian-asymmetric																
0.047	0.839	0.115	0.055	−0.791		1.000			0.070	0.976						
0.047	0.839	0.115	0.055	−0.801		1.000			0.068	0.976	0.018					
0.045	0.834	0.114	0.057	−0.494		1.000			0.122	0.964	0.076	−0.671				
0.045	0.836	0.114	0.058	−0.510		1.000			0.106	0.970	0.286	−0.552	−0.267			
0.045	0.839	0.114	0.057	−0.630		1.000			0.085	0.974	0.220	−0.128	−0.690	0.361		
0.045	0.837	0.112	0.058	−0.547		1.000			0.101	0.970	0.212	−0.806	0.307	−0.610	0.479	
Spline-asymmetric																
0.033	0.849	0.119	0.054	−1.454	0.024	0.919	−0.074	0.100	0.045	0.979						
0.033	0.848	0.119	0.054	−1.720	0.024	0.917	−0.075	0.102	0.035	0.982	0.134					
0.032	0.863	0.117	0.053	−1.038	0.026	0.924	−0.073	0.094	0.054	0.980	0.427	−0.489				
0.031	0.856	0.117	0.056	−0.938	0.026	0.939	−0.063	0.075	0.065	0.977	0.361	−0.808				
0.031	0.857	0.117	0.056	−0.859	0.026	0.942	−0.061	0.071	0.069	0.977	0.430	−0.882	0.390	−0.083		
0.032	0.856	0.117	0.055	−1.063	0.025	0.939	−0.062	0.075	0.055	0.979	0.279	−0.224	−0.191	0.622	−0.491	
Spline & long memory																
0.046	0.760	0.114	0.052		0.010	0.965	−0.032	0.044	0.200							0.507
0.046	0.736	0.112	0.051		0.011	1.075	0.037	−0.094	0.304	−0.315						0.484
0.046	0.724	0.110	0.052		0.012	1.149	0.083	−0.190	0.351	−0.510	0.164					0.485
Spline-asymmetric & long memory																
0.035	0.829	0.119	0.054	−0.431	0.021	0.975	−0.037	0.031	0.179							0.541
0.031	0.849	0.121	0.052	−1.030	0.024	0.931	−0.067	0.085	0.060	0.664						0.496
0.031	0.850	0.121	0.052	−1.034	0.025	0.932	−0.066	0.084	0.056	0.677	0.111					0.501

The rows of Table 11.4 correspond to the rows of Table 11.3. Due to identification restrictions across parameters, the number of parameters in a row do not necessarily correspond to the number of free parameters shown in Table 11.3.

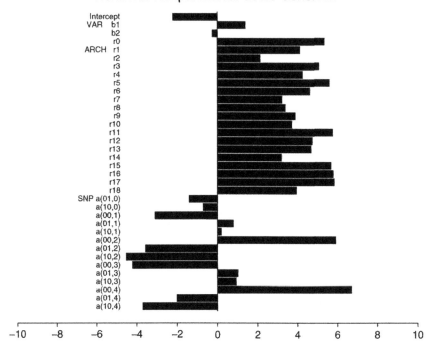

Fig. 11.7. EMM quasi-t-ratios for the stochastic volatility model matched to the nonlinear nonparametric score. The nonlinear nonparametric score is an SNP specification with $L_u = 2, L_r = 18, L_p = 2, K_z = 4, l_z = 0, K_x = 0$, and $I_x = 0$.

The VAR t-ratios and ARCH t-ratios shown in the plot correspond to the equations $\mu_x = b_o + b'x$ and $r_x = \rho_o + \rho'x$ of the SNP specification, respectively. The SNP t-ratios correspond to the coefficients of the polynomial $P(z, x)$ of the SNP specification. A coefficient such as $a(00, 2)$ corresponds to the monomial z^2, one such as a(10, 2) to $z^2 x_1$, a(01, 2) to $z^2 x_2$, and so on. The stochastic volatility specification is $y_t - \mu_y = c_1(y_{t-1} - \mu_y) + c_2(y_{t-2} - \mu_y)$
$$+ \exp{(w_t)}r_y z_t, w_t - \mu_w = a_1(w_{t-1} - \mu_w) + a_2(w_{t-2} - \mu_w) + r_w \tilde{z}_t.$$

The bar chart for the $L_y = 2, L_w = 2$, Gaussian stochastic volatility specification is shown as Fig. 11.7. The ARCH part of the score is fit poorly, as is the SNP part. The quasi-t-ratios are not orthogonal, so that failure to fit the SNP scores could manifest itself as large ARCH quasi-t-ratios and conversely. The spline-transform variant (not shown) does just about as poorly.

The full nonlinear nonparametric score embodies various conditional nonlinearities, such as the asymmetric 'leverage effect' of Nelson (1991) that are discussed in Gallant et al. (1992, 1993). We explore the effects of introducing asymmetry into the stochastic volatility model. A common approach in the stochastic volatility literature (Harvey and Shephard, 1996) is to generate asymmetry by introducing correlations across innovations in the mean and variance equations:

$$y_t - \mu_y = c_1(y_{t-1} - \mu_y) + c_2(y_{t-2} - \mu_y) + \exp(w_t)r_y z_t,$$
$$w_t - \mu_w = a_1(w_{t-1} - \mu_w) + a_2(w_{t-2} - \mu_w) + r_w(\tilde{z}_t + g z_{t-1}),$$

where g is a free parameter to be estimated. This variant does better but still does poorly on the chi-square statistics shown in Table 11.3. The bar chart (not shown) shows large SNP quasi-t-ratios, which suggests that the spline-transform be applied to the asymmetric variant. The model that results is

$$y_t - \mu_y = c_1(y_{t-1} - \mu_y) + c_2(y_{t-2} - \mu_y) + \exp(w_t)r_y T_z(z_t),$$
$$T_z(z_t) = b_{z0} + b_{z1} z_t + b_{z2}(z_t)^2 + b_{z3}I + (z_t)(z_t)^2,$$
$$w_t - \mu_w = a_1(w_{t-1} - \mu_w) + a_2(w_{t-2} - \mu_w) + r_w(\tilde{z}_t + g z_{t-1}).$$

The fit improves but is still inadequate, as indicated by the chi-square statistics shown in Table 11.3.

Finally, we consider long-memory in the variance equation. We estimate with the spline transformation:

$$y_t - \mu_y = c_1(y_{t-1} - \mu_y) + c_2(y_{t-2} - \mu_y) + \exp(w_t^*)r_y T_z(z_t),$$
$$T_z(z_t) = b_{z0} + b_{z1} z_t + b_{z2}(z_t)^2 + b_{z3}I + (z_t)(z_t)^2,$$

$$w_t^* - \mu_w = (1 - \mathscr{L})^{-d} z_{wt},$$

$$z_{wt} = \sum_{j=1}^{L_w} a_j z_{w,t-j} + r_w \tilde{z}_t.$$

We also estimate a model with the spline transformation and cross-correlation in innovations:

$$y_t - \mu_y = c_1(y_{t-1} - \mu_y) + c_2(y_{t-2} - \mu_y) + \exp(w_t^*)r_y T_z(z_t),$$
$$T_z(z_t) = b_{z0} + b_{z1} z_t + b_{z2}(z_t)^2 + b_{z3}I_+(z_t)(z_t)^2,$$
$$w_t^* - \mu_w = (1 - \mathscr{L})^{-d} z_{wt},$$
$$z_{wt} = \sum_{j=1}^{L_w} a_j z_{w,t-j} + r_w(z_t + g\tilde{z}_{t-1}).$$

As seen from the lower two panels of Table 11.3 long memory helps, but, as in fitting to the semiparametric ARCH score, long memory has about the same impact on the objective function as does introducing a few more free lags into the volatility specification. Fig. 11.8 shows the bar chart with long memory for the case $L_w = 2$ and correlated errors. Comparing this figure to Fig. 11.7 shows that the combined effects of the spline transformation, the asymmetry, and the long

T-Ratios of Mean Score, Lw=2, Asymmetric,Spline, Long Memory Nonlinear Nonparametric Score Generator

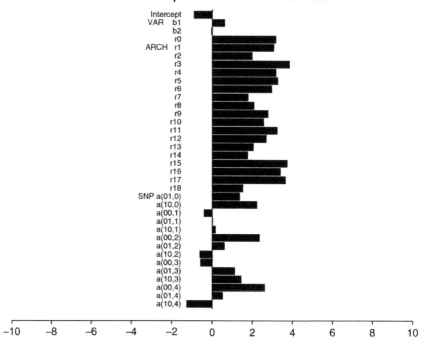

Fig. 11.8. EMM Quasi-t-ratios for the asymmetric, spline-transform stochastic volatility model with a long-memory variance equation matched to the nonlinear nonparametric score. The nonlinear nonparametric score is an SNP specification with $L_u = 2, L_r = 18, L_p = 2, K_z = 4, I_z = 0, K_x = 0$, and $I_x = 0$. The VAR t-ratios and ARCH t-ratios shown in the plot correspond to the equations $\mu_x = b_o + b'x$ and $r_x = \rho o + \rho'x$ of the SNP specification, respectively. The SNP t-ratios correspond to the coefficients of the polynomial $P(z, x)$ of the SNP specification. A coefficient such as $a(00, 2)$ corresponds to the monomial z^2, one such as a(10, 2) to $z^2 x_1$, a(01, 2) to $z^2 x_2$, and so on. The stochastic volatility specification is $y_t - \mu_y = c_1(y_{t-1} - \mu_y) + c_2(y_{t-2} - \mu_y)$
$+ \exp(w_t^*) r_y T_z(z_t), T_z(z_t) = b_{z0} + b_{z1} z_t + b_{z2}(z_t)^2 + b_{z3} I - (z_t)(z_t)^2, w_t^* - \mu_w$
$= (1 - \mathcal{L})^{-d} z_{wt}, z_{wt} = \sum_{j=1}^{L_w} a_j z_{w, t-j} + r_w(\tilde{z}_t + g z_{t-1})$.

memory improves the fit substantially, but despite all of these added complications the model fails to fit both the ARCH and SNP scores.

This, we think, is about as far as one can go and stay within the spirit of the stochastic volatility model. A specification that probably would capture the full complexity of the data is to let the coefficients of the transformation

$$T_z(z_t) = b_{z0} + b_{z1} z_t + b_{z2} z_t^2 + b_{z3} I_+(z_t) z_t^2,$$

depend upon lagged z's and perhaps add a few more unconstrained lag coefficients. However, this degree of complexity is so close to a nonparametric specification that we see little point to it. Why not just fit the series nonparametrically and have done with it?

11.5 Trivariate estimation

Modern asset pricing theory holds that there is a pricing kernel (or marginal rate of substitution) that discounts gross returns to unity. Using methods similar to ours, Andersen and Lund (1997) obtains a good fit of a continuous time stochastic volatility model to high-frequency Treasury returns. As Treasury returns reflect pure nominal pricing kernel movements, Andersen and Lund's findings taken together with asset pricing theory suggest that a stochastic volatility model should be able to account for the co-movements of several assets. As one of the distinguishing features of the EMM method is its ability to accommodate multivariate data, we investigate this possibility using several assets over a shorter, and therefore potentially more homogeneous, time horizon than in the previous section.

Let y_t denote an $M \times 1$ vector containing the first differences (either simple or logarithmic) over a short time interval, a day for instance, of the prices of a financial asset traded on active speculative markets. A multivariate stochastic volatility model for y_t is

$$y_t - \mu_y = \sum_{j=1}^{L_y} C_j(y_{t-j} - \mu_y) + \text{diag}\left[\exp(w_t)\right]R_y z_t,$$

$$w_t - \mu_w = \sum_{j=1}^{L_w} A_j(w_{t-j} - \mu_w) + R_w \tilde{z}_t,$$

where μ_y is an $M \times 1$ vector, the C_j are $M \times M$ matrices for $j = 1, 2, \ldots, L_y$, and R_y is an $M \times M$ upper triangular matrix. Similarly, μ_w is an $M \times 1$ vector, the A_j are $M \times M$ matrices for $j = 1, 2, \ldots, L_w$, and R_w is an $M \times M$ upper triangular matrix. The processes $\{z_t\}$ and $\{\tilde{z}_t\}$ are mutually independent *iid* random variables with mean zero and variance I_M. Throughout, $\exp(\cdot)$ denotes the elementwise exponential of a vector argument, $\text{diag}(v)$ with a vector argument denotes the diagonal matrix with the elements $v_1, \ldots, v_M$ down the diagonal, and $\text{diag}(B)$ with a matrix argument denotes the vector $(b_{11}, \ldots, b_{MM})'$ with the diagonal elements of B as its elements. Thus,

$$\text{diag}[\exp(w_t)] = \begin{bmatrix} e^{w_{1t}} & 0 & \cdots & 0 \\ 0 & e^{w_{2t}} & \ddots & \vdots \\ \vdots & \ddots & \ddots & 0 \\ 0 & \cdots & 0 & e^{w_{Mt}} \end{bmatrix}.$$

The data to which we fit this stochastic volatility model ($M = 3$) consists of 4044 daily observation on three variables: adjusted movements of the Standard and Poor's Composite Price Index, adjusted movements of the \$/DM spot exchange rate, and the adjusted 90-day Euro-Dollar interest rate, 1977–92. In this case $M = 3$, $y_t = (y_{1t}, y_{2t}, y_{3t})'$, and the data set is $\{\tilde{y}_t\}_{t=1}^{4044}$. The raw series consists of the Standard and Poor's Composite Index (SP), the \$/DM exchange rate (DM), and the three-month Euro-dollar interest rate (ED). The three series were collected daily, 4 January 1977–31 December 1992. The stock index and the exchange rate are converted to raw price movements series, $100[\log(SP_t) - \log(SP_{t-1})]$, and $100[\log(DM_t) - \log(DM_{t-1})]$. The two raw price movement series and the raw ED series are then each adjusted for systematic calendar effects. The adjustment procedure is the same as Gallant et al. (1992) except for the use of a robust regression method instead of ordinary least squares.

The estimation treats the three series as strictly stationary. This seems reasonable for stock returns and exchange rate movements, but requires discussion for the interest rate. As is well known, short-term interest rates collected at high frequencies display extreme persistence characteristic of (near) unit-root processes. However, recent empirical results of Aït-Sahalia (1996), and confirmed in Tauchen (1997a), indicate that, although interest rates display little mean revision in the central part of the data, they display substantial mean reversion at very low and very high values. Hence, interest rates appear nonstationary, or nearly so, when considered with linear methodology, when in fact they are stationary when considered with nonlinear methods.

As in Section 11.4, to implement the EMM estimator we require a score generator that approximates these data well. We use the multivariate SNP model as described in Gallant et al. (1992). It is derived along the same lines as set forth in Section 11.4.2 and has the following functional form:

$$f(y \mid x, \theta) = \frac{\{P[R_x^{-1}(y - \mu_x), x^*]\}^2 \phi[R_x^{-1}(y - \mu_x)]}{|\det(R_x)| \int [P(z, x^*)]^2 \phi(z) dz},$$

where

$$\mu_x = b_0 + Bx^*,$$

$$\text{vech}(R_x) = \rho_0 + P|x^*|.$$

vech(R) denotes the elements of the upper triangle of R stored as a column vector, $|x|$ denotes element-wise absolute value, x^* is a vector of lagged values of y_t, and $\phi(z) = (2\pi)^{-M/2} e^{-z'z/2}$. The asterisk indicates that prior to forming lags, the y_t have been centered by subtracting the sample mean, scaled by dividing element-wise by sample standard errors, and then transformed elementwise by the logistic map that takes the interval $(-\infty, \infty)$ into the interval $(-4, 4)$. $P(z, x^*)$ is a polynomial of degree K_z in z whose coefficients are, in turn, polynomials of degree K_x in x^*. μ_x is a function of the first L_u lags in x^* which is accommodated by inserting zeros in B at the appropriate locations; similarly R_x is a function of the first L_r lags in x^* and $P(z, x^*)$ a function of the first L_p lags in x^*. The multivariate model has two additional tuning parameters I_z and I_x that indicate that high order interaction in the polynomial $P(z, x^*)$ have been put to zero: $I_z = 0$ means that no interactions are suppressed, $I_z = 1$ means that the highest order interactions are suppressed, namely those of degree K_z and so on; similarly for K_x. We only allow $P|x^*|$ to contribute to the diagonal of R_x by inserting zeroes in the appropriate elements of P.

As in Section 4, if $K_z = 0, K_x = 0, L_u > 0$, and $L_r > 0$ then the SNP density is a form of ARCH model with Gaussian innovations. If $K_z > 0, K_x = 0, L_u > 0$, and $L_r > 0$ then the SNP density is a form of ARCH model with conditionally homogeneous, non-Gaussian innovations. The SNP model with $K_z > 0$ and $K_x = 0$ can accurately approximate any conditionally homogeneous innovation process by taking K_z large enough. If $K_z > 0, K_x > 0, L_u > 0, L_r > 0$, and $L_p > 0$ then the SNP model can accurately approximate any Markovian, stationary process by taking K_z and K_x large enough, including those that exhibit nonlinearities such as conditional skewness and kurtosis (Gallant et al., 1991).

We fit the SNP model by quasi maximum likelihood following the protocol that is described in Bansal, Gallant, Hussey, and Tauchen (1995) and is summarized in Section 11.4. Following this protocol, we select the model $L_u = 4$, $L_r = 16$, $K_z = 8$, and $I_z = 7$ when innovations are constrained to be homogenous ($K_x = 0, L_p = 1$). The score from this fit we term the 'semiparametric ARCH score'. We also report results for the model $L_u = 4, L_r = 16, L_p = 1$, $K_z = 8, I_z = 7$, $K_x = 2$, and $I_x = 1$, where the homogeneity constraint is dropped, and term the score from this fit the 'nonlinear nonparametric score'. We encountered difficulty fitting the stochastic volatility model to the even larger specification, $L_u = 4, L_r = 16, L_p = 1, K_z = 8$, $I_z = 7, K_x = 3$, and $I_x = 2$, dictated by following the protocol and do not report EMM results for that score. In all cases, the linear VAR model at the core of the SNP hierarchy is constrained to be zero after lag 2, except for lags of the interest rate which go out to lag 4, which reflects our prior knowledge that interest rates display much more complicated patterns of linear persistence than do stock returns or exchange rate movements.

Following the EMM procedure described in Section 11.3 we obtain the chi-square statistics shown in Table 11.5. As seen from the table, the stochastic volatility model fails to approximate the distribution of these data adequately; it is overwhelmingly rejected.

11.6 Conclusion

The standard stochastic volatility model, which has received substantial attention in the literature, is an empirically implausible model for stock returns. Our exhaustive search across many specifications indicates that the model must be extended to include (i) an asymmetric thick-tailed distribution for innovations in the mean equation, (ii) long-term dependence in the volatility equation, and

Table 11.5. Trivariate series: optimized value of the criterion

Score generator (SNP)								SV model			Objective function		
L_u	L_r	L_p	K_z	I_z	K_x	I_x	ℓ_θ	L_y	L_w	ℓ_p	χ^2	df	p-val
4	16	1	8	7	0	0	101	2	1	44	490.306	57	<0.0001
4	16	1	8	7	0	0	101	2	2	47	329.603	54	<0.0001
4	16	1	8	7	2	1	251	2	3	47	4168.470	204	<0.0001

L_u is the number of lags in the linear part of the SNP model; L_r is the number of lags in the ARCH part; L_p the number of lags in the polynomial part, $P(z, x)$. The polynomial $P(z, x)$ is of degree K_z in z, with interactions of degree exceeding $K_z - I_z$ suppressed; likewise, $P(z,x)$ is of degree K_x in x, with interactions of degree exceeding $K_x - I_x$ suppressed. By convention, $L_p = 1$ if $K_x = 0$. ℓ_θ is the number of free parameters associated with the SNP model. L_y is the number of lags in the linear conditional mean specification of the stochastic volatility model, and L_w is the number of lags in the volatility specification. ℓ_p is the number of free parameters of the stochastic volatility model. χ^2 is the EMM objective function scaled to be distributed $\chi^2(\text{df})$ under the maintained assumption of correct specification of the stochastic volatility model.

(iii) cross correlation between innovations in the mean and volatility equations. When introduced individually, each of these extensions improves the fit somewhat. When introduced together, they produce a stochastic volatility model that is quite elaborate and can accommodate features of the data best described as 'semiparametric ARCH'. However, the model still cannot accommodate features that could be described as 'nonlinear nonparametric'. Although not as exhaustive, our investigation for the trivariate data series on stock returns, interest rates, and exchange rates leads to a similar result.

These findings thus cast doubt on the statistical reliability of estimated stochastic volatility models that do not include all three of the extensions. At a minimum, estimates of stochastic volatility models should be accompanied by diagnostic tests in the directions found empirically important here. An even stronger conclusion, which emerges from the failure to fit the nonlinear nonparametric features, is that the stochastic volatility model cannot be made to fit financial market data without losing scientific content. The reason is that the conditional heterogeneity in higher moments exhibited by the stochastic volatility model is imparted solely by the volatility equation and therefore cannot be decoupled from the volatility equation. Without the decoupling, the model is not rich enough to approximate data from financial markets. With a decoupling, the stochastic volatility model becomes akin to a nonparametric specification and there are far more computationally convenient nonparametric estimators. Our findings stand in contrast to results of Kim and Shephard (1994), Geweke (1994), and others who find evidence in favor of fairly standard stochastic volatility models. The reason is that we step outside the narrow confines of stochastic volatility and entertain the possibility of very general and flexible auxiliary models. These models provide the diagnostics discrediting stochastic volatility.

Acknowledgements

This material is based upon work supported by the National Science Foundation. We thank Rob Engle and Jorgen Wolters for helpful remarks at various stages of this research, and we thank the two referees and the editor, Helmut Lutkepohl, for thoughtful remarks.

References

Aït-Sahalia, Y. (1996). Testing continuous-time models of the spot interest rate. *Review of Financial Studies* 9, 385–426.

Andersen, T. G. and Lund, J. (1997). Estimating continuous-time stochastic volatility models. *Journal of Econometrics* 77, 343–79.

——— Sørensen, B. (1996). GMM estimation of a stochastic volatility model: a Monte Carlo study. *Journal of Business and Economic Statistics* 14, 328–52.

Bansal, R., Gallant, A. R., Hussey, R., and Tauchen, G. (1993). Computational aspects of non parametric simulation estimation. In: Belsley, D. A. (ed.), *Computational Techniques for Econometrics and Economic Analysis*, Kluwer Academic Publishers, Boston, MA, 3–22.

——————————(1995). Nonparametric estimation of structural models for high-frequency currency market data. *Journal of Econometrics* 66, 251–87.

Bollerslev, T. and Mikkelsen, H. O. (1996). Modelling and pricing long-memory in stock market volatility. *Journal of Econometrics* 73, 151–84.

Breidt, F. J., Crato, N., and de Lima, P. (1994). Modeling long-memory stochastic volatility. Manuscript. Iowa State University, Ames, IA.

Clark, P. K. (1973). A subordinated stochastic process model with finite variance for speculative prices. *Econometrica* 41, 135–56.

Danielsson, J. (1994). Stochastic volatility in asset prices: estimation with simulated maximum likelihood. *Journal of Econometrics* 61, 375–400.

Ding, Z., Granger, C. W. J., and Engle, R. F. (1993). A long memory property of stock market returns and a new model. *Journal of Empirical Finance* 1, 83–108.

Duffie, D. and Singleton, K. J. (1993). Simulated moments estimation of Markov models of asset prices. *Econometrica* 61, 929–52.

Engle, R. F. and Gonzales-Rivera, G. (1991). Semiparametric ARCH models. *Journal of Business and Economic Statistics* 9, 345–60.

Fenton, V. M. and Gallant, A. R. (1996a). Convergence rates of SNP density estimators. *Econometrica* 64, 719–27.

———(1996b). Qualitative and asymptotic performance of SNP density estimators. *Journal of Econometrics* 74, 77–118.

Gallant, A. R. (1987). Nonlinear Statistical Models. Wiley, New York.

———Hsieh, D. A., and Tauchen, G. (1991). On fitting a recalcitrant series: The pound/dollar exchange rate, 1974–83, In: Barnett, W. A., Powell, J., Tauchen, G. (eds.), *Nonparametric and Semiparametric Methods in Econometrics and Statistics*, Proceedings of the 5th International Symposium in Economic Theory and Econometrics, Cambridge University Press, Cambridge, 199–240.

Gallant, A. R. and Long, J. R. (1997). Estimating stochastic differential equations efficiently by minimum chi-square. *Biometrika*, 84, 125–41.

Gallant, A. R. and Nychka, D. W. (1987). Seminonparametric maximum likelihood estimation. *Econometrica* 55, 363–90.

—— Rossi, P. E., and Tauchen, G. (1992). Stock prices and volume. *Review of Financial Studies* 5, 199–242.

—— —— —— (1993). Nonlinear dynamic structures. *Econometrica* 61, 871–907.

—— Tauchen, G. (1989). Seminonparametric estimation of conditionally constrained heterogeneous processes: asset pricing applications. *Econometrica* 57, 1091–120.

—— —— (1992). A nonparametric approach to nonlinear time series analysis: Estimation and simulation. In: Parzen, E., Brillinger, D., Rosenblatt, M., Taqqu, M., Geweke, J., Gaines, P. (eds.), *New Dimensions in Time Series Analysis, Part II*, Springer, New York, NY, 71–92.

—— —— (1996). Which moments to match? *Econometric Theory* 12, 657–81.

Geweke, J. (1994). Bayesian comparison of econometric models. Manuscript, Federal Reserve Bank, Minneapolis, MN.

Ghysels, E., Harvey, A. C., and Renault, E. (1995). Stochastic volatility. In: Maddala, G.S. (ed.), *Handbook of Statistics, vol. 14, Statistical Methods in Finance*. North-Holland, Amsterdam, forthcoming.

Gourieroux, C., Monfort, A., and Renault, E. (1993). Indirect inference. Journal of *Applied Econometrics* 8, S85–S118.

Granger, C. W. J. and Joyeux, R. (1980). An introduction to long-memory time series models and fractional differencing. *Journal of Time Series Analysis* 1, 15–29.

Harvey, A. C. (1993). Long memory and stochastic volatility. Manuscript, London School of Economics, London.

—— Shephard, N. (1994). Multivariate stochastic variance models. *Review of Economic Studies* 61, 129–58.

—— —— (1996). Estimation of an asymmetric stochastic volatility model for asset returns. *Journal of Business and Economic Statistics* 14, 429–34.

Jacquier, E., Polson, N. G., and Rossi, P. E. (1994). Bayesian analysis of stochastic volatility models. *Journal of Bussiness and Economic Statistics* 12, 371–417.

Kim, S. and Shephard, N. (1994). Stochastic volatility: optimal likilihood inference and comparison with ARCH models. Manuscript, Nuffield College, Oxford.

Mathieu, R. and Schotman, P. (1994). Stochastic volatility and the distribution of exchange rate news, Manuscript, University of Limburg, Maastricht, The Netherlands.

Nelson, D. B. (1991). Conditional heteroskedasticity in asset returns: a new approach. *Econometrica* 59, 347–70.

Schwarz, G. (1978). Estimating the dimension of a model. *Annals of Statistics* 6, 461–4.

Shephard, N. (1995). Statistical aspects of ARCH and stochastic volatility. Manuscript Nuffield College, Oxford.

Sowell, F. (1990). The fractional unit root distribution. *Econometrica* 58, 495–508.

Tauchen, G. (1997a). New minimum chi-square methods in empirical finance. In: Kreps, D. M., Wallis, K. F. (eds.), *Advances in Economics and Econometrics: Theory and Applications, Seventh World Congress*, Cambridge University Press, Cambridge.

—— (1997b). The objective function of simulation estimators near the boundary of the unstable region of the parameter space. Manuscript Duke University, Durham, NC.

—— Pitts, M. (1993). The price variability–volume relationship on speculative markets. *Econometrica* 51, 485–505.

Taylor, S. J. (1986). Modeling Financial Time Series, Wiley, New York, NY.

—— (1994). Modelling stochastic volatility. *Mathematical Finance* 4, 183–204.

Part III
Option pricing

12
Pricing Foreign Currency Options with Stochastic Volatility*

ANGELO MELINO AND STUART M. TURNBULL[†]

This paper investigates the consequences of stochastic volatility for pricing spot foreign currency options. A diffusion model for exchange rates with stochastic volatility is proposed and estimated. The parameter estimates are then used to price foreign currency options and the predictions are compared to observed market prices. We find that allowing volatility to be stochastic results in a much better fit to the empirical distribution of the Canada–U.S. exchange rate, and that this improvement in fit results in more accurate predictions of observed option prices.

12.1 Introduction

Recent attempts to use option models to price foreign currency options have been relatively disappointing. Although observed foreign currency option prices satisfy the boundary conditions that are implied by all option pricing models (Bodurtha and Courtadon (1986)), attempts to specify models that lead to accurate point forecasts of option prices have not been very successful.

Bodurtha and Courtadon (1987) assume a lognormal probability distribution for exchange rates and predict option prices using implied volatilities. The implied volatilities are chosen so as to maximize the correspondence between their model's predictions and the option prices observed on the previous market day. They find that this procedure produces fairly small biases in the average predicted price for most categories of options, although on average they consistently overestimate call and put option, although on average they consistently overestimate call and put option prices. Bodurtha and Courtadon also report that their model produces pricing errors that have a large dispersion. In particular, the average ratio of the absolute forecast error to the actual price is about 13 percent for both the puts and the calls.[1] Melino and Turnbull (1987) question the assumption of lognormality. They consider a class of probability distributions for the exchange rate process which includes the lognormal as a limiting case, and use

---

* Reprinted from *Journal of Econometrics* 45, A. Melino and S. M. Turnbull, 'Pricing Foreign Currency Options with Stochastic Volatility', pp 239–265, Copyright © 1990, with permission from Elsevier.

† Financial support for this paper was provided by the Social Sciences and Humanities Research Council of Canada under Grant 410-87-0850. This paper has benefited from comments by Ken Singleton and from workshop presentations at the National Bureau of Economic Research, Berkeley, and Stanford. Ken Vetzal provided excellent research assistance. We are responsible for any remaining errors.

[1] See tables 13.4b, 5b, and 4a, respectively, in Bodurtha and Courtadon (1987).

historical estimates of volatility to price the options. None of their models perform particularly well. The relatively poor performance of their models arises because the volatility estimates from actual exchange rate data are significantly smaller than those implied by observed option prices.

There are many potential explanations for the poor predictive performance of the foreign currency option models. A leading candidate is misspecification in the assumed distribution of exchange rates. Boothe and Glassman (1987) attempt to determine the appropriate probability distribution with which to describe changes in exchange rates over the period 1973–1984. They report that the distributions of daily and weekly exchange rate changes display kurtosis far in excess of the normal distribution, but find that the normal distribution provides a good approximation to the distribution of quarterly changes in exchange rates. This tendency of the distribution of exchange rate changes to resemble more closely the normal as we take longer differencing intervals suggests that the standard central limit theorems apply to daily exchange rate changes. This casts doubt on models (such as the stable Paretian) which account for the thick tails of the distribution of daily exchange rate changes but have infinite variance. In a similar period, Melino and Turnbull (1987) find evidence that the volatility parameter is highly unstable over time. Such a finding is important because, as noted by Press (1968), McFarland et al. (1982), and Engle (1982), finite but heteroskedastic variances can generate the fat tail feature that seems to characterize exchange rate distributions, but heteroskedastic variances also are consistent with the limiting normal distribution reported by Boothe and Glassman (1987).

The presence of stochastic volatility has important implications for option pricing. The effects of stochastic volatility upon stock option prices have recently been examined by Hull and White (1987), Johnson and Shanno (1987), Scott (1987), and Wiggins (1987). These papers demonstrate that European predicted option prices tend to be less than Black–Scholes option prices for at the money options. If the option is deep in the money, predicted option prices are usually greater than Black–Scholes. For deep out of the money options, the results are sensitive to the parameters of the stochastic process describing changes in volatility and the correlation between changes in volatility and stock price. Cooper et al. (1986) examine the pricing of European foreign currency options. They estimate the parameters of the stochastic process describing changes in volatility and then compare predicted prices to Black–Scholes prices. Their results are similar in nature to those found in the studies on stock options.

In this paper, we focus on obtaining a closer correspondence to the empirical distribution of exchange rates and on the subsequent consequences for option pricing. The first objective of this study is to estimate the parameters of the stochastic process describing changes in exchange rates and volatility, assuming that volatility is stochastic. The fundamental difficulty in the estimation process is that volatility cannot be directly observed. Cooper et al. (1986), Scott (1987), and Wiggins (1987) use a method of moments approach to estimate the parameters. They found that the parameter estimates were sensitive to the moments which they fitted, but they were unable to pool the available information or to test if the different parameter estimates which they obtained were due simply to sampling error. We generalize their approach along the lines of Hansen (1982), so that we can address these issues.

The second objective of this paper is to examine whether the consideration of stochastic volatility translates into important differences in the implied option prices. The estimated parameters for the volatility process and an estimate of the volatility at each point in time are used to price the corresponding currency options. Predictions then are compared to observed option prices, using transactions data from the Philadelphia Exchange (PHLX). Due to very high computing costs, only one foreign currency is considered: the Canadian dollar.

The paper is organized as follows: Section 12.2 reviews briefly the pricing of foreign currency options when volatility is stochastic. The data are examined in Section 12.3. The econometric strategy is described and the estimates of the volatility process are given in Section 12.4. Section 12.5 presents the results of the option pricing model and compares the predicted to the observed option prices. Summary and conclusions are given in Section 12.6.

12.2 The pricing of foreign currency options

We assume the following:

A1. No transactions costs, no differential taxes, no borrowing or lending restrictions, and trading takes place continuously.

A2. The term structure of interest rates in both the domestic and foreign country are flat and nonstochastic.

A3. The underlying state variables are the spot exchange rate (S) and the level of volatility (v).

A4. The transition probabilities for the state variables are summarized by

$$dS = (a + bS)dt + vS^{\beta/2}dZ_s \tag{1}$$

and

$$dv = \mu(v)dt + \sigma(v)dZ_c, \tag{2}$$

where Z_S and Z_c are standard Wiener processes whose increments have instantaneous correlation ρ; a, b, and β are parameters; $\mu(v)$ is the instantaneous mean and $\sigma^2(v)$ is the instantaneous variance of the volatility process. It is assumed that $0 \leq \beta \leq 2$, and that zero is an absorbing barrier for S.

Assumptions A1 and A2 are standard.[2] Economic theory provides little guidance on the choice of state variables or on their equations of motion. Many authors assume that the exchange rate itself is a sufficient statistic for its transition

---

[2] A more complete treatment would also relax A2, include the domestic and foreign interest rates as state variables, and allow for a possible reward for interest rate risk. While conceptually straightforward, allowing for stochastic volatility and stochastic foreign and domestic interest rates presents an imposing computational challenge. We leave this for future research.

probabilities[3] and posit equation (1) with $\beta = 2$ and constant volatility. This model was investigated by Melino and Turnbull (1987), where it was found to be inadequate. The model (i) failed to adequately capture several empirically important features of the distribution of daily exchange rate changes, and (ii) using historical estimates of volatility, it led to predicted option prices that were systematically lower on average than observed transactions prices. Including volatility as a state variable with transition probabilities given by (2) may help account for these inadequacies.

Details about the historical behavior of the Canada–U.S. exchange rate are provided in Section 12.3. At this stage, it is useful to point out three important stylized facts which any descriptive model of exchange rate movements must capture: (a) daily exchange rate changes are virtually unpredictable, (b) squared daily exchange rate changes have a nontrivial dynamic structure that suggests autoregressive conditional heteroskedasticity, and (c) the distribution of daily exchange rate changes has relatively fat tails. The lack of predictability of daily exchange rates can be fit in our specification by drift parameters, a and b, in eq. (1) that are essentially zero.[4] The remaining two features must be accounted for by the diffusion term.

With volatility (v) constant, the process given by (1) does generate exchange rate changes that display conditional heteroskedasticity, that is, heteroskedasticity that depends upon the level of lagged exchange rates, unless $\beta = 0$. Because the exchange rate displays a nontrivial dynamic structure, this conditional heteroskedasticity shows up (*inter alia*) as nonzero auto-correlations of squared exchange rate changes. In addition, the conditional heteroskedasticity leads to fatter tails and higher kurtosis. Therefore, nonstochastic volatility is consistent with the important qualitative features of the exchange rate distribution described above. Nonetheless, it is not satisfactory because it cannot account for the magnitudes that appear in actual data. The values of the autocorrelations of squared daily changes and excess kurtosis that can be generated by (1) depend critically upon both the sample size and the level of volatility. Two limiting arguments can be used to clarify this dependence. For a fixed level of volatility, these values become very large as the sample size increases.[5] However, for a fixed sample size, these values will be virtually zero, if v is small enough. Some simulations that we have performed using estimates of v based on historical

---

[3] For example, Grabbe (1983), Shastri and Tandon (1986), and Bodurtha and Courtadon (1987).

[4] Although economic theory has a good deal to say about what causes exchange rates to move, we have little interest in considering specifications involving more than a linear drift for the exchange rate process because with high frequency data (basically daily) of the sort we plan to use (i) the drift is notoriously difficult to estimate and (ii) the diffusion parameter estimates are fairly robust to the precise specification of the drift (because the centered and uncentered second moments converge). In addition, the drift parameters do not appear explicitly in the pricing equations for the currency options.

[5] For example, consider the case where $\beta = 2$ and we take the initial exchange rate, S_o, as fixed. $E(\Delta S_1^4)/E^2(\Delta S_t^2)$ is unbounded for large t, and, using values of v of the order suggested by the historical estimates, the $(\Delta S_t^2, \Delta S_{t-1}^2)/(\Delta S_t^2)$ goes to a value slightly in excess of 1/3.

data of the Canada–U.S. exchange rate indicate that values of the autocorrelations of squared daily changes and excess kurtosis that can be generated by (1) are virtually zero, even for sample sizes that correspond to 15 years of daily data. Related simulations show that allowing v to be stochastic considerably increases the size of the autocorrelations and excess kurtosis that can be generated.

There are many specifications that one might consider, a priori, for the v process. Our empirical work will assume that volatility changes can be described by

$$d \ln v = (\alpha + \delta \ln v)dt + \gamma dZ_v, \tag{2'}$$

so that $\mu(v) = v(\alpha + \gamma^2/2 + \delta \ln v)$ and $\sigma(v) = \gamma v$. This specification of the volatility process is admittedly ad hoc.[6] It was chosen because it respects the nonnegativity of volatility and because it is tractable. Similar specifications have been suggested by Cooper et al. (1986), Scott (1987), and Wiggins (1987).

Melino and Turnbull (1987) found that the option prices predicted by A1, A2, and eq. (1) with constant volatility (estimated from the historical data) systematically underpredicted observed transactions prices. In their sample, Canadian dollar call options were underpredicted by just over 25%, on average. For the other currencies they examined, predicted call and put option prices ranged from 4% to 22% lower, on average, than corresponding observed option prices. Treating volatility (v) as stochastic and generated by (2') may account for this systematic underprediction.

Given A1 to A4, the price of options written on spot foreign currency can be developed using familiar methods.[7] The option price (C) satisfies the following partial differential equation:

$$\frac{1}{2}(v^2 S^\beta C_{SS} + 2\rho\sigma v S^{\beta/2} C_{Sv} + \sigma^2 C_{vv})$$
$$+ (r_D - r_F)SC_s + (\mu(v) - \lambda\sigma(v))C_v - r_D C + C_t = 0, \tag{3}$$

where r_D and r_F denote the domestic and foreign risk-free rates, respectively, and λ is a risk premium that arises because volatility is not a traded asset.

Note that the drift in the exchange rate does not appear in eq. (3). The derivation of the option price does assume, however, knowledge of all the parameters of the volatility process (including its drift), as well as the level of volatility and the risk premium at each point in time. Section 12.4 describes a method to estimate the parameters and level of the volatility process.

Without an explicit description of endowments, preferences, and technology, it is difficult to say very much about the risk premium. To rule out arbitrage we must require $\lambda = 0$ if $v\sigma(v) = 0$. With specification (2'), however, this constraint is

---

[6] A more general specification of the volatility process would allow for a possible dependence of volatility on days of the week, or perhaps on whether markets were open. We chose not to consider this more general specification because it would introduce formidable difficulties into the econometric estimation and the solution of the predicted option prices.

[7] See Cox, Ingersoll, and Ross (1985).

never binding. Many authors simply assume that λ is identically zero. This follows from the assumption that innovations to exchange rate volatility are uncorrelated with innovations to aggregate consumption. It seems worthwhile to consider more general models for λ that include $\lambda = 0$ as a special case. For computational reasons, it is useful to restrict attention to functional forms for the risk premium that are smooth functions and involve at most the exchange rate, the level of volatility and time. As a first approximation we shall simply assume that λ is a constant.[8] This can be justified if preferences are logarithmic. We will treat the risk premium, λ, as a free parameter in our empirical work and try to infer its value from observed option prices.

When v is constant, (3) simplifies considerably and reduces to the expression derived in Melino and Turnbull (1987). Explicit solutions for the option price satisfying (3) are not available, except for certain special cases. However, eq. (3) can be solved (subject to the appropriate boundary conditions) by numerical methods.

12.3 Data description

Our empirical work requires the following data: (i) the spot Canada–U.S. exchange rate, (ii) the price of exchange rate options written on the Canadian dollar, and (iii) the term structure of interest rates for Canada and the U.S.

Daily data on the spot Canada–U.S. exchange rate for the period January 2, 1975 to December 10, 1986 were obtained from the Bank of Canada. These data refer to rates prevailing at mid-day on the interbank market in Canada. We used these data to identify the stochastic process for the exchange rate. Note that we *did not* use these data directly to price the exchange rate options (see below).

Table 12.1a provides descriptive statistics for the exchange rate over various sample periods. The data are expressed as the number of U.S. cents required to purchase one Canadian dollar. The change in the Canada–U.S. exchange rate tends to display a small negative mean over our sample. The average daily change, however, is swamped by daily volatility as proxied by either the average absolute change or the daily standard deviation. These proxies for volatility are fairly stable if we look at very long samples, but the sharp differences in the estimates obtained from the two shorter samples are too large to be rationalized by sampling error. Changes in the daily Canada–U.S. exchange rate display virtually no skewness, but consistently display positive excess kurtosis.[9]

The dynamic properties of exchange rates are examined in Table 12.1b. The autocorrelations for the level of the Canada–U.S. exchange rate strongly indicate a random walk component. The change in daily exchange rates is virtually white noise. Because of the size of the sample, one can reject the hypothesis that the population autocorrelations of exchange rate changes are exactly zero. However,

---

[8] It would be interesting to investigate alternative models for λ, especially in light of the sensitivity of predicted option prices to λ reported in Section 12.5. We leave this for future research.

[9] Excess kurtosis refers to the value of the kurtosis coefficient in excess of the normal. Cramér (1946, §15.8) calls this the 'coefficient of excess'.

Table 12.1a. Canada–U.S. exchange rate properties, descriptive statistics

Variable	Mean	Standard deviation	Skewness	Excess kurtosis	Minimum value	Maximum value
		75/01/02–86/12/10 (3011 observations)				
S	85.116	8.94	0.37	−0.75	69.498	103.863
ΔS	−0.009	0.197	−0.31	4.98	−1.886	1.073
$(\Delta S)^2$	0.039	0.103	16.30	474.66	0.000	3.556
$\|\Delta S\|$	0.143	0.135	2.51	14.45	0.000	1.886
		75/01/02–80/12/31 (1513 observations)				
S	92.096	6.51	0.26	−1.48	82.590	103.863
ΔS	−0.011	0.207	−0.56	6.27	−1.886	1.073
$(\Delta S)^2$	0.043	0.124	17.41	447.57	0.000	3.556
$\|\Delta S\|$	0.152	0.140	2.89	20.44	0.000	1.886
		81/01/02–86/12/10 (1498 observations)				
S	78.067	4.37	−0.23	−1.46	69.498	84.983
ΔS	−0.007	0.187	0.52	2.83	−0.993	0.920
$(\Delta S)^2$	0.035	0.077	5.59	42.60	0.000	0.851
$\|\Delta S\|$	0.134	0.130	2.02	5.97	0.000	0.923
		83/02/28–84/02/10 (241 observations)				
S	80.979	0.47	−0.74	−0.27	79.853	81.806
ΔS	−0.005	0.101	−0.14	0.30	−0.275	0.329
$(\Delta S)^2$	0.010	0.016	2.87	10.59	0.000	0.109
$\|\Delta S\|$	0.079	0.064	1.12	1.15	0.000	0.329
		84/02/13–85/01/24 (240 observations)				
S	76.796	1.31	1.06	0.34	74.923	80.321
ΔS	−0.020	0.150	0.01	2.12	−0.588	0.636
$(\Delta S)^2$	0.023	0.046	4.81	31.10	0.000	0.405
$\|\Delta S\|$	0.112	0.102	1.81	4.68	0.000	0.636

the estimated autocorrelations are very small which implies there is very little linear structure in the mean of exchange rate changes. By contrast, volatility, as proxied by either the square or the absolute value of daily exchange rate changes, displays a very interesting dynamic structure. The autocorrelations are well below one and they initially damp toward zero. However, the higher autocorrelations stay positive and seem to cluster around a small positive constant for very many more than the twelve autocorrelations reported here. Also, the positive constant around which the higher autocorrelations cluster declined when we looked at shorter subsamples. As pointed out by Schwert (1987), this behavior of the higher autocorrelations indicates a random walk component in both of these proxies for volatility. Note that finding a random walk component in the squared or the absolute daily change does not mean that volatility as defined in eq. (1) has a random walk component. According to our specification, the autocorrelations of these proxies for volatility will depend upon the dynamic structure of volatility *and* the level of exchange rates (unless $\beta = 0$). Therefore, the random walk

Table 12.1b. Canada–U.S. exchange rate, descriptive statistics, 75/01/02–86/12/10

Autocorrelations

	1	2	3	4	5	6	7	8	9	10	11	f12
S	0.999	0.998	0.997	0.996	0.994	0.993	0.992	0.991	0.990	0.988	0.987	0.986
ΔS	0.095	0.006	0.003	0.009	0.064	0.021	0.044	0.002	0.038	-0.007	-0.011	-0.002
$(\Delta S)^2$	0.271	0.149	0.114	0.123	0.076	0.093	0.049	0.058	0.057	0.062	0.055	0.044
$|\Delta S|$	0.232	0.190	0.162	0.164	0.161	0.150	0.122	0.123	0.103	0.092	0.097	0.099

Crosscorrelations $\rho(|\Delta S(t)|,\ \Delta S(t-j))$

-12	-11	-10	-9	-8	-7	-6	-5	-4	-3	-2	-1	0
1	2	3	4	5	6	7	8	9	10	11	12	
0.051	0.042	0.033	-0.009	0.033	0.024	0.034	0.014	0.011	0.053	-0.001	-0.044	-0.104
-0.081	-0.067	-0.077	-0.061	-0.048	-0.033	-0.060	-0.001	-0.035	-0.040	-0.036	-0.020	

component in these proxies for volatility may simply reflect the random walk component in the level of exchange rates. The bottom half of Table 12.1b looks at $\rho(|\Delta S(t)|, \Delta S(t-j))$, the cross-correlations between the absolute daily change and the daily change itself. The correlations between the current absolute daily change and future levels of the daily change are small and display no consistent pattern which implies that the size of absolute changes has no predictive content for subsequent changes in the level of the exchange rate. However, the contemporaneous correlation and the correlation with lagged levels of the daily change are consistently negative and often large. This implies that large declines in the exchange rate are associated with large absolute movements on the current and subsequent days. Increases in the exchange rate, therefore, tend to precede periods of lower volatility.

To price foreign currency options it is necessary to obtain simultaneously sampled data on option prices, spot currency prices, and domestic and foreign interest rates for default-free claims matching the maturities of the option contracts. Our source for simultaneous option prices and currency prices is the transaction surveillance report compiled by the Philadelphia Exchange and described by Bodurtha (1984). For each option trade, the following data are recorded (*inter alia*): the date of the trade, the time of the trade; maturity, exercise price, option price; prevailing bid and ask spot quotes at the time of the trade, and value of the last spot quote reported by Telerate from the interbank market. Our sample of option trades runs from 28 February 1983 to 24 January 1985.

For short-term interest rates, daily closing quotes for 90 and 180 day Canadian and U.S. Treasury bills are used. This data were supplied by the Bank of Canada. For Canada, these data were supplemented by using quotes on 30-, 60-, 90-, and 180-day Treasury bills, collected on a weekly basis and provided by a leading Canadian securities firm.

12.4 Empirical results

12.4.1 Econometric methods

We assume that the model described by eqs. (1) and (2′) holds in calendar (as opposed to market) time. We have no direct measurements on volatility, so inferences about the parameters in (1) and (2′) must be based on a set of unevenly spaced observations $\{S(t_1), \ldots, S(t_n)\}$ on the exchange rate. The uneven spacing reflects weekends, trading holidays, and missing observations.

It does not appear possible to obtain closed form expressions for the exact conditional densities generated by eqs. (1) and (2′), except for certain special cases (such as v constant). Our strategy will be to approximate the continuous time stochastic process for exchange rates and volatility by a discrete time stochastic process. We will then proceed as if the data are generated from the discrete time model to recover parameter estimates.

Define $h_i = t_i - t_{i-1}$ and $h = \min\{h_i\}$. The continuous time process described by (1) and (2′) will be approximated by

$$S(t_i) = ah_i + (1 + bh_i)S(t_{i-1}) + v(t_{i-1})S(t_{i-1})^{\beta/2}h_i^{1/2}e(t_i), \tag{4}$$

$$\ln v(t_i) = \alpha h + (1 + \delta h)\ln v(t_i - h) + \gamma h^{1/2}u(t_i), \tag{5}$$

where

$$\begin{bmatrix} e(t_i) \\ u(t_i) \end{bmatrix} \sim \text{i.i.d.} \quad N_2\left(0, \begin{bmatrix} 1 & \rho \\ \rho & 1 \end{bmatrix}\right).$$

There are an infinity of discrete time models which differ only by terms of order $o(h)$ that converge to (1) and (2) as max $\{h_i\} \to 0.$[10] A priori, it is not clear which of the discrete time models will serve as the best approximation. Eqs. (12.4) and (12.5) display a certain asymmetry because the unobserved volatility process has even spacing, but the exchange rate process has irregular spacing that matches the available data. This asymmetry turns out to be unimportant in our application but serves to simplify our calculations. If $\delta < 0$ and we assume that appropriate initial conditions are satisfied, then the even spacing in the discrete time approximation to the unobserved volatility process leads to the result that volatility will be stationary and, in particular, that

$$\ln v_t \sim N(\mu_v, \sigma_v^2), \tag{6}$$

where

$$\mu_c = -\alpha/\delta \text{ and } \sigma_v^2 = h\gamma^2/\left[1 - (1 + \delta h)^2\right].$$

The quality of the discrete time approximation depends (among other things) upon how tightly sampled are the data. In our application, the mean value of h_i is approximately 1.45 days and h_i never exceeds 5 days. With v constant, it is possible to obtain the exact conditional density for exchange rates and test the quality of the discrete time approximation directly. We did so in previous work (Melino and Turnbull (1987)) and found that the Gaussian quasi-likelihood implied by (4) provided an excellent (and extremely convenient) approximation to the true process.

Define $\theta = (a, b, \alpha, \delta, \gamma, \rho; \beta)$ and $w_i(\theta)$ by

$$w_i(\theta) = \frac{S(t_i) - ah_i - (1 + bh_i)S(t_{i-1})}{[h_i S^\beta(t_{i-1})]^{1/2}}. \tag{7}$$

The w_i represent the one-observation-ahead forecast errors normalized by a term to reflect the contribution of observables to the conditional heteroskedasticity of these forecast errors. Given the discrete time approximation (4), w_i can also be written as

---

[10] Nelson (1989) provides a set of sufficient conditions for a sequence of discrete time models to converge to a well-behaved continuous time limit.

$$w_i(\theta) = v(t_{i-1})e(t_i), \tag{8}$$

so that w_i is the product of two stationary series. In general, the expectation of functions of w_i will depend upon θ. The method of moments estimates the value of θ by matching the computed sample average of these functions of w_i to their expected values. There are infinitely many functions of the w_i that may be considered. In this paper, we consider the following:

$$w_i^m(\theta), \qquad m = 1, 2, 3, \ldots, \tag{9a}$$

$$|w_i^m(\theta)|, \qquad m = 1, 2, 3, \ldots, \tag{9b}$$

$$w_i(\theta)w_{i-j}(\theta), \qquad j = 1, 2, 3, \ldots, \tag{9c}$$

$$|w_i(\theta)w_{i-j}(\theta)|, \qquad j = 1, 2, 3, \ldots, \tag{9d}$$

$$w_i^2(\theta)w_{i-j}^2(\theta), \qquad j = 1, 2, 3, \ldots, \tag{9e}$$

$$|w_i(\theta)||w_{i-j}(\theta), \qquad j = 0, \pm 1, \pm 2, \pm 3, \ldots. \tag{9f}$$

Expressions for the unconditional expectation of these functions are provided in an appendix that is available upon request. The list of moments was chosen with an eye to three criteria: familiarity, identification, and efficiency. The moments in (9a), (9c), and (9e) have been estimated and discussed by various authors, so we began with them. After some Monte Carlo simulations, we realized that including the absolute moments in (9b) and (9d) provided sharp increases in efficiency. These simulations also indicated that the sampling variability of the sample averages of the functions in (9a)–(9b) increase dramatically with m, so we only consider moments up to $m = 4$ in our empirical work. Some of these functions provide information about only a subset of the parameters. For example, the odd powers of w_i all have expectation zero, at the true value of θ. These moments can be used to infer a, b, and β, but they are uninformative about the remaining components of θ. Looking also at the absolute moments allows us to infer the values of μ_v and σ_v^2. The functions in (9c)–(9f) summarize some of the dynamic properties of exchange rates. These properties allow us to distinguish the parameters α, δ, and γ (which appear in μ_v and σ_v^2), allow us to identify ρ, and provide additional information about the remaining parameters. It turns out that consideration of (9f) is essential to uniquely identify ρ. In the appendix, it is shown that

$$E|w_i|w_{i-1} = (2/\pi)^{1/2}\rho\gamma \exp\{2\mu_v + 2\sigma_v^2\}.$$

The sign of this expression is determined entirely by ρ. If $\rho < 0$, for example, then unexpected decreases (increases) in the exchange rate S tend to precede a period with high (low) volatility. The opposite is true if $\rho > 0$.

One way to estimate θ is to choose (judiciously) as many functions from (9) as there are parameters to estimate, and then match the sample averages of these functions to their expected values. This is essentially the approach suggested by Cooper et al. (1986), Scott (1987), and Wiggins (1987). We follow Hansen (1982) who provides a more general framework which allows us to optimally pool the information in as many functions of the w_i as we wish to consider.

Let $f_i(\theta) \in R^p$ denote a vector whose components are functions of w_i drawn from (9) less their unconditional expectations. Define $g_n(\theta)$ by

$$g_n(\theta) = \frac{1}{n} \sum_{i=1}^{n} f_i(\theta). \tag{10}$$

We wish to choose an estimator which makes $g_n(\theta)$ 'small'. More precisely, our estimator is

$$\hat{\theta}_n = \arg \min_{\theta \in \Theta} g'_n(\theta) \hat{W}_n g_n(\theta), \tag{11}$$

where Θ denotes the permissible parameter space and $\hat{W}_n$ is a (possibly random) positive definite weighting matrix. Following previous work (Marsh and Rosenfeld (1983), Melino and Turnbull (1987)) we will minimize the expression given in eq. (11) for a grid of values for β. Under suitable regularity conditions,[11] $\hat{\theta}_n$ will be consistent and asymptotically normal, i.e.

$$n^{1/2}(\hat{\theta}_n - \theta) \sim \text{AN}(0, V_n). \tag{12}$$

The covariance matrix of the asymptotic normal distribution, V_n, can be consistently estimated by

$$\hat{V}_n = (D'_n \hat{W}_n D_n)^{-1} D'_n \hat{W}_n \hat{\Sigma}_n \hat{W}_n D_n (D'_n \hat{W}_n D_n)^{-1}, \tag{13}$$

where $D'_n(\theta)$ is the Jacobian matrix,[12]

---

[11] There are some delicate issues that prevent an immediate mapping into Hansen (1982). If the drift parameters are truly zero (which is not a bad first approximation), then there is a unit root in the level of the exchange rate. Also, because 0 is an absorbing barrier, for some parameter configurations the exchange rate process will not be ergodic. Finally, it is technically very difficult to deal rigorously with the approximation error introduced by using the discrete time model. We refer the reader to Duffie and Singleton (1988) for a discussion of these issues. Although we realize that there are technical difficulties in invoking the usual large sample theory results, simulations indicate that they are a useful guide to the finite sample distribution of g_n. A unit root in the level of the exchange rate would clearly complicate the distribution theory for the drift parameters, but, because they are virtually independent, the asymptotic distribution theory for the remaining parameters should still be a good guide.

[12] Strictly speaking, $dg_n(\theta)/d\theta$ may not exist in any given sample, because the derivatives involving absolute moments have contributions from the individual observations, such as $d|w_i(\theta)|/da$, which are not defined at $w_i(\theta) = 0$. Formally, the derivatives exist almost everywhere, so if we encounter a value of $w_i(\theta) = 0$ during our calculations, we are entitled to set its contribution to $dg_n(\theta)/da$ to anything we like. Because of floating point arithmetic, this situation did arise in our work, and we chose to set the contribution to zero.

$$D'_n(\theta) = \mathrm{d}g_n(\theta)/\mathrm{d}\theta, \tag{14}$$

evaluated at any consistent estimator of θ, and $\hat{\Sigma}_n$ is any consistent estimator of Σ_n given by

$$\Sigma_n = \mathrm{E}\left(\frac{1}{n}\sum_{i=1}^{n}\sum_{j=1}^{n} f_i(\theta)\,f_j(\theta)'\right). \tag{15}$$

Our empirical work uses the Newey–West (1987) estimator of $\hat{\Sigma}_n$.[13] The asymptotic covariance matrix is minimized by choosing $\hat{W}_n = \hat{\Sigma}_n^{-1}$ in which case the expression in (13) also simplifies considerably.

In practice, we fix a value of β and then obtain initial consistent estimators of the remaining components of θ by fitting exactly an initially chosen vector $f_i(\theta)$ with $p = 6$ components. Then we construct a vector $f_i(\theta)$ with a large number ($p = 47$) of components. The initial consistent estimates of θ are used to construct $\hat{\Sigma}_n$ and $\hat{W}_n = \hat{\Sigma}_n^{-1}$, and we again minimize (11) to obtain efficient estimators. Although there is no asymptotic advantage, to reduce the importance of our initial choice of $f_i(\theta)$, we iterate to approximately a fixed point before reporting our results.

12.4.2 Parameter estimates

Parameter estimates for various values of β are reported in Table 12.2. The drift parameters for the exchange rate, a and b, are imprecisely estimated, for all values of β. Although the estimates of b are negative, there is not much evidence of mean-reverting behavior in the level of exchange rates. The parameters of the volatility process are estimated fairly accurately. Allowing volatility to be stochastic appears to generate statistically significant improvements in the fit of the exchange rate distribution. The hypothesis of non-stochastic volatility, $\gamma = 0$, is overwhelmingly rejected for all the models considered. The estimates of δ are negative and significant and the point estimates indicate that shocks to volatility in the Canada–U.S. exchange rate are mostly short-lived, and there is a strong tendency to revert quickly to the mean level of volatility. The half-life of a shock to volatility implied by the parameter estimates is approximately one week. The correlation between innovations to volatility and the level of exchange rates appears to be negative, but the evidence is weak except for the case $\beta = 2$. The point estimates indicate that declines in the Canadian dollar tend to precede periods of high volatility.

---

[13] There was a good deal of serial correlation in the components of $f_i(\theta)$. To decide on the number of autocorrelations to include in the estimate of the covariance matrix, we used the initial consistent estimates of θ and undertook a Monte Carlo study. We generated a collection of samples with 3,000 observations. For each sample, we constructed the Newey–West estimator for different lag lengths (up to 300) and constructed $g_n(\theta)$ as in eq. (10). We then averaged the Newey–West estimators across the samples and compared them to the covariance matrix for $g_n(\theta)$. Based on this comparison, we decided to include 50 autocorrelations in all our subsequent calculations.

Table 12.2. Canada–U.S. exchange rate, parameter estimates,
75/01/02–86/12/10[a]

Beta	a	b	α	δ	γ	ρ	$ng'Wg$
0.0	0.037	$-0.0^3 48$	-0.252	-0.127	0.190	-0.081	41.53
	(0.092)	$(0.0^2 11)$	(0.083)	(0.042)	(0.031)	(0.088)	
1.0	0.042	$-0.0^3 54$	-0.384	-0.091	0.153	-0.110	39.36
	(0.093)	$(0.0^2 11)$	(0.164)	(0.039)	(0.033)	(0.110)	
2.0	0.044	$-0.0^3 57$	-0.745	-0.116	0.192	-0.188	41.33
	(0.087)	$(0.0^2 10)$	(0.204)	(0.032)	(0.028)	(0.090)	

[a] The parameter estimates were obtained from fitting the following moments:

$$w_i^m(\theta), \qquad m = 1, 3,$$
$$|w_i^m(\theta)|, \qquad m = 1, \ldots, 4,$$
$$w_i(\theta)w_{i-j}(\theta), \qquad j = 1, \ldots, 10,$$
$$|w_i(\theta)w_{i-j}(\theta)|, \qquad j = 1, \ldots, 10,$$
$$w_i^2(\theta)w_{i-j}^2(\theta), \qquad j = 1, \ldots, 10,$$
$$|w_i(\theta)||w_{i-j}(\theta), \qquad j = 0, \ldots, 10,$$

Standard errors are in parentheses.

Under the null hypothesis, the minimized value of the quadratic form in eq. (11) has a χ^2 distribution, with degrees of freedom equal to the difference between the number of moments fitted and the number of parameters estimated. All of the models reported in Table 12.2 were estimated from 47 moments, so the χ^2 statistic is approximately equal to its expected value in all cases. There is very little variation in this goodness-of-fit statistic, so that the data appear to be indifferent to the choice of β.

The small χ^2 statistics in Table 12.2 could be due to a good fit or to large sampling error. In either case, the statistic pertains to a model's ability to mimic the moments of w_i, while we are more directly concerned with the moments of exchange rate changes. In order to provide more information about the model's performance, exchange rate data were simulated according to the discrete time model given in eqs. (4) and (5), using the estimated parameter values. For each simulated sample of 3,000 observations, the same summary statistics as those examined in Table 12.1 were calculated. Table 12.3 reports the mean and standard deviation of each statistic across the simulated samples. A good fit to the empirical exchange rate distribution requires the difference between the actual statistic and its mean across the simulated samples to be small, in some meaningful sense. A good statistical fit requires the difference to be small relative to the reported standard deviation. Because the results are virtually identical, only the results corresponding to the $\beta = 2$ case are reported.

The static properties of the exchange rate distribution (i.e. those described in Table 12.1a) are matched very closely. Allowing for stochastic volatility generates the characteristic positive excess kurtosis of daily exchange rate changes and does

Table 12.3. Descriptive statistics from simulated samples (average and standard deviation across simulations)[a]

Variable	Mean	Standard deviation	Skewness	Excess kurtosis	Minimum value	Maximum value
S	85.999	6.29	0.63	−0.12	75.838	101.845
	2.861	1.24	0.56	1.02	2.904	1.547
ΔS	−0.007	0.20	−0.14	5.58	−1.472	1.325
	0.001	0.01	0.33	2.89	0.405	0.303
$(\Delta S)^2$	0.041	0.11	10.64	215.68	0.000	2.694
	0.003	0.02	5.46	267.35	0.000	1.521
$|\Delta S|$	0.142	0.14	2.62	13.05	0.000	1.595
	0.005	0.01	0.46	8.00	0.000	0.389

Autocorrelations

	1	2	3	4	5	6	7	8	9	10	11	12
S	0.998	0.996	0.994	0.993	0.991	0.989	0.987	0.985	0.983	0.982	0.980	0.978
	0.001	0.001	0.002	0.003	0.003	0.004	0.005	0.006	0.006	0.007	0.008	0.008
ΔS	−0.001	0.001	0.004	−0.002	0.001	0.000	0.002	0.000	0.001	−0.002	−0.003	0.001
	0.026	0.026	0.026	0.023	0.028	0.022	0.021	0.019	0.020	0.022	0.020	0.020
$(\Delta S)^2$	0.112	0.092	0.072	0.076	0.125	0.034	0.022	0.018	0.034	0.054	0.004	0.003
	0.087	0.058	0.056	0.076	0.179	0.065	0.027	0.024	0.029	0.046	0.021	0.024
$|\Delta S|$	0.160	0.131	0.105	0.101	0.152	0.055	0.041	0.033	0.051	0.082	0.012	0.011
	0.040	0.031	0.031	0.032	0.041	0.025	0.024	0.024	0.025	0.030	0.021	0.024

Crosscorrelations $p(|\Delta S(t)|, \Delta S(t-j))$

−12	−11	−10	−9	−8	−7	−6	−5	−4	−3	−2	−1	0
1	2	3	4	5	6	7	8	9	10	11	12	
−0.001	0.003	−0.005	−0.001	0.000	0.001	0.001	−0.011	−0.003	−0.002	−0.005	−0.002	−0.065
0.023	0.020	0.025	0.020	0.023	0.021	0.019	0.028	0.026	0.027	0.024	0.028	0.057
−0.047	−0.036	−0.031	−0.027	−0.027	−0.017	−0.015	−0.012	−0.012	−0.008	−0.005	−0.003	
0.023	0.022	0.024	0.023	0.027	0.022	0.023	0.024	0.021	0.028	0.021	0.020	

[a] Number of observations in each sample = 3000. Number of samples = 100. The first row for each statistic is its mean value across the samples, and the second row is its standard deviation. The statistics were calculated from the parameter estimates corresponding to the $\beta = 2$ model.

an excellent job of matching the other moments as well. Fig. 12.1 compares the empirical distribution of exchange rate changes to that of our simulated exchange rates. The correspondence is striking, especially when compared to the normal approximation.

The fit between the actual and the simulated dynamic properties (i.e. those described in Table 12.1b) is good. The simulated level of exchange rates display the characteristic random walk component. The simulated daily change in exchange rates generate essentially zero autocorrelations at all lags. However, the model is unable to fit the small but statistically significant autocorrelation displayed at lag one in the actual data. The model generates serial dependence in the

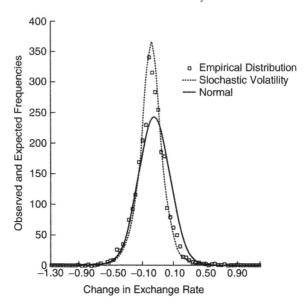

Fig. 12.1. A comparison of actual and predicted exchange rate changes.

squared daily change and the absolute daily change, but there are some notice-
able differences between the actual and predicted autocorrelations. The model
does not capture the large first-order autocorrelation in these proxies for volatility. The model does generate a tendency for the autocorrelations to converge to a
small positive value as the order of the autocorrelations gets large, which indicates a unit root in these proxies for volatility, but it underestimates the limiting
value of these autocorrelations by a large percentage. Since these autocorrelations are not accurately estimated, the discrepancy in fit is not statistically
significant. Nonetheless, a specification which allows volatility to display both
a transitory and a persistent component would be worth exploring in future
research.

12.5 Comparison of actual and predicted option prices

12.5.1 Obtaining daily estimates of volatility

In order to price the foreign currency options, it was necessary to obtain estimates of daily volatility. Our strategy was to apply the Extended Kalman Filter
(EKF), described in Anderson and Moore (1979), to the discrete time model in
Section 12.4. Because the EKF is based on a Taylor series approximation, it is
sensitive to nonlinear transformations of the model. After some experimentation,
eq. (5) was taken as the state transition equation. Eq. (8) was transformed by
taking the logarithm of the absolute value of both sides to obtain the measurement equation, and then the standard Kalman filter was applied. The daily
estimates of volatility were obtained by exponentiating the filtered estimates of

log-volatility produced by the EKF. Simulations based on our estimated parameter values indicate that this procedure produces essentially unbiased estimates of volatility that have a correlation of just over 0.5 with the true volatility process.[14]

12.5.2 Solving the partial differential equation

For European options, solutions to eq. (3) have been derived by Johnson and Shanno (1987), Hull and White (1987), and Cooper et al. (1986). Johnson and Shanno (1987) assume that there exists a marketable asset which is perfectly correlated with volatility. All of these studies use a risk-neutral valuation approach and use Monte Carlo techniques to price the options. To price American options, Monte Carlo techniques cannot be readily used, so other numerical methods must be employed. The alternating directions method algorithm of McKee and Mitchell (1970) was used to solve (3). The accuracy of this algorithm was tested by comparing numerical solutions to the Monte Carlo solutions published in Hull and White (1987).

12.5.3 Empirical results

Descriptive statistics for the actual and predicted option prices are reported in Table 12.4. To reduce computing costs, we considered only the cases $\beta = 0$ and $\beta = 2$. The predicted American option values for the stochastic volatility model are based on the parameter estimates in Table 12.2, and are evaluated at four different values of λ. We also report the European and American option values that are implied by eq. (1) with nonstochastic volatility. For purposes of comparison, these two predicted option values were also evaluated using our daily estimates of volatility.

As in Melino and Turnbull (1987), we find that the constant volatility American and European predicted option prices have standard deviations that are comparable to observed option prices, but that they tend to underestimate the market prices. The constant volatility models underestimate the average price of a put in our sample by about 15%, and the average price of a call by more than 25%.[15] From an investment perspective, pricing errors of this magnitude are enormous. The option prices predicted by the stochastic volatility model show a good deal of sensitivity to the value of λ. Both the mean and the standard deviation of the predicted prices increase as we decrease λ. A pretty close agreement to the observed sample mean and standard deviation of observed option prices is obtained for both values of β and for both calls and puts by choosing $\lambda = -0.1$. For this value of λ, the root mean square error is in all cases at least 20% smaller than those of the constant volatility models.

To examine in more detail the differences between observed option prices (C) and predicted option prices ($\hat{C}$), two cross-sectional regressions were estimated:

---

[14] Adjustments that incorporated the conditional variance of the filtered estimates of log-volatility led to almost identical results.

[15] Note that this underpricing occurs during a sample subperiod where the *ex post* volatility is low compared to its sample average. See Table 13.1.

Table 12.4. Descriptive statistics for actual and predicted option prices

	$\beta = 0$			$\beta = 2$		
	Mean	S.D.	RMSE	Mean	S.D.	RMSE
Call options (2465 observations)						
Stochastic volatility						
$\lambda = 0.1$	0.3318	0.3480	0.2137	0.2985	0.3467	0.2445
$\lambda = 0.0$	0.3870	0.3572	0.1772	0.3499	0.3552	0.2050
$\lambda = -0.1$	0.4550	0.3706	0.1547	0.4183	0.3697	0.1736
$\lambda = -0.2$	0.5360	0.3882	0.1732	0.5039	0.3909	0.1756
Nonstochastic volatility						
American	0.3531	0.3520	0.2037	0.3127	0.3464	0.2342
European	0.3349	0.3289	0.2259	0.2928	0.3198	0.2573
Observed	0.4797	0.3772		0.4797	0.3772	
Put options (1887 observations)						
Stochastic volatility						
$\lambda = 0.1$	0.4968	0.4107	0.2167	0.4607	0.4047	0.2456
$\lambda = 0.0$	0.5544	0.4219	0.1836	0.5164	0.4152	0.2067
$\lambda = -0.1$	0.6234	0.4367	0.1682	0.5853	0.4230	0.1785
$\lambda = -0.2$	0.7000	0.4512	0.1912	0.6698	0.4505	0.1850
Nonstochastic volatility						
American	0.5260	0.4281	0.2081	0.4798	0.4210	0.2369
European	0.5275	0.4291	0.2118	0.4790	0.4213	0.2375
Observed	0.6305	0.4345		0.6305	0.4345	

Test 1:

$$C = \alpha_0 + \alpha_1 \hat{C} + \bar{e},$$

Test 2:

$$C - \hat{C} = \gamma_0 + \gamma_1(S - X)/X + \gamma_2 T + \gamma_3 r_D + \gamma_4 r_F + \bar{e},$$

where S denotes the spot exchange rate, X the exercise price, T the maturity of the option (measured in days), $r_D(r_F)$ the domestic (foreign) rate of interest, and $\bar{e}$ are disturbance terms. In Test 1, a model provides an unbiased estimate of the actual premium if $\alpha_0 = 0$ and $\alpha_1 = 1$. Test 2 is designed to identify if the prediction errors are systematically related to the fundamental inputs used in pricing the options. The interpretation of γ_1 depends upon whether the option is a call or a put. For call options, a positive value of γ_1 means that the model under (over) predicts the price of an option that is in (out of) the money. If γ_2 is positive, then the longer the maturity of the option, the greater the degree of under pricing by the model. If $\gamma_3(\gamma_4)$ is positive, the degree of under pricing is an increasing function of the domestic (foreign) interest rate. If the pricing error is independent of the exercise price, maturity, domestic and foreign interest rates, then $\gamma_1 = \gamma_2 = \gamma_3 = \gamma_4 = 0$.

Strictly speaking, under the null that a model is correctly specified, any discrepancy between observed and predicted option prices must be due to the sampling error in the parameters. The asymptotic normality of the parameter estimates and the mean value approximation can be used to construct asymptotically valid confidence regions for option prices. A formal test would simply check if observed option prices fell in these regions. The computational difficulties caused by the large number of observations on option prices in our sample and the use of American option pricing models which lack closed form solutions preclude our use of this large sample test. Neither Test 1 nor Test 2 should be viewed as formal tests of our option pricing models, but we believe that they provide useful descriptive summaries of each model's performance.

Test 1 A model provides an unbiased estimate of the actual premium if $\alpha_0 = 0$ and $\alpha_1 = 1$. This hypothesis is tested using the Wald statistic which is asymptotically distributed as χ^2 (2). Table 12.5 shows that for all cases the null hypothesis can be overwhelmingly rejected. The slope coefficients tend to be close to one, but the intercepts are positive. In terms of fit and the size of the Wald test statistic, there is some preference for the $\beta = 0$ models, but the differences are not large. The American pricing model with nonstochastic volatility performs slightly better than the European pricing model. Both of these models are dominated by the stochastic volatility models with nonpositive λ. A choice of $\lambda = -0.1$ does reasonably well in all four cases.

Test 2 A number of general comments can be made about the Test 2 results reported in Table 12.6. The results are once again comparable for the two values of β, but with a slight preference for $\beta = 0$. The values of γ_1 and γ_2 vary a great deal across the different models, but they are always smaller for the stochastic volatility models. For $\lambda = -0.1$, the time-to-maturity bias is virtually zero. There is no 'in-the-money' bias for calls, but the model underpredicts the value of 'out-of-the-money' put options. There is considerable evidence that the forecast errors are related to the level of interest rates, which suggests there could be a useful payoff to relaxing our assumption A2. The forecast errors are in all cases negatively related to the level of the domestic (U.S.) interest rate and positively related to the level of the foreign interest rate. A 100 basis point increase in the foreign risk-free rate is associated with a decrease in the forecast error of calls of about 0.07 U.S. cents. In addition to specific biases, we also find that the predictability of the forecast errors from the various models is rather large. The Test 2 regression achieves an R^2 of about 0.3 for calls and 0.2 for puts. The Wald statistic to test the hypothesis $\gamma_0 = \gamma_1 = \gamma_2 = \gamma_3 = \gamma_4 = 0$ is asymptotically distributed as $\chi^2(5)$. All the models are overwhelmingly rejected, although the stochastic volatility models with nonpositive λ fare considerably better than the American or European nonstochastic volatility models. A choice of $\lambda = -0.1$ or $\lambda = -0.2$ seems to be the best.

Table 12.5.[a]

	Call options				Put options			
	Intercept	Slope	Wald statistic	R^2	Intercept	Slope	Wald statistic	R^2
				$\beta = 0$				
$\lambda = 0.1$	0.1515 (0.0107)	0.9893 (0.0290)	223.2	0.8329	0.1470 (0.0196)	0.9732 (0.0196)	59.4	0.8465
$\lambda = 0$	0.1050 (0.0099)	0.9683 (0.0322)	119.4	0.8407	0.1028 (0.0192)	0.9519 (0.0265)	34.4	0.8543
$\lambda = -0.1$	0.0551 (0.0098)	0.9331 (0.0356)	33.1	0.8405	0.0564 (0.0191)	0.9209 (0.0225)	19.5	0.8567
$\lambda = -0.2$	0.0064 (0.0056)	0.8830 (0.0147)	9.6	0.8259	0.0106 (0.0194)	0.8856 (0.0260)	19.5	0.8460
American	0.1367 (0.0115)	0.9716 (0.0270)	158.5	0.8219	0.1432 (0.0201)	0.9265 (0.0267)	53.3	0.8336
European	0.1385 (0.0113)	1.0187 (0.0376)	151.7	0.7891	0.1455 (0.0195)	0.9195 (0.0269)	60.5	0.8249
				$\beta = 2$				
$\lambda = 0.1$	0.1872 (0.0115)	0.9800 (0.0296)	308.8	0.8113	0.1790 (0.0198)	0.9801 (0.0196)	86.2	0.8337
$\lambda = 0$	0.1423 (0.0106)	0.9641 (0.0339)	196.1	0.8241	0.1341 (0.0193)	0.9613 (0.0206)	55.9	0.8439
$\lambda = -0.1$	0.0932 (0.0102)	0.9240 (0.0386)	85.7	0.8202	0.0863 (0.0188)	0.9299 (0.0227)	31.9	0.8469
$\lambda = -0.2$	0.0431 (0.0114)	0.8667 (0.0430)	17.0	0.8065	0.0380 (0.0188)	0.8846 (0.0259)	22.1	0.8415
American	0.1730 (0.0118)	0.9807 (0.0254)	248.9	0.8109	0.1804 (0.0199)	0.9382 (0.0265)	84.2	0.8267
European	0.1744 (0.0115)	1.0427 (0.0362)	238.4	0.7815	0.1814 (0.0199)	0.9376 (0.0265)	84.5	0.8266

[a]Figures in parentheses are standard errors based on Newey and West (1987).

Table 12.6[a]

	γ_0	γ_1	γ_2	γ_3	γ_4	R^2	W_1	W_2
			$\beta = 0$, Call options					
$\lambda = 0.1$	−0.4566 (0.1269)	0.9287 (0.5561)	0.0010 (0.0002)	−5.2475 (1.7973)	9.1446 (2.0150)	0.2991	55.7	251.4
$\lambda = 0$	−0.4853 (0.1264)	0.2760 (0.5571)	0.0007 (0.0002)	−5.7089 (1.7877)	9.6094 (2.0216)	0.2807	40.3	134.9
$\lambda = -0.1$	−0.5186 (0.1265)	−0.4225 (0.5812)	0.0002 (0.0002)	−6.2028 (1.7795)	10.1016 (2.0324)	0.2959	29.2	49.7
$\lambda = -0.2$	−0.5674 (0.1295)	1.0714 (0.6362)	−0.0003 (0.0002)	−6.8263 (1.8060)	10.7970 (2.0796)	0.3571	28.9	32.1
American	−0.1756 (0.1231)	1.1423 (0.5134)	0.0010 (0.0002)	−6.7391 (2.0637)	7.7476 (2.0724)	0.1739	45.9	180.7
European	−0.2179 (0.1288)	3.2686 (0.5455)	0.0013 (0.0003)	−8.0473 (2.1241)	9.3399 (2.1100)	0.2417	96.0	258.1
			$\beta = 0$, Put options					
$\lambda = 0.1$	−0.1931 (0.1813)	3.5060 (0.6969)	0.0012 (0.0003)	−5.2626 (2.5070)	6.3124 (3.1080)	0.2005	80.1	289.8
$\lambda = 0$	−0.2004 (0.1855)	3.8326 (0.6973)	0.0007 (0.0003)	−5.5116 (2.5430)	6.4074 (3.1701)	0.1694	59.0	168.6
$\lambda = -0.1$	−0.2122 (0.1898)	4.1395 (0.7138)	0.0002 (0.0003)	−5.8370 (2.5791)	6.5710 (3.2306)	0.1731	44.0	77.9
$\lambda = -0.2$	−0.2460 (0.1989)	4.2044 (0.7714)	−0.0002 (0.0003)	−6.5607 (2.6665)	7.1929 (3.3616)	0.2125	36.8	37.3
American	0.1177 (0.1755)	3.9614 (0.7100)	0.0011 (0.0003)	−6.7370 (2.5425)	4.5986 (2.9681)	0.1602	64.7	212.0
European	0.1010 (0.1862)	3.9146 (0.7063)	0.0011 (0.0003)	−7.0800 (2.6904)	5.0295 (3.1949)	0.1544	61.6	196.5
			$\beta = 2$, Call options					
$\lambda = 0.1$	−0.4639 (0.1312)	1.3309 (0.5923)	0.0012 (0.0002)	−5.7177 (1.8876)	9.7630 (2.0663)	0.3217	66.9	334.1
$\lambda = 0$	−0.4959 (0.1299)	0.6523 (0.5778)	0.0009 (0.0002)	−6.2292 (1.8336)	10.3249 (2.0327)	0.3038	53.1	209.5
$\lambda = -0.1$	−0.5465 (0.1315)	−0.1461 (0.5933)	0.0004 (0.0002)	−7.1942 (1.9032)	11.3875 (2.1005)	0.3175	39.1	93.9
$\lambda = -0.2$	−0.6606 (0.1330)	−0.9989 (0.6348)	−0.0002 (0.0002)	−8.0873 (1.9191)	12.4316 (2.1323)	0.3840	35.3	36.9
American	−0.1958 (0.1225)	1.7281 (0.5253)	0.0013 (0.0002)	−6.7632 (2.0495)	8.1199 (2.0404)	0.2232	65.9	285.2
European	−0.2345 (0.1276)	4.0929 (0.5564)	0.0016 (0.0002)	−8.0696 (2.1108)	9.6991 (2.0699)	0.3081	136.8	409.7
			$\beta = 2$, Put options					
$\lambda = 0.1$	−0.2206 (0.1312)	3.1163 (0.5923)	0.0014 (0.0002)	−5.7774 (1.8876)	7.1361 (2.0663)	0.2300	88.9	373.8
$\lambda = 0$	−0.2329 (0.1855)	3.4802 (0.6974)	0.0010 (0.0003)	−6.0820 (2.5542)	7.3387 (3.1846)	0.1904	66.3	239.5
$\lambda = -0.1$	−0.2554 (0.1908)	3.8408 (0.7072)	0.0005 (0.0003)	−6.6020 (2.6172)	7.7706 (3.2795)	0.1820	47.6	121.6
$\lambda = -0.2$	−0.2892 (0.1970)	4.1863 (0.7396)	−0.0002 (0.0003)	−7.2382 (2.6743)	8.3600 (3.3756)	0.2312	40.5	51.3
American	0.0779 (0.1755)	3.7563 (0.7100)	0.0014 (0.0003)	−6.8193 (2.5425)	5.2069 (2.9681)	0.1888	78.7	311.9
European	0.0799 (0.1276)	3.7718 (0.5564)	0.0014 (0.0002)	−6.8034 (2.1108)	5.1846 (2.0699)	0.1883	77.7	311.1

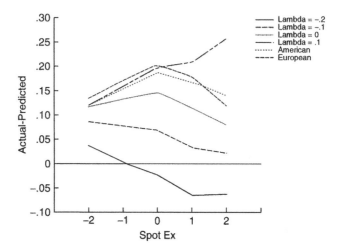

Fig. 12.2. Average pricing errors, call options ($\beta = 2$).

The regression tests indicate that the stochastic volatility models yield significantly better predictions than the usual American or European non-stochastic volatility models. A simple graph shows just how striking is the improvement. In order to examine the relationship between the mispricing of the option and the degree of being in- or out-of-the-money, we plotted $(S - X)$, the exchange rate minus the exercise price, against $(C - \hat{C})$, the observed option price minus its predicted value. To conserve space, we present only the graph made for calls. The graph for puts was qualitatively similar except that it shows more bias. Fig. 12.2 presents the graph corresponding to the $\beta = 2$ model. The $S - X$ axis was divided into a number of intervals with the size of the interval being chosen so as to equalize the number of observations. The graph connects the mean pricing error in each interval.

A similar procedure was used to examine the effects of maturity on the degree of mispricing. The results for calls are provided in Fig. 12.3. They indicate considerably less mispricing by the stochastic volatility models. For the choice $\lambda = -0.1$, there appears to be no systematic relationship between the pricing errors and maturity.

12.6 Conclusions

The standard model for pricing foreign currency options assumes a lognormal probability distribution for exchange rates and that volatility is constant. We have shown that such assumptions are inappropriate: a more plausible hypothesis is that volatility changes stochastically. Our specification of the volatility process provides a much closer fit to the empirical distribution of exchange rate changes than that produced by the lognormal model. It provides a good match to

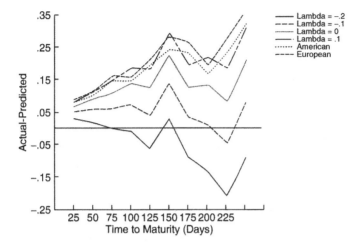

Fig. 12.3. Average pricing errors, call options ($\beta = 2$).

the dynamic properties of exchange rate changes, and an excellent correspondence to the static properties.

The option pricing equation contains a preference term, as volatility is a nontraded asset. It is not obvious a priori what constitutes a reasonable value for the price of volatility risk and many authors simply set it to zero. We treated this price as constant and examined predicted option prices over a grid of four values for this price. In all four cases, we found evidence of systematic prediction error. Nonetheless, for the two negative prices of risk which we examined, the predicted foreign currency option prices provided by the stochastic volatility model provided a striking improvement for all categories of option over the predictions of the standard model.

We conclude that the stochastic volatility model dominates the standard model. It does a superior job of matching the empirical exchange rate distribution and corrects many of the observed biases in predicted option prices. These results have important implications for the risk management of foreign currency option portfolios and the pricing of long-term foreign currency options.[16]

References

Anderson, B. D. O. and Moore, J. B. (1979). Optimal filtering (Prentice-Hall, Englewood Cliffs, NJ).

Bodurtha, J. N. (1984). PHLX currency option surveillance report and OEC exercise history: A data base, Mimeo.

---

[16] See Melino and Turnbull (1988).

Bodurtha, J. N. and Courtadon, G. R. (1986). Efficiency tests of foreign currency options markets. *Journal of Finance* 41, 151–62.

—— —— (1987). Tests of the American option pricing model on the foreign currency options market. *Journal of Financial and Quantitative Analysis* 22, 153–67.

Boothe, P. and Glassman, D. (1987). The statistical distribution of exchange rates. *Journal of International Economics* 22, 297–319.

Cooper, I., Kaplanis, C., Newberger, A., and Schaefer, S. (1986). Option hedging, Mimeo. (London Business School, London).

Cox, J. C., Ingersoll, J. E., and Ross, S. A. (1985). An intertemporal general equilibrium model of asset prices. *Econometrica* 53, 363–84.

Cramér, H. (1946). Mathematical methods of statistics (Princeton University Press, Princeton, NJ).

Duffie, D. and Singleton, K. J. (1988). Simulated moments estimation of diffusion models of asset prices, Mimeo. (GSB, Stanford University, Stanford, CA).

Engle, R. F. (1982). Autoregressive conditional heteroscedasticity with estimates of United Kingdom inflation. *Econometrica* 50, 987–1007.

Grabbe, O. J. (1983). The pricing of call and put options on foreign exchange. *Journal of International Money and Finance* 2, 239–54.

Hansen, L. P. (1982). Large sample properties of generalized method of moments estimators. *Econometrica* 50, 1029–54.

Hull, J. and White, A. (1987). Option pricing when the variance is changing. *Journal of Financial and Quantitative Analysis* 22, 143–51.

McFarland, J. W., Richardson Pettit, R., and Sam Sung, K. (1982). The distribution of foreign exchange price changes: Trading day effects and risk measurement. *Journal of Finance* 37, 693–715.

McKee, S. and Mitchell, A. R. (1970). Alternating direction methods for parabolic equations in two space dimensions with a mixed derivative. *The Computer Journal* 13, 81–6.

Marsh, T. A. and Rosenfeld, E. R. (1983). Stochastic processes for interest rates and equilibrium bond prices. *Journal of Finance* 38, 635–46.

—— —— (1986). Non-trading, market making, and estimates of stock price volatility. *Journal of Financial Economics* 15, 359–72.

Melino, A. and Turnbull, S. M. (1987). The pricing of foreign currency options, Working paper 8720 (Department of Economics, University of Toronto, Toronto).

—— —— (1988). The pricing of long term foreign currency options, Mimeo. (Department of Economics, University of Toronto, Toronto).

Nelson, D. B. (1990). ARCH models as diffusion approximations. *Journal of Econometrics* 45, 7–38.

Newey, W. K. and West, K. D. (1987). A simple, positive semi-definite, heteroskedasticity and autocorrelation consistent covariance matrix. *Econometrica* 55, 703–8.

Press, S. J. (1968). A compound events model for security prices. *Journal of Business* 40, 317–35.

Schwert, G. W. (1987). Effects of model specification on tests for unit roots in macroeconomic data. *Journal of Monetary Economics* 20, 73–103.

Scott, L. O. (1987). Option pricing when the variance changes randomly: Theory, estimation and an application. *Journal of Financial and Quantitative Analysis* 22, 419–38.

Shastri, K. and Tandon, K. (1986). Valuation of foreign currency options: Some empirical tests. *Journal of Financial and Quantitative Analysis* 21, 145–60.

Wiggins, J. B. (1987). Option values under stochastic volatility: Theory and empirical estimates. *Journal of Financial Economics* 19, 351–72.

13

A Closed-Form Solution for Options with Stochastic Volatility with Applications to Bond and Currency Options*

STEVEN L. HESTON[†]

I use a new technique to derive a closed-form solution for the price of a European call option on an asset with stochastic volatility. The model allows arbitrary correlation between volatility and spot-asset returns. I introduce stochastic interest rates and show how to apply the model to bond options and foreign currency options. Simulations show that correlation between volatility and the spot asset's price is important for explaining return skewness and strike-price biases in the Black–Scholes (1973) model. The solution technique is based on characteristic functions and can be applied to other problems.

Many plaudits have been aptly used to describe Black and Scholes's (1973) contribution to option pricing theory. Despite subsequent development of option theory, the original Black–Scholes formula for a European call option remains the most successful and widely used application. This formula is particularly useful because it relates the distribution of spot returns to the cross-sectional properties of option prices. In this article, I generalize the model while retaining this feature.

Although the Black–Scholes formula is often quite successful in explaining stock option prices (Black and Scholes (1972)), it does have known biases (Rubinstein (1985)). Its performance also is substantially worse on foreign currency options (Melino and Turnbull (1990, 1991), Knoch (1992)). This is not surprising, since the Black–Scholes model makes the strong assumption that (continuously compounded) stock returns are normally distributed with known mean and variance. Since the Black–Scholes formula does not depend on the mean spot return, it cannot be generalized by allowing the mean to vary. But the variance assumption is somewhat dubious. Motivated by this theoretical consideration, Scott (1987), Hull and White (1987), and Wiggins (1987) have generalized the model to allow stochastic volatility. Melino and Turnbull (1990, 1991) report that this approach is successful in explaining the prices of currency

* This work was previously published as S. L. Heston (1993), 'A Closed-Form Solution for Options with Stochastic Volatility, with Applications to Bond and Currency Options' *The Review of Financial Studies* 6, 2. Copyright © 1993 Oxford University Press. Reproduced by kind permission.

† I thank Hans Knoch for computational assistance. I am grateful for the suggestions of Hyeng Keun (the referee) and for comments by participants at a 1992 National Bureau of Economic Research seminar and the Queen's University 1992 Derivative Securities Symposium. Any remaining errors are my responsibility.

options. These papers have the disadvantage that their models do not have closed-form solutions and require extensive use of numerical techniques to solve two-dimensional partial differential equations. Jarrow and Eisenberg (1991) and Stein and Stein (1991) assume that volatility is uncorrelated with the spot asset and use an average of Black–Scholes formula values over different paths of volatility. But since this approach assumes that volatility is uncorrelated with spot returns, it cannot capture important skewness effects that arise from such correlation. I offer a model of stochastic volatility that is not based on the Black–Scholes formula. It provides a closed-form solution for the price of a European call option when the spot asset is correlated with volatility, and it adapts the model to incorporate stochastic interest rates. Thus, the model can be applied to bond options and currency options.

13.1 Stochastic volatility model

We begin by assuming that the spot asset at time t follows the diffusion

$$dS(t) = \mu S \, dt + \sqrt{v(t)} S \, dz_1(t), \tag{1}$$

where $z_1(t)$ is a Wiener process. If the volatility follows an Ornstein–Uhlenbeck process (e.g. used by Stein and Stein (1991)),

$$d\sqrt{v(t)} = -\beta\sqrt{v(t)}dt + \delta \, dz_2(t), \tag{2}$$

then Ito's lemma shows that the variance $v(t)$ follows the process

$$dv(t) = [\delta^2 - 2\beta v(t)]dt + 2\delta\sqrt{v(t)}dz_2(t). \tag{3}$$

This can be written as the familiar square-root process (used by Cox, Ingersoll, and Ross (1985))

$$dv(t) = \kappa[\theta - v(t)]dt + \sigma\sqrt{v(t)}dz_2(t), \tag{4}$$

where $z_2(t)$ has correlation ρ with $z_1(t)$. For simplicity at this stage, we assume a constant interest rate r. Therefore, the price at time t of a unit discount bond that matures at time $t + \tau$ is

$$P(t, \ t + \tau) = e^{-r\tau}. \tag{5}$$

These assumptions are still insufficient to price contingent claims because we have not yet made an assumption that gives the "price of volatility risk." Standard arbitrage arguments (Black and Scholes (1973), Merton (1973)) demonstrate that the value of any asset $U(S, v, t)$ (including accrued payments) must satisfy the partial differential equation (PDE)

$$
\frac{1}{2}vS^2\frac{\partial^2 U}{\partial S^2} + \rho\sigma vS\frac{\partial^2 U}{\partial S\partial v} + \frac{1}{2}\sigma^2 v\frac{\partial^2 U}{\partial v^2} + rS\frac{\partial U}{\partial S}
$$
$$
+ \{\kappa[\theta - v(t)] - \lambda(S, v, t)\}\frac{\partial U}{\partial v} - rU + \frac{\partial U}{\partial t} = 0. \tag{6}
$$

The unspecified term $\lambda(S, v, t)$ represents the price of volatility risk, and must be independent of the particular asset. Lamoureux and Lastrapes (1993) present evidence that this term is nonzero for equity options. To motivate the choice of $\lambda(S, v, t)$, we note that in Breeden's (1979) consumption-based model,

$$
\lambda(S, v, t)dt = \gamma\,\mathrm{Cov}[dv, dC/C], \tag{7}
$$

where $C(t)$ is the consumption rate and γ is the relative-risk aversion of an investor. Consider the consumption process that emerges in the (general equilibrium) Cox, Ingersoll, and Ross (1985) model

$$
dC(t) = \mu_c v(t)Cdt + \sigma_c\sqrt{v(t)}Cdz_3(t), \tag{8}
$$

where consumption growth has constant correlation with the spot-asset return. This generates a risk premium proportional to v, $\lambda(S, v, t) = \lambda v$. Although we will use this form of the risk premium, the pricing results are obtained by arbitrage and do not depend on the other assumptions of the Breeden (1979) or Cox, Ingersoll, and Ross (1985) models. However, we note that the model is consistent with conditional heteroskedasticity in consumption growth as well as in asset returns. In theory, the parameter λ could be determined by one volatility-dependent asset and then used to price all other volatility-dependent assets.[1]

A European call option with strike price K and maturing at time T satisfies the PDE (6) subject to the following boundary conditions:

$$
U(S, v, T) = \mathrm{Max}(0, S\text{-}K),
$$
$$
U(0, v, t) = 0,
$$
$$
\frac{\partial U}{\partial S}(\infty, v, t) = 1,
$$
$$
rS\frac{\partial U}{\partial S}(S, 0, t) + \kappa\theta\frac{\partial U}{\partial v}(S, 0, t) \tag{9}
$$
$$
-rU(S, 0, t) + U_t(S, 0, t) = 0,
$$
$$
U(S, \infty, t) = S.
$$

By analogy with the Black–Scholes formula, we guess a solution of the form

---

[1] This is analogous to extracting an implied volatility parameter in the Black–Scholes model.

$$C(S, v, t) = SP_1 - KP(t, T)P_2, \tag{10}$$

where the first term is the present value of the spot asset upon optimal exercise, and the second term is the present value of the strike-price payment. Both of these terms must satisfy the original PDE (6). It is convenient to write them in terms of the logarithm of the spot price

$$x = \ln[S]. \tag{11}$$

Substituting the proposed solution (10) into the original PDE (6) shows that P_1 and P_2 must satisfy the PDEs

$$\begin{aligned} &\frac{1}{2}v\frac{\partial^2 P_j}{\partial x^2} + \rho\sigma v\frac{\partial^2 P_j}{\partial x \partial v} + \frac{1}{2}\sigma^2 v\frac{\partial^2 P_j}{\partial v^2} + (r + u_j v)\frac{\partial P_j}{\partial x} \\ &+ (a_j - b_j v)\frac{\partial P_j}{\partial v} + \frac{\partial P_j}{\partial t} = 0, \end{aligned} \tag{12}$$

for $j = 1, 2$, where

$$u_1 = 1/2, \quad u_2 = -1/2, \quad a = \kappa\theta, \quad b_1 = \kappa + \lambda - \rho\sigma, \quad b_2 = \kappa + \lambda.$$

For the option price to satisfy the terminal condition in Equation (9), these PDEs (12) are subject to the terminal condition

$$P_j(x, v, T; \ln[K]) = 1_{\{x \geq \ln[K]\}}. \tag{13}$$

Thus, they may be interpreted as "adjusted" or "risk-neutralized" probabilities (See Cox and Ross (1976)). The Appendix explains that when x follows the stochastic process

$$\begin{aligned} dx(t) &= [r + u_j v]dt + \sqrt{v(t)}dz_1(t), \\ dv &= (a_j - b_j v)dt + \sigma\sqrt{v(t)}dz_2(t), \end{aligned} \tag{14}$$

where the parameters u_j, a_j, and b_j are defined as before, then P_j is the conditional probability that the option expires in-the-money:

$$P_j(x, v, T; \ln[K]) = \Pr[x(T) \geq \ln[K] \mid x(t) = x, v(t) = v]. \tag{15}$$

The probabilities are not immediately available in closed form. However, the Appendix shows that their characteristic functions, $f_1(x, v, T; \phi)$ and $f_2(x, v, T; \phi)$ respectively, satisfy the same PDEs (12), subject to the terminal condition

$$f_j(x, v, T; \phi) = e^{i\phi x}. \tag{16}$$

The characteristic function solution is

$$f_j(x, \ v, \ t; \ \phi) = e^{C(T-t; \ \phi)+D(T-t; \ \phi)v+i\phi x}, \tag{17}$$

where

$$C(\tau; \ \phi) = r\phi i\tau + \frac{a}{\sigma^2}\left\{(b_j - \rho\sigma\phi i + d)\tau - 2\ln\left[\frac{1 - ge^{d\tau}}{1 - g}\right]\right\},$$

$$D(\tau; \ \phi) = \frac{b_j - \rho\sigma\phi i + d}{\sigma^2}\left[\frac{1 - e^{d\tau}}{1 - ge^{d\tau}}\right],$$

and

$$g = \frac{b_j - \rho\sigma\phi i + d}{b_j - \rho\sigma\phi i - d},$$

$$d = \sqrt{(\rho\sigma\phi i - b_j)^2 - \sigma^2(2u_j\phi i - \phi^2)}.$$

One can invert the characteristic functions to get the desired probabilities:

$$P_j(x, \ v, \ T; \ln[K]) = \frac{1}{2} + \frac{1}{\pi}\int_0^\infty \text{Re}\left[\frac{e^{-i\phi \ln[K]}f_j(x, \ v, \ T; \ \phi)}{i\phi}\right]d\phi. \tag{18}$$

The integrand in Equation (18) is a smooth function that decays rapidly and presents no difficulties.[2]

Equations (10), (17), and (18) give the solution for European call options. In general, one cannot eliminate the integrals in Equation (18), even in the Black–Scholes case. However, they can be evaluated in a fraction of a second on a microcomputer by using approximations similar to the standard ones used to evaluate cumulative normal probabilities.[3]

13.2 Bond options, currency options and other extensions

One can incorporate stochastic interest rates into the option pricing model, following Merton (1973) and Ingersoll (1990). In this manner, one can apply the model to options on bonds or on foreign currency. This section outlines these generalizations to show the broad applicability of the stochastic volatility model. These generalizations are equivalent to the model of the previous section, except that certain parameters become time-dependent to reflect the changing characteristics of bonds as they approach maturity.

To incorporate stochastic interest rates, we modify Equation (1) to allow time dependence in the volatility of the spot asset:

[2] Note that characteristic functions always exist; Kendall and Stuart (1977) establish that the integral converges.
[3] Note that when evaluating multiple options with different strike options, one need not recompute the characteristic functions when evaluating the integral in Equation (18).

$$dS(t) = \mu_S S dt + \sigma_S(t)\sqrt{v(t)}S\, dz_1(t). \tag{19}$$

This equation is satisfied by discount bond prices in the Cox, Ingersoll, and Ross (1985) model and multiple-factor models of Heston (1990). Although the results of this section do not depend on the specific form of σ_S, if the spot asset is a discount bond then σ_S must vanish at maturity in order for the bond price to reach par with probability 1. The specification of the drift term μ_S is unimportant because it will not affect option prices. We specify analogous dynamics for the bond price:

$$dP(t;\ T) = \mu_P P(t;\ T)dt + \sigma_P(t)\sqrt{v(t)}P(t;\ T)\, dz_2(t). \tag{20}$$

Note that, for parsimony, we assume that the variances of both the spot asset and the bond are determined by the same variable $v(t)$. In this model, the valuation equation is

$$\begin{aligned}
&\frac{1}{2}\sigma_S(t)^2 vS^2\frac{\partial^2 U}{\partial S^2} + \frac{1}{2}\sigma_P^2(t)vP^2\frac{\partial^2 U}{\partial P^2} + \frac{1}{2}\sigma^2 v\frac{\partial^2 U}{\partial v^2}\\
&+ \rho_{SP}\sigma_S(t)\sigma_P(t)vSP\frac{\partial^2 U}{\partial S\partial P} + \rho_{Sv}\sigma_S(t)\sigma vS\frac{\partial^2 U}{\partial S\partial v}\\
&+ \rho_{Pv}\sigma_P(t)\sigma vP\frac{\partial^2 U}{\partial P\partial v} + rS\frac{\partial U}{\partial S} + rP\frac{\partial U}{\partial P}\\
&+ (\kappa[\theta - v(t)] - \lambda v)\frac{\partial U}{\partial v} - rU + \frac{\partial U}{\partial t} = 0,
\end{aligned} \tag{21}$$

where ρ_{xy} denotes the correlation between stochastic processes x and y. Proceeding with the substitution (10) exactly as in the previous section shows that the probabilities P_1 and P_2 must satisfy the PDE:

$$\begin{aligned}
&\frac{1}{2}\sigma_x(t)^2 v\frac{\partial^2 P_j}{\partial x^2} + \rho_{xv}(t)\sigma_x(t)\sigma v\frac{\partial^2 P_j}{\partial x\partial v} + \frac{1}{2}\sigma^2 v\frac{\partial^2 P_j}{\partial v^2}\\
&+ u_j(t)v\frac{\partial P_j}{\partial x} + (a_j - b_j(t)v)\frac{\partial P_j}{\partial v} + \frac{\partial P_j}{\partial t} = 0,
\end{aligned} \tag{22}$$

for $j = 1, 2$, where

$$x = \ln\left[\frac{S}{P(t;T)}\right],$$

$$\sigma_x(t)^2 = 1/2\sigma_S(t)^2 - \rho_{SP}\sigma_S(t)\sigma_P(t) + 1/2\sigma_P^2(t),$$

$$\rho_{xv}(t) = \frac{\rho_{Sv}\sigma_S(t)\sigma - \rho_{Pv}\sigma_P(t)\sigma}{\sigma_x(t)\sigma},$$

$$u_1(t) = 1/2\sigma_x(t)^2,\quad u_2(t) = -1/2\sigma_x(t)^2,$$

$$u = \kappa\theta,$$

$$b_1(t) = \kappa + \lambda - \rho_{Sv}\sigma_S(t)\sigma,\quad b_2(t) = \kappa + \lambda - \rho_{Pv}\sigma_P(t)\sigma.$$

Note that Equation (22) is equivalent to Equation (12) with some time-dependent coefficients. The availability of closed-form solutions to Equation (22) will depend on the particular term structure model (e.g. the specification of $\sigma_x(t)$). In any case, the method used in the Appendix shows that the characteristic function takes the form of Equation (17), where the functions $C(\tau)$ and $D(\tau)$ satisfy certain ordinary differential equations. The option price is then determined by Equation (18). While the functions $C(t)$ and $D(\tau)$ may not have closed-form solutions for some term structure models, this represents an enormous reduction compared to solving Equation (21) numerically.

One can also apply the model when the spot asset $S(t)$ is the dollar price of foreign currency. We assume that the foreign price of a foreign discount bond, $F(t; T)$, follows dynamics analogous to the domestic bond in Equation (20):

$$dF(t; T) = \mu_P F(t; T)dt + \sigma_P(t)\sqrt{v(t)}F(t; T)dz_2(t). \tag{23}$$

For clarity, we denote the domestic interest rate by r_D and the foreign interest rate by r_F. Following the arguments in Ingersoll (1990), the valuation equation is

$$\frac{1}{2}\sigma_S(t)^2 vS^2 \frac{\partial^2 U}{\partial S^2} + \frac{1}{2}\sigma_P^2(t)vP^2 \frac{\partial^2 U}{\partial P^2} + \frac{1}{2}\sigma_F^2(t)vF^2 \frac{\partial^2 U}{\partial F^2} + \frac{1}{2}\sigma^2 v \frac{\partial^2 U}{\partial v^2}$$

$$+ \rho_{SP}\sigma_S(t)\sigma_P(t)vSP \frac{\partial^2 U}{\partial S \partial P} + \rho_{SP}\sigma_S(t)\sigma_F(t)vSF \frac{\partial^2 U}{\partial S \partial F}$$

$$+ \rho_{SP}\sigma_P(t)\sigma_F(t)vPF \frac{\partial^2 U}{\partial P \partial F} + \rho_{Sv}\sigma_S(t)\sigma vS \frac{\partial^2 U}{\partial S \partial v} \tag{24}$$

$$+ \rho_{Pv}\sigma_P(t)\sigma vP \frac{\partial^2 U}{\partial P \partial v} + \rho_{Fv}\sigma_F(t)\sigma vF \frac{\partial^2 U}{\partial F \partial v} + r_D S \frac{\partial U}{\partial S} + r_D P \frac{\partial U}{\partial P}$$

$$+ r_F F \frac{\partial U}{\partial F} + (\kappa[\theta - v(t)] - \lambda v)\frac{\partial U}{\partial v} - rU + \frac{\partial U}{\partial t} = 0.$$

Solving this five-variable PDE numerically would be completely infeasible. But one can use Garmen and Kohlhagen's (1983) substitution analogous to Equation (10):

$$C(S, v, t) = SF(t, T)P_1 - KP(t, T)P_2. \tag{25}$$

Probabilities P_1 and P_2 must satisfy the PDE

$$\frac{1}{2}\sigma_x(t)^2 v \frac{\partial^2 P_j}{\partial x^2} + \rho_{xv}(t)\sigma_x(t)\sigma v \frac{\partial^2 p_j}{\partial x \partial v} + \frac{1}{2}\sigma^2 v \frac{\partial^2 P_j}{\partial v^2} + u_j(t)v \frac{\partial P_j}{\partial x}$$

$$+ (a_j - b_j(t)v)\frac{\partial P_j}{\partial v} + \frac{\partial P_j}{\partial t} = 0, \tag{26}$$

for $j = 1, 2$, where

$$x = \ln\left[\frac{SF(t; T)}{P(t; T)}\right],$$

$$\sigma_x(t)^2 = 1/2\sigma_S(t)^2 + 1/2\sigma_P^2(t) + 1/2\sigma_F^2(t) - \rho_{SP}\sigma_S(t)\sigma_P(t)$$
$$+ \rho_{SF}\sigma_S(t)\sigma_F(t) - \rho_{PF}\sigma_P(t)\sigma_F(t),$$

$$\rho_{xv}(t) = \frac{\rho_{Sv}\sigma_S(t)\sigma - \rho_{Pv}\sigma_P(t)\sigma + \rho_{Fv}\sigma_F(t)\sigma}{\sigma_x(t)\sigma},$$

$$u_1(t) = 1/2\sigma_x(t)^2, \quad u_2(t) = -1/2\sigma_x(t)^2,$$

$$a = \kappa\theta,$$

$$b_1(t) = \kappa + \lambda - \rho_{Sv}\sigma_S(t)\sigma - \rho_{Fv}\sigma_F(t)\sigma, \quad b_2(t) = \kappa + \lambda - \rho_{Pv}\sigma_P(t)\sigma.$$

Once again, the characteristic function has the form of Equation (17), where $C(\tau)$ and $D(\tau)$ depend on the specification of $\sigma_x(t)$, $\rho_{xv}(t)$, and $b_j(t)$ (see the Appendix).

Although the stochastic interest rate models of this section are tractable, they would be more complicated to estimate than the simpler model of the previous section. For short-maturity options on equities, any increase in accuracy would likely be outweighed by the estimation error introduced by implementing a more complicated model. As option maturities extend beyond one year, however, the interest rate effects can become more important (Koch (1992)). The more complicated models illustrate how the stochastic volatility model can be adapted to a variety of applications. For example, one could value U.S. options by adding on the early exercise approximation of Barone-Adesi and Whalley (1987). The solution technique has other applications, too. See the Appendix for application to Stein and Stein's (1991) model (with correlated volatility) and see Bates (1992) for application to jump-diffusion processes.

13.3 Effects of the stochastic volatility model options prices

In this section, I examine the effects of stochastic volatility on options prices and contrast results with the Black–Scholes model. Many effects are related to the time-series dynamics of volatility. For example, a higher variance $v(t)$ raises the prices of all options, just as it does in the Black–Scholes model. In the risk-neutralized pricing probabilities, the variance follows a square-root process

$$dv(t) = \kappa^*[\theta^* - v(t)]dt + \sigma\sqrt{v(t)}dz_2(t), \tag{27}$$

where

$$\kappa^* = \kappa + \lambda \quad \text{and} \quad \theta^* = \kappa\theta/(\kappa + \lambda).$$

We analyze the model in terms of this risk-neutralized volatility process instead of the "true" process of Equation (4), because the risk-neutralized process exclusively determines prices.[4] The variance drifts toward a long-run mean of θ^*, with

---

[4] This occurs for exactly the same reason that the Black–Scholes formula does not depend on the mean stock return. See Heston (1992) for a theoretical analysis that explains when parameters drop out of option prices.

Table 13.1. Default parameters for simulation of option prices

$$dS(t) = \mu S\, dt + \sqrt{v(t)}S\, dz_1(t), \tag{10}$$
$$dv(t) = \kappa^*[\theta^* - v(t)]\, dt + \sigma\sqrt{v(t)}\, dz_2(t) \tag{30}$$

Parameter	Value
Mean reversion	$\kappa^* = 2$
Long-run variance	$\theta^* = .01$
Current variance	$v(t) = .01$
Correlation of $z_1(t)$ and $z_2(t)$	$\rho = 0.$
Volatility of volatility parameter	$\sigma = .1$
Option maturity	.5 year
Interest rate	$r = 0$
Strike price	$K = 100$

mean-reversion speed determined by κ^*. Hence, an increase in the average variance θ^* increases the prices of options. The mean reversion then determines the relative weights of the current variance and the long-run variance on option prices. When mean reversion is positive, the variance has a steady-state distribution (Cox, Ingersoll, and Ross (1985)) with mean θ^*. Therefore, spot returns over long periods will have asymptotically normal distributions, with variance per unit of time given by θ^*. Consequently, the Black–Scholes model should tend to work well for long-term options. However, it is important to realize that the implied variance θ^* from option prices may not equal the variance of spot returns given by the "true" process (4). This difference is caused by the risk premium associated with exposure to volatility changes. As Equation (27) shows, whether θ^* is larger or smaller than the true average variance θ depends on the sign of the risk-premium parameter λ. One could estimate θ^* and other parameters by using values implied by option prices. Alternatively, one could estimate θ and κ from the true spot-price process. One could then estimate the risk-premium parameter λ by using average returns on option positions that are hedged against the risk of changes in the spot asset.

The stochastic volatility model can conveniently explain properties of option prices in terms of the underlying distribution of spot returns. Indeed, this is the intuitive interpretation of the solution (10), since P_2 corresponds to the risk-neutralized probability that the option expires in-the-money. To illustrate effects on options prices, we shall use the default parameters in Table 13.1.[5] For comparison, we shall use the Black–Scholes model with a volatility parameter that matches the (square root of the) variance of the spot return over the life of the option.[6] This normalization focuses attention on the effects of stochastic volatility on one option relative to another by equalizing "average" option

---

[5] These parameters roughly correspond to Knoch's (1992) estimates with yen and deutsche mark currency options, assuming no risk premium associated with volatility. However, the mean-reversion parameter is chosen to be more reasonable.
[6] This variance can be determined by using the characteristic function.

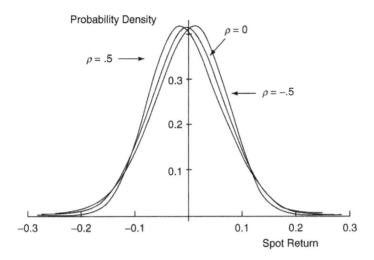

Fig. 13.1. Conditional probability density of the continuously compounded spot return over a six-month horizon. Spot-asset dynamics are $dS(t) = \mu S \, dt + \sqrt{v(t)}S \, dz_1(t)$, where $dv(t) = \kappa^*[\theta^* - v(t)]dt + \sigma\sqrt{v(t)}dz_2(t)$. Except for the correlation ρ between z_1 and z_2 shown, parameter values are shown in Table 13.1. For comparison, the probability densities are normalized to have zero mean and unit variance.

model prices across different spot prices. The correlation parameter ρ positively affects the skewness of spot returns. Intuitively, a positive correlation results in high variance when the spot asset rises, and this "spreads" the right tail of the probability density. Conversely, the left tail is associated with low variance and is not spread out. Figure 13.1 shows how a positive correlation of volatility with the spot return creates a fat right tail and a thin left tail in the distribution of continuously compounded spot returns.[7] Figure 13.2 shows that this increases the prices of out-of-the-money options and decreases the prices of in-the-money options relative to the Black–Scholes model with comparable volatility. Intuitively, out-of-the-money call options benefit substantially from a fat right tail and pay little penalty for an increased probability of an average or slightly below average spot return. A negative correlation has completely opposite effects. It decreases the prices of out-of-the-money options relative to in-the-money options.

The parameter σ controls the volatility of volatility. When σ is zero, the volatility is deterministic, and continuously compounded spot returns have a normal distribution. Otherwise, σ increases the kurtosis of spot returns. Figure 13.3 shows how this creates two fat tails in the distribution of spot returns. As Figure 13.4 shows, this has the effect of raising far-in-the-money

---

[7] This illustration is motivated by Jarrow and Rudd (1982) and Hull (1989).

Price Difference ($)

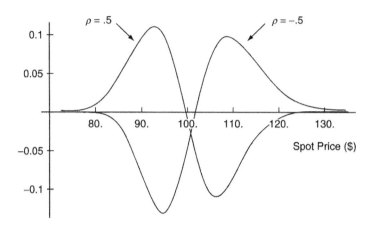

Fig. 13.2. Option prices from the stochastic volatility model minus Black–
Scholes values with equal volatility to option maturity. Except for the
correlation ρ between z_1 and z_2 shown, parameter values are shown in
Table 13.1. When $\rho = -.5$ and $\rho = .5$, respectively, the Black–Scholes
volatilities are 7.10 percent and 7.04 percent, and at-the-money
option values are $2.83 and $2.81.

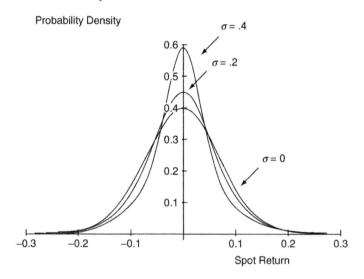

Fig. 13.3. Conditional probability density of the continuously compounded spot
return over a six-month horizon. Spot-asset dynamics are
$dS(t) = \mu S\, dt + \sqrt{v(t)} S\, dz_1(t)$, where $dv(t) = \kappa^*[\theta^* - v(t)]\, dt + \sigma\sqrt{v(t)}\, dz_2(t)$.
Except for the volatility of volatility parameter σ shown, parameter values
are shown in Table 13.1. For comparison, the probability densities
are normalized to have zero mean and unit variance.

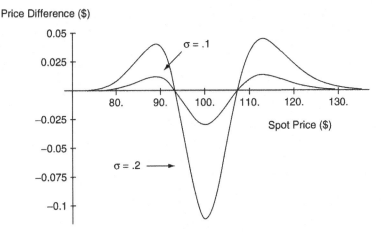

Fig. 13.4. Option prices from the stochastic volatility model minus
Black-Scholes values with equal volatility to option maturity.
Except for the volatility of volatility parameter σ shown,
parameter values are shown in Table 13.1. In both curves,
the Black–Scholes volatility is 7.07 percent and the
at-the-money option value is $2.82.

and far-out-of-the-money option prices and lowering near-the-money prices.
Note, however, that there is little effect on skewness or on the overall pricing of
in-the-money options relative to out-of-the-money options.

These simulations show that the stochastic volatility model can produce a rich
variety of pricing effects compared with the Black–Scholes model. The effects just
illustrated assumed that variance was at its long-run mean, θ^*. In practice, the
stochastic variance will drift above and below this level, but the basic conclusions
should not change. An important insight from the analysis is the distinction
between the effects of stochastic volatility per se and the effects of correlation
of volatility with the spot return. If volatility is uncorrelated with the spot return,
then increasing the volatility of volatility (σ) increases the kurtosis of spot
returns, not the skewness. In this case, random volatility is associated with
increases in the prices of far-from-the-money options relative to near-the-
money options. In contrast, the correlation of volatility with the spot return
produces skewness. And positive skewness is associated with increases in the
prices of out-of-the-money options relative to in-the-money options. Therefore, it
is essential to choose properly the correlation of volatility with spot returns as
well as the volatility of volatility.

13.4 Conclusions

I present a closed-form solution for options on assets with stochastic volatility.
The model is versatile enough to describe stock options, bond options, and

currency options. As the figures illustrate, the model can impart almost any type of bias to option prices. In particular, it links these biases to the dynamics of the spot price and the distribution of spot returns. Conceptually, one can characterize the option models in terms of the first four moments of the spot return (under the risk-neutral probabilities). The Black–Scholes (1973) model shows that the mean spot return does not affect option prices at all, while variance has a substantial effect. Therefore, the pricing analysis of this article controls for the variance when comparing option models with different skewness and kurtosis. The Black–Scholes formula produces option prices virtually identical to the stochastic volatility models for at-the-money options. One could interpret this as saying that the Black–Scholes model performs quite well. Alternatively, all option models with the same volatility are equivalent for at-the-money options. Since options are usually traded near-the-money, this explains some of the empirical support for the Black–Scholes model. Correlation between volatility and the spot price is necessary to generate skewness. Skewness in the distribution of spot returns affects the pricing of in-the-money options relative to-out-of-the money options. Without this correlation, stochastic volatility only changes the kurtosis. Kurtosis affects the pricing of near-the-money versus far-from-the-money options.

With proper choice of parameters, the stochastic volatility model appears to be a very flexible and promising description of option prices. It presents a number of testable restrictions, since it relates option pricing biases to the dynamics of spot prices and the distribution of spot returns. Knoch (1992) has successfully used the model to explain currency option prices. The model may eventually explain other option phenomena. For example, Rubinstein (1985) found option biases that changed through time. There is also some evidence that implied volatilities from options prices do not seem properly related to future volatility. The model makes it feasible to examine these puzzles and to investigate other features of option pricing. Finally, the solution technique itself can be applied to other problems and is not limited to stochastic volatility or diffusion problems.

Appendix: Derivation of the characteristic functions

This appendix derives the characteristic functions in Equation (17) and shows how to apply the solution technique to other valuation problems. Suppose that $x(t)$ and $v(t)$ follow the (risk-neutral) processes in Equation (15). Consider any twice-differentiable function $f(x, v, t)$ that is a conditional expectation of some function of x and v at a later date, T, $g(x(T), v(T))$:

$$f(x, v, t) = E[g(x(T), v(T)) \mid x(t) = x, v(t) = v]. \quad (A1)$$

Ito's lemma shows that

$$
\begin{aligned}
df = &\left(\frac{1}{2} v \frac{\partial^2 f}{\partial x^2} + \rho \sigma v \frac{\partial^2 f}{\partial x \partial v} + \frac{1}{2} \sigma^2 v \frac{\partial^2 f}{\partial v^2} + (r + u_j v) \frac{\partial f}{\partial x} + (a - b_j v) \frac{\partial f}{\partial v} + \frac{\partial f}{\partial t} \right) dt \\
&+ (r + u_j v) \frac{\partial f}{\partial x} dz_1 + (a - b_j v) \frac{\partial f}{\partial v} dz_2.
\end{aligned}
\quad (A2)
$$

By iterated expectations, we know that f must be a martingale:

$$E[df] = 0. \tag{A3}$$

Applying this to Equation (A2) yields the Fokker–Planck forward equation:

$$\frac{1}{2}v\frac{\partial^2 f}{\partial x^2} + \rho\sigma v\frac{\partial^2 f}{\partial x \partial v} + \frac{1}{2}\sigma^2 v\frac{\partial^2 f}{\partial v^2}$$
$$+ (r + u_j v)\frac{\partial f}{\partial x} + (a - b_j v)\frac{\partial f}{\partial v} + \frac{\partial f}{\partial t} = 0 \tag{A4}$$

(see Karlin and Taylor (1975) for more details). Equation (A1) imposes the terminal condition

$$f(x, v, T) = g(x, v). \tag{A5}$$

This equation has many uses. If $g(x, v) = \delta(x - x_0)$, then the solution is the conditional probability density at time t that $x(T) = x_0$. And if $g(x, v) = 1_{\{x \geq \ln[K]\}}$, then the solution is the conditional probability at time t that $x(T)$ is greater than $\ln[K]$. Finally, if $g(x, v) = e^{i\phi x}$, then the solution is the characteristic function. For properties of characteristic functions, see Feller (1966) or Johnson and Kotz (1970).

To solve for the characteristic function explicitly, we guess the functional form

$$f(x, v, t) = \exp[C(T - t) + D(T - t)v + i\phi x]. \tag{A6}$$

This "guess" exploits the linearity of the coefficients in the PDE (A2). Following Ingersoll (1989, p. 397), one can substitute this functional form into the PDE (A2) to reduce it to two ordinary differential equations,

$$-\frac{1}{2}\sigma^2\phi^2 + \rho\sigma\phi iD + \frac{1}{2}D^2 + u_j\phi i - b_jD + \frac{\partial D}{\partial t} = 0,$$
$$r\phi i + aD + \frac{\partial C}{\partial t} = 0, \tag{A7}$$

subject to

$$C(0) = 0, \quad D(0) = 0.$$

These equations can be solved to produce the solution in the text.

One can apply the solution technique of this article to other problems in which the characteristic functions are known. For example, Stein and Stein (1991) specify a stochastic volatility model of the form

$$d\sqrt{v(t)} = [\alpha - \beta\sqrt{v(t)}]dt + \delta dz_2(t), \tag{A8}$$

From Ito's lemma, the process for the variance is

$$dv(t) = [\delta^2 + 2\alpha\sqrt{v} - 2\beta v]dt + 2\delta\sqrt{v(t)}dz_2(t). \tag{A9}$$

Although Stein and Stein (1991) assume that the volatility process is uncorrelated with the spot asset, one can generalize this to allow $z_1(t)$ and $z_2(t)$ to have constant correlation. The solution method of this article applies directly, except that the characteristic functions take the form

$$f_j(x, \ v, \ t; \ \phi) = \exp[C(T - t) + D(T - t)v + E(T - t)\sqrt{v} + \phi x]. \tag{A10}$$

Bates (1992) provides additional applications of the solution technique to mixed jump-diffusion processes.

References

Barone-Adesi, G. and Whaley, R. E. (1987). Efficient Analytic Approximation of American Option Values. *Journal of Finance* 42, 301–20.

Bates, D. S. (1992). Jumps and Stochastic Processes Implicit in PHLX Foreign Currency Options, working paper, Wharton School, University of Pennsylvania.

Black, F. and Scholes, M. (1972). The Valuation of Option Contracts and a Test of Market Efficiency. *Journal of Finance* 27, 399–417.

——— (1973). The Valuation of Options and Corporate Liabilities. *Journal of Political Economy* 81, 637–54.

Breeden, D. T. (1979). An Intertemporal Asset Pricing Model with Stochastic Consumption and Investment Opportunities. *Journal of Financial Economics* 7, 265–96.

Cox, J. C., Ingersoll, J. E., and Ross, S. A. (1985). A Theory of the Term Structure of Interest Rates. *Econometrica* 53, 385–408.

Cox, J. C. and Ross, S. A. (1976). The Valuation of Options for Alternative Stochastic Processes. *Journal of Financial Economics* 3, 145–66.

Eisenberg, L. K. and Jarrow, R. A. (1991). Option Pricing with Random Volatilities in Complete Markets, Federal Reserve Bank of Atlanta Working Paper 91–16.

Feller, W. (1966). *An Introduction to Probability Theory and Its Applications* (Vol. 2), Wiley, New York.

Garman, M. B. and Kohlhagen, S. W. (1983). Foreign Currency Option Values. *Journal of International Money and Finance* 2, 231–7.

Heston, S. L. (1990). Testing Continuous Time Models of the Term Structure of Interest Rates, Ph.D. Dissertation, Carnegie Mellon University Graduate School of Industrial Administration.

——— (1992). Invisible Parameters in Option Prices, working paper, Yale School of Organization and Management.

Hull, J. C. (1989). *Options, Futures, and Other Derivative Instruments* Prentice-Hall, Englewood Cliffs, NJ.

——— White, A. (1987). The Pricing of Options on Assets with Stochastic Volatilities. *Journal of Finance* 42, 281–300.

Ingersoll, J. E. (1989). *Theory of Financial Decision Making* Rowman and Little-field, Totowa, N.J.

——(1990). Contingent Foreign Exchange Contracts with Stochastic Interest Rates, working paper, Yale School of Organization and Management.

Jarrow, R. A. and Rudd, A. (1982). Approximate Option Valuation for Arbitrary Stochastic Processes. *Journal of Financial Economics* 10, 347–69.

Johnson, N. L. and Kotz, S. (1970). *Continuous Univariate Distributions* Houghton Mifflin, Boston.

Karlin, S. and Taylor, H. M. (1975). *A First Course in Stochastic Processes* Academic, New York.

Kendall, M. G. and Stuart, A. (1977). *The Advanced Theory of Statistics* (Vol. 1), Macmillan, New York.

Knoch, H. J. (1992). The Pricing of Foreign Currency Options with Stochastic Volatility, Ph.D. Dissertation, Yale School of Organization and Management.

Lamoureux, C. G. and Lastrapes, W. D. (1993). Forecasting Stock-Return Variance: Toward an Understanding of Stochastic Implied Volatilities. *Review of Financial Studies* 6, 293–326.

Melino, A. and Turnbull, S. M. (1990). The Pricing of Foreign Currency Options with Stochastic Volatility. *Journal of Econometrics* 45, 239–65.

——————(1991). The Pricing of Foreign Currency Options. *Canadian Journal of Economics* 24, 251–81.

Merton, R. C. (1973). Theory of Rational Option Pricing. *Bell Journal of Economics and Management Science* 4, 141–83.

Rubinstein, M. (1985). Nonparametric Tests of Alternative Option Pricing Models Using All Reported Trades and Quotes on the 30 Most Active CBOE Option Classes from August 23, 1976 through August 31, 1978. *Journal of Finance* 40, 455–80.

Scott, L. O. (1987). Option Pricing When the Variance Changes Randomly: Theory, Estimation, and an Application. *Journal of Financial and Quantitative Analysis* 22, 419–38.

Stein, E. M. and Stein, J. C. (1991). Stock Price Distributions with Stochastic Volatility: An Analytic Approach. *Review of Financial Studies* 4, 727–52.

Wiggins, J. B. (1987). Option Values under Stochastic Volatilities. *Journal of Financial Economics* 19, 351–72.

14
A Study Towards a Unified Approach to the Joint Estimation of Objective and Risk Neutral Measures for the Purpose of Options Valuation*

MIKHAIL CHERNOV AND ERIC GHYSELS[†]

Abstract

The purpose of this paper is to bridge two strands of the literature, one pertaining to the objective or physical measure used to model an underlying asset and the other pertaining to the risk-neutral measure used to price derivatives. We propose a generic procedure using simultaneously the fundamental price, S_t, and a set of option contracts $[(\sigma_{it}^I)_{i=1, m}]$ where $m \geq 1$ and σ_{it}^I is the Black–Scholes implied volatility. We use Heston's (1993. Review of Financial Studies 6, 327–343) model as an example, and appraise univariate and multivariate estimation of the model in terms of pricing and hedging performance. Our results, based on the S&P 500 index contract, show dominance of univariate approach, which relies solely on options data. A by-product of this finding is that we uncover a remarkably simple volatility extraction filter based on a polynomial lag structure of implied volatilities. The bivariate approach, involving both the fundamental security and an option contract, appears useful when the information from the cash market reflected in the conditional kurtosis provides support to price long term.

Keywords: Derivative securities; Efficient method of moments; State price densities; Stochastic volatility models; Filtering

* Reprinted from *Journal of Financial Economics* 56, M. Chernov and E. Ghysels, 'A Study Towards a Unified Approach to the Joint Estimation of Objective and Risk Neutral Measures for the Purpose of Options Valuation', pp 407–458, Copyright © 2000, with permission from Elsevier.

† We would like to thank Torben Andersen, Mark Broadie, Stephen Brown, Charles Cao, Jérôme Detemple, Jens Jackwerth, Eric Jacquier, Frank Hatheway, Roger Lee, Kenneth Singleton, and especially Ron Gallant and George Tauchen for invaluable comments and insightful discussions. We also benefited greatly from the comments of Bill Schwert (the Editor) and the Referees who helped us improve the quality of our paper. In addition, we thank the participants of the NBER/NSF Time Series Conference held at the University of Chicago, the RISK Computational and Quantitative Finance conference, the Newton Institute Workshop on Econometrics and Financial Time Series, the Third Annual New England Finance Doctoral Students Symposium and Computational Finance 99 conference both held at NYU, the 9th Derivative Securities Conference at Boston University, and the 1999 Western Finance Association Meetings, as well as seminars at CIRANO, Michigan State, Penn State, Université Libre de Bruxelles, the University of Montreal, the University of Michigan, and the University of Virginia. We are solely responsible for all remaining errors. The material in this paper subsumes two earlier papers: 'What Data Should be Used to Price Options?' and 'Filtering Volatility and Pricing Options: A Comparison of Implied Volatility, GARCH and Stochastic Volatility'.

14.1 Introduction

According to modern asset pricing theory, the value of any asset can be computed as the expectation under the risk-neutral measure of the future cash flows discounted by the pricing kernel. The valuation of any contingent claim, like a European-style option contract, consists of specifying the pricing kernel and determining the appropriate risk-neutral measure transformation. These operations involve several critical steps. First, it should be noted that there is no completely 'model-free' way to proceed.[1] In particular, the characterization of the risk-neutral measure is intimately related to the price of market risk which in turn is determined by the model one adopts to describe the behavior of the fundamental asset underlying the option contract. This step is also inextricably linked to the estimation of parameters which select the data generating process among the class of models considered. There are different sources of data one could use for the purpose of estimating or calibrating parameters and there is certainly an abundant choice as there are many option contracts actively traded and long time series of the fundamental typically available. To further complicate matters it should be noted that many models describing the behavior of the fundamental process feature latent factors such as stochastic volatility. Therefore one faces also the task of using observations to not only estimate parameters but also to filter or extract the unobservable factors.

In recent years we have made considerable progress on various aspects of this research program. We know more about estimating diffusions particularly those involving stochastic volatility or other latent factors.[2] Parallel to this we witnessed the emergence of several studies suggesting schemes to extract risk-neutral measures from option prices (see inter alia references in footnote 2). Considerable effort was also devoted to filters for extracting the latent factors like volatility. These filters either involve options data or underlying fundamentals (but not both jointly).

The purpose of this paper is to bridge two strands of the literature, one pertaining to the objective or physical measure used to model the underlying asset and the other to the risk-neutral measure used to price derivatives. In fact, we start first with estimating both measures *jointly*. This poses several challenges as building a bridge between the objective and risk-neutral world prompts us to think about many new issues which need to be addressed. In addition, it also

---

[1] Even the so-called nonparametric approaches (see for instance Aït-Sahalia and Lo, 1998; Broadie et al., 2000) either implicitly restrict the class of models by imposing regularity conditions to guarantee valid statistical inference or assume an explicit class of models (see for instance Rubinstein, 1994).

[2] Numerous techniques have been proposed for the estimation of continuous time processes pertaining to the pricing of derivative securities. The literature on the estimation of diffusions with or without stochastic volatility and/or jumps, is summarized in a number of surveys and textbooks, including Bates (1996), Campbell et al. (1997), Ghysels et al. (1996), Melino (1994), Renault (1997) and Tauchen (1997).

opens up new possibilities for comparing the information in the underlying fundamental and options data, a theme which has been the subject of many previous studies. Numerous papers have confronted empirical evidence obtained from derivative security markets with results from the underlying and vice versa. In particular, issues related to the informational content of option prices have been examined extensively in the literature (see for instance Christensen and Prabhala (1998) for the most recent example). Our attempt to model the price behavior of fundamental and derivative securities jointly is motivated by the very same issues hitherto raised in the literature. Namely, we want to learn more about the informational content of option prices. We also want to know how we can improve the statistical precision of diffusion parameters by incorporating options.

Our goal is to investigate these questions in a unifying framework. While we use the Heston (1993) model as specific example, it should be stressed at the outset that our analysis is not limited to any particular model. The choice of Heston's model is motivated by two important factors. First, it has closed-form option pricing formula, which represents a considerable computational advantage. Second, because Heston's model features analytic solutions it has received much attention in the literature (see Bakshi et al., 1997, for references), which makes our analysis directly comparable with results previously reported.

Financial theory also suggests that, for stochastic volatility models with two state variables, such as the models of Hull and White (1987), Scott (1987), Wiggins (1987), Heston (1993), and many others, one should consider the fundamental and its derivative contracts jointly to estimate diffusion parameters and price options simultaneously. There are indeed appealing theoretical reasons to pursue this approach, as in a stochastic volatility economy options must be added to create a complete market model (Romano and Touzi, 1997). The complete market model guarantees the existence and uniqueness of the risk-neutral probability density used to price the option contracts. If done judiciously, this challenging task should dominate the use of a single source, whether options or fundamental.

Although no attempts have been made previously to estimate and appraise stochastic volatility models using the joint distribution of fundamentals and options, it is clear that much of the evidence in the literature suggests that we should gain from addressing this issue. For example, a recent paper by Gallant et al. (1998) adopts a strategy similar to ours, though not involving options. They consider the bivariate process of the fundamental and the daily high/low spread, which provides extra information about the course of volatility. In this paper we propose a generic procedure for estimating and pricing options using simultaneously the fundamental price, S_t, and a set of option contracts $[(\sigma_{it}^I)_{i=1,\,m}]$, where $m \geq 1$ and σ_{it}^I is the Black–Scholes implied volatility. Please note that we can, in principle, manage a panel of options, i.e. a time series of cross-sections. The procedure we propose consists of two steps. First, we fit a seminonparametric (henceforth SNP) density of $[S_t, (\sigma_{it}^I)_{i=1,\,m}]$, conditional on its own past

$[S_\tau, \ (\sigma^j_{i\tau})_{i=1, \ m}]$ for $\tau < t$, using market data. Next we simulate the fundamental price and option prices, and calibrate the parameters of the diffusion and its associated option pricing model to fit the conditional density of the market data dynamics. The procedure coined by Gallant and Tauchen (1996) as Efficient Method of Moments (EMM), has been used primarily to estimate diffusions using only the fundamental price process S_t. We extend EMM to incorporate option prices and fundamentals simultaneously. The EMM procedure, which is a simulation-based estimation technique, allows estimating the model parameters under both objective and risk-neutral probability measures if we use simultaneously implied volatilities and the underlying asset data. Indeed, time series of the underlying asset provide parameters under the objective probability measure while risk-neutral parameters can be retrieved from options. Since the model we adopt has a closed-form option pricing formula, we can obtain the volatilities implied by the Black–Scholes formula from the simulated data and contrast them with their counterparts from the real data via the EMM framework. This procedure yields parameter estimates under the risk-neutral measure. Having estimated the risk-neutral and objective measures separately allows us to appraise the typical risk-neutral representations used in the literature. In particular, in order to obtain the closed-form solutions, the standard approach assumes that the linearity of the volatility drift is preserved. We are able to determine if this assumption is consistent with the data.

The task is challenging. Aside from specifying the methodology, we do not know in advance how well our procedure will work in producing better parameter estimates for diffusions. Further, we cannot predict what improvements in option pricing and hedging can be made. We compare univariate and multivariate models in terms of pricing and hedging performance. The univariate specifications consist of models only using the fundamental asset and models using only options data. It should be noted, however, that the knowledge of the estimated model parameters is not sufficient to compute an option price or a hedge ratio. We have to know the latent spot volatility as well. Previous studies treated spot volatility as a parameter and estimated it from the cross-section of options prices taken from the previous trading day. This approach introduces inconsistencies with the model. A recent extension of the SNP/EMM methodology introduced in Gallant and Tauchen (1998) allows us to address the problem. We filter spot volatilities via reprojection. That is, we compute the expected value of the latent volatility process using an SNP density conditioned on the observable processes, such as returns, or options data, or both.

Our results demonstrate the dominance of the univariate approach that relies solely on options. A by-product of this finding is that we uncover a remarkably simple volatility extraction filter based on a polynomial lag structure of implied volatilities. The bivariate approach appears useful when the information from the cash market provides support, through the conditional kurtosis, to price some long-term options.

These findings prompt us to consider alternative volatility filters, such as for instance the one obtained from the GARCH class of models. We examine the quality of various filters through the window of the Black–Scholes (hence-forth BS) option pricing model, which allows us to separate the effects of a particular pricing kernel from the filter's contribution. Interestingly, we find that the role of the pricing kernel is marginal compared to that of filtering spot volatility.

The remainder of the paper is organized as follows. Section 14.2 sets the stage for the analysis of the joint density function of fundamentals and options. We discuss first the issues addressed so far in the literature and present the model we estimate. In Section 14.2 we also provide a brief review of the EMM estimation and reprojection method. Section 14.3 reports the estimation results and exam-ines the mapping from objective to risk-neutral measures, while Section 14.4 evaluates the performance of the estimated models. Section 14.5 studies the role of different volatility filters. The last section concludes. Technical material is covered in several appendices to the paper.

14.2 Joint estimation of the fundamental and option pricing processes

Numerous papers have confronted empirical evidence obtained from deriva-tive security markets with results from the underlying and vice versa. In parti-cular, issues pertaining to the informational content of option prices have been examined extensively in the literature (see Bates, 1996; Canina and Figlewski, 1993; Christensen and Prabhala, 1998; Day and Lewis, 1992; Fleming, 1998; Lamoureux and Lastrapes, 1993, among others). Ait-Sahalia et al. (1997) address essentially the same issue, comparing state-price densities (SPD) implied by time series of the S&P 500 index with the SPD implied by a cross-section of S&P 500 index options. They reject the hypothesis that the two state price densities are the same. As they examine models with volatility specified as a function of the stock price, one can view their result as a rejection of deterministic volatility models. Along the same lines, Dumas et al. (1998) exam-ine the out-of-sample pricing and hedging performance of the same class of volatility models using also S&P 500 options data. Dumas et al. find that 'simpler is better', i.e. deterministic volatility models perform no better than ordinary implied volatility.

Our attempt to model the price behavior of fundamental and derivative secur-ities jointly is motivated by the very same issues raised in the literature. Namely, we want to learn more about the informational content of option prices, as did Canina and Figlewski (1993) and many others. We also want to know how we can improve the statistical precision of diffusion parameters by incorporating options data as did Pastorello et al. (1994), who used at-the-money implied volatilities, replacing latent spot volatility, to estimate the Hull and White (1987) model.[3] Moreover, we also want to assess the advantages of multivariate schemes using

---

[3] Pastorello et al. (1994) did not estimate the joint process as we propose to do in this paper.

financial criteria such as the out-of-sample pricing and hedging performance of models, like Bakshi et al. (1997), Dumas et al. (1998) and Jacquier and Jarrow (1998), among others.

We attempt to investigate these questions in a unifying framework. We use the stochastic volatility (SV) model specified by Heston (1993) for that purpose, though it should be stressed at the outset that our analysis is not limited to this particular model. The Heston model will be covered in a first subsection.

The joint modeling of returns and derivative security prices will present new challenges, which we will discuss in this section. First, we describe the data in Section 14.1.2. Since the EMM procedure is widely used and described elsewhere, notably in Gallant and Tauchen (1998), we will only summarize its major steps in a third subsection. A fourth subsection deals with reprojection methods, an extension of EMM to extract latent volatility processes. The empirical results are discussed in the last two subsections.

14.2.1 The Heston model

Following Heston (1993), we can write the model as

$$dS(t)/S(t) = R \, dt + \sqrt{V(t)} dW_S^*(t) \tag{1}$$

and

$$
\begin{aligned}
dV(t) &= (\theta^* - \kappa^* V(t)) dt + \sigma_V \sqrt{1 - \rho^2} \sqrt{V(t)} dW_V^*(t) \\
&\quad + \sigma_V \rho \sqrt{V(t)} dW_S^*(t),
\end{aligned}
\tag{2}
$$

where the model is stated under the risk-neutral probability measure. Eq. (1) implies that the stock-price process $S(t)$ follows a geometric Brownian motion, with stochastic variance $V(t)$. Eq. (2) states that $V(t)$ follows a square-root mean-reverting process with the long-run mean θ^*/κ^*, speed of adjustment κ^* and variation coefficient σ_V. Imposing the restriction $\sigma_V^2 \leqslant 2\theta$ guarantees that $V(t)$ stays in the open interval $(0, \infty)$ almost surely (see, for instance, Cox et al., 1985). The Brownian motions $W_S^*(t)$ and $W_V^*(t)$ are assumed independent. Eqs. (1) and (2) imply, however, that $Corr_t(dS(t)/S(t), \ dV(t)) = \rho \, dt$. Parameters with asterisks are those that change when the model is rewritten under the objective probability measure. Under the change of measure, the risk-free rate R is substituted by a drift parameter, μ_S, and all asterisks are removed. This model yields the following formula for a price of a call at time t, with time to maturity τ and strike K:

$$C(t, \ \tau, \ K) = S(t)\Pi_1(t, \ \tau, \ S, \ V) - Ke^{-R\tau}\Pi_2(t, \ \tau, \ S, \ V), \tag{3}$$

where the expressions for $\Pi_j, j = 1, \ 2$ are provided in Appendix A.

The common practice of estimating diffusions using the underlying asset and then relying on an option pricing formula has a number of drawbacks. Standard complete market asset pricing theory determines that one has to change the measure, from the objective measure to the risk neutral one.[4] This transformation is often ad hoc. Although continuous time general equilibrium preference-based asset pricing models readily deliver the direct connection from the objective measure to the risk-neutral measure, they often result in rather complex diffusion models for the underlying asset. The complex dynamics arise because the equilibrium asset price process is derived endogenously, based on the discounted flow of dividends, using an endogenously determined risk-neutral rate (see, e.g. Broadie et al. 1997, for such a derivation). It is therefore common to use a simple diffusion for the asset return and volatility dynamics, and assume that the change of drift, which by Girsanov's theorem amounts to changing the measure, maintains the same type of processes.

To further examine the change of measure, let us consider the Radon–Nikodym derivative of the objective probability measure with respect to the risk-neutral one. This derivative can be computed as follows:

$$
\xi_{0,t} = \exp\left(-\frac{1}{2} \int_0^t (\lambda_1^2(u) + \lambda_2^2(u)) \, \mathrm{d}u \right.
$$
$$
\left. - \int_0^t \lambda_1(u) \mathrm{d}W_S(u) - \int_0^t \lambda_2(u) \mathrm{d}W_V(u) \right),
\tag{4}
$$

where $\lambda(t) = (\lambda_1(t), \lambda_2(t))'$ is the vector with the market prices of risk, return and volatility risk, respectively. When we know the parameter values under both measures we can infer $\lambda(t)$. In particular, by Girsanov's theorem we have

$$
\mu_S S(t) - \lambda_1(t)\sqrt{V(t)}S(t) = RS(t)
\tag{5}
$$

and

$$
\theta - \kappa V(t) - \lambda_2(t)\sigma_V\sqrt{1-\rho^2}\sqrt{V(t)} - \lambda_1(t)\sigma_V\rho\sqrt{V(t)} = \theta^* - \kappa^* V(t).
\tag{6}
$$

Therefore,

$$
\lambda_1(t) = \frac{\mu_S - R}{\sqrt{V(t)}}
\tag{7}
$$

and

$$
\lambda_2(t) = \frac{C_1}{\sqrt{V(t)}} - C_2\sqrt{V(t)},
\tag{8}
$$

where

[4] See Harrison and Kreps (1979) and Harrison and Pliska (1981) for further discussion. Arguments about completeness of markets are typically imposed to guarantee the existence of a unique risk-neutral measure.

$$C_1 = \frac{\theta - \theta^* - (\mu_S - R)\sigma_V\rho}{\sigma_V\sqrt{1 - \rho^2}} \tag{9}$$

and

$$C_2 = \frac{\kappa - \kappa^*}{\sigma_V\sqrt{1 - \rho^2}}. \tag{10}$$

Eq. (7) implies that the asset risk premium increases when volatility decreases. This counterintuitive effect of volatility on the risk premium implies arbitrage opportunities. In mathematical terms this effect means that the transformation to the risk neutral measure, described by the Girsanov theorem, may fail. However, it is difficult to verify the conditions of the theorem in this particular case. Rydberg (1997) discusses these issues in more detail.

It is beyond the scope of the current paper to address these deficiencies of the Heston model, since our main focus is to study the joint estimation of risk neutral and objective measures. We employ the standard Heston model for that purpose. In practice, it is unlikely one would have to deal with extremely small volatility values. While the improvement of the Heston model is beyond the scope of the present paper, the condition presented in Eq. (7), above, should be considered by researchers who intend to extend the model for empirical or theoretical reasons. Finally, since our estimation strategy allows us to compute the prices of risk from Eqs. (7) and (8), we will revisit the issues related to the measure transformation in Section 14.2.2, where we discuss the estimation results.

14.2.2 The data
Like many previous studies, we examine the S&P 500 index and the SPX European option contract traded on the index. Our analysis requires both options and returns data. The source of our series is the Chicago Board of Options Exchange (CBOE). The data consist of daily last sale prices of options written on the S&P 500 index, as well as the closing price of the index. Specifically, the dataset contains the date, maturity month, option price, call/put flag, strike, open interest, volume, and the underlying index. There is a 15-min difference between the close of the AMEX, NASDAQ, and NYSE stock markets, where the 500 stocks included in the index are traded, and the Chicago options market. This difference leads to non-synchronicity biases. Harvey and Whaley (1991), and Bakshi et al. (1997), among others, suggest various schemes based on option price quotes or transactions around the 3 PM market close. We control for the possibility of such biases in our simulation procedure, which is discussed below and in Appendix C. The sample covers the time period from November 1985 until October 1994. We set aside the last year of data, November 1993 to October 1994, for the out-of-sample tests, and use the rest for estimation purpose. Plot (A) of Fig. 14.1 displays the S&P 500 series, showing the familiar pattern, including the negative return corresponding to the crash of October 1987. The dashed vertical line represents the end of the estimation sample and the beginning of the data used for the purpose of out-of-sample appraisals of the models.

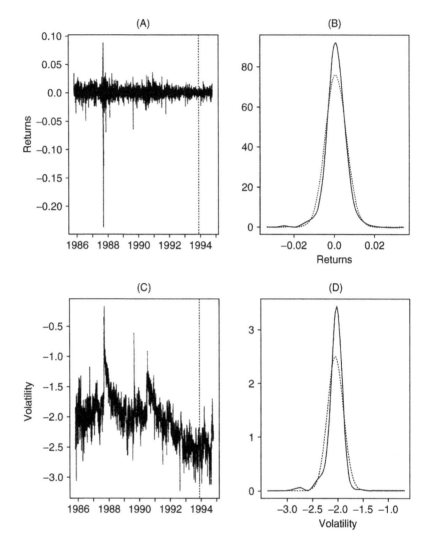

Fig. 14.1. The univariate series and SNP densities. We estimate the SNP
density for the two univariate types of data: (i) the log-returns on the S&P500;
(ii) the log of the BS implied volatilities of the closest to maturity and the
money call options. The data are collected daily, and span the period from
November 1985 to October 1993. The plots to the left are the time series
of the data, the plots to the right are the estimated densities of the series.
The solid line is a plot of an SNP fit, the dashed line is normal density
with the same mean and variance.

Various schemes to extract implied volatilities from options have been suggested in the literature (see, for instance, Bates, 1996, for a survey). We concentrate our attention on the at-the-money (henceforth ATM) calls, where we define at-the-money as $S/K \in [0.97, 1.03]$, for instruments with short maturities, as these are the most liquid instruments. Because of the active trading, the implied volatilities of these contracts should convey the most precise information. Moreover, Harvey and Whaley (1991) note that the ATM volatilities are the most sensitive to changes in the spot volatility rate, since an option's vega is maximized when moneyness is close to 1. To be more precise, we select the calls with the shortest maturities and, in addition to being ATM, we require the option to have the strike as close to the index level as possible, such that $K^* = \mathrm{argmin}_K |S/K - 1|$.[5]

In order to make the observed S&P 500 index and the simulated underlying fundamental data comparable, we adjusted the S&P 500 index for dividends. We took a constant dividend rate, continuously compounded, of 2% which is consistent with Broadie et al. (1997) for example. Therefore, we ignore the lumpiness of the dividend payments, and also conveniently avoid using the historically observed dividends, which would considerably complicate our simulation design. Moreover, since we are dealing with European index options, this issue matters little, as we are only interested in the total flow of dividends paid over the life of the contract. Finally, we used the monthly 3-month T-bill yield from CITIBASE as a proxy for the short-term interest rate. Since the stochastic volatility models we consider assume a constant interest rate, we take the average yield, which is equal to 5.81396%.

Finally, the estimation of SNP density requires the use of stationary and ergodic data. As noted before we will estimate SV models, using three types of data: (i) time series data on the S&P 500 index, (ii) BS volatilities implied by the closest to maturity and at the money calls on the index, and (iii) both data sets jointly. Therefore, the data entries to the SNP estimation routine are the log-returns on the index. Likewise, rather than using the implied volatilities, which are nonnegative, we will work with the log-volatilities. Despite the transformations, we will refer to these data series as S&P 500 and BS volatilities for convenience. Plot (C) of Fig. 14.1 displays the BS implied volatilities. We note that the highest volatility is, not surprisingly, observed at the time of the crash. Moreover, it is also important to note the downward trend in volatility beginning around 1991, and the reversal of this trend in the series coming after the estimation part of our data set. This reversal will make the out-of-sample exercise particularly interesting.[6]

---

[5] Apart from the moneyness filter, several other filters were applied to the data. In particular, observations with a call price missing or equal to zero were dropped. The various filters applied to the data leave us with 1978 observations, which roughly corresponds to 247 observations per year.

[6] The more recent years, which are not covered by our sample, especially the summer and fall of 1998, indicate an upward trending volatility. In other words, the volatility process seems to revert to the mean as assumed in the Heston (1993) model we consider here. It should also be noted that the options contracts on S&P 500 were of American type during a very short period of our sample, namely prior to April 1986. Because we select short maturity contracts, for which the exercise premium is very close to zero, this change should not affect much of our results. Fig. 14.1 also shows that the American option part of our sample, prior to April 1986, does not introduce any abnormal patterns.

14.2.3 The efficient method of moments estimation procedure

Several methods have been proposed to estimate the parameters of stochastic volatility models. These methods include the generalized method of moments (GMM), quasi-maximum likelihood, and various simulation-based procedures, including Bayesian methods and efficient method of moments (see Ghysels et al., 1996, for a literature review). In this paper, we use the Efficient Method of Moments (henceforth EMM) procedure of Gallant and Tauchen (1996), which has already found many applications in the estimation of both continuous time and discrete time stochastic volatility models. Examples include Andersen and Lund (1997), Andersen et al. (1999), Gallant, Hsieh and Tauchen (1997), Gallant et al. (1999), Gallant and Tauchen (1998), Ghysels and Jasiak (1996), Jiang and van der Sluis (1998), and Tauchen (1997). So far, most of these applications only use a single data series, either a short rate process or a stock price (index). There are exceptions, notably Ghysels and Jasiak (1996), who consider the joint process of stock returns and trading volume, and Gallant, Hsu and Tauchen et al. (1999), who as noted before, consider the bivariate process of the fundamental asset and the daily high–low spread. EMM can be divided into two main parts, the estimation of the so-called score generator, which will be discussed first, and the estimation of the diffusion parameters, which will conclude this section.

Suppose the process of interest is denoted ι_t. In our application, this process can be univariate, bivariate, or involving a low-dimensional panel data set. If univariate, the process will include either asset returns or BS implied volatilities. If bivariate the process will include both returns and implied volatilities. In the general case a panel data set is considered which includes the fundamental asset returns series and M option contracts with different moneyness, different maturities, or both, represented by their BS implied volatilities $[(\sigma_{it}^I)_{i=1, M}]$. In a generic context, we assume that ι_t is a vector with L elements. It has a conditional distribution $p(\iota_t | I_t, \Theta)$, where I_t is the information set and Θ represents the parameters of the stochastic volatility model for ι_t. The asymptotically efficient method to estimate Θ is maximum likelihood (MLE), which involves maximizing the function

$$\frac{1}{T}\sum_{t=1}^{T} \log p(\iota_t | I_t, \Theta). \tag{11}$$

Maximizing Eq. (11) is equivalent to solving

$$\frac{1}{T}\sum_{t=1}^{T} \frac{\partial}{\partial \Theta} \log p(\iota_t | I_t, \hat{\Theta}) = 0, \tag{12}$$

where $\partial \log (p(\,\cdot\,|\,\cdot\,))/\partial \Theta$ is the score function. The above expression is the sample equivalent of

$$E\left(\frac{\partial}{\partial \Theta} \log p(\iota_t | I_t, \Theta)\right) = 0. \tag{13}$$

Unfortunately, it is very difficult to obtain the likelihood function for stochastic volatility models. Therefore, it is impossible to compute the score generator $\partial \log(p(\cdot \mid \cdot))/\partial\Theta$. To overcome this challenge, Gallant and Tauchen suggest computing instead a SNP density $f_k(\iota_t \mid X_t, \ \Xi)$, where X_t is the vector of M lags of ι_t and Ξ is the vector of parameters of the SNP model. The index k relates to the dimension of Ξ, and should expand at the appropriate rate as the sample size grows to accomplish MLE asymptotic efficiency (see Gallant and Long, 1997, for further discussion). We provide some specific details regarding the SNP density in Appendix B. Note that EMM can use any score generator which represents the data well. In this paper, we will use the SNP score generator, which is also required for the reprojection procedure described later.

As noted above, EMM has two parts. The first part is the estimation of the auxiliary score generator model. The estimated SNP density provides the input to the second stage of the EMM estimation procedure. More precisely, the SNP score function generates a set of moment conditions. In particular, Θ can be estimated through the moment conditions, or score function, similar to Eq. (13), which in this case will be:

$$m(\Theta, \ \hat{\Xi}) = E\left(\frac{\partial}{\partial\Xi} \log f_k(\iota_t \mid X_t, \ \hat{\Xi})\right) = \int \frac{\partial}{\partial\Xi} \log f_k(\iota_t \mid X_t, \ \hat{\Xi}) \mathrm{d}P(l, \ X, \ \Theta). \quad (14)$$

Since these moment conditions should have mean zero, they can be used as the basis for a GMM-type estimation procedure, which yields the desired estimate for the parameter vector Θ. The moment conditions are easier to compute by simulation instead of computing the integral in Eq. (14) numerically. Hence, we compute sample moments by simulating N observations of ι_t from the SV model.[7] With simulated time series of length N for ι_t, with candidate parameters Θ, the left-hand side of Eq. (12) translates into

$$m_N(\Theta, \ \hat{\Xi}) = \frac{1}{N}\sum_{t=1}^{N}\frac{\partial}{\partial\Xi}\log f_k(\iota_t(\Theta) \mid X_t(\Theta), \ \hat{\Xi}). \quad (15)$$

Then we can formulate the EMM estimator for the parameter vector Θ, using the following quadratic minimization criterion:

$$\hat{\Theta} = \operatorname*{argmin}_{\Theta} m_N(\Theta, \ \hat{\Xi})' W_T m_N(\Theta, \ \hat{\Xi}). \quad (16)$$

Because of the properties of the SNP model,

---

[7] Since the SV model is formulated in continuous time we need to discretize the process to generate simulated paths. We use the explicit order 2.0 weak stochastic differential equation (SDE) discretization scheme, described in Kloeden and Platen (1995 pp. 486–487), to simulate the processes defined in Eqs. (1) and (2). In Appendix C, we provide further details of the scheme employed to create discrete observations. The empirical results reported in the next section are based on simulated samples of size $N = 10,000$.

$$W_T = \frac{1}{T}\sum_{t=1}^{T} \frac{\partial \log f_k(\iota_t|X_t,\ \hat{\Xi})}{\partial \Xi} \frac{\partial \log f_k(\iota_t|X_t,\ \hat{\Xi})}{\partial \Xi'}. \qquad (17)$$

Asymptotically, the EMM estimator is consistent and normal and has, under suitable regularity conditions, the same efficiency as MLE (see Gallant and Tauchen, 1996; Gallant and Long, 1997, for further discussion).

We will focus primarily on the case where ι_t represents a bivariate process of a stock return and a BS implied volatility. The distribution $p(\iota_t|I_t,\ \Theta)$ in this context is implicitly defined by Eqs. (1)–(3). Suppose now that the parameter vector Θ can be written as $(\mu_S,\ \Theta_c,\ \Theta_o,\ \Theta_n)$, where μ_S is the rate of return on the underlying asset under the objective probability measure, Θ_c contains the parameters common to the objective and risk-neutral measure, Θ_o represents the objective probability measure volatility drift parameters, and Θ_n the risk-neutral ones. In Eqs. (1) and (2), these parameter vectors correspond to $\Theta_c = (\sigma_V,\ \rho)$, $\Theta_o = (\theta,\ \kappa)$, and $\Theta_n = (\theta^*,\ \kappa^*)$. The first step consists of simulating the underlying processes from Eqs. (1) and (2) under the objective probability measure for a given set of parameters values for $(\mu_S,\ \Theta_c,\ \Theta_o)$. It should be noted that we simulate the latent volatility process $V(t)$, though it is not part of ι_t since we need to use $V(t)$ to compute the price, $S(t)$. Using the risk-neutral measure parameters $(\Theta_c,\ \Theta_n)$, where the values of Θ_c remain the same, we compute the options price according to Eq. (3) and calculate the BS implied volatilities from these prices. Since we estimate Θ_o and Θ_n separately, we can test certain hypotheses about the transformation from objective to risk-neutral measures.

To obtain the BS volatilities, we need to apply the option pricing formula to the simulated data. This step requires knowing the parameters and choosing time to maturity and strike features of the contract. Obviously, time to maturity is not available in the simulated data. To make the simulated option prices comparable with the observed ones in the actual data, we replicate the maturities from the observed data. In order to decrease the simulation error, the sample size of the simulated data (recall $N = 10,000$) is much larger than the sample of actual data available. Therefore, we cycle through the sequence of observed maturities in the actual data set to cover the entire simulated data set. In particular, for the simulated ith observation, we use the maturity from the mod(i, T), where T is the sample size of the observed data. If the length of the simulated sample is N and a multiple of T, say $N = lT$, then this scheme amounts to replicating the number of times each maturity appears in the observed data by l.

We apply a similar strategy for the strike features of the contracts. In particular, we simulate moneyness instead of strikes, because the simulated sample path of $S(t)$, or price, can be quite different from the observed one. Matching the moneyness with the real data implies the existence of strikes not always observed in the real data sample. Using this strategy preserves the crucial properties of options. Since we can rewrite the option pricing formula in terms of moneyness, the dependence on strike features will be eliminated. We rotate moneyness from the observed data in exactly the same way as maturities to simulate BS implied volatilities.

Finally, it should be noted that the simulation approach described in this section also extends to situations involving only options data, or the more commonly used univariate setup based on returns series. In neither case is it possible to estimate the entire parameter vector Θ, which we wrote as $(\mu_S, \Theta_c, \Theta_o, \Theta_n)$. With options data, we cannot estimate the drift parameter μ_S under the objective measure. Hence, with options we can estimate the parameter vector $(\Theta_c, \Theta_o, \Theta_n)$.[8] When returns series are used we cannot recover the risk neutral volatility parameters, i.e. Θ_n. Hence, only cases with both fundamentals and derivatives will involve the full parameter vector $(\mu_S, \Theta_c, \Theta_o, \Theta_n)$.

14.2.4 Reprojection

Having obtained the EMM estimates of the model parameters $\hat{\Theta}$, we would like to extract the unobserved spot volatility $V(t)$ in order to price options according to Eq. (3). Several filters have been proposed in the literature, all involving the return process exclusively. Harvey et al. (1994) suggest employing the approximate Kalman filter based on a discrete time SV model. The exact filter is derived by Jacquier et al. (1994) in the context of a Bayesian analysis of the same model. Nelson and Foster (1994) demonstrate how diffusion limit arguments apply to the class of EGARCH models, and provide a justification for EGARCH models as filters for instantaneous volatility. Some attempts were made to extend these filters to a multivariate context (see, in particular, Harvey et al., 1994; Jacquier et al., 1995; and Nelson, 1996). These multivariate extensions exclusively use return series, and cannot accommodate derivative security market information. We propose a filtering method based on the reprojection procedure introduced by Gallant and Tauchen (1998). We briefly describe first the method, intuitively, in a generic context and focus on the specific applications we will consider.

Suppose we have a vector process consisting of observable and unobservable time series. For example, observables could be returns, or BS implied volatilities, while the latent spot volatility would be unobservable. Let us denote the vector of contemporaneous and lagged observable variables by x_t, and the vector of contemporaneous unobservable variables by y_t. The filtering problem is equivalent to computing the following conditional expectation

$$\tilde{y}_t = E(y_t|x_t) = \int y_t p(y_t|x_t, \Theta) dy_t, \tag{18}$$

where Θ is the parameter vector. This expectation involves the conditional probability density of y_t given x_t. If we knew the density, we could estimate it

---

[8] Note that options data allow us to estimate the volatility parameter vector under both measures, i.e. both Θ_o and Θ_n. In particular, we proceed along the same lines as in the bivariate case, and simulate that latent volatility process $V(t)$ and the fundamental asset, to compute option prices and obtain implied volatilities. However, since the data is limited to options, and option pricing formulas omit the objective measure drift parameter, we cannot identify μ_S. All other parameters can be identified, since any variation in $(\Theta_c, \Theta_o, \Theta_n)$ affect option prices.

by $\hat{p}(y_t|x_t) = p(y_t|x_t, \hat{\Theta})$. Unfortunately, for SV models there is no analytical expression for the conditional density available. Therefore, we need to estimate this density as $\hat{p}(y_t|x_t) = f_k(\hat{y}_t|\hat{x}_t)$, where $\hat{y}_t$, $\hat{x}_t$ are simulated from the SV model with parameters set equal to $\hat{\Theta}$, and where f_k is again a SNP density. Gallant and Long (1997) show that

$$\lim_{k \to \infty} f_k(\hat{y}_t|\hat{x}_t) = p(y_t|x_t, \hat{\Theta}). \tag{19}$$

Hence, the SNP density converges asymptotically to the true conditional probability density (where convergence is in terms of the Sobolev norm specified by Gallant and Long). Hence, reprojection provides an unbiased estimate of the latent process, namely spot volatility.

The reprojection filtering method takes a multivariate form under three scenarios. These scenarios are, (i) only involving a vector of multiple return series, an approach not considered in this paper but feasible, (ii) only involving a vector of options, as discussed further below and, (iii) a mixture of the previous two scenarios. The latter strategy will be our prime focus here. It should be noted that one can also consider univariate schemes which involve either the return series or the BS implied volatilities. The former univariate scheme would be comparable to the filtering methods of Harvey et al. (1994), Jacquier et al. (1994) and Nelson and Foster (1994). In Section 14.5, we will discuss such univariate volatility filters based on returns data. Univariate schemes only involving options have been proposed informally. Often, though not exclusively, such univariate filters rely on the Black–Scholes model and involve a cross-section of options, treating today's volatility as a parameter. Bakshi et al. (1997), for instance, employ this methodology and obtain volatility estimates which minimize the pricing error of the daily cross-section of options. The reprojection approach applied to a vector of options, such as the second reprojection scheme specified above, is more general since it takes fully advantage of the time series and cross-section data structure. Even the univariate reprojection method using solely an ATM option will result in a time series filter of implied volatilities, which to the best of our knowledge is a filtering scheme for instantaneous volatility which has not been fully exploited so far (and as we will see in the next section performs remarkably good).

In the remainder of this section we will focus exclusively on the applications of filtering using the reprojection method which contains novel features. The specific application can readily be extended to any of the aforementioned generic specifications. There are two novel applications, one of which deals with a bivariate model of returns and an ATM option, and the other which deals with a univariate filter based on options only. The reprojection scheme relies on a one-step-ahead forecast, which is an expectation computed from the distribution of volatility conditional on the contemporaneous and lagged returns, denoted r_t, and lagged implied volatilities: $p(V(t)|r_t, \sigma_{t-1}^I, r_{t-1}, \ldots, \sigma_{t-M}^I, r_{t-M}, \hat{\Theta})$. Hence, $x_t = (r_t, \sigma_{t-1}^I, r_{t-1}, \ldots, \sigma_{t-M}^I, r_{t-M})$ and $y_t = V(t)$ in Eq. (18). The computation of the SNP density for $V(t)$ proceeds in several steps. First, using the estimates $\hat{\Theta}$ one simulates the processes specified in (1) and (2), which produces the series $\{\hat{\sigma}_{t-1}^I, \hat{r}_t, \hat{V}_t\}_{t=1}^N$, in the case of bivariate data, and $\{\hat{\sigma}_{t-1}^I, \hat{V}_t\}_{t=1}^N$, in the univariate case.[9] Let us again denote the vector $(\hat{r}_t, \hat{\sigma}_{t-1}^I, \hat{r}_{t-1}, \ldots, \hat{\sigma}_{t-M}^I, \hat{r}_{t-M})'$ (or $(\hat{\sigma}_{t-1}^I, \ldots, \hat{\sigma}_{t-M}^I)'$ in the univariate case) by $\hat{x}_t$.

Second, since the SNP density has a Gaussian lead term, we need to transform the simulated volatility process which only takes positive values. It would be natural to consider the log-transformation of $\hat{V}_t$, as was done with the implied volatilities data (see Section 14.2.2). However, in this case we need an estimate of the untransformed spot volatility to substitute into the option pricing formula. We conclude this section with the description of a piecewise linear approximation to the log transformation which will allow us to recover spot volatility without any biases.

Consider a first order Taylor expansion of the logarithm of volatility, which we denote by $L(V(t))$. We find the SNP density $f_k(L(\hat{V}_t)|\hat{x}_t)$.[10] From Jensen's inequality, we have that $E(C(V(t))) \leqslant C(E(V(t)))$, for any concave function C. This inequality becomes an equality only if C is linear, hence the use of $L(\cdot)$. As a result, the SNP density fitted to the simulated data produces a mean of $\hat{V}_t$ conditional on the observable vector $\hat{x}_t$, which in turn yields the desired filtered values. The first order Taylor expansion is an approximation and, in theory, can be centered anywhere. One obvious starting point is to compute the Taylor expansion around the mean of simulated $\hat{V}_t$'s. This approximation may be quite inaccurate in the tails of the distribution, however. This drawback is particularly important as the inverse transform may easily result in negative volatilities.[11] Indeed, experiments showed that the first order Taylor expansion centered around the mean of simulated $\hat{V}_t$ resulted in 32% negative volatilities. We therefore took the first order Taylor expansion at different points, yielding a piecewise linear approximation similar to a spline transformation. Further experiments showed that a linear approximation centered around two points yielded roughly 3.6% negative volatilities. Centering the approximation around four points yielded roughly 1.6%. We therefore took a four-point linear spline and centered the first order Taylor expansions around the 8th, 24th, 50th, 76th, and 92nd percentiles of the simulated $\hat{V}_t$ marginal distribution, with break-points at the 16th, 32nd, 68th and 84th percentiles. The remaining few negative values were replaced by a small positive number, namely by 0.0001.

---

[9] To streamline the notation, we use $\hat{V}_t$ for the simulated $V(t)$. Furthermore, since k grows with the sample size N we select a simulation size of 10,000 observations.

[10] Fitting SNP densities in a reprojection exercise requires a slightly different specification since the explanatory variables are exogenous to the dependent variable. Hence, we set M_R equal to 0 (see Appendix B). The SNP code also requires other slight modifications, so that the lags of dependent variables would not be included in the conditioning set as in the standard SNP density specification.

[11] This outcome occurs because the linear transformation imposes lower and upper limits on the range of a volatility, unlike the log-transformation, which can potentially take any value on the real line.

14.3 Empirical results

The discussion of the empirical results is divided into two subsections. We cover the two stages of the EMM procedure. The first stage, which pertains to the SNP density estimation, is covered in a first subsection. The parameter estimates of Heston's model are discussed in a second subsection, along with the computation of the market prices of risk.

14.3.1 SNP density estimation results

The SNP density estimation results are reported in Panel A of Table 14.1. We estimate the SNP density for the three types of data: (i) the log-returns on the S&P500, (ii) the log of the BS implied volatilities of the closest to maturity and ATM call options, and (iii) both series jointly. Rather than report the parameter estimates, we focus instead on the density structures as characterized by the tuning parameters K_z, K_X, M, M_μ, and M_R (see Appendix B for further details). To facilitate the interpretation of the results, Panel B describes the generic features of SNP densities for different combinations of the tuning parameters. In addition, Panel A reports the values of the objective function, s_n, based on the density in Eq. (B.1) found in Appendix B, the values of the Akaike information criterion (AIC), the Hannan and Quinn criterion (HQ), and the Schwarz Bayes information criterion (BIC). Each line reports the best BIC model within each class, as outlined in Panel B. The best model selected by BIC, is in boldface. Comparing Panels A and B of Table 14.1, we note that all series require models with $K_z > 0$, indicating non-Gaussian innovations. The fact that $M_R > 0$ means that we also find ARCH effects, even with BS implied volatilities, in the Hermite polynomial expansions of the SNP densities. We also need autoregressive terms in the mean, since all expansions have $M_\mu > 0$. For BS implied volatilities we need the longest lags in the mean, namely M_μ is set equal to nine. The mean equation for BS volatilities is similar to a conditional second moment equation, which is comparable to the eight lags in the ARCH expansion of the return series (i.e. $M_R = 8$ for S&P 500 return series).[12]

It is worthwhile to examine the estimated density plots. In addition to the raw data, Fig. 14.1 also features plots of the estimated SNP densities for the univariate cases. Fig. 14.2 does the same for the bivariate case involving the joint process of returns and BS implied volatilities. The data section contains a discussion of Plots (A) and (C) in Fig. 14.1. These plots display the S&P 500 series and the corresponding BS implied volatilities. Plots (B) and (D) show the corresponding SNP densities, with a standard normal probability density function (p.d.f.) superimposed with a dashed line. The estimated densities show the familiar peaked, leptokurtic, and weakly skewed patterns. Plot (A) in Fig. 14.2 reports the joint

---

[12] An alternative SNP density specification involving an AR-GARCH lead term has been suggested by Andersen et al. (1999). This alternative specification would be appropriate for discrete-time analogs to the continuous time diffusions, and potentially represents statistical efficiency gains. While these arguments clearly apply to univariate return series, it is not clear that they apply to BS volatilities and the bivariate models. We therefore use the original specification suggested by Gallant and Tauchen (1989).

Table 14.1. The SNP density estimation

We estimate the SNP density for the three types of data: (i) the log-returns on the S&P500; (ii) the log of the BS implied volatilities of the closest to maturity and the money call options; (iii) both series. Panel A reports the structure of the estimated densities and the values of the objective function S_n based on the density in (B.1), the values of the Akaike information criterion (AIC), the Hannan and Quinn criterion (HQ) and the Schwarz Bayes information criterion (BIC). Each line report the best BIC model within each class of density structures. The overall best model selected by BIC is in boldface. Panel B reports possible densities structures, as described in Gallant and Tauchen (1993). Panel C reports the reprojection SNP densities for spot volatility estimated with simulated data from Heston's model with the data of types (i)–(iii) in the conditioning set.

Panel A	Data type	K_z	K_X	M	M_μ	M_R	$S_n(\hat{\Xi})$	AIC	HQ	BIC
	S&P 500	0	0	1	3	0	1.4159	1.4185	1.4211	1.4256
		0	0	1	3	8	1.2140	1.2207	1.2275	1.2392
		9	**0**	**1**	**3**	**8**	**1.1421**	**1.1534**	**1.1649**	**1.1848**
		9	1	1	3	8	1.1371	1.1535	1.1703	1.1991
	BS vol's	0	0	1	9	0	1.0836	1.0893	1.0950	1.1050
		0	0	1	9	5	0.9510	0.9592	0.9676	0.9821
		6	**0**	**1**	**9**	**5**	**0.8183**	**0.8296**	**0.8411**	**0.8610**
		6	3	1	9	5	0.7889	0.8109	0.8335	0.8723
	Joint	0	0	1	4	0	2.4969	2.5077	2.5187	2.5376
		0	0	1	4	4	2.1626	2.1856	2.2092	2.2498
		4	**0**	**1**	**4**	**4**	**1.9942**	**2.0214**	**2.0492**	**2.0970**

Panel B	Parameter K, M_μ, M_R setting	Characterization of l_t
	$K_z = 0$, $K_X = 0$, $M \geqslant 0$, $M_\mu = 0$, $M_R = 0$	iid Gaussian
	$K_z = 0$, $K_X = 0$, $M \geqslant 0$, $M_\mu > 0$, $M_R = 0$	Gaussian VAR
	$K_z > 0$, $K_X = 0$, $M \geqslant 0$, $M_\mu > 0$, $M_R = 0$	non-Gaussian VAR, homogeneous innovations
	$K_z = 0$, $K_X = 0$, $M \geqslant 0$, $M_\mu \geqslant 0$, $M_R > 0$	Gaussian ARCH
	$K_z > 0$, $K_X = 0$, $M \geqslant 0$, $M_\mu \geqslant 0$, $M_R > 0$	non-Gaussian ARCH, homogeneous innovations
	$K_z > 0$, $K_X > 0$, $M > 0$, $M_\mu \geqslant 0$, $M_R \geqslant 0$	general non-linear process, heterogeneous innovations

Panel C	Data type	K_z	K_X	M	M_μ	M_R	$s_n(\hat{\Xi})$	AIC	HQ	BIC
	S&P 500	0	0	1	1	0	0.4601	0.4604	−0.4607	0.4615
		4	0	1	1	0	0.4058	0.4065	0.4073	0.4090
		4	**1**	**1**	**1**	**0**	0.3859	0.3871	0.3886	0.3915
	BS vol's	0	0	1	22	0	−0.8367	−0.8343	−0.8313	−0.8256
		1	0	1	22	0	−0.7889	−0.7864	−0.7833	−0.7773
	Joint	0	0	1	7	0	−25.2651	−25.2618	−25.2578	−25.2498
		8	**0**	**1**	**7**	**0**	30.5975	30.5925	30.5865	30.5747
		8	6	1	7	0	−30.6031	−30.5775	−30.5464	−30.4855

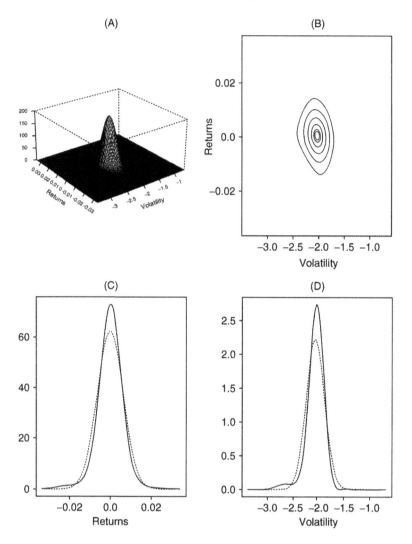

Fig. 14.2. The Bivariate SNP density. We estimate the joint SNP density for the
following series: (i) the log-returns on the S&P500; (ii) the log of the BS
implied volatilities of the closest to maturity and the money call options. The
data are daily, and span the period from November 1985 to October 1993.
Plot (A) shows the perspective plot of the estimated bivariate density; plot
(B) is the contour plot at quantiles 10%, 25%, 50%, 75%, 90%, and 95%;
plots (C) and (D) are the marginal densities of (i) and (ii) correspondingly,
for which the solid line shows the plot of an SNP fit, and the dashed line
shows the normal density with the same mean and variance.

density, Plot (B) gives the contour plot. The marginal densities appear in Plots (C) and (D). The contour plot suggests the presence of slight negative correlation between returns and volatility, which supports the presence of a leverage effect. Hence, in the estimation we imposed the restriction that $\rho \leqslant 0$.

14.3.2 SV model parameter estimates
We turn now to parameter estimates of Heston's SV model. Table 14.2 reports the estimation results. Traditionally, this model is estimated using only returns, so we report this configuration as a benchmark. Then we proceed to the estimation results relying exclusively on options, in the spirit of Pastorello et al. (1994). Next, we consider the structural parameters obtained from matching the moments dictated by the bivariate SNP score. The first observation is that Heston's SV model is rejected in every case, regardless of the data configuration. The standard Normal distribution is used to evaluate the z-statistics, which is an approximation to asymptotically χ^2 distributed test statistics, using GMM-type overidentifying restrictions (see Gallant and Tauchen, 1997, for further discussion).[13] All the z-statistics reported in Table 14.2 are large. The rejections vary dramatically across the rows in Table 14.2, depending on which data is used. In particular, the returns data provide the weakest evidence against the model. However, the precision of the estimates is very poor. For example, the standard error for κ is 0.29. This result is consistent with previous findings (see, for example, Gallant et al., 1997). It is worth noting here that the estimated parameters are annualized, as is typically done in option pricing models. Hence the reported values are quite different from their GARCH counterparts, for instance, which are typically characterized on a daily basis. It is easy to provide the link between them, however, since the SV model allows for temporal aggregation. For example, the value of $\kappa \approx 0.93$ corresponds to $0.93/252 \approx 0.004$ on a daily scale, or roughly 0.996 as the corresponding persistence parameter in a GARCH(1,1) model.

Our major interest goes beyond appraising the model exclusively on the grounds of its statistical properties. Its pricing and hedging features, discussed in the next section, are the primary interest.

There are four parameters which overlap between the first row of Table 14.2, which pertains to parameter estimates obtain from returns data, and the second row, which reports the results obtained using BS implied volatilities. Recall from the discussion in Section 2.3 that, with options data, we can estimate the parameter vector $(\Theta_c, \Theta_o, \Theta_n)$ but not the drift μ_s under the objective measure. Therefore, the parameter vector (Θ_c, Θ_o) is common to the first and second rows of Table 14.2. For all the parameters common to both data sets, we obtain roughly the same point estimates, yet the precision of the estimates are dramatically improved with the second data set. In theory, one would expect that options data should yield more precise diffusion parameter estimates, as almost all estimated parameters are related to the volatility process specified in Eq. (2). Therefore, looking at the process through the observed implied volatilities should

---

[13] Pastorello et al. (1994) did not estimate the joint process as we propose to do in this paper.

Table 14.2. EMM estimation results

We have estimated the stochastic volatility model

$$\frac{dS(t)}{S(t)} = R\,dt + \sqrt{V(t)}\,dW_S^*(t),$$

and

$$dV(t) = (\theta^* - \kappa^* V(t))\,dt + \sigma_V\sqrt{1 - \rho^2}\sqrt{V(t)}\,dW_V^*(t) + \sigma_V\rho\sqrt{V(t)}\,dW_S^*(t),$$

where the model is stated under the risk-free probability measure. We have denoted by asterisks only those parameters, which change when we make a transition to the objective probability measure. With such a change R would have to be substituted by μ_S and all asterisks removed. Three types of data were used in this estimation: (i) the log-returns on the S&P500; (ii) the log of the BS implied volatilities of the closest to maturity and the money call options; (iii) both series. Standard errors are reported in the parentheses, z-statistics testing the model are in the brackets, —denotes unidentifiable parameters. The reported parameter estimates are annualized.

Data type	$\hat{\mu}_S$	$\hat{\theta}$	$\hat{\theta}^*$	$\hat{\kappa}$	$\hat{\kappa}^*$	$\hat{\sigma}_V$	$\hat{\rho}$
S&P 500 [6.863]	0.12767392 (0.00000084)	0.01518484 (0.00514937)	—	0.92586310 (0.29340050)	—	0.06340828 (0.00814696)	-0.01787568 (0.24603696)
Vol [247.447]	—	0.01546074 (0.00017247)	0.00856834 (0.00001727)	0.92803334 (0.00003542)	0.70200229 (0.00019527)	0.06459151 (0.00028325)	-0.01939315 (0.00032025)
Joint [90.328]	0.10190398 (0.00007322)	0.01430366 (0.00005969)	0.00659546 (0.00007541)	0.93086335 (0.00009669)	0.69011763 (0.00026902)	0.06150001 (0.00007698)	-0.01830000 (0.00009685)

give us more precision, an observation also made by Pastorello et al. (1994).[14] Nevertheless, the standard errors we find and report in Table 14.2 are extremely small. Pastorello et al. (1994) report a ratio of roughly 4 to 1 for the standard errors obtained from returns and options data. In Table 14.2, we find standard errors up to 10,000 times smaller, as in the case of κ. Further investigation has revealed to us that one should be very careful with the computation of standard errors. We have discovered that our results are affected by the numerical instabilities in the computation of standard errors, which are computed via the Jacobian equation $(\partial / \partial \Theta')m(\hat{\Theta}, \ \hat{\Xi})$.[15] As there are no analytic expressions for the Jacobian, the derivatives are evaluated numerically. In the EMM code, as with any numerical gradient code, one can change the size of the lower bound on the differencing interval, which is denoted as h. Under normal circumstances, the choice of h should not substantially affect the resulting the standard error computations. We computed standard errors using different values of h. The default value for h in the EMM code is 10^{-7}, which yields the standard errors appearing in Table 14.2. We considered values for h of 10^{-i}, $i = 4$, 5, 6, 7, and 8. We found that deviations from the default value of h yielded in some cases smaller standard errors. For example, for θ we obtained standard errors ranging from 0.00003550 ($h = 10^{-8}$) to 0.00017247 reported as in Table 14.2. In other cases, we obtained substantially larger standard errors, such as the κ values ranging from 0.00003542, reported in Table 14.2 to 0.01496481 ($h = 10^{-5}$). Interestingly, the same sensitivity analysis of the numerical computations applied to the first row of Table 14.2, showed that the standard error computations were invariant to the choice of h when returns data are used. The instability of the computations can therefore only be explained by the considerably more complicated functions involved in computing $(\partial / \partial \Theta')m(\hat{\Theta}, \ \hat{\Xi})$ when options data, and hence an options formula, are used. At this point it is difficult to say which of the errors are correct when options data are used. This subject clearly requires a more thorough investigation. As we are sailing in unchartered waters, this subject surely will require further future research. Finally, to conclude the discussion of the parameter estimates with options data, note the large size of the z-statistic, 247.447, which indicates serious inconsistencies between the model and the data. Specifically, the z-statistic indicates that our model does not explain the information extracted from the options prices.

The model estimated with the joint data set of returns and options is also reported in Table 14.2. Here, we can fit both the objective and risk-neutral density parameters and make direct comparisons with the previous two univariate models. The bivariate model shows an improvement in fit when compared to the options-based approach, the z-statistic is greatly reduced, although the model is still strongly rejected. The precision of the estimates is the best of the different

---

[14] Pastorello et al. (1994) consider the model of Hull and White (1987), and conduct a Monte Carlo study showing the dramatic improvement of parameter estimates when options data are used.
[15] We are grateful to the Referee and to George Tauchen, who helped us to find the source of the computational pitfalls.

configurations, while the point estimates roughly remain the same.[16] The observation regarding the stability of point estimates is important as the bivariate
estimation approach is affected by the non-synchronicity in options and returns
data. This result confirms the observation made in Appendix C, that matching
moments instead of sample paths appears to render any spurious non-synchronicity effects insignificant.

Since we are interested in which type of data we should use to price and hedge
options, we can conclude from Table 14.2 that the returns series should not be
used alone as we can with the univariate data sets, not directly infer the parameters under the risk-neutral probability measure, unless auxiliary assumptions are
made. The two competing data sets which allow us to identify directly the
necessary parameters are the BS implied volatilities and the joint returns and
implied volatilities series. We will therefore focus exclusively on these two alternatives in order to appraise how options are priced, and how well they perform
for the purpose of hedging.

As noted in Section 14.1.1, the complete parameter vector $\hat{\Theta}$ allows us to
compute the prices of risk. The estimated parameters also allow us to estimate
the volatility $V(t)$ via the reprojection procedure. In the next section we will give
the details of the actual implementation. Therefore, we can compute the sample
paths for prices of risk appearing in Eqs. (7) and (8). These parameters are
reported in Fig. 14.3, which has three panels. Plot (A) shows the values of $\lambda_1(t)$
computed with the reprojected volatilities, while Plot (B) does the same for
$\lambda_2(t)$. Plot (C) reproduces the sample path of the actual reprojected volatilities
$\hat{V}(t)$. The first two plots display the time series processes, which represent the
risk adjustments to the Brownian motions W_s and W_v. Realizing that
$dW_v(t) = dW_v^*(t) - \lambda_2(t)dt$, it is clear that the risk-adjusted densities may differ
substantially from the objective Brownian motions. Hence, as it is not possible to
directly simulate processes under the risk neutral measure, one has to be careful
when simulating fundamental processes.

14.4 Assessing pricing and hedging performance

While statistical criteria for model selection are important, financial criteria such
as the out-of-sample pricing and hedging performance, form the basis of our
model selection process. Therefore, we investigate the performance of the alternative model specifications obtained from the previous section. In order to assess
the magnitude of the forecast errors, we use the Black–Scholes valuation model
as a benchmark. All evaluations reported in this section are obtained using the
post-estimation portion of our data set. The estimation sample used in the
preceding section covered November 1985 to October 1993, whereas the sample
used to appraise the models runs from November 1993 to October 1994.[17] Since

---

[16] We have to again express caution, as the observation regarding the numerical complexities
of computing standard errors when options data are used also applies to the bivariate setup.
[17] One could call this genuine out-of-sample approach, as in Dumas et al. (1998) or Jacquier
and Jarrow (1998), unlike the pricing and hedging performance evaluations which rely on in-
sample one-step-ahead forecasts.

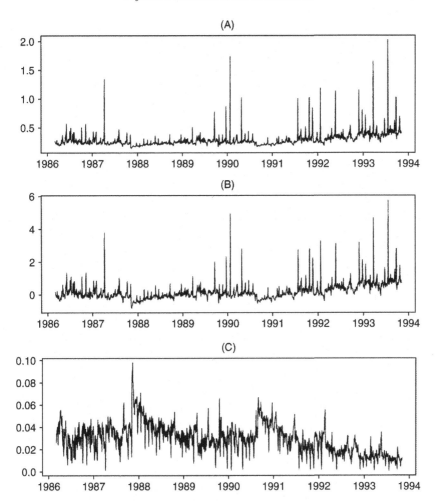

Fig. 14.3. The Market price of risk. The estimation of the Stochastic Volatility model based on bivariate data allows us to compute the market price of risk, $\lambda(t)$. We plot these prices for the entire estimation sample of daily data which span the period from November 1985 to October 1993. Panel (A) reports $\lambda_1(t)$, the market price of the asset risk, see Eq. (7). Panel (B) reports $\lambda_2(t)$, the market price of the volatility risk, see Eq. (8). Panel (C) is the time series of the reprojected volatility, $V(t)$, which was used to compute $\lambda_1(t)$ and $\lambda_2(t)$.

we use out-of-sample data, our results will not be contaminated by in-sample data mining. In our discussion of Plot (B) of Fig. 14.1, which displays the BS implied volatilities, we noted that a downward trend in volatilities, which began around 1991, reversed in the post-estimation part of our data set. This reversal will make the out-of-sample exercise particularly interesting.

A first subsection is devoted to the pricing of options. A second subsection looks at hedging, and we devote a separate subsection to a simple volatility filter for option pricing which emerges from our analysis. The examination of this filter is important given that all model configurations yield roughly the same parameter estimates (recall the results in Table 14.2). Hence, whenever the same option pricing formula is used, the differences in hedging and pricing are mostly due to filtering.

14.4.1 Pricing reliability

The model parameter estimates, the reprojection filters, and Heston's European call pricing formula yield the ingredients needed to price any SPX contract with a particular time to maturity, strike, and cash price for the underlying index. Equipped with these tools, we can compare the call prices predicted by the models with observed prices. In our appraisal, we do not consider in-the-money calls with moneyness greater than 1.03, as there is a very thin market for such options. Furthermore, we separate the calls into twelve groups, according to moneyness and time to maturity. Since the number of contracts varies through time, we assume that each group contains n_t options at time t.

Two measures of pricing errors are considered. The first is an absolute measure, denoted D_a^p, and has a dollar value scale. The second is a relative measure, denoted D_r^p, and reflects percentage deviations. The two measures are defined as follows:

$$D_a^p = \sqrt{\frac{1}{\sum_{t=1}^T n_t} \sum_{t=1}^T \sum_{i=1}^{n_t} (C_{it}^{\text{observed}} - C_{it}^{\text{model}})^2} \qquad (20)$$

and

$$D_r^p = \sqrt{\frac{1}{\sum_{t=1}^T n_t} \sum_{t=1}^T \sum_{i=1}^{n_t} \left(\frac{C_{it}^{\text{observed}} - C_{it}^{\text{model}}}{C_{it}^{\text{observed}}}\right)^2}. \qquad (21)$$

The results are divided in four different categories of moneyness. These are: deep out-of-the-money (OTM) with S/K less than 0.94, OTM with $0.94 < S/K < 0.97$, slightly OTM with $0.97 < S/K < 1$ and slightly in-the-money with $1 < S/K < 1.03$. The last two categories are usually viewed as at-the-money options. Three maturity horizons are considered for the moneyness categories, including short (less than 60 days), medium (between 60 and 180 days) and long (more than 180 days). The respective sample sizes for each of the twelve out-of-sample cells are reported in Table 14.3. For deep OTM options, we have between 313 and 448 contracts to use for computing pricing errors, and slightly fewer for computing hedging errors.[18] For the remaining three moneyness categories, there is a pronounced downward trend in the number of contracts as time-to-maturity

---

[18] The computation of hedging errors, which require contracts with trading activity on two consecutive days, will be discussed in the next subsection.

Table 14.3. Options groups used for evaluating model performance

Moneyness	Pricing sample ($n = 7424$) Days to expiration			Hedging sample ($n = 7132$) Days to expiration		
	< 60	60–180	≥ 180	< 60	60–180	≥ 180
< 0.94	337	448	313	299	437	279
0.94–0.97	1,080	828	168	1,037	818	159
0.97–1.00	1,377	938	195	1,324	930	187
1.00–1.03	1,038	612	90	975	604	83

To assess pricing and hedging performance of alternative model specifications, we separate the call options into twelve groups, sorted by moneyness and time to maturity. Moneyness is computed as the ratio of the current S&P 500 index level and the contract's strike price. The table reports the number of observations in each group. The total number of observations is reported in the headers.

increases. The maximum number of observations is 1,377, and the smallest is 90. Table 14.4 contains the pricing errors, D_a^p and D_r^p, computed for three different model specifications. The first specification, 'BS', prices options with the Black–Scholes model and a volatility estimate based on the previous day ATM option contract (see for instance Bates, 1996, for further discussion on this approach).

The aim of the present exercise is to compare the pricing performance of different models, giving each an equal chance to succeed. Since the implementation of BS is ad hoc, we make every attempt to implement SV in a consistent way, although this task is very difficult. The discussion in Bates (1996) allows us to view the ATM implied volatility as a way to introduce some consistency into the BS implementation. Furthermore, if we price a deep OTM contract based on its volatility implied from the previous day, we will obtain a smaller pricing error. However, this practice does not give an equal chance to results based on an SV formula, which could have been estimated based on OTM contracts as well. Since the focus of the present study is information extraction from ATM options and asset returns, we believe that the proposed scheme allows for a balanced approach to the task.

Next is the specification, denoted 'Vol', calculated using Heston's call price model estimated with a univariate options data set and a univariate reprojection filter. The specification denoted 'Joint' corresponds to the bivariate model. Besides the absolute and relative pricing errors for each of the twelve moneyness/maturity groups, Table 14.4 also reports whether there are any statistically significant differences between the pricing errors computed from these three specifications. We observe that, in general, pricing errors can be large, with absolute dollar values ranging from 5.23 to 0.42. Not surprisingly, large errors occur for longer maturities. The relative errors range from 20.71 to 0.14, with the same pattern.

For our purpose, a comparison across different model specifications is more important. As noted before, to appraise the differences we compute formal tests based on the following set of moment conditions, namely:

Table 14.4. The SV model pricing errors

Moneyness	Model	Pricing Errors Days to expiration						Models	Tests Days to expiration			All groups test
		<60		60–180		≥180			<60	60–180	≥180	
		D_a^p	D_r^p	D_a^p	D_r^p	D_a^p	D_r^p					
<0.94	BS	0.54	4.62	1.56	20.71	3.12	4.93	Vol-BS	3.61***	5.79**	0.29	16.81*
	Vol	0.42	2.01	0.92	12.58	2.26	4.06	Vol-Joint	2.69	10.40*	1.32	24.01*
	Joint	0.44	2.42	1.23	17.35	2.74	4.80	Joint-BS	2.81**	1.30	0.01	5.93**
0.94–0.97	BS	0.82	12.12	1.88	12.35	4.62	0.45	Vol-BS	10.95*	4.17**	17.64*	16.81*
	Vol	0.58	8.39	1.38	7.63	3.41	0.33	Vol-Joint	15.90*	5.42**	11.33*	24.01*
	Joint	0.73	10.79	1.66	9.91	3.86	0.37	Joint-BS	2.10	2.27	8.20*	5.93**
0.97–1.00	BS	1.13	5.78	2.48	0.38	5.23	0.31	Vol-BS	5.72**	19.63*	12.28*	16.81*
	Vol	1.05	4.46	2.20	0.30	4.24	0.24	Vol-Joint	4.93**	38.20*	18.07*	24.01*
	Joint	1.22	4.93	2.48	0.36	4.71	0.27	Joint-BS	3.08***	1.38	5.78**	5.93**
1.00–1.03	BS	1.25	0.14	2.31	0.17	4.63	0.18	Vol-BS	0.07	3.04***	8.16*	16.81*
	Vol	1.35	0.15	2.33	0.16	3.85	0.14	Vol-Joint	11.31*	13.49*	4.19**	24.01*
	Joint	1.40	0.16	2.43	0.17	4.21	0.16	Joint-BS	4.42**	0.07	3.24***	5.93**

We consider post estimation sample data from November 1993 to October 1994 to compute out-of-sample pricing errors. We evaluate three model specifications, according to moneyness and time to maturity. The first is 'BS', which involves pricing options with the Black–Scholes model and a volatility estimate based on the previous day at-the-money option contract. Next is the specification denoted 'Vol' in the table, which involves Heston's call price model estimated using a univariate specification involving options. The specification denoted 'Joint' corresponds to the bivariate specification. The first column is the moneyness category. The next column lists the model specifications. The third column reports the absolute standard error D_a^p (see Eq. (20)) and the relative standard error D_r^p (see Eq. (21)) by each maturity group. The remaining columns report the χ_2^2-statistics from the GMM overidentifying restrictions tests. These tests are aimed to determine whether the means of $((C_{it}^{observed} - C_{it}^{model})/(C_{it}^{observed}))^2$ computed from a pair of model estimates are significantly different. We report results of the tests within each group and overall. *indicates significance at the 1% level, **indicates significance at the 5% level, and ***indicates significance at the 10% level.

$$
\begin{pmatrix}
\left(\sum_{t=1}^{T} n_t\right)^{-1} \sum_{t=1}^{T}\sum_{i=1}^{n_t} ((C_{it}^{\text{observed}} - C_{it}^{\text{vol.model}})/(C_{it}^{\text{observed}}))^2 - m \\[2em]
\left(\sum_{t=1}^{T} n_t\right)^{-1} \sum_{t=1}^{T}\sum_{i=1}^{n_t} ((C_{it}^{\text{observed}} - C_{it}^{\text{joint.model}})/(C_{it}^{\text{observed}}))^2 - m
\end{pmatrix} = \begin{pmatrix} 0 \\ 0 \end{pmatrix}, \qquad (22)
$$

where m is the common mean relative error under the null hypothesis. Computations using the absolute errors could be performed as well, but are not reported here. The common parameter m in Eq. (22) implies that the two pricing errors have the same mean. Rejecting the null hypothesis of a common mean implies that one model is on average superior in producing price estimates. We can proceed in several ways to test the null hypothesis. The errors form a panel data set. On a daily basis, each maturity/moneyness cell contains a total of n_t contracts. The sample data are therefore correlated, which prevents us from considering a simple t-statistic. Instead, we use a GMM-based procedure involving a Newey and West estimator for the covariance matrix. The common mean, m, entails one overidentifying restriction on the moment conditions in (22). Therefore, the overidentifying restrictions test statistic is distributed as a χ^2, with one degree of freedom under the null hypothesis (see Hansen, 1982). The test statistics are reported in Table 14.4. We report overidentifying restrictions test statistics for pairwise comparisons between Vol and BS, Vol and Joint, and finally Joint versus BS. These tests are reported for the three maturity horizons and for each of the moneyness categories. In addition, we also report one joint statistic per moneyness category for pricing errors over all three maturity horizons combined.

The most striking result which emerges from the table is the dominance of the Vol approach. The comparisons of Vol and BS, Vol and Joint are always significant at the 1% level for all moneyness categories, with the three maturities combined. In each of the individual maturity-moneyness cells, we also observe the statistical significance of Vol, though there are exceptions, and most tests are only at the 5% or 10% level. Moreover, in each of the cases in which the over-identification test involving pairwise comparisons of Vol with either BS or Joint are significant, we find that the former has the smallest pricing error. Hence, the estimation of SV models involving only ATM options outperforms BS and the bivariate approach, denoted Joint. Besides yielding superior pricing performance, we observe from the results reported in Table 14.4 that the improvements over Black–Scholes volatility filter range from a 1.21 dollar reduction for OTM long maturity, to a small eight cents for slightly OTM short maturity. The Vol specification outperforms the Joint specification with the largest improvement for the deep OTM long maturity category, although the improvement is only 48 cents. The smallest difference is also in the same moneyness category but has short maturity and is equal to only 2 cents. It is worth emphasizing here that the comparisons between Joint and Vol involved the same call price formula of Heston and, basically, the same parameters (see Table 14.2). Hence, the differences are very much due to the filtering procedures, i.e. the procedure to extract the latent volatility process from the data.

Since the outperformance of the joint reprojection filter by the implied volatility reprojection filter model specification is somewhat surprising, we conducted further tests which are not reported in the table. These additional tests required a departure from the reprojection procedure described in Section 14.2.4. Since the details of the reprojection filter underlying Vol will be discussed in the next section, we focus only on the augmentation from Vol to Joint filtering, where the bivariate filter supplements the options data with returns series. It is not clear from the fitted SNP density in the reprojection routine whether certain individual moments of returns may provide information that enhances the pricing of options. To separate the potential contribution of individual moments, we computed reprojection filters only involving a particular moment of returns in addition to implied volatilities. For instance, to determine whether the mean return has any pricing information, we consider a bivariate filter with implied volatilities and past and concurrent returns. Hence, we ignore the Hermite polynomial expansion terms in the SNP density. This specific filter investigates the improvements brought by the leverage effect in the stock index, not already incorporated in the implied volatilities, to the pricing of European-type contracts. The same strategy can be applied to isolate the informational content of the second, third, and fourth power of returns. These computations reinforced our findings with the SNP reprojection filter, with one potentially important exception. We found that the conditional kurtosis, relying on a filter using a lag operator in the fourth power of returns in addition to implied volatilities, helps to improve the pricing of long maturity slightly in-the-money option contracts. The statistically significant improvement decreased the pricing error from 3.85 to 3.03 dollars.

The general conclusion we can draw so far is that Heston's call price model with a relatively simple volatility filtering scheme, using past options data, yields the most desirable outcome across all three model specifications considered. All models perform relatively well at short maturities, of course. The discrepancies emerge in the cells involving long maturities and OTM contracts. It should be noted that the estimation of the SV models was confined to ATM options. Therefore, one would expect that fitting and filtering with contracts similar to those priced out-of-sample, like OTM contracts, would certainly reduce the pricing errors of the Vol and Joint specifications. We will elaborate on this idea in the concluding section, and delegate this exploration to future research. In Section 14.4, we revisit some of these questions when we consider separating the filtering effects from the pricing kernel effects.

14.4.2 Hedging performance

A common practice for hedging market risk relies on a combination of stocks and options. Many hedging techniques exist, some of which are quite sophisticated and require the simultaneous consideration of several instruments. Many of the sophisticated hedging strategies are difficult to implement in practice (see Figlewski, 1998, for further discussion). We therefore concentrate on a simple minimum variance hedging strategy which uses just one option. In particular, if we want to hedge our position in one call with $N_s(t)$ shares of stock, we choose the number of shares in such a way that the remaining cash position

$$CP(t) = C(t, \tau, K) - N_s(t)S(t) \tag{23}$$

has minimum variance, which is achieved by taking

$$N_s(t) = \Delta_s(t, \tau, K) + \frac{\rho\sigma_v}{S(t)}\Delta_v(t, \tau, K), \tag{24}$$

where

$$\Delta_s(t, \tau, K) = \frac{\partial C(t, \tau, K)}{\partial S} = \Pi_1. \tag{25}$$

Note that this simple formula can be obtained because the SV option price in Eq. (3) is homogeneous of degree one in $S(t)$ and K (for further details, see Nandi, 1998). Finally, we also have that

$$\Delta_v(t, \tau, K) = \frac{\partial C(t, \tau, K)}{\partial V} = S(t)\frac{\partial \Pi_1}{\partial V} - Ke^{-R\tau}\frac{\partial \Pi_2}{\partial V}, \tag{26}$$

The Heston SV model does not account for all sources of risk. For example, this model assumes that the interest rate is constant. Therefore, if we try to unload our position the next day, we will not end up with a zero balance. The hedging error will therefore be

$$H(t + \Delta t) = N_s(t)S(t + \Delta t) + CP(t)e^{R\Delta t} - C(t + \Delta t, \tau - \Delta t, K), \tag{27}$$

where Δt is equal to one day.

We use summary statistics similar to those in the previous subsection to report the hedging performance for each model. In particular, we construct an absolute error (D_a^h) defined as

$$D_a^h = \sqrt{\frac{1}{\sum_{t=1}^{T} n_t}\sum_{t=1}^{T}\sum_{i=1}^{n_t} H_i^2(t)} \tag{28}$$

and comparable relative (D_r^h) measures. To obtain the latter, let us rewrite Eq. (27) as

$$H(t + \Delta t) = CP(t)e^{R\Delta t} - \overline{CP}(t + \Delta t) = \text{Cash}_{t+\Delta t}^{\text{model}} - \text{Cash}_{t+\Delta t}^{\text{observed}}, \tag{29}$$

where $\overline{CP}$ is different from CP because the number of shares was computed in the previous period, not as defined Eq. (23). This yields the relative measure of the hedging error, which is defined as

$$
D_r^h = \sqrt{\frac{1}{\sum_{t=1}^{T} n_t} \sum_{t=1}^{T} \sum_{i=1}^{n_t} \left(\frac{\text{Cash}_{it}^{\text{observed}} - \text{Cash}_{it}^{\text{model}}}{\text{Cash}_{it}^{\text{observed}}} \right)^2}
$$

$$
= \sqrt{\frac{1}{\sum_{t=1}^{T} n_t} \sum_{t=1}^{T} \sum_{i=1}^{n_t} \left(\frac{H_i(t)}{\overline{CP}_i(t)} \right)^2}.
$$

$$(30)$$

The hedging performance comparisons for the BS, Vol and Joint are reported in Table 14.5, again using the classification of 12 moneyness/time-to-maturity cells. The absolute and relative errors are complemented with statistical tests built on moment conditions, similar to Eq. (22), which yield an overidentifying restrictions test. We compute the overidentifying restrictions tests for all individual cells as in Table 14.4, including the grouped maturity tests shown in the last column of Table 14.5. We observe that the Vol specification is again the dominant one, yet not significantly different from both alternatives. In fact, all three specifications perform rather well, and hardly any of the overidentifying restrictions tests are significant, except in four individual cells suggesting some very weak improvements arising from the use of the Vol specification. Overall, we conclude from the results in Table 14.5 that hedging strategies, unlike the pricing errors, appear to be insensitive to model specification.

14.5 Disentangling filtering and pricing kernel effects

To determine the advantages of various filters, we need to construct a situation in which we can separate filtering effects from the pricing formula. In Table 14.4, for instance, the comparison of the Black–Scholes model pricing BS with the Heston model Vol, involves two components, one due to the filtering and the other due to the different pricing formula. In the first subsection, we examine all models through the window of the BS option pricing model, which allows us to separate and appraise the effect of the alternative volatility filters on the pricing of options. In the second subsection, we compare pricing performance of SV, BS, and GARCH option pricing models with their proper pricing formulas. For GARCH models, we follow Duan (1995), who developed a framework for option pricing under a local risk-neutral probability measure. This comparison will allow us to see whether any pricing formula more advanced than the Black–Scholes model adds any improvement in pricing performance. Moreover, this two-tier comparison allows us to separate the role of volatility filtering from that of the pricing kernel in pricing derivative contracts.

Table 14.5. The SV model hedging errors

We consider post estimation sample data from November 1993 to October 1994 to compute out-of-sample hedging errors. We evaluate three model specifications by moneyness and time to maturity. The first is 'BS', which involves pricing options with the Black–Scholes model and a volatility estimate based on the previous day at-the-money option contract. Next is the specification denoted 'Vol' in the table, which involves Heston's call price model estimated using a univariate specification involving options. The specification denoted 'Joint' corresponds to the bivariate specification. The first column is the moneyness category. The next column lists the model specifications. The third column reports the absolute standard error D_a^h (see Eq. (28)) and the relative standard error D_r^h (see Eq. (30)) by each maturity group. The remaining columns report the χ_1^2-statistics from the GMM overidentifying restrictions tests. These tests are aimed to determine whether the means of $((C_{it}^{observed} - C_{it}^{model})/(C_{it}^{observed}))^2$ computed from a pair of model estimates are significantly different. We report results of the tests within each group and overall. *indicates significance at the 1% level, **indicates significance at the 5% level, and ***indicates significance at the 10% level.

Moneyness	Model	Pricing errors days to expiration						Models	Tests Days to expiration			All groups test
		< 60		60–180		≥ 180			< 60	60–180	≥ 180	
		D_a^h	D_r^h	D_a^h	D_r^h	D_a^h	D_r^h					
< 0.94	BS	2.35	0.968	1.33	0.875	1.35	0.067	Vol-BS	0.34	0.01	3.44***	0.89
	Vol	2.43	0.751	1.33	0.881	1.37	0.029	Vol-Joint	0.81	2.24	1.02	1.07
	Joint	2.44	1.525	1.37	1.396	1.36	0.092	Joint-BS	0.47	2.18	0.30	1.10
0.94–0.97	BS	2.04	1.202	1.10	0.804	1.51	0.024	Vol-BS	0.05	0.03	1.76***	0.89
	Vol	2.06	1.064	1.07	0.718	1.62	0.009	Vol-Joint	1.24	0.99	3.75***	1.07
	Joint	2.07	0.470	1.07	0.053	1.61	0.010	Joint-BS	1.65	1.10	1.67	1.10
0.97–1.00	BS	2.26	5.368	1.30	0.013	2.37	0.012	Vol-BS	0.87	1.99	1.07	0.89
	Vol	2.25	1.570	1.30	0.007	2.34	0.009	Vol-Joint	1.00	4.81**	1.77	1.07
	Joint	2.22	0.066	1.30	0.008	2.35	0.009	Joint-BS	1.04	1.69	1.12	1.10
1.00–1.03	BS	1.75	0.005	1.67	0.005	3.97	0.012	Vol-BS	0.01	2.38	1.74	0.89
	Vol	1.77	0.005	1.66	0.005	3.38	0.011	Vol-Joint	1.01	7.20*	1.45	1.07
	Joint	1.77	0.005	1.67	0.005	3.54	0.011	Joint-BS	0.29	0.19	1.39	1.10

14.5.1 Filtering latent spot volatility
We propose to use BS, GARCH, and SV models first as volatility filters, and then, evaluate them via the BS formula. To facilitate the discussion, we introduce the following notation for the filtering schemes (estimators of the $\sqrt{V(t)}$: σ_t^I is the estimate of today's volatility by the previous day's BS implied ATM option, σ_t^G is the estimate of instantaneous volatility using a univariate GARCH(1, 1) model (see below for details), σ_{rt}^R is the estimate of instantaneous volatility via reprojection using a univariate scheme based on returns, and σ_{vt}^R is the estimate of instantaneous volatility via reprojection using a univariate scheme based on BS implied volatility.

Each of these filtering schemes warrant further discussion. Since the univariate Vol specification of Table 14.4 represents the most successful and novel approach, we first discuss the practical implementation of σ_{vt}^R. Constructing a reprojection filter involves a model selection procedure for the tuning parameters of the SNP density, namely K_z, K_X, M, M_μ and M_R. This time, the density is estimated this time with simulated data. To facilitate comparison, we report the reprojection model selection results in Panel C of Table 14.1 along side with the empirical sample results, which appear in Panel A of Table 14.1. Note that the SNP densities applied to the sample data are not comparable to those used in the reprojection. Recall from equation (18) that we are computing a conditional distribution of latent spot volatility given BS implied volatilities. Hence, in the case of Vol the densities reported in Panel A are univariate conditional densities of BS implied volatilities given their own past, whereas in Panel C we fit a conditional reprojection density of latent spot volatilities conditional on implied volatilities. Therefore, we do not expect the SNP densities to coincide. Moreover, the densities in Panel C cannot be autoregressive, involving past latent volatilities. Hence, no AR or ARCH parts appear in the fitted reprojection densities. The tuning parameters are again selected using the BIC criterion. For the reprojection density involving BS implied volatilities, the model specification that minimizes the BIC criterion is a simple linear operator with 22 lags. In Panel C of Table 14.1, we note that M_μ equals 22. Aside from a constant, no other tuning parameters are set to values greater than zero. Hence, the ATM implied volatilities are combined in a weighted historical moving average with a 22-day window.

The filter is remarkably simple, given that we started out with a general specification of a SNP conditional distribution. Table 14.6 lists the filter weights which extract spot volatility from BS implied volatilities. The weights range from 0.25 to 0.03. The intercept is negative, and equal to -0.16. The largest weights in the filter appear at the shorter lags, and the decrease in weights is roughly linear in the lags. Hence, the extraction scheme puts less weight on observations from the options markets that date back about one month, or 22 trading days.

The simplicity of this scheme is rather surprising if one thinks of the complexity of the task. Indeed, alternative filters, such as those proposed by Harvey et al. (1994), Jacquier et al. (1994), and Nelson and Foster (1994), require highly nonlinear functions of returns. Hence, the virtue of using volatility data to predict

Table 14.6. Reprojection model with implied volatilities

The coefficients of the reprojection model used to filter the latent volatility process from the observed past implied volatilities are listed in the table. We also report parameters of AR(22) model for the logarithm of implied volatilities

Lags	Reprojection		AR(22) model	
	Parameters	Std. err.	Parameters	Std. err.
0	−0.16320	0.01043	−1.00038	0.05046
1	0.24514	0.00149	0.45085	0.06300
2	0.20591	0.00144	0.15847	0.06863
3	0.18804	0.00147	−0.03892	0.06936
4	0.16293	0.00154	0.10117	0.06895
5	0.14055	0.00167	0.00499	0.06893
6	0.11489	0.00184	0.00697	0.06887
7	0.09978	0.00203	0.04363	0.06875
8	0.08792	0.00225	−0.04505	0.06827
9	0.07836	0.00253	−0.01029	0.06835
10	0.06675	0.00285	0.01011	0.06821
11	0.05675	0.00321	0.02365	0.06805
12	0.05069	0.00337	−0.08067	0.06818
13	0.04506	0.00365	0.07710	0.06840
14	0.04715	0.00384	0.01280	0.06865
15	0.04298	0.00405	−0.13689	0.06861
16	0.04179	0.00449	0.07321	0.06911
17	0.04882	0.00468	0.05775	0.06927
18	0.04386	0.00503	−0.10836	0.06954
19	0.03987	0.00529	0.12760	0.06964
20	0.03976	0.00554	0.01582	0.07011
21	0.03277	0.00587	−0.13449	0.06957
22	0.03280	0.00629	−0.00279	0.06478

future spot volatility is that one can limit the filter to a linear structure. It should be noted, however, that the construction of the filter is not as simple as running a linear regression model, as spot volatility is a latent process. Therefore, the calculation of the filter weights remains a nontrivial task which cannot be performed by simple regression methods. However, once diffusion parameters are available the task can be completed easily. To clarify this point, suppose that we would consider the simple task of regressing implied rather than spot volatilities on the same window of past implied volatilities. Such a linear regression model is also reported in Table 14.6, with its lag coefficients appearing along side the reprojection filter. The OLS parameter estimates show no resemblance, either numerically or statistically, to extraction filter weights. The difference between the two lag polynomials arises because implied volatility is, unlike spot volatility, related to the expected volatility over the remaining time to maturity of a contract (see, for instance, Hull and White, 1987 or Ghysels et al., 1996).[19] We noted before that to construct volatility estimates based on returns, σ_{rt}^R, Harvey et al. (1994) suggest using the approximate Kalman filter based on a discrete time SV model. The exact filter is derived by Jacquier et al. (1994) in the context of a Bayesian analysis of the same model. Along the same lines, one can use the reprojection approach using EMM applied to returns data. The parameter estimates are reported in Table 14.2, first line. This set of estmiates form the first of two return-based filters we will consider. The reprojection SNP tuning parameters for returns are again reported in Panel C of Table 14.1. Panel C of Table 14.1 also displays the reprojection density of the joint specification. We did not include this filter in the analysis of this section because the SV model using options data was shown to dominate the joint model in terms of pricing.

The next filter, namely σ_t^G, is based on the work of Nelson and Foster (1994) who show that diffusion limit arguments applied to the class of ARCH models provide a justification of ARCH models as filters for instantaneous volatility. To implement this filter, let us consider the GARCH option pricing model specified in Duan (1995). This model is described under the local risk-neutral probability measure by

$$\log S_t / S_{t-1} = R - \frac{1}{2} V(t) + \sqrt{V(t)} \varepsilon_t^* \qquad (31)$$

and

$$V(t) = \alpha_0 + \alpha_1 V(t-1)(\varepsilon_{t-1}^* - c - \lambda)^2 + \beta_1 V(t-1), \qquad (32)$$

where $\varepsilon_t^* \sim N(0, 1)$. Volatility in this case follows a NGARCH(1, 1), which is the conventional GARCH(1, 1) process of Bollerslev (1986) adjusted by the unit risk premium λ. The leverage effect is represented by c, which has an effect similar to that of ρ in Eq. (2).[20] To streamline the presentation we will focus on a GARCH model without leverage effects, and set c equal to zero. However, we did consider both GARCH with and without leverage in our empirical work. Finally, for the GARCH model, Eqs. (31) and (32) suggest to filter volatility, denoted as σ_t^G, using the following recursive relationship

---

[19] Furthermore, this volatility filtering scheme provides insights into the literature that evaluates implied volatilities as estimates of spot volatility. The motivation for the work in this area is the implication of the Hull and White (1997) model that the BS volatility is equal to the average integrated volatility over the remaining life of an option. The conclusions of the studies are somewhat mixed (see Bates, 1996, for a review). The major findings are that implied volatilities are positively biased estimates of the actual volatility, but still contain information about future volatility values.

[20] Note that, we have only one source of uncertainty in the GARCH model. Therefore, c is not a correlation coefficient.

$$\sigma_t^G = \left(\hat{\alpha}_0 + \hat{\alpha}_1 \left(\log\frac{S_{t-1}}{S_{t-2}} - R + \frac{1}{2}\sigma_{t-1}^{G2} - \hat{\lambda}\sigma_{t-1}^G \right)^2 + \hat{\beta}_1 \sigma_{t-1}^{G2} \right)^{1/2}, \qquad (33)$$

where the maximum likelihood estimates are: $\hat{\lambda} = 0.0599$, $\hat{\alpha}_0 = 0.556 \times 10^{-5}$, $\hat{\alpha}_1 = 0.127$, $\hat{\beta}_1 = 0.828$. As is typically the case for these models, the parameters are statistically significant and the models are not rejected by the data using standard diagnostics. The residuals and the squared residuals of the GARCH model are uncorrelated, and Portmanteau tests with up to 24 lags confirm the absence of residual autocorrelation. In particular, the p-values for residuals are equal to 0.212 (up to 6 lags), 0.574 (up to 12 lags), 0.743 (up to 18 lags), and 0.776 (up to 24 lags). The p-values for the squared residuals are equal to 0.928, 0.991, 0.998, and 0.999 respectively.

Fig. 14.4 presents the plots of the filtered volatilities. Panel (A) contrasts the BS implied volatilities and volatilities obtained from the GARCH model according to Eq. (33). Since the GARCH model is specified for daily observations, all the parameters pertain to the daily frequency, and the filtered volatility has daily units of measurement. To make the GARCH filtered volatility comparable to the BS volatilities and the SV-based volatilities, which have yearly units of measurement, we have multiplied the GARCH volatility by $\sqrt{250}$.[21] We see that the two filters of $\sigma_t(\sigma_t^I$ and $\sigma_t^G)$ provide very different forecasts. Panel (B) allows us to evaluate the volatility reprojected from the SV model estimated based on the returns data, σ_{rt}^R. In order to have a common benchmark of comparison with σ_t^G, we also plot σ_t^I in this panel. We note that σ_{rt}^R has a much smaller amplitude in comparison to both σ_t^I and σ_t^G. Finally, panel (B) of Fig. 14.4 also reports the reprojection filter from the SV model estimated with implied volatilities data, σ_{vt}^R. Although the filters in panel (B) are obtained from the same model specification with similar parameters estimates, σ_{rt}^R and σ_{vt}^R yield very different results, indicating that the key feature is not the model itself but the volatility filter it offers. This observation motivates us to consider all of the obtained filters in the framework of a single simple model, namely BS. The next section proceeds with the evaluation of the option pricing quality of the filters.

Table 14.7, Panel A, contains the pricing errors D_a^p and D_r^p. Obviously, GARCH and SV filters are suboptimal schemes here, as they are not used with their corresponding option pricing formula. We consider primarily the relative error term D_r^p, to appraise the differences, though Table 14.7 reports both types of errors. We observe that the GARCH filter σ_t^G is dominated by σ_t^I in every case except for the two long maturity ATM ($0.97 < S/K < 1.03$) groups. The best improvement of the GARCH filter over the implied volatilities is 1.79 dollars for the slightly OTM group, with relative error decreasing from 0.31 to 0.19. The best case of the implied volatility domination over GARCH is OTM medium maturity, where the price improvement is 95 cents with relative error decreasing from 19.62 to 12.35.

---

[21] We know that GARCH models do not temporally aggregate. Therefore, this operation gives us only a rough estimate for the yearly data, which is sufficient for visual comparison.

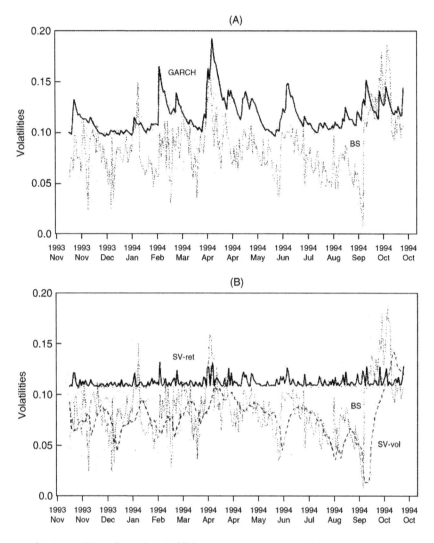

Fig. 14.4. The Filtered volatilities. We plot the volatilities $\hat{\sigma}_t$ which were estimated from different models. Panel (A) shows the volatility obtained from the GARCH model and the previous day Black–Scholes implied volatility. Panel (B) shows the volatility reprojected from the SV model based on the returns series and on the implied volatilities series. It also shows the implied volatilities to have a common benchmark with the GARCH volatility plot in (A).

In this table, the role of volatility filter and particular model specification in option pricing is evaluated separately. In Panel A we consider the pricing performance of various volatility filters by substituting them into the Black–Scholes option valuation formula. In panel B we assess whether the pricing formula associated with a particular volatility filter improves option pricing as compared to the Black–Scholes formula reported in Panel A. We consider three models. The first is 'BS', which is the Black–Scholes model, the second is 'GARCH' model as specified in Duan (1995), and the third, 'SV', is the stochastic volatility model of Heston (1993). The volatility filters considered are: σ_t^I – the estimate of today's volatility by the previous day's 'BS' implied ATM option; σ_t^G – the estimate of instantaneous volatility using the 'GARCH' model; σ_t^R – the estimate of instantaneous volatility via reprojection from 'SV' using a univariate scheme based on returns; σ_{rt}^R is the estimate of instantaneous volatility via reprojection from 'SV' using a univariate scheme based on BS implied volatilities. In Panels A and B, the first column is the moneyness category. The next column in Panel A lists the filters which are used in conjuction with the BS formula, while the second column in Panel B lists the filter/pricing formula combinations. The remaining columns are similar to the ones in Table 14.4. Namely, they report the absolute, D_a^p, and relative, D_r^p, errors by moneyness and maturity categories. GMM overidentifying restrictions tests, which determine whether the means of the relative pricing errors computed from a pair of models are significantly different, are reported next. In Panel A, pairwise tests within each moneyness-maturity group for all possible filters combinations (omitting repetitions) and overall groups tests are reported via the χ_1^2 statistics. The tests in Panel B compare the performance of the filter and pricing formula combinations and their BS formula counterparts from Panel A. The percentiles of the χ_1^2 distribution are: 90th – 2.71, 95th – 3.84, 99th – 6.63.

Panel A

| Moneyness | $\hat{\sigma}_t$ | Pricing errors days to expiration | | | | | | Pairwise tests days to expiration | | | | | | | | | All groups tests | | |
| | | < 60 | | 60–180 | | ≥ 180 | | < 60 | | | 60–180 | | | ≥ 180 | | | | | |
		D_a^p	D_r^p	D_a^p	D_r^p	D_a^p	D_r^p	σ_t^I	σ_t^G	σ_{rt}^R	σ_t^I	σ_t^G	σ_{rt}^R	σ_t^I	σ_t^G	σ_{rt}^R	σ_t^I	σ_t^G	σ_{rt}^R
< 0.94	σ_t^I	0.54	4.62	1.56	20.71	3.12	4.93	3.6	5.0		10.2	12.6		4.8	3.2		42.8	18.9	
	σ_t^G	0.67	6.71	2.35	33.15	3.77	16.49	2.3	4.5		0.5	18.6		4.5	4.4		27.2	53.6	
	σ_t^R	0.44	3.42	1.51	22.89	2.29	13.63	3.5		2.2	5.6		13.4	0.4		3.9	17.5		51.1
	σ_{vt}^R	0.42	2.03	1.01	12.61	3.03	3.65												
0.94–0.97	σ_t^I	0.82	12.12	1.88	12.35	4.62	0.45	30.4	14.6		9.3	0.4		0.0	8.8		42.8	18.9	
	σ_t^G	1.39	21.57	2.83	19.62	4.09	0.45	22.8	37.9		7.6	15.4		11.9	0.0		27.2	53.6	
	σ_t^R	1.08	18.34	2.13	18.93	2.93	0.34	11.7		38.1	4.5		15.8	0.1		11.0	17.5		51.1
	σ_{vt}^R	0.58	8.17	1.57	7.27	4.65	0.46												
0.97–1.00	σ_t^I	1.13	5.78	2.48	0.38	5.23	0.31	22.0	1.7		20.3	1.3		18.0	10.0		42.8	18.9	
	σ_t^G	1.84	12.78	2.66	0.53	3.44	0.19	18.4	22.1		8.1	20.4		28.2	19.4		27.2	53.6	
	σ_t^R	1.57	12.29	2.19	0.51	2.33	0.14	6.0		18.5	2.9		9.0	0.6		26.3	17.5		51.1
	σ_{vt}^R	1.10	4.37	2.60	0.35	5.79	0.33												
1.00–1.03	σ_t^I	1.25	0.14	2.31	0.17	4.63	0.18	29.2	9.8		1.8	8.12		11.0	2.7		42.8	18.9	
	σ_t^G	1.56	0.23	2.29	0.18	2.87	0.11	19.2	22.5		0.7	0.2		16.8	11.3		27.2	53.6	
	σ_t^R	1.35	0.21	1.95	0.16	2.18	0.09	0.7		13.2	1.1		2.2	0.0		16.8	17.5		51.1
	σ_{vt}^R	1.39	0.15	2.61	0.18	4.72	0.18												

Continues

Table 14.7. Continued

Panel B Moneyness	Model-$\hat{\sigma}_t$	Pricing errors days to expiration						Tests: model vs. BS days to expiration			All groups test
		< 60		60–180		≥ 180		< 60	60–180	≥ 180	
		D_a^p	D_r^p	D_a^p	D_r^p	D_a^p	D_r^p				
< 0.94	BS $- \sigma_t^I$	0.54	4.62	1.56	20.71	3.12	4.93				
	GARCH $- \sigma_t^G$	0.98	9.68	5.20	65.58	11.11	47.85	11.02	24.67	5.78	38.75
	SV $- \sigma_{rt}^R$	0.43	3.30	1.41	21.86	1.91	12.42	4.36	22.87	4.49	37.16
	SV $- \sigma_{vt}^R$	0.42	2.01	0.92	12.58	2.26	4.06	0.35	0.01	1.61	3.92
0.94–0.97	BS $- \sigma_t^I$	0.82	12.12	1.88	12.35	4.62	0.45				
	GARCH $- \sigma_t^G$	2.36	36.34	6.28	39.39	12.88	1.37	42.03	17.57	41.35	38.75
	SV $- \sigma_{rt}^R$	1.06	17.99	2.01	18.43	2.54	0.29	39.78	17.23	28.57	37.16
	SV $- \sigma_{vt}^R$	0.58	8.39	1.38	7.63	3.41	0.33	22.20	8.89	30.49	3.92
0.97–1.00	BS $- \sigma_t^I$	1.13	5.78	2.48	0.38	5.23	0.31				
	GARCH $- \sigma_t^G$	3.19	18.03	6.79	1.23	12.33	0.73	13.59	59.65	50.69	38.75
	SV $- \sigma_{rt}^R$	1.54	12.16	2.07	0.49	2.12	0.13	15.81	54.50	24.49	37.16
	SV $- \sigma_{vt}^R$	1.05	4.46	2.20	0.30	4.24	0.24	4.88	85.57	27.24	3.92
1.00–1.03	BS $- \sigma_t^I$	1.25	0.14	2.31	0.17	4.63	0.18				
	GARCH $- \sigma_t^G$	2.93	0.37	6.45	0.48	11.59	0.47	110.64	104.59	30.67	38.75
	SV $- \sigma_{rt}^R$	1.33	0.21	1.87	0.15	2.11	0.08	18.68	69.35	3.86	37.16
	SV $- \sigma_{vt}^R$	1.35	0.15	2.33	0.16	3.85	0.14	6.61	63.22	25.95	3.92

We also studied the performance of the GARCH model with leverage effects. The results are not reported in the table as they are qualitatively similar to the ones without leverage, though slightly and uniformly worse than the results obtained from GARCH without leverage. This observation is yet another example of conflicts between statistical and financial criteria. The leverage parameter in the GARCH model is statistically, though marginally, significant. Yet the resulting filter through the eyes of the Black–Scholes formula worsens the pricing performance. The same observation also applies to SV models, which are rejected on statistical grounds, while GARCH models are not rejected.

Table 14.7 also shows that the reprojection filter based on the model estimated with returns data σ_{rt}^R outperforms σ_t^I only for short maturity deep OTM and for long maturity OTM and ATM calls. The best improvement occurs again for the slightly OTM group, and is equal to 2.90 dollars with the relative error decreasing from 0.31 to 0.14. The best case where BS implied volatility dominates the returns reprojected volatility is the slightly OTM short maturity group with a 44 cents gain, for which the relative error changes from 12.29 to 5.78. The BS $- \sigma_{rt}^R$ specification uniformly dominates BS $- \sigma_t^G$ with the highest gain for the long maturity deep OTM calls equal to \$ 1.48, and the relative error dropping from 16.49 to 13.63. The lowest gain is 21 cents in the short maturity slightly ITM category. BS $- \sigma_{vt}^R$ dominates BS $- \sigma_t^I$ almost uniformly. The exceptions are slightly ITM short and medium maturities, and all long maturities except for deep OTM. However, in these cases, the differences displayed, are not statistically significant. The best improvement, which is equal to 55 cents, occurs in the medium maturity deep OTM group. These observations allow us to make some additional conclusions regarding the relative pricing performance of the four specifications. In particular, BS $- \sigma_t^G$, and therefore BS $- \sigma_{rt}^R$, clearly outperforms BS $- \sigma_{vt}^R$ for long maturity ATM calls. BS $- \sigma_{rt}^R$ also does better for the long maturity OTM group.

We can again conclude that the best volatility filter is σ_{vt}^R, with the exception of pricing long maturity and $0.94 < S/K < 1.03$ calls, for which σ_{rt}^R is the best. Both specifications are SV filters. We can provide several explanations for this result. The first is that long maturity contracts may reflect long memory, which is not taken into account by the models we evaluate in this paper. One would have to consider the long memory models (for SV see Comte and Renault, 1995, and Harvey, 1993; for GARCH models see Baillie et al., 1995). Nevertheless, one could speculate that the SV filters considered here have greater flexibility and capture some of the long memory characteristics. The fact that σ_{rt}^R outperforms σ_{vt}^R at long maturities may be exploited by relying on Backus et al. (1997) and Das and Sundaram (1999), who show that in the SV model kurtosis of returns increases with the time interval, or time to maturity in the option pricing context. Therefore, the volatilities implied from the long maturity contracts have a more pronounced smile effect. This suggests that, for shorter maturities, volatilities implied from the ATM options, as used in our computation of σ_{vt}^R, are a good proxy for all BS implied volatilities. However, this result does not apply to longer maturities. The ATM implied volatilities may be a good reflection of the returns kurtosis for short maturities, but they are not adequate for long maturities. Hence we have to use the fourth power of returns to adequately reflect the kurtosis in pricing long term options. Our results support this theoretical conjecture, especially because the SNP density involved in the returns based reprojection required all the moments of returns up to the fourth moment. This finding also confirms the results reported in the previous section which showed that bivariate returns and options filters dominate σ_{vt}^R only at long maturities. This outcome is due to the kurtosis effect captured by the fourth moment of returns, and is not present in the ATM options at short maturities underlying σ_{vt}^R.

14.5.2 The contribution of the pricing formula

We consider now whether a model generating a particular volatility filter is important for option pricing. In particular, we address the question whether there is any pricing improvement when we use the original pricing formula, relying on SV and GARCH modeling, rather than the Black–Scholes pricing formula. Panel B of Table 14.7 reports the results. Surprisingly, we observe that GARCH option pricing errors are dramatically and uniformly dominated by their BS – σ_t^G counterparts. The GARCH call option value is determined as the expected value of normalized payoff at maturity under the local risk-neutral measure, and can be computed via Monte-Carlo simulations. For our purpose, we adopt paper the empirical martingale simulation strategy proposed by Duan and Simonato (1998). The GARCH with leverage model, not reported in the table, performs roughly the same way. Overall, we need to conclude that the GARCH pricing formula does not perform very well for pricing options. The σ_{rt}^R filter combined with the SV option pricing formulas shows a very different and opposite picture. The SV formula uniformly improves upon its BS counterpart. Contrary to the σ_{rt}^R case, the volatilities-based SV filter substituted into the SV pricing formula shows a mixed picture. In particular, the BS – σ_{vt}^R combination is significantly better in three groups: OTM short maturity, OTM medium maturity, and slightly OTM short maturity. These findings prompt the question of whether the suboptimal BS – σ_t^G dominates GARCH option pricing, and why this result also happens in some of the BS – σ_{vt}^R cases. One possible interpretation is that the parsimony of BS comes into play. The Black–Scholes model appears to be so robust that, when used here with the GARCH volatility filter σ_t^G, for example, it smoothes out the GARCH deficiencies and prices options better.

The general conclusion we can draw from Table 14.7 is that the Heston SV model almost always provides both superior volatility filtering and option pricing. Within the Heston model, the filter specification based on implied volatilities is the best performer, with the exception of long maturity options, which are better priced with σ_{rt}^R. On the other hand, one can notice that the volatility filtering becomes more important than the option pricing formula in which the volatiltiy is subsequently substituted. For example, the differences in pricing errors between BS – σ_{vt}^R and SV – σ_{vt}^R are minimal if compared with pricing errors obtained from other volatility filtering schemes for short and medium maturity options.

14.6 Conclusion

We considered a generic procedure for estimating and pricing options in the context of stochastic volatility models using simultaneously the fundamental price, S_t, and a set of option contracts $[(\sigma_{it}^I)_{i=1, K}]$ where $K \geq 1$ and σ_{it}^I is the Black–Scholes implied volatility. The joint estimation enabled us to recover objective and risk neutral measures simultaneously. This approach, bridging two strands of the literature, opens new possibilities for comparing the information in the underlying fundamental and options data, for conducting tests examining the transformation between the two measures, and investigating the general equilibrium underpinnings of models. Moreover, the bivariate approach involving both the underlying fundamental and an option appears useful for pricing derivatives when the information from the cash market, through the conditional kurtosis of returns, provides support to price options. This result holds for some long term options but the effect is only marginal. However, our results based on the S&P 500 index contract, showed that the univariate approach only involving options dominated for the purpose of pricing. A by-product of this finding is that we uncover a remarkably simple volatility extraction filter based on a polynomial lag structure of implied volatilities. Since the competing model specifications yielded roughly similar diffusion parameter estimates, we found that the filtering of spot volatility is the key ingredient in our procedure. In fact, by comparing various volatility filters, we found that the filter based on implied volatilities performs very well even if it is used in combination with the Black–Scholes formula.

At the general level, our results demonstrate how volatility filters obtained from the same model, and the same parameter estimates, can be very different because alternative filters exploit the information in the panel structure of options and returns differently. Our analysis also shows that financial criteria, like pricing and hedging performance, represent the most valuable selection methods. Models which are rejected using statistical goodness of fit criteria, in our case Heston's model, can be the basis for a relatively effective filter, when effectiveness is measured with respect to pricing. On the contrary, models that fit the data well, like GARCH, might turn out to be quite ineffective when it comes to valuing derivative securities.

Ultimately, financial and statistical criteria need to be reconciled. Heston's model has its obvious limitations, since it assumes that interest and dividend rates are constant. Several extensions of the Heston model have been suggested, including the addition of state variables which determine stochastic interest rates, dividends, and jump components. In particular, Bakshi and Madan (2000) and Duffie et al. (1998) discuss a general framework of jump-diffusions of the affine class which yields analytical option pricing formulas. The generic framework imposes a certain uniformity on the empirical studies in option pricing because the models are easier to compare, given that they are nested in the general model specification.

The methods proposed in this paper can be improved upon in several ways. First, we estimated the continuous time processes using only ATM contracts. It would be worth investigating a specification where more than one option is used, namely a set of option contracts $[(\sigma_{it}^I)_{i=1,K}]$ where some are ATM and others are OTM. This setup will surely improve the pricing of long term OTM options. It would also be intriguing to find out how multivariate filters using several options contracts perform in comparison to the univariate option-based filter. Last but not least, it would be worth exploring the result suggesting that conditional kurtosis information in the cash market improves pricing. One could consider using LEAPS option contracts for such an exploration.

Appendix A: The call options pricing using SV model

We provide the details of the call options pricing formula under the SV model from Bakshi et al. (1997). The call price in Eq. (3) is expressed through $\Pi_j, j = 1, 2$, which are equal to:

$$\Pi_j = \frac{1}{2} + \frac{1}{\pi} \int_0^\infty \mathrm{Re} \frac{e^{-i\phi \ln K} f_j(t, \tau, S(t), V(t); \phi)}{i\phi} \, d\phi \qquad (\text{A.1})$$

and

$$
\begin{aligned}
f_1&(t, \tau, S(t), V(t); \phi) \\
&= \exp\left\{ i\phi R\tau - \frac{\theta^*}{\sigma_V^2} \left[2\ln\left(1 - \frac{[\xi - \kappa^* + (i\phi + 1)\rho\sigma_v](1 - e^{-\xi\tau})}{2\xi} \right) \right] \right. \\
&\quad - \frac{\theta^*}{\sigma_v^2} [\xi - \kappa^* + (i\phi + 1)\rho\sigma_v]\tau + i\phi \ln S(t) \\
&\quad \left. + \frac{i\phi(i\phi + 1)(1 - e^{-\xi\tau})V(t)}{2\xi - [\xi - \kappa^* + (1 + i\phi)\rho\sigma_v](1 - e^{-\xi\tau})} \right\},
\end{aligned}
\qquad (\text{A.2})
$$

where

$$\xi = \sqrt{[k^* - (1 + i\phi)\rho\sigma_v]^2 - i\phi(i\phi + 1)\sigma_v^2}, \qquad (\text{A.3})$$

and

$$
\begin{aligned}
f_2&(t, \tau, S(t), V(t); \phi) \\
&= \exp\left\{ i\phi R\tau - \frac{\theta^*}{\sigma_v^2} \left[2\ln\left(1 - \frac{[\psi - \kappa^* + i\phi\rho\sigma_v](1 - e^{-\psi\tau})}{2\psi} \right) \right] \right. \\
&\quad - \frac{\theta^*}{\sigma_v^2} [\psi - \kappa^* + i\phi\rho\sigma_v]\tau + i\phi \ln S(t) \\
&\quad \left. + \frac{i\phi(i\phi - 1)(1 - e^{-\psi\tau})}{2\psi - [\psi - k^* + i\phi\rho\sigma_v](1 - e^{-\psi\tau})} V(t) \right\},
\end{aligned}
\qquad (\text{A.4})
$$

and

$$\psi = \sqrt{[k^* - i\phi\rho\sigma_v]^2 - i\phi(i\phi - 1)\sigma_v^2} \qquad (A.5)$$

Appendix B: SNP density estimation

SNP is a method of nonparametric time series analysis which employs a Hermite polynomial series expansion to approximate the conditional density of a multivariate process. An appealing feature of this expansion is that it is a nonlinear nonparametric model that directly nests the Gaussian VAR model, the semiparametric VAR model, the Gaussian ARCH model, and the semiparametric ARCH model. The SNP model is fitted using conventional maximum likelihood methods, together with a model selection strategy that determines the appropriate degree of the polynomial.

The SNP method is based on the notion that a Hermite expansion can be used as a general purpose approximation to a density function. Here, it is employed in the form $f_k(z_t|X_t, \Xi) \propto [P_K(z_t, X_t)^2]\phi(z_t)$, where $P_K(\cdot)$ denotes a multivariate polynomial of degree K_z and $\phi(z)$ denotes the standard normal, possibly multivariate, probability density function (p.d.f.). The process X_t is the vector of M lags of the process of interest. The index k denotes the dimension of Ξ, which expands as the sample size increases (see discussion in Section 2.1). Since $f_k(z)$, as the distribution proxy, has to integrate to 1, the constant of proportionality is the inverse of $N_K(X_t) = \int [P_K(s, X_t)^2]\phi(s)\mathrm{d}s$. To achieve a unique representation, the constant term of the polynomial part is set equal to one.

First of all, let us note that if the process of interest $\iota \sim N(\mu, \Sigma = RR')$, where R is an upper triangular matrix, then $\iota = Rz + \mu$ and

$$f_k(\iota|X_t, \Xi) = \frac{1}{N_K(X_t)} \frac{[P_K(z_t, X_t)^2]\phi(z_t)}{|det(R)|}, \qquad (B.1)$$

where $\Xi = (a_{ij}, \mu, R)$ and is estimated by QML.

The mean μ at time t depends on M_μ lags of ι: $\mu_t^X = b_0 + BX_t$. R_t^X also depends on M_R lags of the process of interest, when an ARCH leading term is present. A Hermite polynomial is used to expand the density around the leading Gaussian density, namely

$$P_K(z_t, X_t) = \sum_{i=0}^{K_z} a_i(X_t) z^i = \sum_{i=0}^{K_z} \left(\sum_{j=0}^{K_X} a_{ij} X_t^j \right) z^i. \qquad (B.2)$$

As discussed above, we set a_{00} equal to 1 for the uniqueness of the representation. The subscript K denotes the vector (K_X, K_z, M). According to Andersen and Lund (1996), if the leading term is specified carefully, $M = 1$ generally suffices in the univariate SNP setting.

When K_z is set equal to zero, one obtains normal distributions. When K_z is positive and $K_X = 0$, one obtains a density which is conditionally homogeneous with respect to X. Finally, when both K_z and K_X are positive, we obtain conditionally heterogeneous classes of densities.

The optimal values of K, (as well as M_μ and M_R), are chosen based on standard criterions and tests, such as AIC, BIC and HQ model selection criteria. Gallant and Tauchen (1993) provide a table which matches values of the parameters K, M_μ, M_R, to popular time series models. We reproduce this table here (Table 14.8). Typically, BIC is used to select the model specification. We follow this strategy in Table 14.1, Panels A and C.

Appendix C: Details of the SDE discretization scheme

The discussion in this appendix is based on Kloeden and Platen (1995), to which we refer the reader for additional details.

The EMM estimation procedure requires the process under study to be simulated. It is impossible to simulate the actual process if it does not have an analytical solution, which is the case for Heston's model. Therefore, to simulate the process at hand, we need to discretize the process specified in Eqs. (1) and (2). The discretizations are based on the truncation of the Ito–Taylor expansion formula. The more terms we use, the more accurate is the expansion. The Ito–Taylor formula also involves the derivatives of the drift and diffusion coefficients with respect to the process of interest. Hence, an approximation of these derivatives may be advisable to improve computational efficiency. The discretization schemes mainly differ in the number of terms that one keeps and the way one approximates, or fails to approximate, the above-mentioned derivatives. For the following reasons, we choose to work with the explicit order 2.0 weak discretization scheme.

Each strong scheme of order p is a weak scheme of order $2p$. Schemes are classified as weak if they approximate moments rather than sample paths of a diffusion. Strong schemes, on the other hand, approximate sample paths. Moreover, strong schemes require more time to simulate, and since we match moments instead of sample paths in our estimation, we use a weak scheme. The order of the scheme determines the quality of an approximation. We say that a discrete approximation $Y(\Delta t) = (S_n, V_n)'$ of the process $X = (S(t), V(t))'$ converges weakly with order $p > 0$ to X at time T as $\Delta t \to 0$ if, for each moment M, there exists a positive constant C which does not depend on Δt, and a finite $\Delta_0 t$ such that

$$|M(X_T) - M(Y_T(\Delta t))| \leq C\Delta t^p \tag{C.1}$$

for any $\Delta t \in (0, \Delta_0 t)$. In our case $p = 2$, which yields a faster convergence than the commonly used Euler discretization, a weak scheme of order 0.5. Note that, following the tradition in the option pricing literature, we estimate the annualized parmeters, taking $\Delta t = 1/252$. Kloeden and Platen show that, under standard regularity conditions, the moments of the diffusions exist provided the initial value is a constant (see Kloeden and Platen, 1995, Theorem 4.5.4). The discretization scheme guarantees that the moments of the discretized processes also exist. Therefore, it is legitimate to implement the moments matching procedure.

The term "explicit" in the discretization scheme refers to the derivatives approximation method. In case of deterministic differential equations, this method works similar to the Runge–Kutta methods. Since this method imposes fewer computational burdens than the implicit scheme, it is often preferable to use.

This approach also allows us to control for the non-synchronicity bias discussed in the data section. We can show that by matching moments instead of sample paths, the error introduced by the differential in stock prices over the fifteen minute closing interval has a negligible impact on the estimation of the moments. We simulate the fundamental process as being observed at 4:00 pm, or time T, and we use these simulated values to substitute in the implied volatility function, $I(S_t, V_t)$, implicitly based on the option price, which is observed at 4:15 pm, or time $T + \delta t$. We will use the Ito–Taylor expansion formula to compute the error introduced by this operation. The EMM procedure matches the moments of the function $I(\cdot)$. Therefore, we have to assess the size of the error for all possible moments $E(I^n(\cdot))$. Since it is a sufficiently smooth function, we can approximate it with polynomials based on $(S_t, V_t)'$ to any degree of accuracy. Hence, in our discussion, we will consider $E(f(S_t, V_t))$ for any smooth function f. In particular, according to Theorem 5.5.1 of Kloeden and Platen (1995), we can write:

$$
\begin{aligned}
f(S_{T+\delta t}, V_{T+\delta t}) = &\, f(S_T, V_T) + f_{(0)}(S_T, V_T) \int_T^{T+\delta t} \mathrm{d}u \\
&+ f_{(1)}(S_T, V_T) \int_T^{T+\delta t} \mathrm{d}W_s(u) \\
&+ f_{(2)}(S_T, V_T) \int_T^{T+\delta t} \mathrm{d}W_v(u) \\
&+ f_{(1,1)}(S_T, V_T) \int_T^{T+\delta t} \int_T^v \mathrm{d}W_s(u)\mathrm{d}W_s(v) \quad\quad \text{(C.2)} \\
&+ f_{(2,2)}(S_T, V_T) \int_T^{T+\delta t} \int_T^v \mathrm{d}W_v(u)\mathrm{d}W_v(v) \\
&+ f_{(1,2)}(S_T, V_T) \int_T^{T+\delta t} \int_T^v \mathrm{d}W_s(u)\mathrm{d}W_v(v) \\
&+ f_{(2,1)}(S_T, V_T) \int_T^{T+\delta t} \int_T^v \mathrm{d}W_s(u)\mathrm{d}W_v(v) + \mathrm{o}(\delta t),
\end{aligned}
$$

where $f_{(\cdot)}$ are the Ito coefficient functions (Kloeden and Platen, 1995, 5.3). As we already mentioned, we are interested in the accuracy of the moments. Therefore, we have to compute $E(f(S_{T+\delta t}, V_{T+\delta t}))$:

$$E(f(S_{T+\delta t}, V_{T+\delta t}))$$
$$= E(f(S_T, V_T)) + E(f_{(0)}(S_T, V_T))\delta t + o(\delta t)$$
$$= E(f(S_T, V_T)) + E\left(\frac{\partial}{\partial t} + \mu_s S \frac{\partial}{\partial S} + (\theta - \kappa V)\frac{\partial}{\partial V}\right.$$
$$\left. + \frac{1}{2}VS^2\frac{\partial^2}{\partial S^2} + \sigma_V \rho VS \frac{\partial^2}{\partial S \partial V} + \frac{1}{2}\sigma_v^2 V \frac{\partial^2}{\partial V}\right) f(S_T, V_T)\delta t + o(\delta t) \qquad (C.3)$$
$$= E(f(S_T, V_T)) + o(\delta t).$$

The last equality follows from the fact that the expected value of the infinitesimal generator $f_{(0)}(S_T, V_T)$ of the process specified in Eqs. (1) and (2) is equal to zero (see, for instance, Hansen and Scheinkman, 1995). Since the interval δt is relatively small, at 1/96th of the simulation interval Δt, substituting $f(S_{T+\delta t}, V_{T+\delta t})$ by $f(S_T, V_T)$ in the implied volatility moments matching procedure introduces only a negligable error.

References

Aït-Sahalia, Y. and Lo, A. (1998). Nonparametric estimation of state-price densities implicit in financial prices. *Journal of Finance* 53, 499–548.

——— Wang, Y., and Yared, F. (1997). Do options markets correctly price the probabilities of movements of the underlying asset? Unpublished discussion paper. University of Chicago, IL.

Andersen, T. G., Chung, H.-J., and Sørensen, B. E. (1999). Efficient method of moments estimation of a stochastic volatility model: a Monte Carlo study. *Journal of Econometrics* 91, 61–87.

——— Lund, J. (1996). The short rate diffusion revisited: an investigation guided by the efficient method of moments. Unpublished discussion paper, Northwestern University, Evanston, IL.

——— ——— (1997). Estimating continuous-time stochastic volatility models of the short-term interest rate. *Journal of Econometrics* 77, 343–77.

Backus, D., Foresi, S., Li, K., and Wu, L. (1997). Accounting for biases in Black–Scholes. Unpublished discussion paper, New York University.

Bakshi, G., Cao, C., and Chen, Z. (1997). Empirical performance of alternative option pricing models. *Journal of Finance* 52, 2003–49.

——— Madan, D. B. (2000). Spanning and derivative-security valuation. *Journal of Financial Economics* 55.

Bates, D. S. (1996). Testing option pricing models. In: Maddala, G. S., Rao, C. R. (eds.), *Handbook of Statistics, Vol. 14*. Elsevier, Amsterdam.

Bollerslev, T. (1986). Generalized autoregressive conditional heteroscedasticity. *Journal of Econometrics* 31, 307–27.

Broadie, M., Detemple, J., Ghysels, E., and Tòrres, O. (1997). American options with stochastic volatility and dividends: a nonparametric approach. *Journal of Econometrics*, forthcoming.

Campbell, J., Lo, A., and MacKinlay, C. (1997). The Econometrics of Financial Markets. Princeton University Press, Princeton, NJ.

Canina, L. and Figlewski, S. (1993). The informational content of implied volatility. *Review of Financial Studies* 6, 659–81.

Comte, F. and Renault, E. (1995). Long memory continuous time stochastic volatility models. Paper presented at the HFDF-I Conference, Zurich.

Cox, J., Ingersoll, J. E., and Ross, S. A. (1985). A theory of the term structure of interest rates. *Econometrica* 53, 385–408.

Christensen, B. J. and Prabhala, N. R. (1998). The relation between implied and realized volatility. *Journal of Financial Economics* 50, 125–50.

Das, S. and Sundaram, R. (1999). Of smiles and smirks: a term-structure perspective. *Journal of Financial and Quantitative Analysis* 34, 211–40.

Day, T. and Lewis, C. (1992). Stock market volatility and the information content of stock index options. *Journal of Econometrics* 52, 267–87.

Duan, J. C. (1995). The GARCH option pricing model. *Mathematical Finance* 5, 13–32.

——— Simonato, J. G. (1998). Empirical martingale simulation for asset prices. *Management Science* 44, 1218–33.

Duffie, D., Pan, J., and Singleton, K. J. (1998). Transform analysis and option pricing for affine jump-diffusions. *Econometrica*, forthcoming.

Dumas, B., Fleming, J., and Whaley, R. E. (1998). Implied volatility functions: empirical tests. *Journal of Finance* 53, 2059–106.

Figlewski, S. (1998). Derivatives risks, old and new. Wharton–Brookings Papers on Financial Services I.

Fleming, J. (1998). The quality of market volatility forecasts implied by S&P 100 index option prices. *Journal of Empirical Finance* 5, 317–45.

Gallant, A. R., Hsieh, D. A., and Tauchen, G. (1997). Estimation of stochastic volatility models with diagnostics. *Journal of Econometrics* 81, 159–92.

——— Hsu, C.-T., and Tauchen, G. (1999). Using daily range data to calibrate volatility diffusions and extract the forward integrated variance, *Review of Economics and Statistics*, 81, 617–31.

——— Long, J. R. (1997). Estimating stochastic differential equations efficiently by minimum chi-square. *Biometrika* 84, 125–41.

——— Tauchen, G. (1989). Seminonparametric estimation of conditionally constrained heterogeneous processes: asset pricing applications. *Econometrica* 57, 1091–120.

——— ——— (1993). S. P. A program for nonparametric time series analysis. Version 8.3, User's Guide. University of North Carolina, Chapel Hill, unpublished discussion paper.

——— ——— (1996). Which moments to match?. *Econometric Theory* 12, 657–81.

——— ——— (1997). E. M. A program for Efficient Method of Moments estimation. Version 1.4, User's guide. Unpublished discussion paper. Duke University, Durham, NC.

Gallant, A. R. and Tauchen, G. (1998). Reprojecting partially observed systems with application to interest rate diffusions. *Journal of American Statistical Association* 93, 10–24.

Ghysels, E., Harvey, A. C., and Renault, E. (1996). Stochastic volatility. In: Maddala, G. S., Rao, C. R. (eds.), *Handbook of Statistics, Vol. 14*. Elsevier, Amsterdam.

——— Jasiak, J. (1996). Stochastic volatility and time deformation. Unpublished discussion paper, Centre interuniversitaire de recherche en analyse des organisations (CIRANO) Montreal.

Hansen, L. P. (1982). Large sample properties of generalized method of moments estimators. *Econometrica* 50, 1029–54.

Hansen, L. P. and Scheinkman, J. (1995). Back to the future: generating moment implications for continuous-time Markov processes. *Econometrica* 63, 767–804.

Harrison, M and Kreps, D. M. (1979). Martingales and arbitrage in multiperiod securities markets. *Journal of Economic Theory* 20, 381–408.

—— Pliska, S. (1981). Martingales and stochastic integrals in the theory of continuous trading. *Stochastic Processes and Their Applications* 11, 215–60.

Harvey, A. C. (1993). Long memory in stochastic volatility. Unpublished discussion paper. London School of Economics.

—— Ruiz, E., and Shephard, N. (1994). Multivariate stochastic variance models. *Review of Economic Studies* 61, 247–64.

Harvey, C. R. and Whaley, R. E. (1991). S&P 100 index option volatility. *Journal of Finance* 46, 1551–61.

Heston, S. L. (1993). A closed-form solution for options with stochastic volatility with applications to bond and currency options. *Review of Financial Studies* 6, 327–43.

Hull, J. and White, A. (1987). The pricing of options on assets with stochastic volatilities. *Journal of Finance* 42, 281–300.

Jacquier, E. and Jarrow, R. A. (1998). Model error in contingent claim models: dynamic evaluation. *Journal of Econometrics* forthcoming.

—— Polson, N. G., and Rossi, P. E. (1994). Bayesian analysis of stochastic volatility models (with discussion). *Journal of Business and Economic Statistics* 12, 371–417.

—— —— (1995). Stochastic volatility: univariate and multivariate extensions. Unpublished discussion paper, Boston College.

Jiang, G. and van der Sluis, P. (1998). Pricing stock options under stochastic volatility and interest rates with efficient method of moments estimation. Unpublished discussion paper, University of Groningen, Netherlands.

Kloeden, P. E. and Platen, E. (1995). Numerical Solution of Stochastic Differential Equations. Springer, New York, NY.

Lamoureux, C. G. and Lastrapes, W. D. (1993). Forecasting stock-return variance: toward an understanding of stochastic implied volatilities. *Review of Financial Studies* 6, 293–326.

Melino, A. (1994). Estimation of continuous-time models in finance. In: Sims, C. A. (ed.), *Advances in Econometrics*. Cambridge University Press, Cambridge.

Nandi, S. (1998). How important is the correlation between returns and volatility in a stochastic volatility model? Emprical evidence from pricing and hedging in the S&P 500 index options market. *Journal of Banking and Finance* 22, 589–610.

Nelson, D. B. and Foster, D. P. (1994). Asymptotic filtering theory for univariate ARCH models. *Econometrica* 62, 1–41.

—— —— (1996). Asymptotic filtering theory for multivariate ARCH models. *Journal of Econometrics* 62, 1–41.

Pastorello, S., Renault, E., and Touzi, N. (1994). Statistical inference for random variance option pricing. *Journal of Business and Economic Statistics*, forthcoming.

Renault, E. (1997). Econometric models of option pricing errors. In: Kreps, D. M., Wallis, K. F. (eds.), *Advances in Economics and Econometrics: Theory and Applications, Seventh World Congress, Vol. 3*. Cambridge University Press, Cambridge.

Romano, M. and Touzi, N. (1997). Contingent claims and market completeness in a stochastic volatility model. *Mathematical Finance* 7, 399–412.

Rubinstein, M. (1994). Implied binomial trees. *Journal of Finance* 49, 771–818.

Rydberg, T. H. (1997). A note on the existence of unique equivalent martingale measures in a Markovian setting. *Finance and Stochastics* 1, 251–7.

Scott, L. O. (1987). Option pricing when the variance changes randomly: theory, estimation, and an application. *Journal of Financial and Quantitative Analysis* 22, 419–38.

Tauchen, G. (1997). New minimum chi-square methods in empirical finance. In: Kreps, D. M., Wallis, K. F. (eds.), *Advances in Economics and Econometrics: Theory and Applications, Seventh World Congress, Vol. 3.* Cambridge University Press, Cambridge.

Wiggins, J. B. (1987). Option values under stochastic volatility: theory and empirical estimates. *Journal of Financial Economics* 19, 351–72.

Part IV
Realised variation

15
The Distribution of Realized
Exchange Rate Volatility*

TORBEN G. ANDERSEN, TIM BOLLERSLEV,
FRANCIS X. DIEBOLD, AND PAUL LABYS[†]

Using high-frequency data on deutschmark and yen returns against the dollar, we construct model-free estimates of daily exchange rate volatility and correlation that cover an entire decade. Our estimates, termed realized volatilities and correlations, are not only model-free, but also approximately free of measurement error under general conditions, which we discuss in detail. Hence, for practical purposes, we may treat the exchange rate volatilities and correlations as observed rather than latent. We do so, and we characterize their joint distribution, both unconditionally and conditionally. Noteworthy results include a simple normality-inducing volatility transformation, high contemporaneous correlation across volatilities, high correlation between correlation and volatilities, pronounced and persistent dynamics in volatilities and correlations, evidence of long-memory dynamics in volatilities and correlations, and remarkably precise scaling laws under temporal aggregation.

Keywords: Forecasting; High-frequency Data; Integrated volatility; Long-memory; Quadratic variation; Realized volatility; Risk management.

* This work was previously published as T. G. Andersen, T. Bollerslev, F. X. Diebold, and P. Labys (2001), 'The Distribution of Exchange Rate Volatility', *Journal of the American Statistical Association* 96, 453. Copyright © 2001 American Statistical Association. Reproduced by kind permission.

† This work was supported by the National Science Foundation. The authors are grateful to Olsen and Associates for making the intraday exchange rate quotations available. The authors thank participants at the 1999 North American and European Meetings of the Econometric Society, the Spring 1999 National Bureau of Economic Research Asset Pricing Meeting, the 2000 Western Finance Association Meeting, and seminars at Boston University, Chicago, Columbia, Georgetown, International Monetary Fund, Johns Hopkins, New York University, and London School of Economics (LSE), as well as the editor, associate editor, two anonymous referees, Dave Backus, Michael Brandt, Rohit Deo, Rob Engle, Clive Granger, Lars Hansen, Joel Hasbrouck, Ludger Hentschel, Cliff Hurvich, Blake LeBaron, Richard Levich, Bill Schwert, Rob Stambaugh, George Tauchen, and Stephen Taylor. Much of this paper was written while Diebold was visiting the Stern School of Business, New York University, whose hospitality is gratefully acknowledged.

15.1 Introduction

It is widely agreed that although daily and monthly financial asset returns are approximately unpredictable, return *volatility* is highly predictable, a phenomenon with important implications for financial economics and risk management (e.g. Bollerslev, Engle, and Nelson 1994). Of course, volatility is inherently unobservable, and most of what we know about volatility has been learned either by fitting parametric econometric models such as generalized autoregressive conditional heteroscedasticity (GARCH), by studying volatilities implied by options prices in conjunction with specific option pricing models such as Black–Scholes, or by studying direct indicators of volatility such as ex post squared or absolute returns. However, all of those approaches, valuable as they are, have distinct weaknesses. For example, the existence of competing parametric volatility models with different properties (e.g. GARCH versus stochastic volatility) suggests misspecification; after all, at most *one* of the models could be correct, and surely, *none* is strictly correct. Similarly, the well-known smiles and smirks in volatilities implied by Black–Scholes prices for options written at different strikes provide evidence of misspecification of the underlying model. Finally, direct indicators, such as ex post squared returns, are contaminated by noise, and Andersen and Bollerslev (1998*a*) documented that the variance of the noise is typically very large relative to that of the signal.

In this article, we introduce a new and complementary volatility measure, termed realized volatility. The mechanics are simple—we compute daily realized volatility simply by summing intraday squared returns—but the theory is deep: By sampling intraday returns sufficiently frequently, the realized volatility can be made arbitrarily close to the underlying integrated volatility, the integral of instantaneous volatility over the interval of interest, which is a natural volatility measure. Hence for practical purposes, we may treat volatility as observed, which enables us to examine its properties directly, using much simpler techniques than the complicated econometric models required when volatility is latent.

Our analysis is in the spirit of and extends earlier contributions of French, Schwert, and Stambaugh (1987), Hsieh (1991), Schwert (1989, 1990), and, more recently, Taylor and Xu (1997). We progress, however, in important directions. First, we provide rigorous theoretical underpinnings for the volatility measures for the general case of a special semimartingale. Second, our analysis is explicitly multivariate; we develop and examine measures not only of return variance, but also of covariance. Finally, our empirical work is based on a unique high-frequency dataset that consists of 10 years of continuously recorded 5-min returns on two major currencies. The high-frequency returns allow us to examine *daily* volatilities, which are of central concern in both academia and industry. In particular, the persistent volatility fluctuations of interest in risk management, asset pricing, portfolio allocation, and forecasting are very much present at the daily horizon.

We proceed as follows. In Section 15.2 we provide a formal and detailed justification for our realized volatility and correlation measures as highly accurate estimates of the underlying quadratic variation and covariation, assuming only that returns evolve as special semimartingales. Among other things, we relate our realized volatilities and correlations to the conditional variances and correlations common in the econometrics literature and to the notion of integrated variance common in the finance literature, and we show that they remain valid in the presence of jumps. Such background is needed for a serious understanding of our volatility and correlation measures, and it is lacking in the earlier literature on which we build. In Section 15.3, we discuss the high-frequency deutschmark–U.S. dollar (DM/$) and yen–U.S. dollar (yen/$) returns that provide the basis for our empirical analysis, and we also detail the construction of our realized daily variances and covariances. In Section 15.4 and 15.5, we characterize the unconditional and conditional distributions of the daily volatilities, respectively, including long-memory features. In Section 15.6, we explore issues related to temporal aggregation, with particular focus on the scaling laws implied by long memory, and we provide concluding remarks in Section 15.7.

15.2 Volatility measurement: theory

In this section we develop the foundations of our volatility and covariance measures. When markets are open, trades may occur at any instant. Therefore, returns as well as corresponding measures of volatility may, in principle, be obtained over arbitrarily short intervals. We, therefore, model the underlying price process in continuous time. We first introduce the relevant concepts, after which we show how the volatility measures may be approximated using high-frequency data, and we illustrate the concrete implications of our concepts for standard Itô and mixed jump–diffusion processes.

15.2.1 Financial returns as a special semimartingale
Arbitrage-free price processes of practical relevance for financial economics belong to the class of special semimartingales. They allow for a unique decomposition of returns into a local martingale and a predictable finite variation process. The former represents the "unpredictable" innovation, whereas the latter has a locally deterministic drift that governs the instantaneous mean return, as discussed in Back (1991).

Formally, for a positive integer T and $t \in [0, T]$, let $\mathcal{F}_t$ be the σ field that reflects the information at time t, so that $\mathcal{F}_s \subseteq \mathcal{F}_t$ for $0 \leq s \leq t \leq T$, and let P denote a probability measure on $(\Omega, P, \mathcal{F})$, where Ω represents the possible states of the world and $\mathcal{F} \equiv \mathcal{F}_T$ is the set of events that are distinguishable at time T. Also assume that the information filtration $(\mathcal{F}_t)_{t \in [0, T]}$ satisfies the usual conditions of P completeness and right continuity. The evolution of any arbitrage-free logarithmic price process, p_k, and the associated continuously compounded return over $[0, t]$ may then be represented as

$$p_k(t) - p_k(0) = M_k(t) + A_k(t), \tag{1}$$

where $M_k(0) = A_k(0) = 0$, M_k is a local martingale, and A_k is a locally integrable and predictable process of finite variation. For full generality, we define p_k to be inclusive of any cash receipts such as dividends and coupons, but exclusive of required cash payouts associated with, for example, margin calls.

The formulation (1) is very general and includes all specifications used in standard asset pricing theory. It includes, for example, Itô, jump, and mixed jump–diffusion processes, and it does not require a Markov assumption. It can also accommodate long memory, either in returns or in return volatility, as long as care is taken to eliminate the possibility of arbitrage first noted by Meheswaran and Sims (1993), using, for example, the methods of Rogers (1997) or Comte and Renault (1998).

Without loss of generality, each component in Equation (1) may be assumed to be cadlag (right continuous with left limits). The corresponding caglad (left continuous with right limits) process is now p_{k-}, defined as $p_{k-}(t) \equiv \lim_{s \to t, s \leq t} p_k(s)$ for each $t \in [0, T]$, and the jumps are $\Delta p_k \equiv p_k - p_{k-}$ or

$$\Delta p_k(t) \equiv p_k(t) - \lim_{s \to t, \, s \leq t} p_k(s). \tag{2}$$

By no arbitrage, the occurrence and size of jumps are unpredictable, so M_k contains the (compensated) jump part of p_k along with any infinite variation components, whereas A_k has continuous paths. We may further decompose M_k into a pair of local martingales, one with continuous and infinite variation paths, M^c, and another of finite variation, ΔM, representing the compensated jump component so that $M_k = M_k^c + \Delta M_k$. Equation (1) becomes

$$p_k(t) - p_k(0) = M_k^c(t) + \Delta M_k(t) + A_k(t). \tag{3}$$

Finally, we introduce some formal notation for the returns. For concreteness, we normalize the unit interval to be one trading day. For $m \cdot T$ a positive integer, indicating the number of return observations obtained by sampling prices m times per day, the return on asset k over $[t - 1/m, t]$ is

$$r_{k, \, (m)}(t) \equiv p_k(t) - p_k(t - 1/m), \qquad t = 1/m, \ 2/m, \ \ldots, \ T. \tag{4}$$

Hence, $m > 1$ corresponds to high-frequency intraday returns, whereas $m < 1$ indicates interdaily returns.

15.2.2 Quadratic variation and covariation

Development of formal volatility measures requires a bit of notation. For any semimartingale X and predictable integrand H, the stochastic integral $\int H dX = \{ \int_0^t H(s) dX(s) \}_{t \in [0, T]}$ is well defined, and for two semimartingales X and Y, the quadratic variation and covariation processes, $[X, X] = ([X, X])_{t \in [0, T]}$ and $[X, Y] = ([X, Y])_{t \in [0, T]}$, are given by

$$[X, X] = X^2 - 2 \int X_- dX, \tag{5a}$$

$$[X, Y] = XY - \int X_- dY - \int Y_- dX, \tag{5b}$$

where the notation X_- means the process whose value at s is $\lim_{u \to s, \, u < s} X_u$; see Protter (1990, sections 2.4–2.6). These processes are semimartingales of finite variation on $[0, T]$. The following properties are important for our interpretation of these quantities as volatility measures. For an increasing sequence of random partitions of $[0, T]$, $0 = \tau_{m,0} \le \tau_{m,1} \le \cdots$, so that $\sup_{j \ge 1}(\tau_{m,j+1} - \tau_{m,j}) \to 0$ and $\sup_{j \ge 1} \tau_{m,j} \to T$ for $m \to \infty$ with probability 1, we have for $t \wedge \tau \equiv \min(t, \tau)$ and $t \in [0, T]$,

$$\lim_{m \to \infty} \{ X(0) Y(0) + \sum_{j \ge 1} [X(t \wedge \tau_{m,j}) - X(t \wedge \tau_{m,j-1})]$$
$$\times [Y(t \wedge \tau_{m,j}) - Y(t \wedge \tau_{m,j-1})] \} \to [X, Y]_t, \tag{6}$$

where the convergence is uniform on $[0, T]$ in probability. In addition, we have that

$$[X, Y]_0 = X(0) Y(0), \tag{7a}$$

$$\Delta[X, Y] = \Delta X \Delta Y, \tag{7b}$$

$$[X, X] \text{ is an increasing process.} \tag{7c}$$

Finally, if X and Y are locally square integrable local martingales, the covariance of X and Y over $[t - h, t]$ is given by the expected increment to the quadratic covariation,

$$\text{Cov}(X(t), Y(t) | \mathcal{F}_{t-h}) = E([X, Y]_t | \mathcal{F}_{t-h}) - [X, Y]_{t-h}. \tag{8}$$

15.2.3 Quadratic variation as a volatility measure

Here we derive specific expressions for the quadratic variation and covariation of arbitrage-free asset prices, and we discuss their use as volatility measures in light of the properties (6)–(8). The additive decomposition (3) and the fact that the predictable components satisfy $[A_k, A_j] = [A_k, M_j] = 0$, for all j and k, imply that

$$[p_k, p_j]_t = [M_k, M_j]_t$$
$$= [M_k^c, M_j^c]_t + \sum_{0 \le s \le t} \Delta M_k(s) \Delta M_j(s). \tag{9}$$

We convert this cumulative volatility measure into a corresponding time series of incremental contributions. Letting the integer $h \ge 1$ denote the number of trading days over which the volatility measures are computed, we define the time series of h-period quadratic variation and covariation, for $t = h$, $2h, \ldots, T$, as

$$\text{Qvar}_{k,h}(t) \equiv [p_k,p_k]_t - [p_k,p_k]_{t-h}, \tag{10a}$$

$$\text{Qcov}_{kj,h}(t) \equiv [p_k,p_j]_t - [p_k,p_j]_{t-h}. \tag{10b}$$

Equation (9) implies that the quadratic variation and covariation for asset prices depend solely on the realization of the return innovations. In particular, the conditional mean is of no import. This renders these quantities model-free: regardless of the specific arbitrage-free price process, the quadratic variation and covariation are obtained by cumulating the instantaneous squares and cross-products of returns, as indicated by (6). Moreover, the measures are well defined even if the price paths contain jumps, as implied by (7), and the quadratic variation is increasing, as required of a cumulative volatility measure.

Equation (8) implies that the *h*-period quadratic variation and covariation are intimately related to, but distinct from, the conditional return variance and covariance. Specifically,

$$\text{Var}(p_k(t)|\mathscr{F}_{t-h}) = E[\text{Qvar}_{k,h}(t)|\mathscr{F}_{t-h}], \tag{11a}$$

$$\text{Cov}(p_k(t),p_j(t)|\mathscr{F}_{t-h}) = E[\text{Qcov}_{kj,h}(t)|\mathscr{F}_{t-h}]. \tag{11b}$$

Hence, the conditional variance and covariance diverge from the quadratic variation and covariation, respectively, by a zero-mean error. This is natural because the conditional variance and covariance are ex ante concepts, whereas the quadratic variation and covariation are ex post concepts. One can think of the quadratic variation and covariation as unbiased for the conditional variance and covariance, or conversely. Either way, the key insight is that, unlike the conditional variance and covariance, the quadratic variation and covariation are in principle *observable* via high-frequency returns, which facilitates the analysis and forecasting of volatility using standard statistical tools. Shortly we exploit this insight extensively.

15.2.4 Approximating the quadratic variation and covariation
Equation (6) implies that we may approximate the quadratic variation and covariation directly from high-frequency return data. In practice, we fix an appropriately high sampling frequency and cumulate the relevant intraday return products over the horizon of interest. Concretely, using the notation in Equation (4) for prices sampled *m* times per day, we define for $t = h, 2h, \ldots, T$,

$$\text{var}_{k,h}(t; m) = \sum_{i=1,\ldots,mh} r_{k,(m)}^2(t-h+(i/m)), \tag{12a}$$

$$\text{cov}_{kj,h}(t; m) = \sum_{i=1,\ldots,mh} r_{k,(m)}(t-h+(i/m)) \\ \times r_{j,(m)}(t-h+(i/m)). \tag{12b}$$

We call the observed measures in (12) the time-t realized h-period volatility and covariance. Note that for any fixed sampling frequency m, the realized volatility and covariance are directly observable, in contrast to their underlying theoretical counterparts, the quadratic variation and covariation processes. For sufficiently large m, however, the realized volatility and covariance provide arbitrarily good approximations to the quadratic variation and covariation, because for all $t = h, 2h, \ldots, T$ we have

$$\operatorname*{plim}_{m \to \infty} \operatorname{var}_{k,h}(t; m) = \operatorname{Qvar}_{k,h}(t), \tag{13a}$$

$$\operatorname*{plim}_{m \to \infty} \operatorname{cov}_{kj,h}(t; m) = \operatorname{Qcov}_{kj,h}(t). \tag{13b}$$

Note that the realized volatility measures $\operatorname{var}_{k,h}(t; m)$ and $\operatorname{cov}_{kj,h}(t; m)$ converge as $m \to \infty$ to $\operatorname{Qvar}_{k,h}(t)$ and $\operatorname{Qcov}_{kj,h}(t)$, but generally do not converge to the corresponding time $t - h$ conditional return volatility or covariance, $E[\operatorname{Qvar}_{k,h}(t)/\mathscr{F}_{t-h}]$ and $E[\operatorname{Qcov}_{kj,h}(t)/\mathscr{F}_{t-h}]$. Standard volatility models focus on the latter, which require a model for the return generating process. Our realized volatility and covariance, in contrast, provide unbiased estimators of the conditional variance and covariance, without taking a stand on any underlying model.

15.2.5 Integrated volatility for Itô processes

Much theoretical work assumes that logarithmic asset prices follow a univariate diffusion. Letting W be a standard Wiener process, we write $dp_k = \mu_k dt + \sigma_k dW$ or, more formally,

$$p_k(t) - p_k(t - 1) \equiv r_k(t) = \int_{t-1}^{t} \mu_k(s)ds + \int_{t-1}^{t} \sigma_k(s)dW(s). \tag{14}$$

For notational convenience, we suppress the subscript m or h when we consider variables measured over the daily interval ($h = 1$). For example, we have $r_k(t) \equiv r_{k,(1)}(t)$ and $\operatorname{Qcov}_{kj,1}(t) \equiv \operatorname{Qcov}_{kj}(t)$.

Our volatility measure is the associated quadratic variation process. Standard calculations yield

$$\operatorname{Qvar}_k(t) = [p_k, p_k]_t - [p_k, p_k]_{t-1} = \int_{t-1}^{t} \sigma^2(s)ds. \tag{15}$$

The expression $\int_{t-1}^{t} \sigma^2(s)ds$ defines the so-called integrated volatility, which is central to the option pricing theory of Hull and White (1987) and further discussed in Andersen and Bollerslev (1998a) and Barndorff-Nielsen and Shephard (1998). They note that, under the pure diffusion assumption, $r_k(t)$ conditional on $\operatorname{Qvar}_k(t)$ is normally distributed with variance $\int_{t-1}^{t} \sigma^2(s)ds$.

These results extend to the multivariate setting. If $W = (W_1, \ldots, W_d)$ is a d-dimensional standard Brownian motion and $(\mathscr{F}_t)_{t \in [0, T]}$ denotes its completed

natural filtration. Then, by martingale representation, any locally square integrable price process of the Itô form can be written as (Protter 1990, theorem
4.42),

$$p_k(t) - p_k(0) = \int_0^t \mu_k(s)ds + \sum_{i=1}^d \int_0^t \sigma_{k,i}(s)dW_i(s). \tag{16}$$

This result is related to the fact that any continuous local martingale, H, can be
represented as a time change of a Brownian motion, that is, $H(t) = B([H, H]_t)$,
a.s. (Protter 1990, theorem 2.41). That flexibility allows this particular specification to cover a large set of applications. Specifically, we obtain

$$\text{Qvar}_k(t) = \sum_{i=1}^d \int_{t-1}^t \sigma_{k,i}^2(s)ds, \tag{17a}$$

$$\text{Qcov}_{kj}(t) = \sum_{i=1}^d \int_{t-1}^t \sigma_{k,i}(s)\sigma_{j,i}(s)ds. \tag{17b}$$

The $\text{Qvar}_k(t)$ expression provides a natural multivariate concept of integrated
volatility, and we may correspondingly denote $\text{Qcov}_{kj}(t)$ as the integrated covariance. As a special case of this framework, we may assign a few of the orthogonal
Wiener components to be common factors and the remaining components to be
pure idiosyncratic error terms. This produces a continuous-time analog to the
discrete-time factor volatility models of Diebold and Nerlove (1989) and King,
Sentana, and Wadhwani (1994).

   Within this pure diffusion setting, stronger results may be obtained. Foster
and Nelson (1996) constructed a volatility filter based on a weighted average of
past squared returns that extracts the instantaneous volatility perfectly in
the continuous record limit. There are two main differences between their
approach and ours. From a theoretical perspective, their methods rely critically
on the diffusion assumption and extract instantaneous volatility, whereas
ours are valid for the entire class of arbitrage-free models, but extract only
cumulative volatility over an interval. Second, from an empirical perspective,
various market microstructure features limit the frequency at which returns can
be productively sampled, which renders infeasible a Foster-Nelson inspired
strategy of extracting instantaneous volatility estimates for a large number of
time points within each trading day. Consistent with this view, Foster and Nelson
applied their theoretical insights only to the study of volatility filters based on
daily data.

   The distribution of integrated volatility also has been studied by previous
authors, notably, Gallant, Hsu, and Tauchen (1999), who proposed an intriguing
reprojection method for direct estimation of the relevant distribution given a
specific parametric form for the underlying diffusion, whereas Chernov and
Ghysels (2000) applied similar techniques, exploiting options data as well. Our

high-frequency return methodology, in contrast, is simpler and more generally applicable, requiring only the special semi-Martingale assumption.

15.2.6 Volatility measures for pure jump and mixed jump–diffusion processes

Jump processes have particularly simple quadratic covariation measures. The fundamental semimartingale decomposition (1) reduces to a compensated jump component and a finite variation term,

$$p_k(t) = p_k(0) + M_k(t) + \int_0^t \mu_k(s)ds, \tag{18}$$

where $\mu_k(t)$ denotes the instantaneous mean and the innovations in $M_k(t)$ are pure jumps. The specification covers a variety of scenarios in which the jump process is generated by distinct components,

$$M_k(t) = \sum_{i=1}^{J} \sum_{0 \le s \le t} \kappa_{k,i}(s)\Delta N_{k,i}(s) - \int_0^t \mu_k(s)ds, \tag{19}$$

where $\Delta N_{k,i}(t)$ is an indicator function for the occurrence of a jump in the ith component at time t, while the (random) $k_{k,i}(t)$ term determines the jump size. From property (7),

$$\text{Qcov}_{kj}(t) = \sum_{i=1}^{J} \sum_{t-1 \le s \le t} \kappa_k(s)\kappa_j(s)\Delta N_k(s)\Delta N_j(s). \tag{20}$$

Andersen, Benzoni, and Lund (2000), among others, argued the importance of including both time-varying volatility and jumps when modeling speculative returns over short horizons, which can be accomplished by combining Itô and jump processes into a general jump–diffusion

$$p_k(t) - p_k(0) = \int_0^t \mu_k(s)ds + \int_0^t \sigma_k(s)dW(s) + \sum_{0 \le s \le t} \kappa_k(s)\Delta N_k(s). \tag{21}$$

The jump–diffusion allows for a predictable stochastic volatility process $\sigma_k(t)$ and a jump processes, $\kappa_k(t)N_k(t)$ with a finite conditional mean. The quadratic covariation follows directly from Equations (9) and (10):

$$\text{Qcov}_{kj}(t) = \int_{t-1}^{t} \sigma_k(s)\sigma_j(s)ds + \sum_{t-1 \le s \le t} \kappa_k(s)\kappa_j(s)\Delta N_k(s)\Delta N_j(s). \tag{22}$$

It is straightforward to allow for a d-dimensional Brownian motion, resulting in modifications along the lines of Equations (13)–(15), and the formulation readily accommodates multiple jump components, as in (19) and (20).

15.3 Volatility measurement: data

Our empirical analysis focuses on the bilateral DM/\$ and yen/\$ spot exchange rates, which are attractive candidates for examination because they represent the two main axes of the international financial system. We first discuss our choice of 5-min returns to construct realized volatilities, and then explain how we handle weekends and holidays. Finally, we detail the actual construction of the volatility measures.

15.3.1 On the use of 5-min returns

In practice, the discreteness of actual securities prices can render continuous-time models poor approximations at very high sampling frequencies. Furthermore, tick-by-tick prices are generally only available at unevenly spaced time points, so the calculation of evenly spaced high-frequency returns necessarily relies on some form of interpolation among prices recorded around the endpoints of the given sampling intervals. It is well known that this nonsynchronous trading or quotation effect may induce negative autocorrelation in the interpolated return series. Moreover, such market microstructure biases may be exacerbated in the multivariate context if varying degrees of interpolation are employed in the calculation of the different returns.

Hence a tension arises in the calculation of realized volatility. On the one hand, the theory of quadratic variation of special semimartingales suggests the desirability of sampling at very high frequencies, striving to match the ideal of continuously observed frictionless prices. On the other hand, the reality of market microstructure suggests not sampling *too* frequently. Hence a good choice of sampling frequency must balance two competing factors; ultimately it is an empirical issue that hinges on market liquidity. Fortunately, the markets studied in this article are among the most active and liquid in the world, permitting high-frequency sampling without contamination by microstructure effects. We use a sampling frequency of 288 times per day ($m = 288$, or 5-min returns), which is high enough such that our daily realized volatilities are largely free of measurement error (see the calculations in Andersen and Bollerslev 1998a), yet low enough such that microstructure biases are not a major concern.

15.3.2 Construction of 5-min DM/\$ and yen/\$ Returns

The two raw 5-min DM/\$ and yen/\$ return series were obtained from Olsen and Associates. The full sample consists of 5-min returns covering 1 December 1986, through 30 November 1996, or 3,653 days, for a total of $3,653 \times 288 = 1,052,064$ high-frequency return observations. As in Müller et al. (1990) and Dacorogna, Müller, Nagler, Olsen, and Pictet (1993), the construction of the returns utilizes the interbank FX quotes that appeared on Reuter's FXFX page during the sample period. Each quote consists of a bid and an ask price together with a "time stamp" to the nearest even second. After filtering the data for outliers and other anomalies, the price at each 5-min mark is obtained by linearly interpolating from the average of the log bid and the log ask for the two closest ticks. The continuously compounded returns are then simply the change in these

5-min average log bid and ask prices. Goodhart, Ito, and Payne (1996) and Danielsson and Payne (1999) found that the basic characteristics of 5-min FX returns constructed from quotes closely match those calculated from transactions prices, which are only available on a very limited basis.

It is well known that the activity in the foreign exchange market slows decidedly over the weekend and certain holiday periods; see, for example, Andersen and Bollerslev (1998*b*) and Müller et al. (1990). So as not to confound the distributional characteristics of the various volatility measures by these largely deterministic calendar effects, we explicitly excluded a number of days from the raw 5-min return series. Whenever we did so, we always cut from 21:05 GMT on one night to 21:00 GMT the next evening, to keep the daily periodicity intact. This definition of a "day" is motivated by the daily ebb and flow in the FX activity patterns documented by Bollerslev and Domowitz (1993). In addition to the thin trading period from Friday 21:05 GMT until Sunday 21:00 GMT, we removed several fixed holidays, including Christmas (24–26 December), New Year's (31 December – 2 January), and July Fourth. We also cut the moving holidays of Good Friday, Easter Monday, Memorial Day, July Fourth (when it falls officially on 3 July), and Labor day, as well as Thanks-giving and the day after. Although our cuts do not capture all the holiday market slowdowns, they do succeed in eliminating the most important such daily calender effects.

Finally, we deleted some returns contaminated by brief lapses in the Reuter's data feed. This problem manifests itself in long sequences of zero or constant 5-min returns in places where the missing quotes have been interpolated. To remedy this, we simply removed the days containing the 15 longest DM/\$ zero runs, the 15 longest DM/\$ constant runs, the 15 longest yen/\$ zero runs, and the 15 longest yen/\$ constant runs. Because of the overlap among the four different sets of days defined by these criteria, we actually removed only 51 days. All in all, we were left with 2,449 complete days, or $2,449 \times 288 = 705,312$ 5-min return observations, for the construction of our daily realized volatilities and covariances.

15.3.3 Construction of DM/\$ and yen/\$ daily realized volatilities

We denote the time series of 5-min DM/\$ and yen/\$ returns by $r_{D,(288)}(t)$ and $r_{y,(288)}(t)$, respectively, where $t = 1/288, 2/288, \ldots, 2,449$. We then form the corresponding 5-min squared return and cross-product series $(r_{D,(288)}(t))^2$, $(r_{y,(288)}(t))^2$, and $r_{D,(288)}(t) \cdot r_{y,(288)}(t)$. The statistical properties of the squared return series closely resemble those found by Andersen and Bollerslev (1997*a*, *b*) with a much shorter 1-year sample of 5-min DM/\$ returns. Interestingly, the basic properties of the 5-min cross-product series, $r_{D,(288)}(t) \cdot r_{y,(288)}(t)$, are similar. In particular, all three series are highly persistent and display strong intraday calendar effects, the shape of which is driven by the opening and closing of the different financial markets around the globe during the 24-hour trading cycle.

Now, following (12), we construct the realized h-period variances and covariances by summing the corresponding 5-min observations across the h-day horizon. For notational simplicity, we suppress the dependence on the fixed sampling frequency ($m = 288$), and define $vard_{t,h} \equiv \text{var}_{D,h}(t; 288)$, $vary_{t,h} \equiv \text{var}_{y,h}(t; 288)$, and $cov_{t,h} \equiv cov_{Dy,h}(t; 288)$. Furthermore, for daily measures ($h = 1$), we suppress the subscript h, and simply write $vard_t$, $vary_t$, and cov_t. Concretely, we define for $t = 1, 2, \ldots, [T/h]$,

$$vard_{t,h} \equiv \sum_{j=1, \ldots, 288 \cdot h} (r_{D,(288)}(h \cdot (t-1) + j/288))^2, \tag{23a}$$

$$vary_{t,h} \equiv \sum_{j=1, \ldots, 288 \cdot h} (r_{y,(288)}(h \cdot (t-1) + j/288))^2, \tag{23b}$$

$$\begin{aligned} cov_{t,h} \equiv \sum_{j=1, \ldots, 288 \cdot h} & r_{D,(288)}(h \cdot (t-1) + j/288) \\ & \cdot r_{y,(288)}(h \cdot (t-1) + j/288). \end{aligned} \tag{23c}$$

In addition, we examine several alternative, but related, measures of realized volatility derived from those in (23), including realized standard deviations, $stdd_{t,h} \equiv vard_{t,h}^{1/2}$ and $std\, y_{t,h} \equiv vary_{t,h}^{1/2}$, realized logarithmic standard deviations, $lstdd_{t,h} \equiv 1/2 \cdot \log{(vard_{t,h})}$ and $lstdy_{t,h} \equiv 1/2 \cdot \log{(vary_{t,h})}$, and realized correlations, $corr_{t,h} \equiv cov_{t,h}/(stdd_{t,h} \cdot stdy_{t,h})$. In Sections 15.4 and 15.5 we characterize the unconditional and conditional distributions of the daily realized volatility measures, whereas Section 15.6 details our analysis of the corresponding temporally aggregated measures ($h > 1$).

15.4. The unconditional distribution of daily realized FX volatility

The unconditional distribution of volatility captures important aspects of the return process, with implications for risk management, asset pricing, and portfolio allocation. Here we provide a detailed characterization.

15.4.1 Univariate unconditional distributions

The first two columns of the first panel of Table 15.1 provide a standard menu of moments (mean, variance, skewness, and kurtosis) that summarizes the unconditional distributions of the daily realized volatility series, $vard_t$ and $vary_t$, and the top panel of Figure 15.1 displays kernel density estimates of the unconditional distributions. It is evident that the distributions are very similar and extremely right skewed. Evidently, although the realized daily volatilities are constructed by summing 288 squared 5-min returns, the pronounced heteroscedasticity in intraday returns renders the normal distribution a poor approximation.

The standard deviation of returns is measured on the same scale as the returns, and thus provides a more readily interpretable measure of volatility. We present summary statistics and density estimates for the two daily realized standard deviations, $stdd_t$ and $stdy_t$, in columns three and four of the first panel of Table 15.1 and the second panel of Figure 15.1. The mean daily realized standard

Table 15.1. Statistics that summarize unconditional distributions of realized DM/$ and yen/$ volatilities

	$vard_{t,h}$	$vary_{t,h}$	$stdd_{t,h}$	$stdy_{t,h}$	$lstdd_{t,h}$	$lstdy_{t,h}$	$cov_{t,h}$	$corr_{t,h}$
Daily, $h = 1$								
Mean	0.529	0.538	0.679	0.684	−0.449	−0.443	0.243	0.435
Variance	0.234	0.272	0.067	0.070	0.120	0.123	0.073	0.028
Skewness	3.711	5.576	1.681	1.867	0.345	0.264	3.784	−0.203
Kurtosis	24.090	66.750	7.781	10.380	3.263	3.525	25.250	2.722
Weekly, $h = 5$								
Mean	2.646	2.692	1.555	1.566	0.399	0.405	1.217	0.449
Variance	3.292	3.690	0.228	0.240	0.084	0.083	0.957	0.022
Skewness	2.628	2.769	1.252	1.410	0.215	0.382	2.284	−0.176
Kurtosis	14.200	14.710	5.696	6.110	3.226	3.290	10.020	2.464
Biweekly, $h = 10$								
Mean	5.297	5.386	2.216	2.233	0.759	0.767	2.437	0.453
Variance	10.440	11.740	0.389	0.403	0.072	0.070	2.939	0.019
Skewness	1.968	2.462	1.063	1.291	0.232	0.380	1.904	−0.147
Kurtosis	7.939	11.980	4.500	5.602	3.032	3.225	7.849	2.243
Triweekly, $h = 15$								
Mean	7.937	8.075	2.717	2.744	0.964	0.977	3.651	0.455
Variance	22.330	22.770	0.560	0.546	0.069	0.064	5.857	0.018
Skewness	2.046	2.043	1.033	1.177	0.208	0.400	1.633	−0.132
Kurtosis	9.408	8.322	4.621	4.756	2.999	3.123	6.139	2.247
Monthly, $h = 20$								
Mean	10.590	10.770	3.151	3.179	1.116	1.127	4.874	0.458
Variance	34.090	36.000	0.671	0.671	0.062	0.059	8.975	0.017
Skewness	1.561	1.750	0.906	1.078	0.295	0.452	1.369	−0.196
Kurtosis	5.768	6.528	3.632	4.069	2.686	2.898	4.436	2.196

deviation is about 68 basis points, and although the right skewness of the distributions has been reduced, the realized standard deviations clearly remain non-normally distributed.

Interestingly, the distributions of the two daily realized logarithmic standard deviations, $lstdd_t$ and $lstdy_t$, in columns five and six of the first panel of Table 15.1 and in the third panel of Figure 15.1, appear symmetric, with skewness coefficients near zero. Moreover, normality is a much better approximation for these measures than for the realized volatilities or standard deviations, because the kurtosis coefficients are near 3. This is in accord with the findings for monthly volatility aggregates of daily equity index returns in French, Schwert, and Stambaugh (1987), as well as evidence from Clark (1973) and Taylor (1986).

Finally, we characterize the distribution of the daily realized covariances and correlations, cov_t and $corr_t$, in the last columns of the first panel of Table 15.1 and the bottom panel of Figure 15.1. The basic characteristics of the unconditional distribution of the daily realized covariance are similar to those of the daily realized volatilities—they are extremely right skewed and leptokurtic. In con-

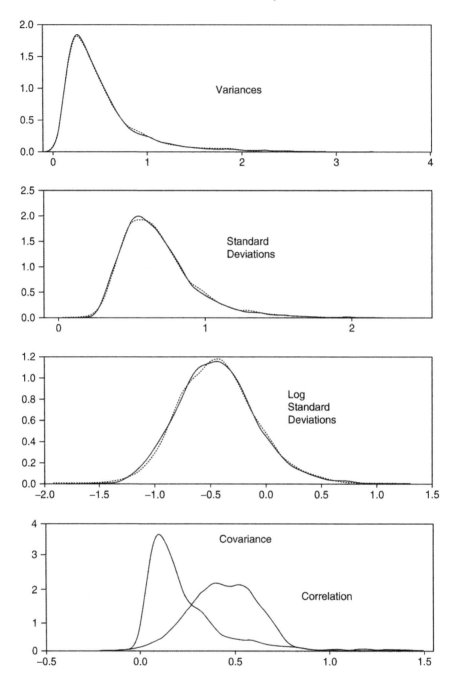

Fig. 15.1. Distribution of daily realized exchange rate volatilities
and correlations.

trast, the distribution of the realized correlation is approximately normal. The mean realized correlation is positive (.43), as expected, because both series respond to U.S. macroeconomic fundamentals. The standard deviation of the realized correlation (.17) indicates significant intertemporal variation in the correlation, which may be important for short-term portfolio allocation and hedging decisions.

15.4.2 Multivariate unconditional distributions

The univariate distributions characterized in the foregoing text do not address relationships that may exist among the different measures of variation and covariation. Key issues relevant in financial economic applications include, for example, whether and how $lstdd_t$, $lstdy_t$, and corr$_t$ move together. Such questions are difficult to answer using conventional volatility models, but they are relatively easy to address using our realized volatilities and correlations.

   The sample correlations in the first panel of Table 15.2, along with the $lstdd_t$ – $lstdy_t$ scatterplot in the top panel of Figure 15.2, clearly indicate a strong positive association between the two exchange rate volatilities. Thus, not only do the two exchange rates tend to move together, as indicated by the positive means for cov$_t$ and corr$_t$, but so too do their volatilities. This suggests factor structure, as in Diebold and Nerlove (1989) and Bollerslev and Engle (1993).

   The correlations in the first panel of Table 15.2 and the corr$_t$ – $lstdd_t$ and corr$_t$ – $lstdy_t$ scatterplots in the second and third panels of Figure 15.2 also indicate positive association between correlation and volatility. Whereas some nonlinearity may be operative in the corr$_t$ – $lstdd_t$ relationship, with a flattened response for both very low and very high $lstdd_t$ values, the corr$_t$ – $lstdy_t$ relationship appears approximately linear. To quantify further this volatility effect in correlation, we show in the top panel of Figure 15.3 kernel density estimates of corr$_t$ when both $lstdd_t$ and $lstdy_t$ are less than −.46 (their median value) and when both $lstdd_t$ and $lstdy_t$ are greater than −.46. Similarly, we show in the bottom panel of Figure 15.3 the estimated corr$_t$ densities conditional on the more extreme volatility situation in which both $lstdd_t$ and $lstdy_t$ are less than −.87 (their 10th percentile) and when both $lstdd_t$ and $lstdy_t$ are greater than .00 (their 90th percentile). It is clear that the distribution of realized correlation shifts rightward when volatility increases. A similar correlation effect in volatility was documented for international equity returns by Solnik, Boucrelle, and Le Fur (1996). Of course, given that the high-frequency returns are positively correlated, some such effect is to be expected, as argued by Ronn (1998), Boyer, Gibson, and Loretan (1999), and Forbes and Rigobon (1999). However, the magnitude of the effect nonetheless appears noteworthy.

   To summarize, we have documented a substantial amount of variation in volatilities and correlation, as well as important contemporaneous dependence measures. We now turn to dynamics and dependence, which characterize the conditional, as opposed to unconditional, distribution of realized volatility and correlation.

Table 15.2. Correlation matrices of realized DM/\$ and yen/\$ volatilities

	$vary_{t,h}$	$stdd_{t,h}$	$stdy_{t,h}$	$lstdd_{t,h}$	$lstdy_{t,h}$	$cov_{t,h}$	$corr_{t,h}$
Daily, $h = 1$							
$var\,d_t$	0.539	0.961	0.552	0.860	0.512	0.806	0.341
$vary_t$	1.000	0.546	0.945	0.514	0.825	0.757	0.234
std d_t	—	1.000	0.592	0.965	0.578	0.793	0.383
$stdy_t$	—	—	1.000	0.589	0.959	0.760	0.281
lstd d_t	—	—	—	1.000	0.604	0.720	0.389
lstd y_t	—	—	—	—	1.000	0.684	0.294
cov_t	—	—	—	—	—	1.000	0.590
Weekly, $h = 5$							
$vard_{t,h}$	0.494	0.975	0.507	0.907	0.495	0.787	0.311
$vary_{t,h}$	1.000	0.519	0.975	0.514	0.908	0.761	0.197
$stdd_{t,h}$	—	1.000	0.545	0.977	0.545	0.789	0.334
$stdy_{t,h}$	—	—	1.000	0.555	0.977	0.757	0.220
$lstdd_{t,h}$	—	—	—	1.000	0.571	0.748	0.336
$lstdy_{t,h}$	—	—	—	—	1.000	0.718	0.235
$cov_{t,h}$	—	—	—	—	—	1.000	0.617
Biweekly, $h = 10$							
$vard_{t,h}$	0.500	0.983	0.503	0.931	0.490	0.776	0.274
$vary_{t,h}$	1.000	0.516	0.980	0.514	0.923	0.772	0.170
$stdd_{t,h}$	—	1.000	0.533	0.982	0.531	0.780	0.293
$stdy_{t,h}$	—	—	1.000	0.544	0.981	0.762	0.188
$lstdd_{t,h}$	—	—	—	1.000	0.556	0.753	0.300
$lstdy_{t,h}$	—	—	—	—	1.000	0.726	0.202
$cov_{t,h}$	—	—	—	—	—	1.000	0.609
Triweekly, $h = 15$							
$vard_{t,h}$	0.498	0.982	0.505	0.931	0.497	0.775	0.255
$vary_{t,h}$	1.000	0.522	0.984	0.525	0.939	0.763	0.146
$stdd_{t,h}$	—	1.000	0.538	0.983	0.539	0.787	0.277
$stdy_{t,h}$	—	—	1.000	0.551	0.984	0.756	0.155
$lstdd_{t,h}$	—	—	—	1.000	0.564	0.765	0.285
$lstdy_{t,h}$	—	—	—	—	1.000	0.727	0.162
$cov_{t,h}$	—	—	—	—	—	1.000	0.605
Monthly, $h = 20$							
$vard_{t,h}$	0.479	0.988	0.484	0.952	0.479	0.764	0.227
$vary_{t,h}$	1.000	0.501	0.988	0.509	0.953	0.747	0.109
$stdd_{t,h}$	—	1.000	0.512	0.988	0.511	0.775	0.241
$stdy_{t,h}$	—	—	1.000	0.527	0.988	0.741	0.112
$lstdd_{t,h}$	—	—	—	1.000	0.533	0.763	0.245
$lstdy_{t,h}$	—	—	—	—	1.000	0.719	0.115
$cov_{t,h}$	—	—	—	—	—	1.000	0.596

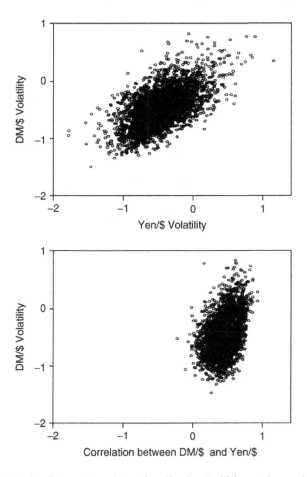

Fig. 15.2. Bivariate scatterplots of realized volatilities and correlations.

15.5 The conditional distribution of daily realized FX volatility

The value of financial derivatives such as options is closely linked to the expected volatility of the underlying asset over the time until expiration. Improved volatility forecasts should, therefore, yield more accurate derivative prices. The conditional dependence in volatility forms the basis for such forecasts. That dependence is most easily identified in the daily realized correlations and logarithmic standard deviations, which we have shown to be approximately unconditionally normally distributed. To conserve space, we focus our discussion on those three series.

It is instructive first to consider the time series plots of the realized volatilities and correlations in Figure 15.4. The wide fluctuations and strong persistence

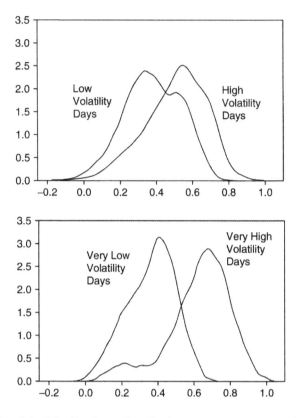

Fig. 15.3. Distributions of realized correlations: low volatility
versus high volatility days.

evident in the *lstdd*ₜ and *lstdy*ₜ series are, of course, manifestations of the well-documented return volatility clustering. It is, therefore, striking that the time series plot for corrₜ shows equally pronounced persistence, with readily identifiable periods of high and low correlation.

The visual impression of strong persistence in the volatility measures is confirmed by the highly significant Ljung–Box tests reported in the first panel of Table 15.3. (The .001 critical value is 45.3.) The correlograms of *lstdd*ₜ, *lstdy*ₜ, and corrₜ in Figure 15.5 further underscore the point. The autocorrelations of the realized logarithmic standard deviations begin around .6 and decay very slowly to about .1 at a displacement of 100 days. Those of the realized correlations decay even more slowly, reaching just .31 at the 100-day displacement. Similar results based on long series of daily absolute or squared returns from other markets have been obtained previously by a number of authors, including Ding, Granger, and Engle (1993). The slow decay in Figure 15.5 is particularly noteworthy, however, in that the two realized daily volatility series span "only" 10 years.

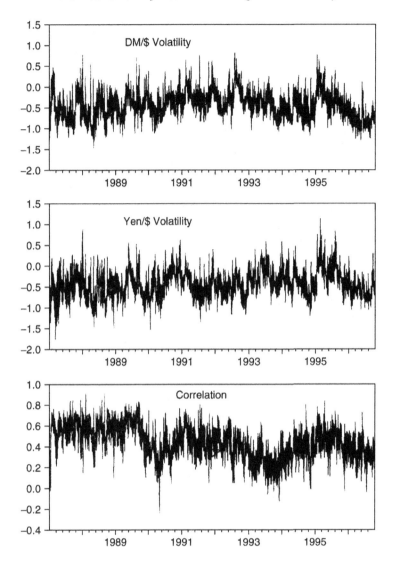

Fig. 15.4. Time series of daily realized volatilities and correlation.

The findings of slow autocorrelation decay may seem to indicate the presence of a unit root, as in the integrated GARCH model of Engle and Bollerslev (1986). However, Dickey–Fuller tests with 10 augmentation lags soundly reject this hypothesis for all of the volatility series. (The test statistics range from −9.26 to −5.59, and the .01 and .05 critical values are −2.86 and −3.43.) Although unit roots may be formally rejected, the very slow autocorrelation decay coupled with the negative signs and slow decay of the estimated augmentation lag coefficients in the Dickey–Fuller regressions suggest that long memory of a non-unit-root

Table 15.3. Dynamic dependence measures for realized DM/\$ and yen/\$ volatilities

	$vard_{t,h}$	$wary_{t,h}$	$stdd_{t,h}$	$stdy_{t,h}$	$lstdd_{t,h}$	$lstdy_{t,h}$	$cov_{t,h}$	$corr_{t,h}$
Daily, $h=1$								
LB	4539.300	3257.200	7213.700	5664.700	9220.700	6814.100	2855.200	12197.000
$\hat{d}$	0.356	0.339	0.381	0.428	0.420	0.455	0.334	0.413
Weekly, $h=5$								
LB	592.700	493.900	786.200	609.600	930.000	636.300	426.100	2743.300
$\hat{d}$	0.457	0.429	0.446	0.473	0.485	0.496	0.368	0.519
Biweekly, $h=10$								
LB	221.200	181.000	267.900	206.700	305.300	203.800	155.400	1155.600
$\hat{d}$	0.511	0.490	0.470	0.501	0.515	0.507	0.436	0.494
Triweekly, $h=15$								
LB	100.700	108.000	122.600	117.300	138.300	112.500	101.600	647.000
$\hat{d}$	0.400	0.426	0.384	0.440	0.421	0.440	0.319	0.600
Monthly, $h=20$								
LB	71.800	69.900	83.100	70.900	94.500	66.000	78.500	427.300
$\hat{d}$	0.455	0.488	0.440	0.509	0.496	0.479	0.439	0.630

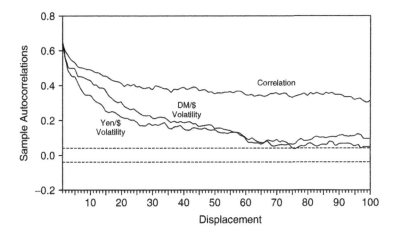

Fig. 15.5. Sample autocorrelations of realized volatilities correlation.

variety may be present. Hence, we now turn to an investigation of fractional integration in the daily realized volatilities.

As noted by Granger and Joyeux (1980), the slow hyperbolic decay of the long-lag autocorrelations or, equivalently, the log-linear explosion of the low-frequency spectrum are distinguishing features of a covariance stationary fractionally integrated, or $I(d)$, process with $0 < d < \frac{1}{2}$. The low-frequency spectral behavior also forms the basis for the log-periodogram regression estimation procedure proposed by Geweke and Porter-Hudak (1983) and refined by Robinson (1994, 1995), Hurvich and Beltrao (1994) and Hurvich, Deo, and Brodsky (1998). In particular, let $I(\omega_j)$ denote the sample periodogram at the jth Fourier frequency, $\omega_j = 2\pi j/T, j = 1, 2, \ldots, [T/2]$. The log-periodogram estimator of d is then based on the least squares regression

$$\log[I(\omega_j)] = \beta_0 + \beta_1 \cdot \log(\omega_j) + u_j, \tag{24}$$

where $j = 1, 2, \ldots, n$, and $\hat{d} \equiv -\hat{\beta}_1/2$. The least squares estimator of β_1, and hence $\hat{d}$, is asymptotically normal and the corresponding standard error, $\pi \cdot (24 \cdot n)^{-1/2}$, depends only on the number of periodogram ordinates used. Although the earlier proofs for consistency and asymptotic normality of the log-periodogram regression estimator rely on normality, Deo and Hurvich (1998) and Robinson and Henry (1999) showed that these properties extend to non-Gaussian, possibly heteroscedastic, time series as well. Of course, the actual value of the estimate of d depends upon the choice of n. Although the formula for the theoretical standard error suggests choosing a large n to obtain a small standard error, doing so produces bias in the estimator, because the relationship underlying (24), in general, holds only for frequencies close to zero. Following Taqqu and Teverovsky (1996), we therefore graphed and examined $\hat{d}$ as a function of n, looking for a flat region in which we are plagued by neither high variance (n too small) nor high bias (n too large). Our subsequent choice of $n = [T^{4/5}]$, or $n = 514$, is consistent with the optimal rate of $O(T^{4/5})$ established by Hurvich, Deo, and Brodsky (1998).

The estimates of d are given in the first panel of Table 15.3. The estimates are highly statistically significant for all eight volatility series, and all are fairly close to the "typical value" of .4. These estimates for d are also in line with the estimates based on longer time series of daily absolute and squared returns from other markets reported by Granger, Ding, and Spear (1997), and the findings based on a much shorter 1-year sample of intraday DM/$ returns reported in Andersen and Bollerslev (1997b). This suggests that the continuous-time models used in much of theoretical finance, where volatility is assumed to follow an Ornstein–Uhlenbeck type process, are misspecified. Nonetheless, our results are constructive, in that they also indicate that parsimonious long-memory models should be able to accommodate the long-lag autoregressive effects.

Having characterized the distributions of the daily realized volatilities and correlations, we now turn to longer horizons.

15.6 Temporal aggregation and scaling laws

The analysis in the preceding sections focused on the distributional properties of daily realized volatility measures. However, many practical financial problems invariably involve longer horizons. Here we examine the distributional aspects of the corresponding multiday realized variances and correlations. As before, we begin with an analysis of unconditional distributions, followed by an analysis of dynamics and dependence, including a detailed examination of long memory as it relates to temporal aggregation.

15.6.1 Univariate and multivariate unconditional distributions

In the lower panels of Table 15.1 we summarize the univariate unconditional distributions of realized volatilities and correlations at weekly, biweekly, tri-weekly, and monthly horizons ($h = 5, 10, 15$, and 20, respectively), implying samples of length 489, 244, 163, and 122. Consistent with the notion of efficient capital markets and serially uncorrelated returns, the means of $vard_{t,h}, vary_{t,h}$, and $cov_{t,h}$ grow at the rate h, while the mean of the realized correlation, $corr_{t,h}$, is largely invariant to the level of temporal aggregation. In addition, the growth of the variance of the realized variances and covariance adheres closely to h^{2d+1}, where d denotes the order of integration of the series, a phenomenon we discuss at length subsequently. We also note that even at the monthly level, the unconditional distributions of $vard_{t,h}, vary_{t,h}$, and $cov_{t,h}$ remain leptokurtic and highly right skewed. The basic characteristics of $stdd_{t,h}$ and $stdy_{t,h}$ are similar, with the means increasing at rate $h^{1/2}$. The unconditional variances of $lstdd_{t,h}$ and $lstdy_{t,h}$, however, *decrease* with h, but again at a rate linked to the fractional integration parameter, as we document subsequently.

Next, turning to the multivariate unconditional distributions, we display in the lower panels of Table 15.2 the correlation matrices of all volatility measures for $h = 5, 10, 15$, and 20. Although the correlation between the different measures drops slightly under temporal aggregation, the positive association between the volatilities, so apparent at the 1-day return horizon, is largely preserved under temporal aggregation. For instance, the correlation between $lstdd_{t,h}$ and $lstdy_{t,h}$ ranges from a high of .604 at the daily horizon to a low of .533 at the monthly horizon. Meanwhile, the volatility effect in correlation is somewhat reduced by temporal aggregation; the sample correlation between $lstdd_{t,1}$ and $corr_{t,1}$ equals .389, whereas the one between $lstdd_{t,20}$ and $corr_{t,20}$ is .245. Similarly, the correlation between $lstdy_{t,h}$ and $corr_{t,h}$ and $corr_{t,h}$ drops from .294 for $h = 1$ to .115 for $h = 20$. Thus, whereas the long-horizon correlations remain positively related to the level of volatility, the lower values suggest that the benefits to international diversification may be the greatest over longer investment horizons.

15.6.2 Conditional distribution: dynamic dependence, fractional integration, and scaling

Andersen, Bollerslev, and Lange (1999) showed that, given the estimates obtained at the daily level, the integrated volatility should, in theory, remain strongly serially correlated and highly predictable, even at the monthly level. The Ljung–Box statistics for the realized volatilities in the lower panels of Table 15.3 provide strong empirical backing. Even at the monthly level, or $h = 20$, with only 122 observations, all of the test statistics are highly significant. This contrasts with previous evidence that finds little evidence of volatility clustering for monthly returns, such as Baillie and Bollerslev (1989) and Christoffersen and Diebold (2000). However, the methods and/or data used in the earlier studies may produce tests with low power.

The estimates of d reported in Section 4 suggest that the realized daily volatilities are fractionally integrated. The class of fractionally integrated models is self-similar, so that the degree of fractional integration is invariant to the sampling frequency (see, e.g., Beran 1994). This strong prediction is borne out by the estimates for d for the different levels of temporal aggregation reported in the lower panels of Table 15.3. All of the estimates are within two asymptotic standard errors of the average estimate of .391 obtained for the daily series, and all are highly statistically significantly different from both zero and unity.

Another implication of self-similarity concerns the variance of partial sums. In particular, let

$$[x_t]_h \equiv \sum_{j=1,\dots,h} x_{h\cdot(t-1)+j} \tag{25}$$

denote the h-fold partial sum process for x_t, where $t = 1, 2, \dots, [T/h]$. Then, as discussed by, Beran (1994) and Diebold and Lindner (1996), among others, if x_t is fractionally integrated, the partial sums obey a scaling law,

$$\mathrm{Var}([x_t]_h) = c \cdot h^{2d+1}. \tag{26}$$

Of course, by definition $[vard_t]_h \equiv vard_{t,h}$ and $[vary_t]_h \equiv vary_{t,h}$, so the variance of the realized volatilities should grow at rate h^{2d+1}. This implication is remarkably consistent with the values for the unconditional sample (co)variances reported in Table 15.1 and a value of d around .35–.40. Similar scaling laws for power transforms of absolute FX returns have been reported in a series of articles initiated by Müller et al. (1990).

The striking accuracy of our scaling laws carries over to the partial sums of the alternative volatility series. The left panel of Figure 15.6 plots the logarithm of the sample variances of the partial sums of the realized logarithmic standard deviations versus the log of the aggregation level; that is, $\log(\mathrm{Var}([lstdd_t]_h))$ and $\log(\mathrm{Var}([lstdy_t]_h))$ against $\log(h)$ for $h = 1, 2, \ldots, 30$. The linear fits implied by (26) are validated. Each of the slopes is very close to the theoretical value of $2d + 1$ implied by the log-periodogram estimates for d, further solidifying the notion of long-memory volatility dependence. The estimated slopes in the top and bottom panels are 1.780 and 1.728, respectively, corresponding to values of $\hat{d}$ of .390 and .364.

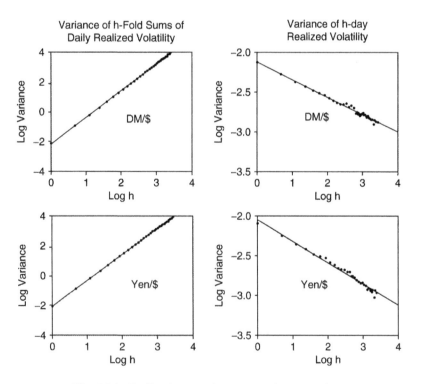

Fig. 15.6. Scaling laws under temporal aggregation.

Because a nonlinear function of a sum is not the sum of the nonlinear function, it is not clear whether $lstdd_{t,h}$ and $lstddy_{t,h}$ will follow similar scaling laws. The estimates of d reported in Table 15.3 suggest that they should. The corresponding plots for the logarithm of the h-day logarithmic standard deviations $\log(\text{Var}(lstdd_{t,h}))$ and $\log(\text{Var}(lstdy_{t,h}))$ against $\log(h)$, for $h = 1, 2, \ldots, 30$, in the right panel of Figure 15.6, lend empirical support to this conjecture. Interestingly, however, the lines are downward sloped.

To understand why these slopes should be negative, assume that the returns are serially uncorrelated. The variance of the temporally aggregated return should then be proportional to the length of the return interval, that is, $E(\text{var}_{t,h}) = b \cdot h$, where $\text{var}_{t,h}$ refers to the temporally aggregated variance as defined in the preceding text. Also, by the scaling law (26), $\text{Var}(\text{var}_{t,h}) = c \cdot h^{2d+1}$. Furthermore, assume that the corresponding temporally aggregated logarithmic standard deviations, $lstd_{t,h} \equiv 1/2 \cdot \log(\text{var}_{t,h})$, are normally distributed at all aggregation horizons h with mean μ_h and variance σ_h^2. Of course, these assumptions agree closely with the actual empirical distributions summarized in Table 15.1. It then follows from the properties of the log-normal distribution that

$$E(\text{var}_{t,h}) = \exp(2\mu_h + 2\sigma_h^2) = b \cdot h, \tag{27a}$$

$$\begin{aligned}\text{Var}(\text{var}_{t,h}) &= \exp(4\mu_h)\exp(4\sigma_h^2)[\exp(4\sigma_h^2) - 1] \\ &= c \cdot h^{2d+1},\end{aligned} \tag{27b}$$

and solving for the variance of the log standard deviation yields

$$\text{Var}(lstd_{t,h}) \equiv \sigma_h^2 = \log(c \cdot b^{-2} \cdot h^{2d-1} + 1). \tag{28}$$

With $2d - 1$ slightly negative, this explains why the sample variances of $lstd\,d_{t,h}$ and $lstd\,y_{t,h}$ reported in Table 15.1 decrease with the level of temporal aggregation, h. Furthermore, by a log-linear approximation,

$$\log[\text{Var}(lstd_{t,h})] \approx a + (2d - 1) \cdot \log(h), \tag{29}$$

which explains the apparent scaling law behind the two plots in the right panel of Figure 15.6, and the negative slopes of approximately $2d - 1$. The slopes in the top and bottom panels are $-.222$ and $-.270$, respectively, and the implied d values of $.389$ and $.365$ are almost identical to the values implied by the scaling law (26) and the two left panels of Figure 15.6.

15.7 Summary and concluding remarks

We first strengthened the theoretical basis for measuring and analyzing time series of realized volatilities constructed from high-frequency intraday returns, and then we put the theory to work, examining a unique dataset that consists of

10 years of 5-min DM/$ and yen/$ returns. We found that the distributions of realized daily variances, standard deviations, and covariances are skewed to the right and leptokurtic, but that the distributions of logarithmic standard deviations and correlations are approximately Gaussian. Volatility movements, moreover, are highly correlated across the two exchange rates. We also found that the correlation between the exchange rates (as opposed to the correlation between their volatilities) increases with volatility. Finally, we confirmed the wealth of existing evidence of strong volatility clustering effects in daily returns. However, in contrast to earlier work, which often indicates that volatility persistence decreases quickly with the horizon, we find that even monthly realized volatilities remain highly persistent. Nonetheless, realized volatilities do not have unit roots; instead, they appear to be fractionally integrated and, therefore, very slowly mean-reverting. This finding is strengthened by our analysis of temporally aggregated volatility series, whose properties adhere closely to the scaling laws implied by the structure of fractional integration.

A key conceptual distinction between this article and the earlier work on which we build—Andersen and Bollerslev (1998a), in particular—is the recognition that realized volatility is usefully viewed as the object of intrinsic interest, rather than simply a postmodeling device to be used to evaluate parametric conditional variance models such as GARCH. As such, it is of interest to examine and model realized volatility directly. This article is a first step in that direction, providing a nonparametric characterization of both the unconditional and conditional distributions of bivariate realized exchange rate volatility.

It will be of interest in future work to fit parametric models directly to realized volatility, and in turn to use them for forecasting in specific financial contexts. In particular, our findings suggest that a multivariate linear Gaussian long-memory model is appropriate for daily realized logarithmic standard deviations and correlations. Such as model could result in important improvements in the accuracy of volatility and correlation forecasts and related value-at-risk type calculations. This idea is pursued in Andersen, Bollerslev, Diebold, and Labys (2000).

References

Andersen, T. G., Benzoni, L., and Lund, J. (2000). Estimating Jump-Diffusions for Equity Returns, unpublished manuscript, Northwestern University, Dept. of Finance, J. L. Kellogg Graduate School of Management.

Andersen, T. G. and Bollerslev, T. (1997a). Intraday Periodicity and Volatility Persistence in Financial Markets. *Journal of Empirical Finance* 4, 115–158.

——(1997b). Heterogeneous Information Arrivals and Return Volatility Dynamics: Uncovering the Long-Run in High Frequency Returns. *Journal of Finance* 52, 975–1005.

——(1998a). Answering the Skeptics: Yes, Standard Volatility Models Do Provide Accurate Forecasts. *International Economic Review* 39, 885–905.

——(1998b). DM-Dollar Volatility: Intraday Activity Patterns, Macroeconomic Announcements, and Longer-Run Dependencies. *Journal of Finance* 53, 219–265.

—— Bollerslev, T., Diebold, F. X., and Labys, P. (2000). Modeling and Forecasting Realized Volatility, unpublished manuscript, Northwestern University, Duke University, and University of Pennsylvania.

—— Lange, S. (1999). Forecasting Financial Market Volatility: Sample Frequency vis-à-vis Forecast Horizon. *Journal of Empirical Finance* 6, 457–77.

Back, K. (1991). Asset Prices for General Processes. *Journal of Mathematical Economics* 20, 317–95.

Baillie, R. T., and Bollerslev, T. (1989). The Message in Daily Exchange Rates: A Conditional Variance Tale. *Journal of Business and Economic Statistics* 7, 297–305.

Barndorff-Nielsen, O. E. and Shephard, N. (1998). Aggregation and Model Construction for Volatility Models, unpublished manuscript, Nuffield College, Oxford, UK.

Beran, J. (1994). *Statistics for Long-Memory Processes*, New York: Chapman and Hall.

Bollerslev, T., and Domowitz, I. (1993). Trading Patterns and Prices in the Interbank Foreign Exchange Market. *Journal of Finance* 48, 1421–43.

—— Engle, R. F. (1993). Common Persistence in Conditional Variances. *Econometrica* 61, 166–87.

—— —— Nelson, D. B. (1994). ARCH Models, in *Handbook of Econometrics* (Vol. IV), (eds.) Engle, R. F. and D. McFadden, Amsterdam: North-Holland, 2959–3038.

Boyer, B. H., Gibson, M. S., and Loretan, M. (1999). Pitfalls in Tests for Changes in Correlations, IFS Discussion Paper No. 597, Federal Reserve Board.

Chernov, M. and Ghysels, E. (2000). A Study Towards a Unified Approach to the Joint Estimation of Objective and Risk Neutral Measures for the Purpose of Options Valuation. *Journal of Financial Economics* 56, 407–58.

Christoffersen, P. F. and Diebold, F. X. (2000). How Relevant is Volatility Forecasting for Risk Management?. *Review of Economics and Statistics* 82, 12–22.

Clark, P. K. (1973). A Subordinated Stochastic Process Model with Finite Variance for Speculative Prices. *Econometrica* 41, 135–55.

Comte, F. and Renault, E. (1998). Long Memory in Continuous-Time Stochastic Volatility Models. *Mathematical Finance* 8, 291–323.

Dacorogna, M. M., Müller, U. A., Nagler, R. J., Olsen, R. B., and Pictet, O. V. (1993). A Geographical Model for the Daily and Weekly Seasonal Volatility in the Foreign Exchange Market. *Journal of International Money and Finance* 12, 413–38.

Danielsson, J. and Payne, R. (1999). Real Trading Patterns and Prices in Spot Foreign Exchange Markets, unpublished manuscript, London School of Economics, Financial Markets Group.

Deo, R. and Hurvich, C. M. (1998). On the Log Periodogram Regression Estimator of the Memory Parameter in Long Memory Stochastic Volatility Models. *Econometric Theory*, forthcoming.

Diebold, F. X. and Lindner, P. (1996). Fractional Integration and Interval Prediction. *Economics Letters* 50, 305–13.

—— Nerlove, M. (1989). The Dynamics of Exchange Rate Volatility: A Multivariate Latent Factor ARCH Model. *Journal of Applied Econometrics* 4, 1–22.

Ding, Z., Granger, C. W. J., and Engle, R. F. (1993). A Long Memory Property of Stock Market Returns and a New Model. *Journal of Empirical Finance* 1, 83–106.

Engle, R. F. and Bollerslev, T. (1986). Modeling the Persistence of Conditional Variances. *Econometric Reviews* 5, 1–50.

Forbes, K. and Rigobon, R. (1999). No Contagion, Only Interdependence: Measuring Stock Market Co-Movements, Working Paper 7267, National Bureau of Economic Research.

Foster, D. P. and Nelson, D. B. (1996). Continuous Record Asymptotics for Rolling Sample Variance Estimators. *Econometrica* 64, 139–74.

French, K. R., Schwert, G. W., and Stambaugh, R. F. (1987). Expected Stock Returns and Volatility. *Journal of Financial Economics* 19, 3–29.

Gallant, A. R., Hsu, C.-T., and Tauchen, G. (1999). Using Daily Range Data to Calibrate Volatility Diffusions and Extract the Forward Integrated Variance. *Review of Economics and Statistics* 81, 617–31.

Geweke, J. and Porter-Hudak, S. (1983). The Estimation and Application of Long Memory Time Series Models. *Journal of Time Series Analysis* 4, 221–38.

Goodhart, C., Ito, T., and Payne, R. (1996). One Day in June 1993: A Study of the Working of the Reuters 2000–2 Electronic Foreign Exchange Trading System, in *The Microstructure of Foreign Exchange Markets*, (eds.) Frankel, J. A., Galli, G., and Giovannini, A., Chicago: University of Chicago Press, 107–79.

Granger, C. W. J., Ding, Z., and Spear, S. (1997). Stylized Facts on the Temporal and Distributional Properties of Daily Data From Speculative Markets, unpublished manuscript, University of California, San Diego, Dept. of Economics.

——Joyeux, R. (1980). An Introduction to Long Memory Time Series Models and Fractional Differencing. *Journal of Time Series Analysis* 1, 15–39.

Hsieh, D. A. (1991). Chaos and Nonlinear Dynamics: Application to Financial Markets. *Journal of Finance* 46, 1839–77.

Hull, J. and White, A. (1987). The Pricing of Options on Assets with Stochastic Volatilities. *Journal of Finance* 42, 381–400.

Hurvich, C. M. and Beltrao, K. I. (1994). Automatic Semiparametric Estimation of the Memory Parameter of a Long-Memory Time Series. *Journal of Time Series Analysis* 15, 285–302.

——Deo, R., and Brodsky, J. (1998). The Mean Squared Error of Geweke and Porter Hudak's Estimator of the Memory Parameter of a Long-Memory Time Series. *Journal of Time Series Analysis* 19, 19–46.

King, M., Sentana, E., and Wadhwani, S. (1994). Volatility and Links Between National Markets. *Econometrica* 62, 901–33.

Meheswaran, S. and Sims, C. A. (1993). Empirical Implications of Arbitrage-Free Asset Markets, in *Models, Methods and Applications of Econometrics: Essays in Honor of A. R. Bergstrom*, (ed.), P. C. B. Phillips, Cambridge, MA: Blackwell, 301–16.

Müller, U. A., Dacorogna, M. M., Olsen, R. B., Pictet, O. V., Schwarz, M., and Morgenegg, C. (1990). Statistical Study of Foreign Exchange Rates, Empirical Evidence of a Price Change Scaling Law, and Intraday Analysis. *Journal of Banking and Finance* 14, 1189–208.

Protter, P. E. (1990). *Stochastic Integration and Differential Equations: A New Approach*, New York: Springer-Verlag (third printing, 1995).

Robinson, P. M. (1994). Semiparametric Analysis of Long-Memory Time Series. *The Annals of Statistics* 22, 515–39.

——(1995). Long-Periodogram Regression of Time Series with Long-Range Dependence. *The Annals of Statistics* 23, 1048–72.

——Henry, M. (1999). Long and Short Memory Conditional Heteroskedasticity in Estimating the Memory Parameter of Levels. *Econometric Theory* 19, 299–336.

Rogers, L. C. G. (1997). Arbitrage with Fractional Brownian Motion. *Mathematical Finance* 7, 95–105.

Ronn, E. (1998). The Impact of Large Changes in Asset Prices on Intra-Market Correlations in the Stock and Bond Markets, unpublished manuscript, University of Texas, Austin, Dept. of Finance.

Schwert, G. W. (1989). Why does Stock Market Volatility Change Over Time?. *Journal of Finance* 44, 1115–154.

——(1990). Stock Market Volatility. *Financial Analysts Journal*, May–June, 23–34.

Solnik, B., Boucrelle, C., and Le Fur, Y. (1996). International Market Correlation and Volatility. *Financial Analysts Journal*, September–October, 17–34.

Taqqu, M. S. and Teverovsky, V. (1996). Semi-Parametric Graphical Estimation Techniques for Long-Memory Data, in *Time Series Analysis in Memory of E. J. Hannan*, (eds.) Robinson, P. M. and Rosenblatt, M., New York: Springer-Verlag, pp. 420–32.

Taylor, S. J. (1986). *Modelling Financial Time Series*, Chichester: Wiley.

——Xu, X. (1997). The Incremental Volatility Information in One Million Foreign Exchange Quotations. *Journal of Empirical Finance* 4, 317–40.

16
Econometric Analysis of Realized Volatility and its use in Estimating Stochastic Volatility Models*

OLE E. BARNDORFF-NIELSEN

AND

NEIL SHEPHARD

Summary. The availability of intraday data on the prices of speculative assets means that we can use quadratic variation-like measures of activity in financial markets, called realized volatility, to study the stochastic properties of returns. Here, under the assumption of a rather general stochastic volatility model, we derive the moments and the asymptotic distribution of the realized volatility error—the difference between realized volatility and the discretized integrated volatility (which we call actual volatility). These properties can be used to allow us to estimate the parameters of stochastic volatility models without recourse to the use of simulation-intensive methods.

Keywords: Kalman filter; Leverage; Lévy process; Power variation; Quadratic variation; Quarticity; Realized volatility; Stochastic volatility; Subordination; Superposition

16.1 Introduction

16.1.1 Stochastic volatility

In the stochastic volatility (SV) model for log-prices of stocks and for log-exchange-rates a basic Brownian motion is generalized to allow the volatility term to vary over time. Then the log-price $y^*(t)$ follows the solution to the stochastic differential equation (SDE)

$$\mathrm{d}y^*(t) = \{\mu + \beta\sigma^2(t)\}\,\mathrm{d}t + \sigma(t)\,\mathrm{d}w(t), \tag{1}$$

where $\sigma^2(t)$, the *instantaneous* or *spot volatility*, will be assumed (almost surely) to have locally square integrable sample paths, while being stationary and stochastically independent of the standard Brownian motion $w(t)$. We shall label μ the drift and β the risk premium. Over an interval of time of length $\Delta > 0$ returns are defined as

$$y_n = y^*(\Delta n) - y^*\{(n-1)\Delta\}, \quad n = 1, 2, \ldots, \tag{2}$$

* This work was previously published as O. E. Barndorff-Nielsen and N. Shephard (2002), 'Non-Gaussian Ornstein-Uhlenbeck-Based Models and Some of their Uses in Financial Economics (with Discussion)', *Journal of the Royal Statistical Society B* 64, Part 2. Copyright © Blackwell Publishing. Reproduced by kind permission.

which implies that, whatever the model for σ^2, it follows that

$$y_n | \sigma_n^2 \sim N(\mu\Delta + \beta\sigma_n^2, \sigma_n^2),$$

where

$$\sigma_n^2 = \sigma^{2*}(n\Delta) - \sigma^{2*}\{(n-1)\Delta\}$$

and

$$\sigma^{2*}(t) = \int_0^t \sigma^2(u)\,du.$$

In econometrics $\sigma^{2*}(t)$ is called *integrated volatility*, whereas we call σ_n^2 *actual volatility*. Both definitions play a central role in the probabilistic analysis of SV models. Reviews of the literature on this topic are given in Taylor (1994), Shephard (1996) and Ghysels et al. (1996), whereas statistical and probabilistic aspects are studied in detail in Barndorff-Nielsen and Shephard (2001a). One of the key results in this literature (Barndorff-Nielsen and Shephard, 2001a) is that if we write (when they exist) ξ, ω^2 and r respectively as the mean, variance and the autocorrelation function of the process $\sigma^2(t)$ then

$$\left.\begin{array}{l} E(\sigma_n^2) = \xi\Delta, \\ \text{var}(\sigma_n^2) = 2\omega^2 r^{**}(\Delta), \\ \text{cov}(\sigma_n^2, \sigma_{n+s}^2) = \omega^2 \diamond r^{**}(\Delta s), \end{array}\right\} \tag{3}$$

where

$$\diamond r^{**}(s) = r^{**}(s + \Delta) - 2r^{**}(s) + r^{**}(s - \Delta), \tag{4}$$

and

$$\begin{array}{l} r^*(t) = \int_0^t r(u)\,du, \\ r^{**}(t) = \int_0^t r^*(u)\,du, \end{array} \tag{5}$$

i.e. the second-order properties of $\sigma^2(t)$ completely determine the second-order properties of actual volatility.

One of the most important aspects of SV models is that $\sigma^{2*}(t)$ can be exactly recovered using the entire path of $y^*(t)$. In particular, for the above SV model the quadratic variation is $\sigma^{2*}(t)$, i.e. we have

$$[y^*](t) = \plim_{q\to\infty} \left[\Sigma\{y^*(t_{i+1}^q) - y^*(t_i^q)\}^2 \right] = \sigma^{2*}(t) \tag{6}$$

for any sequence of partitions $t_0^q = 0 < t_1^q < \ldots < t_{m_r}^q = t$ with $\sup_i (t_{i+1}^q - t_i^q) \to 0$ for $q \to \infty$. Here plim denotes the probability limit of the sum. This is a powerful result for it does not depend on the model for instantaneous volatility nor the drift terms in the SDE for log-prices given in equation (1). The quadratic variation estimation of integrated volatility has recently been highlighted, following the initial draft of Barndorff-Nielsen and Shephard (2001*a*) and the concurrent independent work of Andersen and Bollerslev (1998*a*), by Andersen, Bollerslev, Diebold and Labys (2001) and Maheu and McCurdy (2001) in foreign exchange markets and Andersen, Bollerslev, Diebold and Ebens (2001) and Areal and Taylor (2002) in equity markets. See also the contribution of Comte and Renault (1998).

In practice, although we often have a continuous record of quotes or transaction prices, at a very fine level the SV model is a poor fit to the data. This is due to market microstructure effects (e.g. discreteness of prices, bid–ask bounce, irregular trading etc.; see Bai et al. (2000)). As a result we should regard the above quadratic variation result as indicating that we can estimate actual volatility, e.g. over a day, reasonably accurately by sums of squared returns, say, by using periods of 30 min but keeping in mind that taking returns over increasingly finer time periods will lead to the introduction of important biases. Hence the limit argument in quadratic variation is interesting but of limited direct practical use on its own. Suppose instead that we have fixed M intraday observations during each day; then the sum of squared intraday changes over a day is

$$\{y\}_n = \sum_{j=1}^{M} \left[y^* \left\{ (n-1)\Delta + \frac{\Delta j}{M} \right\} - y^* \left\{ (n-1)\Delta + \frac{\Delta(j-1)}{M} \right\} \right]^2, \qquad (7)$$

which is an estimate of σ_n^2. It is a consistent estimate as $M \to \infty$, while it is unbiased when μ and β are 0. In econometrics $\{y\}_n$ has recently been labelled *realized volatility*, and we shall follow that convention here. Andersen, Bollerslev, Diebold and Labys (2001), Andersen, Bollerslev, Diebold and Ebens (2001) and Andersen et al. (2000) have empirically studied the properties of $\{y\}_n$ in foreign exchange and equity markets (earlier, less formal work on this topic includes Poterba and Summers (1986), Schwert (1989), Taylor and Xu (1997) and Christensen and Prabhala (1998)). In their econometric analysis they have regarded $\{y\}_n$ as a very accurate estimate of σ_n^2. Indeed they often regard the estimate as basically revealing the true value of actual volatility so that $y_n / \sqrt{\{y\}_n}$ is virtually Gaussian. So far no measure of error has been obtained which indicates the difference between $\{y\}_n$ and σ_n^2. We shall show that this difference is approximately mixed Gaussian, can be substantial and that more accurate estimates of σ_n^2 are readily available if we are willing to use a model for $\sigma^2(t)$. Andreou and Ghysels (2001) have independently approximated the properties of realized volatility using the methods of Foster and Nelson (1996) in their study of rolling estimators of the spot volatility $\sigma^2(t)$.

In this paper we shall discuss a simple way of formally bridging the gap between realized and actual volatility, providing a discussion of the properties of $\{y\}_n$ which has so far been lacking in the literature. Inevitably for finite M these properties will depend on the dynamics of the instantaneous volatility as well as the drift term in the SDE for log-prices. This must be the case, for the shorthand of ignoring the small sample effects of estimating σ_n^2 with the consistent $\{y\}_n$ is only valid for infeasibly large values of M.

In particular the contribution of our paper will be to allow us

(a) to derive the asymptotic distribution of $(\{y\}_n - \sigma_n^2)\sqrt{M}$ for large M, showing that this does not depend on μ and β, and is statistically sensible,

(b) to analyse the properties of realized volatility by assuming that $\mu = \beta = 0$ as the corresponding error has been shown to be small,

(c) to understand the exact second-order properties of $\{y\}_n$ when $\mu = \beta = 0$,

(d) to use the models for instantaneous volatility to provide *model-based* estimates of actual volatility (rather than model-free estimates which assume $M \to \infty$) using the series of realized volatility measurements when $\mu = \beta = 0$ (these model-based estimates can be based on past, current or historical sequences of realized volatilities) and

(e) to estimate the parameters of SV models by using simple and rather accurate statistical procedures when $\mu = \beta = 0$.

16.1.2 Empirical example

To illustrate some of the empirical features of realized volatility we have used the same return data as employed by Andersen, Bollerslev, Diebold and Labys (2001), although Appendix A will describe the slightly different adjustments that we have made to deal with some missing data. This US dollar–German Deutschmark series covers the 10-year period from 1 December 1986, until 30 November 1996. Every 5 min it records the most recent quote to appear on the Reuters screen. It has been kindly supplied to us by Olsen and Associates in Zurich and preprocessed by Tim Bollerslev. It will be used throughout our paper to illustrate the results that we shall develop. In Fig. 16.1(a) we have drawn the correlogram of the squared 5-min returns over the 10 years' sample. It shows the well-known very strong diurnal effect (the x-axis is drawn in days). This will be discussed in detail in Section 6 but for now will be ignored entirely. Fig. 16.1(b) shows the correlogram of realized volatility, $\{y\}_n$, computed using $M = 288$ (i.e. based on 5-min data) and again using the whole 10 years of data. The graph starts out at around 0.6, decays very quickly for a number of days and then decays at a slower rate. Fig. 16.1(c) shows a cumulative version of the squared 5-min returns drawn on a small scale, while in Fig. 16.1(d) the same cumulative function is drawn over a larger timescale. It is the daily increments of this process which make up realized volatility.

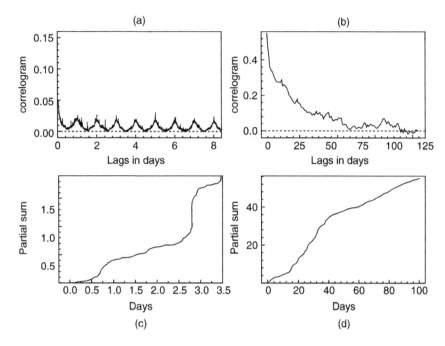

Fig. 16.1. Summary statistics for Olsen group's 5-min changes data:
(a) autocorrelation function of 5-min returns; (b) autocorrelation function
of realized volatility; (c) cumulative sum of squared 5-min changes over
a short interval; (d) cumulative sum of squared 5-min changes over a
long interval.

16.1.3 Outline of the paper

The outline of the rest of the paper is as follows. In Section 16.2 we discuss the basic approach in the most straightforward set-up where μ and β are 0, providing the second-order properties of realized volatility. These can be used in estimating the value of actual volatility from a time series of realized volatilities. This is discussed in Section 16.3, which also contains a discussion of using the realized volatilities to provide estimates of continuous SV models. Section 16.4 gives an empirical illustration of the methods developed in the previous two sections. Section 16.5 provides the asymptotic distribution of $(\{y\}_n - \sigma_n^2)\sqrt{M}$, covering the case where there is drift and a risk premium. This section shows that the effect on realized volatility of the drift and the risk premium is extremely small. Section 16.6 studies diurnal effects and leverage extensions. Section 16.7 concludes, whereas Appendix A contains a discussion of the data set that is used in this paper together with a proof of lemma 1 and theorem 1.

16.2 Relating actual to realized volatility

16.2.1 Generic results

Actual volatility σ_n^2 plays a crucial role in SV models. It can be estimated using realized volatility $\{y\}_n$, given in equation (7). Here we discuss this in the simplest context where $\mu = \beta = 0$, delaying our discussion of the effect on $\{y\}_n$ of the drift and risk premium until Section 16.5. In that section we shall show that the effect is minor and so the results that we develop here will still be important in that wider case.

In SV models we can always make the decomposition

$$\{y\}_n = \sigma_n^2 + u_n, \quad \text{where } u_n = \{y\}_n - \sigma_n^2. \tag{8}$$

Here we call u_n the *realized volatility error*, which has the property that $E(u_n | \sigma_n^2) = 0$. Hence realized volatility is an unbiased estimator of actual volatility. We know that as $M \to \infty$ then $\{y\}_n \to \sigma_n^2$, almost surely, so it is also consistent. However, the purpose of this section is to discuss the properties of $\{y\}_n$ for finite M. We can see that

$$E(\{y\}_n) = \Delta\xi, \quad \text{var}(\{y\}_n) = \text{var}(u_n) + \text{var}(\sigma_n^2), \quad \text{cov}(\{y\}_n, \{y\}_{n+s}) = \text{cov}(\sigma_n^2, \sigma_{n+s}^2).$$

Further, writing

$$\sigma_{j,n}^2 = \sigma^{2*}\left\{(n-1)\Delta + \frac{\Delta j}{M}\right\} - \sigma^{2*}\left\{(n-1)\Delta + \frac{\Delta(j-1)}{M}\right\}$$

we have that

$$u_n \overset{\mathcal{L}}{=} \sum_{j=1}^{M} \sigma_{j,n}^2(\varepsilon_{j,n}^2 - 1),$$

where $\varepsilon_{j,n} \sim^{\text{IID}} N(0, 1)$ and independent of $\{\sigma_{j,n}^2\}$. It is clear that $\{u_n\}$ is a weak white noise sequence which is uncorrelated with the actual volatility series $\{\sigma_n^2\}$.

Now, unconditionally,

$$\begin{aligned}
\text{var}(u_n) &= 2ME\{(\sigma_{1,n}^2)^2\} \\
&= 2M\{\text{var}(\sigma_{1,n}^2) + E(\sigma_{1,n}^2)^2\},
\end{aligned} \tag{9}$$

for $\sigma_{1,n}^2$ has the same marginal distribution as each element of $\{\sigma_{j,n}^2\}$. In general we have from equations (3) that

$$\begin{aligned}
E(\sigma_{1,n}^2) &= \Delta M^{-1}\xi, \\
\text{var}(\sigma_{1,n}^2) &= 2\omega^2 r^{**}(\Delta M^{-1}).
\end{aligned} \tag{10}$$

Hence we can compute $\text{var}(u_n)$ for all SV models when $\mu = \beta = 0$. In turn, having established the second-order properties of σ_n^2 and u_n, we can immediately use the results in Whittle (1983) to provide best linear prediction and smoothing results for the unobserved actual volatilities σ_n^2 from the time series of realized volatilities $\{y\}_n$. The only issues which remain on this front are computational. Otherwise this covers all covariance stationary models for $\sigma^2(t)$—including long memory processes.

One of the implications of the result given above is that

$$(\text{corr}(\{y\}_n, \{y\}_{n+s}) = \frac{\text{cov}(\sigma_n^2, \sigma_{n+s}^2)}{\text{var}(u_n) + \text{var}(\sigma_n^2)}$$

$$= \frac{\omega^2 \Diamond r^{**}(\Delta s)}{2M^{-1}\{2\omega^2 M^2 r^{**}(\Delta M^{-1}) + (\Delta \xi)^2\} + 2\omega^2 r^{**}(\Delta)}.$$

Notice that

$$\text{corr}(y_n^2, y_{n+s}^2) = \frac{\omega^2 \Diamond r^{**}(\Delta s)}{2\{2\omega^2 r^{**}(\Delta) + (\Delta \xi)^2\} + 2\omega^2 r^{**}(\Delta)}$$

can be derived from this result, for $\{y\}_n = y_n^2$ when $M = 1$. Hence the decay rates in the autocorrelation function of $\{y\}_n$, σ_n^2 and y_n^2 are the same in general but the correlation varies considerably, being the highest for σ_n^2, followed by $\{y\}_n$ and lowest for y_n^2.

In practice we tend to use realized volatility measures with M being moderately large. Hence it is of interest to think of a central limit approximation to the distribution of u_n. This will depend on the limit of $t^{-2}r^{**}(t)$ as $t \to 0$ from above. Now, by Taylor series expansion

$$r^{**}(t) = r^{**}(0+) + tr^*(0+) + \frac{1}{2}t^2 r(0+) + o(t^2) = \frac{1}{2}t^2 r(0+) + o(t^2).$$

This means that the limit of $t^{-2}r^{**}(t)$ is $\frac{1}{2}$. A consequence of this is that

$$\lim_{M \to \infty} \{M^2 \text{var}(\sigma_{1,n}^2)\} = \Delta^2 \omega^2, \tag{11}$$

implying that, as $M \to \infty$,

$$\text{var}(u_n \sqrt{M}) = \text{var}\{(\{y\}_n - \sigma_n^2)\sqrt{M}\} \to 2\Delta^2(\omega^2 + \xi^2).$$

This is an important result. We have moved away from the standard consistency result of $\{y\}_n \to \sigma_n^2$ in probability as $M \to \infty$, which follows from familiar quadratic variation results. Now we have the more refined measure of the uncertainty of this error term.

16.2.2 Simple example

Suppose that the volatility process has the autocorrelation function $r(t) = \exp(-\lambda|t|)$. Here we recall two classes of processes which have this property. The first is the constant elasticity of variance (CEV) process which is the solution to the SDE

$$d\sigma^2(t) = -\lambda\{\sigma^2(t) - \xi\}dt + \omega\sigma(t)^\eta db(\lambda t), \qquad \eta \in [1,\ 2],$$

where $b(t)$ is standard Brownian motion uncorrelated with $w(t)$. Of course the special case of $\eta = 1$ delivers the square-root process, whereas when $\eta = 2$ we have Nelson's generalized autoregressive conditional heteroscedastic diffusion. These models have been heavily favoured by Meddahi and Renault (2002) in this context. The second process is the non-Gaussian Ornstein–Uhlenbeck (OU) process which is the solution to the SDE

$$d\sigma^2(t) = -\lambda\sigma^2(t)dt + dz(\lambda t), \tag{12}$$

where $z(t)$ is a Lévy process with non-negative increments. These models have been developed in this context by Barndorff-Nielsen and Shephard (2001a). In Fig. 16.2 we have drawn a curve to represent a simulated sample path of σ_n^2 from

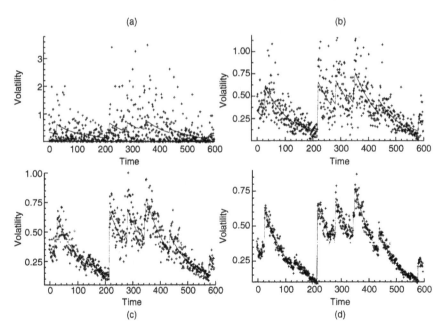

Fig. 16.2. Actual σ_n^2 (——) and realized $\{v\}_n(+)$ (with M varying) volatility based on a Γ (4, 8) OU process with $\lambda = -\log(0.98)$ and $\Delta = 1$ (this implies $\xi = 0.5$ and $\xi\omega^{-2} = 8$): (a) $M = 1$; (b) $M = 12$; (c) $M = 48$; (d) $M = 288$.

an OU process where $\sigma^2(t)$ has a $\Gamma(4, 8)$ stationary distribution, $\lambda = -\log(0.98)$ and $\Delta = 1$, along with the associated realized volatility (depicted by using crosses) computed using a variety of values of M. We see that as M increases the precision of realized volatility increases, whereas Fig. 16.2(d) shows that the variance of the realized volatility error increases with the volatility, a result which we shall come back to in Section 5 where the asymptotic distribution that we develop for $u_n\sqrt{M}$ will reflect this feature.

For both CEV and OU models

$$r^{**}(t) = \lambda^{-2}\{\exp(-\lambda|t|) - 1 + \lambda t\}$$

and

$$\Diamond r^{**}(\Delta s) = \lambda^{-2}\{1 - \exp(-\lambda\Delta)\}^2 \exp\{-\lambda\Delta(s - 1)\}, \quad s > 0.$$

This implies that

$$E(\sigma_n^2) = \Delta\xi,$$

$$\mathrm{var}(\sigma_n^2) = \frac{2\omega^2}{\lambda^2}\{\exp(-\lambda\Delta) - 1 + \lambda\Delta\}$$

and

$$\mathrm{corr}(\sigma_n^2, \sigma_{n+s}^2) = d\exp t\{-\lambda\Delta(s - 1)\}, \quad s = 1, 2, \ldots, \tag{13}$$

where

$$d = \frac{\{1 - \exp(-\lambda\Delta)\}^2}{2\{\exp(-\lambda\Delta) - 1 + \lambda\Delta\}} \leqslant 1.$$

Finally

$$\begin{aligned}
\mathrm{var}(u_n) &= 2M\{\mathrm{var}(\sigma_{1,\,n}^2) + E(\sigma_{1,\,n}^2)^2\} \\
&= 2M[2\omega^2\lambda^{-2}\{\exp(-\lambda\Delta/M) - 1 + \lambda\Delta M^{-1}\} + (\Delta M^{-1})^2\xi^2].
\end{aligned} \tag{14}$$

Importantly this analysis implies that actual volatility has the autocorrelation function of an autoregressive moving average (ARMA) model of order $(1, 1)$. Its autoregressive root is $\exp(-\lambda\Delta)$, which will be typically close to 1 unless Δ is very large, whereas the moving average root is also determined by $\exp(-\lambda\Delta)$ but must be found numerically. A graph of the moving average root against $\exp(-\lambda\Delta)$ is given in Fig. 16.3(a) and shows that for a wide range of the autoregressive root the moving average root is around 0.265. Likewise Fig. 16.3(b)

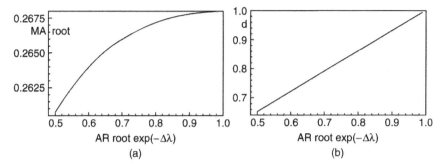

Fig. 16.3. (a) Moving average root plotted against autoregressive root $\exp(-\Delta\lambda)$ for the ARMA(1, 1) representation and (b) d in the expression for $\mathrm{corr}(\sigma_n^2, \sigma_{n+s}^2)$ against autoregressive root $\exp(-\Delta\lambda)$.

shows a plot of d against $\exp(-\lambda\Delta)$ and indicates a rapid decline in this coefficient as the autoregressive root falls. In particular, in financial econometrics the literature suggests that volatility is quite persistent, which would imply that d should be close to 1. Thus, if t is recorded in days and Δ is set to 1 day, then empirically reasonable values of λ will imply that d should be close to 1.

In turn the autocorrelation function for σ_n^2 implies that the squares of returns have autocorrelations of the form

$$\mathrm{corr}(y_n^2, y_{n+s}^2) = c' \exp\{-\lambda\Delta(s-1)\}, \tag{15}$$

where

$$\frac{1}{3} \geqslant \frac{1}{3} d \geqslant c' = \frac{\{1 - \exp(-\lambda\Delta)^2\}}{6\{\exp(-\lambda\Delta) - 1 + \lambda\Delta\} + 2(\lambda\Delta)^2(\xi/\omega)^2} \geqslant 0.$$

This means that y_n^2 also has a linear ARMA(1, 1) representation. Further, it has the same autocorrelation function as the familiar generalized autoregressive conditional heteroscedastic model that is used extensively in econometrics (see, for example, Bollerslev et al. (1994)). Finally, the autoregressive root of the ARMA representation is the same for y_n^2 as for σ_n^2; however, the moving average root of the square changes is much larger in absolute value. The implication is that the correlograms for y_n^2 will be less clear than if we had observed the correlograms of the σ_n^2. This can be most easily seen by noting that for small λ

$$c' \simeq \frac{1 - \lambda\Delta}{3 + 2(\xi/\omega)^2},$$

which is much smaller than d which is approximately $1 - \lambda\Delta$. For example, if $\xi = \omega$, then c' will be approximately 0.2 for daily data.

16.2.3 Extension of the example: superpositions

The OU or CEV volatility models are often too simple to fit accurately the types of dependence structures that we observe in financial economics. This can be seen Fig. 16.1(b) which displays the autocorrelation function of realized volatility for the Olsen group's 5-min data. This graph shows a relatively quick initial decline in the autocorrelation function, followed by a slower decay. This single observation is sufficient to dismiss the OU and CEV models.

One mathematically tractable way of improving the flexibility of the volatility model is to let the instantaneous volatility be the sum, or superposition, of independent OU or CEV processes. As the processes do not need to be identically distributed, this offers plenty of flexibility while still being mathematically tractable. Superpositions of such processes also have potential for modelling long-range dependence and self-similarity in volatility. This is discussed in the OU case in Barndorff-Nielsen and Shephard (2001*a*) and in more detail by Barndorff-Nielsen (2001) who formalizes the use of superpositions as a way of modelling long-range dependence. This follows earlier related work by Granger (1980), Barndorff-Nielsen et al. (1990), Cox (1991), Ding and Granger (1996), Engle and Lee (1999), Shephard (1996), pages 36–37, Andersen and Bollerslev (1997*a*), Barndorff-Nielsen (1998) and Comte and Renault (1998).

Consider volatility based on the sum of J independent OU or CEV processes,

$$\sigma^2(t) = \sum_{i=1}^{J} \tau^{(i)}(t),$$

where the $\tau^{(i)}(t)$ process has the memory parameter λ_i. We assume that

$$E\{\tau^{(i)}(t)\} = w_i\xi,$$
$$\operatorname{var}\{\tau^{(i)}(t)\} = w_i\omega^2,$$

where $\{w_i \geqslant 0\}$ and $\sum_{i=1}^{J} w_i = 1$, implying that $E\{\sigma^2(t)\} = \xi$ and $\operatorname{var}\{\sigma^2(t)\} = \omega^2$. The implication is that

$$\operatorname{cov}\{\sigma^2(t),\ \sigma^2(t+s)\} = \sum_{i=1}^{J} \operatorname{cov}\{\tau^{(i)}(t),\ \tau^{(i)}(t+s)\} = \omega^2 \sum_{i=1}^{J} w_i \exp\left(-\lambda_i|s|\right).$$

Hence the autocorrelation function of instantaneous volatility can have components which are a mix of quickly and slowly decaying components. For fixed J the statistical identification of this model (imposing a constraint like $\lambda_1 < \ldots < \lambda_J$) is a consequence of the form of the autocorrelation function and the uniqueness of the Laplace transformation.

The linearity of the superposition of OU processes means that actual volatility has the form $\sigma_n^2 = \sum_{i=1}^{J} \tau_n^{(i)}$ where

$$\tau_n^{(i)} = \tau^{(i)*}(n\Delta) - \tau^{(i)*}\{(n-1)\Delta\}$$

and

$$\tau^{(i)*}(t) = \int_0^t \tau^{(i)}(u)\mathrm{d}u.$$

The key feature is that each $\tau_n^{(i)}$ has an ARMA(1, 1) representation of the type discussed earlier. As the autocovariance function of a sum of independent components is the sum of the autocovariances of the terms in the sum, we can compute the autocorrelation function of σ_n^2 without any new work. Computationally it is helpful to realize that the sum of uncorrelated ARMA(1, 1) processes can be fed into a linear state space representation when combined with decomposition (8). The only new issue is computing

$$\mathrm{var}(u_t) = 2M\{\mathrm{var}(\sigma_{1,n}^2) + E(\sigma_{1,n}^2)^2\}.$$

Clearly $E(\sigma_{1,n}^2) = \xi\Delta M^{-1}$ whereas

$$\mathrm{var}(\sigma_{1,n}^2) = \sum_{i=1}^{J} \mathrm{var}(\tau_{1,n}^{(i)}) = 2\omega^2 \sum_{i=1}^{J} w_i r_i^{**}(\Delta M^{-1})$$

$$= 2\omega^2 \sum_{i=1}^{J} \frac{w_i}{\lambda_i^2}\{\exp(-\lambda_i\Delta M^{-1}) - 1 + \lambda_i\Delta M^{-1}\}.$$

$$= 2\omega^2 \sum_{i=1}^{J} \frac{w_i}{2\lambda_i^2}(\lambda_i\Delta M^{-1})^2 + o(M^{-2})$$

Importantly, for large M this expression simplifies and so we again obtain

$$\mathrm{var}(u_n\sqrt{M}) \to 2\Delta^2(\omega^2 + \xi^2), \qquad \text{as} \quad M \to \infty.$$

16.3 Efficiency gains: model-based estimators of volatility

16.3.1 State space representation

If $\sigma^2(t)$ is an OU or CEV process then σ_n^2 has an ARMA(1, 1) representation and so it is computationally convenient to place decomposition (8) into a linear state space representation (see, for example, Harvey (1989), chapter 3, and Hamilton (1994), chapter 13). In particular we write $\alpha_{1n} - \sigma_n^2 - \Delta\xi$ and $u_n - \sigma_u v_{1n}$; then the state space representation is explicitly

$$\{y\}_n = \Delta\xi + (1\ 0)\,\alpha_n + \sigma_u v_{1n},$$

$$\alpha_{n+1} = \begin{pmatrix} \phi & 1 \\ 0 & 0 \end{pmatrix}\alpha_n + \begin{pmatrix} \sigma_\sigma \\ \sigma_\sigma\theta \end{pmatrix}v_{2n}, \tag{16}$$

where v_n is a zero-mean, white noise sequence with an identity covariance matrix. The parameters ϕ, θ and σ_σ^2 represent the autoregressive root, the moving average root and the variance of the innovation to this process, whereas σ_u^2 is found from equations (9) and (10). Software for handling linear state space models is available in Koopman et al. (1999). Having constructed this representation we can use a Kalman filter to estimate unbiasedly and efficiently (in a linear sense) σ_n^2 by prediction (i.e. the estimate of σ_n^2, using $\{y\}_1, \ldots, \{y\}_{n-1}$) and smoothing (i.e. the estimate of σ_n^2, using $\{y\}_1, \ldots, \{y\}_T$ where T is the sample size). By-products of the Kalman filter are the mean-square errors of these *model-based* (i.e. they depend on the assumption that σ_n^2 has an ARMA(1, 1) representation) estimators.

Table 16.1 reports the mean-square error of the model-based predictor and smoother of actual volatility, as well as the corresponding result for the model-free raw realized volatility (the mean-square errors of the model-based estimators will be above the figures quoted towards the very start and end of the sample, for we have quoted steady state quantities). The results in the lefthand block of Table 16.1 correspond to the model which was simulated in Fig. 16.2, whereas the other blocks vary the ratio of ξ to ω^2. The exercise is repeated for two values of λ.

Table 16.1. Exact mean-square error (steady state) of the estimators
of actual volatility[†]

M	Results for $\xi = 0.5$ and $\xi\omega^{-2} = 8$			Results for $\xi = 0.5$ and $\xi\omega^{-2} = 4$			Results for $\xi = 0.5$ and $\xi\omega^{-2} = 2$		
	Smoother	Predictor	$\{y\}_n$	Smoother	Predictor	$\{y\}_n$	Smoother	Predictor	$\{y\}_n$
$\exp(-\Delta\lambda) = 0.99$									
1	0.0134	0.0226	0.624	0.0209	0.0369	0.749	0.0342	0.0625	0.998
12	0.00383	0.00792	0.0520	0.00586	0.0126	0.0624	0.00945	0.0211	0.0833
48	0.00183	0.00430	0.0130	0.00276	0.00692	0.0156	0.00440	0.0116	0.0208
288	0.000660	0.00206	0.00217	0.000967	0.00343	0.00260	0.00149	0.00600	0.00347
$\exp(-\Delta\lambda) = 0.9$									
1	0.0345	0.0456	0.620	0.0569	0.0820	0.741	0.0954	0.148	0.982
12	0.0109	0.0233	0.0520	0.0164	0.0396	0.0624	0.0259	0.0697	0.0832
48	0.00488	0.0150	0.0130	0.00707	0.0260	0.0156	0.0108	0.0467	0.208
288	0.00144	0.00966	0.00217	0.00195	0.0178	0.00260	0.00280	0.0338	0.00347

[†] The first two estimators are model based (smoother and predictor) and the third is model free (realized volatility $\{y\}_n$). These measures are calculated for different values of $\omega^2 = \text{var}\{\sigma^2(t)\}$ and λ, keeping $\xi = E\{\sigma^2(t)\}$ fixed at 0.5.

The main conclusion from the results in Table 16.1 is that model-based approaches can potentially lead to very significant reductions in mean-square error, with the reductions being highest for persistent (low value of λ) volatility processes with high values of $\xi\omega^{-2}$. Even for moderately large values of M the model-based predictor can be more accurate than realized volatility, sometimes by a considerable amount. This is an important result from a forecasting viewpoint. However, when there is not much persistence and M is very large, this result is reversed and realized volatility can be moderately more accurate. The smoother is always substantially more accurate than realized volatility, even when M is very large and there is not much memory in volatility. This suggests that model-based methods may be particularly helpful in estimating historical records of actual volatility. Finally, we should place some *caveats* on these conclusions. These results represent a somewhat favourable set-up for the model-based approach. In these calculations we have assumed knowledge of the second-order properties of volatility whereas in practice we shall have to build such a model and then to estimate it, inducing additional biases that we have not reported on.

16.3.2 Estimating parameters: a numerical illustration

Estimating the parameters of continuous time SV models is known to be difficult owing to our inability to compute the appropriate likelihood function. This has prompted the development of a sizable collection of methods to deal with this problem. A very incomplete list of references includes Gourieroux et al. (1993), Gallant and Long (1997), Kim et al. (1998), Elerian et al. (2001) and Sørensen (2000). Here we study a simple approach based on the realized volatilities. The closest reference to ours in this respect is Bollerslev and Zhou (2001) who use a method-of-moments approach based on assuming that the actual volatility process $\{\sigma_n^2\}$ is observed via the quadratic variation estimator, i.e. they assume that there is no realized volatility error.

Table 16.2 shows the result of a small simulation experiment which investigates the effectiveness of the quasi-likelihood estimation methods based on the time series of realized volatility. The quasi-likelihood is constructed using the output of the Kalman filter. It is suboptimal for it does not exploit the non-Gaussian nature of the volatility dynamics, but it provides a consistent and asymptotically normal set of estimators. This follows from the fact that the Kalman filter builds the Gaussian quasi-likelihood function for the ARMA representation of the process, where the noise in the representation is both white and strong mixing (strong mixing follows from Sørensen (2000) and Genon-Catalot et al. (2000) who showed that if the volatility is strong mixing then squared returns are strong mixing). This means that we can immediately apply the asymptotic theory results of Francq and Zakoïan (2000) in this context so long as $\sigma^2(t)$ is strong mixing. Further the estimation takes only around 5 s on a Pentium III notebook computer.

The set-up of the simulation study uses 500 daily observations where the volatility is an OU process with a gamma marginal distribution. Table 16.2 varies

Table 16.2. Monte Carlo estimates of the 0.1- and 0.9-quantiles of the maximum quasi-likelihood estimator of an SV model with OU volatility†

M	Quantiles for the following parameter values:					
	$\lambda = 0.01$	$\xi = 0.5$	$\omega^2 = \xi/8 = 0.0625$	$\lambda = 0.01$	$\xi = 0.5$	$\omega^2 = \xi/4 = 0.125$
1	0.00897, 1.76	0.318, 0.659	0.00751, 0.152	0.00750, 0.400	0.272, 0.752	0.0172, 0.225
12	0.00891, 0.0409	0.341, 0.669	0.0130, 0.0759	0.00789, 0.0367	0.265, 0.751	0.0197, 0.168
48	0.00920, 0.0348	0.339, 0.672	0.0134, 0.0715	0.00920, 0.0320	0.266, 0.727	0.0199, 0.149
288	0.00928, 0.0336	0.334, 0.674	0.0130, 0.0755	0.00906, 0.0299	0.269, 0.731	0.0207, 0.152
	$\lambda = 0.1$	$\xi = 0.5$	$\omega^2 = \xi/8 = 0.0625$	$\lambda = 0.1$	$\xi = 0.5$	$\omega^2 = \xi/4 = 0.125$
1	0.0451, 1.57	0.400, 0.573	0.0271, 0.151	0.0505, 0.312	0.374, 0.599	0.0548, 0.226
12	0.0725, 0.165	0.420, 0.572	0.0383, 0.0847	0.0713, 0.158	0.397, 0.593	0.0717, 0.170
48	0.0748, 0.152	0.421, 0.566	0.0397, 0.0829	0.0754, 0.148	0.398, 0.592	0.0763, 0.163
288	0.0792, 0.141	0.425, 0.572	0.0410, 0.0788	0.0755, 0.136	0.403, 0.619	0.0774, 0.176

† The volatility model has $\sigma^2(t) \sim \Gamma(\nu, a)$ with 500 daily observations, which implies $\xi = \nu a^{-1}$ and $\omega^2 = \nu a^{-2}$. The true value of ξ is always fixed at 0.5, while ω^2 and λ vary. M denotes the number of intraday observations used. 1000 replications are used in the study.

the value of M. When $M = 1$ this corresponds to using the classical approach of squared daily returns. When M is higher we are using intraday data. The results suggest that the intraday data allow us to estimate the parameters much more efficiently. Indeed when M is large the estimators have very little bias and turn out to be quite close to being jointly Gaussian. The experiment also suggests that when λ is larger, which corresponds to the process having less memory, then the estimates of ξ and ω^2 are sharper. Taken together the results are quite encouraging for they are based on only 2 years of data but suggest that we can construct quite precise estimates of these models with this.

16.4 Empirical illustration

To illustrate some of these results we have fitted a set of superposition-based OU or CEV SV models to the realized volatility time series constructed from the 5-min exchange rate return data discussed in Section 16.1. Here we use the quasi-likelihood method to estimate the parameters of the model: ξ, ω^2, $\lambda_1, \ldots, \lambda_J$ and $w_1, \ldots, w_J$. We do this for a variety of values of M, starting with $M = 6$, which corresponds to working with 4-h returns. The resulting parameter estimates are given in Table 16.3. For the moment we shall focus on this case.

The fitted parameters suggests a dramatic shift in the fitted model as we go from $J = 1$ to $J = 2$ or $J = 3$. The more flexible models allow for a factor which has quite a large degree of memory, as well as a more rapidly decaying component or two. A simple measure of fit of the model is the Box–Pierce statistic, which shows a large jump from a massive 302 when $J = 1$, down to an acceptable number for a superposition model.

To provide a more detailed assessment of the fit of the model we have drawn a series of graphs in Fig. 16.4. Except where explicitly noted we have computed the

Table 16.3. Fit of the superposition of J volatility processes for an SV model based on realized volatility computed using $M = 6$, $M = 18$ and $M = 144^{\dagger}$

M	J	ξ	ω^2	λ_1	λ_2	λ_3	w_1	w_2	Quasi-likelihood	BP
6	3	0.4783	0.376	0.0370	1.61	246	0.212	0.180	−113258	11.2
6	2	0.4785	0.310	0.0383	3.76	—	0.262	—	−113261	11.3
6	1	0.4907	0.358	1.37	—	—	—	—	−117397	302
18	3	0.460	0.373	0.0145	0.0587	3.27	0.0560	0.190	−101864	26.4
18	2	0.460	0.533	0.0448	4.17	—	0.170	—	−101876	26.5
18	1	0.465	0.497	1.83	—	—	—	—	−107076	443
144	3	0.508	4.79	0.0331	0.973	268	0.0183	0.0180	−68377	15.3
144	2	0.509	0.461	0.0429	3.74	—	0.212	—	−68586	23.3
144	1	0.513	0.374	1.44	—	—	—	—	−76953	765

† We do not record w_J as this is 1 minus the sum of the other weights. The estimation method is quasi-likelihood using output from a Kalman filter. BP denotes the Box–Pierce statistic, based on 20 lags, which is a test of serial dependence in the scaled residuals.

graphs using the $J = 3$ fitted model, although there would be very little difference if we had taken $J = 2$. Fig. 16.4(a) draws the computed realized volatility $\{y\}_n$, together with the corresponding smoothed estimate of actual volatility using the fitted SV model. We can see that realized volatility is much more jagged than the smoothed quantity. In Fig. 16.4(b) we have drawn a kernel-based estimate of the log-density of log(realized volatility). The bandwidths were taken to be $1.06\hat{\sigma}T^{-1/5}$, where T is the sample size and $\hat{\sigma}$ is the empirical standard deviation of log(realized volatility) (this is an optimal choice against a mean-square error loss for Gaussian data, e.g. Silverman (1986)) while we have chosen the range of the display to match the upper and lower 0.05% of the data—so trimming very little of the data. Andersen, Bollerslev, Diebold and Labys (2001) have suggested that the marginal distribution of realized volatility is closely approximated by a log-normal distribution when M is high, and that this would support a model for actual volatility which is log-normal. Such models go back to Clark (1973) and Taylor (1986). However, when we draw the corresponding fitted log-normal log-density, choosing the parameters by using maximum likelihood based on the smoothed realized volatilities as data, we see that the fit is poor. The same holds for the inverse Gaussian log-density. This is also drawn on Fig. 16.4(b), but is so close to the fit of the log-normal curve that it is extremely difficult to tell the difference between the two curves. Inverse Gaussian models for volatility were suggested by Barndorff-Nielsen and Shephard (2001*a*). The rejection of the log-normal and inverse Gaussian marginal distributions for realized volatility itself seems conclusive here. However, when we carry out the same action on the smoothed realized volatilities this rejection no longer holds, implying that the realized volatility error matters greatly here. The kernel-based estimate of the log-density of the logarithmic smoothed estimates is very much in line with the log-normal or inverse Gaussian hypothesis. This seems to extend the observations of Andersen, Bollerslev, Diebold and Labys (2001) in at least two directions:

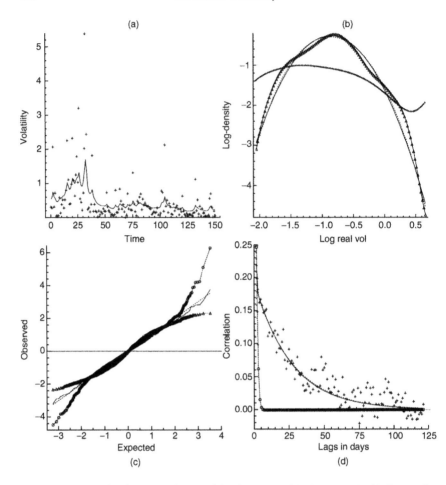

Fig. 16.4. Results from the SV model using $M = 6$ (4-h returns): (a) first 150 observations of $\{y\}_n (+)$ and smoothed estimates of σ_n^2 (———); (b) kernel-based estimates of the density of $\log(\{y\}_n)(+)$ and log-smoothed $\log(\sigma_n^2)(\Delta)$, and the log-normal (———) and inverse Gaussian (. . . . . . .) fits; (c) QQ-plot for y_n scaled by estimated σ_n, using $\sqrt{\{y_n\}}(\Delta)$, predicted ($\circ$) and smoothed (———) volatility (. . . . . . ., 45° line); (d) autocorrelation function of $\{y_n\}(+)$ and the fit of OU SV models with $J = 1(\circ)$, $J = 2$ (———) and $J = 3$ (. . . . . . .).

(a) our model-based estimated actual volatility is fitted well, not just by the log-normal distribution, but equally well by the inverse Gaussian distribution;

(b) by using a model-based smoother the above stylized fact can be deduced using quite a low value of M.

Of course we have yet to see whether these results continue to hold as M increases.

Fig. 16.4(c) draws a QQ-plot of returns y_n divided by a number of estimates of σ_n. If the SV model holds correctly and there is no measurement error then these variables should be Gaussian and the QQ-plot should appear on a 45° line. Fig. 16.4(c) indicates that when we scale returns by realized volatility the returns are highly non-Gaussian, whereas when we use the smoothed estimate then the model seems to fit extremely well. If we replace the smoothed estimate by the predictor of actual volatility, then we see that the fit is as poor as the plot based on the realized volatility. Overall, Fig. 16.4(c) again confirms the fit of the model, which suggests that when $M = 6$ the difference between realized and smoothed volatility is important.

Fig. 16.4(d) shows the corresponding autocorrelation function for the realized volatility series together with the corresponding empirical correlogram. We see from Fig. 16.4(d) that when $J = 1$ we are entirely unable to fit the data, as its autocorrelation function starts at around 0.6 and then decays to 0 in a couple of days. A superposition of two processes is much better, picking up the longer-range dependence in the data. The superpositions of two and three processes give very similar fits; indeed in the graph they are hardly distinguishable.

We next ask how these results vary as M increases. We reanalyse the situation when $M = 144$, which corresponds to working with 10-min returns. Table 16.3 contains the estimated parameters for this problem. They suggest that moving to a superposition of three processes has an important effect on the fit of the model. Again the fitted models indicate that the volatility has elements which have a substantial memory, whereas other components are much more transitory. An important feature of Table 16.3 is the jump in the value of the estimated ω^2 when we move to having $J = 3$. This is caused by the third component which has a very high value of λ, which does not overly change the variance of the actual volatility.

The fit of the model can also be seen from Fig. 16.5. This broadly shows the same results as Fig. 16.4 except for the following. Realized volatility is now less jagged, and so the smoothed estimator of actual volatility and realized volatility are much more in line. The plots of the estimated log-densities show that realized and smoothed volatilities are again closer, with both being quite well fitted by the log-normal and inverse Gaussian distributions. The smoothed estimators are still more closely approximated than the realized volatilities, however. The QQ-plots for realized and smoothed volatility are roughly similar, whereas the plot for prediction is still not satisfactory. This indicates that the uncertainty of predicting volatility 1 day ahead is substantial. Finally, the autocorrelation functions show an improvement in fit as we go from $J = 2$ to $J = 3$ in the SV model.

We finish this section by briefly repeating this exercise with an intermediate value of M, taking $M = 18$, which corresponds to working with returns calculated over 80-min periods. The results are given in Table 16.3. They, and the corresponding plots not reproduced here, are very much in line with the previous graphs with the smoothed estimates of actual volatility performing well, although the QQ-plot is not as good as it was when we used 4-h data.

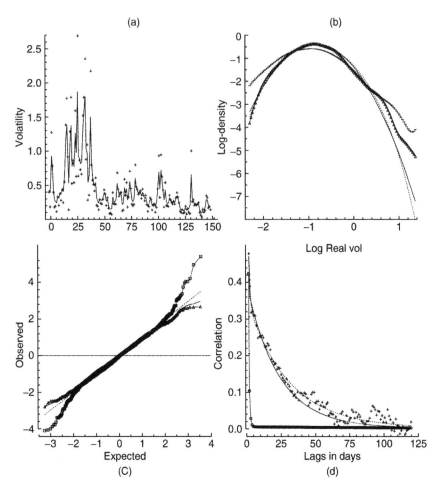

Fig. 16.5. Results from the fit of the SV model using $M = 144$ (10-min returns):
(a) $\{y_n\}(+)$ together with the smoothed estimator of σ_n^2 (——); (b) estimates of
the log-density $\log(\{y\}_n)$ (_-⁻) and smoothed estimates of $\log(\sigma_n^2)(\Delta)$, and the lognormal (——) and inverse Gaussian ($\ldots\ldots$) fits; (c) QQ-plot for the standardized returns (——, smoothed; $\square$, prediction; Δ, $\{y\}_n$; $\ldots\ldots$, $45°$ line); (d)
autocorrelation function of $\{y\}_n(+)$ and the fit of OU SV models with
$J = 1(\circ)$, $J = 2$ (——) and $J = 3$ ($\ldots\ldots$).

16.5 Asymptotic distribution of realized volatility error

16.5.1 The theory

In Section 16.2 we derived the mean and variance of the realized volatility error
for a continuous time SV model when $\mu = \beta = 0$. Although it is possible to derive
the corresponding result when $\mu \neq 0$ but $\beta = 0$, adapting to the risk premium case

seems difficult. Instead we take an asymptotic route. In this section we obtain a limit theory for

$$(\{y\}_n - \sigma_n^2)\sqrt{M},$$

which covers the case of a drift and risk premium.

Theorem 1 For the SV model (1) suppose that the volatility process σ^2 is of locally bounded variation (i.e. with probability 1 the paths of σ^2 are of bounded variation on any compact subinterval of $[0, \infty)$). Then, for any positive Δ and $M \to \infty$

$$(\{y\}_n - \sigma_n^2) \Big/ \sqrt{2 \sum_{j=1}^{M} (\sigma_{j,\,n}^2)^2} \xrightarrow{L} N(0, 1), \tag{17}$$

where

$$\sigma_{j,\,n}^2 = \sigma^{2*}\left\{(n-1)\Delta + \frac{\Delta j}{M}\right\} - \sigma^{2*}\left\{(n-1)\Delta + \frac{\Delta(j-1)}{M}\right\}.$$

Furthermore,

$$\Delta^{-1} M \sum_{j=1}^{M} (\sigma_{j,\,n}^2)^2 \to \sigma_n^{[4]} \qquad \text{almost surely} \tag{18}$$

where

$$\sigma_n^{[4]} = \int_{(n-1)\Delta}^{n\Delta} \sigma^4(s)\mathrm{d}s$$

In particular, then, the limiting law of $\sqrt{M}(\{y\}_n - \sigma_n^2)$ is a normal variance mixture.

Proof The proof of theorem 1 is given in Appendix A.
  This theorem implies that

$$\sqrt{M}(\{y\}_n - \sigma_n^2)|\sigma_n^{[4]} \xrightarrow{L} N(0, 2\Delta\sigma_n^{[4]}), \tag{19}$$

which has the important implication that we can strengthen the usual quadratic variation result that the drift and risk premium has no effect on the limit of $\{y\}_n$ to the result that the asymptotic distribution of $(\{y\}_n - \sigma_n^2)\sqrt{M}$ does not depend on μ or β. Thus the effect on realized volatility of the drift and risk premium is of only *third order*, which suggests that it may be safe to ignore it in many cases.

Theorem 1 also implies that we would expect the variance of the realized volatility error to depend positively on the level of volatility. We have already seen an example of this in the simulated data in Fig. 16.2. Further, the marginal distribution of the realized volatility error should be thicker than normal owing to the normal variance mixture (19) averaged over the random $\sigma_n^{[4]}$. We call $\sigma_n^{[4]}$ the *actual quarticity*, whereas the associated $\sigma^4(t)$ is the *spot quarticity*.
We should note that

$$\sum_{j=1}^{M} (\sigma_{j,n}^2)^2$$

is the realized volatility of $\sigma^{2*}(t)$. Of course the limit, as $M \to \infty$, of this realized volatility is 0; however, theorem 1 shows that the scaled

$$M \sum_{j=1}^{M} (\sigma_{j,n}^2)^2$$

has a stochastic limit. This is a special case of a more general lemma that we prove in Appendix A on what we call *power variation*.

Lemma 1 Assume that $\tau(t)$ is of locally bounded variation. Then, for $M \to \infty$ and r a positive integer,

$$\Delta^{-r+1} M^{r-1} \sum_{j=1}^{M} \tau_j^r \to \tau^{r*}(\Delta) \qquad \text{almost surely} \qquad (20)$$

where

$$\tau_j = \tau^*(jM^{-1}\Delta) - \tau^*\{(j-1)M^{-1}\Delta\}$$

and

$$\tau^{r*}(t) = \int_0^t \tau^r(s)\, ds.$$

The proof of lemma 1 is given in Appendix A.
We report fully on the implications of this result, and various possible extensions, in Barndorff-Nielsen and Shephard (2001c). One of these extensions is that, again writing

$$y_{j,n} = y^*\{(n-1)\Delta + j\Delta M^{-1}\} - y^*\{(n-1)\Delta + (j-1)\Delta M^{-1}\},$$

it can be shown that the *realized quarticity*

$$\frac{1}{3} M \Delta^{-1} \sum_{j=1}^{M} y_{j,n}^4 \to \sigma_n^{[4]} \qquad \text{almost surely,}$$

which is also the limit for $M \to \infty$ of $M\Delta^{-1} \sum_{j=1}^{M} (\sigma_{j,n}^2)^2$. Consequently, the former—known—sum can be used instead of the latter—unknown—sum in the denominator on the left-hand side of the key limiting result (17). In particular

$$(\{y\}_n - \sigma_n^2) \Big/ \sqrt{\left(\frac{2}{3} \sum_{j=1}^{M} y_{j,n}^4\right)} \xrightarrow{\mathcal{L}} N(0, 1).$$

Following the first draft of this paper we have used Monte Carlo methods to study the finite sample behaviour of this asymptotic approximation. Results are reported in Barndorff-Nielsen and Shephard (2001*b*). These experiments suggest that we need quite large values of M for the result to be reliable; however, a better performance is obtained by transforming the approximation on to the log-scale. Then the approximation becomes

$$\{\log(\{y\}_n) - \log(\sigma_n^2)\} \Big/ \sqrt{\left\{\frac{2}{3} \frac{\sum_{j=1}^{M} y_{j,n}^4}{\left(\sum_{j=1}^{M} y_{j,n}^2\right)^2}\right\}} \xrightarrow{\mathcal{L}} N(0, 1).$$

This seems to be quite accurate even for moderate values of M. Following the developments of this paper, our further work on power variation has recently been reported in Barndorff-Nielsen and Shephard (2001*c*).

Finally we note that theorem 1 requires that τ is of locally bounded variation. In the OU case this is easily checked for we know that

$$\tau(t) = \exp(-\lambda t)\tau(0) + \int_0^t \exp\{-\lambda(t-s)\} \, \mathrm{d}z(\lambda s).$$

16.5.2 Application

Suppose that our interest is in estimating μ and β, knowing that

$$y_n | \sigma_n^2 \sim N(\mu + \beta \sigma_n^2, \ \sigma_n^2).$$

A naïve approach would be to regress returns on a constant and the sequence of feasible realized volatilities to produce a simple regression-based estimator. Such an estimator will be both biased and inconsistent owing to an *errors-in-variables* effect of mismeasuring actual volatility by using realized volatility (see Hendry

(1995), chapter 12, for a discussion of this in a historical context). The bias is determined by the variance of $\{y\}_n - \sigma_n^2$, which we have seen is $O(M^{-1})$ even in the presence of drift and risk premium. A smaller bias would result if we use a model-based estimator of actual volatility, instead of the simpler realized volatility. We saw in Section 16.2 that this can substantially reduce the variance, and this will carry over to the bias reduction of the regression-based estimator.

An alternative strategy is to employ an instrumental variable approach. This requires us to find an estimator of σ_n^2 which does not rely on data at time n but is correlated with σ_n^2. A model-free candidate for this task is

$$\widehat{\sigma_n^2} = \frac{1}{2}(\{y\}_{n-1} + \{y\}_{n+1}),$$

the average of contiguous realized volatilities. If actual volatility is temporally dependent, the theory developed in Section 16.2 shows that $\widehat{\sigma_n^2}$ will be correlated with σ_n^2 and so is a valid instrument. Of course, within the context of a model, the best instrument will be the jack-knife estimator, which is the best linear estimator of σ_n^2 given

$$\{y\}_1, \{y\}_2, \ldots, \{y\}_{n-1}, \{y\}_{n+1}, \ldots, \{y\}_T.$$

This is readily computed for models which can be placed within a linear state space form. A final approach to dealing with this issue is to append an extra measurement equation to the linear state space form (16) and to estimate μ and β at the same time as other parameters in a fully specified model.

16.6 Extensions

16.6.1 Diurnal effects and actual volatility

An important aspect of the realized volatility series is that it is not very sensitive to the substantial and complicated intraday diurnal pattern in volatility that is found in many empirical studies (e.g. Andersen and Bollerslev (1997*b*, 1998*b*)) as well as being clear from Fig. 16.1(a). To understand this it is helpful to think of the spot volatility as the sum of a (potentially unknown) deterministic diurnal component $\sigma_\psi^2\{\text{mod}(t, \Delta)\}$ where Δ represents a day, plus a stochastic process $\sigma_\lambda^2(t)$; then we have

$$\sigma^2(t) = \sigma_\psi^2\{\text{mod}(t, \Delta)\} + \sigma_\lambda^2(t).$$

Hence in this model the spot volatility has a repeating intraday (i.e. diurnal) component, but does not have a day of the week or monthly seasonal component. As a result

$$\sigma_n^2 = c + \sigma_{n,\lambda}^2,$$

where

$$c = \int_0^\Delta \sigma_\psi^2 \{\mathrm{mod}(u, \ \Delta)\} \, du$$

and

$$\sigma_{n, \lambda}^2 = \sigma_\lambda^{2*}(n) - \sigma_\lambda^{2*}(n-1),$$

and

$$\sigma_\lambda^{2*}(t) = \int_0^t \sigma_\lambda^2(u) \, du.$$

In this structure the dynamics of realized volatility are unaffected by a diurnal effect. Of course, in practice this additive structure should be regarded as holding only approximately, in which case the diurnal effect may not be completely ignorable. However, in this paper we shall neglect this deficiency.

16.6.2 Leverage

This analysis has not included a leverage term in the model. This can be added in various ways. We follow Barndorff-Nielsen and Shephard (2001a) in parameter-izing the effect as

$$dy^*(t) = \{\mu + \beta\sigma^2(t)\} \, dt + \sigma(t) \, dw(t) + \rho d\bar{z}(\lambda t),$$

where we assume that $\bar{z}(t) = z(t) - E\{z(t)\}$ and $z(t)$ is a Lévy process potentially correlated with $\sigma^2(t)$. The corresponding quadratic variation for this process is

$$[\, y^*](t) = \sigma^{2*}(t) + \rho^2[\bar{z}](\lambda t),$$

whereas the realized volatility error

$$u_n = (\{\, y^0\}_n - \sigma_n^2) + \rho^2(\{\bar{z}\}_n - [\bar{z}]_n) + 2\rho c_n,$$

where

$$y^0(t) = \int_0^t \sigma(t) \, dw(t),$$

$$c_n = \sum_{j=1}^M \bar{z}_{j,\,n} \varepsilon_{j,\,n} \sigma_{j,\,n}$$

$$\{y^0\}_n - \sigma_n^2 = \sum_{j=1}^M \sigma_{j,\,n}^2(\varepsilon_{j,\,n}^2 - 1),$$

using the generic realized volatility notation that was developed in Section 16.2. Here the three terms which make up u_n are zero meaned and uncorrelated when we assume that $\mu = \beta = 0$. The only task is to calculate the variances of each of the terms.

The new terms are straightforward to study once we have the following lemma which relates a Lévy process to its quadratic variation and realized volatility.

Lemma 2 Let t be fixed and let $z(t)$ be a Lévy process with finite fourth cumulant. Then, defining

$$\{z\}(t) = \sum_{j=1}^{M} [z(jtM^{-1}) - z\{(j-1)tM^{-1}\}]^2,$$

we have that

$$E\left\{\begin{array}{c} z(t) \\ \{z\}(t) \\ [z](t) \end{array}\right\} = t\left(\begin{array}{c} \kappa_1 \\ \kappa_2 \\ \kappa_2 \end{array}\right),$$

$$\mathrm{cov}\left\{\begin{array}{c} z(t) \\ \{z\}(t) \\ [z](t) \end{array}\right\} = t\left(\begin{array}{ccc} \kappa_2 & \kappa_3 & \kappa_3 \\ \kappa_3 & \kappa_4 + 3\kappa_2^2 tM^{-1} & \kappa_4 \\ \kappa_3 & \kappa_4 & \kappa_4 \end{array}\right),$$

where κ_r denotes the rth cumulant of $z(1)$. An implication is that $\{z\}(t) - [z](t)$ has zero mean, whereas

$$\mathrm{var}\langle\{z\}(t) - [z](t)\rangle = 3k_2^2 t^2 M^{-1}.$$

Proof Most of the results follow immediately, recognizing that the rth cumulant of $z(t)$ is $t\kappa_r$. This is a consequence of the Lévy–Khintchine representation. The only piece of this result which is not trivial is

$$\begin{aligned} \mathrm{var}[\{z\}(t)] &= M\mu_4\{z(tM^{-1})\} \\ &= M[\kappa_4\{z(tM^{-1})\} + 3\kappa_2\{z(tM^{-1})\}^2] \\ &= M(tM^{-1}\kappa_4 + 3t^2 M^{-2}\kappa_2^2). \end{aligned}$$

Here $\mu_4\{\cdot\}$ and $\kappa_4\{\cdot\}$ denote the fourth centred moment and cumulant respectively.

We achieve our desired result immediately for

$$M\mathrm{cov}\left(\begin{array}{c} \{\bar{z}\}_n - [\bar{z}]_n \\ \{y^0\}_n - \sigma_n^2 \\ c_n \end{array}\right) \rightarrow \Delta^2\left(\begin{array}{ccc} 3\kappa_2^2 & 0 & 0 \\ 0 & 2(\omega^2 + \xi^2) & 0 \\ 0 & 0 & \kappa_2\xi \end{array}\right),$$

as $M \to \infty$. Repeating the pattern we had before, no new issues arise when we allow for a drift or a risk premium for their effect will be small compared with the other terms. Of course, the central limit theory that we developed in Section 16.5 will apply to $(\{y^0\}_n - \sigma_n^2)\sqrt{M}$ not to $(\{y\}_n - [y]_n)\sqrt{M}$.

Trivially this analysis also deals with the situation of a model which is an SV process plus jumps, where the volatility is not correlated with the jumps.

16.7 Conclusion

In this paper we have studied the statistical properties of realized volatility in the context of SV models. Our results are entirely general, providing both a central limit theory approximation as well as an exact second-order analysis. These results can be used, in conjunction with a model for the dynamics of volatility, to produce a more accurate estimate of actual volatility. Further, a simple quasi-likelihood results which could be used to perform computationally quite simple estimation. Potentially they allow us to exploit the availability of high frequency data in financial economics, giving us relatively simple and efficient ways of estimating these stochastic processes.

Finally, in our empirical work we have taken Δ to be 1 day. This choice is entirely ad hoc. Another possibility is to look simultaneously at several different Δ-values. This may have virtue as a way of checking the fit of the model, as well as allowing potentially more efficient estimation. However, we have yet to explore this issue. To do so it would be convenient to have a functional limit theorem for $(\{y\}_n - \sigma_n^2)$.

Acknowledgements

Barndorff-Nielsen's work is supported by the Centre for Analytical Finance, which is funded by the Danish Social Science Research Council, and by the Centre for Mathematical Physics and Stochastics, which is funded by the Danish National Research Foundation. Neil Shephard's research is supported by the UK's Economic and Social Research Council through grant R00023839. All the calculations made in this paper are based on software written by the second author using the Ox language of Doornik (2001) combined with the state space software library described by Koopman et al. (1999). We thank Michel M. Dacorogna for allowing us to use Olsen's high frequency exchange rate data in our study and Tim Bollerslev for supplying us with a semicleaned version of these data. The comments of Tim Bollerslev, Frank Gerhard, Nour Meddahi, Enrique Sentana and the two excellent referees on an initial draft were particularly helpful.

Appendix A

This appendix has three subsections. First we discuss some of the aspects of the data that we use in the paper. Second we give a proof of lemma 1, whereas in the third subsection we prove theorem 1.

A.1 Data appendix

The Olsen group have kindly made available to us a data set which records every 5 min the most recent quote to appear on the Reuters screen from 1 December 1986, until 30 November 1996. When prices are missing they have interpolated them. Details of this processing are given in Dacorogna et al. (2001). The same data set was analysed by Andersen, Bollerslev, Diebold and Labys (2001). We follow the extensive work of Torben Andersen and Tim Bollerslev on this data set, who removed much of the times when the market is basically closed. This includes almost all of the weekends, and they have taken out most US holidays. The result is what we shall regard as a single time series of length 705 313 observations. Although many of the breaks in the series have been removed, sometimes there are sequences of very small price changes caused by, for example, unmodelled non-US holidays or data feed breakdowns. We deal with this by adding a Brownian bridge simulation to sequences of data where at each time point the absolute change in a 5-min period is below 0.01%, i.e., when this happens, we interpolate prices stochastically, adding a Brownian bridge with a standard deviation of 0.01 for each time period. By using a bridge process we are not affecting the long run trajectory of prices, and the effect on realized volatility is very small indeed. We have used this stochastic method here to be consistent with our other work on this topic where this effect is important. It is illustrated in Fig. 16.6, which shows the first 500 observations in the US dollar–Deutschmark series that we have used in this paper and another series which is for the yen–dollar comparison. Later stretches of the data have fewer breaks in them, but this graph illustrates the effects of our intervention. Clearly our approach is ad hoc. However, a proper statistical modelling of these breaks is very complicated because of their many causes and the fact that our data set is enormous.

A.2 Proof of lemma 1

Recall for the process τ that we use the notation

$$\tau^*(t) = \int_0^t \tau(s)\mathrm{d}s$$

and

$$\tau_j = \tau^*(jM^{-1}\Delta) - \tau^*\{(j-1)M^{-1}\Delta\}.$$

Proof By the definition of τ_j, for every j there is a c_j such that

$$\inf_{(j-1)M^{-1}\Delta \leq s \leq jM^{-1}\Delta} \{\tau(s)\} \leq c_j \leq \sup_{(j-1)M^{-1}\Delta \leq s \leq jM^{-1}\Delta} \{\tau(s)\}$$

and

$$\tau_j = c_j\Delta M^{-1}. \qquad (21)$$

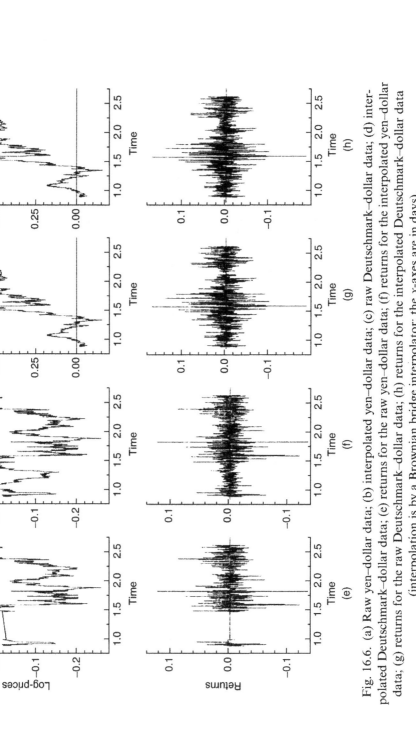

Fig. 16.6. (a) Raw yen–dollar data; (b) interpolated yen–dollar data; (c) raw Deutschmark–dollar data; (d) interpolated Deutschmark–dollar data; (e) returns for the raw yen–dollar data; (f) returns for the interpolated yen–dollar data; (g) returns for the raw Deutschmark–dollar data; (h) returns for the interpolated Deutschmark–dollar data (interpolation is by a Brownian bridge interpolator; the *x*-axes are in days).

The local bounded variation of τ implies that τ^r is locally bounded and Riemann integrable. Consequently

$$\Delta^{-r+1} M^{r-1} \sum_{j=1}^{M} \tau_j^r = \sum_{j=1}^{M} c_j^r \Delta M^{-1} \to \int_0^{\Delta} \tau^r(s)\,\mathrm{d}s = \tau^{r*}(\Delta). \qquad \square$$

The fact that τ^r is Riemann integrable is perhaps not immediately obvious. However, we recall that a bounded function f is Riemann integrable on an interval $[0, t]$ if and only if the set of discontinuity points of f has Lebesgue measure 0 (see Hobson (1927), pp. 465–6, Munroe (1953), p. 174, theorem 24.4, or Lebesgue (1902)). In our case the latter property follows immediately from the bounded variation of τ (any function of bounded variation is the difference between an increasing and a decreasing function and any monotone function has at most countably many discontinuities).

A.3 Proof of theorem 1

We first recall some definitions. Consider the SV model

$$y^*(t) = \mu t + \beta \tau^*(t) + \int_0^t \tau^{1/2}(s)\,\mathrm{d}w(t),$$

with τ positive, stationary and independent of w (we have switched our notation for the volatility as it simplifies our later derivation). Now writing u and $\{y\}$ for u_1 and $\{y\}_1$ we have

$$u = \{y\} - \tau^*(\Delta) = \sum_{j=1}^{M} y_j^2 - \tau^*(\Delta)$$

where

$$y_j = y^*(jM^{-1}\Delta) - y^*\{(j-1)M^{-1}\Delta\}.$$

Conditionally on $\tau_1, \ldots, \tau_M$, the increments $y_1, \ldots, y_M$ are independent, and

$$y_j \overset{\mathcal{L}}{=} N(\mu M^{-1}\Delta + \beta\tau_j,\ \tau_j).$$

Thus, conditionally, y_j^2 is non-central χ^2 distributed with cumulant function

$$C\{\zeta \ddagger y_j^2 | \tau_j\} = -\frac{1}{2}\log(1 - 2\mathrm{i}\tau_j\zeta) + \mathrm{i}v_j\zeta(1 - 2\mathrm{i}\tau_j\zeta)^{-1}$$

where $\mathrm{i} = \sqrt{-1}$ and

$$v_j = (\mu M^{-1}\Delta + \beta\tau_j)^2. \tag{22}$$

Consequently

$$C\{\zeta \ddagger u | \tau_1, \ldots, \tau_M\} = -\sum_{j=1}^{M}\left\{\frac{1}{2}\log(1 - 2\mathrm{i}\tau_j\zeta) - \mathrm{i}v_j\zeta(1 - 2\mathrm{i}\tau_j\zeta)^{-1} + \mathrm{i}\tau_j\zeta\right\}.$$

By Taylor's formula with remainder (see, for instance, Barndorff-Nielsen and Cox (1989), formula 6.122) we find, provided that

$$2|\zeta| \max_{1 \leqslant j \leqslant M} (\tau_j) < 1,$$

that

$$\frac{1}{2}\log(1 - 2\mathrm{i}\tau_j\zeta) - \mathrm{i}v_j\zeta(1 - 2\mathrm{i}\tau_j\zeta)^{-1} + \mathrm{i}\zeta\tau_j = \zeta^2\{\tau_j^2 Q_{0j}(\zeta) + 2v_j\tau_j Q_{1j}(\zeta)\} - \mathrm{i}v_j\zeta,$$

where

$$Q_{0j}(\zeta) = 2\int_0^1 \frac{1 - s}{(1 - 2\mathrm{i}\tau_j\zeta s)^2}\,\mathrm{d}s$$

and

$$Q_{1j}(\zeta) = 2\int_0^1 \frac{1 - s}{(1 - 2\mathrm{i}\tau_j\zeta s)^3}\,\mathrm{d}s.$$

Hence

$$C\{\zeta \ddagger u | \tau_1, \ldots, \tau_M\} = \mathrm{i}\zeta \sum_{j=1}^{M} v_j - \zeta^2 \sum_{j=1}^{M} \{\tau_j^2 Q_{0j}(\zeta) + 2v_j\tau_j Q_{1j}(\zeta)\}. \qquad (23)$$

Proof Note first that expression (18) follows from lemma 1. Next, rewrite equation (23) as

$$C\{\zeta \ddagger u | \tau_1, \ldots, \tau_M\} = \mathrm{i}\zeta \sum_{j=1}^{M} v_j - \zeta^2 \sum_{j=1}^{M} (\tau_j^2 + 2v_j\tau_j) - \zeta^2 \sum_{j=1}^{M} [\tau_j^2 \{Q_{0j}(\zeta) - 1\}$$

$$+ 2v_j\tau_j\{Q_{1j}(\zeta) - 1\}]$$

$$= \frac{1}{2}\zeta^2 \times 2 \sum_{j=1}^{M} \tau_j + R(\zeta),$$

where

$$R(\zeta) = i\zeta \sum_{j=1}^{M} v_j - 2\zeta^2 \sum_{j=1}^{M} v_j \tau_j - \zeta^2 \sum_{j=1}^{M} [\tau_j^2 \{Q_{0j}(\zeta) - 1\} + 2v_j \tau_j \{Q_{1j}(\zeta) - 1\}].$$

Thus, to verify expression (17) we must show that

$$\sum_{j=1}^{M} v_j \bigg/ \sqrt{\sum_{j=1}^{M} \tau_j^2} \to 0,$$

$$\sum_{j=1}^{M} v_j \tau_j \bigg/ \sum_{j=1}^{M} \tau_j^2 \to 0,$$

$$\sum_{j=1}^{M} \tau_j^2 \left[Q_{0j} \left\{ \zeta \bigg/ \sqrt{\left(2 \sum_{j=1}^{M} \tau_j^2 \right)} \right\} - 1 \right] \bigg/ \sum_{j=1}^{M} \tau_j^2 \to 0$$

and

$$\sum_{j=1}^{M} v_j \tau_j \left[Q_{1j} \left\{ \zeta \bigg/ \sqrt{\left(2 \sum_{j=1}^{M} \tau_j^2 \right)} \right\} - 1 \right] \bigg/ \sum_{j=1}^{M} \tau_j^2 \to 0$$

or, equivalently, by expression (20), that

$$\sqrt{M} \sum_{j=1}^{M} v_j \to 0,$$

$$M \sum_{j=1}^{M} v_j \tau_j \to 0, \tag{24}$$

$$M \sum_{j=1}^{M} \tau_j^2 \left[Q_{0j} \left\{ \zeta \bigg/ \sqrt{\left(2 \sum_{j=1}^{M} \tau_j^2 \right)} \right\} - 1 \right] \to 0$$

and

$$M \sum_{j=1}^{M} v_j \tau_j \left[Q_{1j} \left\{ \zeta \bigg/ \sqrt{\left(2 \sum_{j=1}^{M} \tau_j^2 \right)} \right\} - 1 \right] \to 0. \tag{25}$$

We have

$$\sqrt{M} \sum_{j=1}^{M} v_j = M^{-1/2} \left(\Delta^2 \mu^2 + 2\mu\Delta\beta \sum_{j=1}^{M} \tau_j + \beta^2 M \sum_{j=1}^{M} \tau_j^2 \right),$$

which tends to 0 on account of expression (20). Furthermore, also by expression (20) we find that

$$M \sum_{j=1}^{M} v_j \tau_j = M^{-1} \mu^2 \Delta^2 \sum_{j=1}^{M} \tau_j + 2\mu\Delta\beta \sum_{j=1}^{M} \tau_j^2 + \beta^2 M \sum_{j=1}^{M} \tau_j^3 \to 0.$$

Finally, to show expressions (24) and (25) we first note that, by equation (21), the local boundedness of τ and expression (20),

$$\tau_j \Big/ \sqrt{\sum_{j=1}^{M} \tau_j^2} = \sqrt{M}\tau_j \Big/ \sqrt{\left(M \sum_{j=1}^{M} \tau_j^2 \right)}$$

$$= M^{-1/2} \Delta c_j \Big/ \sqrt{\left(M \sum_{j=1}^{M} \tau_j^2 \right)} = O(M^{-1/2})$$

uniformly in j. Hence

$$Q_{0j} \left\{ \zeta \Big/ \sqrt{\left(2 \sum_{j=1}^{M} \tau_j^2 \right)} \right\} - 1 \to 0 \tag{26}$$

and

$$Q_{1j} \left\{ \zeta \Big/ \sqrt{\left(2 \sum_{j=1}^{M} \tau_j^2 \right)} \right\} - 1 \to 0 \tag{27}$$

uniformly in j. Moreover, again using expression (20), we have

$$M \sum_{j=1}^{M} (\tau_j^2 + v_j \tau_j) = (1 + \Delta^2 \mu^2) M \sum_{j=1}^{M} \tau_j^2 + 2\Delta\mu\beta M \sum_{j=1}^{M} \tau_j^3 + \beta^2 M \sum_{j=1}^{M} \tau_j^4 = O(1)$$

and expressions (24) and (25) follow from this and expressions (26) and (27).

References

Andersen, T. G. and Bollerslev, T. (1997a). Heterogeneous information arrivals and return volatility dynamics: uncovering the long-run in high frequency returns. *Journal of Finance* 52, 975–1005.

——(1997b). Intraday periodicity and volatility persistence in financial markets. *Journal of Emperical Finance* 4, 115–58.

——(1998a). Answering the skeptics: yes, standard volatility models do provide accurate forecasts. *International Economic Review* 39, 885–905.

Andersen, T. G. and Bollershev, T. (1998b). Deutsche mark-dollar volatility: intraday activity patterns, macro-economic announcements, and longer run dependencies. *Journal of Finance* 53, 219–65.

—— Diebold, F. X., and Ebens, H. (2001). The distribution of realized stock return volatility. *Journal of Empirical Finance* 61, 43–76.

—— —— Labys, P. (2000). Exchange rate returns standardised by realised volatility are (nearly) Gaussian. *Multi-national Finance Journal* 4, 159–79.

—— (2001). The distribution of exchange rate volatility. *Journal of the American Statistical Association* 92, 42–55.

Andreou, E. and Ghysels, E. (2001). Rolling-sampling volatility estimators: some new theoretical, simulation and empirical results. *Journal of Business, Economic Statistics* 19, in the press.

Areal, N. M. P. C. and Taylor, S. J. (2002). The realised volatility of FTSE-100 futures prices. *Journal of Futures Markets* 22, 627–48.

Bai, X., Russell, J. R., and Tiao, G. C. (2000). Beyond Merton's utopia: effects of non-normality and dependence on the precision of variance estimates using high-frequency financial data. Unpublished. Graduate School of Business, University of Chicago, Chicago.

Barndorff-Nielsen, O. E. (1998). Processes of normal inverse Gaussian type. *Financial Stochastics* 2, 41–68.

—— (2001). Superposition of Ornstein-Uhlenbeck type processes. *Theory Probability Application* 45, 175–194.

—— Cox, D. R. (1989). *Asymptotic Techniques for Use in Statistics*. London: Chapman and Hall.

—— Jensen, J. L., and Sørensen, M. (1990). Parametric modelling of turbulence. *Phil. Trans. R. Soc. Lond.*, 332, 439–55.

—— Shephard, N. (2001a). Non-Gaussian Ornstein–Uhlenbeck-based models and some of their uses in financial economics (with discussion). *Journal of the Royal Statistical Society*, B, 63, 167–241.

—— (2001b). How accurate is the asymptotic approximation to the distribution of realised volatility? To be published.

—— (2001c). Realised power variation and stochastic volatility. Unpublished. Nuffiled College, Oxford.

Bollerslev, T., Engle, R. F., and Nelson, D. B. (1994). ARCH models. In *The Handbook of Econometrics*, vol. 4 (eds Engle, R. F. and D. McFadden), pp. 2959–3038. Amsterdam: North-Holland.

—— Zhou, H. (2001). Estimating stochastic volatility diffusion using conditional moments of integrated volatility. *Journal of Econometrics*, to be published.

Christensen, B. J. and Prabhala, N. R. (1998). The relation between implied and realized volatility. *Journal of Empirical Finance* 37, 125–50.

Clark, P. K. (1973). A subordinated stochastic process model with fixed variance for speculative prices. *Econometrica* 41, 135–56.

Comte, F. and Renault, E. (1998). Long memory in continuous-time stochastic volatility models. *Mathematical Finance* 8, 291–323.

Cox, D. R. (1991). Long-range dependence, non-linearity and time irreversibility. *Journal of Time Series Analysis* 12, 329–35.

Dacorogna, M. M., Gencay, R., Muller, U. A., Olsen, R. B., and Pictet, O. V. (2001). *An Introduction to High-frequency Finance*. San Diego: Academic Press.

Ding, Z. and Granger, C. W. J. (1996). Modeling volatility persistence of speculative returns: a new approach. *Journal of Econometrics* 73, 185–215.

Doornik, J. A. (2001). *Ox: Object Oriented Matrix Programming, 3.0.* London: Timberlake.

Elerian, O., Chib, S., and Shephard, N. (2001). Likelihood inference for discretely observed non-linear diffusions. *Econometrica* 69, 959–93.

Engle, R. F. and Lee, G. G. J. (1999). A permanent and transitory component model of stock return volatility. In *Cointegration, Causality, and Forecasting: a Festschrift in Honour of Clive W. J. Granger* (eds.) Engle, R. F. and White, H., ch. 20, 475–97. Oxford: Oxford University Press.

Foster, D. P. and Nelson, D. B. (1996). Continuous record asymptotics for rolling sample variance estimators. *Econometrica* 64, 139–74.

Francq, C. and Zakoïan, J.-M. (2000). Covariance matrix estimation for estimators of mixing weak ARMA models. *Journal of Statistical Planning and Finance* 83, 369–94.

Gallant, A. R. and Long, J. R. (1997). Estimating stochastic differential equations efficiently by minimum chisquare. *Biometrika* 84, 125–41.

Genon-Catalot, V., Jeantheau, T., and Larédo, C. (2000). Stochastic volatility as hidden Markov models and statistical applications. *Bernoulli* 6, 1051–79.

Ghysels, E., Harvey, A. C., and Renault, E. (1996). Stochastic volatility. In *Statistical Methods in Finance* (eds.) Rao, C. R. and Maddala, G. S., 119–91. Amsterdam: North-Holland.

Gourieroux, C., Monfort, A., and Renault, E. (1993). Indirect inference. *Journal of Applied Econometrics* 8, S85–S118.

Granger, C. W. J. (1980). Long memory relationships and the aggregation of dynamic models. *Journal of Econometrics* 14, 227–38.

Hamilton, J. D. (1994). *Time Series Analysis.* Princeton: Princeton University Press.

Harvey, A. C. (1989). *Forecasting, Structural Time Series Models and the Kalman Filter.* Cambridge: Cambridge University Press.

Hendry, D. F. (1995). *Dynamic Econometrics.* Oxford: Oxford University Press.

Hobson, E. W. (1927). *The Theory of Functions of a Real Variable and the Theory of Fourier's Series*, 3rd edn. Cambridge: Cambridge University Press.

Kim, S., Shephard, N., and Chib, S. (1998). Stochastic volatility: likelihood inference and comparison with ARCH models. *Review of Economic Studies* 65, 361–93.

Koopman, S. J., Shephard, N., and Doornik, J. A. (1999). Statistical algorithms for models in state space using Ssf-Pack 2.2. *Journal of Econometrics* 2, 107–66.

Lebesgue, H. (1902). Integrale, longuer, aire. *Ann. Math. Pura Applic.*, 7, 231–359.

Maheu, J. M. and McCurdy, T. H. (2001). Nonlinear features of realised FX volatility. *Review of Economic Statistics* 83, to be published.

Meddahi, N. and Renault, E. (2002). Temporal aggregation of volatility models. *Journal of Econometrics*, to be published.

Munroe, M. E. (1953). *Introduction to Measure and Integration.* Cambridge: Addison-Wesley.

Poterba, J. and Summers, L. (1986). The persistence of volatility and stock market fluctuations. *American Economic Review* 76, 1124–41.

Schwert, G. W. (1989). Why does stock market volatility change over time. *Journal of Finance* 44, 1115–53.

Shephard, N. (1996). Statistical aspects of ARCH and stochastic volatility. In *Time Series Models in Econometrics, Finance and Other Fields* (eds.) Cox, D. R., Hinkley, D. V., and O. E. Barndorff-Nielsen, 1–67. London: Chapman and Hall.

Silverman, B. W. (1986). *Density Estimation for Statistical and Data Analysis.* London: Chapman and Hall.

Sørensen, M. (2000). Prediction based estimating equations. *Econometrics Journal* 3, 123–47.

Taylor, S. J. (1986). *Modelling Financial Time Series.* Chichester: Wiley.

——— (1994). Modelling stochastic volatility. *Math. Finan.*, 4, 183–204.

——— Xu, X. (1997). The incremental volatility information in one million foreign exchange quotations. *Journal of Empirical Finance* 4, 317–40.

Whittle, P. (1983). *Prediction and Regulation* 2nd edn. Oxford: Blackwell.

Author Index

Subject Index

Printed in the United States
By Bookmasters